OKANAGAN UNIV/COLLEGE LIBRARY

D0506712

K

13

Sociological Debates

Thinking about
'The Social'

CARLTON UNIVERSITY COLLEGE
LIBRARY
BRITISH COLUMBIA

Sociological Debates

Thinking about
'The Social'

edited by

FLOYA ANTHIAS

PROFESSOR OF SOCIOLOGY AND
HEAD OF SOCIOLOGY
UNIVERSITY OF GREENWICH

and

MICHAEL P. KELLY

PROFESSOR OF SOCIAL SCIENCES AND
HEAD OF THE SCHOOL OF SOCIAL SCIENCES
UNIVERSITY OF GREENWICH

 Greenwich University Press

Selection, arrangement and introduction © Greenwich University Press 1995

All rights reserved. No part of this publication may be reproduced, stored in a retrieval system, or transmitted in any form or by any means, electronic, mechanical, photocopying, recording, or otherwise without the prior permission of the publisher.

First published in 1995 by
Greenwich University Press
Unit 42
Dartford Trade Park
Hawley Road
Dartford
Kent DA1 1PF
United Kingdom

British Library Cataloguing-in-Publication Data
A CIP catalogue record for this book is available from the British Library

ISBN 1 874529 55 8

Designed and produced for Greenwich University Press by
Angela Allwright and Kirsten Brown.

Printed in Great Britain by The Bath Press, Avon.

Every effort has been made to trace all the copyright holders, but if any have been inadvertently overlooked the publishers will be pleased to make the necessary arrangements at the earliest opportunity.

Contents

Introduction

Thinking about 'The Social'

Social theory is at the heart of sociology and at the same time is practised, albeit using a 'natural' attitude (Schutz 1970), by all individuals in society. All conscious thinking humans use some form of theory because theory is about understanding. It is impossible to make sense of the world around us without theory. Theory guides the way we understand, interpret and examine the world. Experience, sensations, and the perception of external reality are brought together into a coherent whole and understood by using theory. Sociologists who develop sociological theory are attempting to devise a more systematic, comprehensive and rigorous way of doing this than the ordinary common-sense methods which all people use. Therefore, social theory is both something that all human beings unselfconsciously practise in their day to day lives, and also a set of concepts and tools which sociologists (as well as other social scientists) rigorously and consciously develop to aid understanding of the social world. What is of particular interest, and sometimes a specific difficulty about social theory is that it has to embrace both the scientific aspect of social theorising *and* these common-sense understandings of the world. It has to confront the fact that common sense and theory in a formal academic sense interact with each other.

This presents a dilemma because sociologists, most of them in academic life, but some of them practitioners in a range of other professions, lay claim to some privileged domain of knowledge and understanding. Though they may be correct in this, social theory is what all human beings do in their every day lives. They perceive, understand, explain and interpret the world around them and the actions of others, and attribute meaning both to the immediate social world and that beyond their immediate lives.

This paradox lies at the heart of the sociological enterprise which has claimed for itself a specific and thereby specialised area of study. Out of this have emerged a series of specific methods and sociological orientations which attempt to grapple with the development of more precise and fruitful approaches to the social world or to develop what we call the *sociological imagination*. This term, first coined by C. Wright Mills (1959), refers to the ability to transcend common-sense understandings of the world and develop a deeper comprehension of the world around us.

In spite of the fact that all humans naturally engage in theorising, students coming to sociology, even for the second time (say after A levels in Britain), but certainly those coming to it for the first time, often find themselves intimidated by the highly intellectualised and difficult (and sometimes turgid) vocabularies they have to learn. They may also be concerned by the 'new language' skills they will need to acquire as well as the 'attitude' they will have to learn to adopt, adapting their 'natural' attitude to theorising to the special 'stock of knowledge' (Schutz 1970) of the sociological territory and its practitioners.

Demystifying the theoretical enterprise is thus the initial task of helping first year students to find their way into sociology. One of the things a first year theory course must try to do is make transparent the ability of all of us to make theoretical statements and to have legitimacy in expressing our views and understandings of 'the social'. The second thing a theory course must do is make clear that not any old statement can count as a contribution to theory. So students need to learn the importance of presenting an argument that is coherent and which marshals conceptual and other forms of evidence; the claims need to be formulated in a way which persuades, provokes or enlightens through applying certain rules regarding the effective formulation of an argument or point of view.

This anthology aims to introduce students interested in sociological thought to some of the main concerns and debates in sociology with a focus on the classical writers. The book brings together readings, some of them by the generally acknowledged great writers in sociology like Durkheim, Marx, Weber, Simmel and others, as well as some commentaries made by more contemporary writers. The book originally arose out of a lecture programme given to first year sociology students at the University of Greenwich. Over many years one of the editors (FA) has confronted the problem of introducing undergraduates to the complexities of sociological ideas. One solution has been to introduce students to original texts and ask students therefore to make acquaintance directly with some of the most important and path-breaking sociological writing. Obviously this is both potentially and in reality full of problems, if only because some of the texts are written in an outmoded language and are sometimes poor translations of originals written in French or German. Also there is no doubt that some of the writing is intrinsically difficult (although our students have often claimed that they are less difficult than some of the contemporary exegeses found in textbooks!). Despite this, we regard the exercise as vital in the acquisition of sociological knowledge.

The book is organised around the theme of 'the individual and society' or, alternatively, the dilemmas posed in sociology by the focus on structure on the one hand and human action or agency on the other. This theme draws together the problem of reconciling an understanding of human action with the understanding of social structure. For many sociologists this relationship between agency (human volition, free will and individualism) and structure (the social forces often called society which impact on and affect people's every day lives) is at the heart of sociology. Which comes first, the individual or society? What is society itself? Is it a collection of individuals only, or is it something more, made up of the billions and billions of actions of millions and millions of individuals. Which determines what? This central problem of the individual and society emerged as sociology developed as a discipline during the period of industrialisation in Europe and America in the nineteenth century. The developments in sociology around a set of related questions emerged in the context of the growth of industrial capitalism and the unfolding of what has been termed 'modernity'. Commentators recognised that society was changing rapidly. The ties of tradition, of family and religion appeared to be breaking down. The 'individual' in this new type of society seemed cut loose from those arrangements which previously seemed to establish the social bonds between human beings and social organisation. The role of the individual and the role of society and the relationship between the two became an important sociological preoccupation.

Sociology cannot be understood without contextualising it within the Enlightenment and modernity. The social context of the rise of capitalism, the French Revolution and the period called the Age of Reason are crucial elements also. Enlightenment Thought (1700–1775 approximately) involved three central beliefs : the belief in the power of reason, the belief in progress and the belief in science. It stood against dogma and intolerance and superstition: it was anti-tradition. The central figures included Hobbes and Locke, Saint Simon and Rousseau, Hume, Kant and Smith.

Clearly, society was changing very rapidly and the traditional ways in which human communities were organised were also changing rapidly. The so-called classical sociological writers all tried in various ways to understand both what was going on in these changes and the relationship of the individual and society within these processes. These classical writers produced rather different answers and explanations, but out of the common attempt a unified discipline of sociology may be regarded as having arisen.

In terms of the development of sociology, Auguste Comte, who coined the term 'sociology' saw it as the crowning achievement of the Enlightenment. He regarded sociology as embracing the study of the development of the human mind and the development of human societies. He argued that societies passed through three critical stages of development: the theological stage, the metaphysical stage and the scientific or positive stage. In the theological stage human ideas were dominated by superstition, magic and religion. In the metaphysical stage human conduct was governed by philosophical concerns and an attempt to discover and understand the natural world. In the positive stage, however, the search for ultimate causes was abandoned in favour of understanding how things worked.

There is another sense in which social theory and sociology are products of the Enlightenment and the development of the modern world. Sociology has sought to answer questions about the nature of what modern as opposed to traditional societies consist of, what knowledge as against ignorance means, and the role of science in human development. It has not been possible, however, to include all the relevant Enlightenment thinkers in this volume. However, the predominant theme of social change and modernity has been critical to the way our teaching, and this volume has developed.

The aim has been to consciously avoid a textbook approach to social theory and to make students aware of the diversity of sociological positions. On the other hand, the aim is also to contextualise social theory in terms of modernity and the Enlightenment. However, what we regard as either the most important, and sometimes, the least accessible writings have been included. As in all collections, it has been necessary to select and these readings do not provide, obviously, an exhaustive listing of material that could be used on such a course.

We believe that it is important to locate the arguments made in the context of growing social divisions and a fragmentary social structure, and to show students the androcentric and Eurocentric nature of social theorising as it emerged in Western Europe. What strikes the sociologist today, in fact, is the absence in these writings of concern with gender and 'race' issues and this classical Reader will be followed by a second one which examines some of the pitfalls sociological theory (or to be more precise 'social theory') faces when confronted by contributions from feminism and anti-racist approaches to society.

It is important that students coming to sociology should be aware of the Eurocentrism and androcentrism in social theory. Briefly, androcentricity involves a male-oriented approach that is concerned with public life and excludes women, treating social institutions and practices in an ungendered manner. Eurocentricity is found in the view that society is a boundary maintaining system with certain fundamental characteristics (this excludes the consideration of differing forms). The model of 'society' used is Western and the assumption is that there is an agreement on what is meant by referring to such aspects of life as 'the family'. Sociology, for example, rarely considers the implications of the diversity of cultures and ethnicities both within and across social formations.

Gender and 'race' in sociology are themes that are singularly lacking in the early conceptions of the sociological enterprise. For example, the notion of class, favoured by the early writers, finds difficulty in explaining gender and 'race' inequalities. There is a problem of thinking about the class position of women and particularly the problem of thinking about the class position of racialised women and men. The 1980s saw an explosion of writings which provided the necessary correction to these as well as alternative formulations of the central parameters of study for the sociologist. There will be a follow-up anthology which explores the ways in which sociology has theorised social divisions, particularly those of gender, 'race' and class. However, in this volume a short introduction to the androcentrism of sociology as it emerged in the nineteenth and developed in the twentieth century is included in a paper by Sandra Harding (1986).

An issue that concerns sociologists today (as well as those hostile to the sociological enterprise!) is the use to which sociological theorising can be put and the role it can play in society. There are various views of the role of our social theories, whether those used by us in our every day lives or those used in the practice of academic sociology: to reveal on the one and to conceal on the other hand. The sociological approach stemming from Comte saw the role of social theory to be one of scientifically revealing the real nature of events as well as their causes. There is also another position that holds that social theory can be defined as a form of ideology, stemming from capitalism, whose task essentially is to obfuscate reality, that is to conceal (Therborn 1976). Some writers additionally make a distinction between those that reveal and those that conceal (Mannheim 1960; Althusser 1971).

Within Marxism and other forms of the sociology of knowledge (see Hamilton 1974) there is a long tradition of seeing theory and ideas as always linked to social position or the social and political interests of the people or social groups who produce ideas. This approach forces us to ask questions of a theory's origins: who is saying it, when it is said, and to whom? It asks us to interrogate the underlying social interests that are promoted by its formulation and application. The thoroughgoing critique of foundationalism found in postmodern theory additionally urges us to abandon the idea of the possibility of developing totalising theories (Lyotard 1984) and asks us to locate theoretical concepts within their local social habitat.

Whatever we may think of these alternative explanations of the role of theory and whatever we may understand by postmodern theory and by cultural relativist approaches to knowledge, there is one factor which relates to all forms of communication and knowledge production that appears incontrovertible. The location of individuals within the schema of power relations means that the voices of the powerful are much more audible and carry further, blocking out the voices of the weaker subjects or not allowing them to speak at all even when they have found their voice. This view of social theory as needing to be contextualised within the interests and power positions of social places, groups or individuals derives largely from a Marxist influence, but also from debates around interpretative sociology and postmodernist forms of cultural relativism.

The tradition stemming from August Comte has been characterised as deeply conservative (Nisbett 1967). And yet, there is a view at large (particularly in the tabloid press!) that sociology is a discipline with generally anti-orthodox views, questioning and debunking existing power relations. There is certainly this endemic potential in a subject matter that continuously asks the practitioner and the audience to no longer take for granted that which is part of the everyday understandings in societies. It calls upon us to reflect upon the processes of creation of what we take as 'natural', thereby denaturalizing and allowing scrutiny of what we hold most dear and most unchangeable. But sociology is rooted in a deeply conservative tradition of dealing with the problem of order and instability, of providing explanation and possible solutions to the social problems of industrial capitalism. Hence the concern with class, with alienation, with anomie, with the 'pathologies' of modern society and the celebration and the critique that is found within the writings of Durkheim, Weber, Simmel and other key thinkers of the nineteenth century.

Sociology grew out of the concerns of the Enlightenment with providing an analysis steeped in reason and exploration of the emerging social developments, transformations and conflicts at the social and political level. Sociology was dedicated to understanding the bases and structures of modern society and how it differed from earlier forms of social organisation tied to the idea of traditional social forms. Hence, the evolutionary schemas that underpin the typologies (expressed often as a series of dichotomies or polarities) found in many of the central sociological texts up until the 1950s with the work of Parsons (1951), and beyond. The distinction between simple and complex appears as a neutral statement and yet is echoed in the distinction between traditional and modern, mechanical and organic, traditional and rational, community and association, rural and urban that lie at the heart of a range of sociological positions.

The diverse ways in which the polarity between the traditional and the modern (however that was defined and wherever, chronologically, it was to be located) was conceptualised led to the development of core ideas about the central characteristics of the modern social, political and moral order in the work of a number of key thinkers. Durkheim, Weber and Marx constitute what some have referred to as the Holy Trinity of Sociology or, alternatively, three White men (views differ about the extent to which they were also three wise men!). The concerns of the Enlightenment and the rise of sociology are clearly related in the concern of sociology with progress, science and social order.

The three versions found in Durkheim, Weber, Marx and others of the major characteristics and distinguishing features of modern society gave rise to three different forms of sociology (to quote Ted Benton 1977) with common philosophical traditions underlying them: a different interpretation arising out of similar intellectual concerns although different political ones.

The idea of the distinctiveness of the 'social' is found most clearly in the work of Emile Durkheim (1858–1917). For Durkheim, modern society saw a shift from the importance of the collective conscience to the rise of 'the cult of the individual', from social bonds based on similarity to social bonds, in both a more potentially fraught but also more potentially gelling harmonious unison, arising out of the differentiation and specialisation of tasks and functions in society. For Durkheim, the potential for divisions also grew hand in hand with the growth of organic complementarity. Anomic and other pathological features could, or indeed would develop within this highly differentiated social arrangement.

The place of Durkheim in sociological thought is pivotal in asserting the distinctiveness of social reality. Durkheim believed that the 'social' constituted a distinctive object of study and that sociology therefore had a distinctive subject matter. He also upheld the use of the scientific method, a method common to all the 'sciences'. A further central idea was a belief in the progressive development of societies which were treated as organic wholes. Durkheim is well known for the importance he gave to distinguishing ideas from 'facts'. Social facts he tells us 'are things and should be treated as things.' Social facts are: (a) External to us (b) 'Resistant to our will' (c) They are 'general' (d) They constrain us and are not reducible to individuals. Durkheim additionally made a distinction between normal and pathological social facts.

Max Weber (1864–1920) saw the distinctiveness of the 'modern' to lie in the development of rational forms of action and organisation emerging out of the growth of rational forms of orientation. The growth of rationality and rationalisation, the twin concepts, ousted traditional modes of thought and behaviour. The potential in this was greater control of resources and greater efficiency in their technical management, but also the demise of the more 'human' forms of social interaction and the growth of 'disenchantment' and insidious bureaucratization. Where, for Durkheim, the modern grew out of population growth and density, which led to a requirement for new ways of interacting in order to lower competition, for Weber it was the growth of rational economic action that epitomised the new social order of industrial capitalism. The concept of social action in the work of Weber, on the other hand, was a concern with the study of society as constituted through social action and he upheld the belief in a distinctive method to the social sciences (including history and sociology), and in the role of interpretation and understanding meaning.

Karl Marx (1818–1883) saw modern society expressed in the ways in which humans organised the production of material life and the movement to capitalist production. Its key features were to be found in the conversion of labour to labour power (indicating the depersonalisation of relations in the production process), the growth of a money economy and a waged labourer class. This latter would eventually become the 'undertaker' of the very system that gave rise to it. The core feature of modern society lay in the wage labour-employer relationship, or proletariat-capitalist relationship. This was a relationship of exploitation and concomitantly of domination—politically, intellectually and economically. The forms of alienation that Marx wrote about in his early work were related to the mystification of the relations of domination and exploitation through the notion of free exchange and free wage labour. These processes individuated the work-force and deprived it of the sense of a common human endeavour.

There are a number of ideas and questions that may be drawn out of the various readings presented in this volume. These are the ideas and questions around which we have built our teaching and which, arguably, constitute some of the central dilemmas of sociology in the sense that nearly all academic work done in the name of sociology will be seeking in one way or another to answer one or more of these questions. One key set of questions revolves around the issue of the nature of society, or put another way, the nature of the social. As indicated earlier, is society merely a collection of the different individual humans who happen to be alive at any given moment? Is it the sum of their actions? Is it a mere aggregate of such enormous complexity that it cannot be understood? Or is society something worthy of analysis in its own right and which is more than the sum of its parts and which has its own qualities and characteristics, patterns and structures? Related to this is the extent to which individuals can determine the course of their own lives and constitute society and the extent and ways in which social structures, practices and values have their own dynamic, limiting the role that individuals can play in their constitution and development.

A second and closely related set of questions is found around the issue of the nature of the connections between different aspects of society or what may be called the various bits and pieces that make up society. What are the different types of relationship between individuals, on the one hand, and also what are the relationships between the institutions, organisations, nations, 'racialised' groupings, ethnic groupings, religions, cultures and so on, on the other hand. Society is made up of a multiplicity of different components overlapping, interlocking and into which humans relate in various ways. A central issue here is that not all individuals or groups in society have equal power or equal resources for pursuing their ends. The inequalities and the struggles over power and material resources are key, recurrent themes in sociology. The existence of interdependency in society has to be seen in the context of diversity, differentiation and unequal power relations.

A third set of questions relate to the fact that society is not something static. Society changes all the time and in a sense is like a living thing. People are born every day, people die every day and the nature of the structures, the patterns, the institutions and the organisations change day on day, year on year, century on century. Sometimes the processes of change appear to us as violent and dramatic. Sometimes they appear rapid, sometimes they appear to be much more gradual. Sociology is interested in what leads to and what drives these changes. It is also concerned with some of the contradictions found in these processes between groups that struggle to change society and those that are concerned with maintaining existing structures and relations. Related to this is the issue of the ways in which 'social stability' and 'social change' may be conceptualised and indeed whether the differentiation made between 'stability' and 'change' is able to understand the dynamic nature of social relations.

Floya Anthias and Michael P. Kelly
September 1995

References

Althusser, L. (1971) *Lenin and Philosophy and other essays*, New Left Books.

Benton, T. (1977) *The Philosophical Foundations of the Three Sociologies*, Routledge and Kegan Paul.

Hamilton, P. (1974) *Knowledge and Social Structure*, Routledge and Kegan Paul.

Lyotard, J. (1984) *The Postmodern Condition*, University of Minneaplolis Press.

Mannheim, K. (1960) *Ideology and Utopia*, Routledge and Kegan Paul.

Mills, C. W. (1959) *The Sociological Imagination,* Penguin.

Nisbett, R. (1967) *The Sociological Tradition*, Heinemann.

Parsons, T. (1951) *The Social System*, Routledge and Kegan Paul.

Therborn, G. (1976) *Science, Class and Society*, New Left Books.

Schutz, A. (1970) *On Phenomenology and Social Relations*, University of Chicago Press.

The following are useful texts:

Bauman, Z. (1990) *Thinking Sociologically*, Blackwell.

Hall, S. and Gieben, Bram (eds) (1992) *Formations of Modernity*, OU Polity.

Bocock, R. and Thompson, K. (eds) (1992) *Social and Cultural Forms of Modernity*, OU Polity.

Giddens, A. (1993) *Sociology*, Polity.

Giddens, A. (1971) *Capitalism and Modern Social Theory*, Cambridge University Press, (new edition now available).

Lee, D. and Newby H. (1983) *The Problem of Sociology*, Hutchinson.

Craib, I. (1992) *Modern Social Theory*, Harvester Wheatsheaf.

Johnson, T., Dandeker, C. and Ashworth, C. (1984) *The Structure of Social Theory*, Macmillan.

Publisher's note

The contents of the readings in this anthology have been reproduced as they appear in the publications from which they are taken. In the majority of cases footnotes and bibliographic material are included, the exceptions being where they are of excessive length.

The Individual and Society

1.   Freedom and Dependence
Zygmunt Bauman

Being free and unfree at the same time is perhaps the most common of our experiences. It is also, arguably, the most confusing. No doubt it is one of the most profound puzzles of the human condition which sociology attempts to unravel. Indeed, much in the history of sociology may be explained as an on-going effort to solve this puzzle.

I am free: I can choose and I do make my own choices. I can go on reading this book or I can stop reading it and make myself a cup of coffee. Or forget it all and go for a walk. More than that; I can abandon the whole project of studying sociology and obtaining a college degree, and start looking for a job instead. Because I can do all those things, going on reading this book and sticking to my original intention to study sociology and to graduate are surely the results of my choices; they are courses of action I have selected from among available alternatives. Making decisions testifies to my freedom. Indeed, **freedom** means the ability to decide and choose.

Even if I do not spend much time thinking about my choices and take my decisions without properly surveying alternative courses of action, now and again I am reminded of my freedom by others. I am told, 'This has been your decision, no one but you is responsible for the consequences', or, 'No one forced you to do so, you have only yourself to blame!' If I do something which other people do not allow or normally abstain from doing (if, so to speak, I break a rule), I may be punished. The punishment will confirm that I am *responsible* for what I have done; it will confirm that I could, if I wanted to, refrain from breaking the rule. I could, for example, arrive promptly at the tutorial instead of making myself absent without good reason. Sometimes I am told of my freedom (and hence of my responsibility) in a form which I may find more difficult to accept than in previous examples. I may be told, for instance, that remaining unemployed is entirely my own fault and that I could make a living if only I tried hard enough. Or that I could have become an altogether different person if only I had stretched myself more and applied myself more earnestly to my task.

If these last examples were not enough to make me pause and wonder whether I am indeed free and in control of my life (I might have looked for a job in earnest but not have been able to find one as there was none on offer; or I might have tried hard to enter a different career, yet been barred entry to where I wished to go), I have surely experienced many other situations which showed me in no unclear way that my freedom is, in fact, limited. Such situations taught me that to decide on my own what goal to pursue, and to have an intention to pursue it with all my heart, is one thing; it is an entirely different thing, however, to be able to act on my words and reach the purpose I sought.

Zygmunt Bauman: 'Freedom and Dependence' from *THINKING SOCIOLOGICALLY* (Basil Blackwell Limited, 1990), pp. 20-36.

First of all, I learn that other people may strive for the same goals as I do, but not all can reach them, since the amount of available prizes is limited, that is, smaller than the number of people pursuing them. If this is the case, I will find myself engaged in a competition, the outcome of which will not wholly depend on my efforts alone. I may, for example, compete for a college place, only to find out that there are twenty candidates for every place available, and that most of them have all the qualifications required and use their freedom sensibly — do precisely the things which prospective students are prompted and expected to do. In addition, I will find that the results of my actions and theirs depend on someone else — on people who decide how many places are available and judge the skills and the efforts of the applicants. Such people set the rules of the game; they are, at the same time, the referees: they have the last say in the selection of the winner. They possess the right of discretion — their own freedom to choose and to decide, this time about my own and my competitors' fate. Their freedom seems to draw the boundaries of mine. I depend on the way they decide their own actions — because their freedom to choose introduces an element of uncertainty in my own situation. It is a factor over which I have no control and which nevertheless heavily influences the outcome of my efforts. I am dependent on them because they are in control of this uncertainty. At the end of the day, it is they who pronounce the verdict as to whether my efforts have been good enough and justify my admission.

Secondly, I learn that my determination and goodwill are just not enough if I lack the means to act upon my decision and see it through. I may, for example, 'follow the jobs' and decide to move to the South of the country where jobs are abundant, but then find that house prices and rents in the South are exorbitant and much beyond my means. Or I may wish to escape the squalor of inner-city dwellings and move to a healthier, greener area of the suburbs, yet again find out than I cannot afford the move because houses in better and more-coveted locations cost more than I can afford. Again, I may be dissatisfied with the kind of education my children are offered in their school and wish them to be better taught than they are. Yet there are no other schools available in the area where I live and I am told that if I wish to secure a better education for my children I ought to send them to a richer, better-equipped private school and pay the fees, often higher than my total income. What all such examples (as well as many others you can easily supply yourself) demonstrate is that freedom of choice does not by itself guarantee freedom to act effectively on one's choice; still less does it secure freedom to attain the intended results. To be able to act freely, I need resources in addition to free will.

Most commonly, such resources are money. But they are not the only resources on which freedom of action depends. I may find out that freedom to act on my wishes depends not on what I *do*, or not even on what I *have*, but on what I *am*. For example, I may be refused entry to a certain club, or employment in a certain office, because of my qualities — lice race, or sex, or age, or ethnicity, or nationality. None of these attributes depends on my will or action, and no amount of freedom will enable me to change them. Alternatively, my access to the club, or the employment, or the school may depend on my past achievements (or lack of them) — acquired skills, or a diploma, or the length of previous service, or the nature of my accumulated experience, or the local dialect I learned in my childhood and never bothered to refine. In such cases, I may conclude that the requirements do not coincide with the principle of my free will and responsibility for my actions, as the absence of skill or a distinguished service record are the lasting consequences of my past choices. And yet there is nothing I can do now to change it. My freedom today is limited by my freedom of yesterday; I am '**determined**' — constrained in my present freedom — by my past actions.

Thirdly, I may find out (as I surely will, sooner or later) that as I was, say, born British and as English is my mother tongue, I feel most comfortable, most at home in Britain and among English-speaking people. Elsewhere, I am not sure what the effects of my action would be, I am uncertain what to do and thus feel unfree. I cannot communicate easily, I do not understand the meaning of things other people do, and I am not sure what I should do myself to express my own intentions and achieve the results I am after. I experience a similarly upsetting feeling in many other situations — not just when visiting another country. Coming from a working-class family, I may feel ill at ease among rich, middle-class neighbors. Or being a Catholic, I may find that I cannot live according to more libertarian, relaxed habits which accept divorces and abortions as ordinary facts of life. Had I time to think about experiences of this kind, I would probably come to the conclusion that the group in which I feel most at home also sets limits to my freedom — makes me dependent on it for my freedom. It is inside this group that I am capable of exercising my freedom most fully (that means that only inside this group can I assess the situation correctly and select the course of action that the others approve of and that fits the situation well). The very fact that I am adjusted so well to the conditions of action inside the group to which I belong, however, constrains my freedom of action in the vast and poorly charted, often off-putting and frightening space beyond the confines of that group. Having trained me in its ways and means, my group enables me to practise my freedom. Yet by the same token it limits this practice to its own territory.

As far as my freedom goes, therefore, the group of which I am member plays an ambivalent role. On one hand it *enables* me to be free; on the other it *constrains* me by drawing the borders of my freedom. It enables me to be free as it imparts the sort of desires which are both acceptable and 'realistic' inside my group, teaches me to select the ways of acting which are appropriate to the pursuit of such desires, and gives me the ability to read the situation properly and hence to orient myself correctly to the actions and intentions of others who influence the outcome of my efforts. At the same time it fixes the territory within which my freedom may be properly exercised, as all the many assets I owe to it, all the invaluable skills I acquired from my group turn from advantages into liabilities the moment I venture beyond the boundary of my own group and find myself in an environment where different desires are promoted, different tactics are deemed appropriate, and the connections between other people's conduct and their intentions are not like those I have come to expect.

This is not, however, the only conclusion I would have drawn, had I been able and willing to think through my experience. I would discover something more bewildering still: that usually the very group which plays such an ambivalent and yet crucial role in my freedom is not one which I have myself freely chosen. I am a member of such a group because I was born into it. The territory of my freedom itself is not a matter of free choice. The group which made me a free person and which continues to guard the realm of my freedom took command over my life (my desires, my purposes, the actions I would take and the actions I would refrain from, etc.) uninvited. Becoming a member of that group was not an act of my freedom. On the contrary, it was a manifestation of my **dependence**. I never decided to be French, or to be black, or to be middle-class. I may accept my fate with equanimity or resignation; or I may make it into destiny: relish it, enthusiastically embrace it, and decide to make the best of it — advertising my Frenchness, feeling proud of the beauty of being black, or living my life carefully and prudently as a decent middle-class person is expected to. If I want, however, to change what the group made me and to become someone else, I will have to exert myself to the utmost. The change would require much more effort, self-sacrifice, determination and endurance than are normally needed for living placidly and obediently in conformity with the upbringing offered by the group into which one was born. I will find then that my own group is the most awesome adversary I must conquer to win my fight. The contrast between the ease of swimming with the stream and the difficulty of changing sides is the secret of that hold which my natural group has over me; it is the secret of my dependence on my group.

If I look closely and try to write down an inventory of all those things I owe to the group to which I — for better or worse — belong, I'll end up with quite a long list. For the sake of brevity I may divide all the items on the list into four broad categories. First, the distinction I make between the **ends** worth pursuing and those that are not worth my trouble. If I happened to be born into a middle-class family, the chances are that gaining a higher education would seem to me an indispensable condition of a proper, successful, satisfying life — yet if chance made me a working-class child, the odds are that I would agree to leave school early, aiming at a job which does not necessarily call for a lengthy study, but which would allow me to 'enjoy life' right away, and later perhaps to support my family. And so I take from my group the purpose to which I should apply my capacity for 'free choice'. Second, the **means** I use in pursuing whatever end my group has taught me to pursue. These means are also supplied by the group, and once supplied they form my 'private capital', which I can use in my efforts: the speech and the 'body language' with which I communicate my intentions to others, the intensity with which I apply myself to some ends as distinct from others, and — in general — the forms of conduct considered appropriate to the task in hand. Third, the criteria of **relevance**, the art of distinguishing between things or people relevant and irrelevant to the project I set out to complete. My group guides me to set apart my allies from my enemies or rivals as well as from those who are neither, and whom I may therefore leave out of the account, disregard and treat with disdain. Last but not least, my 'map of the world' — things charted on my map as against such things as may be visible on other people's maps but on my map are represented only by blank spaces. Among other roles such a map plays in my life, it selects the set of conceivable life itineraries — the set of realistic **life-projects** — suitable for 'people like me'. All in all, I owe to my group quite a lot; all that enormous knowledge which helps me through the day and without which I would be totally unable to conduct my daily business.

In most cases, as a matter of fact, I am not aware that I possess all that knowledge. If asked, for example, what the code is through which I communicate with other people and decipher the meaning of their actions towards me, I would, in all probability, be taken aback; I probably would not quite understand what I had been asked to do, and when I did comprehend the question, I would not be able to explain that code (much as I am incapable of explaining the simplest rules of grammar, while using the language they guide competently, fluently and with little difficulty). All the same, the knowledge required to fight my way through daily tasks and challenges is somewhere within me. I somehow have it at my disposal, if not in the form of *rules* I can recite, then as a set of practical *skills* I use effortlessly day by day throughout my life.

It is thanks to such knowledge that I feel secure and need not look far for the right thing to do. If I am in command of all that knowledge without in fact being aware of it, it is because I acquired most of its basic precepts in my early childhood, time of which one does not remember much. And so I can say little, if anything, about the way I acquired that knowledge, dipping into my own experience or personal recollections. It is precisely thanks to this forgetting of my origins that my knowledge is so well settled, that it has such a powerful grip over me, that I take it for granted as the 'natural' thing and seldom feel like questioning it. To find out how the knowledge of everyday life is in fact produced and then 'handed in' by the group, I need to consult results of research conducted by professional psychologists and sociologists. When I consult them, I find the results are often disturbing. What seemed to be obvious, evident, and natural is now revealed as a collection of beliefs which have no more than the authority of one group among many to stand on.

Perhaps no one has contributed more to our understanding of this **internalization** of group standards than the American social psychologist **George Herbert Mead**. To describe the process of acquisition of the essential skills of social life the concepts he coined are mainly used. Most famous among these are the concepts of **I and Me**, which refer to the duality of the self, to its split into two: an external part (more exactly, a part that is seen by the person as coming from outside, from the society which surrounds it, in the form of demands to be met and patterns to be followed), the 'Me' of the self, and another part, the 'I', which is the self's inner core, from where those external, social demands and expectations are scrutinized, assessed, taken stock of and ultimately spelled out. The role played by the group in shaping the self is accomplished through the 'Me' part. Children learn that they are looked upon, evaluated, chastised, prompted to behave in a particular way, pushed into line if they depart from the required way. This experience sediments in the child's growing self as an image of the *expectations* the others have of him or her. They — the others — obviously have a way of distinguishing between a proper and an improper conduct. They approve of the proper behaviour and punish the wrong one as a *deviation* from the norm. Memories of rewarded and penalized actions blend gradually into the unconscious understanding of the *rule* — of what is and what is not expected — into the 'Me', which is nothing other than the self's image of the others' image of itself. Moreover, the 'others' are not just any others who happen to be around. From the multitude of people with whom the child comes into contact, some are picked up by the self as *significant others* — those whose evaluations and responses count more than anybody else's, being more persistently or more poignantly felt, and hence more effective.

From what has been said so far a wrong conclusion may be drawn, that the development of the self through learning and training is a passive process; that it is the others and only they who do the job, that the child is filled with instructions and — with the help of stick or carrot — cajoled, pressed and drilled into following them obediently. The truth of the matter is, however, different. The self develops in an interaction between the child and its environment. Activity and initiative mark both sides of the interaction. It could hardly be otherwise. One of the first discoveries every child must make is that the 'others' differ among themselves. They rarely see eye to eye, they give commands which clash with each other and cannot be obeyed at the same time. In many cases, satisfying one command cannot but mean defying another. One of the first skills the child must learn is to discriminate and select, which cannot be acquired unless supported by the ability to resist and withstand pressure, take a stand, act against at least some of the external forces. In other words, the child learns to *choose* and to take *responsibility* for his or her own action. The 'I' part of the self represents precisely these abilities. Because of the contradictory and inconsistent content of the 'Me' (contradictory signals about the expectations of various significant others), the 'I' must stand aside, at a distance, look at the external pressures internalized in the 'Me' as if from outside; scan them, classify and evaluate. In the end, it is the 'I' which makes the choice and thus becomes the true, rightful 'author' of the ensuing action. The stronger the 'I', the more *autonomous* becomes the *personality* of the child. The strength of the 'I' expresses itself in the persons's ability and readiness to put the social pressures internalized in the 'Me' to the test, check their true power and their limits, challenge them — and bear the consequences.

A crucial task in the separation of the 'I' from the 'Me' (that is, in the emergent ability of the self to visualize, scrutinize and monitor the demands of the significant others) is performed by the child's activity of *role playing*. By playfully assuming the roles of the others, for instance the father or mother, and experimenting with their behaviour (including their conduct towards the child itself), the child learns the art of looking at action as at an *assumed* role, something one can do or not do; action means doing what the situation requires, and it may change with the situation. This somebody, who acts, is not truly me — not the 'I'. As children grow and their knowledge of various roles accumulates, they may engage in *games*, which, unlike the playing, include the element of cooperation and coordination with other role players. Here the child experiments with the art most central to a truly autonomous self: that of selecting the appropriate course of action in response to the action of others and to lure or force the others to act as one would wish them to. Through play and games, the child simultaneously acquires habits and skills instilled by the social world outside, and the ability to act in that world as a free — an autonomous and responsible — person. In the course of this acquisition, a child develops the peculiar ambiguous attitude which we all know well; *having* a self (looking at one's own behaviour as if from outside, praising it or disapproving of it, attempting to control and, if necessary, correct it), and *being* a self (asking myself, 'what am I really like?' and 'Who am I?', occasionally rebelling against a model other people try to impose upon my life, and striving instead to achieve what I think of as 'the authentic life', life conforming to my true identity). I experience the contradiction between freedom and dependence as an inner conflict between what I wish to do and what I feel obliged to do because of what the significant others have made, or intend to make, of me.

The significant others do not mould the child's self out of nothing; rather, they impress their image on the 'natural' (pre-social or, more precisely, pre-educational) predispositions of the child. Though such natural predispositions — *instincts* or *drives* — play on the whole a lesser role in human life than in the life of the other animals, they are still present in the biological endowment of each newly born human being. What instincts there are, is a moot question. The scholars differ in their opinions, and their views range from an attempt to explain most of the ostensibly socially induced conduct by biological determinants, to the belief in the almost unlimited potential of the social processing of human behaviour. Still, most scholars would support the claim of a society to its right to set and enforce standards of acceptable behaviour, as well as the argument which backs up this claim: that socially administered training is indispensable because the natural predispositions of men make cohabitation either impossible or unacceptably coarse and dangerous. Most scholars agree that the pressure of some natural drives is particularly powerful and hence must be dealt with, one way or the other, by any human group. *Sexual* and *aggressive* drives are most often named as those which groups may omit to control only at their peril. Scholars point out that were such drives given a free rein, they would result in conflicts of an intensity no group could bear and render social life all but impossible.

All surviving groups must have developed, so we are told, effective ways of taming, bridling, suppressing or otherwise controlling manifestations of such drives. **Sigmund Freud**, the founder of **psychoanalysis**, suggested that the whole process of self-development and the social organization of human groups may be interpreted in the light of the need, and the practical effort required, to control the expression of socially dangerous drives, particularly the sexual and the aggressive instincts. Freud suggested that the instincts are never annihilated; they cannot be destroyed, they can only be 'repressed', driven into the subconscious. What keeps them in that limbo is the **superego**, the internalized knowledge of demands and pressures exerted by the group. The superego has been metaphorically described by Freud as a 'garrison left in a conquered city' by the victorious army of society, in order to keep the suppressed instincts — the subconscious — in permanent obedience. The **ego** itself is hence permanently suspended between two powers: the instincts which have been driven into the subconscious yet remain potent and rebellious, and the superego (akin to Mead's 'Me'), which presses the ego (akin to Mead's 'I') to keep the drives subconscious and prevent their escape from confinement. **Norbert Elias**, the German-British sociologist who followed up Freud's hypotheses with comprehensive historical research, has suggested that the experience of the self we all have arises precisely from such double pressure to which we are all exposed. Our previously mentioned ambiguous attitude towards out respective selves is the result of the ambivalent position in which the two pressures, acting in opposite directions, cast us. Living in a group, *I* have to control *myself*. The self is something to be controlled, and I am the one to control it . . .

That all societies control the natural predispositions of their members and strain to contain the range of permissible interactions is beyond question. What is less certain is whether only the morbid, anti-social aspects of the natural endowment are suppressed in the process (though this is exactly what the powers speaking in the name of society aver). As far as we know, there is no conclusive evidence that human beings are naturally aggressive and therefore must be bridled and tamed. What tends to be interpreted as the outburst of natural aggression is more often than not an outcome of callousness or hatred — both attitudes traceable to their social rather than genetic origin. In other words, while it is true that groups train and control the conduct of their members, it does not necessarily follow that they make such conduct more humane and moral. It only means that, as a result of this drilling and surveillance and correcting, the conduct better conforms to the patterns recognized as proper for a given kind of social group and enforced by it.

The processes of the 'I' and 'Me' formation, of the suppression of instincts and the production of the superego, are often given the name of **socialization**. I have been socialized (that is, transformed into a being capable of living in society) inasmuch as I have been made, through internalizing social pressures, fit to live and act in a group; inasmuch as I have acquired the skills to behave in the way society allows, and thus to be 'free', to bear the responsibility for my action. Those significant others who played such an important role in the acquisition of these skills may therefore be seen as the socializing agents. But who are they? We have seen that the force which truly operates in the development of the self is the child's *image* of the intentions and expectations other people have, not necessarily the intentions and expectations they themselves entertain; and that the child itself performs the selection of significant others from among the many persons who appear within its vision. True, the child's freedom to select is not complete; some 'others' may force their way into the child's world more effectively than other 'others', and interfere with the selection. And yet while growing in a world populated by groups acting at cross purposes and pursuing different modes of life, the child can hardly avoid choosing; if the demands of others are contradictory and cannot be met at the same time, some of them must be paid more attention than others and so assigned more significance.

The need to assign significance (relevance) *differentially* is not confined to the plight of the child. You and I experience this need virtually daily. Day by day I must select between the demands of family, friends or bosses, each wishing me to do something at the same time. I have to risk the displeasure of some friends whom I cherish and respect in order to placate some others whom I like equally strongly. Whenever I express political views, I can be pretty sure that some people I know and care about would not like them and would bear a grudge against me for expressing them. There is little I can do to ward off such unpleasant consequences of my choices. Assigning relevance means, unavoidably, assigning irrelevance; selecting some people as significant means, inescapably, proclaiming someone else insignificant, or at least less significant. This very often means risking someone's resentment. The risk grows with the degree to which the environment in which I live is **heterogeneous** — conflict-ridden, split into groups of diverging ideals and modes of life.

Making a selection of significant others in such an environment means choosing one group among many as my **reference group**; a group against which I measure my own behaviour, which I accept as the standard for my whole life or a particular aspect of life. From what I know of the reference group of my choice, I will evaluate my behaviour and draw conclusions about its worthiness, its quality. I will derive from the knowledge the comforting feeling that what I am doing is right, or the unpleasant awareness that my action should have been different from what it was. I will try to follow the example of the reference group in the way I speak, in the words I use, in the way I dress. I will try to learn from the group whether and in what circumstances to be bold or irreverent, and when to go along obediently with the shared standards. From the image I hold of my reference group I will draw advice concerning the things which are worth my attention and such as are beneath me. All this I will do as if I sought the approval of my reference group; as if I wished to obtain its acceptance of me as its member, as 'one of them', its satisfaction with my style of life; as if I were trying to avoid the harsh measures the reference group may apply to bring me into line or retaliate for my rule-breaking.

And yet it is by and large *my* selection and analyses, conclusions and actions which make the reference group such a potent agent in shaping my conduct. Often the groups themselves are blissfully unaware of my attention, of my efforts to imitate what I think is their mode of life and apply what I think is their standards. Some of the groups, to be sure, may be justly called **normative reference groups** — as they do indeed, at least on occasion, set the norms for my conduct, watch what I do and thus are in a position to 'normatively influence' my actions by rewarding or punishing them, confirming or correcting. Particularly prominent among such groups are the family, friends in whose company I spend a large part of my time, my teachers, my superiors in the place of my work, my neighbors whom I cannot avoid meeting frequently and from whom I cannot easily hide. Being in a position to respond to my action does not make them, however, automatically my reference groups. They become such only when selected by me — when I respond to their attention with assigning them significance, when I care for their wardenship. I may still disregard their pressure (even if at my own peril) and choose to follow the standards they condemn. I may, for instance, deliberately defy my neighbours' ideas about the proper design of front gardens, or about the kind of people one should receive at home and the time of the day they should be received. I may also challenge my friends' dislike of overdoing the study and their preference for taking it easy as far as one's duties are concerned. I may 'play it cool' when deep involvement and passion are called for by the group. In order to exercise their normative influence, even the normative reference groups therefore need my consent to treat them as my reference groups and, for one reason or another, to refrain from resisting their pressure, to conform to their demands.

My decision to be bound is all the more in evidence in the case of **comparative reference groups** — groups of which I am not a member, as I remain, so to speak, beyond the reach. I see the comparative groups without being seen by them. Assigning relevance is in this case one-sided: I consider their actions and standards significant, while they hardly pay any attention to my existence. Because of the distance between us, they are often physically incapable of invigilating and evaluating my actions; for that reason they cannot punish me for my deviation, but neither can they reward me for my conformity. Since, thanks to the mass media and television in particular, all of us are more and more exposed to the flood of information about the diverse ways of life, everything points to the increasing role of comparative reference groups in shaping contemporary selves. The mass media transmit information about reigning

11

fashions and latest styles with enormous speed, and reach the most distant corners of the world. By the same token, they also stamp authority on the patterns they make visually accessible: surely modes of life that deserve to be shown on such media and to be watched by millions of people around the world are worth consideration and, if possible, imitation . . . .

I believe our discussion so far has conveyed the right impression that the process of socialization is not confined to the childhood experience. In fact, it never ends; it goes on throughout one's life, always bringing freedom and dependence into a complex interaction with each other. Sociologists sometimes speak of the **secondary socialization**, to distinguish the continuous transformation of the self which takes place in later life from the internalization of elementary social skills in childhood. They focus attention on situations in which the insufficiency or inadequacy of the former — the **primary** — socialization happens to be dramatically exposed and sharply brought into relief: when, for instance, a person emigrates to a distant country with strange customs and unfamiliar language, and so must not only acquire new skills, but unlearn the old ones which have now turned into a handicap; or when a person brought up in remote countryside migrates to a large city and feels lost and helpless among the dense traffic, rushing crowds and the indifference of passers-by and neighbours. It has been suggested that radical changes of this kind are likely to cause acute anxiety and, indeed, high incidence of nervous breakdowns and even mental ailments. It has also been pointed out that a situation of secondary socialization with equally dramatic consequences may be brought about by the change in external social conditions, rather than mobility of the individual. Sudden economic depression, the onset of mass unemployment, outbreak of war, destruction of life savings by rampant inflation, loss of security through withdrawal of the right to a benefit or on the contrary a rapid rise in prosperity and opportunities for improvement, opening up new, unthought-of possibilities — all provide examples of such cases. They all 'invalidate' the achievements of preceding socialization and require a radical restructuring of one's behaviour, which in its turn calls for new skills and new knowledge.

Examples of both kinds help us to visualize the problems brought about by secondary socialization, as they present them in their sharpest and most acute form. Yet in a less spectacular mode each of us confronts the secondary socialization problems virtually daily; most certainly we experience them whenever we change a school, go to university or leave it, take up a new job, change from being a single to a married person, acquire a house of our own, move house, become parents, turn into old-age pensioners, and so on. It is perhaps better to think of socialization as a continuing process, rather than to split it into two separate stages. The dialectics of freedom and dependence starts at birth and ends only with death.

The balance between the two partners in this continuous dialectical relationship shifts, however. In early childhood there is little, if any, freedom to choose the group one is dependent on. One is born into a particular family, locality, neighbourhood, class or country. One is assumed, without being asked, to be a member of a particular nation or one of the two socially accepted sexes. With age (that means with a growing collection of skills and resources of action) the choice widens; some dependencies may be challenged and rejected, others sought and assumed voluntarily. And yet freedom is never complete. Remember that all of us tend to become determined by our own past actions; because of them, we find ourselves at every moment in a position in which some choices, however attractive, are unattainable, while the costs of change are exorbitant and off-putting. There is too much to be 'de-learned', too many habits to be forgotten. The skills and resources which could be acquired only at an earlier stage were neglected at that time, and now it is too late to make up for the lost opportunity. By and large, we find the feasibility and the likelihood of a 'new break' increasingly remote beyond a certain age.

Neither is the balance the same for all human beings. Remember the role which the available resources play in making choice a viable, realistic proposition. Remember too the role of the 'horizons' set by the original social location for later life-projects and such ends as one may find attractive enough to pursue. It is enough to consider the role of these two factors, to understand that while all people are free and cannot but be free (that is, they are bound to take responsibility for whatever they do), some are more free than others: their horizons (range of choice) are wider, and once they have made up their minds as to the kind of life-project they wish to pursue, they have most of the resources (money, connections, education, refined speech habits, etc) such a project requires; they are freer than others to desire, to act upon their wishes, and to achieve the results they want.

We can say that the ratio between freedom and dependence is an indicator of the relative position a person, or a whole category of persons, occupies in society. What we call privilege appears, under closer scrutiny, a higher degree of freedom and a lesser degree of dependence. The obverse is true for those who bear the name of disprivileged.

2. Individual and Society in Eighteenth and Nineteenth Century Views of Life: An Example of Philosophical Sociology

Georg Simmel

1. Individual life as the basis of the conflict between individual and society

The really practical problem of society is the relation between its forces and forms and the individual's own life. The question is not whether society exists only in the individuals or also outside of them. For even if we attribute "life," properly speaking, only to individuals, and identify the life of society with that of its individual members, we must still admit the existence of conflict between the two. One reason for this conflict is the fact that, in the individuals themselves, social elements fuse into the particular phenomenon called "society." "Society" develops its own vehicles and organs by whose claims and commands the individual is confronted as by an alien party. A second reason results from another aspect of the inherency of society in the individual. For man has the capacity to decompose himself into parts and to feel any one of these as his proper self. Yet each part may collide with any other and may struggle for the dominion over the individual's actions. This capacity places man, insofar as he feels himself to be a social being, into an often contradictory relation with those among his impulses and interests that are *not* preempted by his social character. In other words, the conflict between society and individual is continued in the individual himself as the conflict among his component parts. Thus, it seems to me, the basic struggle between society and individual inheres in the general form of individual life. It does not derive from any single, "anti-social," individual interest.

Society strives to be a whole, an organic unit of which the individuals must be mere members. Society asks of the individual that he employ all his strength in the service of the special function which he has to exercise as a member of it; that he so modify himself as to become the most suitable vehicle for this function. Yet the drive toward unity and wholeness that is characteristic of the individual himself rebels against this role. The individual strives to be rounded out in himself, not merely to help to round out society. He strives to develop his full capacities, irrespective of the shifts among them that the interest of society may ask of him. This conflict between the whole, which imposes the one-sidedness of partial function upon its elements, and the part, which itself strives to be a whole, is insoluble. No house can be built of houses, but only of specially formed stones; no tree can grow from trees, but only from differentiated cells.

2. Individual egoism vs. individual self-perfection as an objective value

The formulation presented seems to me to describe the contrast between the two parties much more comprehensively than does its customary reduction to the

Reprinted with the permission of The Free Press, an imprint of Simon & Schuster from *THE SOCIOLOGY OF GEROG SIMMEL* translated and edited by Kurt H. Wolff. Copyright © 1950, copyright renewed 1978 by The Free Press.

egoism-altruism dichotomy. On the one hand, the individual's striving for wholeness appears as egoism, which is contrasted with the altruism of his ordering himself into society as a selectivity formed social member of it. Yet on the other hand, the very quest of society is an egoism that does violence to the individual for the benefit and utility of the many, and that often makes for an extremely one-sided individual specialization, and even atrophy. Finally, the individual's urge toward self-perfection is not necessarily an expression of egoism. It may also be an objective ideal whose goal is by no means success in terms of happiness and narrowly personal interests but a super-personal value realized in the personality.

What has just been suggested — and what will be elaborated presently — appears to me to exemplify a very significant stage in the development of cultural-philosophical consciousness. It also throws new light on the ethics of the individual and, indirectly, on the ethics of society. It is popularly held that all intentions which do not break through the orbit of the individual existence and interest are of an egoistic nature, and that egoism is overcome only when concern shifts toward the welfare of the Thou or of society. Yet it is already some time that a deeper reflection on the values of life has ascertained a third alternative, most impressively perhaps in the figures of Goethe and Nietzsche (though not in any abstract formula). It is the possibility that the perfection of the individual as such constitutes an objective value, quite irrespective of its significance for any other individuals, or in merely accidental connection with it. This value, moreover, may exist in utter disregard for the happiness or unhappiness of this individual himself, or may even be in conflict with them. What a person represents in terms of strength, nobility of character, achievement, or harmony of life, is very often quite unrelated to what he or others "get out" of these qualities. All that can be said about them is that the world is enriched by the existence in it of a valuable human being who is perfect in himself. Certainly, his value often consists in his practical devotion to other individuals or groups; but to limit it to this would be to proceed by an arbitrary moralistic dogma. For, beauty and perfection of life, the working upon oneself, the passionate efforts to obtain ideal goods, do not always result in happiness. These efforts and aims are inspired by certain world values, and may have no other effect than to create and maintain a particular attitude in the individual consciousness.

Countless times, the individual craves situations, events, insights, achievements, in whose particular existence or general nature he simply sees ultimately satisfactory aims. Occasionally the content of such cravings may be the improvement or well-being of others. But not necessarily: the aim is striven after for the sake of its own realization; and, therefore, to sacrifice others or even oneself may not be too high a price. "*Fiat justitia, pereat mundus*"; the fulfilment of divine will merely because it is divine; the fanaticism of the artist, completion of whose work makes him forget any other consideration, altruistic or egoistic; the political idealist's enthusiasm for a constitutional reform that renders him entirely indifferent to the question of how the citizens would fare under it — these are examples of purely objective valuations that permeate even the most trivial contents. The acting individual feels himself to be only the object or executor — who at bottom is accidental — of the task his cause puts to him. The passion for this cause is as little concerned with the I, Thou, or society as the value of the state of the world can be measured in terms of the world's pleasure or suffering (although it can, of course, be partly so measured). Yet, evidently, the claims made by individuals or groups, insofar as they, too, are agents of ultimate values, do not necessarily coincide with the individual's striving after such objective values. Particularly if he tries to realize a value either in himself or in an accomplishment that is unappreciated socially, the super-egoistic nature of his procedure is not rewarded by society. Society claims the individual for itself. It wants to make of him a form that it can incorporate into its own structure. And this societal claim is often so incompatible with the claim imposed on the individual by his striving after an objective value, as only a purely egoistic claim can be incompatible with a purely social one.

3. The social vs. the human

The stage reached by the interpretation presented certainly goes beyond the customary contrast between egoism and altruism, as I have already pointed out. But even this interpretation cannot resolve the basic contrast between individual and society. And a related contrast that deals with the same content but springs from another ultimate world view is suggested by the modern analysis of certain sociological concepts.

Society — and its representative in the individual, social-ethical conscience — very often imposes a specialization upon him. I have already called attention to the fact that this specialization not only leaves undeveloped, or destroys, his harmonious wholeness. What is more, it often foists contents on the individual that are wholly inimical to the qualities usually called general-human. Nietzsche seems to have been the first to feel, with fundamental distinctness, the difference between the interest of humanity, of mankind, and the interest of society. Society is but one of the forms in which mankind shapes the contents of its life, but it is neither essential to all forms nor is it the only one in which human development is realized. All purely objective realms in which we are involved in whatever way — logical cognition or metaphysical imagination, the beauty of life or its image in the sovereignty of art, the realms of religion or of nature — none of these, to the extent to which they become our intimate possessions, has intrinsically and essentially anything whatever to do with "society." The human values that are measured by our greater or smaller stakes in these ideal realms have a merely accidental relation to social values, however often they intersect with them.

On the other hand, purely personal qualities — strength, beauty, depth of thought, greatness of conviction, kindness, nobility of character, courage, purity of heart — have their autonomous significance which likewise is entirely independent of their social entanglements. They are values of human existence. As such they are profoundly different from social values, which always rest upon the individual's *effects*. At the same time, they certainly are elements, both as effects and causes, of the social process. But this is only one side of their significance — the other is the intrinsic fact of their existence in the personality. For Nietzsche, this, strictly speaking, *immediate* existence of man is the criterion by which the level of mankind must be gauged at any given moment. For him, all social institutions, all giving and receiving by which the individual becomes a social being, are mere preconditions or consequences of his own nature. It is by virtue of this intrinsic nature that he constitutes a stage in the development of mankind.

17

Yet utilitarian-social valuation does not entirely depend on this intrinsic nature. It also depends on other individuals' responses to it. Thus, the individual's value does not wholly reside in himself: part of it he receives as the reflection of processes and creations in which his own nature has fused with beings and circumstances outside of him. It is on the basis of this relation between him and others that ethics (above all, Kantian ethics) has shifted the ground on which to appraise man, from his deeds to his attitude. Our value lies in our good will — a certain quality of the ultimate springs of our action that must be left undefined. It lies behind all appearance of our actions which, along with the effects they may have, are its mere consequences. They sometimes express it correctly, sometimes distort it — since they are mere "phenomena," they have but an accidental relationship to this fundamental value, good will itself.

Kant's position was expanded, or conceived more profoundly, by Nietzsche. He translated the Kantian contrast between attitude and success of external action (which already had freed the value of the individual from its social dependence) into the contrast between the existence and the effect of man in general. For Nietzsche, it is the qualitative *being* of the personality which marks the stage that the development of mankind has reached; it is the highest exemplars of a given time that carry humanity beyond its past. Thus Nietzsche overcame the limitations of merely social existence, as well as the valuation of man in terms of his sheer effects. It thus is not only quantitatively that mankind is more than society. Mankind is not simply the sum of all societies: it is an entirely different synthesis of the same elements that in other syntheses result in societies. Mankind and societies are two different vantage points, as it were, from which the individual can be viewed. They measure him by different standards, and their claims on him may be in violent conflict. What ties us to mankind and what we may contribute to the development of mankind — religious and scientific contributions, inter-family and international interests, the aesthetic perfection of personality, and purely objective production that aims at no "utility" — all this, of course, may on occasion also help develop the historical society of which we are members. But, essentially, it is rooted in claims that go far beyond any given society and that serve the elevation and objective enrichment of the type "man" itself. They may even be in pointed conflict with the more specific claims of the group that for any given man represents "his society."

In many other respects, however, society promotes a leveling of its members. It creates an average and makes it extremely difficult for its members to go beyond this average merely through the individual excellence in the quantity or quality of life. Society requires the individual to differentiate himself from the humanly general, but forbids him to stand out from the socially general. The individual is thus doubly oppressed by the standards of society: he may not transcend them either in a more general or in a more individual direction. In recent historical periods, these conflicts into which he falls with his political group, with his family, with his economic association, with his party, with his religious community, etc., have eventually become sublimated into the abstract need, as it were, for individual freedom. This is the general category that came to cover what was common in the various complaints and self-assertions of the individual against society.

3. Human Interdependencies — Problems of Social Bonds

Norbert Elias

Affective bonds

The concept of figuration puts the problem of human interdependencies into the very heart of sociological theory. What makes people bonded to and dependent on each other? This problem is too wide-ranging and many-sided to be treated thoroughly within the confines of this book. People's dependencies on each other are obviously not always the same in all societies at different stages of development. We can, however, try to focus on one or two universal forms of dependence, and to show briefly how people's interdependencies change as societies become increasingly differentiated and stratified.

The opinion is widely held that man's biological characteristics — in contrast to those of subhuman forms of life — play no part in the formation of societies. For example, one type of sociological theory postulates that human norms are essential in integrating society. In fact, this makes it seem as though man's biological equipment made no contribution towards his dependence on other people. Norms are unquestionably not biologically fixed. We have already shown how it is a human characteristic that the grip of inborn forms of behaviour can be relaxed, enabling human societies to develop without mankind developing as a biological species. This too could be taken to mean that man's biological endowments play no part in the formation of his social bonds. If it is simply taken for granted — as it is by Talcott Parsons[1] — that human personality structure is independent of social structure, then it is not surprising that the fact that the human body is a source of 'motivating energies', that it can serve as a 'reward object' yielding 'gratification', is taken as further evidence of the independence of the individual. Parsons is not the only theoretician to take the privacy and individuality of every person's bodily sensations as evidence that man is by nature in effect a self-contained and solitary being. In this case, the conception of man as a lone individual being is so strong that it is often forgotten that each person's striving for gratification is directed towards other people from the very outset. Nor is gratification itself derived entirely from one's own body — it depends a great deal on other people too. Indeed this is one of the universal interdependencies which bind people together.

Moreover, it would certainly be wrong to imagine that this elementary and biologically based dependence on others is confined to the satisfaction of *sexual* needs. There is a profusion of evidence to show that over and above the immediate gratification of their sexual needs, people look to others for the fulfilment of a whole gamut of emotional needs. It is unnecessary here to delve into the question of whether the remarkably diverse and subtle emotional bonds which people enter into with each other are

Norbert Elias: 'Human Interdependencies — Problems of Social Bonds' from *WHAT IS SOCIOLOGY?*, translated by Stephen Mennell and Grace Morrissey (Hutchinson, 1970), pp. 134–157.

libidinous in origin. There is good reason to believe that people need to be emotionally stimulated by other people even when their sexual valencies are firmly connected in a lasting relationship. This can best be conveyed by picturing a person as having many valencies at any given time. All these are directed towards other people, and some will already be firmly connected with them. But other valencies will be free and open, searching for people with whom to form linkages and bonds. The concept of open emotional valencies which are directed towards other people helps towards replacing the image of man as 'Homo clausus' with that of 'open people'.[2]

This can be illustrated by a simple example. Think of a person who has lost someone he loves through death. This example demonstrates how necessary it is to reorganize our perception if we are to understand the durability typical of elementary emotional bonds between people. When we speak of sexual bonds we are singling out and emphasizing a central but relatively brief and transitory aspect of human relationships. The possibility of emotional durability above and beyond the sexual act is characteristic of human emotional bonds. So is the possibility of there being very strong emotional bonds of many kinds without any sexual overtones.

The categories which were appropriate to research into relatively lower levels of integration are inadequate for research into the human and social level of integration. When a beloved person dies, it does not mean that something has happened in the social 'outside world' of the survivor, which acts as an external cause on his 'inner self'; it will not even do to say that something happened 'there' of which the effect is felt 'here'. Such categories cannot express the emotional relationship between the survivor and the person he loved. The latter's death means that the survivor has lost a part of himself. One of the valencies in the figuration of his attached and unattached valencies had become fixed to the other person. Now that person is dead. An integral part of his self, his 'I-and-we' images, has been broken off.

The valency which had become attached to the other person is torn out. As a result, the particular figuration of all the survivor's valencies is altered and the balance of his whole web of personal relationships is changed. His relationship with another person who had previously occupied only a marginal place in the figuration of his valencies may become much warmer than before. There may be some cooling-off in his relations with others who performed a special function for him in his relationship with the dead person, perhaps by acting as catalysts or as benevolent bystanders. So it would be true to say that when a much-loved person dies, the total figuration of the survivor's valencies and the whole balance of his web of relationships will be changed.

The example draws attention back to everyone's fundamental directedness to other people. In subhuman society this directedness manifests itself in more or less stereotyped and rigid modes of behaviour. In human society these have been lost, but the directedness itself has never disappeared — that is, the deeply-rooted emotional need of every human being for the society of other members of his species. Sexuality is only the strongest, most demonstrative manifestation of this need. Biologically determined instincts are still present, but they can be greatly modified by learning, experience, and the processes of sublimation. There is little justification for regarding the biological constitution of man as something which is relevant only to the 'individual', not to 'society' and to which accordingly no attention need be paid in the study of sociology.

Airing such problems is chiefly important in helping to settle the question of what binds people to each other and forms the foundation of their interdependence. Sociologists are accustomed to looking at human bonds mainly from the 'they' perspective. For example, it is possible to do as Durkheim did and view human bonds chiefly in the context of increasing job specialization, which makes people more and more dependent on each other. These insights are important, but the bonds to which they refer are still merely economic. It is impossible, however, to deal adequately with the problem of people's social bonds, especially their emotional ones, if only relatively impersonal interdependencies are taken into account. In the realm of sociological theory a fuller picture can be gained only by including personal interdependencies, and above all emotional bonds between people, as agents which knit society together.

The significance of these personal aspects of human bonds may not be entirely clear if the only illustration used is that of a single person's nexus of relationships. Nevertheless, it is essential to return to this one person's web of personal relationships, to see how it appears from his point of view — how it feels from the 'I' perspective. This alone makes it possible to understand a whole range of more widely spreading interdependencies based on personal emotional bonds. In small social units containing comparatively few people, every single person's web of personal relationships may include all the other people in the unit. The figuration of each person's attached and unattached valencies will certainly differ from that of everyone else. Yet as long as the unit is small, the figuration will include the whole tribe. As social units become bigger and more stratified, new forms of emotional bond will be found. As well as interpersonal bonds there will be bonds connecting people to the symbols of larger units, to coats of arms, to flags and to emotionally-charged concepts.

In this way, people are emotionally bound together through the medium of symbols. This kind of bond is no less significant for human interdependence than the bonds created, as mentioned above, by growing specialization. The emotional valencies which bind people together, whether directly by face-to-face relationships or indirectly by their attachment to common symbols, form a separate level of bonds. Blended with other more impersonal types of bond, they underlie the extended 'I-and-we' consciousness, which hitherto has always seemed indispensable in binding together not only small tribes but large social units like nation-states encompassing many millions of people. People's attachment to such large social units is often as intense as their attachment to a person they love. The individual who has formed such a bond will be as deeply affected when the social unit to which he is devoted is conquered or destroyed, debased or humiliated, as when a beloved person dies. One of the biggest gaps in the older theories in contemporary sociology is that they mostly investigated the 'they' perspectives of society, hardly ever using precise conceptual tools to investigate the 'I-and-we' perspectives.

Political and economic bonds

Most sociological statements today refer primarily to societies which are organized as states or tribes. Yet it is hardly ever justifiable to select these particular types of society as the basis for everything that is said about 'society' or social systems *in general*. Why not choose the village or the town as a model of society, or (as was often done in the nineteenth century) human society as a whole? What makes complexes like states and tribes so important that it is almost taken for granted that they are what is meant whenever reference is made to social 'wholes'?

In trying to answer such questions, the first point to make is that states and tribes are to a considerable extent objects of common identification — objects to which many individual valencies are bonded. Yet why do emotional bonds to state-societies — which nowadays are nation-states — take priority over bonds to other figurations? At other stages of social development, towns, tribes or even villages have taken priority in the same way. What are the common features of the various figurations which at different stages of development have bound individuals to them by this type of predominating emotional bond?

First of all, these units all seem to have exercised comparatively strict control over the use of physical violence in relationships between their members. At the same time, they have allowed, and often encouraged, their members to use physical violence against non-members. *To date, sociology has lacked any clear conception of the common features of this type of solidaristic grouping at different levels of social development.* Its function is obvious: it knits people together for common purposes — the common defence of their lives, the survival of their group in the face of attacks by other groups and, for a variety of reasons, attacks in common on other groups. Thus the primary function of such an alliance is either physically to wipe out other people or to protect its own members from being physically wiped out. Since the potential of such units for attack is inseparable from their potential for defence, they may be called 'attack-and-defence units' or 'survival units'. At the present stage of social development they take the form of nation-states. In the future they may be amalgamations of several former nation-states.[3] In the past they were represented by city-states or the inhabitants of a stronghold. Size and structure vary: the function remains the same. At every stage of development, wherever people have been bound and integrated into units for attack and defence, this bond has been stressed above all others. This survival function, involving the use of physical force against others, creates interdependencies of a particular kind. It plays a part in the figurations people form, perhaps no greater but also no more negligible than 'occupational' bonds. Though it cannot be reduced to a function of 'economics', neither is it separable from it.

Given the range of his experiences, a nineteenth-century European might be expected to perceive the immediate danger of people starving to death as a result of unequal distribution of power within a state, while the risk of being subjugated or killed by an external enemy might seem to him only marginal. So Marx was a man typical of his age in perceiving, albeit more sharply and clearly than anyone before him, the interdependencies arising out of the division of labour in the production of means of subsistence and other goods. In consequence he was also able to grasp more clearly than his predecessors the structure of the conflict associated with the monopoly of the means of production by certain groups. Yet it was equally typical that he should fail to perceive that the danger of one group of people being subjugated or physically annihilated by another was highly significant as a basis for certain kinds of integration and interdependence. Marx observed a particular stage in the development of industrial society. Corresponding to this stage was his belief that the functions and power resources of the state could be explained as deriving from the functions and power resources of the bourgeois entrepreneurial groups. Ultimately he believed that they derive also from the class interests of those social groups to whom we owe the meaning of the concepts of 'the economy' and 'economics'. For at the time Marx was writing it was still a relatively new idea that certain forms of interdependence — those most closely connected with the specialized business activities of the entrepreneurial strata — possessed laws of their own and were to some extent autonomous with respect to all other social activities. This sphere of activity was described by the then relatively new term 'the economy'. On the one hand, the recognition of its autonomy was associated with the development of the new science of economics. On the other hand, the theoretical exposition of the autonomy of 'economic' functional nexuses and their autonomy within the overall context of a state-society was most closely linked with the demand of the wealthy and rising English middle classes for freedom from state intervention in their own enterprises. They demanded that 'economic' laws — the free play of supply and demand — should be allowed to take their own 'natural' course.

To the rising entrepreneurial bourgeoisie, struggling to free itself from intervention by governments whose members were still drawn mainly from the pre-industrial aristocracy, it may indeed have appeared that the 'economy' possessed absolute functional autonomy from the 'state'. This idea found symbolic expression in the development of the nascent science's name. From 'political economy', symbolizing that the economic sphere is a subdivision of the political, was derived 'economics', the symbolic expression of the idea that as society develops, an independent economic sphere emerges with immanent, autonomous laws of its own. The claim of the bourgeois entrepreneurs that the 'economy' *ought* to be autonomous and free from state intervention became metamorphosed. From it developed the idea that the economy, as a sphere within the functional nexus of a state-society, actually *was* quite autonomous. This set of liberal ideas was clearly reflected in Marx's conception of the relationship between the economy and the state. It led him to think of the 'economic' sphere as an autonomous self-contained functional nexus with laws of its own, but within the functional nexus of the whole society. Both the entrepreneurial bourgeoisie and the science of economics claimed that the state obviously *ought* to be an institution for the protection of bourgeois interests. Accordingly, Marx depicted the organization of the state as though it actually did nothing but that, and had no function other than defending bourgeois economic interests. In other words, he took over an ideology derived from the bourgeois science of economics, changing its sign, so to speak, from plus to minus. From the point of view of the working class, the defence of bourgeois interests seemed pernicious; therefore the organization of the state must seem pernicious too.

Analysed more closely in the light of developmental sociology,[4] it is clear that the development of political and economic structures were two quite inseparable aspects of the development of the whole functional nexus of society. Closely associated with the development of political institutions were many processes leading to the lengthening of chains of social interdependence. Among these processes were the growing 'economic' division of labour and the superseding of limited local markets and enterprises as nodal points of the social network by much larger ones. The institutions of the state were capable of guaranteeing the safety of traders and their goods, now transported over longer and longer distances, of ensuring that contracts were fulfilled, of levying import duties to protect infant industries from foreign competition, and much besides. In their turn, the development of political institutions was closely associated with the spreading networks of trade and industry. From a sociological point of view, the development of the state and political organization and of the occupational structure were indivisible aspects of the development of one and the same functional nexus. In fact, these so-called separate 'spheres' of society are none other than the integrating and the differentiating aspects respectively in the development of the same web of interdependence. Every so often, the functional differentiation of society lurches forward, outstripping the development of the integrating and coordinating institutions of the time. In the industrialization of England, the great leap forward just before and after 1800 is an example of how processes of differentiation can overreach themselves in this way. The corresponding development of coordinating institutions was notoriously slow. This situation became intellectually enshrined in the idea that the 'economic sphere' can be regarded as the engine of all social development. However, the development of the economy without corresponding development of the state and political organization is as unthinkable as the latter without the former, since both are part of developing webs of interdependence. The conceptual separation of these two spheres, and the absolute autonomy of the respective social sciences dealing with them, are a leftover from the period defined 'ideologically' as that of economic liberalism. Sociologically speaking, that was, as we have said, *a period during which the functional differentiation of chains of interdependence outpaced the corresponding process of integration.* If, instead of the traditional model of 'spheres', one of increasing or decreasing functional differentiation and integration is used, an immediate advance is made. It leads to a sociological conception of society, displacing the extremely artificial image of society as a hotch-potch of adjacent but unconnected spheres, of which first one and then another is singled out as the true driving force behind social development.

Both the theoretical and the practical effects of correcting these habits of thought will be far-reaching. At this point we need mention just one implication. As long as the 'economic sphere' is pictured as functioning more or less autonomously in and for itself within the overall context of the state-society, social stratification is liable to be portrayed in terms of this separation of spheres. Thus stratification in industrial societies is seen in terms of social classes and their conflicts of interest, which are determined primarily by economic factors. This conception corresponds fairly accurately to the grandstand view of the strata which are themselves involved. From this perspective it appears as if their power struggles are simply about the distribution of economic chances, about the changing balance between wages and profits.

Yet here, too, closer study reveals the inadequacy of the idea that the tensions and conflicts between the two great classes in industrial society — the industrial working class and the industrial bourgeoisie — can be explained by focusing on 'economic' chances to the exclusion of all the other chances subject to dispute. When compared with what can actually be observed, this is plainly misleading. On closer examination, the problem appears to concern the distribution of power throughout the length and breadth and on every level of multi-level industrial state-societies. For example, one of its aspects is the distribution of power chances on the level of the individual factory. Which groups in factories have access to positions of command, carrying responsibility for coordination and integration? And which groups do not? People occupying the position of employer are interdependent with people in the position of worker, because of the particular functional relationship between the two positions. But their reciprocal dependencies are not the same — the power weightings are not equally distributed. Even at this level, the problem does not merely concern how the income available in the business for sharing amongst the groups occupying various positions is actually divided between them. The distribution of these 'economic' chances is itself a function of the greater balance of power — the distribution of power chances between these groups. The balance of power within an industrial concern is not, however, expressed solely in the distribution of 'economic' chances, but also through the distribution of chances for the members of one of these groups to control, command and dismiss the others in the course of their work.

Bearing in mind the distribution of power between capitalists and workers which Marx witnessed in the England of the first half of the nineteenth century, it is quite understandable that he paid almost exclusive attention to analysing the distribution of economic chances. A considerable part of the labour force was living at bare subsistence level. The workers were minimally organized at factory level and even less at the higher levels of the national state. In any case, Marx's concept of class applied to only one level. As he saw it, the only point of contact between working and capitalist classes was in the places of production; their contact was solely the result of the nature of their positions in the production process. In his day, workers and employers never met on any other level, since neither group had any effective unifying organizations on higher levels of integration in society, let alone any national or party organizations. So it was understandable that his conception of class referred only to specific groups of positions in the production process. Nor has this analysis lost its relevance as industrial societies have developed further. But now it can be seen more clearly that the analysis, though indispensable, is incomplete. Even in Marx's time, the balance of power in the factory between workers and employers was not completely self-contained; it did make some difference whether, or how far, the then agents of the state cast their weight into the scales for the benefit of one side or the other. As industrial societies have developed, the trend has been for the importance of disputes, skirmishes, compromises and settlements at the factory level to decline relative to those at higher levels of integration, notably in the most central institutions of the state, like parliament and the government.

It is therefore necessary to correct the traditional one-level conception of class seemingly based entirely on the distribution of economic chances. A conception of class is needed which takes into account the fact that functionally and organizationally interdependent disputes between workers and employers are enacted on many levels of integration other than that of the factory. They are acted out especially at the highest level of integration of a state-society. This new conception must take into account that in all the more developed societies the two organized classes are nowadays far more integrated into these state organizations than they were in Marx's day. In fact both these industrial classes have become ruling classes, because they are represented on all the various levels of integration of industrial society — on the local and regional as well as the national level. The distribution of power between the two classes is still very unequal, especially at factory level, but not as unequal as in Marx's day. And tensions of a new kind are emerging alongside those which Marx noted at a time when these social classes could still be regarded as homogeneous, one-layer social formations at factory level. These new tensions occur between the rulers and the ruled, and do not preclude tensions between people who represent the same class at different levels of integration.

The often neglected relationship of processes of integration and differentiation is very useful in studying long-term social change. These processes are not so complicated as they often appear. This is an example of how difficulties are due more to theoretical confusion than to the complexity of the subject matter itself. There is a whole range of relatively simple possibilities for analysing long-term processes of social integration and differentiation. When considering integration, one possibility is to ascertain the number of hierarchically graded levels of integration found in the societies being structurally analysed. It will be found that if different societies have the same number of levels, they will also have other structural similarities. There are equally simple methods of analysing stages of differentiation. One is to determine the number of occupations for which a society has distinct names. Of course, this source material is not always available or accessible, but many of the sources which are available have not yet been tapped.

This simple method of determining with greater precision the stage the division of labour has reached at a given time throws a curious light on what we rather one-sidedly designate 'processes of industrialization'. Compared with every kind of pre-industrial society, and especially with medieval societies, the number of occupational groups distinguished by name in industrial societies is astounding. Not only that, but the number increases at a rate unknown in earlier times. For the individual, the significance of this is that he becomes caught up in ever-lengthening chains of interdependence which for him constitute functional nexuses beyond his control. At the same time it means that, in comparison with earlier societies, power chances will be less unevenly distributed, and that the reliance of interdependent positions on each other will become relatively less one-sided and more reciprocal. Yet it also means that as functional differentiation makes people on many levels interdependent, they simultaneously become more dependent on the centre for their coordination and integration. People who have access to and who occupy coordinating and integrating positions will clearly have great power chances at their disposal. Consequently, though integrating and coordinating social positions are indispensable, one of the main problems in highly differentiated societies is how to maintain effective institutional control over them. How can it be socially guaranteed that the occupants of such positions do not to any great extent subordinate their 'it' and 'they' functions to their own purposes?

Notes

1. Talcott Parsons, 'Psychology and sociology', in John Gillin (ed.), *For a Science of Social Man*, New York, 1954, p. 84. Here Parsons establishes that 'the structure of the personality is a kind of "mirror-image" of the structure of the social object-system', and then, as a kind of warning, immediately adds that 'We should be very careful in the interpretation of these statements. They clearly do not mean that a personality as a system is simply a reflection of the social situation at the time. This would be a negation of the postulate of the independence of the personality system.' He makes no attempt to explain how the idea of personality as a mirror-image of society is to be harmonized with his postulating the independence of the individual. The two assertions simply stand side by side in Parsons's system of arguments, never really reconciled.

2. This constellation of problems is dealt with in more detail in Norbert Elias, 'Sociology and Psychiatry', in S. H. Foulkes and G. S. Prince (eds.), *Psychiatry in a Changing Society*, London, 1969, pp. 117–44.

3. This problem will remain until all former attack-and-defence units have been effectively integrated into one — mankind.

4. See Elias, *Über den Prozess der Zivilisation*, 2nd ed., Berne and Munich, 1969.

4. Social Construction Theory: Problems in the History of Sexuality

Carole S. Vance

Different degrees of social construction

The widespread use of social construction as a term and as a paradigm obscures the fact that constructionist writers have used this term in diverse ways. It is true that all reject transhistorical and transcultural definitions of sexuality and suggest instead that sexuality is mediated by historical and cultural factors. But a close reading of constructionist texts shows that social construction spans a theoretical field of what might be constructed, ranging from sexual acts, sexual identities, sexual communities, the direction of sexual desire (object choice) to sexual impulse or sexuality itself.

At minimum, all social construction approaches adopt the view that physically identical sexual acts may have varying social significance and subjective meaning depending on how they are defined and understood in different cultures and historical periods. Because a sexual act does not carry with it a universal social meaning, it follows that the relationship between sexual acts and sexual identities is not a fixed one, and it is projected from the observer's time and place to others at great peril. Cultures provide widely different categories, schemata, and labels for framing sexual and affective experiences. The relationship of sexual act and identity to sexual community is equally variable and complex. These distinctions, then, between sexual acts, identities, and communities are widely employed by constructionist writers.

A further step in social construction theory posits that even the direction [of] sexual desire itself, for example, object choice or hetero/homosexuality, is not intrinsic or inherent in the individual but is constructed. Not all constructionists take this step; for some, the direction of desire and erotic interest are fixed, although the behavioural *form* this interest takes will be constructed by prevailing cultural frames, as will the subjective experience of the individual and the social significance attached to it by others.

The most radical form of constructionist theory is willing to entertain the idea that there is no essential, undifferentiated sexual impulse, 'sex drive' or lust', which resides in the body due to physiological functioning and sensation. Sexual impulse itself is constructed by culture and history. In this case, an important constructionist question concerns the origins of these impulses, since they are no longer assumed to be intrinsic or, perhaps, even necessary. This position, of course, contrasts sharply with more middle-ground constructionist theory which implicitly accepts an inherent sexual impulse which is then constructed in terms of acts, identity, community, and object choice. The contrast between middle-ground and radical positions make it evident that

Carole S. Vance: 'Social Construction Theory: Problems in the History of Sexuality', in A. van Kooten Niekerk and T. van der Meer (eds) HOMOSEXUALITY, WHICH HOMOSEXUALITY?, (London, GMP Publishers, 1989), pp. 18–19, 21–24. Reproduced in SOCIAL AND CULTURAL FORMS OF MODERNITY, edited by R. Bocock and K. Thompson (OU Polity Press, 1992).

constructionists may well have arguments with each other, as well as with essentialists. Each degree of social construction points to different questions and assumptions, possibly to different methods, and perhaps to different answers. . . .

The instability of sexuality as a category

Because they were tied to essentialist assumptions which posited biological and physiological factors as influential in determining the contours of sexuality, sexological and biomedical paradigms of sexuality nevertheless offered one advantage: sexuality enjoyed the status of a stable, ongoing, and cohesive entity. The constructionist paradigm more flexibly admits variability in behavior and motive over time and place. But to the extent that social construction theory grants that sexual acts, identities and even desire are mediated by cultural and historical factors, the object of study — sexuality — becomes evanescent and threatens to disappear. If sexuality is constructed differently at each time and place, can we use the term in a comparatively meaningful way? . . .

Some social constructionists explicitly encourage the total deconstruction of the category of the sexual, for example, Foucault. Others have not taken this theoretical position, though it remains implicit in their work. For, if sexuality is constituted differently in different times and places, it follows that behaviors and relations seen as sexual by us (contemporary Euro-Americans) may not be by others, and vice versa. . .

The role of the body

Social construction's greatest strength lies in its violation of our folk knowledge and scientific ideologies that would frame sexuality as 'natural', determined by biology and the body. This violation makes it possible, indeed compels us to raise questions that a naturalizing discourse would obscure and hide. Social constructionists have been even-handed in this endeavor, dethroning the body in all fields — in heterosexual history as well as in lesbian and gay history. At first, we greeted this development with good cheer, happy to be rid of the historical legacy of 19th-century spermatic and ovarian economies, women's innate sexual passivity, and the endless quest to find the hormonal cause of homosexuality. Yet the virtue of social construction may also be its vice.

Has social construction theory, particularly variants which see 'sexual impulse', 'sex drive', or 'lust' as created, made no room for the body, its functions, and physiology? As sexual subjects, how do we reconcile constructionist theory with the body's visceral reality and our own experience of it? If our theory of sexuality becomes increasingly disembodied, does it reach the point of implausibility, even for us? And if we wish to incorporate the body within social construction theory, can we do so without returning to essentialism and biological determinism?

Let me discuss these points more concretely by giving an example from my own work on female circumcision. . . . [This topic] illuminates the difficulty of thinking about the relationship of sexuality to the body and has much to offer for other body issues.

Briefly, female circumcision is an umbrella term for traditional customs carried out in various Middle Eastern and African countries. These customs involve the surgical alteration and removal of female genital tissue, usually performed by midwives and female kin. The procedures vary in severity and range from removing part or all of the clitoris (simple circumcision) to removing the labia (excision). In infibulation, the most radical form of surgery, the clitoris and labia are excised, and the vaginal opening is sutured to reduce its circumference, making heterosexual penetration impossible and thus guaranteeing virginity. These operations are done at different ages and for different reasons — to promote hygiene and fertility, to render women aesthetically more feminine and thus marriageable, and to promote virginity. It is important to understand that these procedures are widespread and in local terms thought to be required by religion or custom.

In the past ten years, an intense conversation has developed between Western and Third-World feminists over these practices. It is not my goal here to thoroughly describe this debate, or to suggest, by examining Western views, that we enjoy a privileged vantage point or right to intervene. What interests me here is how we think about these practices and the body in less guarded moments. . . . We tend to think about the effects of these customs, particularly on sexual functioning. We draw on a physiological model of Masters and Johnson, which places the clitoris at the center of female sexual response and orgasm. We reason that removal of part or all of the clitoris interferes with orgasm, perhaps making it impossible. That is, we are universalizing a physiological finding made on American subjects without much thought.

The Enlightenment and the Nature of Modernity:
The Social and Intellectual Origins of Sociology

5. [Extracts from] The Enlightenment and the Birth of Social Science

Peter Hamilton

Before looking at the content and context of the key ideas of the Enlightenment, let us set them out in a concise form here. They make up what sociologists call a 'paradigm', a set of interconnected ideas, values, principles, and facts which provide both an image of the natural and social world, and a way of thinking about it. The 'paradigm' of the Enlightenment — its 'philosophy' and approach to key questions — is a combination of a number of ideas, bound together in a tight cluster. It includes some elements which may even appear to be inconsistent — probably because, like many intellectual movements, it united people whose ideas had many threads in common but differed on questions of detail. As a minimum, however, all the *philosophes* would have agreed on the following list:

1. *Reason* — the *philosophes* stressed the primacy of *reason* and rationality as ways of organizing knowledge, tempered by experience and experiment. In this they took over the 'rationalist' concept of reason as the process of rational thought, based upon clear, innate ideas independent of experience, which can be demonstrated to any thinking person, and which had been set out by Descartes and Pascal in the seventeenth century. However, the *philosophes* allied their version of rationalism with *empiricism*.

2. *Empiricism* — the idea that all thought and knowledge about the natural and social world is based upon empirical facts, things that all human beings can apprehend through their sense organs.

3. *Science*—the notion that scientific knowledge, based upon the experimental method as developed in the scientific revolution of the seventeenth century, was the key to expanding *all* human knowledge.

4. *Universalism* — the concept that reason and science could be applied to any and every situation, and that their principles were the same in every situation. Science in particular produces general laws which govern the entire universe, without exception.

5. *Progress* — the idea that the natural and social condition of human beings could be improved, by the application of science and reason, and would result in an ever-increasing level of happiness and well-being.

6. *Individualism* — the concept that the individual is the starting point for all knowledge and action, and that individual reason cannot be subjected to a higher authority. Society is thus the sum or product of the thought and action of a large number of individuals.

Peter Hamilton: Extracts from 'The Enlightenment and the Birth of Social Science' from *FORMATIONS OF MODERNITY*, edited by Stuart Hall and Bram Gieben (Polity Press in association with Blackwell Publishers and The Open University), pp. 21–34. Reproduced by permission of Basil Blackwell Limited.

7. *Toleration* — the notion that all human beings are essentially the same, despite their religious or moral convictions, and that the beliefs of other races or civilizations are not inherently inferior to those of European Christianity.

8. *Freedom* — an opposition to feudal and traditional constraints on beliefs, trade, communication, social interaction, sexuality, and ownership of property (although as we shall see the extension of freedom to women and the lower classes was problematic for the *philosophes*).

9. *Uniformity of human nature* — the belief that the principal characteristics of human nature were always and everywhere the same.

10. *Secularism* — an ethic most frequently seen in the form of virulent anti-clericalism. The *philosophes'* opposition to traditional religious authority stressed the need for secular knowledge free of religious orthodoxies.

It would be possible to add other ideas to this list or to discuss the relative importance of each. However, the above list provides a good starting point for understanding this complex movement, and for making connections between its characteristic concerns and the emergence of sociology. Each of these central ideas weaves its way through the account that follows, and all form part of the new social sciences which emerged in the nineteenth century.

What was the Enlightenment?

A simple answer to this question would separate out at least eight meanings of the Enlightenment:

1. A characteristic bundle of ideas.

2. An intellectual movement.

3. A communicating group or network of intellectuals.

4. A set of institutional centres where intellectuals clustered — Paris, Edinburgh, Glasgow, London, etc.

5. A publishing industry, and an audience for its output.

6. An intellectual fashion.

7. A belief-system, world-view, or *Zeitgeist* (spirit of the age).

8. A history and a geography.

All of these are overlapping aspects of the same general phenomenon, and they remind us that it is ultimately futile to try to pin down a single definitive group, set of ideas, or cluster of outcomes and consequences, which can serve as *the* Enlightenment. There were many aspects to the Enlightenment, and many *philosophes*, so what you will find here is an attempt to map out some broad outlines, to set some central ideas in their context, and to indicate some important consequences.

In its simplest sense the Enlightenment was the creation of a new framework of ideas about man, society and nature, which challenged existing conceptions rooted in a traditional world-view, dominated by Christianity. The key domain in which

Enlightenment intellectuals challenged the clergy, who were the main group involved in supporting existing conceptions of the world, concerned the traditional view of nature, man and society which was sustained by the Church's authority and its monopoly over the information media of the time.

These new ideas were accompanied by and influenced in their turn many cultural innovations in writing, printing, painting, music, sculpture, architecture and gardening, as well as the other arts. Technological innovations in agriculture and manufactures, as well as in ways of making war, also frame the social theories of the Enlightenment. We have no space to explore such matters here, except to point out that the whole idea of a professionalized discipline based on any of these intellectual or cultural pursuits was only slowly emerging, and that as a consequence an educated man or woman of the eighteenth-century Enlightenment saw him or herself as able to take up any or all of them which caught his or her interest. The notion that Enlightenment knowledge could be strictly compartmentalized into bounded domains, each the province of certificated 'experts', would have been completely foreign to Enlightenment thinkers. The 'universalism' which thus characterized the emergence of these ideas and their cultural counterparts assumed that any educated person could in principle know everything. This was in fact a mistaken belief. Paradoxically, the Enlightenment heralded the very process — the creation of specialized disciplines presided over by certificated experts — which appears to negate its aim of universalized human knowledge. Such a 'closing-off' of knowledge by disciplinary boundaries occurred earlier than anywhere else in the natural sciences, those models of enlightened knowledge so beloved of the *philosophes*. The main reason for this was that science produced specialist languages and terminologies, and relied in particular upon an increasingly complex mathematical language, inaccessible to even the enlightened gentleman-*philosophe*. Denis Diderot (1713–84), a key figure in the movement, noted perceptively in 1756 that the mathematical language of Newton's *Principia Mathematica* is 'the veil' which scientists 'are pleased to draw between the people and nature' (quoted in Gay, 1973b, p.158).

However much they might have wanted to extend the benefits of enlightened knowledge, the *philosophes* helped the process by which secular intellectual life became the province of a socially and economically defined group. They were the first people in western society outside of the Church to make a living (or more properly a *vocation*) out of knowledge and writing. As Roy Porter has put it, 'the Enlightenment was the era which saw the emergence of a secular intelligentsia large enough and powerful enough for the first time to challenge the clergy' (Porter, 1990, p.73).

In the next section, I want to locate the Enlightenment in its social, historical, and geographical context.

1. The social, historical and geographical location of the Enlightenment

When we use the term 'the Enlightenment' it is generally accepted that we refer to a period in European intellectual history which spans the time from roughly the first quarter to the last quarter of the eighteenth century. Geographically centred in France, but with important outposts in most of the major European states, 'the Enlightenment' is composed of the ideas and writings of a fairly heterogeneous group, who are often called by their French name *philosophes*. It does not exactly correspond to our modern 'philosopher', and is perhaps best translated as 'a man of letters who is also a freethinker'. The *philosophes* saw themselves as cosmopolitans, citizens of an enlightened intellectual world who valued the interest of mankind above that of country or clan. As the French *philosophe* Diderot wrote to Hume in 1768: 'My dear David, you belong to all nations, and you'll never ask an unhappy man for his birth-certificate. I flatter myself that I am, like you, citizen of the great city of the world' (quoted in Gay, 1973a, p. 13). The historian Edward Gibbon (1737–94) stressed the strongly European or 'Euro-centric' nature of this *universalistic* cosmopolitanism: 'it is the duty of a patriot to prefer and promote the exclusive interest and glory of his native country; but a philosopher may be permitted to enlarge his views, and to consider Europe as a great republic, whose various inhabitants have attained almost the same level of politeness and cultivation' (quoted in Gay, 1973a, p.13). Gibbon even composed some of his writings in French, because he felt that the ideas with which he wanted to work were better expressed in that language than in his own.

The Enlightenment was the work of three overlapping and closely linked generations of *philosophes*. The first, typified by Voltaire (1694–1778) and Charles de Secondat, known as Montesquieu (1689–1755), were born in the last quarter of the seventeenth century: their ideas were strongly influenced by the writings of the English political philosopher John Locke (1632–1704) and the scientist Isaac Newton (1642–1727), whose work was fresh and controversial whilst both *philosophes* were still young men. The second generation includes men like David Hume (1711–76), Jean-Jacques Rousseau (1712–78), Denis Diderot (1713–84), and Jean d'Alembert (1717–83), who combined the fashionable anti-clericalism and the interest in scientific method of their predecessors into what Gay calls 'a coherent modern view of the world'. The third generation is represented by Immanuel Kant (1724–1804), Adam Smith (1723–90), Anne Robert Turgot (1727–81), the Marquis de Condorcet (1743–94), and Adam Ferguson (1723–1816), and its achievement is the further development of the Enlightenment world-view into a series of more specialized proto-disciplines: epistemology, economics, sociology, political economy, legal reform. It is to Kant that we owe the slogan of the Enlightenment — *sapere aude* ('dare to know') — which sums up its essentially secular intellectual character.

Of course there is a danger in applying the term 'the Enlightenment' too loosely or broadly, to the whole of intellectual life in eighteenth-century Europe, as if the movement was one which touched every society and every intellectual elite of this period equally. As Roy Porter emphasizes in an excellent short study of recent work on the Enlightenment, the Enlightenment is an amorphous, hard-to-pin-down and constantly shifting entity (Porter, 1990). It is commonplace for the whole period to be referred to as an 'Age of Enlightenment', a term which implies a general process of society awakening from the dark slumbers of superstition and ignorance, and a notion certainly encouraged by the *philosophes* themselves, although it is one which perhaps poses more questions than it resolves. Kant wrote an essay *'Was ist Aufklärung?'* (What is Enlightenment?), which actually says 'if someone says "are we living in an enlightened age today?" the answer would be, "No: but ... we *are* living in an Age of Enlightenment" '. The French *philosophes* referred to their time as *'le siècle des lumières'* (the century of the enlightened), and both Scottish and English writers of the time talked about 'Enlightened' thinking.

Certainly the metaphor of the 'light of reason', shining brightly into all the dark recesses of ignorance and superstition, was a powerful one at the time: but did the process of Enlightenment always and everywhere have the same meaning? One recent historical study of Europe in the eighteenth century has suggested that the Enlightenment is more 'a tendency towards critical inquiry and the application of reason' than a coherent intellectual movement (Black, 1990, p.208).

In fact, if we look at such indicators as the production and consumption of books and journals, the Enlightenment was a largely French and British (or more properly Scottish) intellectual vogue, although one whose fashionable ripples extended out to Germany, Italy, the Habsburg Empire, Russia, the Low Countries and the Americas. But its centre was very clearly Paris, and it emerged in the France of Louis XV (1710–74), during the first quarter of the eighteenth century.

By the last quarter of the eighteenth century, Enlightenment ideas were close to having become a sort of new intellectual orthodoxy amongst the cultivated élites of Europe. This orthodoxy was also starting to give way to an emergent 'pre-Romanticism' which placed greater emphasis on sentiment and feeling, as opposed to reason and scepticism. However, the spirit of enlightened and critical rationalism was quite an influential factor in the increasing disquiet about how *ancien régime* France was being run, which began to set in after about 1770 (Doyle, 1989, p.58). It helped to encourage a mood of impending disaster which led inexorably towards the French Revolution of 1789, a topic to which we shall return in Section 5. If we need to find a historical end to the Enlightenment, it could be said to be the French Revolution — but even that is a controversial notion.

Although the Enlightenment was in reality a sort of intellectual fashion which took hold of the minds of intellectuals throughout Europe, rather than a consciously conceived project with any institutionalized form, there is one classic example of a cooperative endeavour among the *philosophes:* the great publishing enterprise called the *Encyclopédie*.

2. The *Encyclopédie*

In order to explain the influence of this massive publication, it is worth reminding ourselves that by the mid-eighteenth century French was the language of all of educated Europe, except for England and Spain (and even in those two countries any self-respecting member of the educated elite would have had a good knowledge of the language). As a Viennese countess put it, '. . . in those days the greater part of high society in Vienna would say: I speak French like Diderot, and German . . . like my nurse' (Doyle, 1989, p.58).

The universality of French as the language of reason and ideas explains in part the Europe-wide popularity of the *Encyclopédie* — where the intellectual fashion for treating all aspects of human life and the natural world as open to rational study is displayed in astonishing depth.

The cooperative endeavour which produced the *Encyclopédie* parallels another distinctive feature of the Enlightenment — the learned society committed to the pursuit of knowledge, whose prototypes were the Académie française (est. 1635) and the Royal Society of London (est. 1645). Such organizations were the first modern social institutions devoted to the study of the arts and sciences. The most distinctive break with the past came about because the members of such academies believed in the grounding of knowledge in experience as opposed to secular authority, religious dogma, or mysticism.

Science was the supreme form of knowledge for the *philosophes* because it seemed to create secure truths based on observation and experiment. Their confidence in scientific method was such that they believed it was a force for enlightenment and progress: there was in principle no domain of life to which it could not be applied. They believed that a new man was being created by this scientific method, one who understands, and by his understanding masters nature.

The *Encyclopédie* represented this belief in the beneficial effects of science put into practice. It was also the product of an intellectual society — 'a society of men of letters and artisans' as Denis Diderot, one of its main editors, described it. Its purpose was summed up by Kant's definition of Enlightenment: 'man realising his potential through the use of his mind' (quoted in Gay, 1973a, p.21).

The concept of the *Encyclopédie* was originally based on an English work, Ephraim Chambers's *Cyclopaedia or Universal Dictionary of Arts and Sciences* (1728). Although initially intended to be a translation of this popular and successful work, it soon became an original work in its own right, after Denis Diderot and Jean d'Alembert (a scientifically inclined *philosophe*) took over the editorship for its publisher, Le Breton. Virtually all of the major *philosophes* contributed to it, and its influence was very widespread in eighteenth-century Europe.

There are two striking characteristics of the *Encyclopédie* from our point of view. Firstly, in creating a plan for the enterprise — a way of linking all the articles together in a coherent manner — the decision was taken to place man at the centre. As Diderot said (in an entry in the *Encyclopédie* under the heading 'Encyclopédie'), what he and his associates wanted for the *Encyclopédie* was a plan or design that would be 'instructive and grand' — something which would order knowledge and information as 'a grand and noble avenue, stretching into the distance, and along which one would find other avenues, arranged in an orderly manner and leading off to isolated and remote objects by the easiest and quickest route' (*Encyclopédie*, Volume V, 1755).

Secondly, the *Encyclopédie* is truly 'universalistic' in its approach. Diderot and his colleagues wanted it to be the sort of work from which, should a disaster overtake civilization, all human knowledge could be reconstructed. As a result, it is a vast publication: it took over twenty years to be published, from 1751 to 1772, and amounts to seventeen volumes of text and twelve volumes of plates.

The pre-eminence in the eighteenth century of French as the language of culture and of ideas made the *Encyclopédie* a widely-known work — some 50 per cent of the 25,000 copies in various editions which sold before 1789 were purchased outside of France. It is not surprising perhaps that from a modern standpoint this endeavour should seem to support the idea of an 'Enlightenment project', the notion that a planned and influential intellectual movement, designed to popularize certain key notions to do with science, reason and progress, was at work in the eighteenth century. But from the evidence available on those who purchased copies of it, the *Encyclopédie* sold more because of its critical and irreverent notoriety than for any specific programme or project which it represented (Doyle, 1989. p.52). What is more, it is clear that the term 'Encyclopedism' was quite widely used at the time as a synonym for the refusal to accept anything uncritically.

Indeed, a key feature of the whole Enlightenment period is the influence of a wide range of individual writers on educated and cultivated opinion. Thinkers such as Voltaire, Montesquieu, Diderot, Hume, Smith, Ferguson, Rousseau, and Condorcet — to mention only some of the most notable — produced a large collection of novels, plays, books, pamphlets and essays which became bestsellers amongst an audience which was avid for new and exciting ideas, and receptive to the notion that the application of reason to the affairs of men would encourage a general advance of civilization. This audience was not however dominated by the 'new' social groups, the emergent middle classes of manufacturers and merchants, but by members of more traditional élite groups — nobles, professionals (especially lawyers), academics and the clergy. The idea of disciplinary demarcation was foreign to such people, for whom the ideal of Renaissance Man was the archetype of cultivated knowledge — a person whose knowledge and understanding enabled him or her to pick up a book on physics, read a text of Tacitus, design a Palladian villa, paint a *Mona Lisa*, or compose a sonnet with equal facility. They had for the most part received a classical education (in French colleges of the mid-eighteenth century, for example, four hours a day were given over to the study of the classics), but also some introduction to the sciences. Men (and the much smaller number of women educated to the same level) would expect to understand and participate in the spread of knowledge about new ideas, whether in the field of moral philosophy or physical science. Yet women, though they played a major part in the development and diffusion of Enlightenment ideas, found themselves in a contradictory position in the application of such ideas to their social condition. We shall return to this in Section 5.

3. Tradition and modernity

The *philosophes* took a very clear position in their writings on certain important transitions underway within European society. These involved the move from a traditional social order and a traditional set of beliefs about the world to new forms of social structure and ways of thinking about the world which were distinctively modern. The modernity of these modes of thought lay in the innovative way in which the *philosophes* sought to demolish and replace *established* forms of knowledge dependent on religious authority, such as the biblical account of the creation of the world, with those new forms of knowledge which depended upon experience, experiment and reason — quintessentially, science.

Until the eighteenth century, what passed in Europe for knowledge about the creation of the world, about man's place in that world, about nature and society, and about man's duties and destiny, was dominated by the Christian churches. Knowledge was continually referred to scriptural sources in the Bible, and was transmitted through the religious institutions of universities, colleges, religious orders, schools and churches. A typical visual representation of the traditional world-view shows heaven and earth as physically contiguous. Even Bossuet's *Histoire Universelle* (Universal History) of 1681 began its account of human history over the previous 6,000 years with Adam and Eve's departure from the Garden of Eden, and did not mention the Chinese once. Yet, as Voltaire pointed out (in his *Lettres Philosophiques*), the Chinese could trace their civilization back through '36 recorded eclipses of the sun to a date earlier than that which we normally attribute to the Flood'.

The astronomic discoveries in the sixteenth and seventeenth centuries of Kepler and Copernicus about the nature of the universe, the observations of Galileo concerning the movements of the planets, the lessons of empirical science, and the increasingly common accounts of distant and exotic societies available through travellers' tales, combined to provide an effective scientific and empirical base from which to challenge traditional cosmologies (a cosmology is an intellectual picture or model of the universe) founded upon Christian belief, which placed the earth at the centre of the universe, and Christendom at the centre of the world. This was fertile ground for the *philosophes*, who opposed traditional religious authority and the false knowledge which it ordained.

The particular form in which Enlightenment anti-traditionalism appears, then, is as a debunking of outmoded, scripturally-based concepts of the universe, the earth and human society. Although we must be clear that many of the *philosophes* were in fact believers in a God, or at least a divine entity, this did not prevent much of their writing from heaping scorn upon religious teaching, and being virulently anti-clerical. The *philosophes* challenged the traditional role of the clergy as the keepers and transmitters of knowledge: because the wished to redefine what was socially important knowledge, to bring it outside of the sphere of religion, and to provide it with a new meaning and relevance. As a result, they typically presented traditional religious world-views as attempts to keep people in a condition of ignorance and superstition, and thus reserved much of the most pointed of their intellectual attacks for key elements in what they saw as the ideological window-dressing of the Church, such as miracles and revelations.

Religious ideas and knowledge also underpinned the absolute claim to power exercised by the French, Austrian and German kings, and the Russian Czar, and were also used, in a modified form, to support the claim on the British throne of the Hanoverians. Some of the *philosophes* were quite explicitly antithetical to 'despotism' (the Enlightenment's code-word for absolutism); others were more equivocal about the virtue of a strong monarch, and both Voltaire and Diderot were virtually apologists for the absolutist regimes of Frederick the Great of Prussia, and Catherine the Great of Russia.

The ideas developed and disseminated by the *philosophes* touched critically upon nearly all aspects of the traditional societies in which they operated, and sought to question virtually all (the condition of women being, perhaps, the main exception) of the forms which that society took. One of the main sources of their approach to the critique of traditional society is found in their enthusiasm for science, and the notions of progress and reason for which it seemed to provide a guarantee. We shall return to the connection between the Enlightenment and the emergence of modern science in [Section 3.1].

4. Social orders and social structure

Despite their secular radicalism, the ideas of the typical *philosophes* were not as subversive of the traditional social structure in which they lived as might have been the case. There is perhaps a simple reason for this: self-interest. The English historian Edward Gibbon described himself as fortunate to have been placed by the lottery of life amongst a cultured and leisured élite, the 'polished and enlightened orders of society', which he contrasts with the condition of the masses:

> The most numerous portion of it [society] is employed in constant and useful labour. The select few, placed by fortune above necessity, can, however, fill up their time by the pursuits of interest or glory, by the improvements of their estate or of their understanding, by the duties, the pleasures, and even the follies of social life.
>
> (Gibbon, 1966, p.207)

Most of the *philosophes* came from the higher orders of society. Many were of noble birth, whilst some came from the gentry classes or from a professional milieu. Montesquieu, for example, was a great landowner in the Bordeaux region of France. Diderot and Rousseau came from the traditional middle class — Diderot's father was a master-cutler, Rousseau's a watchmaker.

Peter Gay describes the *philosophes* as a 'solid, respectable clan of revolutionaries' (Gay, 1973a, p.9). Most were born into a cultured élite, and in the main their works were circulated amongst other members of that élite. It was not until almost the eve of the French Revolution, in the 1780s, that a new social group emerged, concerned with popularizing Enlightenment ideas (Darnton, 1979).

This new group was composed largely of lower-middle-class hack journalists and other writers, who supplied the growing number of popular newspapers with a diet of scandal mixed up with simplified Enlightenment ideas. Their audiences were the disaffected and propertyless lower middle classes, for whom the traditional social structure had little to offer.

The traditional social structure of eighteenth-century Europe was essentially based upon the ownership of land and landed property. It was a society composed of orders, rather than economically defined classes, although class formations were beginning to appear. The great noble landowners formed the dominant ruling order (of which a Louis XV or a George III was simply a leading member), and although there was considerable variation within Europe over the extent of their political power — in France, for example, feudal rights over land still remained, whilst in Russia serfdom was the norm on the great estates — they dominated an economy in which at least 80 per cent of the population derived their employment and income from agriculture in one form or another.

Beneath the landed nobility there existed a stratum of 'traditional' professional orders which had changed little since the feudal period — lawyers, clerics, state officials, etc. — and also a stratum of small landowners or gentry-farmers. In France the latter group (the *hobereaux,* or gentry) was quite numerous, but often possessed only modest means. Frequently reasonably well-educated, they were the social group from which many of the lesser figures of the Enlightenment emerged, for an acceptable profession for this social group was that of 'writer'. There was an emergent and growing 'new' middle class involved in new forms of manufacture and trade, as well as the traditional merchant order of feudalism, which included the quite large numbers of urban craftsmen — from the wealthy goldsmiths, perfumiers or tailors who worked for the nobility, through to an assortment of printers, furniture makers, or carriage makers, down to the modest shoemaker or mason. Below the urban middle class was to be found a large class of domestic servants, and a small urban working class, supplemented on a daily or seasonal basis by day labourers from the countryside. Peasants or smallholders made up the great mass of the population — in mid-eighteenth century France they probably accounted for eighteen of the twenty million or so of the population.

In eighteenth-century France, these social orders were represented as three 'Estates' — Clergy, Nobility, and the 'Third Estate', which comprised everyone else, from wealthiest bourgeois to poorest peasant. Some *philosophes* were members of the Second Estate, which perhaps also indicates why they should be less explicitly subversive of the traditional social order than of the traditional religious order.

For the lower orders of European eighteenth-century society, the Enlightenment had apparently little to offer. Voltaire was fond of describing the peasantry in terms which put them hardly above the beasts of the field, in order to criticize the sort of social system which reduced men to such a level of ignorance and bestiality. However, he showed little interest in a levelling of social distinction. Few indeed of the *philosophes* were interested in the greater involvement of the great mass of the population in the government of society, for the most part favouring a system *à la* Great Britain, where political power was extended to the propertied classes and the landed gentry, but not beyond.

The Enlightenment certainly propagated concepts of equality, (limited) democracy and emancipation. But in the societies in which it flourished its ultimately revolutionary implications were not grasped by (or meant to be extended to) the mass of poor and uneducated people. None the less. ruling élites in particular saw the ideas of the Enlightenment as a threat to the established order. Because they discerned in it certain dangerous and revolutionary elements, both secular and religious authorities tried to control the spread of Enlightenment culture. However, the *philosophes* themselves refused to believe that they were rebels or revolutionaries: they thought that progress could come about within the existing social order by the spread of their ideas among men of influence. As Diderot once said, their aim was to 'change the general way of thinking', and was revolutionary only insofar as it sought 'the revolution which will take place in the minds of men' (quoted in Eliot and Stern, 1979, p.44).

5. Women and Enlightenment: the salon

Although there were some wealthy and powerful women manifestly involved in the propagation of its principles — Catherine the Great of Russia was one of its staunchest supporters at one stage — the Enlightenment was essentially promoted and prosecuted, at least in its public face, by a male intellectual élite. Women figured as either silent partners in the intellectual enterprises of their more famous consorts (Voltaire spent much time performing scientific experiments with the aid of his mistress Madame du Châtelet, whilst much of what we know of the intellectual society of the times comes from Diderot's voluminous correspondence with his mistress, Sophie Volland), or as the (frequently brilliant) hostesses of the regular salons and soirées where the *philosophes* and other members of the cultivated élites would meet.

The institution of the salon had begun in seventeenth-century Paris, the invention of the Marquise de Rambouillet in 1623, who created 'a space in which talented and learned women could meet with men as intellectual equals, rather than as exceptional prodigies' (Anderson and Zinsser, 1990, vol.II, p.104). Yet the salon proved to be a rather double-edged sword in the expansion of women's rights. Although many of those set up in imitation of Mme de Rambouillet's were presided over by women who, like her, refused sexual liaisons so as to free themselves for a role beyond that of wife or courtesan, many salons were also the locus for affairs between talented or titled men and intellectual women, and the reputation of all *salonières* (chaste or otherwise) was affected: it was assumed that relations between men and women, however intellectual or artistic they might appear, could not remain platonic.

References

Anderson, B. and Zinsser, J. (1990) *A History of their Own: Women in Europe from Prehistory to the Present,* 2 vols, Harmondsworth, Penguin.

Black, J. (1990) *Eighteenth Century Europe 1700–1789,* London, Macmillan.

Brinton, C. (1930) 'The Revolutions', *Encyclopaedia of the Social Sciences,* vol.1, Macmillan, New York.

Darnton, R. (1979) *The Business of Enlightenment. A Publishing History of the Encyclopédie 1775–1800,* Cambridge, Mass., Harvard University Press.

Doyle, W. (1989) *The Oxford History of the French Revolution.* Oxford, Clarendon Press.

Eliot, S. and Stern, B. (eds) (1979) *The Age of Enlightenment: An Anthology of Eighteenth Century Texts,* London, Ward Lock Educational.

Gay, P. (1973a) *The Enlightenment: An Interpretation. Vol. 1: The Rise of Modern Paganism,* London, Wildwood House.

Gay, P. (1973b) *The Enlightenment: An Interpretation. Vol .2: The Science of Freedom,* London, Wildwood House.

Gibbon, E. (1966) *Memoirs of my Life* (ed. by G. A. Bonnard), London, Nelson.

Hampson, N. (1969) *The Enlightenment,* Harmondsworth, Penguin.

Nisbet, R. (1967) *The Sociological Tradition,* London, Heinemann.

Porter, R. (1990) *The Enlightenment,* London, Macmillan.

Sorel, A. (1969) *Europe and The French Revolution: The Political Traditions of the Old Regime* (first published 1885), London, Collins.

Taylor, K. (1975) *Henri Saint-Simon 1760–1825: Selected Writings on Science, Industry and Social Organisation,* London, Croom Helm.

Thompson, K. (1976) *Auguste Comte: The Foundation of Sociology,* London, Nelson.

6. The Metropolis and Mental Life
Georg Simmel

The deepest problems of modern life derive from the claim of the individual to preserve the autonomy and individuality of his existence in the face of overwhelming social forces, of historical heritage, of external culture, and of the technique of life. The fight with nature which primitive man has to wage for his *bodily* existence attains in this modern form its latest transformation. The eighteenth century called upon man to free himself of all the historical bonds in the state and in religion, in morals and in economics. Man's nature, originally good and common to all, should develop unhampered. In addition to more liberty, the nineteenth century demanded the functional specialization of man and his work; this specialization makes one individual incomparable to another, and each of them indispensable to the highest possible extent. However, this specialization makes each man the more directly dependent upon the supplementary activities of all others. Nietzsche sees the full development of the individual conditioned by the most ruthless struggle of individuals; socialism believes in the suppression of all competition for the same reason. Be that as it may, in all these positions the same basic motive is at work: the person resists to being leveled down and worn out by a social-technological mechanism. An inquiry into the inner meaning of specifically modern life and its products, into the soul of the cultural body, so to speak, must seek to solve the equation which structures like the metropolis set up between the individual and the super-individual contents of life. Such an inquiry must answer the question of how the personality accommodates itself in the adjustments to external forces. This will be my task today.

The psychological basis of the metropolitan type of individuality consists in the *intensification of nervous stimulation* which results from the swift and uninterrupted change of outer and inner stimuli. Man is a differentiating creature. His mind is stimulated by the difference between a momentary impression and the one which preceded it. Lasting impressions, impressions which differ only slightly from one another, impressions which take a regular and habitual course and show regular and habitual contrasts — all these use up, so to speak, less consciousness than does the rapid crowding of changing images, the sharp discontinuity in the grasp of a single glance, and the unexpectedness of onrushing impressions. These are the psychological conditions which the metropolis creates. With each crossing of the street, with the tempo and multiplicity of economic, occupational and social life, the city sets up a deep contrast with small town and rural life with reference to the sensory foundations of psychic life. The metropolis exacts from man as a discriminating creature a different amount of consciousness than does rural life. Here the rhythm of life and sensory mental imagery flows more slowly, more habitually, and more evenly. Precisely in this connection the sophisticated character of metropolitan psychic life becomes understandable — as over against small town life which rests more upon deeply felt

Reprinted with the permission of The Free Press, an imprint of Simon & Schuster from *THE SOCIOLOGY OF GEORG SIMMEL*, translated and edited by Kurt H. Wolff, pp. 409–424. Copyright © 1950, copyright renewed 1978 by The Free Press.

and emotional relationships. These latter are rooted in the more unconscious layers of the psyche and grow most readily in the steady rhythm of uninterrupted habituations. The intellect, however, has its locus in the transparent, conscious, higher layers of the psyche; it is the most adaptable of our inner forces. In order to accommodate to change and to the contrast of phenomena, the intellect does not require any shocks and inner upheavals; it is only through such upheavals that the more conservative mind could accommodate to the metropolitan rhythm of events. Thus the metropolitan type of man — which, of course, exists in a thousand individual variants — develops an organ protecting him against the threatening currents and discrepancies of his external environment which would uproot him. He reacts with his head instead of his heart. In this an increased awareness assumes the psychic prerogative. Metropolitan life, thus, underlies a heightened awareness and a predominance of intelligence in metropolitan man. The reaction to metropolitan phenomena is shifted to that organ which is least sensitive and quite remote from the depth of the personality. Intellectuality is thus seen to preserve subjective life against the overwhelming power of metropolitan life, and intellectuality branches out in many directions and is integrated with numerous discrete phenomena.

The metropolis has always been the seat of the money economy. Here the multiplicity and concentration of economic exchange gives an importance to the means of exchange which the scantiness of rural commerce would not have allowed. Money economy and the dominance of the intellect are intrinsically connected. They share a matter-of-fact attitude in dealing with men and with things; and, in this attitude, a formal justice is often coupled with an inconsiderate hardness. The intellectually sophisticated person is indifferent to all genuine individuality, because relationships and reactions result from it which cannot be exhausted with logical operations. In the same manner, the individuality of phenomena is not commensurate with the pecuniary principle. Money is concerned only with what is common to all: it asks for the exchange value, it reduces all quality and individuality to the question: How much? All intimate emotional relations between persons are founded in their individuality, whereas in rational relations man is reckoned with like a number, like an element which is in itself indifferent. Only the objective measurable achievement is of interest. Thus metropolitan man reckons with his merchants and customers, his domestic servants and often even with persons with whom he is obliged to have social intercourse. These features of intellectuality contrast with the nature of the small circle in which the inevitable knowledge of individuality as inevitably produces a warmer tone of behavior, a behavior which is beyond a mere objective balancing of service and return. In the sphere of the economic psychology of the small group it is of importance that under primitive conditions production serves the customer who orders the good, so that the producer and the consumer are acquainted. The modern metropolis, however, is supplied almost entirely by production for the market, that is, for entirely unknown purchasers who never personally enter the producer's actual field of vision. Through this anonymity the interests of each party acquire an unmerciful matter-of-factness; and the intellectually calculating economic egoisms of both parties need not fear any deflection because of the imponderables of personal relationships. The money economy dominates the metropolis; it has displaced the last survivals of domestic production and the direct barter of goods; it minimizes, from day to day, the amount of work ordered by customers. The matter-of-fact attitude is obviously so intimately interrelated with the money economy, which is dominant in the metropolis, that nobody can say whether the intellectualistic mentality first promoted the money economy or whether the latter determined the former. The metropolitan way of life is certainly the most fertile soil for this reciprocity, a point which I shall document merely by citing the dictum of the most eminent English constitutional historian: throughout the whole course of English history, London has never acted as England's heart but often as England's intellect and always as her moneybag!

In certain seemingly insignificant traits, which lie upon the surface of life, the same psychic currents characteristically unite. Modern mind has become more and more calculating. The calculative exactness of practical life which the money economy has brought about corresponds to the ideal of natural science: to transform the world into an arithmetic problem, to fix every part of the world by mathematical formulas. Only money economy has filled the days of so many people with weighing, calculating, with numerical determinations, with a reduction of qualitative values to quantitative ones. Through the calculative nature of money a new precision, a certainty in the definition of identities and differences, an unambiguousness in agreements and arrangements has been brought about in the relations of life-elements — just as externally this precision has been effected by the universal diffusion of pocket watches. However, the conditions of metropolitan life are at once cause and effect of this trait. The relationships and affairs of the typical metropolitan usually are so varied and complex that without the strictest punctuality in promises and services the whole structure would break down into an inextricable chaos. Above all, this necessity is brought about by the aggregation of so many people with such differentiated interests, who must integrate their relations and activities into a highly complex organism. If all clocks and watches in Berlin would suddenly go wrong in different ways, even if only by one hour, all economic life and communication of the city would be disrupted for a long time. In addition an apparently mere external factor: long distances, would make all waiting and broken appointments result in an ill-afforded waste of time. Thus, the technique of metropolitan life is unimaginable without the most punctual integration of all activities and mutual relations into a stable and impersonal time schedule. Here again the general conclusions of this entire task of reflection become obvious, namely, that from each point on the surface of existence — however closely attached to the surface alone — one may drop a sounding into the depth of the psyche so that all the most banal externalities of life finally are connected with the ultimate decisions concerning the meaning and style of life. Punctuality, calculability, exactness are forced upon life by the complexity and extension of metropolitan existence and are not only most intimately connected with its money economy and intellectualistic character. These traits must also color the contents of life and favor the exclusion of those irrational, instinctive, sovereign traits and impulses which aim at determining the mode of life from within, instead of receiving the general and precisely schematized form of life from without. Even though sovereign types of personality, characterized by irrational impulses, are by no means impossible in the city, they are, nevertheless, opposed to typical city life. The passionate hatred of men like Ruskin and Nietzsche for the metropolis is understandable in these terms. Their natures discovered the value of life alone in the unschematized existence which cannot be defined with precision for all alike. From the same source of this hatred of the metropolis surged their hatred of money economy and of the intellectualism of modern existence.

The same factors which have thus coalesced into the exactness and minute precision of the form of life have coalesced into a structure of the highest impersonality; on the other hand, they have promoted a highly personal subjectivity. There is perhaps no psychic phenomenon which has been so unconditionally reserved to the metropolis as has the blasé attitude. The blasé attitude results first from the rapidly changing and closely compressed contrasting stimulations of the nerves. From this, the enhancement of metropolitan intellectuality, also, seems originally to stem. Therefore, stupid people who are not intellectually alive in the first place usually are not exactly blasé. A life in boundless pursuit of pleasure makes one blasé because it agitates the nerves to their strongest reactivity for such a long time that they finally cease to react at all. In the same way, through the rapidity and contradictoriness of their changes, more harmless impressions force such violent responses, tearing the nerves so brutally hither and thither that their last reserves of strength are spent; and if one remains in the same milieu they have no time to gather new strength. An incapacity thus emerges to react to new sensations with the appropriate energy. This constitutes that blasé attitude which, in fact, every metropolitan child shows when compared with children of quieter and less changeable milieus.

This physiological source of the metropolitan blasé attitude is joined by another source which flows from the money economy. The essence of the blasé attitude consists in the blunting of discrimination. This does not mean that the objects are not perceived, as is the case with the half-wit, but rather that the meaning and differing values of things, and thereby the things themselves, are experienced as insubstantial. They appear to the blasé person in an evenly flat and gray tone; no one object deserves preference over any other. This mood is the faithful subjective reflection of the completely internalized money economy. By being the equivalent to all the manifold things in one and the same way, money becomes the most frightful leveler. For money expresses all qualitative differences of things in terms of "how much?" Money, with all its colorlessness and indifference, becomes the common denominator of all values; irreparably it hollows out the core of things, their individuality, their specific value, and their incomparability. All things float with equal specific gravity in the constantly moving stream of money. All things lie on the same level and differ from one another only in the size of the area which they cover. In the individual case this coloration, or rather discoloration, of things through their money equivalence may be unnoticeably minute. However, through the relations of the rich to the objects to be had for money, perhaps even through the total character which the mentality of the contemporary public everywhere imparts to these objects, the exclusively pecuniary evaluation of objects has become quite considerable. The large cities, the main seats of the money exchange, bring the purchasability of things to the fore much more impressively than do smaller localities. That is why cities are also the genuine locale of the blasé attitude. In the blasé attitude the concentration of men and things stimulate the nervous system of the individual to its highest achievement so that it attains its peak. Through the mere quantitative intensification of the same conditioning factors this achievement is transformed into its opposite and appears in the peculiar adjustment of the blasé attitude. In this phenomenon the nerves find in the refusal to react to their stimulation the last possibility of accommodating to the contents and forms of metropolitan life. The self-preservation of certain personalities is brought at the price of devaluating the whole objective world, a devaluation which in the end unavoidably drags one's own personality down into a feeling of the same worthlessness.

Whereas the subject of this form of existence has to come to terms with it entirely for himself, his self-preservation in the face of the large city demands from him a no less negative behavior of a social nature. This mental attitude of metropolitans toward one another we may designate, from a formal point of view, as reserve. If so many inner reactions were responses to the continuous external contacts with innumerable people as are those in the small town, where one knows almost everybody one meets and where one has a positive relation to almost everyone, one would be completely atomized internally and come to an unimaginable psychic state. Partly this psychological fact, partly the right to distrust which men have in the face of the touch-and-go elements of metropolitan life, necessitates our reserve. As a result of this reserve we frequently do not even know by sight those who have been our neighbors for years. And it is this reserve which in the eyes of the small-town people makes us appear to be cold and heartless. Indeed, if I do not deceive myself, the inner aspect of this outer reserve is not only indifference but, more often than we are aware, it is a slight aversion, a mutual strangeness and repulsion, which will break into hatred and fight at the moment of a closer contact, however caused. The whole inner organization of such an extensive communicative life rests upon an extremely varied hierarchy of sympathies, indifferences, and aversions of the briefest as well as of the most permanent nature. The sphere of indifference in this hierarchy is not as large as might appear on the surface. Our psychic activity still responds to almost every impression of somebody else with a somewhat distinct feeling. The unconscious, fluid and changing character of this impression seems to result in a state of indifference. Actually this indifference would be just as unnatural as the diffusion of indiscriminate mutual suggestion would be unbearable. From both these typical dangers of the metropolis, indifference and indiscriminate suggestibility, antipathy protects us. A latent antipathy and the preparatory stage of practical antagonism effect the distances and aversions without which this mode of life could not at all be led. The extent and the mixture of this style of life, the rhythm of its emergence and disappearance, the forms in which it is satisfied — all these, with the unifying motives in the narrower sense, form the inseparable whole of the metropolitan style of life. What appears in the metropolitan style of life directly as dissociation is in reality only one of its elemental forms of socialization.

This reserve with its overtone of hidden aversion appears in turn as the form or the cloak of a more general mental phenomenon of the metropolis: it grants to the individual a kind and an amount of personal freedom which has no analogy whatsoever under other conditions. The metropolis goes back to one of the large developmental tendencies of social life as such, to one of the few tendencies for which an approximately universal formula can be discovered. The earliest phase of social formations found in historical as well as in contemporary social structures is this: a relatively small circle firmly closed against neighboring, strange, or in some way antagonistic circles. However, this circle is closely coherent and allows its individual members only a narrow field for the development of unique qualities and free, self-responsible movements. Political and kinship groups, parties and religious associations begin in this way. The self-preservation of very young associations requires the establishment of strict boundaries and a centripetal unity. Therefore they cannot allow the individual freedom and unique inner and outer development. From this stage social development proceeds at once in two different, yet corresponding, directions. To the extent to which the group grows — numerically, spatially, in significance and in content of life — to the same degree the group's direct, inner unity loosens, and the rigidity of the original demarcation against others is softened through mutual relations and connections. At the same time, the individual gains freedom of movement, far beyond the first jealous delimitation. The individual also gains a specific individuality to which the division of labor in the enlarged group gives both occasion and necessity. The state and Christianity, guilds and political parties, and innumerable other groups have developed according to this formula, however much, of course, the special conditions and forces of the respective groups have modified the general scheme. This scheme seems to me distinctly recognizable also in the evolution of individuality within urban life. The small-town life in Antiquity and in the Middle Ages set barriers against movement and relations of the individual toward the outside, and it set up barriers against individual independence and differentiation within the individual self. These barriers were such that under them modern man could not have breathed. Even today a metropolitan man who is placed in a small town feels a restriction similar, at least, in kind. The smaller the circle which forms our milieu is, and the more restricted those relations to others are which dissolve the boundaries of the individual, the more anxiously the circle guards the achievements, the conduct of life, and the outlook of the individual, and the more readily a quantitative and qualitative specialization would break up the framework of the whole little circle.

The ancient *polis* in this respect seems to have had the very character of a small town. The constant threat to its existence at the hands of enemies from near and afar effected strict coherence in political and military respects, a supervision of the citizen by the citizen, a jealousy of the whole against the individual whose particular life was suppressed to such a degree that he could compensate only by acting as a despot in his own household. The tremendous agitation and excitement, the unique colorfulness of Athenian life, can perhaps be understood in terms of the fact that a people of incomparably individualized personalities struggled against the constant inner and outer pressure of a de-individualizing small town. This produced a tense atmosphere in which the weaker individuals were suppressed and those of stronger natures were incited to prove themselves in the most passionate manner. This is precisely why it was that there blossomed in Athens what must be called, without defining it exactly, "the general human character" in the intellectual development of our species. For we maintain factual as well as historical validity for the following connection: the most extensive and the most general contents and forms of life are most intimately connected with the most individual ones. They have a preparatory stage in common, that is, they find their enemy in narrow formations and groupings the maintenance of which places both of them into a state of defense against expanse and generality lying without and the freely moving individuality within. Just as in the feudal age, the "free" man was the one who stood under the law of the land, that is, under the law of the largest social orbit, and the unfree man was the one who derived his right merely from the narrow circle of a feudal association and was excluded from the larger social orbit — so today metropolitan man is "free" in a spiritualized and refined sense, in contrast to the pettiness and prejudices which hem in the small-town man. For the reciprocal reserve and indifference and the intellectual life conditions of large circles are never felt more strongly by the individual in their impact upon his independence than in the thickest crowd of the big city. This is because the bodily proximity and narrowness of space makes the mental distance only the more visible. It is obviously only the obverse of this freedom if, under certain circumstances, one nowhere feels as lonely and lost as in the metropolitan crowd. For here as elsewhere it is by no means necessary that the freedom of man be reflected in his emotional life as comfort.

It is not only the immediate size of the area and the number of persons which, because of the universal historical correlation between the enlargement of the circle and the personal inner and outer freedom, has made the metropolis the locale of freedom. It is rather in transcending this visible expanse that any given city becomes the seat of cosmopolitanism. The horizon of the city expands in a manner comparable to the way in which wealth develops; a certain amount of property increases in a quasi-automatical way in ever more rapid progression. As soon as a certain limit has been passed, the economic, personal, and intellectual relations of the citizenry, the sphere of intellectual predominance of the city over its hinterland, grow as in geometrical progression. Every gain in dynamic extension becomes a step, not for an equal, but for a new and larger extension. From every thread spinning out of the city, ever new threads grow as if by themselves, just as within the city the unearned increment of ground rent, through the mere increase in communication, brings the owner automatically increasing profits. At this point, the quantitative aspect of life is transformed directly into qualitative traits of character. The sphere of life of the small town is, in the main, self-contained and autarchic. For it is the decisive nature of the metropolis that its inner life overflows by waves into a far-flung national or international area. Weimar is not an example to the contrary, since its significance was hinged upon individual personalities and died with them; whereas the metropolis is indeed characterized by its essential independence even from the most eminent individual personalities. This is the counterpart to the independence, and it is the price the individual pays for the independence, which he enjoys in the metropolis. The most significant characteristic of the metropolis is this functional extension beyond its physical boundaries. And this efficacy reacts in turn and gives weight, importance, and responsibility to metropolitan life. Man does not end with the limits of his body or the area comprising his immediate activity. Rather is the range of the person constituted by the sum of effects emanating from him temporally and spatially. In the same way, a city consists of its total effects which extend beyond its immediate confines. Only this range is the city's actual extent in which its existence is expressed. This fact makes it obvious that individual freedom, the logical and historical complement of such extension, is not to be understood only in the negative sense of mere freedom of mobility and elimination of prejudices and petty philistinism. The essential point is that the particularity and incomparability, which ultimately every human being possesses, be somehow expressed in the working-out of a way of life. That we follow the laws of our own nature — and this after all is freedom — becomes obvious and convincing to ourselves and to others only if the expressions of this nature differ from the expressions of others. Only our unmistakability proves that our way of life has not been superimposed by others.

Cities are, first of all, seats of the highest economic division of labor. They produce thereby such extreme phenomena as in Paris the renumerative occupation of the *quatorzième*. They are persons who identify themselves by signs on their residences and who are ready at the dinner hour in correct attire, so that they can be quickly called upon if a dinner party should consist of thirteen persons. In the measure of its expansion, the city offers more and more the decisive conditions of the division of labor. It offers a circle which through its size can absorb a highly diverse variety of services. At the same time, the concentration of individuals and their struggle for customers compel the individual to specialize in a function from which he cannot be readily displaced by another. It is decisive that city life has transformed the struggle with nature for livelihood into an inter-human struggle for gain, which here is not granted by nature but by other men. For specialization does not flow only from the competition for gain but also from the underlying fact that the seller must always seek to call forth new and differentiated needs of the lured customer. In order to find a source of income which is not yet exhausted, and to find a function which cannot readily be displaced, it is necessary to specialize in one's services. This process promotes differentiation, refinement, and the enrichment of the public's needs, which obviously must lead to growing personal differences within this public.

All this forms the transition to the individualization of mental and psychic traits which the city occasions in proportion to its size. There is a whole series of obvious causes underlying this process. First, one must meet the difficulty of asserting his own personality within the dimensions of metropolitan life. Where the quantitative increase in importance and the expense of energy reach their limits, one seizes upon qualitative differentiation in order somehow to attract the attention of the social circle by playing upon its sensitivity for differences. Finally, man is tempted to adopt the most tendentious peculiarities, that is, the specifically metropolitan extravagances of mannerism, caprice, and preciousness. Now, the meaning of these extravagances does not at all lie in the contents of such behavior, but rather in its form of "being different," of standing out in a striking manner and thereby attracting attention. For many character types, ultimately the only means of saving for themselves some modicum of self-esteem and the sense of filling a position is indirect, through the awareness of others. In the same sense a seemingly insignificant factor is operating, the cumulative effects of which are, however, still noticeable. I refer to the brevity and scarcity of the inter-human contacts granted to the metropolitan man, as compared with social intercourse in the small town. The temptation to appear "to the point," to appear concentrated and strikingly characteristic, lies much closer to the individual in brief metropolitan contacts than in an atmosphere in which frequent and prolonged association assures the personality of an unambiguous image of himself in the eyes of the other.

The most profound reason, however, why the metropolis conduces to the urge for the most individual personal existence — no matter whether justified and successful —

appears to me to be the following: the development of modern culture is characterized by the preponderance of what one may call the "objective spirit" over the "subjective spirit." This is to say, in language as well as in law, in the technique of production as well as in art, in science as well as in the objects of the domestic environment, there is embodied a sum of spirit. The individual in his intellectual development follows the growth of this spirit very imperfectly and at an ever increasing distance. If, for instance, we view the immense culture which for the last hundred years has been embodied in things and in knowledge, in institutions and in comforts, and if we compare all this with the cultural progress of the individual during the same period — at least in high status groups — a frightful disproportion in growth between the two becomes evident. Indeed, at some points we notice a retrogression in the culture of the individual with reference to spirituality, delicacy, and idealism. This discrepancy results essentially from the growing division of labor. For the division of labor demands from the individual an ever more one-sided accomplishment, and the greatest advance in a one-sided pursuit only too frequently means dearth to the personality of the individual. In any case, he can cope less and less with the overgrowth of objective culture. The individual is reduced to a negligible quantity, perhaps less in his consciousness than in his practice and in the totality of his obscure emotional states that are derived from this practice. The individual has become a mere cog in an enormous organization of things and powers which tear from his hands all progress, spirituality, and value in order to transform them from their subjective form into the form of a purely objective life. It needs merely to be pointed out that the metropolis is the genuine arena of this culture which outgrows all personal life. Here in buildings and educational institutions, in the wonders and comforts of space-conquering technology, in the formations of community life, and in the visible institutions of the state, is offered such an overwhelming fullness of crystallized and impersonalized spirit that the personality, so to speak, cannot maintain itself under its impact. On the one hand, life is made infinitely easy for the personality in that stimulations, interests, uses of time and consciousness are offered to it from all sides. They carry the person as if in a stream, and one needs hardly to swim for oneself. On the other hand, however, life is composed more and more of these impersonal contents and offerings which tend to displace the genuine personal colorations and incomparabilities. This results in the individual's summoning the utmost in uniqueness and particularization, in order to preserve his most personal core. He has to exaggerate this personal element in order to remain audible even to himself. The atrophy of individual culture through the hypertrophy of objective culture is one reason for the bitter hatred which the preachers of the most extreme individualism, above all Nietzsche, harbor against the metropolis. But it is, indeed, also a reason why these preachers are so passionately loved in the metropolis and why they appear to the metropolitan man as the prophets and saviors of his most unsatisfied yearnings.

If one asks for the historical position of these two forms of individualism which are nourished by the quantitative relation of the metropolis, namely, individual independence and the elaboration of individuality itself, then the metropolis assumes an entirely new rank order in the world history of the spirit. The eighteenth century found the individual in oppressive bonds which had become meaningless — bonds of a political, agrarian, guild, and religious character. They were restraints which, so to speak, forced upon man an unnatural form and outmoded, unjust inequalities. In this situation the cry for liberty and equality arose, the belief in the individual's full freedom of movement in all social and intellectual relationships. Freedom would at once permit the noble substance common to all to come to the fore, a substance which nature had deposited in every man and which society and history had only deformed. Besides this eighteenth-century ideal of liberalism, in the nineteenth century, through Goethe and Romanticism, on the one hand, and through the economic division of labor, on the other hand, another ideal arose: individuals liberated from historical bonds now wished to distinguish themselves from one another. The carrier of man's values is no longer the "general human being" in every individual, but rather man's qualitative uniqueness and irreplaceability. The external and internal history of our time takes its course within the struggle and in the changing entanglements of these two ways of defining the individual's role in the whole of society. It is the function of the metropolis to provide the arena for this struggle and its reconciliation. For the metropolis presents the peculiar conditions which are revealed to us as the opportunities and the stimuli for the development of both these ways of allocating roles to men. Therewith these conditions gain a unique place, pregnant with inestimable meanings for the development of psychic existence. The metropolis reveals itself as one of those great historical formations in which opposing streams which enclose life unfold, as well as join one another with equal right. However, in this process the currents of life, whether their individual phenomena touch us sympathetically or antipathetically, entirely transcend the sphere for which the judge's attitude is appropriate. Since such forces of life have grown into the roots and into the crown of the whole of the historical life in which we, in our fleeting existence, as a cell, belong only as a part, it is not our task either to accuse or to pardon, but only to understand.*

* The content of this lecture by its very nature does not derive from a citable literature. Argument and elaboration of its major cultural-historical ideas are contained in my *Philosophie des Geldes* [The Philosophy of Money; München und Leipzig: Duncker und Humblot, 1900].

7.   Modernity — An Incomplete Project
Jürgen Habermas

In 1980, architects were admitted to the Biennial in Venice, following painters and filmmakers. The note sounded at this first Architecture Biennial was one of disappointment. I would describe it by saying that those who exhibited in Venice formed an avant-garde of reversed fronts. I mean that they sacrificed the tradition of modernity in order to make room for a new historicism. Upon this occasion, a critic of the German newspaper, *Frankfurter Allgemeine Zeitung*, advanced a thesis whose significance reaches beyond this particular event; it is a diagnosis of our times: "Postmodernity definitely presents itself as Antimodernity." This statement describes an emotional current of our times which has penetrated all spheres of intellectual life. It has placed on the agenda theories of postenlightenment, postmodernity, even of posthistory.

From history we know the phrase, "The Ancients and the Moderns." Let me begin by defining these concepts. The term "modern" has a long history, one which has been investigated by Hans Robert Jauss.[1] The word "modern" in its Latin form "modernus" was used for the first time in the late 5th century in order to distinguish the present, which had become officially Christian, from the Roman and pagan past. With varying content, the term "modern" again and again expresses the consciousness of an epoch that relates itself to the past of antiquity, in order to view itself as the result of a transition from the old to the new.

Some writers restrict this concept of "modernity" to the Renaissance, but this is historically too narrow. People considered themselves modern during the period of Charles the Great in the 12th century, as well as in France of the 17th century at the time of the famous "Querelle des Anciens et des Modernes." That is to say, the term "modern" appeared and reappeared exactly during those periods in Europe when the consciousness of a new epoch formed itself through a renewed relationship to the ancients — whenever, moreover, antiquity was considered a model to be recovered through some kind of imitation.

The spell which the classics of the ancient world cast upon the spirit of later times was first dissolved with the ideals of the French Enlightenment. Specifically, the idea of being "modern" by looking back to the ancients changed with the belief, inspired by modern science, in the infinite progress of knowledge and in the infinite advance towards social and moral betterment. Another form of modernist consciousness was formed in the wake of this change. The romantic modernist sought to oppose the antique ideals of the classicists; he looked for a new historical epoch and found it in the idealized Middle Ages. However, this new ideal age, established early in the 19th century, did not remain a fixed ideal. In the course of the 19th century, there emerged out of this romantic spirit that radicalized consciousness of modernity which freed

Jürgen Habermas: 'Modernity — An Incomplete Project', in *POSTMODERN CULTURE*, edited by Hal Foster (Bay Press/Pluto Press, 1985), pp. 3–15.

itself from all specific historical ties. This most recent modernism simply makes an abstract opposition between tradition and the present; and we are, in a way, still the contemporaries of that kind of aesthetic modernity which first appeared in the midst of the 19th century. Since then, the distinguishing mark of works which count as modern is "the new" which will be overcome and made obsolete through the novelty of the next style. But, while that which is merely "stylish" will soon become outmoded, that which is modern preserves a secret tie to the classical. Of course, whatever can survive time has always been considered to be a classic. But the emphatically modern document no longer borrows this power of being a classic from the authority of a past epoch; instead, a modern work becomes a classic because it has once been authentically modern. Our sense of modernity creates its own self-enclosed canons of being classic. In this sense we speak, e.g., in view of the history of modern art, of classical modernity. The relation between "modern" and "classical" has definitely lost a fixed historical reference.

The discipline of aesthetic modernity

The spirit and discipline of aesthetic modernity assumed clear contours in the work of Baudelaire. Modernity then unfolded in various avant-garde movements and finally reached its climax in the Café Voltaire of the dadaists and in surrealism. Aesthetic modernity is characterized by attitudes which find a common focus in a changed consciousness of time. This time consciousness expresses itself through metaphors of the vanguard and the avant-garde. The avant-garde understands itself as invading unknown territory, exposing itself to the dangers of sudden, shocking encounters, conquering an as yet unoccupied future. The avant-garde must find a direction in a landscape into which no one seems to have yet ventured.

But these forward gropings, this anticipation of an undefined future and the cult of the new mean in fact the exaltation of the present. The new time consciousness, which enters philosophy in the writings of Bergson, does more than express the experience of mobility in society, of acceleration in history, of discontinuity in everyday life. The new value placed on the transitory, the elusive and the ephemeral, the very celebration of dynamism, discloses a longing for an undefiled, immaculate and stable present.

This explains the rather abstract language in which the modernist temper has spoken of the "past." Individual epochs lose their distinct forces. Historical memory is replaced by the heroic affinity of the present with the extremes of history — a sense of time wherein decadence immediately recognizes itself in the barbaric, the wild and the primitive. We observe the anarchistic intention of blowing up the continuum of history, and we can account for it in terms of the subversive force of this new aesthetic consciousness. Modernity revolts against the normalizing functions of tradition; modernity lives on the experience of rebelling against all that is normative. This revolt is one way to neutralize the standards of both morality and utility. This aesthetic consciousness continuously stages a dialectical play between secrecy and public scandal; it is addicted to a fascination with that horror which accompanies the act of profaning, and yet is always in flight from the trivial results of profanation.

On the other hand, the time consciousness articulated in avant-garde art is not simply ahistorical; it is directed against what might be called a false normativity in history.

The modern, avant-garde spirit has sought to use the past in a different way; it disposes those pasts which have been made available by the objectifying scholarship of historicism, but it opposes at the same time a neutralized history which is locked up in the museum of historicism.

Drawing upon the spirit of surrealism, Walter Benjamin constructs the relationship of modernity to history in what I would call a posthistoricist attitude. He reminds us of the self-understanding of the French Revolution: "The Revolution cited ancient Rome, just as fashion cites an antiquated dress. Fashion has a scent for what is current, whenever this moves within the thicket of what was once." This is Benjamin's concept of the *Jetzizeit*, of the present as a moment of revelation; a time in which splinters of a messianic presence are enmeshed. In this sense, for Robespierre, the antique Rome was a past laden with momentary revelations.[2]

Now this spirit of aesthetic modernity has recently begun to age. It has been recited once more in the 1960s; after the 1970s, however, we must admit to ourselves that this modernism arouses a much fainter response today than it did fifteen years ago. Octavio Paz, a fellow traveller of modernity, noted already in the middle of the 1960s that "the avant-garde of 1967 repeats the deeds and gestures of those of 1917. We are experiencing the end of the idea of modern art." The work of Peter Burger has since taught us to speak of "post-avant-garde" art; this term is chosen to indicate the failure of the surrealist rebellion.[3] But what is the meaning of this failure? Does it signal a farewell to modernity? Thinking more generally, does the existence of a post-avant-garde mean there is a transition to that broader phenomenon called postmodernity?

This is in fact how Daniel Bell, the most brilliant of the American neoconservatives, interprets matters. In his book, *The Cultural Contradictions of Capitalism*, Bell argues that the crises of the developed societies of the West are to be traced back to a split between culture and society. Modernist culture has come to penetrate the values of everyday life; the life-world is infected by modernism. Because of the forces of modernism, the principle of unlimited self-realization, the demand for authentic self-experience and the subjectivism of a hyperstimulated sensitivity have come to be dominant. This temperament unleashes hedonistic motives irreconcilable with the discipline of professional life in society, Bell says. Moreover, modernist culture is altogether incompatible with the moral basis of a purposive, rational conduct of life. In this manner, Bell places the burden of responsibility for the dissolution of the Protestant ethic (a phenomenon which had already disturbed Max Weber) on the "adversary culture." Culture in its modern form stirs up hatred against the conventions and virtues of everyday life, which has become rationalized under the pressures of economic and administrative imperatives.

I would call your attention to a complex wrinkle in this view. The impulse of modernity, we are told on the other hand, is exhausted; anyone who considers himself avant-garde can read his own death warrant. Although the avant-garde is still considered to be expanding, it is supposedly no longer creative. Modernism is dominant but dead. For the neoconservative the question then arises: how can norms arise in society which will limit libertinism, reestablish the ethic of discipline and work? What new norms will put a brake on the levelling caused by the social welfare state so that the virtues of individual competition for achievement can again dominate? Bell sees a religious revival to be the only solution. Religious faith tied to a faith in tradition will provide individuals with clearly defined identities and existential society.

Cultural modernity and societal modernization

One can certainly not conjure up by magic the compelling beliefs which command authority. Analyses like Bell's, therefore, only result in an attitude which is spreading in Germany no less than in the States: an intellectual and political confrontation with the carriers of cultural modernity. I cite Peter Steinfels, an observer of the new style which the neoconservatives have imposed upon the intellectual scene in the 1970s:

> The struggle takes the form of exposing every manifestation of what could be considered an oppositionist mentality and tracing its "logic" so as to link it to various forms of extremism: drawing the connection between modernism and nihilism. . . between government regulation and totalitarianism, between criticism of arms expenditures and subservience to communism, between Women's liberation or homosexual rights and the destruction of the family. . . between the Left generally and terrorism, anti-semitism, and fascism. . .[4]

The *ad hominen* approach and the bitterness of these intellectual accusations have also been trumpeted loudly in Germany. They should not be explained so much in terms of the psychology of neoconservative writers; rather, they are rooted in the analytical weaknesses of neoconservative doctrine itself.

Neoconservative shifts onto cultural modernism the uncomfortable burdens of a more or less successful capitalist modernization of the economy and society. The neoconservative doctrine blurs the relationship between the welcomed process of societal modernization on the one hand, and the lamented cultural development on the other. The neoconservative does not uncover the economic and social causes for the altered attitudes towards work, consumption, achievement and leisure. Consequently, he attributes all of the following — hedonism, the lack of social identification, the lack of obedience, narcissism, the withdrawal from status and achievement competition — to the domain of "culture." In fact, however, culture is intervening in the creation of all these problems in only a very indirect and mediated fashion.

In the neoconservative view, those intellectuals who still feel themselves committed to the project of modernity are then presented as taking the place of those unanalyzed causes. The mood which feeds neoconservatism today in no way originates from discontent about the antinomian consequences of a culture breaking from the museums into the stream of ordinary life. This discontent has not been called into life by modernist intellectuals. It is rooted in deep-seated reactions against the process of *societal* modernization. Under the pressures of the dynamics of economic growth and the organizational accomplishments of the state, this social modernization penetrates deeper and deeper into previous forms of human existence. I would describe this subordination of the life-worlds under the system's imperatives as a matter of disturbing the communicative infrastructure of everyday life.

Thus, for example, neopopulist protests only express in pointed fashion a widespread fear regarding the destruction of the urban and natural environment and of forms of human sociability. There is a certain irony about these protests in terms of neoconservatism. The tasks of passing on a cultural tradition, of social integration and of socialization require adherence to what I call communicative rationality. But the occasions for protest and discontent originate precisely when spheres of communicative action, centered on the reproduction and transmission of values and norms, are penetrated by a form of modernization guided by standards of economic and administrative rationality — in other words, by standards of rationalization quite different from those of communicative rationality on which those spheres depend. But neoconservative doctrines turn our attention precisely away from such societal processes: they project the causes, which they do not bring to light, onto the plane of a subversive culture and its advocates.

To be sure, cultural modernity generates its own aporias as well. Independently from the consequences of *societal* modernization and within the perspective of *cultural* development itself, there originate motives for doubting the project of modernity. Having dealt with a feeble kind of criticism of modernity — that of neoconservatism — let me now move our discussion of modernity and its discontents into a different domain that touches on these aporias of cultural modernity — issues that often serve only as a pretense for those positions which either call for a postmodernity, recommend a return to some form of premodernity, or throw modernity itself overboard.

The project of Enlightenment

The idea of modernity is intimately tied to the development of European art, but what I call "the project of modernity" comes only into focus when we dispense with the usual concentration upon art. Let me start a different analysis by recalling an idea from Max Weber. He characterized cultural modernity as the separation of the substantive reason expressed in religion and metaphysics into three autonomous spheres. They are: science, morality and art. These came to be differentiated because the unified world-views of religion and metaphysics fell apart. Since the 18th century, the problems inherited from these older world-views could be arranged so as to fall under specific aspects of validity: truth, normative rightness, authenticity and beauty. They could then be handled as questions of knowledge, or of justice and morality, or of taste. Scientific discourse, theories of morality, jurisprudence, and the production and criticism of art could in turn be institutionalized. Each domain of culture could be made to correspond to cultural professions in which problems could be dealt with as the concern of special experts. This professionalized treatment of the cultural tradition brings to the fore the intrinsic structures of each of the three dimensions of culture. There appear the structures of cognitive-instrumental, of moral-practical and of aesthetic-expressive rationality, each of these under the control of specialists who seem more adept at being logical in these particular ways than other people are. As a result, the distance grows between the culture of the experts and that of the larger public. What accrues to culture through specialized treatment and reflection does not immediately and necessarily become the property of everyday praxis. With cultural rationalization of this sort, the threat increases that the life-world, whose traditional substance has already been devalued, will become more and more impoverished.

The project of modernity formulated in the 18th century by the philosophers of the Enlightenment consisted in their efforts to develop objective science, universal morality and law, and autonomous art according to their inner logic. At the same time, this project intended to release the cognitive potentials of each of these domains from their esoteric forms. The Enlightenment philosophers wanted to utilize this accumulation of specialized culture for the enrichment of everyday life — that is to say, for the rational organization of everyday social life.

Enlightenment thinkers of the cast of mind of Condorcet still had the extravagant expectation than the arts and sciences would promote not only the control of natural forces but also understanding of the world and of the self, moral progress, the justice of institutions and even the happiness of human beings. The 20th century has shattered this optimism. The differentiation of science, morality and art has come to mean the autonomy of the segments treated by the specialist and their separation from the hermeneutics of everyday communication. This splitting off is the problem that has given rise to efforts to "negate" the culture of expertise. But the problem won't go away: should we try to hold on to the *intentions* of the Enlightenment, feeble as they may be, or should we declare the entire project of modernity a lost cause? I now want to return to the problem of artistic culture, having explained why, historically, aesthetic modernity is only a part of cultural modernity in general.

The false programs of the negation of culture

Greatly oversimplifying, I would say that in the history of modern art one can detect a trend towards ever greater autonomy in the definition and practice of art. The category of "beauty" and the domain of beautiful objects were first constituted in the Renaissance. In the course of the 18th century, literature, the fine arts and music were institutionalized as activities independent from sacred and courtly life. Finally, around the middle of the 19th century an aestheticist conception of art emerged, which encouraged the artist to produce his work according to the distinct consciousness of art for art's sake. The autonomy of the aesthetic sphere could then become a deliberate project: the talented artist could lend authentic expression to those experiences he had in encountering his own de-centered subjectivity, detached from the constraints of routinized cognition and everyday action.

In the mid-19th century, in painting and literature, a movement began which Octavio Paz finds epitomized already in the art criticism of Baudelaire. Color, lines, sounds and movement ceased to serve primarily the cause of representation; the media of expression and the techniques of production themselves became the aesthetic object. Theodor W. Adorno could therefore begin his *Aesthetic Theory* with the following sentence: "It is now taken for granted that nothing which concerns art can be taken for granted any more; neither art itself, nor art in its relationship to the whole, nor even the right of art to exist." And this is what surrealism then denied: *das Existenzrecht der Kunst als Kunst*. To be sure, surrealism would not have challenged the right of art to exist, if modern art no longer had advanced a promise of happiness concerning its own relationship " to the whole" of life. For Schiller, such a promise was delivered by aesthetic intuition, but not fulfilled by it. Schiller's *Letters on the Aesthetic Education of Man* speaks to us of a utopia reaching beyond art itself. But by the time of Baudelaire, who repeated this *promesse de bonheur* via art, the utopia of reconciliation with society had gone sour. A relation of opposites had come into being; art had become a critical mirror, showing the irreconcilable nature of the aesthetic and the social worlds. The modernist transformation was all the more painfully realized, the more art alienated itself from life and withdrew into the untouchableness of complete autonomy. Out of such emotional currents finally gathered those explosive energies which unloaded in the surrealist attempt to blow up the autarkical sphere of art and to force a reconciliation of art and life.

But all those attempts to level art and life, fiction and praxis, appearance and reality to one plane; the attempts to remove the distinction between artifact and object of use, between conscious staging and spontaneous excitement; the attempts to declare everything to be art and everyone to be an artist, to retract all criteria and to equate aesthetic judgment with the expression of subjective experiences — all these undertakings have proved themselves to be sort of nonsense experiments. These experiments have served to bring back to life, and to illuminate all the more glaringly, exactly those structures of art which they were meant to dissolve. They gave a new legitimacy, as ends in themselves, to appearance as the medium of fiction, to the transcendence of the artwork over society, to the concentrated and planned character of artistic production as well as to the special cognitive status of judgments of taste. The radical attempt to negate art has ended up ironically by giving due exactly to these categories through which Enlightenment aesthetics had circumscribed its object domain. The surrealists waged the most extreme warfare, but two mistakes in particular destroyed their revolt. First, when the containers of an autonomously developed cultural sphere are shattered, the contents get dispersed. Nothing remains from a desublimated meaning or a destructured form; an emancipatory effect does not follow.

Their second mistake has more important consequences. In everyday communication, cognitive meanings, moral expectations, subjective expressions and evaluations must relate to one another. Communication processes need a cultural tradition covering all spheres — cognitive, moral-practical and expressive. A rationalized everyday life, therefore, could hardly be saved from cultural impoverishment through breaking open a single cultural sphere — art — and so providing access to just one of the specialized knowledge complexes. The surrealist revolt would have replaced only one abstraction.

In the spheres of theoretical knowledge and morality, there are parallels to this failed attempt of what we might call the false negation of culture. Only they are less pronounced. Since the days of the Young Hegelians, there has been talk about the negation of philosophy. Since Marx, the question of the relationship of theory and practice has been posed. However, Marxist intellectuals joined a social movement; and only at its peripheries were there sectarian attempts to carry out a program of the negation of philosophy similar to the surrealist program to negate art. A parallel to the surrealist mistakes becomes visible in these programs when one observes the consequences of dogmatism and of moral rigorism.

A reified everyday praxis can be cured only by creating unconstrained interaction of the cognitive with the moral-practical and the aesthetic-expressive elements.

Reification cannot be overcome by forcing just one of those highly stylized cultural spheres to open up and become more accessible. Instead, we see under certain circumstances a relationship emerge between terroristic activities and the over-extension of any one of these spheres into other domains: examples would be tendencies to aestheticize politics, or to replace politics by moral rigorism or to submit it to the dogmatism of a doctrine. These phenomena should not lead us, however, into denouncing the intentions of the surviving Enlightenment tradition as intentions rooted in a "terroristic reason."[5] Those who lump together the very project of modernity with the state of consciousness and the spectacular action of the individual terrorist are no less short-sighted than those who would claim that the incomparably more persistent and extensive bureaucratic terror practiced in the dark, in the cellars of the military and secret police, and in camps and institutions, is the *raison d'être* of the modern state, only because this kind of administrative terror makes use of the coercive means of modern bureaucracies.

Alternatives

I think that instead of giving up modernity and its project as a lost cause, we should learn from the mistakes of those extravagant programs which have tried to negate modernity. Perhaps the types of reception of art may offer an example which at least indicates the direction of a way out.

Bourgeois art had two expectations at once from its audiences. On the one hand, the layman who enjoyed art should educate himself to become an expert. On the other hand, he should also behave as a competent consumer who uses art and relates aesthetic experiences to his own life problems. This second, and seemingly harmless, manner of experiencing art has lost its radical implications exactly because it had a confused relation to the attitude of being expert and professional.

To be sure, artistic production would dry up, if it were not carried out in the form of a specialized treatment of autonomous problems and if it were to cease to be the concern of experts who do not pay so much attention to exoteric questions. Both artists and critics accept thereby the fact that such problems fall under the spell of what I earlier called the "inner logic" of a cultural domain. But this sharp delineation, this exclusive concentration on one aspect of validity alone and the exclusion of aspects of truth and justice, break down as soon as aesthetic experience is drawn into an individual life history and is absorbed into ordinary life. The reception of art by the layman, or by the "everyday expert," goes in a rather different direction than the reception of art by the professional critic.

Albrecht Wellmer has drawn my attention to one way that an aesthetic experience which is not framed around the experts' critical judgments of taste can have its significance altered: as soon as such an experience is used to illuminate a life-historical situation and is related to life problems, it enters into a language game which is no longer that of the aesthetic critic. The aesthetic experience then not only renews the interpretation of our needs in whose light we perceive the world. It permeates as well our cognitive significations and out normative expectations and changes the manner in which all these moments refer to one another. Let me give an example of this process.

This manner of receiving and relating to art is suggested in the first volume of the work *The Aesthetics of Resistance* by the German-Swedish writer Peter Weiss. Weiss describes the process of reappropriating art by presenting a group of politically motivated, knowledge-hungry workers in 1937 in Berlin.[6] These were young people who, through an evening high-school education, acquired the intellectual means to fathom the general and social history of European art. Out of the resilient edifice of this objective mind, embodied in works of art which they saw again and again in the museums in Berlin, they started removing their own chips of stone, which they gathered together and reassembled in the context of their own milieu. This milieu was far removed from that of traditional education as well as from the then existing regime. These young workers went back and forth between the edifice of European art and their own milieu until they were able to illuminate both.

In examples like this which illustrate the reappropriation of the expert's culture from the standpoint of the life-world, we can discern an element which does justice to the intentions of the hopeless surrealist revolts, perhaps even more to Brecht's and Benjamin's interests in how art works, which having lost their aura, could yet be received in illuminating ways. In sum, the project of modernity has not yet been fulfilled. And the reception of art is only one of at least three of its aspects. The project aims at a differentiated relinking of modern culture with an everyday praxis that still depends on vital heritages, but would be impoverished through mere traditionalism. This new connection, however, can only be established under the condition that social modernization will also be steered in a different direction. The life-world has to become able to develop institutions out of itself which set limits to the internal dynamics and imperatives of an almost autonomous economic system and its administrative complements.

If I am not mistaken, the chances for this today are not very good. More or less in the entire Western world a climate has developed that furthers capitalist modernization processes as well as trends critical of cultural modernism. The disillusionment with the very failures of those programs that called for the negation of art and philosophy has come to serve as a pretense for conservative positions. Let me briefly distinguish the antimodernism of the "young conservatives" from the premodernism of the "old conservatives" and from the postmodernism of the neoconservatives.

The "young conservatives" recapitulate the basic experience of aesthetic modernity. They claim as their own the revelations of a decentered subjectivity, emancipated from the imperatives of work and usefulness, and with this experience they step outside the modern world. On the basis of modernistic attitudes they justify an irreconcilable antimodernism. They remove into the sphere of the far-away and the archaic the spontaneous powers of imagination, self-experience and emotion. To instrumental reason they juxtapose in Manichean fashion a principle only accessible through evocation, be it the will to power or sovereignty, Being or the Dionysiac force of the poetical. In France this line leads from Georges Bataille via Michel Foucault to Jacques Derrida.

The "old conservatives" do not allow themselves to be contaminated by cultural modernism. They observe the decline of substantive reason, the differentiation of science, morality and art, the modern world view and its merely procedural rationality, with sadness and recommend a withdrawal to a position *anterior* to modernity. Neo-Aristotelianism, in particular, enjoys a certain success today. In view of the problematic of ecology, it allows itself to call for a cosmological ethic. (As belonging to this school, which originates with Leo Strauss, one can count the interesting works of Hans Jonas and Robert Spaemann.)

Finally, the neoconservatives welcome the development of modern science, as long as this only goes beyond its sphere to carry forward technical progress, capitalist growth and rational administration. Moreover, they recommend a politics of defusing the explosive content of cultural modernity. According to one thesis, science, when properly understood, has become irrevocably meaningless for the orientation of the life-world. A further thesis is that politics must be kept as far aloof as possible from the demands of moral-practical justification. And a third thesis asserts the pure immanence of art, disputes that it has a utopian content, and points to its illusory character in order to limit the aesthetic experience to privacy. (One could name here the early Wittgenstein, Carl Schmitt of the middle period, and Gottfried Benn of the late period.) But with the decisive confinement of science, morality and art to autonomous spheres separated from the life-world and administered by experts, what remains from the project of cultural modernity is only what we would have if we were to give up the project of modernity altogether. As a replacement one points to traditions which, however, are held to be immune to demands of (normative) justification and validation.

This typology is like any other, of course, a simplification, but it may not prove totally useless for the analysis of contemporary intellectual and political confrontations. I fear that the ideas of antimodernity, together with an additional touch of premodernity, are becoming popular in the circles of alternative culture. When one observes the transformations of consciousness within political parties in Germany, a new ideological shift (*Tendenzwende*) becomes visible. And this is the alliance of postmodernists with premodernists. It seems to me that there is no party in particular that monopolizes the abuse of intellectuals and the position of neoconservatism. I therefore have good reason to be thankful for the liberal spirit in which the city of Frankfurt offers me a prize bearing the name of Theodor Adorno, a most significant son of this city, who as philosopher and writer has stamped the image of the intellectual in our country in incomparable fashion, who, even more, has become the very image of emulation for the intellectual.

Translated by Seyla Ben-Habib

References

1. Jauss is a prominent German literary historian and critic involved in "the aesthetics of reception," a type of criticism related to reader-response criticism in this country. For a discussion of "modern" see Jauss, *Asthetische Normen und geschichtliche Reflexion in der Querelle des Anciens et des Modernes* (Munich, 1964). For a reference in English see Jauss, "History of Art and Pragmatic History," *Toward an Aesthetic of Reception*, trans. Timothy Bahti (Minneapolis: University of Minnesota Press, 1982), pp. 46–8. [Ed.]

2. See Benjamin, "Theses on the Philosophy of History," *Illuminations*, trans. Harry Zohn (New York: Schocken, 1969), p. 261. [Ed.]

3. For Paz on the avant-garde see in particular *Children of the Mire: Modern Poetry from Romanticism to the Avant-Garde* (Cambridge: Harvard University Press, 1974), pp. 148–64. For Bürger see *Theory of the Avant-Garde* (Minneapolis: University of Minnesota Press, Fall 1983). [Ed.]

4. Peter Steinfels, *The Neoconservatives* (New York: Simon and Schuster, 1979), p. 65.

5. The phrase "to aestheticize politics" echoes Benjamin's famous formulation of the false social program of the fascists in "The Work of Art in the Age of Mechanical Reproduction." Habermas's criticism here of Enlightenment critics seems directed less at Adorno and Max Horkheimer than at the contemporary *nouveaux philosophes* (Bernard-Henri, Lèvy, etc.) and their German and American counterparts. [Ed.]

6. The reference is to the novel *Die Asthetik des Widerstands* (1975-8) by the author perhaps best known here for his 1965 play *Marat/Sade*. The work of art "reappropriated" by the workers is the Pergamon altar, emblem of power, classicism and rationality. [Ed.]

This essay was originally delivered as a talk in September 1980 when Habermas was awarded the Theodor W. Adorno prize by the city of Frankfurt. It was subsequently delivered as a James Lecture of the New York Institute for the Humanities at New York University in March 1981 and published under the title "Modernity Versus Postmodernity" in *New German Critique* 22 (Winter, 1981).

8. The Development of Sociological Theory
Anthony Giddens

When they first start studying sociology, many people are puzzled by the diversity of perspectives they encounter. Sociologists do not have an agreed theoretical standpoint; they quite often argue among themselves about how we should go about studying human behaviour and how research results might best be interpreted. Why should this be? Why can't sociologists agree with one another more consistently, as natural scientists seem able to do?

The answer to these questions is bound up with the very nature of sociology itself. Sociology is about our own lives and our own behaviour, and studying ourselves is the most complex and difficult endeavour we can undertake. In all academic disciplines — including the natural sciences — there is far more disagreement over theoretical approaches than over empirical research, because empirical work can be directly checked, and repeated if there are varying views about its factual findings. Theoretical disputes are always partly dependent on interpretation, and can rarely be decisively settled in the same way. In sociology, the difficulties inherent in subjecting our own behaviour to study further complicate this problem. Hence theoretical controversies and debates occupy a central place in the discipline.

In this chapter, we shall analyse the development of the major **theoretical approaches** in sociology, identifying the dilemmas to which they point. We shall start by looking at the views of some of the founders of modern sociology — for many of the ideas they pioneered are still influential — before considering the theoretical approaches which dominate the discipline today and going on to discuss some of the problems they raise.

Early origins

Human beings have always been curious about the sources of their own behaviour, but for thousands of years our attempts to understand ourselves relied on ways of thinking passed down from generation to generation and expressed in religious terms. The systematic study of human behaviour and human society is a relatively recent development, whose beginnings can be found in the late eighteenth century. The background to the new approach was the series of sweeping changes, referred to many times in this book, associated with industrialization and urbanism. The shattering of traditional ways of life prompted the attempt to develop a new understanding of both the social and the natural worlds.

Auguste Comte

No single individual, of course, can found a whole discipline, and there were many contributors to early sociological thinking. Pride of place is usually given to the French

Anthony Giddens: 'The Development of Sociological Theory' from *SOCIOLOGY* (2nd revised edition; Polity Press, 1994), pp. 705-710. © Anthony Giddens 1989, 1993. Reproduced by permission of Basil Blackwell Limited.

author Auguste Comte (1789–1857), if only because he actually coined the word 'sociology'. Comte originally used the term 'social physics' to refer to the new field of study, but other writers were also beginning to use that term, and he wanted to distinguish his views from theirs, so he invented a new word to describe the subject he wished to establish. Comte regarded sociology as the last science to develop, but as the most significant and complex of all sciences. He believed it should contribute to the welfare of humanity; in the later part of his career, he drew up ambitious plans for the reconstruction of French society in particular and human societies in general.

Emile Durkheim

Comte's work had a direct influence on another French writer, Emile Durkheim (1858–1917). Although he drew on aspects of Comte's writings, Durkheim thought much of his work too speculative and vague, believing that Comte had not successfully carried out his programme — to establish sociology on a scientific basis. To become scientific, according to Durkheim, sociology must study 'social facts'. That is to say, it must pursue the analysis of social institutions with the same objectivity as scientists study nature. Durkheim's famous first principle of sociology is: 'study social facts as *things*!' By this he means that social life can be analysed as rigorously as objects or events in nature.

Like all the major founders of sociology, Durkheim was preoccupied with the changes transforming society. He tried to understand these changes in terms of the development of the **division of labour** (the growth of ever more complex distinctions between different occupations) as part of industrialization. Durkheim argues that the division of labour gradually replaces religion as the main basis of social cohesion. As the division of labour expands, people become more and more dependent on one another, because each person needs goods and services that those in other occupations supply. According to Durkheim, processes of change in the modern world are so rapid and intense that they give rise to major social difficulties, which he linked to **anomie**. Anomie is the feeling of aimlessness or purposelessness provoked by certain social conditions. Traditional moral controls and standards, which used to be supplied by religion, are largely broken down by modern social development, and this leaves many individuals in modern societies with the feeling that their day-to-day lives lack meaning.

One of Durkheim's most famous studies is concerned with the analysis of suicide (Durkheim, 1952; originally published 1897). Suicide seems to be a purely personal act; it appears to be entirely the outcome of extreme personal unhappiness. Durkheim shows, however, that social factors have a fundamental influence on suicidal behaviour — anomie being one of these influences. Suicide rates show regular patterns from year to year, and these patterns have to be explained sociologically. Many objections can be raised against aspects of Durkheim's study, but it remains a classic work whose relevance to sociology today is by no means exhausted.

Karl Marx

The ideas of Karl Marx contrast quite sharply with those of Comte and Durkheim. Marx was born in Germany in 1818, and died in England in 1883. Although originally trained in German traditions of thought, he spent much of his life in Britain and produced his major works there. Marx was not able to pursue a university career, since as a young man his political activities had brought him into conflict with the German authorities. After a brief stay in France he settled permanently in exile in Britain.

Marx's writings cover a diversity of areas. Even his sternest critics regard his work as of significance to the development of sociology, but Marx did not see himself as a 'sociologist'. Much of his writing concentrates on economic issues, but since he is always concerned to connect economic problems to social institutions, his work is rich in sociological insights.

Marx's viewpoint is founded on what he calls the **materialist conception of history**. According to him, it is not the ideas or values which human beings hold that are the main sources of social change. Rather, social change is prompted primarily by economic influences. These are linked to the conflicts between classes that provide the motive power of historical development. In Marx's words: 'All human history thus far is the history of class struggles' (Marx and Engels, 1968, p. 35).

Though he writes about various phases of history, Marx concentrates his attention on change in modern times. For him, the most important changes involved in the modern period are bound up with the development of **capitalism**. Capitalism is a system of production that contrasts radically with previous economic orders in history, involving as it does the production of goods and services sold to a wide range of consumers. Those who own capital — factories, machines and large sums of money — form a ruling class. The mass of the population make up a class of wage-workers, or working class, who do not own the means of their own livelihood, but have to find employment provided by the owners of capital. Capitalism is thus a class system, in which conflict between classes is a common occurrence.

According to Marx, capitalism will in future be supplanted by socialism or communism (he used these words interchangeably), and in socialist society there will be no classes. Marx does not mean by this that all inequalities between individuals will disappear; rather, societies will no longer be split into a small class which monopolizes economic and political power and the large mass of people who benefit little from the wealth their labour creates. The economic system will come under communal ownership, and a more egalitarian and participatory social order will be established.

For Marx, the study of the development and likely future of capitalism was to provide the means of actively transforming it through political action. Marx's sociological observations were thus closely related to a political programme. However valid Marx's writings themselves may or may not be, this programme has had a far-reaching effect on the twentieth-century world. Until recently, more than a third of the world's population lived in societies whose governments claimed to derive their inspiration from Marx's ideas.

It is important to try to approach the study of Marx's work in an unprejudiced way. This is not easy, because the widespread influence of Marx's writings has produced major differences of opinion about their value. Even those strongly influenced by Marx have used them in varying ways — there are large differences among the views of those who call themselves 'Marxists'. In spite of the fall of Communism in Eastern Europe, Marx's ideas, used in a critical and selective way, are likely to remain an important intellectual resource in the social sciences.

Max Weber

Like Marx, Max Weber (1864–1920) cannot simply be labelled as a 'sociologist' — his interests and concerns ranged across many disciplines. He was born in Germany, and spent the whole of his academic career there. Weber was somewhat depressive in character, and for much of his life was unable to sustain a full-time teaching post in a university; but a private income allowed him to devote himself to scholarship. He was an individual of quite extraordinarily wide learning. His writings covered the fields of economics, law, philosophy and comparative history, as well as sociology, and much of his work was concerned with the development of modern capitalism. He was influenced by Marx, but was also strongly critical of some of Marx's major views. He rejected the materialist conception of history, and saw class conflict as less significant than Marx. In Weber's view, ideas and values have as much impact as economic conditions on social change.

Some of Weber's most important writings are concerned with analysing the distinctiveness of Western society and culture, as compared to those of other major civilizations. He produced extensive studies of the traditional Chinese empire, India and the Near East (Weber, 1951, 1958, 1952), and in the course of these researches made major contributions to the sociology of religion. Comparing the leading religious systems in China and India with those of the West, Weber concluded that certain aspects of Christian beliefs strongly influenced the rise of capitalism.

One of the most persistent concerns of Weber's work is the study of **bureaucracy**. A bureaucracy is a large-scale organization divided into offices and staffed by officials of varying ranks; large industrial firms, government organizations, hospitals and schools are examples. Weber believed the advance of bureaucracy to be an inevitable feature of our era. It makes possible the efficient running of large-scale organizations, but poses problems for effective democratic participation in modern societies. Bureaucracy involves the rule of experts, whose decisions are taken without much reference to those affected by them.

Weber's contributions range over many other areas, including the study of the development of cities, systems of law, types of economy and the nature of classes. He also wrote extensively on the overall character of sociology itself. Weber was more cautious than either Durkheim or Marx in claiming sociology to be a science. According to him, it is misleading to imagine that we can study people using the same procedures as are applied to investigating the physical world. Humans are thinking, reasoning beings; we attach meaning and significance to most of what we do, and any discipline that deals with human behaviour must acknowledge this.

Later developments

While the origins of sociology were mainly European, this century the subject has become firmly established worldwide, and some of the most important developments have taken place in the United States. The work of George Herbert Mead (1863–1931), a philosopher teaching at the University of Chicago, has had an important influence on the development of sociological theory. Mead emphasized the centrality of language and of symbols as a whole in human social life. The perspective he developed later came to be called **symbolic interactionism**. Mead gave more attention to analysing small-scale social processes than to the study of overall societies.

Talcott Parsons (1902–79) was the most prominent American sociological theorist of the postwar period. He was a prolific author, who wrote on many empirical areas of sociology as well as theory. He made contributions to the study of the family, bureaucracy, the professions and the study of politics, among other areas. He was one of the main contributors to the development of **functionalism**, a theoretical approach originally pioneered by Durkheim and Comte. According to the functionalist viewpoint, in studying any given society, we should look at how its various 'parts', or institutions, combine to give that society continuity over time.

European thinkers continue to be prominent in the latter-day development of sociological theory, however. An approach which has achieved particular prominence is **structuralism**, which links sociological analysis closely to the study of language. Structuralist thought was originally pioneered in linguistics, and was then imported into the social sciences by the anthropologist Claude Lévi-Strauss (1908–). But its origins can also be traced back to Durkheim and Marx.

The Subject Matter of Sociology: Discovering 'The Social'

9. [Extracts from] The Enlightenment and the Birth of Social Science

Peter Hamilton

Human nature and human society

It is arguable that the sociological ideas developed by the Enlightenment were preoccupied with the advancement of freedom and humanity.

In this section, the emergence of a specifically modern approach to the scientific study of man in society will be analysed, as it appears principally in the work of two Enlightenment writers, Montesquieu (Charles de Secondat), and Adam Ferguson.

. . . Mere curiosity, scepticism and a belief that scientific principles could be applied to human affairs were not enough. The distinctive character of the emergent social sciences was given them by the commitment of their practitioners to *social change,* to a transformation of human affairs by means of extending man's understanding of himself.

Revolution and Reformation

In the emergence of distinctively modern societies, the social and political transformations which occurred in the American and French Revolutions of 1776 and 1789 appear to be intimately linked. They are widely represented as the thresholds between traditional and modern society, symbolizing the end of feudalism and absolutism, and the rise of the bourgeoisie as the dominant class in capitalist society, as well as major steps along the roads to both liberal democracy and totalitarianism. But what is the precise nature of the relationship between the Enlightenment and the French and American Revolutions? This topic has been hotly debated for the last 200 years, and we are not going to resolve it in this chapter. Our concerns are more with some of the implications of these Revolutions for the emergence of sociology and the other social sciences as institutionalized disciplines.

The American Revolution and the War of Independence which followed it (1776–83) appeared to prove that a new Republic could be created, that it could defeat a powerful monarchy and that it could encapsulate Enlightenment ideas. A number of the central figures of the new American Republic — notably Thomas Jefferson, Benjamin Franklin, John Adams, and Alexander Hamilton — were *philosophes* in the sense of being part of the wider circle of intellectuals in touch with the key figures of the Enlightenment. The Republic's constitution enshrined a number of central precepts of the Enlightenment: the uniformity of human nature (equality), tolerance, freedom of thought and expression, the separation of powers. It owed a lot to Montesquieu's ideas about the social basis of political order, to Hume's conception of the universality of

Peter Hamilton: 'Human Nature and Human Society', 'Revolution and Reformation' and 'The Birth of Sociology: Saint Simon and Comte' from *FORMATIONS OF MODERNITY*, edited by Stuart Hall and Bram Gieben (Polity Press in association with Blackwell Publishers and The Open University), pp. 46-57. Reproduced by permission of Basil Blackwell Limited.

human nature, and to Voltaire's concern with freedom of thought. Yet like most products of the Enlightenment it had its dark side: slavery paradoxically remained legal (Jefferson was himself a plantation owner and a slave-master).

The success of the American Revolution — helped to no small degree by aid from the French state, as part of its long struggle with Britain for European dominance — encouraged those in France who wished to see an end to the 'despotism' of absolute monarchy in Europe.

It was widely thought at the time that the French Revolution was in part at least a by-product of the dangerous ideas proposed by the *philosophes*. As Catherine the Great of Russia wrote in 1794 to the Baron Grimm:

> Do you remember that the late King of Prussia claimed to have been told by Helvétius that the aim of the *philosophes* was to overturn all thrones, and that the *Encyclopédie* was written with no other end in view than to destroy all kings and all religions? Do you also remember that you never wished to be included among the *philosophes*? Well, you were right . . . The sole aim of the whole movement, as experience is proving, is to destroy.

Yet, as we have noted, the *philosophes* for the most part thought that progress could come about within the existing social order. As Diderot once said, their aim was revolutionary only insofar as it sought 'the revolution which will take place in the minds of men' (quoted in Eliot and Stern, 1979, p.44). Indeed, Voltaire believed in the necessity of absolute monarchs (like Louis XV, whose historiographer-royal he became) because only they would have the power to sweep away the institutions and outmoded laws which kept men in a state of ignorance and superstition.

In Britain, Edmund Burke (1729–97), a political theorist of the Whig party, put forward what was to be an influential conservative interpretation of the Enlightenment, which saw it as an intellectual or philosophic conspiracy, fomented by a 'literary cabal', and designed to destroy Christianity, and in the process bring down the French state. To support his case he used the example of the Bavarian *Illuminati*. There had been a notorious conspiracy by a group of Enlightenment-influenced intellectuals in Bavaria — the *Illuminati* — to use freemasonry to bring down the Church-dominated government of the German principality in 1787.

In his widely read *Reflections on the Revolution in France* (1790), Burke laid responsibility for the Revolution squarely at the door of the *philosophes*. He told the French that there was nothing fundamentally wrong with the *ancien régime*, and that they had no need to bring the monarchy down: 'You had the elements of a constitution very nearly as good as could be wished . . . but you chose to act as if you had never been moulded into civil society and had everything to begin anew' (quoted in Doyle, 1989, p.166).

Burke's ideas were vigorously contested by Thomas Paine (1737–1809), amongst others, in his *Rights of Man*, a strong case for the republican argument, and one which stressed that the French were creating a new constitution on the basis of Enlightenment thinking — rational, equitable, based on natural law and scientific principles. The debate between Burke and Paine was linked quite closely to a wider political struggle over parliamentary reform in England, and continued until about 1800. Although Paine's ideas were highly influential in Britain, in Europe Burke's argument that societies were very unwise to abandon heritage and established traditions struck a strong chord — particularly among the cultivated and ruling élites who perceived that the example of the French Revolution threatened their own vested interests.

In one sense, the *philosophes* were a key factor in the French Revolution. As Albert Sorel, writing a century later would say:

> The Revolutionary situation was a result of the faults of the Government, but the philosophes gave it leaders, cadres, a doctrine, direction, the temptation of illusions and the irresistible momentum of hope. They did not create the causes of the Revolution, but they made them manifest, actuated them, gave them emotive force, multiplied them and quickened their pace. The writings of the philosophes were not responsible for the disintegration of the ancien régime: it was because it was disintegrating of its own accord that their influence promoted the Revolution.
>
> (Sorel, 1969, pp.238–9; first published 1885)

As Sorel and many historians since have made very clear, the conditions for revolution existed at least as early as the reign of Louis XV: only a certain sense of optimism that his successor would put things right, founded in the residual legitimacy of the monarchy for most of the French, delayed the events which finally occurred in 1789. Despite the *philosophes'* own protestations to the contrary, the Enlightenment was a radical force in undermining the legitimacy of the *ancien régime*. The main factor in this was the great popularity of Enlightenment thinking among the educated élites. We have noted the virtual explosion in the number of books, newspapers, journals, literary societies, and subscription libraries between 1725 and 1789. This provoked a growth in the number of state censors, from 41 in 1720 to 148 by 1789. The expulsion of the Jesuit order in 1764 as a result of a long dispute between the order and the French *Parlements* (which seriously disrupted the French educational system: about a quarter of the French *collèges* were run by Jesuits) also gave a boost to the mounting tide of irreligion and to demands for greater religious tolerance, largely emanating from the *philosophes*. The Church itself tried to stem this tide by publishing refutations of philosophic impieties, and getting pious laymen in positions of authority to suppress dissent, but of course as a result it only succeeded in encouraging the wider debate of central issues of Enlightenment thought.

The French Revolution became, as the historian William Doyle has said, 'an opportunity for enlightened men to bring about a more rational, just and humane organisation of the affairs of mankind'. The National Assembly, which launched the Revolution in 1789, included 'the cream of the country's intelligentsia, who consciously saw themselves as the products and the instruments of the triumph of Enlightenment. All over France men of similar background rallied to them, inspired by the same ideals' (Doyle, 1989, p.393). The revolutionary constitution which that Assembly produced in 1791 was directly based upon ideas first enunciated in *De l'Esprit des Lois* by Montesquieu, especially those relating to the separation of powers between executive, legislature and judiciary.

It would be misleading to see the French Revolution as no more than the putting into practice of the intellectual principles of the Enlightenment. As Mounier, the moderate royalist leader of 1789, argued much later, 'it was not the influence of those principles which created the Revolution, it was on the contrary the Revolution which created their influence' (quoted in Hampson, 1969, p.256).

As a socio-political event, the French Revolution stands at the threshold of the modern world, and that world is arguably inconceivable without it, for it transformed men's outlook on the nature and organization of society. If we then look at the chief architects of that Revolution, and ask from where their own outlook was derived, we come back to the main figures of the Enlightenment — to Voltaire, Montesquieu, Diderot, Rousseau, Condorcet, Bejamin Franklin.

It is in the areas of civil law, parliamentary control of taxation, the liberties of the press and of the individual, religious tolerance, and the wholesale sweeping away of feudal laws and obligations ('privilege') that the influence of the Enlightenment on the Revolution is clearest. The *philosophes* believed that 'men would live with greater happiness and dignity if their social institutions were determined by what was considered reasonable or scientific rather than regulated by prescription' (Hampson 1969, p.252). With this went the assumption that men had certain inalienable rights, such as unrestricted freedom of access to information, freedom of speech, freedom from arbitary arrest, and freedom of economic activity. Taken overall, they appear as the Revolution's drive to institutionalize a greater degree of social, political and economic equality within the state, to counter the natural inequality of man which underpinned the whole complex system of law, taxation and local government of the *ancien régime*. Yet, at least in its early stages, the ideal of equality was a limited one, and not as radical as it might appear. What the revolutionaries of 1789–91 wanted was an opening up of French society to those men — essentially the educated, cultivated 'gentlemen' who had been some of the main consumers of Enlightenment thought — then excluded from power and influence. In many ways they wanted a society like that of England, where a limited democracy was available.

The Revolution took a different turn after 1792, entering a clear second phase and becoming both more radically republican and Rousseauist in its form. The Republic was engaged in a war against numerous absolutist or monarchist states on its frontiers (Austria, Prussia, Holland, Spain, Britain) and internally against those who opposed the increasingly democratic and totalitarian directions which its institutions were taking. It had progressively less to do with the basic principles of the *philosophes*, and became closer in spirit to the ideas of Jean-Jacques Rousseau, with the Republic represented as a sort of Ideal City, and society seen as a means for reinforcing the morality of its members. The execution of Louis XVI in 1793, and the Terror unleashed against many of those who had been the main supporters of the Revolution of 1789, seemed to many outside of France to be proof that the Enlightenment had created a monster. Many European intellectuals — Kant among them — were repelled by the violence of the Revolution, and the increasingly belligerent nationalism of France.

The latter history of the Revolution, and its transformation into a new form of absolutism under Napoleon, thus helped to accelerate a move away from the ideals of the Enlightenment. Only those measures which helped national efficiency (e.g. internal free trade, technical education) remained. Basic liberties, such as freedom of the press and freedom from arbitrary arrest, were suspended. The Enlightenment as a force for progress and intellectual change was effectively at an end. Nevertheless, the intellectual principles which it had institutionalized amongst the cultivated élite survived, and formed the basis of a new set of reflections upon the ordering of a post-revolutionary society.

The birth of sociology: Saint-Simon and Comte

Although the Revolution and its aftermath carried away with it some of the 'momentum of hope' engendered by the Enlightenment, the intellectual advances it brought in ways of thinking about man and society were not jettisoned in the process. Other intellectual fashions — especially, in the more conservative forms of Romanticism, a return to a belief in order and tradition — held sway, but the palpable advances of the natural sciences and their progressive institutionalization as professionalized disciplines continued to provide a model for the social sciences to follow. The social changes which the French Revolution had brought in its train — notably the emergence of an economically powerful middle class — also provided a new social force in the constitution of civil society, and with it the creation of new social theories which could make sense of the new directions in which an emergent 'modern' and 'industrial' society was heading.

Although a properly professionalized sociology was not to appear until the latter half of the nineteenth century, it is in the carry-over of ideas and concepts from the Enlightenment into the 'classical sociology' formulated in the first decades of the nineteenth century that we can discern its roots. In the writings and activities of Saint-Simon and Comte, a theory was elaborated about the emergent 'industrial society' forming itself in post-revolutionary Europe, and this constituted an agenda of interests for the new science of sociology which was still being debated by Emile Durkheim and Max Weber in the 1890s.

Saint-Simon

When Henri de Saint-Simon (1760–1825) set out to construct a new science of society from the wreckage of the Enlightenment, he saw himself as carrying the *philosophes'* ideas on to a new plane: 'The philosophy of the eighteenth century has been critical and revolutionary; that of the nineteenth century will be inventive and constructive' (quoted in Taylor, 1975, p.22).

Saint-Simon was a typical product of the Enlightenment. From a noble family, he received an education steeped in the classics, the new science of Newton, and the writings of the *philosophes*, typical of the second half of the eighteenth century. As he later wrote: 'Our education achieved its purpose: it made us revolutionaries' (quoted in Taylor, 1975, p.14).

Saint-Simon narrowly escaped becoming a victim of the Terror before a series of successful financial speculations made him (briefly) a rich man. He used the leisure this brought him to follow and even finance courses in the study of science and physiology, the latter because he held the view that a new science of society — a 'social physiology' — would be necessary if order and stability were to become possible again. Saint-Simon came to believe that modern society was threatened by the forces of anarchy and revolution, and that society would only progress beyond this stage if science and industry were put at the service of mankind through a major social reorganization. Scientists would become the new religious leaders because, as human thought had become more enlightened since the Middle Ages, the Catholic clergy could no longer demonstrate the spiritual power required to hold society together. Saint-Simon proposed a 'religion of Newton' organized on both national and international levels, with the world's most eminent scientists and artists at its head. Temporal power would belong with the property owners, representatives of the new industrial class.

Although these notions received relatively little attention, Saint-Simon's ideas about the need for a science of man and society became progressively more influential as war and social disorder engulfed Europe in the first two decades of the nineteenth century. His *Memoire sur la Science de l'Homme* (Memoir on the Science of Man) and *Travail sur la Gravitation Universelle* (Work on Universal Gravitation), both written in 1813, received wide recognition as an appeal to found a new social science which would counteract the forces of conflict and disorder. As a result of this and later work, Saint-Simon became a key figure in the 'liberal' political movements of post-Napoleonic Europe. In his journal *L'Industrie*, Saint-Simon used the term 'liberal' to describe economic and political values which were in favour of greater freedom for manufacture and trade, and a bigger say in how the country was run for those who owned factories and other businesses.

Comte

Auguste Comte (1798–1857) was the first person to use the term 'sociology' to describe the scientific study of society. Comte's work has been presented as a synthesis of the writings of key Enlightenment figures such as Montesquieu, the physiocratic economist Turgot, and Condorcet, and of his erstwhile patron and collaborator, Saint-Simon. Although the *philosophes* clearly inspired Comte, his work in defining the subject matter and methods of the new science — sociology — goes far beyond them, and offers a clear link to the professionalized discipline of the twentieth century (Thompson, 1976, p.6).

Comte wished to create a naturalistic science of society capable of both explaining its past and predicting its future. He developed a theory which has many affinities with those of the Enlightenment *philosophes*, in that it proposed a series of stages (The Law of Human Progress or the Law of Three Stages), through which society has progressed. Unlike the stadial (staged) theories of Ferguson or Smith however, his notion of development was based on the idea of a development of the human mind, and societal stages thus mirrored these developments in terms of social organization, types of social unit and forms of social order. Like the *philosophes*, he saw society as developing progressively through the emancipation of the human intellect. Where he differed from them most substantially was in the notion that societies are in effect like giant biological organisms. Their evolution and development thus follow well-defined, law-like stages, much as the development of an animal follows a clear pattern.

Comte believed that sociology was the study of such patterns of societal evolution, and that it would proceed through an analysis of both static and dynamic aspects of social organization. He distinguished these two not by empirical criteria, but ethodologically.

Static and dynamic, order and progress are always present in an interconnected way, and thus their differentiation in any empirical context is always a matter of methodological distinction, based on theoretical concepts. It is often very hard to make a purely empirical distinction between these elements in a given situation, where the point at which progress ends and order begins becomes a matter of interpretation. Comte's insight is that these distinctions are theoretical, rather than simple observations.

Like Saint-Simon, Comte used ideas about the function of religion as a sort of social cement which binds societies together. Language also performs this function, but without some form of religion (adapted to the stage of society in which it is found) governments would possess no legitimacy, and society would be torn apart by factional violence. Comte also used a further notion, derived essentially from the Scottish Enlightenment, to explain social order — the division of labour. Men are:

> bound together by the very distribution of their occupations; and it is this distribution which causes the extent and growing complexity of the social organism.

> The social organization tends more and more to rest on an exact estimate of individual diversities, by so distributing employments as to appoint each one to the destination he is most fit for, from his own nature . . . from his education and his position, and, in short, from all his qualifications; so that all individual organizations, even the most vicious and imperfect . . . may finally be made use of for the general good.
> (Comte, *Cours de Philosophie Positive*, 1830–2, vol.II; quoted in Thompson, 1976)

Many of Comte's ideas are remarkably close in spirit to the sociology developed by Emile Durkheim at the end of the nineteenth century: especially his emphasis on the clear definition of sociology's subject matter, and on the methodological principles underlying the new science — observation, experimentation, comparison. Durkheim was also concerned with the role of religion in generating social cohesion or solidarity, in the role of the division of labour within industrial societies, and in the forms of solidarity which modern societies required. Indeed, all of Durkheim's most characteristic ideas have close affinities with those of Comte and Saint-Simon, although it is also quite evident that Durkheim departed from their perspective in a number of respects. But the crucial point is that Emile Durkheim provided theories, methodologies and subject matter for the earliest institutionalization of sociology as a university-based discipline. With Comte and Saint-Simon, then, we are at one of the crucial bridges between the ideas of the Enlightenment and those of modern sociology. They provided the conduit along which certain central principles of the Enlightenment's world-view flowed into modern sociology.

Conclusion

The Enlightenment, which its proponents saw as spreading reason like light, played a critically important part in the emergence of the social sciences. It formed the first stage in the forging of a modern conception of society as an entity open to human agency, whose workings are in principle open to our scrutiny. It created the elements from which intellectuals could begin to construct an image of society which reflected human interests. The *philosophes* certainly believed that human agency, if properly informed by enlightened self-knowledge, was perfectly capable of controlling society — for what was the latter but the aggregated wills of individual men and women? We can be sceptical about the extent to which they really wanted to change society as a result of that self-knowledge, and there is little doubt that most of the major figures in the movement wished only for the end of absolutist rule, and for a political regime which extended if only in a limited way the liberties of the social orders from which they issued.

It is also clear that, like all knowledge, that of the Enlightenment spilled over from the narrow cup into which it was poured by the *philosophes*, and washed over those for whom it was not originally intended, being taken up by a wide range of popularizers and political activists of many hues. When the great rupture between traditional and modern society first took shape in the French Revolution, the jettisoning of traditional values based on Christianity and absolutism must have seemed to many people a logical outcome of the radical programme of the Enlightenment — its hatred of religious orthodoxy and the clergy, its opposition to the political controls of the absolutist state, and its egalitarian ideology. Having prepared — even unwittingly — the ground for Revolution, it is not surprising that the Enlightenment's central ideas were tarred by the ruling élites of post-1815 Europe with the brush of sedition, subversion, and disorder. Indeed, it is a paradox of some magnitude that whilst the Enlightenment never developed a coherent theory or model of the society from which it issued, it produced enough elements of a *critique* of that society to help it along the way to an eventual demise.

How does the Enlightenment link to later stages in the emergence of a science of society? To begin with, we can assess its impact as an early and rather rickety sociological 'paradigm' — a cluster of interconnected ideas which were influential in the ways people thought about the social world and human relationships. If we think of Kant's motto *sapele aude* — dare to know — we can capture the essence of this new approach, this new paradigm. For the first time, man could 'dare to know' about the social arrangements under which he lived, rather than have them presented to him through the obscuring haze of a religious ideology. By knowing about these social arrangements, their operation would become clear, and thus open to change. Much in the same way as knowing about the cause of smallpox enabled man to devise a way of preventing it, it seemed to the *philosophes* self-evident that knowing about the cause of a social injustice, like religious persecution, would enable men to stop it occurring. Rather than a model of society, the Enlightenment had a model of how to think about social arrangements. Its practitioners were not loth to use the term 'society', but rarely even approached a definition of what could be meant by the word. The nearest the *philosophes* got to achieving a modern concept of society is thus the Scottish Enlightenment's ideas about human civilization going through a series of stages, which become the progressive unveiling of the uniformity of human nature. Ferguson's concept of 'civil society' thus appears as a setting in which the uniformity of human nature is finally allowed to operate as a set of arrangements for conducting the business of a nation in an enlightened fashion. It is in 'civil society' that the division of labour enables human nature to work most efficiently, and without unnecessary restraint.

We must not forget that the Enlightenment also encompassed medical, scientific, technological and other innovations, and that as a result it was widely thought of as part of a society-wide process of improving human life. It also made a big impact on education and therefore came to be part of the body of knowledge and ideas which were passed on in the process of schooling. In a general sense, once ways of thinking have been changed, they rarely go back to an earlier state. If I tell you something important which you did not already know, it will be hard for you to forget it. Those who thought and wrote about the society which emerged from the ashes of Revolutionary France, like Saint-Simon and Comte, could not escape their upbringing, which was steeped in the ideas and learning of the *philosophes*. They could not forget the Enlightenment, but they could react against it, and attempt to surpass it. The very thing that was deficient in Enlightenment thought — its inability to provide a coherent explanatory model of the society in which it existed — was precisely the thing that Saint-Simon and Comte tried to improve. They used the concept of society to describe the new combination of people, institutions, social groups and manufacturing processes which was emerging from the wreckage of the traditional European world. But their aim was not merely to describe and understand: like the *philosophes* their objective was to change society. Saint-Simon and Comte wished to see created the 'industrial society' dealt with in their writings.

By contrast, most *philosophes* stopped short of a properly worked out model of society, because they held an essentially 'individualist' conception of man, and because their social theory hardly needed the explicit conception of society as an entity. Once we 'know' that all men share a uniform human nature, it appears possible to construct an explanation of the behaviour of a multitude of people by simply aggregating individual characteristics (as a way of explaining social behaviour, this approach is known by the term 'methodological individualism'). Saint-Simon and Comte went beyond this to write quite explicitly about society as an entity which can be 'known' independently of individual men, as a force which can coerce and constrain individuals to behave in certain ways. Their ideas were influenced both by the traditionalism and romanticism of their time (a sort of reaction to the Enlightenment idea that man is a self-sufficient individual), and by the success of life-sciences such as biology and medicine, in which understanding the interconnections of organic processes played a crucial role. In Comte's work, man becomes subject to society once more, no longer self-sufficient but pushed and pulled by the twin forces of statics and dynamics. Comte presents society as a system which obeys certain laws — the laws which his positive sociology was established to study. His approach is often called 'organicism' because it uses the idea of society as a huge organism, as something more than the sum of its parts. If we take out one unit of that society — a particular person, for instance — we can know something about him or her, but not about how the whole society operates. But in the Enlightenment model, that person is a microcosm of society: by studying him or her we can build a picture about how society as a whole will operate — there are no 'laws of society' which are independent of the individual.

The history of sociology since the Enlightenment can be presented as the tension between the two approaches to society outlined above: one based in the *philosophes'* idea that society is no more than an aggregate of individuals, the other in Comte's idea that society is a superindividual entity, with a life of its own. Such a tension appears in the approaches of the central figures of nineteenth-century sociology, from J.S.Mill and Herbert Spencer to Emile Durkheim and Max Weber. Durkheim developed his own version of organicism, whilst Weber's approach recast the 'methodological individualism' of the Enlightenment in a modern form.

The Enlightenment, then, is one of the starting points for modern sociology. Its central themes formed the threshold of modern thinking about society and the realm of the social. Perhaps of equal importance is that it signalled the appearance of the secular intellectual within western society, a figure whose role is intimately bound up with the analysis and critique of society. It is from that role that emerged, amongst other intellectual positions, the modern conception of the professional sociologist, based in a specific institution. It may be that we have to thank Comte for the name 'sociology', but it is arguably to the Enlightenment that we should turn to see the emergence of the profession of sociologist.

References

Anderson. B. and Zinsser, J. (1990) *A History of their Own: Women in Europe from Prehistory to the Present,* 2 vols, Harmondsworth, Penguin.

Black, J. (1990) *Eighteenth Century Europe 1700–1789,* London, Macmillan.

Brinton, C. (1930) 'The Revolutions', *Encyclopaedia of the Social Sciences,* vol.1. Macmillan, New York.

Darnton, R. (1979) *The Business of Enlightenment. A Publishing History of the Encyclopédie 1775–1800,* Cambridge, Mass., Harvard University Press.

Doyle, W. (1989) *The Oxford History of the French Revolution,* Oxford, Clarendon Press.

Eliot, S. and Stern, B. (eds) (1979) *The Age of Enlightenment: An Anthology of Eighteenth Century Texts,* London, Ward Lock Educational.

Gay, P. (1973a) *The Enlightenment: An Interpretation. Vol. 1: The Rise of Modern Paganism,* London, Wildwood House.

Gay, P. (1973b) *The Enlightenment: An Interpretation. Vol .2: The Science of Freedom,* London, Wildwood House.

Gibbon, E. (1966) *Memoirs of my Life* (ed. by G. A. Bonnard), London, Nelson.

Hampson, N. (1969) *The Enlightenment,* Harmondsworth, Penguin.

Nisbet, R. (1967) *The Sociological Tradition,* London, Heinemann.

Porter, R. (1990) *The Enlightenment,* London, Macmillan.

Sorel, A. (1969) *Europe and The French Revolution: The Political Traditions of the Old Regime* (first published 1885), London, Collins.

Taylor, K. (1975) *Henri Saint-Simon 1760–1825: Selected Writings on Science, Industry and Social Organisation,* London, Croom Helm.

Thompson, K. (1976) *Auguste Comte: The Foundation of Sociology ,* London, Nelson.

10. The Social Element of Suicide

Emile Durkheim

Usually when collective tendencies or passions are spoken of, we tend to regard these expressions as mere metaphors and manners of speech with no real signification but a sort of average among a certain number of individual states. They are not considered as things, forces *sui generis* which dominate the consciousness of single individuals. None the less this is their nature, as is brilliantly[5] shown by statistics of suicide. The individuals making up a society change from year to year, yet the number of suicides is the same so long as the society itself does not change. The population of Paris renews itself very rapidly; yet the share of Paris in the total of French suicides remains practically the same. Although only a few years suffice to change completely the personnel of the army, the rate of military suicides varies only very slowly in a given nation. In all countries the evolution of collective life follows a given rhythm throughout the year; it grows from January to about July and then diminishes. Thus, though the members of the several European societies spring from widely different average types, the seasonal and even monthly variations of suicide take place in accordance with the same law. Likewise, regardless of the diversity of individual temperaments, the relation between the aptitude for suicide of married persons and that of widowers and widows is identically the same in widely differing social groups, from the simple fact that the moral condition of widowhood everywhere bears the same relation to the moral constitution characteristic of marriage. The causes which thus fix the contingent of voluntary deaths for a given society or one part of it must then be independent of individuals, since they retain the same intensity no matter what particular persons they operate on. One would think that an unchanging manner of life would produce unchanging effects. This is true; but a way of life is something, and its unchanging character requires explanation. If a way of life is unchanged while changes occur constantly among those who practise it, it cannot derive its entire reality from them.

It has been thought that this conclusion might be avoided through the observation that this very continuity was the work of individuals and that, consequently, to account for it there was no need to ascribe to social phenomena a sort of transcendency in relation to individual life. Actually, it has been said, "anything social, whether a word of a language, a religious rite, an artisan's skill, an artistic method, a legal statute or a moral maxim is transmitted and passes from an individual parent, teacher, friend, neighbor, or comrade to another individual."[6]

Doubtless if we had only to explain the general way in which an idea or sentiment passes from one generation to another, how it is that the memory of it is not lost, this explanation might as a last resort be considered satisfactory.[7] But the transmission of facts such as suicide and, more broadly speaking, such as the various acts reported by

Reprinted with permission of The Free Press, an imprint of Simon & Schuster, and Routledge, from *SUICIDE: A STUDY IN SOCIOLOGY* by Emile Durkheim, translated by John A. Spaulding and George Simpson. Copyright © 1951, copyright renewed by 1979 by The Free Press.

moral statistics, has a very special nature not to be so readily accounted for. It relates, in fact, not merely in general to a certain way of acting, *but to the number of cases in which this way of acting is employed*. Not merely are there suicides every year, but there are as a general rule as many each year as in the year preceding. The state of mind which causes men to kill themselves is not purely and simply transmitted, but — something much more remarkable — transmitted to an equal number of persons, all in such situations as to make the state of mind become an act. How can this be if only individuals are concerned? The number as such cannot be directly transmitted. Today's population has not learned from yesterday's the size of the contribution it must make to suicide; nevertheless, it will make one of identical size with that of the past, unless circumstances change.

Are we then to imagine that, in some way, each suicide had as his initiator and teacher one of the victims of the year before and that he is something like his moral heir? Only thus can one conceive the possibility that the social suicide-rate is perpetuated by way of interindividual traditions. For if the total figure cannot be transmitted as a whole, the units composing it must be transmitted singly. According to this idea, each suicide would have received his tendency from some one of his predecessors and each act of suicide would be something like the echo of a preceding one. But not a fact exists to permit the assumption of such a personal filiation between each of these moral occurrences statistically registered this year, for example, and a similar event of the year before. As has been shown above, it is quite exceptional for an act to be inspired in this way by another of like nature. Besides, why should these ricochets occur regularly from year to year? Why should the generating act require a year to produce its counterpart? Finally, why should it inspire a single copy only? For surely each model must be reproduced only once on the average, or the total would not be constant. Such an hypothesis, as arbitrary as it is difficult to conceive, we need discuss no longer. But if it is dropped, if the numerical equality of annual contingents does not result from each particular case producing its counterpart in the ensuing period, it can only be due to the permanent action of some impersonal cause which transcends all individual cases.

The terms therefore must be strictly understood. Collective tendencies have an existence of their own; they are forces as real as cosmic forces, though of another sort; they, likewise, affect the individual from without, though through other channels. The proof that the reality of collective tendencies is no less than that of cosmic forces is that this reality is demonstrated in the same way, by the uniformity of effects. When we find that the number of deaths varies little from year to year, we explain this regularity by saying that mortality depends on the climate, the temperature, the nature of the soil, in brief on a certain number of material forces which remain constant through changing generations because independent of individuals. Since, therefore, moral acts such as suicide are reproduced not merely with an equal but with a greater uniformity, we must likewise admit that they depend on forces external to individuals. Only, since these forces must be of a moral order and since, except for individual men, there is no other moral order of existence in the world but society, they must be social. But whatever they are called, the important thing is to recognize their reality and conceive of them as totality of forces which cause us to act from without, like the physico-chemical forces to which we react. So truly are they things *sui generis* and not mere verbal entities that they may be measured, their relative sizes compared, as is done with the intensity of electric currents or luminous foci. Thus, the basic proposition that social facts are objective, a proposition we have had the opportunity to prove in another work[8] and which we consider the fundamental principle of the sociological method, finds a new and especially conclusive proof in moral statistics and above all in the statistics of suicide. Of course, it offends common sense. But science has encountered incredulity whenever it has revealed to men the existence of a force that has been overlooked. Since the system of accepted ideas must be modified to make room for the new order of things and to establish new concepts, men's minds resist through mere inertia. Yet this understanding must be reached. If there is such a science as sociology, it can only be the study of a world hitherto unknown, different from those explored by the other sciences. This world is nothing if not a system of realities.

But just because it encounters traditional prejudices this conception has aroused objections to which we must reply.

First, it implies that collective tendencies and thoughts are of a different nature from individual tendencies and thoughts, that the former have characteristics which the latter lack. How can this be, it is objected, since there are only individuals in society? But, reasoning thus, we should have to say that there is nothing more in animate nature than inorganic matter, since the cell is made exclusively of inanimate atoms. To be sure, it is likewise true that society has no other active forces than individuals; but individuals by combining form a psychical existence of a new species, which consequently has its own manner of thinking and feeling. Of course the elementary qualities of which the social fact consists are present in germ in individual minds. But the social fact emerges from them only when they have been transformed by association since it is only then that it appears. Association itself is also an active factor productive of special effects. In itself it is therefore something new. When the consciousness of individuals, instead of remaining isolated, becomes grouped and combined, something in the world has been altered. Naturally this change produces others, this novelty engenders other novelties, phenomena appear whose characteristic qualities are not found in the elements composing them.

This proposition could only be opposed by agreeing that a whole is qualitatively identical with the sum of its parts, that an effect is qualitatively reducible to the sum of its productive causes; which amounts to denying all change or to making it inexplicable. Someone has, however, gone so far as to sustain this extreme thesis, but only two truly extraordinary reasons have been found for its defense. First, it has been said that "in sociology we have through a rare privilege intimate knowledge both of that element which is our individual consciousness and of the compound which is the sum of consciousness in individuals"; secondly, that through this two-fold introspection "we clearly ascertain that if the individual is subtracted nothing remains of the social."[9]

The first assertion is a bold denial of all contemporary psychology. Today it is generally recognized that psychical life, far from being directly cognizable, has on the contrary profound depths inaccessible to ordinary perception, to which we attain only gradually by devious and complicated paths like those employed by the sciences of the external world. The nature of consciousness is therefore far from lacking in mystery for the future. The second proposition is purely arbitrary. The author may of course state that in his personal opinion nothing real exists in society but what is individual, but proofs supporting this statement are lacking and discussion is therefore impossible. It would be only too easy to oppose to this the contrary feeling of a great many persons, who conceive of society not as the form spontaneously assumed by individual nature on expanding outwardly, but as an antagonistic force restricting individual natures and resisted by them! What a remarkable intuition it is, by the way, that lets us know directly and without intermediary both the element — the individual — and the compound, society? If we had really only to open our eyes and take a good look to perceive at once the laws of the social world, sociology would be useless or at least very simple. Unfortunately, facts show only too clearly the incompetence of consciousness in this matter. Never would consciousness have dreamt, of its own accord, of the necessity which annually reproduces demographic phenomena in equal numbers, had it not received a suggestion from without. Still less can it discover their causes, if left to its own devices.

But by separating social from individual life in this manner, we do not mean that there is nothing psychical about the former. On the contrary, it is clear that essentially social life is made up of representations. Only these collective representations are of quite another character from those of the individual. We see no objection to calling sociology a variety of psychology, if we carefully add that social psychology has its own laws which are not those of individual psychology. An example will make the thought perfectly clear. Usually the origin of religion is ascribed to feelings of fear or reverence inspired in conscious persons by mysterious and dreaded beings; from this point of view, religion seems merely like the development of individual states of mind and private feelings. But this over-simplified explanation has no relation to facts. It is enough to note that the institution of religion is unknown to the animal kingdom, where social life is always very rudimentary, that it is never found except where a collective organization exists, that it varies with the nature of societies, in order to conclude justifiably that exclusively men in groups think along religious lines. The individual would never have risen to the conception of forces which so immeasurably surpass him and all his surroundings, had he known nothing but himself and the physical universe. Not even the great natural forces to which he has relations could have suggested such a notion to him; for he was originally far from having his present knowledge of the extent of their dominance; on the contrary, he then believed that he could control them under certain conditions.[10] Science taught him how much he was their inferior. The power thus imposed on his respect and become the object of his adoration is society, of which the gods were only the hypostatic form. Religion is in a word the system of symbols by means of which society becomes conscious of itself; it is the characteristic way of thinking of collective existence. Here then is a great group of states of mind which would not have originated if individual states of consciousness had not combined, and which result from this union and are superadded to those which derive from individual natures. In spite of the minutest possible analysis of the latter, they will never serve to explain the foundation and development of the strange beliefs and practices from which sprang totemism, the origin of naturism from it and how naturism itself became on the one hand the abstract religion of Jahwe, on the other, the polytheism of the Greeks and Romans, etc. All we mean by affirming the distinction between the social and the individual is that the above observations apply not only to religion, but to law, morals, customs, political institutions, pedagogical practices, etc., in a word to all forms of collective life.[11]

Another objection has been made, at first glance apparently more serious. Not only have we admitted that the social states of mind are qualitatively different from individual ones, but that they are in a sense exterior to individuals. We have not even hesitated to compare this quality of being external with that of physical forces. But, it is objected, since there is nothing in society except individuals, how could there be anything external to them?

If the objection were well founded we should face an antinomy. For we must not lose sight of what has been proved already. Since the handful of people who kill themselves annually do not form a natural group, and are not in communication with one another, the stable number of suicides can only be due to the influence of a common cause which dominates and survives the individual persons involved. The force uniting the conglomerate multitude of individual cases, scattered over the face of the earth, must necessarily be external to each of them. If it were really impossible for it to be so, the problem would be insoluble. But the impossibility is only apparent.

First, it is not true that society is made up only of individuals; it also includes material things, which play an essential role in the common life. The social fact is sometimes so far materialized as to become an element of the external world. For instance, a definite type of architecture is a social phenomenon; but it is partially embodied in houses and buildings of all sorts which, once constructed, become autonomous realities, independent of individuals. It is the same with the avenues of communication and transportation, with instruments and machines used in industry or private life which express the state of technology at any moment in history, of written language, etc. Social life, which is thus crystallized, as it were, and fixed on material supports, is by just so much externalized, and acts upon us from without. Avenues of communication which have been constructed before our time give a definite direction to our activities, depending on whether they connect us with one or another country. A child's taste is formed as he comes into contact with the monuments of national taste bequeathed by previous generations. At times such monuments even disappear and are forgotten for centuries, then, one day when the nations which reared them are long since extinct, reappear and begin a new existence in the midst of new societies. This is the character of those very social phenomena called Renaissances. A Renaissance is a portion of social life which, after being, so to speak, deposited in material things and remaining long latent there, suddenly reawakens and alters the intellectual and moral orientation of peoples who had had no share in its construction. Doubtless it could not be reanimated if living centers of consciousness did not exist to receive its influence; but these individual conscious centers would have thought and felt quite differently if this influence were not present.

The same remark applies to the definite formulae into which the dogmas of faith are precipitated, or legal precepts when they become fixed externally in a consecrated form. However well digested, they would of course remain dead letters if there were no one to conceive their significance and put them into practice. But though they are not self-sufficient, they are none the less in their own way factors of social activity. They have a manner of action of their own. Juridical relations are widely different depending on whether or not the law is written. Where there is a constituted code, jurisprudence is more regular but less flexible, legislation more uniform but also more rigid. Legislation adapts itself less readily to a variety of individual cases, and resists innovations more strongly. The material forms it assumes are thus not merely ineffective verbal combinations but active realities, since they produce effects which would not occur without their existence. They are not only external to individual consciousness, but this very externality establishes their specific qualities. Because these forms are less at the disposal of individuals, individuals cannot readily adjust them to circumstances, and this very situation makes them more resistant to change.

Of course it is true that not all social consciousness achieves such externalization and materialization. Not all the aesthetic spirit of a nation is embodied in the works it inspires; not all of morality is formulated in clear precepts. The greater part is diffused. There is a large collective life which is at liberty; all sorts of currents come, go, circulate everywhere, cross and mingle in a thousand different ways, and just because they are constantly mobile are never crystalized in an objective form. Today, a breath of sadness and discouragement descends on society; tomorrow, one of joyous confidence will uplift all hearts. For a while the whole group is swayed towards individualism; a new period begins and social and philanthropic aims become paramount. Yesterday cosmopolitanism was the rage, today patriotism has the floor. And all these eddies, all these fluxes and refluxes occur without a single modification of the main legal and moral precepts, immobilised in their sacrosanct forms. Besides, these very precepts merely express a whole sub-jacent life of which they partake; they spring from it but do not supplant it. Beneath all these maxims are actual, living sentiments, summed up by these formulae but only as in a superficial envelope. The formulae would awake no echo if they did not correspond to definite emotions and impressions scattered through society. If, then, we ascribe a kind of reality to them, we do not dream of supposing them to be the whole of moral reality. That would be to take the sign for the thing signified. A sign is certainly something; it is not a kind of supererogatory epiphenomenon; its role in intellectual development is known today. But after all it is only a sign.[12]

But because this part of collective life has not enough consistency to become fixed, it none the less has the same character as the formulated precepts of which we were just speaking. *It is external to each average individual taken singly*. Suppose some great public danger arouses a gust of patriotic feeling. A collective impulse follows, by virtue of which society as a whole assumes axiomatically that private interests, even those usually regarded most highly, must be wholly effaced before the common interest. And the principle is not merely uttered as an *ideal*; if need be it is literally applied. Meanwhile, take a careful look at the average body of individuals. Among very many of them you will recapture something of this moral state of mind, though infinitely attenuated. The men who are ready to make freely so complete a self-abnegation are rare, even in time of war. *Therefore there is not one of all the single centers of consciousness who make up the great body of the nation, to whom the collective current is not almost wholly exterior, since each contains only a spark of it.*

The same thing is observable in respect to even the stablest, most fundamental moral sentiments. Every society, for example, has a respect for the life of man in general, the intensity of which is determined by and commensurate with, the relative[13] weight of the penalties attached to homicide. The average man, on the other hand, certainly feels something of the same sort, but far less and in a quite different way from society. To appreciate this difference, we need only compare the emotion one may individually feel at sight of the murderer or even of the murder, and that which seizes assembled crowds under the same circumstances. We know how far they may be carried if unchecked. It is because, in this case, anger is collective. The same difference constantly appears between the manner in which society resents these crimes and the way in which they affect individuals; that is, between the individual and the social form of the sentiment offended. Social indignation is so strong that it is very often satisfied only by supreme expiation. The private person, however, provided that the victim is unknown or of no interest to him, that the criminal does not live near and thus constitute a personal threat to him, though thinking it proper for the crime to be punished, is not strongly enough stirred to feel a real need for vengeance. He will not take a step to discover the guilty one; he will even hesitate to give him up. Only when public opinion is aroused, as the saying goes, does the matter take on a different aspect. Then we become more active and demanding. But it is opinion speaking through us; we act under the pressure of the collectivity, not as individuals.

Indeed, the distance between the social state and its individual repercussions is usually even greater. In the above case, the collective sentiment, in becoming individualized, retained, at least among most people, strength enough to resist acts by which it is offended; horror at the shedding of human blood is sufficiently deeply enrooted in most consciences today to prevent the outburst of homicidal thoughts. But mere misappropriation, quiet, non-violent fraud, are far from inspiring us with equal aversion. Not many have enough respect for another's rights to stifle in the germ every wish to enrich themselves fraudulently. Not that education does not develop a certain distaste for all unjust actions. But what a difference between this vague, hesitant feeling, ever ready for compromise, and the categorical, unreserved and open stigma with which society punishes theft in all shapes! And what of so many other duties still less rooted in the ordinary man, such as the one that bids us contribute our just share to public expense, not to defraud the public treasury, not to try to avoid military service, to execute contracts faithfully, etc.? If morality in all these respects were only guaranteed by the uncertain feelings of the average conscience, it would be extremely unprotected.

So it is a profound mistake to confuse the collective type of a society, as is so often done, with the average type of its individual members. The morality of the average man is of only moderate intensity. He possesses only the most indispensable ethical principles to any decided degree, and even they are far from being as precise and authoritative as in the collective type, that is, in society as a whole. This, which is the very mistake committed by Quételet, makes the origin of morality an insoluble problem. For since the individual is in general not outstanding, how has a morality so far surpassing him succeeded in establishing itself, if it expresses only the average of individual temperaments? Barring a miracle, the greater cannot arise from the lesser. If the common conscience is nothing but the most general conscience, it cannot rise above the vulgar level. But then whence come the lofty, clearly imperative precepts which society undertakes to teach its children, and respect for which it enforces upon its members? With good reason, religions and many philosophies with them have regarded morality as deriving its total reality only from God. For the pallid, inadequate sketch of it contained in individual consciences cannot be regarded as the original type. This sketch seems rather the result of a crude, unfaithful reproduction, the model for which must therefore exist somewhere outside individuals. This is why the popular imagination, with its customary over-simplicity assigns it to God. Science certainly could waste no time over this conception, of which it does not even take cognizance.[14] Only, without it no alternative exists but to leave morality hanging unexplained in the air or make it a system of collective states of conscience. Morality either springs from nothing given in the world of experience, or it springs from society. It can only exist in a conscience; therefore, if it is not in the individual conscience it is in that of the group. But then it must be admitted that the latter, far from being confused with the average conscience, everywhere surpasses it.

Observation thus confirms our hypothesis. The regularity of statistical data, on the one hand, implies the existence of collective tendencies exterior to the individual, and on the other, we can directly establish this exterior character in a considerable number of important cases. Besides, this exteriority is not in the least surprising for anyone who knows the difference between individual and social states of consciousness. By definition, indeed, the latter can reach none of us except from without, since they do not flow from our personal predispositions. Since they consist of elements foreign to us[15] they express something other than ourselves. To be sure in so far as we are solidary with the group and share its life, we are exposed to their influence; but so far as we have a distinct personality of our own we rebel against and try to escape them. Since everyone leads this sort of double existence simultaneously, each of us has a double impulse. We are drawn in a social direction and tend to follow the inclinations of our own natures. So the rest of society weighs upon us as a restraint to our centrifugal tendencies, and we for our part share in this weight upon others for the purpose of neutralizing theirs. We ourselves undergo the pressure we help to exert upon others. Two antagonistic forces confront each other. One, the collective force, tries to take possession of the individual; the other, the individual force, repulses it. To be sure, the former is much stronger than the latter, since it is made of a combination of all the individual forces; but as it also encounters as many resistances as there are separate persons, it is partially exhausted in these multifarious contests and reaches us disfigured and enfeebled. When it is very strong, when the circumstances activating it are of frequent recurrence, it may still leave a deep impression on individuals; it arouses in them mental states of some vivacity which, once formed, function with the spontaneity of instinct; this happens in the case of the most essential moral ideas. But most social currents are either too weak or too intermittently in contact with us to strike deep roots in us; their action is superficial. Consequently, they remain almost completely external. Hence, the proper way to measure any element of a collective type is not to measure its magnitude within individual consciences and to take the average of them all. Rather, it is their sum that must be taken. Even this method of evaluation would be much below reality, for this would give us only the social sentiment reduced by all its losses through individuation.

So there is some superficiality about attacking our conception as scholasticism and reproaching it for assigning to social phenomena a foundation in some vital principle or other of a new sort. We refuse to accept that these phenomena have as a substratum the conscience of the individual, we assign them another; that formed by all the individual consciences in union and combination. There is nothing substantival or ontological about this substratum, since it is merely a whole composed of parts. But it is just as real, nevertheless, as the elements that make it up; for they are constituted in this very way. They are compounds, too. It is known today that the ego is the resultant of a multitude of conscious states outside the ego; that each of these elementary states, in turn, is the product of unconscious vital units, just as each vital unit is itself due to an association of in-animate particles. Therefore if the psychologist and the biologist correctly regard the phenomena of their study as well founded, merely through the fact of their connection with a combination of elements of the next lower order, why should it not be the same in sociology? Only those have the right to consider such a basis inadequate who have not renounced the hypothesis of a vital force and of a substantive soul. Nothing is more reasonable, then, than this proposition at which such offense has been taken;[16] that a belief or social practice may exist independently of its individual expressions. We clearly did not imply by this that society can exist without individuals, an obvious absurdity we might have been spared having attributed to us. But we did mean: 1. that the group formed by associated individuals has a reality of a different sort from each individual considered singly; 2. that collective states exist in the group from whose nature they spring, before they affect the individual as such and establish in him in a new form a purely inner existence.

Such a way of considering the individual's relations to society also recalls the idea assigned the individual's relations with the species or the race by contemporary zoologists. The very simple theory has been increasingly abandoned that the species is only an individual perpetuated chronologically and generalized spacially. Indeed it conflicts with the fact that the variations produced in a single instance become specific only in very rare and possibly doubtful cases.[17] The distinctive characteristics of the race change in the individual only as they change in the race in general. The latter has therefore some reality whence come the various shapes it assumes among individual beings, far from its consisting simply of a generalization of these beings. We naturally cannot regard these doctrines as finally demonstrated. But it is enough for us to show that our sociological conceptions, without being borrowed from another order of research, are indeed not without analogies to the most positive sciences.

Notes

5. However, such statistics are not the only ones to do so. All the facts of moral statistics imply this conclusion.

6. Tarde, *La sociologie élémentaire*, in *Annales de l'Institut international de sociologie*, p. 213.

7. We say "as a last resort" for the essence of the problem could not be solved in this way. The really important thing if this continuity is to be explained is to show not merely how customary practices of a certain period are not forgotten in a subsequent one, but how they

preserve their authority and continue to function. The mere fact that new generations may know by way of transmissions solely between individuals, what their ancestors did, does not mean that they have to do the same. What does oblige them, then? The respect for custom, the authority of past generations? In that case the cause of the continuity is no longer individuals serving as vehicles for ideas or practices, but the highly collective state of mind which causes ancestors to be regarded with an especial respect among a certain people. And this state of mind is imposed on individuals. Like the tendency to suicide, this state of mind in a given society even has a definite intensity, depending on the greater or lesser degree with which individuals conform to tradition.

8. See *Règles de la méthode sociologique*, ch. II.

9. Tarde, *op. cit.*, in *Annales de l'Institut de sociol.*, p. 222.

10. See Frazer, *Golden Bough*, p. 9 ff.

11. Let us add, to avoid any misunderstanding, that despite all the above we do not admit that there is a precise point at which the individual comes to an end and the social realm commences. Association is not established and does not produce its effects all at once; it requires time and there are consequently moments at which the reality is indeterminate. Thus we pass without interval from one order of facts to the other; but this is no reason for not distinguishing them. Otherwise nothing in the world would be distinct, since there are no distinct genera and evolution is continuous.

12. We do not expect to be reproached further after this explanation with wishing to substitute the exterior for the interior in sociology. We start from the exterior because it alone is immediately given, but only to reach the interior. Doubtless the procedure is complicated; but there is no other unless one would risk having his research apply to his personal feeling concerning the order of facts under investigation instead of to this factual order itself.

13. To discover whether this sentiment of respect is stronger in one society or another, not only the intrinsic violence of the repressive measures should be considered, but the position of the penalty in the penal scale. Premeditated murder is punished solely by death, today as in past centuries. But today unadorned punishment by death has a greater relative significance; for it is the supreme punishment, whereas heretofore it could be aggravated. And since these aggravations were not then applied to ordinary murder, it follows that the latter was the object of lesser reprobation.

14. Just as the science of physics involves no discussion of the belief in God, the creator of the physical world, so the science of morals involves no concern with the doctrine which beholds the creator of morality in God. The question is not of our competence; we are not bound to espouse any solution. Secondary causes alone need occupy out attention.

15. See above, p. 39 and p. 310.

16. See Tarde, *op. cit.*, p. 212.

17. See Delage, *Structure du protoplasme, passim*; Weissmann, *L'hérédité* and all the theories akin to Weissmann's.

11. The Definitions of Sociology and of Social Action

Max Weber

Sociology (in the sense in which this highly ambiguous word is used here) is a science which attempts the interpretive understanding of social action in order thereby to arrive at a causal explanation of its course and effects. In 'action' is included all human behaviour when and in so far as the acting individual attaches a subjective meaning to it. Action in this sense may be either overt or purely inward or subjective; it may consist of positive intervention in a situation, or of deliberately refraining from such intervention or passively acquiescing in the situation. Action is social in so far as, by virtue of the subjective meaning attached to it by the acting individual (or individuals), it takes account of the behaviour of others and is thereby oriented in its course.[3]

The methodological foundations of sociology [4]

1. 'Meaning' may be of two kinds. The term may refer first to the actual existing meaning in the given concrete case of a particular actor, or to the average or approximate meaning attributable to a given plurality of actors; or secondly to the theoretically conceived *pure type*[5] of subjective meaning attributed to the hypothetical actor or actors in a given type of action. In no case does it refer to an objectively 'correct' meaning or one which is 'true' in some metaphysical sense. It is this which distinguishes the empirical sciences of action, such as sociology and history, from the dogmatic disciplines in that area, such as jurisprudence, logic, ethics, and esthetics, which seek to ascertain the 'true' and 'valid' meanings associated with the objects of their investigation.

2. The line between meaningful action and merely reactive behaviour to which no subjective meaning is attached, cannot be sharply drawn empirically. A very considerable part of all sociologically relevant behaviour, especially purely traditional behaviour, is marginal between the two. In the case of many psychophysical processes, meaningful, i.e. subjectively understandable, action is not to be found at all; in others it is discernible only by the expert psychologist. Many mystical experiences which cannot be adequately communicated in words are, for a person who is not susceptible to such experiences, not fully understandable. At the same time the ability to imagine one's self performing a similar action is not a necessary prerequisite to understanding; 'one need not have been Caesar in order to understand Caesar.' For the verifiable accuracy [6] of interpretation of the meaning of a phenomenon, it is a great help to be able to put one's self imaginatively in the place of the actor and thus sympathetically to participate in his experiences, but this is not an essential condition of meaningful interpretation. Understandable and non-understandable components of a process are often intermingled and bound up together.

Reprinted with the permission of The Free Press, an imprint of Simon & Schuster from *THE THEORY OF SOCIAL AND ECONOMIC ORGANIZATION* by Max Weber, translated by A.M. Henderson and Talcott Parsons. Edited by Talcott Parsons. Copyright © 1947, renewed 1975 by Talcott Parsons.

3. All interpretation of meaning, like all scientific observation, strives for clarity and verifiable accuracy of insight and comprehension (*Evidenz*). The basis for certainty in understanding can be either rational, which can be further subdivided into logical and mathematical, or it can be of an emotionally empathic or artistically appreciative quality. In the sphere of action things are rationally evident chiefly when we attain a completely clear intellectual grasp of the action-elements in their intended context of meaning. Empathic or appreciative accuracy is attained when, through sympathetic participation, we can adequately grasp the emotional context in which the action took place. The highest degree of rational understanding is attained in cases involving the meanings of logically or mathematically related propositions; their meaning may be immediately and unambiguously intelligible. We have a perfectly clear understanding of what it means when somebody employs the proposition $2 \times 2 = 4$ or the Pythagorean theorem in reasoning or argument, or when someone correctly carries out a logical train of reasoning according to our accepted modes of thinking. In the same way we also understand what a person is doing when he tries to achieve certain ends by choosing appropriate means on the basis of the facts of the situation as experience has accustomed us to interpret them. Such an interpretation of this type of rationally purposeful action possesses, for the understanding of the choice of means, the highest degree of verifiable certainty. With a lower degree of certainty, which is, however, adequate for most purposes of explanation, we are able to understand errors, including confusion of problems of the sort that we ourselves are liable to, or the origin of which we can detect by sympathetic self-analysis.

On the other hand, many ultimate ends or values toward which experience shows that human action may be oriented, often cannot be understood completely, though sometimes we are able to grasp them intellectually. The more radically they differ from our own ultimate values, however, the more difficult it is for us to make them understandable by imaginatively participating in them. Depending upon the circumstances of the particular case we must be content either with a purely intellectual understanding of such values or when even that fails, sometimes we must simply accept them as given data. Then we can try to understand the action motivated by them on the basis of whatever opportunities for approximate emotional and intellectual interpretation seem to be available at different points in its course. These difficulties apply, for instance, for people not susceptible to the relevant values, to many unusual acts of religious and charitable zeal; also certain kinds of extreme rationalistic fanaticism of the type involved in some forms of the ideology of the 'rights of man' are in a similar position for people who radically repudiate such points of view.

The more we ourselves are susceptible to them the more readily can we imaginatively participate in such emotional reactions as anxiety, anger, ambition, envy, jealousy, love, enthusiasm, pride, vengefulness, loyalty, devotion, and appetites of all sorts, and thereby understand the irrational conduct which grows out of them. Such conduct is 'irrational,' that is, from the point of view of the rational pursuit of a given end. Even when such emotions are found in a degree of intensity of which the observer himself is completely incapable, he can still have a significant degree of emotional understanding of their meaning and can interpret intellectually their influence on the course of action and the selection of means.

For the purposes of a typological scientific analysis it is convenient to treat all irrational, affectually determined elements of behaviour as factors of deviation from a conceptually pure type of rational action. For example a panic on the stock exchange can be most conveniently analysed by attempting to determine first what the course of action would have been if it had not been influenced by irrational affects; it is then possible to introduce the irrational components as accounting for the observed deviations from this hypothetical course. Similarly, in analysing a political or military campaign it is convenient to determine in the first place what would have been a rational course, given the ends of the participants and adequate knowledge of all the circumstances. Only in this way is it possible to assess the causal significance of irrational factors as accounting for the deviations from this type. The construction of a purely rational course of action in such cases serves the sociologist as a type ('ideal type') which has the merit of clear understandability and lack of ambiguity. By comparison with this it is possible to understand the ways in which actual action is influenced by irrational factors of all sorts, such as affects[7] and errors, in that they account for the deviation from the line of conduct which would be expected on the hypothesis that the action were purely rational.

Only in this respect and for these reasons of methodological convenience, is the method of sociology 'rationalistic.' It is naturally not legitimate to interpret this procedure as involving a 'rationalistic bias' of sociology, but only as a methodological device. It certainly does not involve a belief in the actual predominance of rational elements in human life, for on the question of how far this predominance does or does not exist, nothing whatever has been said. That there is, however, a danger of rationalistic interpretations where they are out of place naturally cannot be denied. All experience unfortunately confirms the existence of this danger.

4. In all the sciences of human action, account must be taken of processes and phenomena which are devoid of subjective meaning,[8] in the role of stimuli, results, favouring or hindering circumstances. To be devoid of meaning is not identical with being lifeless or non-human; every artifact, such as for example a machine, can be understood only in terms of the meaning which its production and use have had or will have for human action; a meaning which may derive from a relation to exceedingly various purposes. Without reference to this meaning such an object remains wholly unintelligible.[9] That which is intelligible or understandable about it is thus its relation to human action in the role either of means or of end; a relation of which the actor or actors can be said to have been aware and to which their action has been oriented. Only in terms of such categories is it possible to 'understand' objects of this kind. On the other hand processes or conditions, whether they are animate or inanimate, human or non-human, are in the present sense devoid of meaning in so far as they cannot be related to an intended purpose. That is to say they are devoid of meaning if they cannot be related to action in the role of means or ends but constitute only the stimulus, the favouring or hindering circumstances.[10] It may be that the incursion of the Dollart at the beginning of the twelfth century[11] had historical significance as a stimulus to the beginning of certain migrations of considerable importance. Human mortality, indeed the organic life cycle generally from the helplessness of infancy to that of old age, is naturally of the very greatest sociological importance through the various ways in

which human action has been oriented to these facts. To still another category of facts devoid of meaning belong certain psychic or psychophysical phenomena such as fatigue, habituation, memory, etc.; also certain typical states of euphoria under some conditions of ascetic mortification; finally, typical variations in the reactions of individuals according to reaction-time, precision, and other modes. But in the last analysis the same principle applies to these as to other phenomena which are devoid of meaning. Both the actor and the sociologist must accept them as data to be taken into account.

It is altogether possible that future research may be able to discover non-understandable uniformities underlying what has appeared to be specifically meaningful action, though little has been accomplished in this direction thus far. Thus, for example, differences in hereditary biological constitution, as of 'races,' would have to be treated by sociology as given data in the same way as the physiological facts of the need of nutrition or the effect of senescence on action. This would be the case if, and in so far as, we had statistically conclusive proof of their influence on sociologically relevant behaviour. The recognition of the causal significance of such factors would naturally not in the least alter the specific task of sociological analysis or of that of the other sciences of action, which is the interpretation of action in terms of its subjective meaning. The effect would be only to introduce certain non-understandable data of the same order as others which, it has been noted above, are already present, into the complex of subjectively understandable motivation at certain points. Thus it may come to be known that there are typical relations between the frequency of certain types of teleological orientation of action or of the degree of certain kinds of rationality and the cephalic index or skin colour or any other biologically inherited characteristic.

5. Understanding may be of two kinds: the first is the direct observational understanding[12] of the subjective meaning of a given act as such, including verbal utterances. We thus understand by direct observation, in this sense, the meaning of the proposition $2 \times 2 = 4$ when we hear or read it. This is a case of the direct rational understanding of ideas. We also understand an outbreak of anger as manifested by facial expression, exclamations or irrational movements. This is direct observational understanding of irrational emotional reactions. We can understand in a similar observational way the action of a woodcutter or of somebody who reaches for the knob to shut a door or who aims a gun at an animal. This is rational observational understanding of actions.

Understanding may, however, be of another sort, namely explanatory understanding. Thus we understand in terms of *motive* the meaning an actor attaches to the proposition twice two equals four, when he states it or writes it down, in that we understand what makes him do this at precisely this moment and in these circumstances. Understanding in this sense is attained if we know that he is engaged in balancing a ledger or in making a scientific demonstration, or is engaged in some other task of which this particular act would be an appropriate part. This is rational understanding of motivation, which consists in placing the act in an intelligible and more inclusive context of meaning.[13] Thus we understand the chopping of wood or aiming of a gun in terms of motive in addition to direct observation if we know that the woodchopper is working for a wage or is chopping a supply of firewood for his own use or possibly is doing it for recreation. But he might also be 'working off' a fit of rage, an irrational case. Similarly we understand the motive of a person aiming a gun if we know that he has been commanded to shoot as a member of a firing squad, that he is fighting against an enemy, or that he is doing it for revenge. The last is affectually determined and thus in a certain sense irrational. Finally we have a motivational understanding of the outburst of anger if we know that it has been provoked by jealousy, injured pride, or an insult. The last examples are all affectually determined and hence derived from irrational motives. In all the above cases the particular act has been placed in an understandable sequence of motivation, the understanding of which can be treated as an explanation of the actual course of behaviour. Thus for a science which is concerned with the subjective meaning of action, explanation requires a grasp of the complex of meaning in which an actual course of understandable action thus interpreted belongs.[14] In all such cases, even where the processes are largely affectual, the subjective meaning of the action, including that also of the relevant meaning complexes, will be called the 'intended' meaning.'[15]. This involves a departure from ordinary usage, which speaks of intention in this sense only in the case of rationally purposive action.

6. In all these cases understanding involves the interpretive grasp of the meaning present in one of the following contexts: (a) as in the historical approach, the actually intended meaning for concrete individual action; or (b) as in cases of sociological mass phenomena the average of, or an approximation to, the actually intended meaning; or (c) the meaning appropriate to a scientifically formulated pure type (an ideal type) of a common phenomenon. The concepts and 'laws' of pure economic theory are examples of this kind of ideal type. They state what course a given type of human action would take if it were strictly rational, unaffected by errors or emotional factors and if, furthermore, it were completely and unequivocally directed to a single end, the maximization of economic advantage. In reality, action takes exactly this course only in unusual cases, as sometimes on the stock exchange; and even then there is usually only an approximation to the ideal type.[16]

Notes

3.   In this series of definitions Weber employs several important terms which need discussion. In addition to *Verstehen*, which has already been commented upon, there are four important ones: *Deuten*, *Sinn*, *Handeln*, and *Verhalten*. *Deuten* has generally been translated as 'interpret.' As used by Weber in this context it refers to the interpretation of subjective states of mind and the meanings which can be imputed as intended by an actor. Any other meaning of the word 'interpretation' is irrelevant to Weber's discussion. The term *Sinn* has generally been translated as 'meaning'; and its variations, particularly the corresponding adjectives, *sinnhaft*, *sinnvoll*, *sinnfremd*, have been dealt with by appropriately modifying the term meaning. The reference here again is always to features of the content of subjective states of mind or of symbolic systems which are ultimately referable to such states of mind.

The terms *Handeln* and *Verhalten* are directly related. *Verhalten* is the broader term referring to any mode of behaviour of human individuals, regardless of the frame of reference in terms of which it is analysed. 'Behaviour' has seemed to be the most appropriate English equivalent. *Handeln*, on the other hand, refers to the concrete phenomenon of human behaviour only in so far as it is capable of 'understanding,' in

Weber's technical sense, in terms of subjective categories. The most appropriate English equivalent has seemed to be 'action.' This corresponds to the editor's usage in *The Structure of Social Action* and would seem to be fairly well established. 'Conduct' is also closely similar and has sometimes been used. *Deuten*, *Verstehen*, and *Sinn* are thus applicable to human behaviour only in so far as it constitutes action or conduct in this specific sense. (ed).

4. Weber's text is organized in a somewhat unusual manner. He lays down certain fundamental definitions and then proceeds to comment upon them. The definitions themselves are in the original printed in large type, the subsidiary comments in smaller type. For the purposes of this translation it has not seemed best to make a distinction in type form, but the reader should be aware that the numbered paragraphs which follow a definition or group of them are in the nature of comments, rather than the continuous development of a general line of argument. This fact accounts for what is sometimes a relatively fragmentary character of the development and for the abrupt transition from one subject to another. Weber apparently did not intend this material to be 'read' in the ordinary sense, but rather to serve as a reference work for the clarification and systematization of theoretical concepts and their implications. While the comments under most of the definitions are relatively brief, under the definitions of Sociology and of Social Action, Weber wrote what is essentially a methodological essay. This makes sec I out of proportion to the other sections of this and the following chapters. It has, however, seemed best to retain Weber's own plan for the subdivision of the material. (ed).

5. Weber means by 'pure type' what he himself generally called and what has come to be known in the literature about his methodology as the 'ideal type.' The reader may be referred for general orientation to Weber's own Essay (to which he himself refers below), *Die Objektivität sozialwissenschaftlicher Erkenntnis*; to two works of Dr. Alexander von Schelting, 'Die logische Theorie der historischen Kulturwissenschaften von Max Weber' (*Archiv fuer Sozialwissenschaft*, vol. xlix), and *Max Webers Wissenschaftslehre*; and to the editor's *Structure of Social Action*, chap. xvi. A somewhat different interpretation is given in Theodore Abel, *Systematic Sociology in Germany*, chap. iv. (ed).

6. This is an imperfect rendering of the German term *Evidenz*, for which, unfortunately, there is no good English equivalent. It has hence been rendered in a number of different ways, varying with the particular context in which it occurs. The primary meaning refers to the basis on which a scientist or thinker becomes satisfied of the certainty or acceptability of a proposition. As Weber himself points out, there are two primary aspects of this. On the one hand a conclusion can be 'seen' to follow from given premises by virtue of logical, mathematical, or possibly other modes of meaningful relation. In this sense one 'sees' the solution of an arithmetical problem or the correctness of the proof of a geometrical theorem. The other aspect is concerned with empirical observation. If an act of observation is competently performed, in a similar sense one 'sees' the truth of the relevant descriptive proposition. The term *Evidenz* does not refer to the process of observing, but to the quality of its result, by virtue of which the observer feels justified in affirming a given statement. Hence 'certainty' has seemed a suitable translation in some contexts, 'clarity' in others, 'accuracy' in still others. The term 'intuition' is not usable because it refers to the process rather than to the result. (ed).

7. A term now much used in psychological literature, especially that of Psychoanalysis. It is roughly equivalent to 'emotion' but more precise. (ed).

8. The German term is *sinnfremd*. This should not be translated by 'meaningless'' but interpreted in the technical context of Weber's use of *Verstehen* and *Sinndeutung*. The

essential criterion is the impossibility of placing the object in question in a complex of relations on the meaningful level. (ed).

9. *Unverstehbar.*

10. Surely this passage states too narrow a conception of the scope of meaningful interpretation. It is certainly not *only* in terms such as those of the rational means-end schema, that it is possible to make action understandable in terms of subjective categories. This probably can actually be called a source of rationalistic bias in Weber's work. In practice he does not adhere at all rigorously to this methodological position. For certain possibilities in this broader field, see the editor's *Structure of Social Action*, chaps. vi and xi. (ed).

11. A gulf of the North Sea which broke through the Netherlands coast, flooding an area. (ed).

12. Weber here uses the term *aktuelles Verstehen*, which he contrasts with *erklärendes Verstehen*. The latter he also refers to as *motivationsmaessig*. 'Aktuell' in this context has been translated as 'observational.' It is clear from Weber's discussion that the primary criterion is the possibility of deriving the meaning of an act or symbolic expression from immediate observation without reference to any broader context. In *erklärendes Verstehen*, on the other hand, the particular act must be placed in a broader context of meaning involving facts which cannot be derived from immediate observation of a particular act or expression. (ed).

13. The German term is *Sinnzusammenhang*. It refers to a plurality of elements which form a coherent whole on the level of meaning. There are several possible modes of meaningful relation between such elements, such as logical consistency, the esthetic harmony of a style, or the appropriateness of means to an end. In any case, however, a *Sinnzusammenhang* must be distinguished from a system of elements which are causally interdependent. There seems to be no single English term or phrase which is always adequate. According to variations in the context, 'context of meaning,' 'complex of meaning,' and sometimes 'meaningful system' have been employed. (ed).

14. On the significance of this type of explanation for casual relationship. See para. 6, pp. 96 ff. below in the present section.

15. The German is *gemeinter Sinn*. Weber departs from ordinary usage not only in broadening the meaning of this conception. As he states at the end of the present methodological discussion, he does not restrict the use of this concept to cases where a clear self-conscious awareness of such meaning can be reasonably attributed to every individual actor. Essentially, what Weber is doing is to formulate an operational concept. The question is not whether in a sense obvious to the ordinary person such an intended meaning 'really exists,' but whether the concept is capable of providing a logical framework within which scientifically important observations can be made. The test of validity of the observations is not whether their object is immediately clear to common sense, but whether the results of these technical observations can be satisfactorily organized and related to those of others in a systematic body of knowledge. (ed).

16. The scientific functions of such construction have been discussed in the author's article in the *Archiv für Sozialwissenschaft*, vol. xix, pp. 64 ff.

12. Sociology and the Growth of Industrial Society

David Lee and Howard Newby

Although it is possible to trace retrospectively a 'sociological' tradition of thought whic hgoes back to the time of the Ancient Greeks, the word itself — an unhappy amalgam of Latin and Greek roots — is said to have been first coined by the Frenchman, Auguste Comte, as recently as the beginning of the nineteenth century. Like so many words, 'sociology' was introduced in response to a need. It was not a coincidence that sociology began to emerge as a recognized form of enquiry at the beginning of the nineteenth century for there was widespread agreement among observers and commentators at this time that Northern Europe and North America were passing through the most profound transformation of society in the history of mankind. This rupture was regarded as being so profound and so unique that most of the hitherto taken-for-granted assumptions about society and social relationships were thrown into confusion and doubt. We are referring here to the effects of the so-called twin 'revolutions' — the Industrial Revolution of England (and later elsewhere) which occurred roughly between 1780 and 1840 and the Democratic Revolutions of the United States of America in 1776 and France in 1789. Rightly or wrongly, these revolutions were viewed as having precipitated quite unprecedented changes in the organization of society. The tremendous social, economic, political and *ideological* ferment which they provoked forced a whole range of thinkers to come to terms with trying to explain these changes in an apparently novel and distinctive way — a way which we can now call, loosely, sociology.

In many respects we are all, individually and collectively, still trying to come to terms with the kind of society which was forged during this period. The social problems which have been left in its wake remain all around us. And as sociologists we are still trying to grapple with the sociological problems which so concerned the 'founding fathers' of the discipline. This is why this chapter is aimed at conveying something of the flavour of the changes which the early sociologists were trying to explain, principally those which occurred in England between 1750 and 1850 and in France, Germany and the United States somewhat later.

In the previous chapter we referred to the kind of society which emerged in this period as 'industrial society' and, indeed, this period is often referred to as the Industrial Revolution. But this begs some very important questions. Although all the early 'sociologists' were agreed that *something* unique and important had happened during this period, they were by no means in agreement about what, precisely, it was. They characterized the 'great transformation' in different ways and therefore, not surprisingly, sought different explanations of what they observed. From these different explanations we can trace the founding of the main theoretical traditions in sociology.

David Lee and Howard Newby: 'Sociology and the Growth of Industrial Society' from *THE PROBLEM OF SOCIOLOGY: AN INTRODUCTION TO THE DISCIPLINE* (Hutchinson Education, 1983). Reprinted by permission of Routledge.

The important and distinctive features of this period can be interpreted in (at least) four different ways, as representing the growth of:

a)   industrialism

b)   capitalism

c)   urbanism

d)   liberal democracy.

A moment's reflection will, of course, show that the first three are closely related interpretations of the *economic* transformations of the 'Industrial' Revolution. The fourth bears upon responses to the political transformations wrought by the 'Democratic' Revolutions. In the remainder of this chapter, then, we will deal with each of these in turn and examine their significance for the rise of sociology.

Industrialism

What, asks Eric Hobsbawm in his book *The Age of Revolution,*

> does the phrase '[the] industrial revolution broke out' mean? It means that some time in the 1780s, and for the first time in human history, the shackles were taken off the productive power of human societies which henceforth became capable of the constant, rapid and up to the present limitless multiplication of men, goods and services. (Hobsbawm 1962, p. 45)

Typically when we refer to the Industrial Revolution we are concerned with the transformation of the British economy from one based primarily upon agriculture to one based primarily upon manufacture. With this transformation came the changes to which Hobsbawm refers — changes in the technology of production (for example, new machines) and changes in the social relationships which surround the organization of production (for example, the factory system). It is important to recognize that industrialism is not the same phenomenon as capitalism. Although the two are often merged together, and while we can indeed recognize that in the case of Britain they were closely connected, capitalism clearly predated the Industrial Revolution (see the following section). The same could also be said of urbanism, since there are plenty of examples of cities in the pre-industrial world. However, the growth of cities was obviously accelerated by the Industrial Revolution, just as the Industrial Revolution also aided the spread of the spirit of capitalism.

In some respects the early Industrial Revolution appears a rather modest and insignificant event. It was originally based upon the workshop rather than the factory and was technically rather primitive. New methods of manufacture were founded largely upon the application of simple ideas and devices, often by no means expensive and within the means of the relatively humble artisan or skilled craftsman, but which could, nevertheless, produce striking results. At the centre of the Industrial Revolution was the industry which illustrates this process rather well: the cotton industry. As Hobsbawm again points out, this time in another of his books, *Industry and Empire*:

> Whoever says Industrial Revolution says cotton. . . . The British Industrial
> Revolution was by no means only cotton, or Lancashire or even textiles,
> and cotton lost its primacy within it after a couple of generations. Yet
> cotton was the pacemaker of industrial change, and the basis of the first
> regions which could not have existed but for industrialisation, and which
> expressed a new form of society, industrial capitalism. (Hobsbawm 1969,
> p. 56)

Cotton manufacture in Britain had grown along with the cycle of international trade
during the eighteenth century. The technical problems involved in industrializing
cotton production related to the imbalance between spinning and weaving. While
weaving had been considerably speeded up by the invention of the 'flying shuttle' in
the 1730s, it was not until the 1780s that cotton could be spun in sufficient quantities
and at a sufficient speed to supply the weavers. By this time the 'spinning jenny', the
'water frame' and the 'mule' had more than restored the balance, the latter two
implying production in new (manu)'factories'. The introduction of power looms for
weaving at the beginning of the nineteenth century also placed weaving in factories
and virtually completed the technological revolution in cotton manufacture.

For over fifty years 'cotton was king' — even by the 1830s cotton accounted for over
half of total British exports. Cotton mills came to epitomize the new 'factory system',
a system which was, without any doubt, revolutionary:

> A new industrial system based on a new technology thus emerged with
> remarkable speed and ease among the rainy farms and villages of
> Lancashire. . . . It represented a new economic relationship between men,
> a new system of production, a new rhythm of life, a new society, a new
> historical era, and contemporaries were aware of it almost from the start.
> (Hobsbawm 1969, pp. 64, 65)

Soon this new factory system spread elsewhere. Technological changes in cotton
manufacture both provoked and were provoked by changes in the chemical and
engineering industries. The widespread introduction of steam power not only created
a new market for machines but in turn stimulated the iron industry and provided an
expanded market for coal. In all of these sectors the growth of industrialism brought
with it new forms of social organization and new patterns of work, of which two
examples follow.

The division of labour

The predominant method of production before the Industrial Revolution was by
handicraft. The productive unit was often the family with work being carried out in or
adjacent to the family home. Production would also take place *sequentially* — that is,
each sequence in the process of production would only be carried out once the previous
one had been completed and thus, by and large, a single worker or family unit would
see the whole process through from beginning to end. The revolutionary impact of the
Industrial Revolution was such, however, that it brought about the change

a) from handicraft to machine production; and

b) from the family to the factory as a unit of production.

This enabled production to be carried out *concurrently* — that is, *all* the processes of production could be carried out *simultaneously*, by machine if necessary.

The Industrial Revolution therefore brought about a tremendous increase in the *division of labour* and this change in the organization of production was in itself sufficient to create a vast increase in productivity — as Adam Smith, the founder of modern economics, set out with great clarity in his book, *The Wealth of Nations*, published in 1776. This increase in the division of labour, and especially mechanized labour, totally transformed the worker's experience of work. The workers, particularly women and children in the early years of textile manufacture, were taken out of the familiar environment of the home and placed in the new impersonal factory, which imposed a regularity, a routine and a monotony that was quite unlike the pre-industrial rhythms of work, which had been largely unaffected by such a rational division of labour. The new factory system

> inspired such visions as working men narrowed and dehumanised into 'operatives' or 'hands' before being dispensed with altogether by completely 'self-acting' (automated) machinery. . . . The 'factory' with its logical flow of processes, each a specialised machine tended by a specialised 'hand' all linked together by the inhuman and constant pace of the 'engine' and the discipline of mechanisation . . . *was* a revolutionary form of work. (Hobsbawm 1969, p. 68)

The tyranny of the clock

Organizing the processes of production in such a way that could take place concurrently involved a careful attention to the pacing and timing of machines in order to obtain the maximum possible production in the shortest possible time. Time therefore became money. The Industrial Revolution not only brought about an increase in the division of labour but it also brought about the tyranny of the clock. We see the beginning of a trend which reaches its apotheosis in the twentieth-century specialism of 'time-and-motion' study.

The historian E. P. Thompson has written a famous paper, entitled 'Time, work-discipline and industrial capitalism' (1967), which traces the changes in the apprehension of time which parallel the new industrial system. Thompson notes that, in the pre-industrial world, work rhythms were determined by the necessities of the job — the changing seasons in agriculture, the changing tides in fishing, and so on. The notion of time which arises in such contexts is called by Thompson 'task-orientation'. He proposes three points concerning this perception of time:

1   There is a sense in which this form of time is more humanly comprehensible than work 'by the clock' because it is based upon what is an observed necessity.

2   Second, a community in which 'task-orientation' prevails exhibits little demarcation between 'work' and 'leisure'. As Thompson puts it:

> Social intercourse and labour are intermingled — the working-day lengthens or contracts according to the task — and there is no great sense

of conflict between labour and 'passing the time of day'. (Thompson 1967, p. 60)

3   Third, to those who are accustomed to labour timed by the clock, workers whose attitude to time is based upon 'task-orientation' will appear lazy, wasteful and lacking in urgency.

With the rise of industrialism, as Thompson puts it, 'Time is now currency: it is not passed but spent'. The changes in manufacturing technique demanded a greater synchronization of labour and a greater punctuality and exactitude in the routine of daily work. Much of this was an anathema to the pre-industrial worker, whose perception of time was dominated by 'task-orientation'. Hence we find the characteristic irregularity of labour patterns before the coming of large-scale, machine-powered industry. It is not therefore surprising that one of the major social conflicts which emerged from the Industrial Revolution concerned the control of time — conflicts over the limitation of the 'working day' (the Ten Hour Movement) and conflicts over the payment of 'over-time'. Similarly workers, brought up under the assumptions of 'task-orientation', were subject to massive indoctrination on the folly or 'wasting' time by their employers, a moral critique of idleness which stemmed from the Puritan work ethic and which sought to inculcate the new time discipline. Thompson is insistent, however, that this conflict over the use and perception of time is not *only* a product of industrialism, but also of *capitalism*:

> What we are examining here are not only changes in manufacturing technique which demand greater synchronisation of labour and a greater exactitude in time-routines in *any* society; but also these changes as they were lived through in the society of nascent industrial capitalism. We are concerned simultaneously with time-sense in its technological conditioning, and with time-measurement as a means of labour exploitation. (Thompson 1967, p. 74)

Thompson's reference to exploitation here introduces a wholly separate aspect of the 'transformation', the spread of production for profit on the basis of wage labour. It was a development which, although it accompanied the growth of industrialism, calls for the discussion of a distinct set of views.

Capitalism and the Industrial Revolution

We will be examining the precise nature of capitalism later in this book when we encounter the theories of Karl Marx, and so at this stage we will give only a brief definition of what is meant by this term. Capitalism is first and foremost a system of economic production for a *market* organized around the principle of *profit*. On both counts capitalism differed from the form of society which preceded it, namely feudalism. Under feudalism production was primarily for *subsistence* (with only the surplus over and above subsistence needs being disposed of on the market) and organized around the principle of *use*. Capitalism, however, as the very word suggests, was founded on the investment of capital in the process of production in the expectation that it would eventually yield a return in the form of a profit. The size of this profit was to be regulated, according to Adam Smith, by the conditions of the market for the goods which were produced — that is, by the so-called 'laws' of supply and demand, although we shall see later in this book that many of the founding fathers of sociology (and not only Marx) challenged this view and argued that these 'laws' were in fact dependent upon certain prior *social* arrangements.

It is important to realize that this capitalist system of production did *not* arrive with the Industrial Revolution, although the latter certainly promoted and spread it. In Britain the most thoroughgoing and innovative commercial capitalist system began in agriculture, symbolized by the Agricultural Revolution of the eighteenth century. This revolution ensured the destruction of the peasantry, the most prosperous of whom became *capitalist* (commercial) farmers, producing not for their own subsistence but for the market, while the poorer majority became landless farm labourers, employed on the farms in much the same way that workers were later to be employed in the factories. Capitalist agriculture was ushered in by, for the most part, the 'improving' landowners of the seventeenth and eighteenth centuries, some of whom like Lord 'Turnip' Townsend were to become as famous for their innovations as James Watt or Richard Arkwright were later to become in the sphere of industrial production. It was these landowners who were in the forefront of the movement which epitomizes the transition from feudalism to capitalism in agriculture: enclosure. Enclosure involved the rearranging of open fields and/or common land into self-contained privately owned holdings enclosed by hedges, walls or fences. This enabled capitalist entrepreneurs to proceed with profit maximization on their own holdings unhindered by the customs and traditions of the village community as a whole. Those on the margins of agricultural production — small-holders, cottagers — often lost their crucial rights over common land to graze their animals and to forage for timber. They were left pauperized and landless. Enclosure itself may only have been part of this process, but the sum total of these changes in agriculture was that social relationships in the countryside became utterly transformed. While previously they were bound by custom and common rights, they now became dominated by what Marx was later to call *cash-nexus* — that is, by payment for commodities. Thus landowners extracted a *rent* from their tenant farmers, who in turn made *profits* from the sale of agricultural produce on the market. Farmers also purchased labour in the labour market whose conditions determined the payment of workers in the form of a *wage*. In each case the payment (at least in theory) was fixed by the so-called 'hidden hand' of the market. These cash-nexus relationships between employer and employee were thus characterized as impersonal and contractual.

The successful establishment of a capitalist agriculture was a crucial prerequisite of the growth of industrialism, principally for two reasons:

1. It enabled the growing proportion of the population who were not engaged in the production of food to be adequately fed and to obtain their food from the market. Of course 'adequately' is here very much a relative term — it means little more than 'allowed them to be kept alive'. It is a matter of vociferous argument among historians as to whether the standard of living of the working population rose or fell during the early years of industrialization (see Hobsbawm 1964, chapter 5) but there is no doubt that the new breed of industrial workers were allowed to subsist and little more. This in itself, however, was sufficient to enable industrialization to proceed.

110

2. Second, the rise of a capitalist agriculture enabled thousands of (near-destitute) ex-peasants and rural workers to be released for employment elsewhere in the expanding industries in the towns. It was they who provided a plentiful pool of labour for the Industrial Revolution and who flocked to the towns in search of employment and higher wages.

The Industrial Revolution was therefore capitalist in its nature, even though industrialism and capitalism must be understood as quite separate concepts. The spread of capitalism into industry had exactly the same effects upon social relationships as it had previously engendered in the countryside. The relationship between industrial employers and employees also became primarily based upon cash-nexus — the wage — and the very impersonality of this, together with the manifest short-term conflict of interest between wages and profits, were quite capable of producing the social and political turmoil which also accompanied the Industrial Revolution (see Thompson 1963). This new, impersonal, economically regulated system also produced a very common cultural response over this period — what Raymond Williams (1973) has called 'retrospective regret'. There was a constant harking back to a largely mythical 'Golden Age' of the pre-industrial era, when the land was alleged, by such influential writers as William Cobbett, to have been peopled by merrie rustics and a happy beef-eating yeomanry. Much of the unrest during the early decades of the nineteenth century was based on a demand for a return to this Golden Age and a restoration of the rights and duties which were believed to have accompanied it. As we shall see in the [following two chapters], one important tradition in sociology emerged from this cultural response, founded in a critique of the de-humanizing aspects of industrial capitalism.

These new social relationships also brought forth new social groupings. The word 'class', for example, began to achieve a general currency (see Williams R. 1960; Briggs 1967). Hitherto it had meant little more than 'classification' (like so many butterflies); now it was to take on entirely new meanings in the wake of the large-scale economic and social changes of the late eighteenth and early nineteenth centuries. As Asa Briggs points out:

> There was no dearth of social conflicts in pre-industrial society, but they were not conceived of at the time in straight class terms. The change in nomenclature in the late eighteenth and early nineteenth centuries reflected a basic change not only in men's ways of viewing society but in society itself. (Briggs 1967, p. 43)

In the wake of the Industrial Revolution the language of 'class' became commonplace. To the Victorian 'class' was an obvious social fact and the word was used in common parlance without any of today's reticence or apology. When it came to matters of 'class' each person 'knew their place', for each 'class' was identified by its principal means of monetary return.

a) First, there was the upper class, who maintained a virtual monopoly on the ownership of land and who lived off rent. As the nineteenth century proceeded, members of the upper class were to find it increasingly difficult to live in the style to which they were accustomed without recourse to other forms of income than the rents from their estates (unless they were fortunate enough to own the land upon which the new industrial cities were founded). They came also to rely upon the mineral wealth beneath their land and their profitable ventures into various forms of industrial and commercial enterprise.

b) Second, there was the middle class, who owned little or no land — but since the new methods of factory production required very little land, this was not an insuperable problem. Their importance lay in the provision of *capital* and since Britain was moving more and more towards a capitalist, industrial economy they were clearly in the ascendancy. Such *parvenus* or *nouveaux riches* (as the landed aristocracy somewhat disdainfully referred to them in a language which few of the new middle class could understand) provided a political threat to the upper class which was not finally settled until the repeal of the Corn Laws in 1846.

c) Third, there was the working class, who owned neither land nor capital, but who sold the power of their labour in return for a wage. As they became massed together in even larger conglomerations in factories and in cities, so the spectre of class conflict first began to haunt the minority of society who comprised the other two groups. This particularly applied to the great urban centres where, increasingly, manufacture was taking place. As the cities expanded they seemed to threaten the very bonds of society. The cities exemplified *the* key social problem of the age as perceived by the upper and middle classes — the problem of social *order*.

Urbanism

As in the case of capitalism, urbanism did not arrive with the Industrial Revolution. There are plenty of examples of pre-industrial cities, which go back to the ancient civilizations of the East, Ancient Greece and Rome and the urban centres of medieval Europe. However, industrialization promoted urbanization and also transformed the character of cities.

In pre-industrial Europe the city usually possessed one or more of the following four functions:

1   Cities were garrisons, centres of military protection for the surrounding countryside and often fortified against attack.

2   They were also centres of administration, both secular and ecclesiastical. Thus the city often retained the functions — and the functionaries — of political, religious and economic control.

3   Cities were also centres of trade — and so contained a significant proportion of merchants. Since, during the medieval period, travel across land was usually far slower and more hazardous than travel by sea, the major trading cities were seaports or cities with easy access to the sea by river.

4   Finally cities were the centres of craft manufacture. This principally involved the production of those articles which were necessities of life in predominantly agrarian societies — tools and implements, clothes, furniture, etc. This ensured that the social and economic connections between the city and the surrounding countryside never diverged very far, since both the city and the countryside depended upon each other for the provision of goods and services.

It was this fourth function of the medieval city which was to expand and dominate the process of urbanization during the late eighteenth and early nineteenth centuries. For this reason those cities which were largely dependent upon the other three functions were bypassed by the Industrial Revolution. In England, for example, medieval urban centres gave way to the new cities which arose from villages and small market towns like Manchester, Leeds, Birmingham and Sheffield. Only London managed to retain the pre-eminence which it had enjoyed before the Industrial Revolution had begun. In 1750 London had been one of only two cities in Britain with a population of over 50,000 (the other was Edinburgh), but by 1801 there were eight such cities and by 1851 there were twenty-nine, including nine with a population of over 100,000. By 1851, in fact, almost one-third of the population lived in towns with more than 50,000 inhabitants.

The cities attracted such a flow of population partly, as we have seen, because the commercialization of agriculture was expelling the rural poor and leaving a large rural population surplus to the requirements of capitalist agriculture. This rural surplus population was also, however, attracted to the towns by the prospects of a higher standard of living ('streets paved with gold') in the expanding and buoyant manufacturing sector of the economy. The consequent process of urbanization proceeded at such a pace that it was impossible for the amenities of the cities to keep pace with them. Housing was jerry-built close to factories and was frequently damp and insanitary (though perhaps no less so than the equally dilapidated rural hovels that most of their inhabitants had left behind). The crowding together of such large numbers of people also increased the risks to public health (especially in the absence of running water and adequate sewerage) and it was not long before epidemics of typhoid, cholera and other diseases swept through the major cities, especially after 1830.

These epidemics seemed to encapsulate the fear in which the city was held by the vast majority of the upper and middle classes during the first half of the nineteenth century. Despite the fact that the city was not a novel form of social organization, in Britain, at least, there was a widespread assumption on the part of 'responsible' opinion that they were mere temporary necessities which would have no lasting degree of permanence. Evidence for this was culled from the many examples to be found in classical and biblical literature of the rise and eventual fall of city states and of the accompanying decadence of their civilizations. There was, however, no room for complacency. As the nineteenth century advanced, the industrial city showed disturbingly few signs of the decline which the many classical and biblical allusions had predicted. And added to this came a further worry which developed into almost a nineteenth-century upper- and middle-class obsession: that the rise of the city represented a fundamental threat to *social order*.

In many respects this worry was well founded. Urbanization did destroy the established pattern of social relationships in what had hitherto been a small-scale and predominantly agrarian society. The city, by comparison, seemed to consist of a massive conglomeration of working people — a 'great wen', in Cobbett's famous epithet on London — oozing disease, vice and pauperism. The city, it was believed, brought about the breakdown of the *personal* relationships and modes of social control which had characterized the dealings between the classes in the countryside. As we shall see in the [following two chapters], virtually the entire spectrum of the nineteenth-century propertied classes feared that the growth of the city would mean a 'loss of community' and result in society as a whole becoming much less stable. In the city the classes would become segregated and isolated from each other and the 'vertical ties' of community life would be broken. All of this did not augur well for continued social order.

At the beginning of the nineteenth century the typical reaction to the growth of the industrial city was voiced by the poet and essayist, Robert Southey:

> A manufacturing poor is more easily instigated to revolt. They have no local attachments . . . a manufacturing populace is always rife for rioting . . . . Governments who found their prosperity upon manufactures sleep upon gunpowder.

Rife for rioting, sleep upon gunpowder: these powerful images expressed the common fear of some volcanic process at work in the city which would unleash chaos and anarchy upon the world. It was a widely held view among the upper and middle classes that a fundamental transformation of society had taken place and one with which they were ill equipped to cope. Overlying this was a revulsion based upon a more humane response. The rise of German and English romanticism taught that in the city man was separated from nature. Therefore the city was 'unnatural' and its inhabitants were dehumanized. The prevailing emotion here was not so much fear as pity. So in addition to the city being 'rife for rioting', there was an additional view, to which many nineteenth-century liberals attested, that the city was also a place where people lacked fulfilling and authentic personal social relationships. In 1844 Frederick Engels, in typically colourful language, expressed this view very well:

> The very turmoil of the streets has something repulsive, something against which human nature rebels. . . . And still they crowd by one another as though they had nothing in common, nothing to do with one another, and their only agreement is a tacit one, that each keep to his own side of the pavement, so as not to delay the opposing streams of the crowd, while it occurs to no man to honour another with so much as a glance. The brutal indifference, the unfeeling isolation of each in his private interest becomes the more repellent and offensive, the more these individuals are crowded together, within a limited space. And, however much one may be aware that this isolation of the individual, this narrow self-seeking is the fundamental principle of our society everywhere, it is nowhere so shamelessly barefaced, so self-conscious as just here in the crowding of the great city. The dissolution of mankind into nomads, of which each one has a separate principle, the world of atoms, is here carried to its utmost extreme. (in Coleman 1973, pp. 108–9)

As we shall see in the [following two chapters], this kind of imagery was extremely influential on the perspective on the city taken by the early sociologists.

Liberal democracy

Finally, let us turn from the interpretation of economic change to that of political change. The Industrial Revolution brought with it new forms of social organization in the factory and prompted the rapid growth of cities, but it was elsewhere, in the revolutions of the United States of America and France, that a transformation in political *ideas* was also brought about. Both the American Revolution in its Declaration of Independence and the French Revolution with its rallying cry of 'liberty, equality and fraternity' raised in a fundamental way a number of crucial issues which remain relevant to the conduct of politics and society today. Robert Nisbet, in his book *The Sociological Tradition* (1967), lists these issues as follows:

1. *Tradition versus reason.* The American and French Revolutions posed in a stark form the issue of whether society should be organized according to tradition — that is, according to ideas and values handed down from the past — or whether it was possible to organize society rationally according to some generally accepted principles embodied in a code of law.

2. *Religion versus the state.* One, but only one, dimension of the American and French Revolutions was the attempt to escape from the omnipotence and dogma of the medieval church, including its associated authority over the morality of individual behaviour. An important aspect of the ideal of creating a rational social order was that large areas of society hitherto under the authority of the church should become secularized and that, in particular, the church should be divorced from the ultimate secular authority of the state (embodied, in most cases, in the monarch).

3. *The nature of property.* Property rights became redefined so that those who could lay claim to property were divested of any obligations over how they used it. Thus ideas such as *noblesse oblige* and other such obligations which were imposed upon property holders in medieval times lost much of their significance, especially legal significance. Instead the law became concerned only with establishing a title to property — what the property owner then did with it was left to the freedom of the individual. This was an essential element of the law if the transition to an unfettered market economy was to take place successfully. The interpretation of freedom as freedom of the *individual* was crucial if this was to be carried out successfully.

4. *Relations between social classes.* Labour, as we have seen, became merely a kind of property under capitalism, over which an employer gained title by virtue of a *contract*. This contractual relationship characterized the new era. It applied equally to inanimate property rights and relationships between the social classes where contracts embodied the elements of cash-nexus referred to earlier in this chapter.

5. *Egalitarianism.* In the desire to cast off the yoke of feudal restrictions on individual liberty it was but a short step to conceive of all men as being born equal. 'This truth', as the American Declaration of Independence put it, was henceforth 'taken to be self-evident'.

The significance of these political notions for the development of sociology cannot be over estimated. They acted like a catalyst upon the currents of speculation and unrest stirred up by the urbanism and industrialization occurring in Britain and elsewhere.

Hence the consequences of putting into practice the principles underlying the French and American Revolutions were carefully monitored — both in these countries themselves and abroad. Soon major divisions of opinion had become evident: on one hand various streams of 'progressive' thought greeted the transformations with more or less optimism; on the other writers and commentators offered a largely pessimistic and conservative account of such fundamental political and social changes.

We must now examine certain aspects of these divisions more closely for the debate did not continue to be centred solely around questions of preference. Rival political evaluations of contemporary events encouraged, indeed, relied upon rival *explanations* of them. In this brief account we shall concentrate on three major instances where connection between a recognizable political position and a definite theoretical attitude to industrial society is obvious.

We begin with two 'progressive' accounts.

Classical liberalism

The classical statements of the liberal position in politics drew upon various doctrines stressing the sanctity of the individual person. One of the clearest expressions of this sanctity is contained in the assertions of the American Declaration of Independence that individuals are possessed of certain 'inalienable rights' among which are life, liberty and the pursuit of happiness'. Another particularly influential version of this outlook argued that political institutions should be treated as akin to a contract between *equal* partners. Rousseau, for example, expounded the view that political organization of mankind was the result of an actual social contract. In establishing it individuals had emerged from a state of natural savagery to cede some of their personal sovereignty. They had done so in order to create the more effective guarantee that government *ought* to provide of their remaining rights as individuals. The corollary of this emphasis on individual rights was that *each should be free to pursue his (or, less readily, her) own happiness unless it impinged on the happiness of another.*

The merit that liberals saw in the new order lay precisely in the fact that after centuries of tyranny this freedom would at last be possible. The political upheavals attending it were portrayed as an unshackling of the human spirit from centuries of unnatural and often tyrannical restraint. In future the main role of the state would merely be one of providing a useful arrangement whereby conflicting individual interests would be reconciled.

Now, underneath the idealism and optimism to be found in all versions of liberalism was an already established theory of what the human world is, or ought to be, like. It was portrayed as consisting of self-contained individuals, each with certain built-in passions, motives and faculties. Moreover it was assumed that man (*sic*) by nature is a *rational* animal: that his distinguishing and crowning faculty is the ability to think and reason logically from a dispassionate examination of the merits of a case. It was the exercise of reason which had enabled European nations to progress thus far on the road to civilization. The removal of traditional restraints was now urgently necessary and desirable as the next step in the development of reason.

116

Of course, because of the growing economic dominance of Britain, the liberal credo of the rising British (especially the English) 'middle' class attracted a growing amount of attention from all European social thinkers and critics. Admittedly, the theoretical basis of the 'English System', as it was called, was in some ways merely a variant of the general efforts of European Enlightenment thought to free itself from accounts of natural and social phenomena that still relied on theology, intuition or mere tradition. In their place, as Saint-Simon and Comte in France were to propose, should come a positive', that is, a rational-scientific study of human affairs. But for the British, human affairs meant especially *business* affairs, that is, the 'wealth of nations'. Their versions of classical liberalism put especial emphasis on the removal of all obstacles — whether created by tradition or the state — to the growth of trade and profits. Hence the development in Britain of a style of liberal positive or positivist theory which seemed particularly suited to the prosecution of such matters. It is usually referred to as *utilitarian rationalism* or simply *utilitarianism*.

To be sure, the term 'utilitarianism' itself was not coined until quite late in the history of the theory, in association with the moral doctrines of Jeremy Bentham, J. S. Mill and their followers. (As such the utilitarian enjoined law givers and moralists to observe the famous precept of the 'greatest happiness of the greatest number'.) The underlying view of society which it represented had appeared from much earlier on, however, in the writings of Thomas Hobbes, John Locke, James Mill, Adam Smith and many others. Each of these writers was to give the meaning of human rationality a distinctive twist by interpreting all actions as the product of self-interest and the egoistic pursuit of satisfaction and happiness. Out went notions of morality, duty or altruism as causes of human behaviour. All arrangements should be understood as a matter of the calculation and exchange of advantage or 'utility' as it was to become known.

In the hands of the utilitarian theorists the liberal idea of the self-contained sovereign individual was taken to the point where it actually threatened the account of politics which it was intended to support. This possibility was one which Thomas Hobbes had noted in his treatise, *The Leviathan*, at the end of the seventeenth century. If everyone pursued their own ends with scant regard for others, would we not end up with a state of what he called 'a war of all against all'? This chilling vision of chaos and anarchy began to acquire an ominous ring by the beginning of the nineteenth century. It seemed very plausible in the turmoil accompanying industrialization. Hence, what some writers have called 'the Hobbesian problem of order' achieved a peculiar relevance during this period.

This was the first of a number of 'unpleasant surprises' — to use J. B. Burrow's telling phrase which the rationalist, particularly the utilitarian rationalist, account of human society was to spring on itself. And herein lay a matter of tremendous importance for both the early and the later history of sociological work. But before we can take the point further we must examine some other theories born of rather different political attitudes to the new order.

Utopian socialism

In reaction to utilitarianism a new set of ideas, equally 'progressive' but based upon other premises, began to take hold — the utopian socialism of Claude de Saint-Simon in France and Robert Owen in Britain. The utopian socialists made their case by simply pushing the arguments of classical liberalism beyond the point where most liberals were prepared to go. According to Robert Owen.

> The primary and necessary object of all existence is to be happy, but happiness cannot be obtained individually; it is useless to expect isolated happiness; all must partake of it or the few will never enjoy it. (Hobsbawm 1962, p. 286)

The utopian socialists therefore accepted the force of Hobbes's argument. The uninhibited pursuit of self-interest would indeed, they believed, lead to a war of all against all. They therefore rejected the doctrine of the self-contained individual, arguing that human beings were naturally communal and that the greatest happiness of the greatest number could only be achieved collectively. Hence the idea of Owen, for example, was to create co-operative enterprises and 'communist' (in the literal sense) colonies away from the corrupting influences of industrial capitalism. Owen converted his utopia into reality in his settlement of New Lanark in Scotland.

It is important to be clear about the exact sense in which utopian socialism can be described as 'progressive'. Its proponents rejected the nineteenth century because they rejected the dehumanizing nature of *capitalism*. But they quite accepted the growth of *industrialism* as a necessary step in the evolution of mankind. New Lanark, for example, was to serve as an example of the benefits of the new processes of production while at the same time avoiding the reduction of human relationships to those of the cash-nexus.

Liberal democracy: the conservative reaction

Ranged against both of these two 'progressive' reactions to industrialism there stood *classical conservatism*. Notoriously conservatism was not so much a coherent and explicit set of ideas but a gut feeling. Edmund Burke was its most influential exponent in Britain and it is possible to discern in his writing some or all of the following:

1. *An attack upon rationalism.* Instead conservatism placed the emphasis upon instinct, tradition, religious faith and the intractable quality of 'human nature'. Conservatives were thus initially suspicious of liberal democracy or of allowing any semblance of political control to pass to the 'swinish multitude' of the cities and factories.

2. *A belief in the immutability of history.* Radical change was an impossibility because 'the weight of perpetuity' was impossible to cast off. Society was a product of its history and could only proceed in a manner commensurate with that of history.

3. *Society as an organism.* Conservatives regarded the internal relationships of society as 'organic' — that is, based upon mutual dependence. This particularly applied to relations between classes. Like any other organism, society was therefore resistant to rapid change and could only 'evolve' slowly and patiently in a manner which did not create any social disequilibrium and social pathology.

Attempts to create revolution were thus not only unwelcome but self-defeating. The growth of cities was also deplored since they provoked both 'disequilibrium' (conflict) and 'pathology' (crime, vice, disease).

4. *Urban industrialism as a 'loss of community'.* Conservatives shared this perception with the utopian socialists, with whom they combined to attack the growth of cities. They did so, however, in a literally 'reactionary' manner by desiring to return to the pre-industrial Golden Age ruled over by a protective and benevolent squirearchy. They yearned for the certainties of a society composed of identifiable 'natural orders' before the confusing and threatening onset of urbanism and industrialism.

Conclusion: industrialism, politics and sociology

Liberalism, socialism and conservatism, then, were overtly 'political' responses to the novel changes which occurred in North America and Northern Europe between 1750 and 1850. Buried within them, however, were recognizable if embryonic theories of how this new form of society worked. And although the writers concerned usually began by speaking about the nature of the new society and the direction of its development, they rapidly found themselves pronouncing on human nature in general and the basis of the bond between individual and society in particular. Gradually the widespread faith in a scientific approach to politics and society brought these assumptions to the surface so that they became a matter of debate in themselves.

In this respect, the influence of liberalism was of great importance, probably outweighing that of either socialism or conservatism. This may seem a somewhat surprising remark particularly, in view of the significance which socialism has come to assume in the modern political context. We concede, too, that it cuts across the lines of a debate on this very issue which is evident among historians of sociology. On one hand a well-known study by Nisbet presents the thesis that much of the nineteenth-century sociology was inspired by a largely conservative and hence hostile attitude to political and industrial revolution as described in this chapter (Nisbet 1967). Zeitlin, on the other hand, has argued that real creative ferment in sociology, the so-called classical period of the late nineteenth and early twentieth centuries, could only take place under the influence of socialism — specifically the scientific socialism of Karl Marx and counter-reactions to it (Zeitlin 1971). It is not, however, our intention to challenge the validity of these interpretations but to supplement them. They do, after all, concentrate attention on the motives which impelled social enquiry forward rather than the issues with which it dealt. The emphasis in this book is rather different. Our main interest we have said is in the emergence of sociology as a discipline, one which despite much internal controversy and diversity may be defended as unified by a distinctive agenda of common problems. Such an approach is bound to recognize the special position of the liberal rationalist outlook:

1. It offered an interpretation of industrialism which was acceptable to aspiring political movements and social groups in several important European states. It was to become the dominant belief system in Britain, the most prosperous and industrialized of these states throughout the nineteenth century. The attention of serious speculative thinkers was bound to be drawn to it even when they themselves were not directly imbued with its assumptions.

119

2. It represented the dominant form through which people retained at least a nominal belief in the Enlightenment ideal; that in the light of reason the course of human history and the character of political society might be improved. The very idea of a social science was merely an extension of this view and the work of some of sociology's 'founding fathers' may be read as a rearguard effort to defend the Enlightenment ideal against encroaching Unreason (Hughes H. S. 1959).

3. The most fundamental factor, though, lay not in the various aspirations which liberalism expressed but in the successive defects which were uncovered in its *theory* of both human nature and human society. The limitations of the concept of reason — and in particular the limitations of the utilitarian theory of rational self-interest — were brought out in two main ways:

    a) Though it claimed to be a theory with universal applications, it clearly could not account for the diversity of customs and moral rules which Europeans encountered as their influence and trade spread over the globe. What then was the origin of moral rules, especially the 'irrational' but entrenched practices of savage and barbarian societies?

    b) There was also the problem of the 'lower orders' in the industrial nations themselves. It was not simply that the improvident moral habits of the poor represented a puzzling phenomenon to the apostles of self-interest. It was also that the existence of inequality itself was neither anticipated nor adequately explained by a theory of rational choice (cf. MacPherson 1969).

We shall find these two themes, the origin and effectiveness of moral rules and the causes and consequences of inequality, recurring very frequently in the following pages.

Despite these difficulties, liberalism and utilitarianism represented a remarkable intellectual achievement. Their importance for the history of sociological thought lay in the fact that they stressed the intimate connection between the ways in which individuals make choices and the nature of society. Subsequent theorists in the sociological tradition never denied this. What they did object to was the particular assumption that self-interest is the only ingredient in the making of choices or that only choices involving self-interest may be considered rational. Nor did they consider it to be true that individuals are invariably the most knowledgeable judges of what constitutes their self-interest, nor always act rationally in order to pursue it. For many 'choices' are not based upon complete freedom of will but are constrained by 'society' at large. Choice, therefore, always depends upon antecedent social conditions — and this became the focus of the sociological critique of utilitarianism. Thus, while theories of behaviour based on rational self-interest developed into modern economics, sociology took a different path, investigating the social conditions under which various choices are made and in which particular kinds of rationality thrive. 'Society' rather than 'the individual' became the focus of attention.

13. Five Sources of Androcentrism in Social Inquiry

Sandra Harding

In their introduction to *Another Voice: Feminist Perspectives on Social Life and Social Science*, an early collection of feminist criticisms of the social sciences, Marcia Millman and Rosabeth Moss Kanter identify six problematic assumptions that have directed sociological research.[2] Because these assumptions appear in other social sciences as well, we can use five of their six categories to grasp the depth and extent of the feminist charge that masculine bias in social inquiry has consistently made women's lives invisible, that it has distorted our understanding of women's and men's interactions and beliefs and the social structures within which such behaviors and beliefs occur. (The sixth assumption concerns the goals of social inquiry, an issue I shall take up later.) It is useful to focus here on an early set of feminist criticisms of the social sciences as a basis for reviewing what is generally accepted by feminist scholars today. The Millman and Kanter analyses have been elaborated and refined, but these scholars of the 1970s identified problems that have remained crucial areas of feminist concern.

First, they point out that "important areas of social inquiry have been overlooked because of the use of certain conventional field-defining models" (p. ix). For example, the role of emotion in social life and social structure tends to become invisible in sociological analyses that focus exclusively on the role of Weberian rationality. Sociological images of the social actor tend to feature only two types of humans, for neither of whom are self-consciousness of feeling and emotions a crucial element in beliefs and behaviors: either the "conscious, cognitive actor . . . consciously wanting something (e.g., money or status) and consciously calculating the merit of various means toward an end," or the "unconscious, emotional actor . . . 'driven' or 'prompted' by a limited number of 'instincts,' 'impulses,' or 'needs' to achieve, affiliate, or do any number of things that merely surface as ends or means."[3] In neither case is awareness of feeling or emotion seen as significant in the reasons for or causes of people's actions and beliefs, or as an element of social structure, and yet such consciousness of feeling appears to be an obvious and important element in our own and others' beliefs and behaviors. We can wonder if this tendency to ignore the social role of conscious emotion is exacerbated by the combination of a cultural stereotype and a second *sociological* assumption. On the one hand, gender stereotypes present only women as motivated by conscious feelings and emotions; men are supposed to be motivated by calculation of instrumental or other "rational" considerations. On the other hand, social science assumes that it is primarily men's activities and beliefs that create social structure. Are not both men and women often motivated to adopt beliefs and behaviors, to support policies and institutions, by an awareness of their own feelings of love, affinity, anger, or repugnance?

Sandra Harding: 'Five Sources of Androcentrism in Social Inquiry' from *THE SCIENCE QUESTION IN FEMINISM* (Open University Press, 1986), pp. 85-93.

Second, "sociology has focused on public, official, visible, and/or dramatic role players and definitions of the situation; yet unofficial, supportive, less dramatic, private, and invisible spheres of social life and organization may be equally important" (p. x). Such restrictive notions of the field of social action can distort our understanding of social life. For instance, they tend to make invisible the ways in which women have gained informal power. They hide the informal systems of men's sponsorship and patronage, that both ensure coveted career paths for professional men and isolate women employees — thereby circumventing the overt goals of affirmative action programs. They obscure the ways in which the accomplishments of "geniuses" in the history of art, literature, politics, and the sciences have been made possible only through an analytically invisible substructure of women's support systems and social networks (p. 33). They make invisible the role of social interactions in local settings in community life — the settings where women predominate — in shaping those communitywide interactions and policies where men appear the creators of social structure (p. xii).

Third, "sociology often assumes a 'single society' with respect to men and women, in which generalizations can be made about all participants, yet men and women may actually inhabit different social worlds" and this difference is not taken into account (p. xiii). Jessie Bernard has argued, for example, that the same marriage may constitute two different realities for the husband and the wife; this fact invalidates generalizations about marriage and family life that do not identify and account for the differences in position and interests.[4] Similarly, economist Heidi Hartmann points to the "battle between the genders" within the family over housework, which is responsible for giving women and men different interests in a wide array of public policy issues.[5] Additional analyses reveal many other kinds of interactions and institutions where women more than men are forced to lower expectations and rationalize discomfort in order to gain economic or social/political benefits.

The single-society issue in sociology is related to conceptual problems in the social sciences noted by other feminists. The common assumption that a particular social structure or kind of behavior is functional for the agents or the society usually ignores the misfit between women's consciousness, desires, and needs and the roles assigned to women.[6] Beyond and across adjustments to race and class hierarchies, women are forced to accommodate their natures and activities to restrictions they have not chosen. The gap between their consciousness and the expected behaviors they exhibit is what has made the consciousness-raising achievements of the women's movement such an important scientific as well as political resource. Male-dominated social orders are not functional for women, but one cannot easily detect that fact simply by observing women's behaviors.

Equally problematic implications arise from the suggestion in anthropology that the models of social structure — indeed of the very boundaries of the social — assumed by men in all cultures appear to be peculiarly consistent with the anthropological models of Western masculine investigators.[7] Social actors who are women appear to make significantly different and broader assumptions about what constitutes social interaction and social structure than do either the men in their own culture or (masculine) social scientists. Pertinent to our interests is the apparent fact that much of what men count as nature — as outside of culture — is part of culture for women.

Sociologist Dorothy Smith has analyzed the fit between, on the one hand, administrative models of social structure and the administrative personalities and interests to which men of all classes in our culture aspire, and, on the other hand, the conceptual structure of sociology.[8] She argues that the conceptual apparatus of sociology is part of the conceptual apparatus of ruling in societies with our kind of primarily masculine and administrative "rulers." For instance, she points out that the sociological category "housework" has been made part of a conceptual scheme wherein all human activity is either work or leisure, a dichotomy that more accurately describes men's lives than women's. Child-raising, cooking, house care, and the like are certainly both work in the sense of socially useful labor *and* leisure in the sense of oft-chosen and pleasurable activity, but for women they are both more and less than these categories can capture. Child-care in particular seems distorted by this dichotomy. It is less than babysitting, which has the fixed hours, limited responsibilities, and economic return (albeit a low one) of wage labor. But its value to women and, indeed, to society is far more than that of a bridge game, a trip to the beach, or most kinds of wage labor.

Moreover, in industralized societies, it is convenient for the administrator-rulers to divide all human activities into time spent at work for others for pay and time spent at leisure, which it is the individual's responsibility to organize and maintain. Since leisure is regarded as a matter of private, individual choice, only labor for others — at best — requires social support. Welfare-state capitalism has had to accommodate itself to increasing demands for public support of women, children, the aged, sick and unemployed, yet policy-makers and analysts will tend to see these as merely social programs in contrast to the truly political programs directing wage-labor and foreign policy. Smith argues that sociology's replication of the conceptual categories of industrial capitalism makes sociology part of the ruling of our kind of society. (We might further ask whether Marxism's tendency to insist that the fundamental locus of politics is in the economic world — narrowly construed as the world of production — does not also replicate and thus support industrial capitalism's conceptual world.[9] Smith's arguments appear applicable to many of the conceptual frameworks of other social sciences as well. Far from inhabiting a single society, women and men appear to live in different worlds. But it is only the men's world that social science takes to be the social world.

Fourth, "in several fields of study, sex is not taken into account as a factor in behavior, yet sex may be among the most important explanatory variables" (p. xiv; from the theoretical perspective of my study, it is gender difference, not sex difference, with which Millman and Kanter are concerned). There is, for example, the failure to analyze the impact of the gender of the classroom teacher or the physician on the interactions these people have with girls and boys, women and men, and the failure to examine the effect of stereotypical masculine models of the artist, the scientist, or the successful person on women's motivation to enter traditional masculine fields and to be recognized as successful in them.

As my parenthetical remark in the preceeding paragraph suggests, confusingly but intimately intertwined with discussions of sex as a variable in social action are the issues of gender as a variable in history and in contemporary social life. Historian Joan

Kelly-Gadol indicates that feminist scholars in history, too, have shown that the "sex" of social actors has been ignored as an explanatory variable, even though it is probably the single most significant variable in history. Her point is not that biological differences between the sexes have primarily determined the course of history; rather, she is elaborating Simone de Beauvoir's claim that "woman is made, not born." Social constructions of sexuality and gender have been responsible for assigning women and men to different roles in social life. Thus men, too, are "made, not born," and they are also distinctively men in the gender-specific sense — not accurately presented as representative of "humanity." Kelly-Gadol argues that history has been shaped not only by distinctively masculine needs and desires but also by the socially constructed activities of women; thus studies assuming that women's natures and activities are fundamentally biologically determined and that men's socially created natures and activities are entirely responsible for social patterns doubly distort women, men, and social life.[10] Millman and Kanter point out, "When male sociologists (or men in general) look at a meeting of a board of trustees and see only men, they think they are observing a sexually neutral or sexless world rather than a masculine world" (p. xiv). If we substitute "genderless" for "sexless," we can see that the problem these critics are addressing is that only women are assumed to be the bearers of gender and only men the bearers of culture.

Fifth, "certain methodologies (frequently quantitative) and research situations (such as having male social scientists studying worlds involving women) may systematically prevent the elicitation of certain kinds of information, yet this undiscovered information may be the most important for explaining the phenomenon being studied" (p. xv). Criticism of an excessive preference for quantitative measures certainly does not originate with feminists. What is new in the feminist criticisms is the suspicion mentioned earlier that the preference for dealing with variables rather than persons "may be associated with an unpleasantly exaggerated masculine style of control and manipulation" (p. xvi).

The impact of the gender of the researcher on the adequacy of the results of inquiry has several dimensions. There is the obvious problem that for social reasons men do not have real access to many women-centered aspects of social life, either in our society or in other cultures. Such indirect access as they gain is primarily through masculine informants whose knowledge of women's activities is both limited and shaped by local ideological beliefs; if they do gain direct access, their presence changes the situation they are observing or the responses they elicit beyond the changes expected in interview or participant-observer situations. In part, this series of methodological problems explains the excessive focus in social science on the official, visible, and/or dramatic performers and social situations, for it is primarily these actors and this world to which (masculine) observers have access, and it is these actors and this world that masculine informants think most important in the cultures studied.

The historical dimensions of this problem are the subject of constant comment in anthropology, for the classic ethnographies were primarily collected by men who had either little or only distorted access to "native" women informants and to women's activities.[11] Thus the existing reports of what women actually believe and do now or at any other time in history must be regarded as far less reliable than the reports of men's beliefs and activities. The latter are also questionable, however: men are as gendered as are women, and everyone knows that men report to each other different aspects of their beliefs, desires, and behaviors than they report to women. Selective and distorted communication therefore occurs *between* men as well as between men and women. All these methodological limitations raise again the question of the suspicious fit between the concepts and theories favored by social science and those favored by men in every culture.

The five foregoing highlights of feminist criticisms do not pretend to provide a complete list of the ways in which it is clear that distinctively masculine bias has permeated the social sciences. There are more problems in sociology than the present brief account can address; in psychology, anthropology, history, and economics as well, biases peculiar to the subject matters and methodologies of each field similarly distort understandings of the social order.[12] But this outline is sufficient to indicate that feminist criticisms do severely challenge social science's self-perceived attempts to be value-neutral, objective, and dispassionate. As I have already suggested, it is not at all clear that these problems are solely the consequences of social science's different subject matter, variable complexity, and immaturity relative to the natural sciences.

More important to this study is that all these problems reappear in the favored philosophies, histories, and sociologies of natural science — in the *social* studies of science, as well as in popular understandings of science. Important areas of the social aspects of natural science, too, "have been overlooked because of conventional field-defining models." Traditional social studies of natural science, too, have focused on the "public, official, visible, and/or dramatic" at the expense of perhaps equally important "unofficial, supportive, less dramatic, private, and invisible spheres of social life and organization." The social studies of science, too, often assume, "a 'single society' in which generalizations can be made about all participants, yet men and women may actually inhabit different social worlds" in the natural sciences. In the social studies of science, too, gender "is not taken into account as a factor in behavior yet may be among the most important explanatory variables." Finally, methodologies and research situations in the natural sciences, too, "may systematically prevent the elicitation of certain kinds of information" that "may be the most important for explaining the phenomenon being studied."

I have argued that contrary to the dogmas of empiricism, the same kinds of analytical categories are appropriate for understanding science and society, and that science is not just a particular set of sentences or a unique method but a comprehensive set of meaningful social practices. If self-understandings of the nature and purposes of science shape the practices of science, then — contrary to empiricist dogma — the kinds of beliefs physics and chemistry tend to produce should be explained in the same ways that we explain the kinds of beliefs produced through anthropological, sociological, psychological, economic, political, and historical inquiry.

Notes

2. Millman and Kanter (1975). Subsequent page references to this collection appear in the text.

3. Arlie Hochschild, "The Sociology of Feeling and Emotion: Selected Possibilities," in Millman and Kanter (1975, 281).

4. Jessie Bernard, "The Myth of the Happy Marriage," in Vivian Gornick and Barbara K. Moran, *Woman in Sexist Society: Studies in Power and Powerlessness* (New York: Basic Books, 1971).

5. Hartmann (1981a).

6. See Westkott (1979).

7. See Ardener (1972; Smith (1974).

8. Smith (1974; 1977; 1979; 1981).

9. Balbus (1982) is one critic who makes this point.

10. Kelly-Gadol (1976).

11. See, e.g., Leacock's (1982) discussion of this issue.

12. For more extensive analyses of feminist criticisms of the social sciences, see Anderson (1983); Bernard (1981); and the frequent review essays in *Signs* (1975 *et. seq.*).

Durkheim and
Sociological Method

14. What is a Social Fact?
Emile Durkheim

Before inquiring into the method suited to the study of social facts, it is important to know which facts are commonly called "social." This information is all the more necessary since the designation "social" is used with little precision. It is currently employed for practically all phenomena generally diffused within society, however small their social interest. But on that basis, there are, as it were, no human events that may not be called social. Each individual drinks, sleeps, eats, reasons; and it is to society's interest that these functions be exercised in an orderly manner. If, then, all these facts are counted as "social" facts, sociology would have no subject matter exclusively its own, and its domain would be confused with that of biology and psychology.

But in reality there is in every society a certain group of phenomena which may be differentiated from those studied by the other natural sciences. When I fulfil my obligations as brother, husband, or citizen, when I execute my contracts, I perform duties which are defined, externally to myself and my acts, in law and in custom. Even if they conform to my own sentiments and I feel their reality subjectively, such reality is still objective, for I did not create them; I merely inherited them through my education. How many times it happens, moreover, that we are ignorant of the details of the obligations incumbent upon us, and that in order to acquaint ourselves with them we must consult the law and its authorized interpreters! Similarly, the church-member finds the beliefs and practices of his religious life ready-made at birth; their existence prior to his own implies their existence outside of himself. The system of signs I use to express my thought, the system of currency I employ to pay my debts, the instruments of credit I utilize in my commercial relations, the practices followed in my profession, etc., function independently of my own use of them. And these statements can be repeated for each member of society. Here, then, are ways of acting, thinking, and feeling that present the noteworthy property of existing outside the individual consciousness.

These types of conduct or thought are not only external to the individual but are, moreover, endowed with coercive power, by virtue of which they impose themselves upon him, independent of his individual will. Of course, when I fully consent and conform to them, this constraint is felt only slightly, if at all, and is therefore unnecessary. But it is, nonetheless, an intrinsic characteristic of these facts, the proof thereof being that it asserts itself as soon as I attempt to resist it. If I attempt to violate the law, it reacts against me so as to prevent my act before its accomplishment, or to nullify my violation by restoring the damage, if it is accomplished and reparable, or to make me expiate it if it cannot be compensated for otherwise.

Reprinted with the permission of The Free Press, an imprint of Simon and Schuster from *THE RULES OF SOCIOLOGICAL METHOD* by Emile Durkheim, translated by Sarah A. Solovay and John H. Mueller. Edited by George E. G. Catlin. Copyright © 1938 by George E.G. Catlin; copyright renewed 1966 by Sarah A. Solovay, John H. Mueller, and George E.G. Catlin.

In the case of purely moral maxims, the public conscience exercises a check on every act which offends it by means of the surveillance it exercises over the conduct of citizens, and the appropriate penalties at its disposal. In many cases the constraint is less violent, but nevertheless it always exists. If I do not submit to the conventions of society, if in my dress I do not conform to the customs observed in my country and in my class, the ridicule I provoke, the social isolation in which I am kept, produce, although in an attenuated form, the same effects as a punishment in the strict sense of the word. The constraint is nonetheless efficacious for being indirect. I am not obliged to speak French with my fellow-countrymen nor to use the legal currency, but I cannot possibly do otherwise. If I tried to escape this necessity, my attempt would fail miserably. As an industrialist, I am free to apply the technical methods of former centuries; but by doing so, I should invite certain ruin. Even when I free myself from these rules and violate them successfully, I am always compelled to struggle with them. When finally overcome, they make their constraining power sufficiently felt by the resistance they offer. The enterprises of all innovators, including successful ones, come up against resistance of this kind.

Here, then, is a category of facts with very distinctive characteristics: it consists of ways of acting, thinking, and feeling, external to the individual, and endowed with a power of coercion, by reason of which they control him. These ways of thinking could not be confused with biological phenomena, since they consist of representations and of actions; nor with psychological phenomena, which exist only in the individual consciousness and through it. They constitute, thus, a new variety of phenomena; and it is to them exclusively that the term "social" ought to be applied. And this term fits them quite well, for it is clear that, since their source is not in the individual, their substratum can be no other than society, either the political society as a whole or some one of the partial groups it includes, such as religious denominations, political, literary, and occupational associations, etc. On the other hand, this term "social" applies to them exclusively, for it has a distinct meaning only if it designates exclusively the phenomena which are not included in any of the categories of facts that have already been established and classified. These ways of thinking and acting therefore constitute the proper domain of sociology. It is true that, when we define them with this word "constraint," we risk shocking the zealous partisans of absolute individualism. For those who profess the complete autonomy of the individual, man's dignity is diminished whenever he is made to feel that he is not completely self-determinant. It is generally accepted today, however, that most of our ideas and our tendencies are not developed by ourselves but come to us from without. How can they become a part of us except by imposing themselves upon us? This is the whole meaning of our definition. And it is generally accepted, moreover, that social constraint is not necessarily incompatible with the individual personality.[1]

Since the examples that we have just cited (legal and moral regulations, religious faiths, financial systems, etc.) all consist of established beliefs and practices, one might be led to believe that social facts exist only where there is some social organization. But there are other facts without such crystallized form which have the same objectivity and the same ascendency over the individual. These are called "social currents." Thus the great movements of enthusiasm, indignation, and pity in a crowd do not originate in any one of the particular individual consciousness. They come to each one of us from without and can carry us away in spite of ourselves. Of course, it may happen that, in abandoning myself to them unreservedly, I do not feel the pressure they exert upon me. But it is revealed as soon as I try to resist them. Let an individual attempt to oppose one of these collective manifestations, and the emotions that he denies will turn against him. Now, if this power of external coercion asserts itself so clearly in cases of resistance, it must exist also in the first-mentioned cases, although we are unconscious of it. We are then victims of the illusion of having ourselves created that which actually forced itself from without. If the complacency with which we permit ourselves to be carried along conceals the pressure undergone, nevertheless it does not abolish it. Thus, air is no less heavy because we do not detect its weight. So, even if we ourselves have spontaneously contributed to the production of the common emotion, the impression we have received differs markedly from that which we would have experienced if we had been alone. Also, once the crowd has dispersed, that is, once these social influences have ceased to act upon us and we are alone again, the emotions which have passed through the mind appear strange to us, and we no longer recognize them as ours. We realize that these feelings have been impressed upon us to a much greater extent than they were created by us. It may even happen that they horrify us, so much were they contrary to our nature. Thus, a group of individuals, most of whom are perfectly inoffensive, may, when gathered in a crowd, be drawn into acts of atrocity. And what we say of these transitory outbursts applies similarly to those more permanent currents of opinion on religious, political, literary, or artistic matters which are constantly being formed around us, whether in society as a whole or in more limited circles.

To confirm this definition of the social fact by a characteristic illustration from common experience, one need only observe the manner in which children are brought up. Considering the facts as they are and as they have always been, it becomes immediately evident that all education is a continuous effort to impose on the child ways of seeing, feeling, and acting which he could not have arrived at spontaneously. From the very first hours of his life, we compel him to eat, drink, and sleep at regular hours; we constrain him to cleanliness, calmness, and obedience; later we exert pressure upon him in order that he may learn proper consideration for others, respect for customs and conventions, the need for work, etc. If, in time, this constraint ceases to be felt, it is because it gradually gives rise to habits and to internal tendencies that render constraint unnecessary; but nevertheless it is not abolished, for it is still the source from which these habits were derived. It is true that, according to Spencer, a rational education ought to reject such methods, allowing the child to act in complete liberty; but as this pedagogic theory has never been applied by any known people, it must be accepted only as an expression of personal opinion, not as a fact which can contradict the aforementioned observations. What makes these facts particularly instructive is that the aim of education is, precisely, the socialization of the human being; the process of education, therefore, gives us in a nutshell the historical fashion in which the social being is constituted. This unremitting pressure to which the child is subjected is the very pressure of the social milieu which tends to fashion him in its own image, and of which parents and teachers are merely the representatives and intermediaries.

It follows that sociological phenomena cannot be defined by their universality. A thought which we find in every individual consciousness, a movement repeated by all individuals, is not thereby a social fact. If sociologists have been satisfied with defining them by this characteristic, it is because they confused them with what one might call their reincarnation in the individual. It is, however, the collective aspects of the beliefs, tendencies, and practices of a group that characterize truly social phenomena. As for the forms that the collective states assume when refracted in the individual, these are things of another sort. This duality is clearly demonstrated by the fact that these two orders of phenomena are frequently found dissociated from one another. Indeed, certain of these social manners of acting and thinking acquire, by reason of their repetition, a certain rigidity which on its own account crystallizes them, so to speak, and isolates them from the particular events which reflect them. They thus acquire a body, a tangible form, and constitute a reality in their own right, quite distinct from the individual facts which produce it. Collective habits are inherent not only in the successive acts which they determine but, by a privilege of which we find no example in the biological realm, they are given permanent expression in a formula which is repeated from mouth to mouth, transmitted by education, and fixed even in writing. Such is the origin and nature of legal and moral rules, popular aphorisms and proverbs, articles of faith wherein religious or political groups condense their beliefs, standards of taste established by literary schools, etc. None of these can be found entirely reproduced in the applications made of them by individuals, since they can exist even without being actually applied.

No doubt, this dissociation does not always manifest itself with equal distinctness, but its obvious existence in the important and numerous cases just cited is sufficient to prove that the social fact is a thing distinct from its individual manifestations. Moreover, even when this dissociation is not immediately apparent, it may often be disclosed by certain devices of method. Such dissociation is indispensable if one wishes to separate social facts from their alloys in order to observe them in a state of purity. Currents of opinion, with an intensity varying according to the time and place, impel certain groups either to more marriages, for example, or to more suicides, or to a higher or lower birthrate, etc. These currents are plainly social facts. At first sight they seem inseparable from the forms they take in individual cases. But statistics furnish us with the means of isolating them. They are, in fact, represented with considerable exactness by the rates of births, marriages, and suicides, that is, by the number obtained by dividing the average annual total of marriages, births, suicides, by the number of persons whose ages lie within the range in which marriages, births, and suicides occur.[2] Since each of these figures contains all the individual cases indiscriminately, the individual circumstances which may have had a share in the production of the phenomenon are neutralized and, consequently, do not contribute to its determination. The average, then, expresses a certain state of the group mind (*l'âme collective*).

Such are social phenomena, when disentangled from all foreign matter. As for their individual manifestations, these are indeed, to a certain extent, social, since they partly reproduce a social model. Each of them also depends, and to a large extent, on the organopsychological constitution of the individual and on the particular circumstances in which he is placed. Thus they are not sociological phenomena in the strict sense of the word. They belong to two realms at once; one could call them sociopsychological. They interest the sociologist without constituting the immediate subject matter of sociology. There exist in the interior of organisms similar phenomena, compound in their nature, which form in their turn the subject matter of the "hybrid sciences," such as physiological chemistry, for example.

The objection may be raised that a phenomenon is collective only if it is common to all members of society, or at least to most of them — in other words, if it is truly general. This may be true; but it is general because it is collective (that is, more or less obligatory), and certainly not collective because general. It is a group condition repeated in the individual because imposed on him. It is to be found in each part because it exists in the whole, rather than in the whole because it exists in the parts. This becomes conspicuously evident in those beliefs and practices which are transmitted to us ready made by previous generations; we receive and adopt them because, being both collective and ancient, they are invested with a particular authority that education has taught us to recognize and respect. It is, of course, true that a vast portion of our social culture is transmitted to us in this way; but even when the social fact is due in part to our direct collaboration, its nature is not different. A collective emotion which bursts forth suddenly and violently in a crowd does not express merely what all the individual sentiments had in common; it is something entirely different, as we have shown. It results from their being together, a product of the actions and reactions which take place between individual consciousnesses; and if each individual consciousness echoes the collective sentiment, it is by virtue of the special energy resident in its collective origin. If all hearts beat in unison, this is not the result of a spontaneous and pre-established harmony but rather because an identical force propels them in the same direction. Each is carried along by all.

We thus arrive at the point where we can formulate and delimit in a precise way the domain of sociology. It comprises only a limited group of phenomena. A social fact is to be recognized by the power of external coercion which it exercises or is capable of exercising over individuals, and the presence of this power may be recognized in its turn either by the existence of some specific sanction or by the resistance offered against every individual effort that tends to violate it. One can, however, define it also by its diffusion within the group, provided that, in conformity with our previous remarks, one takes care to add as a second and essential characteristic that its own existence is independent of the individual forms it assumes in its diffusion. This last criterion is perhaps, in certain cases, easier to apply than the preceding one. In fact, the constraint is easy to ascertain when it expresses itself externally by some direct reaction of society, as is the case in law, morals, beliefs, customs, and even fashions. But when it is only indirect, like the constraint which an economic organization exercises, it cannot always be so easily detected. Generality combined with externality may, then, be easier to establish. Moreover, this second definition is but another form of the first; for if a mode of behavior whose existence is external to individual consciousnesses becomes general, this can only be brought about by its being imposed upon them.[3]

133

But these several phenomena present the same characteristic by which we defined the others. These "ways of existing" are imposed on the individual precisely in the same fashion as the "ways of acting" of which we have spoken. Indeed, when we wish to know how a society is divided politically, of what these divisions themselves are composed, and how complete is the fusion existing between them, we shall not achieve our purpose by physical inspection and by geographical observations; for these phenomena are social, even when they have some basis in physical nature. It is only by a study of public law that a comprehension of this organization is possible, for it is this law that determines the organization, as it equally determines our domestic and civil relations. This political organization is, then, no less obligatory than the social facts mentioned above. If the population crowds into our cities instead of scattering into the country, this is due to a trend of public opinion, a collective drive that imposes this concentration upon the individuals. We can no more choose the style of our houses than of our clothing — at least, both are equally obligatory. The channels of communication prescribe the direction of internal migrations and commerce, etc., and even their extent. Consequently, at the very most, it should be necessary to add to the list of phenomena which we have enumerated as presenting the distinctive criterion of a social fact only one additional category, "ways of existing"; and, as this enumeration was not meant to be rigorously exhaustive, the addition would not be absolutely necessary.

Such an addition is perhaps not necessary, for these "ways of existing" are only crystallized "ways of acting." The political structure of a society is merely the way in which its component segments have become accustomed to live with one another. If their relations are traditionally intimate, the segments tend to fuse with one another, or, in the contrary case, to retain their identity. The type of habitation imposed upon us is merely the way in which our contemporaries and our ancestors have been accustomed to construct their houses. The methods of communication are merely the channels which the regular currents of commerce and migrations have dug, by flowing in the same direction. To be sure, if the phenomena of a structural character alone presented this permanence, one might believe that they constituted a distinct species. A legal regulation is an arrangement no less permanent than a type of architecture, and yet the regulation is a "physiological" fact. A simple moral maxim is assuredly somewhat more malleable, but it is much more rigid than a simple professional custom or a fashion. There is thus a whole series of degrees without a break in continuity between the facts of the most articulated structure and those free currents of social life which are not yet definitely molded. The differences between them are, therefore, only differences in the degree of consolidation they present. Both are simply life, more or less crystallized. No doubt, it may be of some advantage to reserve the term "morphological" for those social facts which concern the social substratum, but only on condition of not overlooking the fact that they are of the same nature as the others. Our definition will then include the whole relevant range of facts if we say: *A social fact is every way of acting, fixed or not, capable of exercising on the individual an external constraint; or again, every way of acting which is general throughout a given society, while at the same time existing in its own right independent of its individual manifestations.*[4]

Notes

1. We do not intend to imply, however, that all constraint is normal. We shall return to this point later.

2. Suicides do not occur at every age, and they take place with varying intensity at the different ages in which they occur.

3. It will be seen how this definition of the social fact diverges from that which forms the basis of the ingenious system of M. Tarde. First of all, we wish to state that our researches have nowhere led us to observe that preponderant influence in the genesis of collective facts which M. Tarde attributes to imitation. Moreover, from the preceding definition, which is not a theory but simply a résumé of the immediate data of observation, it seems indeed to follow, not only that imitation does not always express the essential and characteristic features of the social fact, but even that it never expresses them. No doubt, every social fact is imitated; it has, as we have just shown, a tendency to become general, but that is because it is social, i.e., obligatory. Its power of expansion is not the cause but the consequence of its sociological character. If, further, only social facts produced this consequence, imitation could perhaps serve, if not to explain them, at least to define them. But an individual condition which produces a whole series of effects remains individual nevertheless. Moreover, one may ask whether the word "imitation" is indeed fitted to designate an effect due to a coercive influence. Thus, by this single expression, very different phenomena, which ought to be distinguished, are confused.

4. This close connection between life and structure, organ and function, may be easily proved in sociology because between these two extreme terms there exists a whole series of immediately observable intermediate stages which show the bond between them. Biology is not in the same favorable position. But we may well believe that the inductions on this subject made by sociology are applicable to biology and that, in organisms as well as in societies, only differences in degree exist between these two orders of facts.

15. The Ways and Means of Sociology
Zygmunt Bauman

Chapter by chapter, we have travelled together through the world of daily experience we share. Sociology was invited to accompany us as our guide: if our own daily concerns and problems marked the itinerary, sociology was offered the task of commenting on what we see and do. As on any guided tour, we hoped that our guide would make sure that we did not miss anything of importance and would bring to our attention things which if left to ourselves we would be liable to pass by unnoticed. We also expected the guide to explain to us things we knew only superficially — tell us stories about them we did not know. We hoped that at the end of our guided tour we would know more and understand things better than we did at the start; when we again go through our daily business of life after this trip, we should be better equipped to cope with the problems we face. Not that our attempts to solve them will necessarily be more successful; but at least we will know what the problems are and what their solution, if at all feasible, requires.

I think that sociology as we have come to know it during our tour acquitted itself reasonably well of the task we asked it to perform; but then, it would have disappointed us if we were expecting it to do more than provide us with a **commentary**, a series of explanatory footnotes to our daily experience. Commentary is exactly what sociology has to offer. Sociology is a refinement on that knowledge we possess and employ in our daily life — inasmuch as it brings into the open some finer distinctions and some not immediately evident connections which an unaided eye would fail to locate. Sociology charts more details on our 'world map'; it also extends the map beyond the horizon of our own daily experience, so that we can see how the territories we inhabit fit into the world we have had no chance to explore ourselves. The difference between what we know without sociology and what we know after we have heard its comments is not the difference between error and truth (though, let us admit, sociology may happen to correct our opinions here or there); it is, rather, the difference between believing that what we experience can be described and explained in one way and in one way only, and knowing that the possible — and plausible — interpretations are plentiful. Sociology, one may say, is not the end of our search for understanding, but an inducement to go on searching and an obstacle to that state of self-satisfaction in which curiosity wilts and the search grinds to a halt. It has been said that the best service sociology may offer is to 'prod sluggish imagination' — by showing apparently familiar things from unexpected angles and thus undermining all routine and self-confidence.

Generally however, two very different expectations are held regarding the services that sociology — as 'social science' (that is, as a body of knowledge which claims superiority over mere views and opinions and is believed to possess reliable, trustworthy, correct information about how things *truly* are) — can and should render.

Zygmunt Bauman: 'The Ways and Means of Sociology' from *THINKING SOCIOLOGICALLY* (Basil Blackwell Limited, 1990), pp. 214-232.

One expectation puts sociology on a par with other kinds of expertise that promise to tell us what our problems are, what to do about them and how to get rid of them. Sociology is viewed as a sort of DIY briefing, or a textbook teaching the art of life: how to get what we want, how to jump over or by-pass anything that may stand in our way. What such an expectation boils down to is a hope that once we know how various elements of our situation depend on each other, we will be free to control that situation, to subordinate it to our purposes or at least force it to serve these purposes better. This is, after all, what **scientific knowledge** is all about. We hold it in such high esteem because we believe that the wisdom it supplies is of the kind that allows one to *predict* how things will turn out; and that the ability to predict the turn of events (and thus also the consequences of one's own action) will enable one to act freely and rationally — that is, to make such moves and only such moves as are guaranteed to bring the desired results.

Another expectation is closely related to the former one, but it throws open the assumptions underlying the instrumental usefulness idea — premises that the former expectation did not need to spell out. To be in control of the situation must mean, one way or another, luring, forcing or otherwise causing other people (who are always part of that situation) to behave in a way that helps us to get what we want. As a rule, control over the situation cannot but mean also control over other people (this is how the art of life is normally presented, after all — as the way 'to win friends and influence people'). In the second expectation this desire to control others comes to the fore. The services of sociology are enlisted in the hope that they will assist those efforts to create order and evict chaos which we found in a previous chapter to be a distinctive mark of our modern times. By exploring the inner springs of human actions, sociologists are expected to provide practically useful information about the way things ought to be arranged in order to elicit the kind of behaviour one would wish people to demonstrate; or, alternatively, to eliminate any conduct that the designed model of order makes unsuitable. So the factory owners may ask sociologists how to prevent strikes, commanders of armed forces occupying a foreign land may ask them how to fight the guerrillas, policemen may commission practical proposals on how to disperse crowds and keep potential rioters at bay, managers of trading companies may demand the best means to seduce prospective customers into buying their products, public relation officers may inquire how to make the politicians who hired them more popular and electable, the politicians themselves may seek advice on the methods of preserving law and order — that is, making their subjects obey the law, preferably willingly, but also when they do not like what they must obey.

What all such demands amount to is that sociologists should offer advice on how to reduce the freedom of some people so that their choice be confined and their conduct more predictable. A knowledge is wanted of how to transform the people in question from *subjects* of their own action into *objects* of other people's actions; how to implement in practice a sort of 'snooker ball' model of human action, in which what people do is wholly determined by pressures applied from outside. The more human action approximated such a 'snooker ball' movement, the more useful sociological services would be for the intended purpose. Even if people cannot stop being choosers and decision-makers, the external context of their actions should be so manipulated as to make it utterly improbable that the choices and decisions they make go against the wishes of the manipulators.

By and large, such expectations amount to the demand that sociology be *scientific*, that it shape its activity, and thus its products, after the pattern of established sciences which we all hold in high esteem because of their amply demonstrated practical usefulness — the tangible benefits it brings. Sociology ought to deliver recipes as exact, practically useful and effective as those offered by, say, physics or chemistry. From their inception those and similar sciences have been aimed at gaining a clearly defined kind of knowledge: such as may lead eventually to full mastery over the object of their study. That object, construed as 'nature', was denied its own will and purpose, so that it could without compunction be subordinated fully to the will and purpose of human beings wishing to exploit it for the better satisfaction of their own needs. The language of science used to describe its 'natural' objects was carefully purified of all terms referring to purpose or meaning; what remained after such a purge was an 'objective' language, a language construing its objects as far as they receive, not generate, action; as objects buffeted by external forces, invariably described as 'blind', that is, not aimed at any specific end and devoid of any intention. So described, the natural world was conceived as a 'free for all': a virgin territory waiting to be tilled and transformed into a purposefully designed plot better suited to human habitation. The objectivity of science expressed itself in reporting its findings in an unemotional, technical language that emphasized the unbridgeable gap between human bearers of ends and nature, destined to be shaped and moulded in accordance with such ends. The declared purpose of science was to aid the 'mastery of human kind over nature'.

The world was explored with this purpose in mind. Nature was to be studied so that human craftsmen would know how to give it the shape they desired (think, for instance, of sculptors and the slabs of marble they wish to transform into the likeness of a human figure. To implement their purpose, they must first know the inner qualities of the stone. There are only certain directions in which one can apply force to cut and chip the marble without breaking it. In order to impose on the marble the form they carry in their heads — to subordinate the stone to their designs — the sculptors must learn how to recognize such directions. The knowledge they seek would subordinate the dead stone to their will and allow them to reshape it in accordance with their ideas of harmony and beauty). This is how scientific knowledge was constructed: to *explain* the object of science was to acquire the ability to *predict* what would happen if this or that took place; with such an ability to predict, one would be *able to act* — that is, to impress upon a fragment of now conquered and docile reality the design that will better serve the selected purpose. Reality was seen as, first and foremost, a resistance to human purposeful activity. The aim of science was to find out how that resistance could be broken. The resulting conquest of nature would mean the emancipation of humanity from natural constraints; the enhancement, so to speak, of our collective freedom.

All knowledge worth its salt was exhorted and expected to match this model of science. Any kind of knowledge aspiring to public recognition, a place in the academic world, a share in public resources had to prove that it was like the natural sciences, that it could deliver a similarly useful, practical instruction which would permit us to make the world better suited to human purposes. The pressure to conform to the standard established by the natural sciences was enormous and virtually impossible to resist. Even if the role of the architects or draughtsmen of the social order did not cross their minds, even if the only thing they wanted was to comprehend the human condition more fully, the founding fathers of sociology could not but tacitly or overtly accept the dominant model of science as the prototype of 'good knowledge' and of the pattern of all comprehension. They had therefore to demonstrate that one could devise for the study of human life and activity methods as precise and objective as those which had been deployed by the sciences of nature; and that an equally exact and objective knowledge may result. They had to prove that sociology could elevate itself to the status of science and hence be admitted to the academic family on an equal footing with its older and trend-setting members.

This need goes a long way towards explaining the shape sociological discourse acquired once it settled down in the company of other sciences in the world of academic teaching and research. The effort to make sociology 'scientific' dominated the discourse; the task occupied the pride of place among the concerns of the participants. There were three strategies with which the budding academic sociology could respond to the challenge. All three were tried, and all three subsequently converged in the shape the established sociology assumed.

The first strategy is best illustrated by the teachings of the founder of academic sociology in France, **Emile Durkheim**. Durkheim took for granted that there was a model of science, shared by all areas of knowledge aspiring to scientific status. That model was characterized first and foremost by its *objectivity*, that is, by its treating the object of study as strictly separate from the studying subject, as a thing 'out there', which can be subjected to the gaze of the researcher, observed and described in strictly neutral and detached language. As all science behaves in the same way, scientific disciplines differ from each other only by directing the same kind of objective scrutiny to separate areas of reality; the world, so to speak, is divided into plots, each researched by a scientific discipline of its own. Researchers are all the same, they all command the same kind of technical skills and engage in an activity subjected to the same rules and code of behaviour. And the reality they study is the same for them all, always composed of things 'out there' waiting to be observed, described and explained. What sets scientific disciplines apart from each other is solely the division of the territory of investigation. Various branches of science divide the world between themselves, each one taking care of its own fragment, its own 'collection of things'.

If this is what sciences do, then for sociology to find a place in science — to become a science — it must find a section of the world which the extant scientific disciplines have not yet appropriated. Like a seafaring explorer, sociology should discover a continent over which no one has yet claimed sovereignty, so that it can establish its own uncontested domain of scientific competence and authority. To put it simply, sociology as a science and as a separate, sovereign, scientific discipline can only be legitimized if a hitherto neglected 'collection of things' is found that is still waiting to be subjected to the scientific gaze.

Durkheim suggested that specifically *social* facts — collective phenomena that do not belong to any person in particular (like shared beliefs and patterns of behaviour) — may be treated as such *things* and studied in an objective, detached fashion as other things are. Indeed, such phenomena appear to individuals like you and me much the same as the rest of the reality 'out there': they are tough and stubborn and independent of our will to recognize them as we cannot wish them away. They are there whether we know of them or not, much like a table or chair that occupies a certain place in my room whether or not I look at it or think of it. Moreover, I may ignore their presence only at my own peril. If I behave as if they did not exist, I would be severely punished (if I ignore the *natural* law of gravity and leave the room through the window rather than through the door, I'll suffer punishment — break a leg or an arm. If I ignore a *social* norm — the law and moral injunction against thieving — I'll also suffer punishment; I'll be put in jail or ostracized by my fellows). In fact, I learn of the presence of a social norm the hard way: when I breach it and hence inadvertently 'trigger' the punitive sanctions against me.

We can say, therefore, that social phenomena, though they obviously would not exist without human beings, do not reside *inside* human beings as individuals, but *outside* them. Together with nature and its inviolable laws, they constitute a vital part of the objective environment of every human being, of the outer conditions of any human action and human life as a whole. There would be no point in learning about those social phenomena by asking people subjected to their force (one cannot really study the law of gravity by collecting the opinions of people who must walk instead of flying). The information one may obtain by asking people would anyway be hazy, partial and misleading: the people to whom we address our questions have little to tell us, as they did not invent or create the phenomena under study, they found them already in place and ready made, and more often than not confronted them (that is, were made aware of their presence) but briefly and fragmentarily. So one must study social facts directly, objectively, 'from outside', by systematic observation; precisely as one studies the rest of the things 'out there'.

In one important respect, Durkheim agreed, social facts differ from the facts of nature. The connection between violating the law of nature and the damage that follows it is automatic: it has not been introduced by human design (or, for that matter, by anyone's design). The connection between violating the norm of society and the sufferings of norm-breakers is, on the contrary, 'human-made'. Certain conduct is punished because society condemns it and not because the conduct itself causes harm to its perpetrator (thus, stealing does no harm to the thief and may even be beneficial to him; if the thief suffers in its consequence, it is only because social sentiments militate against thieving). This difference, however, does not detract from the 'thing-like' character of social norms or from the feasibility of their objective study. The opposite is the case: it further adds to the norms' 'thing-like' nature, as they appear to be the real material and efficient causes of the regularity and non-randomness of human conduct and therefore of the social order itself. Such 'thing-like' social facts, and not the states of mind or emotions of individuals (such as are avidly studied by psychologists) offer the genuine explanation of human conduct. Wishing to describe correctly and to explain human behaviour, the sociologist is thus entitled (and exhorted) to by-pass the individual psyche, intentions, and private meanings that only the individuals themselves can tell us about — and that for this reason are bound to remain non-observable, impenetrable 'mysteries of the human soul' — and concentrate instead on studying phenomena which can be observed from outside and would in all probability look the same to any observer watching them.

This is one of the possible strategies one can follow to make a case for the scientific status of sociology. A very different strategy is associated with the work of **Max Weber**. The idea that there is one and only one way of 'being scientific' and that therefore sociology should selflessly imitate the practices of natural science is emphatically rejected. Instead, Weber proposes that sociological practice, without losing the precision expected from scientific knowledge, should be as different from that of the natural sciences as the human reality investigated by sociology is from the non-human world studied by the science of nature.

Human reality is different — indeed, unique — in that human actors put **meaning** in their actions. They have motives; they act in order to reach the ends they set for themselves. It is such ends that explain their actions. For this reason, human actions, unlike the spatial movements of physical bodies or chemical reactions, need to be understood rather than explained. More precisely, to explain human action means to *understand* it: to grasp the meaning invested into it by the actor.

That human actions are meaningful, and hence call for a special kind of investigation, was not Weber's discovery. On the contrary, this idea served long before as the foundation of **hermeneutics** — the theory and practice of 'recovery of meaning' embedded in a literary text, or a painting, or any other product of a human creative spirit. Hermeneutical investigations struggled in vain to attain scientific status. The theorists of hermeneutics found it difficult to demonstrate that the method, and the findings, of hermeneutical study may be as objective as the methods and results of science purport to be: that is, that one can codify the method of hermeneutical investigation so precisely that any researcher following the rules would have to arrive to the same conclusions. Such a scientific ideal seemed to the hermeneuticians unattainable. It seemed that in order to understand its meaning the interpreters of the text must 'put themselves in the author's place', see the text through the author's eyes, think the author's thoughts; in brief, try to be, to think, to reason, to feel like the author (such an effort to 'transfer' oneself into the life and spirit of the author, to relive and copy the author's experience, was called **empathy**). This requires a genuine congeniality with the author and the powerful exercise of the imagination; and the results would not depend on a uniform method *anybody* can apply with equal success, but on the *unique* talents of a single interpreter. Thus the whole procedure of interpreting belongs more to the arts than to science. If interpreters come forward with sharply different interpretations, one may choose one of the competing proposals because it is richer, more perceptive, profound, aesthetically pleasing or otherwise more satisfying than the rest; but these are not reasons that allow us to say that the interpretation we prefer is *true*, while the ones we do not like are *false*. And an assertion which cannot be definitely corroborated as true, or proved wrong, cannot belong to science.

And yet Weber insisted that, being an investigation of human acts aimed at their understanding (that is, striving like hermeneutics to grasp their meaning), sociology can still reach the level of **objectivity** that is the distinctive mark of scientific knowledge. In other words, he insisted that sociology can, and should, achieve the objective knowledge of subjective human reality.

Not all human actions may be so interpreted, to be sure, as much of our activity is either traditional or affective — guided by habits or emotions. In both cases the action is *unreflective*: when I act out of anger or follow a routine, I do not calculate my action nor pursue particular ends; I do not design nor monitor my action as a means leading to a specific end. Traditional and affective actions are determined by factors my mind does not control — much like natural phenomena; and like natural phenomena, they are best comprehended when their cause is pointed out. What requires an understanding of meaning rather than a causal explanation are *rational* actions, that is *reflective* actions, *calculated* actions, actions that are consciously conceived and controlled and aimed at a consciously considered end (the 'in order to' actions). If traditions are manifold and emotions are thoroughly personal and idiosyncratic, the *reason* we deploy to measure our ends against the means we select in order to achieve them is common to all human beings. So I can wrest meaning out of the action I observe not by guessing what has been going on in the actors' heads, not by 'thinking their thoughts' (in other words, not by empathy), but by matching to the action a motive that makes sense and thus renders the action meaningful to me and to any other observer. Your hitting your fellow student in rage may fail to make sense to me if I happen to be a placid person who never experiences strong emotions. But if I see you 'burning the candle', late into the night and writing an essay, I can easily make sense of what I see (and so can anyone else) because I know that writing essays is an excellent, tested means of acquiring knowledge.

What Weber seemed to assume, in short, was that one rational mind may recognize itself in another rational mind; that as long as the studied actions are rational (calculated, following a purpose) they can be rationally understood: explained by postulating a meaning, not a cause. Sociological knowledge need not therefore be inferior to science. On the contrary, it has a clear advantage over science in that it can not only describe but also *understand* its objects — the human objects. However thoroughly explored, the world described by science stays meaningless (one can know everything about the tree, but one cannot 'understand' the tree). Sociology goes further than science — it recovers the *meaning* of the reality it studies.

There was also a third strategy aimed at lifting social study to the status of science: to show that, like science, sociology has direct and effective **practical** applications. This strategy has been applied with particular zeal by the pioneers of sociology in the United States of America — a country prominent for its pragmatic frame of mind and viewing practical success as the supreme criterion of value and, in the end, also of truth. Unlike their European colleagues, the first American sociologists had little time for theorizing about the nature of their enterprise; they did not concern themselves with the philosophical justification of sociological practice. Instead, they earnestly set out to demonstrate that the kind of knowledge sociological research can provide can be used in exactly the same way as scientific knowledge has been used for years with spectacular results: it can be employed to make predictions and to 'manipulate' reality, to change it in a way that agrees with our needs and intentions whatever they may be and however they have been defined and selected.

The third strategy concentrated on developing the methods of *social diagnosis* (surveys showing in detail the exact state of affairs in certain areas of social life) and the general theory of human behaviour (that is, of the factors that determine such behaviour; it was hoped that an exhaustive knowledge of such factors might render human conduct predictable and manipulable). From the start, sociology was given a practical edge. The edge was pressed against recognized social problems like rising criminality, juvenile delinquency, alcoholism, prostitution, the weakening of family ties, etc. Sociology grounded its bid for social recognition in a promise to assist the administration of social processes in the way geology and physics assist the builders of skyscrapers. In other words, sociology put itself at the service of the construction and maintenance of social order. It shared the concerns of social administrators, of people set on the task of managing other people's conduct. The promise of practical usefulness was addressed and taken up by ever new areas of managerial activity. The services of sociologists were deployed to defuse antagoism and prevent conflicts in factories and mines, to facilitate the adaptation of young soldiers in war-weary army units, to help the promotion of new commercial products, to rehabilitate former criminals, to increase the effectiveness of social welfare provisions.

This strategy came closest to Francis Bacon's formula 'to subdue nature by submission'; it blended truth with usefulness, information with control, knowledge with power. It accepted the power-holders' challenge to prove the validity of sociological knowledge by the practical benefits it may bring to the management of social order, to the solution of 'problems' as seen and articulated by the managers of order. By the same token, sociology that pursued such a strategy had to adopt the managerial perspective: to view society 'from the top', as an object of manipulation, as resistant material whose inner qualities must be known better in order to be made more pliable and more receptive to the shape one may wish to give it.

The merger of sociological and managerial interests may have endeared sociology to state, industrial or military administrations, but it exposed it to the criticism of those who perceived power control from the top as a threat to the values they cherished, and particularly to individual freedom and communal self-management. The critics pointed out that the pursuit of discussed strategy amounts to taking sides and an active support for the extant asymmetry of social power. It is not true — they insisted — that the knowledge and practical precepts proferred by sociology may serve equally well anyone that might wish to use them, and therefore may be seen as neutral and non-partisan. Not everyone can use knowledge construed from the managerial perspective; its application, after all, demands resources that only the managers command and can deploy. Sociology thus enhances the control of those who are already in control; it further shifts the stakes in favour of those who already enjoy a better hand. The cause of inequality and social injustice is thereby served.

Sociology therefore attracted controversy. Its work is subjected to pressures that are hard to reconcile. What one side asks sociology to do the other sees as an abomination and is determined to resist. The blame for controversiality cannot be put solely at sociology's door. Sociology falls victim to a real social conflict, an inner contradiction tearing apart society at large; a contradiction it is in no position to resolve.

The contradiction resides in the very project of *rationalization* inherent in modern society. Rationality is a two-edged sword. On the one hand, it helps human individuals to gain more control over their own actions. Rational calculation, as we have seen, may gear action better to the actor's ends and thus increase its effectiveness. On the whole, it seems that rational individuals are more likely to achieve their ends than such individuals as do not plan, calculate and monitor their actions. Put in the service of the individual, rationality may increase the scope of individual freedom. On the other hand, once applied to the environment of individual action — to the organization of the society at large — rational analysis may well limit the range of the individuals' choices or diminish the pool of means from which the individuals may draw to pursue their ends. It may achieve an exactly opposite effect: constrain individual freedom. So the possible applications of rationality are intrinsically incompatible and doomed to remain controversial.

The controversy that surrounds sociology only reflects the Janus-faced nature of rationality. There is little sociology can do to repair it, and so the controversy is likely to continue. The power-holders will go on accusing sociology of undermining their hold over their subjects and inciting what they see as social unrest and subversion. People defending their way of life against the stifling constraints imposed by the resourceful powers that be will go on being nonplussed or aggrieved when they see sociologists as counsellors and acolytes of their erstwhile adversaries. In each case, the virulence of the accusation will reflect the current intensity of conflict.

Attacked on two fronts, sociology finds its scientific status widely questioned. Its adversaries are vitally interested in delegitimizing the validity of sociological knowledge, and the denial of scientific status serves the purpose well. It is perhaps this double assault, such as few other branches of scholarship face, that makes sociologists so sensitive about the issue of their own status as scientists, and prompts ever renewed attempts to convince both academic opinion and the wider public that the knowledge sociologists produce can claim the truth value of the standard ascribed to scientific findings. Attempt remain inconclusive. They also turn attention away from the genuine service sociological thinking may offer to daily life.

All knowledge, being an orderly vision, a vision of order, contains an interpretation of the world. It does not, as we often believe, reflect things as they are by themselves; things are, rather, called into being by the knowledge we have; it is as if our raw, inchoate sensations condensed into things by sifting into containers our knowledge has prepared for them in the form of categories, classes, types. The more knowledge we have, the more things we see — the greater number of different things we discern in the world. Or, rather, to say, 'I have more knowledge' and 'I distinguish more things in the world' means the same. If I study the art of painting, my heretofore indiscriminate impression of 'redness' splits into an ever growing number of specific and highly distinct members of the 'family of red colours': I now see differently Adrianople red, flame red, hellebore red, Indian red, Japanese red, carmine, crimson, ruby, scarlet, cardinal red, sanguine, vermilion, damask, Naples red, Pompeian red, Persian red and a constantly increasing number of other reds. The difference between a person untrained, ignorant in arts, and an expert, a schooled artist or art critic, will express itself in the first person's inability to see the colours which for the second person appear blatantly (and 'naturally') distinct and separate. It may also express itself in the second person losing the first person's ability to see 'redness' as such, to perceive all the objects painted with various shades of red as being of the same colour.

In all areas, acquisition of knowledge consists of learning how to make new discriminations, how to make the uniform discrete, how to render distinctions more specific, split large classes into smaller ones, so that the interpretation of experience gets richer and more detailed. Often we hear of the education people possess being measured by the richness of the vocabulary they deploy (by how many words their language contains). Things may be described as 'nice' — but their 'niceness' may be made more specific, and then it transpires that things so described may be experienced as 'nice' for various reasons — for being enjoyable, or savoury, or kind, or suitable, or tasteful, or 'doing the right thing'. It seems that richness of experience and vocabulary grow together.

Language does not come into life 'from outside', to report what has already happened. Language is in life from the start. Indeed, we may say that language is *a form of life*, and every language — English, Chinese, Portuguese, working-class language, 'posh' language, the 'official' language of civil servants, the argot of the underworld, the jargon of adolescent gangs, the language of art critics, of sailors, of nuclear physicists, or surgeons or miners — is a form of life in its own right. Each brings together a map of the world (or a specific section of the world) and a code of behaviour — with the two orders, the two planes of discrimination (one of perception and another of behavioural practice), parallel and coordinated. Inside each form of life, the map and the code intertwine. We can think of them separately, but in practice we cannot pull them apart. Distinctions made between the names of things reflect our perception of the difference in their qualities — and hence also in their uses and in our actions towards them; but our recognition of the difference in quality reflects the discrimination we make in our actions towards them and the expectations from which our actions follow. Let us recall what we have found out already: to understand is to know how to go on. And vice versa: if we know how to go on, we have understood. It is precisely this overlapping, this harmony between the two — the way we act and the way we see the world — that makes us suppose that the differences are in the things themselves, that the world around us is by itself divided into separate parts distinguished by our language, that the names 'belong' to the named things.

Forms of life are many. Each one, of course, differs from another; their distinctions, after all, are what makes them into separate forms of life. But they are not separated from each other by impermeable walls; they should not be thought of as self-enclosed, sealed worlds, with inventories of contents all of their own, with all objects they contain belonging to them and to them alone. Forms of life are orderly, shared patterns — but often superimposed on each other. They overlap and vie for selected areas of the total life experience. They are, so to speak, different selections and alternative arrangements of the same portions of the total world and the same items drawn from the shared pool. In the course of one day, I move through many forms of life; but wherever I move, I carry a piece of other forms of life with me (so that the way I act in the research team where I work is 'tainted' by the regional and local particularities of the form of life of which I partake in my private life; my participation in that neighbourhood-bound form of life, in its turn, bears traces of a particular religious congregation to which I belong and whose life I share — and so on). In every form of life through which I pass in the course of my life I share knowledge and behavioural codes with a different set of people; and each of them might have a unique combination of forms of life of which he or she partakes. For this reason, no form of life is 'pure'; neither is it static, given once and for all. My entry into a form of life is not a passive process of rote learning on my part; not a process of twisting and moulding and trimming my ideas and my skills so that they conform to the rigid rules to which I now intend to submit myself. My entry into a form of life changes the form of life I enter; we *both* change, I bring with me a sort of dowry (in the shape of other forms of life which I carry in me) which transforms the contents of the form of life to which I am a newcomer, so that after my entry this form of life is different from before. And so it changes all the time. Each act of entry (of learning, of mastering and practising the language which constitutes a form of life) is a creative act: an act of transformation. To put this another way: languages, like the communities that share them, are wide-open and dynamic entities. They can exist only in a state of constant change.

This is why problems of understanding constantly arise (as well as the threats of confusion, of breakdown in communication). Renewed attempts to make communication foolproof (by 'freezing' the interpretations the language contains through enforcing a clear-cut, obligatory definition of every word) do not and cannot help, as the practitioners of language with their own and distinct interpretations constantly bring different sets of forms of life into interaction. In the course of such interaction, meanings undergo a subtle, yet steady and unavoidable change. They acquire new colouring, come to be associated with referents from which they used to be distant, displace older meanings and pass through many other changes that cannot but change the language itself. We can say that the process of communication — that action aimed at achieving joint understanding, at thrashing out the differences, at agreeing on interpretation — prevents any form of life from staying put. To grasp this amazing quality of the forms of life, think of whirls in a stream; each looks as if it had a steady shape and therefore 'remained the same', held its 'identity', over a protracted period of time — and yet, as we well know, it cannot keep a single molecule of water for more than a few seconds, its substance being in a state of permanent flux. In case you think this is a weakness of the whirl, and that it would be better for its security — for its 'survival' — if the flow of water in the river were stopped, remember that such an event would mean the 'death' of the whirl. It cannot 'live' (it cannot keep its shape, its form of separate and persistent identity) without a constant influx and outflow of ever new quantities of water (which, by the way, always carry somewhat different inorganic and organic ingredients).

We can say that languages, or forms of life, like whirls, or like rivers themselves, stay alive and preserve their identity, their **relative autonomy**, precisely because they are flexible, permanently in flux, able to absorb new material and let out the 'used up' one. This means, however, that forms of life (all languages, all bodies of knowledge) would die were they ever to become closed, stiff and repellent to change. They would not survive their final codification and that precision which prompts the attempts at codification. To put it differently, languages and knowledge in general need ambivalence to remain alive, to retain cohesion, to be of use.

And yet powers concerned with ordering the 'messy' reality cannot but view that ambivalence as an obstacle to their aims. They naturally tend to freeze the whirl, to bar all unwelcome input into the knowledge they control, to seal the 'form of life' for which they wish to secure monopoly. The search for unambiguous knowledge ('certain' thanks to the lack of competition) and the effort to make reality orderly, hospitable to self-assured, effective action, blend into one. To want full control over the situation is to strive for a clear-cut 'linguistic map' in which the meanings of words are not in doubt and never contested, in which each word unmistakably points to its referent and this one and only link is binding on all who use it. For these reasons, ambivalence of knowledge constantly prompts efforts to 'fix' certain knowledge as obligatory and unquestionable — as **orthodoxy**; to force through a belief that this knowledge and this knowledge alone is faultless, beyond reproach, or at any rate better (more trustworthy, reliable and useful) than its competitors; and to degrade by the same token the alternative forms of knowledge to the inferior, derisible status of superstition, prejudice, bias or manifestation of ignorance — but in any case a **heresy**, a condemnable deviation from the truth.

Such a double-pronged effort (to secure the position of the orthodoxy and to prevent or eliminate heresy) has control over interpretation as its objective. The power in question aims at gaining an exclusive right to decide which of the possible interpretations ought to be chosen and made binding as the *true* one (in the definition of truth, many of the competing versions may be false, but only one can be correct; errors are plentiful, while there is but one truth; the presumption of monopoly, of exclusivity, of non-competition is contained in the very idea of truth). The quest for monopoly of power expresses itself in casting the proponents of an alternative in the role of dissidents, in general *intolerance* of the pluralism of opinion, censorship and in extreme cases persecution (as in the burning of heretics by the Inquisition, the shooting of dissenters during Stalinist purges and of prisoners of conscience under contemporary dictatorial regimes).

By its nature sociology is singularly ill suited to the 'closing down' and 'sealing' job. Sociology is an extended commentary on the experience of daily life; an interpretation which feeds on other interpretations and is in turn fed into them. It does not compete, but shares forces with other discourses engaged in the interpretation of human experience (like literature, art, philosophy). If anything, thinking sociologically undermines the trust in the exclusivity and completeness of any interpretation. It brings into focus the plurality of experiences and forms of life; it shows each as an entity in its own right, a world with a logic of its own, while at the same time exposing the sham of its ostensible self-containment and self-sufficiency. Sociological thinking does not stem, but facilitates the flow and exchange of experiences. To put it bluntly, it adds to the volume of ambivalence as it saps the effort to 'freeze the flux' and shut the entry points. From the point of view of powers obsessed with the order they have designed, sociology is part of the 'messiness' of the world; a problem, rather than a solution.

The great service sociology is well prepared to render to human life and human cohabitation is the promotion of mutual understanding and tolerance as a paramount condition of shared freedom. Sociological thinking cannot but promote the understanding that breeds tolerance and the tolerance that makes understanding possible. In the words of the American philosopher Richard Rorty, 'if we take care of freedom, truth and goodness will take care of themselves'. Sociological thinking helps the cause of freedom.

16.   The Form of Explanatory Accounts
Anthony Giddens

In nineteenth-century social philosophy and social theory positivism was in the ascendant, if positivism is taken to mean two things. First, a conviction that all 'knowledge', or all that is to count as 'knowledge', is capable of being expressed in terms which refer in an immediate way to some reality, or aspects of reality that can be apprehended through the senses. Second a faith that the methods and logical structure of science, as epitomized in classical physics, can be applied to the study of social phenomena. In the writings of Comte and Marx alike, the science of social life was to complete the freeing of the human spirit from religious dogmas and the customary, unexamined beliefs men had about themselves. I have already talked of the erosion in the twentieth century of faith in scientific knowledge as the exemplar of all knowledge, and of the ranking of human cultures according to how far they have progressed towards the attainment of scientific rationalism. With the tempering, or loss, of the conviction that scientific knowledge is the highest form of knowledge, and the only sort worth striving to attain, has come a reappraisal of traditional and habitual beliefs and modes of action, whose earlier dismissal is seen as a compound of unthinking custom and blind prejudice.

In philosophy, one result was a massive split between two streams of thought in the 1920s and 1930s. On the one hand, logical positivism arose as a more radical defence of the privileged status of scientific knowledge than had ever been developed before. On the other hand, in phenomenology and linguistic philosophy, the authority of commonsense was resurrected and placed in the forefront as both a topic of study and a resource for study. The phenomenological philosophers have sought to effect a critique of natural science by arguing that its claims to knowledge are secondary to, and dependent upon, ontological premises of the natural attitude. Linguistic philosophy, on the other hand, has not generated any such critique, but rather has tended to cut itself off from the philosophy of science by insisting that there exists a logical disparity between the world of men and the world of nature, and confining its attentions to the former. Both phenomenology and linguistic philosophy culminate in a critique of social science, however, from the point of view of the 'natural attitude'.

The technical defence of commonsense by phenomenological and 'ordinary language' philosophers, in so far as this is directed towards explicating problems of the social sciences, converges with what might be regarded as a very common commonsense attitude towards them. This expresses the idea that the findings of social science, and especially of sociology, are bound to be unremarkable, since they cannot do more than redescribe what we must already know as participants in social life — thus, as a philosopher I have already quoted puts it, sociologists' accounts of social conduct must 'seem unnecessary and pretentious'. Such a view is normally dismissed fairly casually by social scientists themselves, who offer two reasons for its rebuttal. One is that even

Anthony Giddens: 'The Form of Explanatory Accounts' from *NEW RULES OF SOCIOLOGICAL METHOD* (Polity Press, 1993), pp. 130-135. Reproduced by permission of Basil Blackwell Limited.

if it were true that sociology merely 'describes', or 'redescribes', what actors already know about their actions, no specific person can possess detailed knowledge of anything more than the particular sector of society in which he participates, so that there still remains the task of making into an explicit and comprehensive body of knowledge that which is only known in a partial way by lay actors themselves. However, most would go on to add, it is in any case not true that their endeavours can be no more than descriptive in character, and it is their principal task to correct and improve upon notions which are used by actors themselves in interpreting their own actions and the action of others. I think that this is indeed so. But, in the face of the critiques developed in the interpretative sociologies which I discussed in [Chapter 1], the claim demands detailed elucidation. Such elucidation confronts an array of epistemological problems of considerable complexity.

Positivistic dilemmas

Comte coined both the terms 'positive philosophy' and 'sociology', thus establishing a conjunction which, if it did not serve to accomplish the practical social reforms he envisaged, nonetheless consolidated an intellectual tradition which, as transposed by Durkheim, became dominant in sociology into recent times. The thesis that there can be a 'natural science of society' which, whatever the differences between human conduct and occurrences in nature, would involve explanatory schemes of the same logical form as those established in the natural sciences, has been elaborated in various guises since Durkheim's time. But the latter's *Rules of Sociological Method* remains perhaps the boldest expression of such a view, and although it is not my intention to consider the theme of that work in any detail, it is worth briefly characterizing the framework of inductive method that it advocates. According to Durkheim, the object of sociology is to construct theories about human conduct inductively on the basis of prior observations about that conduct: these observations, which are made about externally 'visible' characteristics of conduct, are necessarily 'pre-theoretical' since it is out of them that theories are born. Such observations, it is held, have no particular connection with the ideas actors have about their own actions and those of others; it is incumbent upon the observer to make every possible effort to separate himself from commonsense notions held by actors themselves, because these frequently have no basis in fact. In Durkheim's presentation of this kind of standpoint, the social scientist is instructed to formulate his concepts for himself, at the outset of his research, and to break away from those current in everyday life. The concepts of everyday activity, Durkheim says, 'merely express the confused impression of the mob'; 'if we follow common use,' he continues, 'we risk distinguishing what should be combined, or combining what should be distinguished, thus mistaking the real affinities of things, and accordingly misapprehending their nature.' The investigations which the social scientist makes have to deal with 'comparable facts' whose 'natural affinities' cannot be distinguished by the 'superficial examination that gives rise to ordinary terminology'. The assumption that there are discriminable 'natural affinities' of objects (physical or social), which pre-exist and determine what the observer does in describing and classifying those objects, appears throughout Durkheim's writings. What this actually leads to is classification by fiat, which has, not surprisingly, disturbed many of his readers. Thus, for example, having dismissed commonsense notions of suicide as irrelevant to his study, Durkheim proceeded to establish a new definition of the phenomenon, as he put it, 'to determine the order of facts to be studied under the name of suicides'.

The ideas worked out in *Suicide* are thus supposely based upon the initial formulation of the nature of suicide, defined as 'all cases of death resulting directly or indirectly from a positive or negative act of the victim himself, which he knows will produce this result'. But, it has been argued by critics, this definition is impossible to apply. One reason given for this is that Durkheim was unable to observe the distinctions entailed in his own formulation because virtually all of his analyses involve the use of suicide statistics, and it seems rather unlikely that the officials who constructed those statistics understood by 'suicide' what Durkheim proposed the term should be used to mean by the social scientist. But the more radical claim has also been made by some of the critics mentioned in [Chapter 1] that a concept of 'suicide' such as might be employed in social analysis must be constructed out of detailed descriptions of relevant commonsense concepts used by actors themselves. Now I shall want to affirm subsequently that the problem of 'adequacy', involving the relation between everyday language and social scientific metalanguages, is an issue of basic importance. But no useful end is served by supposing that, in place of the 'external affinities' between social phenomena that Durkheim sought, we can merely substitute ideations. While such a view is quite different in substance from the Durkheimian sort of programme, replacing naturalism by idealism, in logical form it is quite similar to it. For it is an assumption of both that social science has to be founded upon descriptions of 'reality' that are 'pre-theoretical' in character. In the case of those influenced by phenomenology and ethnomethodology, this is a 'reality' composed of ideas, rather than 'external' characteristics of conduct. Once we have ascertained what this reality 'is' — e.g., 'suicide' as defined as a phenomenon by members of society — we are supposedly in a position to build up generalizatons on that basis, although there is some considerable difference of opinion about what kind of generalizations these will be.

In so far as they concern general matters of epistemology, the issues involved here can be illuminated by reference to the long-standing debate over the status of 'observational statements' in the philosophy of natural science. What Feigl calls the 'orthodox' view of natural science, as formulated by those influenced by logical positivism, runs roughly as follows. Scientific theories are hypothetico-deductive systems. The formulation of theories involves several levels of conceptual differentiation: at the highest level, abstract postulates which cannot be given a precise definition in terms of their empirical content, but only in terms of their logical relations with other postulates. The concepts contained in theoretical generalizations are distinct from the terms of the observation language, which refer to the sensory 'soil' of observation as given in experience. Hence there have to be correspondence rules which specify the relations that pertain between the language of observation and the language of theory. According to the view just outlined, as well as to earlier-established variants of empiricism, the 'data' of experience force upon us definite modes of description and classification of the world of 'outer reality'. This implies two claims: that it is feasible and necessary to search for some sort of ultimate foundations of scientific knowledge which are 'certain'; and that these foundations have to be located in some area of experience which can be described or categorized in a language which is theoretically neutral. The quest for unassailable 'foundations' of empirical knowledge is one which has occupied Western philosophers since Descartes, and has been pursued in modern times by empiricists and phenomenologists alike. Both come up with answers that presuppose an essentially passive relation between subject and object: in the first case, the bedrock is found in sense-experience, in the second, it is found in ideations that are regarded as distinct from experience and instead inform it. The first, however, having located its 'starting point' in sensory experience, finds diffculty in explaining the nature of theoretical categories, which do not stand in any discernible relation of isomorphy with sense-data, and hence it becomes necessary to introduce correspondence rules which connect the content of one to the content of the other. But this had never been satisfactory, for the nature of correspondence rules has proved to be highly elusive. The other view, having located the foundations of knowledge in the ideal categories that are immediately available to the ego, finds the reverse difficulty — that of reconstituting the world of sensory experience itself.

Each of the claims mentioned in the above paragraph can be disputed. Most traditional schools of philosophy have proceeded on the assumption that our choice of a 'starting-point' is decisively important to scientific knowledge, since the 'foundations' determine the character of all that is built upon them. But there can be no 'foundations' of knowledge that are unshakeably secure, or which are not theory-impregnated. The idea of a 'protocol language' — as Quine once put it, a 'fancifully fancyless medium of unvarnished news' — depends upon what Popper sardonically labels the 'bucket theory of knowledge': the human mind is treated as if it were a sort of container, empty at birth, into which material pours through our senses, and in which it accumulates. All immediate experience, if it is held, is thus received as sense-data. There are many objections that can be made to this, as Popper indicates in his devastating critique. Statements which refer to 'sensory observation' cannot expressed in a theoretically neutral observation language; the differentiation between the latter and theoretical language is a relative one, within a framework of a pre-existing conceptual system.

17.   Empiricism

Terry Johnson, Christopher Dandeker
and Clive Ashworth

As with other sociological perspectives considered in this book, the analysis of empiricism takes as a central theme the problem, 'What is social structure?' We have already indicated that this theme can be broken down into two interrelated questions: what is the nature of social reality?; and, how can we know it?

As should be clear from the [introductory chapter], sociological answers to these questions cannot help but draw and contribute to arguments that have philosophical implications. Unfortunately, these arguments have all too often become the specialised preserve of philosophers rather than being directly confronted by sociologists. Moreover the degree to which this has been so has been reinforced by the dominance of empiricism in social scientific thinking. As we shall see, empiricism in social science has been marked by an 'anti-philosophical' attitude, which has had the effect of imposing a particular set of hidden assumptions, on sociological theorising. One consequence of this rejection of 'philosophical' issues is that we are forced to go to the empiricist philosophers of science in order to find a discussion of the assumptions underlying the empiricist strategy in sociology.[1] Such philosophy of science is of particular importance for us, as it is there that *positivism* has been most fully developed and refined; that is, the doctrine that the methods of the natural sciences can be transferred, with only minor if any modification, to the social sciences.[2]

The strategy and tensions of empiricism

Our consideration of the empiricist strategy starts with a paradox: namely, that while the solutions to the dilemmas of knowledge are, like those of any other strategy, infused with philosophically relevant arguments, the distinguishing feature of empiricism is its attempt to eradicate all 'philosophical' concerns from sociology (and the sciences generally). Such concerns are either denigrated as 'metaphysical' or are made acceptable by their transformation into technical, 'methodological' problems; a specialist concern of specialist methodologists. As we shall see, the paradox leads to a rejection of 'philosophy' that is just as 'philosophical' or 'metaphysical' as those strategies that are rejected.[3]

At the core of the empiricist strategy is a view of reality as constituted by material things. Knowledge of such reality is seen to be rooted in the sensory experiences that mediate the relations between nervous system and events in the physical world. For the empiricist, then, experience is sensorily based, and knowledge remains tied to these foundations. The concepts and generalisations of science are, therefore, merely shorthand summaries of particular, albeit repeated, observations; that is to say, such statements are *nominal*. Reference to any reality beyond particular observations

Copyright © 1984 Johnson, R., Dandeker, C. and Ashworth, C., from *THE STRUCTURE OF SOCIAL THEORY*. Reprinted with permission of Macmillan Press Limited and St Martin's Press, Incorporated.

always involves, for the empiricist, a confusion between general concepts and particular realities; it is a confusion that, it is claimed, characterises all forms of objectivism in the rationalist and substantialist traditions. Empiricism also departs from subjectivist assumptions in suggesting that scientific observations of social reality can be expressed in an objective language; that is, a language that reflects the real world. The two elements of the empiricist strategy constitutes its commitment to *materialism* and *nominalism*.

Classical empiricism (often referred to as 'vulgar' by contemporary social scientists) regards knowledge as the product of observations; often referred to as the process of induction. In modern forms of empiricism this view has to some extent been supplanted, or at least complemented by 'deductivism'. Deductivist strategies suggest that knowledge results from the imaginative insights of the observer controlled by rigorous empirical test. These views constitute only a modification of classical empiricism, as the principles of nominalism and materialism are still adhered to. The imaginative insight must be presented in a logically consistent and empirically testable form: i.e. hypotheses that state what observable events would verify or refute them. Induction and deductivism have, then, constituted the main foundations of empiricism in sociological thinking, ranging from what, on the one hand, has been called 'abstracted empiricism', to holistic functionalism on the other.[4] The strategic assumptions which maintain the basic conditions of empiricism are both dogmatic and essentially unstable, leading to the creation of a proliferating field of tensions within the tradition.

At the centre of empiricism is the view that experience provides the sole and secure source of knowledge. This assumption both eliminates from science all philosophical questions concerning how it is we know reality, and at the same time is itself a debatable philosophical assertion.[5] In empiricism, therefore, science and metaphysics are both connected and *dis*connected. As we have argued, metaphysics are allowed into science in accordance with the rules of empiricism; that is, in a hypothetical testable form; yet once allowed in, such imaginative insights open up empiricism to questions that undermine a strategy based entirely on experience as the sole source of knowledge. As a result, the empiricist strategy is always vulnerable to criticism directed from the alternative strategies, a process that has been particularly marked in sociology during the last decade or so, undermining the pre-eminent position of empiricism in the discipline.[6]

The tensions in empiricism stem from the central part played by experience in the strategy. Two main issues arise, and involve two senses of the term 'objectivity'. First, if concepts are 'shorthand' summaries of experience, then in what sense may we say that concepts refer to entities beyond any particular experience? Projects within empiricism equivocate on this issue because their commitment to the existence of an objective material world, external to the human subject, is undercut by the view that knowledge of the world is confined to what is available in experience. This results in difficulties in sustaining coherent distinctions and connections between experiences, events that are being experienced, and the causal mechanisms that produce such events. Indeed, empiricism's initial commitment to an external objective world (and thus its association with the central concerns of *substantialism*) has been whittled away during its historical development from the sixteenth to the twentieth century.[7] The commitment has remained, but not the means necessary to sustain it. As a result, points of contact with the subjectivist strategy have been strengthened.

Second, empiricism suggests that the objectivity or truth of theories is secured through testing them and their competitors against experiences that are themselves theory-neutral and are not, therefore, matters of individual and/or 'uncontrollable' interpretations. Yet as subjectivists have argued, the possibility of describing experience in language that is theory-neutral is itself a matter of dispute in the philosophy of science. Consequently, many empiricists have been forced to accept the idea that reality is never confronted *directly*, but only through agreed conventions as to what reality is taken to be for the purpose of a particular experimental test.[8]

However, empiricist projects in sociological theorising have only fairly recently begun to come to terms with such tensions inherent in the development of their strategy.

Empiricism and positivism

Of central and particular significance for the development of empiricism in sociological theory have been the attempts to transfer natural scientific principles to the study of social reality. This 'positivistic' attitude involves two sets of contentious issues: first, the assertion that the empiricist interpretation of scientific knowledge — namely the construction of laws based on experience — provides an adequate account of the natural sciences; and second, whether natural scientific procedures are in any sense directly applicable to the problem of studying social reality.

Let us clarify what is meant by the term 'positivism'. Positivism is most frequently used to refer to the extension of empiricist models of natural science to the field of human action, by arguing for either a methodological or substantive unity of the two. The claim for methodological unity leads to behaviourism, while the latter implies reductionist explanations, i.e. the explanation of human action in terms of either 'heredity' or 'environment'.

Positivism in sociology is particularly associated with the behaviourist approach to social action. The claim that, unlike natural events, human action is meaningful both to the participants and the observer is rejected by behaviourists, as a ground for radically distinguishing between the natural and social sciences, on the basis of method, for they believe that the 'mental' or 'psychic' components of human action should be translated into behavioural statements; that all the scientific observer can know of human action is the actual behaviour that takes place, and that observable behaviour is as amenable to study by scientific method as any 'objective' natural phenomenon. While the behavioural approach in the social sciences need not necessarily involve the reduction of social action to physical or biological conditions, it is consistent with the view that the methods of all sciences are basically the same, allowing for variations in experimental potential and degree of precision, etc.

The impact of behaviourism in the social sciences is well illustrated by the work of Skinner.[9] His approach rests on the idea that in the scientific analysis of human behaviour all reference to unobservable entities and processes such as mind, motive and imagination, must be eliminated. Such entities are not 'publicly observable'. Indeed, for science, they do not exist. All that can be publicly observed is the behaviour of the human organism under varying conditions or stimuli. The methods used to study human behaviour are, therefore, logically similar to those of the natural sciences.

Skinner goes further in suggesting that the behaviour of all living species may be understood in terms of the same basic primary laws. These may be derived from the experimental study of rats, pigeons, and other relatively simple organisms, and applied to the (only apparently) more complex human activities, such as religious worship, language, human aggression, etc.

The search for such laws of behaviour involves determining the experimental conditions under which particular types of behaviour occur. The model of explanation employed is one of an atomistic chain of stimuli and responses through time, aided by the concept of 'reinforcement'. It has been found that a rat will emit an 'operant response' — for example, press a bar — when such behaviour is rewarded (i.e. reinforced) by a food pellet. Indeed, the bar will continue to be pressed even when such behaviour is no longer immediately rewarded by food pellets, especially when pressing the bar has been so rewarded only occasionally and not at every instance. The rat will try again because the intermittent patterns of reward suggest the 'next time' may well be the *one* producing a reward. (The application of this to 'compulsive' gambling on a fruit machine is fairly obvious.) The strength of the conditioned response (i.e. its persistence after rewards cease) can be measured precisely.

However, the problems of tautology in this scheme seem inescapable. Thus, it is argued, the bar is pressed when no food is presented because such behaviour has been 'reinforced'; yet the opposite behaviour can be similarly explained by the argument that reinforcement has faded. As we are not told what reinforcement is in terms other than the pattern of behaviour it produces, the persuasiveness of the argument rests solely on the *predictive* value of such experimental techniques.[10] Indeed, rather like shock therapy, such explanations are supported by the view that they 'work' — i.e. behaviour can be controlled and calculated — rather than by any argument as to why they work. The 'strength' of a conditioned response is thus defined in terms of the persistence of behaviour, rather than of processes such as 'motive' or 'drive'.

However, of greatest importance in applying such methods to the social sciences — the application of Skinnerian methods to human behaviour — is the difficulty entailed in controlling the environment of a human subject. The experimental method developed in the study of animals assumes that to control the material environment is to control the stimuli producing behavioural responses. The major criticism of Skinnerian technique is that because human subjects are capable of reflection, of reflecting upon past events and future possibilities, the material conditions of action in specific experimental conditions do not exhaust the stimuli that may be present for any particular actor who has the capacity to think beyond the immediate situation. In short, the explanation of human action must take into account an interpretative process which is not directly accessible to such controlled observation.

Notes

1. General discussions of empiricism may be found in L. Kolakowski, *Positivist Philosophy* (Harmondsworth: Penguin, 1972); G. Novack, *Empiricism and its Evolution* (New York: Pathfinder Press, 1969).

2. See A. Giddens, 'Positivism and its Critics', in T. Bottomore and R. Nisbet, *A History of Sociological Analysis* (London: Heinemann, 1979) pp. 237–86; Kolakowski, *Positivist Philosophy*; P. Achinstein and S. F. Barker, *The Legacy of Logical Positivism* (Baltimore: Johns Hopkins Press, 1969); C. G. A. Bryant, 'Positivism Reconsidered', *Sociological Review*, 23 2 1975; R. Bernstein, *Restructuring of Social and Political Theory* (Oxford: Blackwell, 1976) pp. 1–55.

3. Metaphysics may be viewed either as meaningless, as in Ayer's empiricism, or as meaningful but non-scientific as in Popper. See A. J. Ayer, *Language, Truth and Logic* (Harmondsworth: Penguin, 1971); K. Popper, *Conjectures and Refutations* (London: Routledge & Kegan Paul, 1963).

4. On these variations in empiricist explanation, see E. Nagel, *The Structure of Science* (London: Routledge & Kegan Paul, 1961); C. G. Hempel, *Aspects of Scientific Explanation* (Glencoe, Ill.: Free Press, 1965); A. Ryan, *The Philosophy of the Social Sciences* (London: Macmillan, 1970); R. Keat and J. Urry, *Social Theory as Science* (London: Routledge & Kegan Paul, 1975) pp. 9–22, 67–87; T. Benton, *Philosophical Foundations of the Three Sociologies* (London: Routledge & Kegan Paul, 1977) pp. 46–77.

5. See Trent Schroyer, *The Critique of Domination: Origins and Development of Critical Theory* (New York: Braziller, 1973).

6. This has led, in recent years, to a number of attempts to reconstruct the bases of sociological theorising: see A. W. Gouldner, *The Coming Crisis of Western Sociology* (London: Heinemann, 1971); Bernstein, *Restructuring of Social and Political Theory*; Keat and Urry, *Social Theory as Science*; Benton, *Philosophical Foundations*; and A. Giddens, *New Rules of Sociological Method* (London: Hutchinson, 1976), *Central Problems in Social Theory* (London: Macmillan, 1979) and *A Contemporary Critique of Historical Materialism* (London: Macmillan, 1981).

7. On these points see R. Bhaskar, *A Realist Theory of Science* (Leeds: Leeds Books, 1975) and *Possibility of Naturalism* (Brighton: Harvester, 1979).

8. On conventionalism and problems of theory-neutral observation languages, see Bernstein, *Restructurings*, pp. 4–7; Keat and Urry, *Social Theory*, pp. 46–65; Benton, *Philosophical Foundations*, pp. 73–6.

9. On Skinner, and problems of Behaviourism generally, see B. F. Skinner, *Verbal Behaviour* (London: Methuen, 1957) and *About Behaviourism* (London: Cape, 1974); N. Chomsky, *Language and Mind* (New York: Harcourt Brace Jovanovich, 1968); A. Koestler, *Ghost in the Machine* (London: Hutchinson, 1967); S. Mennell, *Sociological Theory: Uses and Unities* (Sunbury: Nelson, 1974) pp. 9–13.

10. D. and J. Willer, *Systematic Empiricism – A Critique of a Pseudo-Science* (Englewood Cliffs: Prentice Hall, 1973); C. Wright Mills, *The Sociological Imagination* (Oxford University Press, 1959) pp. 60–86, and; The Ideology of Social Pathologists', in Wright Mills, *Power, Politics and People* (Oxford University Press, 1967) pp. 525–52.

18. Auguste Comte and Positivist Sociology
Ted Benton

Central to this chapter will be a consideration of that conception of the nature of scientific sociology which has had the greatest influence both on the practice of social scientists and on their conceptions of what they do. This is the positivist philosophy — or 'positivism' — usually associated with the name of Auguste Comte. I have already said a little about the positivist conception of the relationship between philosophy and the social sciences, and in this chapter I propose to discuss the leading doctrines of the positivist philosophy, as expounded by Comte himself. But Comte's positivism was not a closed and finally elaborated system of ideas. On the contrary, it and its relatives have been subjected to a continuous process of revision, development and sophistication up to the present day, and so I shall devote part of my [third and fourth chapters] to giving some account of these latter-day developments before advancing the more fundamental criticisms of positivist doctrine.

Although Comte coined the term 'positivisme', he was by no means a profoundly original thinker, either in philosophy or sociology, and it will be necessary to approach his work through a prior discussion of the philosophical tradition to which he belonged, and the traditions of social thought which informed his work. It is also necessary, if Comte's particular combination of philosophical and social thought is to be understood, to speak a little of the economic and political situation in the France of the early nineteenth century.

Epistemology

The aspect of Comte's philosophy with which I shall be centrally concerned is his contribution to 'epistemology', or the philosophical theory of knowledge. The principal questions of epistemology, as I mentioned in [chapter 1], are questions as to the nature and scope of human knowledge: what can be known with certainty, and what must be left to faith, or opinion? What is the proper source or foundation of knowledge? A central pre-occupation in epistemology, I argued (though it is by no means always explicit), is the search for criteria by which to distinguish scientific knowledge from the non-scientific.

Although there is a popular tendency in the history of ideas to search for the precursors of modern ideas earlier and yet earlier in the Middle Ages, I shall not follow it. The posing of these questions, as part of a systematic onslaught on traditional forms of knowledge and their credentials, was neither widespread nor did it have a major impact on the development of knowledge itself until the sixteenth and seventeenth centuries. The target of the onslaught was the enormous intellectual achievement of the late Middle Ages: a synthesis of Catholic theology and Aristotelian/Ptolemaic cosmology, which was achieved, in its main outlines, during the thirteenth century by

Ted Benton: 'Auguste Comte and Positivist Sociology' from *PHILOSOPHICAL FOUNDATIONS OF THE THREE SOCIOLOGIES* (Routledge & Kegan Paul Ltd, 1977) pp. 18-26. Reproduced by permission of Routledge.

St Thomas Aquinas among other leading Catholic theologians. The doctrines of the Church, the teachings of the scholastics in the universities (themselves predominantly subordinated to the task of educating the future priesthood), and the established medical beliefs and practices of the time all fell within the framework of this colossal intellectual monument. The new movement in philosophy was intimately connected with innovations in scientific knowledge and constituted a challenge to the intellectual authority of tradition, divine revelation and faith, at least in those spheres being opened up to scientific knowledge. And this challenge was not, of course, a purely 'intellectual' one. It had social and political implications of the most profound kind. Descartes, for instance, who was one of the leaders in this persistent scepticism, demonstrated his clear awareness of its political implications by hastily denying them.

> I could in no way approve those cloudy and unquiet spirits who, being called neither by birth nor fortune to the handling of public affairs, are forever reforming the state in imagination; and, if I thought that there was the least thing in what I have written to bring me under suspicion of such folly, I should deeply regret its publication.[1]

This was written in 1637, and it is likely that Descartes had the Inquisition, which had so recently arrested Galileo and forced him to recant his heliocentric astronomical views, very much in mind. To question the intellectual authority of the Church and the scholastics was to question the authority of an institution which was an enormous political power in itself; but more than this it was to challenge the main ideological support of the monarchical form of government. Of course, not all of the philosophical radicals of this period were also political radicals — some found ways of combining political conservatism with intellectual radicalism, whilst many more, like Descartes, disguised their radicalism in their published writings. My point is, rather, that irrespective of the openly avowed political views of individual philosophers, the overall significance of the new tendencies in philosophical thought could not be anything but subversive of the established political and intellectual order.

Of course, to challenge the — by now rather ramshackle — edifice of medieval ideas, the philosophers of the sixteenth and seventeenth centuries needed to be able to point to new, firmer foundations upon which to begin the work of reconstruction or they must run the risk of being discounted as nihilists. There were, speaking very loosely, two main alternatives to faith and revelation as sources and foundations of knowledge: reason and experience. The first alternative reason — might seem to be not so radical after all, since Thomist philosophy had been quite explicitly an attempt to give Christian belief a rational foundation and defence. But what was distinctive about the rationalism of Descartes was the democratic and individualistic form which the demand for rational defence took. At the very start of his *Discourse on Method* he suggests that 'the power of judging rightly, and of separating what is true from what is false (which is generally called good sense or reason), is equal by nature in all men'.[2] All men, it follows, have the power to submit established doctrine to the test of critical reason (though Descartes denies the propriety of just this, a little later in the text).[3] And the author of the *Meditations* is an isolated individual, seated by his fire, subjecting everything he has hitherto taken for granted to systematic doubt. This is no mere accident of style, but symptomatic of the form taken by the problem of knowledge in the thought of both rationalist and empiricist philosophers. The central question is: what certainty can the individual human subject have concerning the world about him? Not only can the existence of God and the external world be the objects of doubt, but even the existence of other persons. Descartes's answer to the central question, that 'whatever I perceive very clearly and distinctly is true', implies that the 'natural light of reason' is capable of shining in the mind of each secluded individual.

Similarly, for the empiricists, knowledge is founded on the experience of a typified individual subject, and the scope and limits of human knowledge are defined in terms of a psychological theory of the scope and limits of the human mind. Although modern empiricists tend to abandon adherence to such a psychological theory, knowledge for them remains logically tied to the experience of the human subject.

Both the rationalists and the empiricists more or less self-consciously produced their new conceptions of knowledge and its foundation as a defence of the claims of science as a (or sometimes 'the') source of genuine knowledge. For the rationalists the criteria of certain knowledge, the standards by which all knowledge-claims must be judged were plainly drawn from logic and mathematics, whilst for the empiricists it was the experiment and observation which they took to be responsible for the contemporary advances in physical science, that they placed at the centre of their account of knowledge. But though both major tendencies or traditions in the theory of knowledge had, at least in their earlier phases, a close relationship to the sciences, they tended to conceive of this relationship differently. By now the affinity between empiricism and the under-labourer conception on the one hand, and rationalism and the master-scientist conception on the other, should be apparent.

Empiricism

The major philosophical tendency to which positivism belongs is empiricism. Positivism is a variant form of empiricism, along with phenomenalism, pragmatism, operationalism, empirio-criticism, logical empiricism and others. I shall mention some of these more modern variants again in [chapters 3 and 4], but for the moment it should be sufficient to give a broad — and necessarily oversimple — characterisation of the leading doctrines of empiricism as a philosophical tendency and to give some indication of its historical significance up to the time of Comte.

'Seeing is believing'; 'the proof of the pudding is in the eating'; 'I saw it with my own eyes . . .'. These are the common-sense attitudes which empiricism articulates into a philosophical theory. Central to empiricism, then, is the conception of a human subject whose beliefs about the external world are worthy of the description 'knowledge' only if they can be put to the test of experience. In classical seventeenth- and eighteenth-century empiricism this doctrine is not clearly distinguished from the proposition that all genuine knowledge has its source or origin in experience. Locke, for instance, devoted the first book of his *Essay* to refuting the doctrine that 'there are in the understanding certain innate principles . . . which the soul receives in its very first being . . .', on the assumption, presumably, that to admit such principles would be to admit the possibility of true propositions not subject to the court of experience (an odd assumption for Locke, since Francis Bacon had already identified the innate contents of the mind as a fundamental source of error). But most empiricists have been prepared to countenance at least one class of statements whose truth or falsity is independent of experience: these are analytic truths, or 'relations of ideas' as Hume called them. They are true or false 'by definition' or by virtue of the meanings of the terms which make them up. Sometimes such statements are referred to as 'conceptual' statements, and contrasted with 'factual' statements whose truth or falsity is establishable by experience. There is much debate within empiricism about which statements to include in the conceptual or analytical category, some arguing that the propositions of mathematics, for instance, are all of them analytic (and therefore tell us nothing about the world), others arguing, as did Mill, that mathematical propositions are factual. The modern empiricist W. V. Quine has even gone so far as to suggest that there are no analytic propositions at all, arguing that statements simply differ in the degree to which they are protected from rejection on the basis of experience.[4] But despite this disagreement there is a central doctrine which I shall take as the touchstone of empiricism: that there is no knowledge *a priori* ('prior to' or independent of experience) which is at the same time informative about the world, as distinct from our ideas, or the meanings of the terms we use.

Empiricists also differ in the kind and strength of the links they assert between knowledge and the experience upon which it is based. For the classical empiricists an elementary associationist psychology provided the framework for conceiving of this link. The mind was thought of as the initially empty and passive receptor of impressions or 'ideas' through the organs of sense. Ideas so received (or received by the mind's reflection upon its own operations) were the basic units upon which the mind could perform such operations as abstraction, combination, generalisation, etc. to yield systematic propositional knowledge of the world. Later empiricists who dispensed with this psychological theory tended to search for logical links between the meanings of terms, sentences, or whole systems of sentences, on the one hand, and possible confirming or disconfirming observations on the other.

A final source of variation in empiricist theories of knowledge has to do with the content they give to concepts like 'experience', 'perception', or 'observations'. For Francis Bacon (not in the fullest sense an empiricist, but certainly one of its most important forerunners) 'experience' involved practical attempts to change nature, setting ideas to work. The concept of experience in empiricist thought subsequently became progressively attenuated through the metaphor of impressions on a plain sheet to that of an inner display of mental images which serve rather to cut off the subject from knowledge of his environment than to inform him of its constitution.

The history of empiricism[5]

Because of this variability of empiricist doctrine, it is extremely difficult to generalise about its historical significance. In Britain from the mid-sixteenth century an empirical tendency of thought seems to have become dominant among the mathematicians, scientists, craftsmen and merchants who were receptive to new scientific ideas which were rapidly being introduced from the continent. Men such as Robert Recorde, Thomas Digges, John Dee, Nicholas Culpeper, William Gilbert and a host of others were active, not only in translating important scientific works into the vernacular, but in making important contributions of their own to mathematics, astronomy, magnetism, medicine and so on. Perhaps, in part, because of the scholastic resistance to the new knowledge in the universities, and the 'college of physicians', and also because of the resistance on the part of these vested interests to the popular spread of knowledge ('Vile men would, prelate-like, have knowledge hid'),[6] science developed in England outside the universities under the patronage of the merchants, and in close relationship with the crafts, manufactures and methods of transport of the day. Scientists learned from these practices and also, with an eye to the practical application of their knowledge, co-operated to provide free scientific education to the popular classes. It is also beyond question that the newly prevailing current of Protestantism was connected with this combined flowering of science, commerce and manufacture (though the precise form of this connection is very much a matter of debate).[7]

The philosopher (and corrupt politician), Francis Bacon (1561–1627) was able to articulate and combine these existing practical knowledges and scientific traditions with Protestant theology into an intellectual system which, once the power of the monarchy and the bishops was challenged by the Civil War, was a powerful influence on the development of science and industry and of social reform. In particular, his achievement was to appropriate the rigorous separation between God and nature which was central to Protestant theology to serve as a justification for the free exploration by experimental methods of the latter domain, unhampered by theological restrictions. This separation of the two domains enabled Bacon and his empiricist successors to defend the autonomy of the sciences whilst at the same time giving 'to faith that which is faith's'.[8] Science was given further ethical justification in terms of its contribution to the glorification of God through knowledge of his creation and, more importantly, in terms of a conception of human progress through the application of science in trade and manufacture. It is not surprising, therefore, that many of the most politically radical of the parliamentarians — including the Digger, Winstanley and the Leveller, Overton — together with a group supported by Pym who proposed state patronage for scientific research and massive educational reform, were the bearers of Bacon's ideas. Another of Bacon's intellectual legatees, the political philosopher Hobbes, was by no means a radical, though it is not without significance that his combination of the empiricist theory of knowledge with a mechanical-materialist causal theory of perception and of mental functions such as memory led him to be attacked as an atheist.

The work of the post-revolutionary philosopher, John Locke, can be understood as a compromise between conflicting tendencies, granting (with doubtful consistency) certainty to our knowledge of the existence of God, yet at the same time advancing the claims of the natural sciences. Only in the work of the Irish philosopher, Bishop George Berkeley (1683–1753) do we find empiricism turned back upon itself, historically speaking, to provide a defence for theology and a critique of science. For Berkeley, since all the mind is directly aware of are its own ideas, there can be no justification in experience for the claim that these ideas are 'representations' or 'copies' of a material world outside us. We must, rather, suppose that our ideas are produced in our minds by a beneficent creator.

Enlightenment and revolution in France [9]

In the eighteenth century the centre of the stage, philosophically speaking, is taken by Enlightenment France. Here the rationalist epistemology and the cosmology of Descartes rapidly came under challenge from the physical theory and empiricist epistemology connected with the names of Newton and Locke. The sensationalist philosopher Condillac played the leading role in popularising these intellectual currents in France, and the enormously influential philosophers grouped around the *Encyclopédie* were all to a greater or lesser degree followers of Locke. The empiricist epistemology was, for many of them, combined with atheism and materialism. D'Holbach even turns Locke's own argument against obscurantism in science against theology. 'Theology is nothing but ignorance of natural causes reduced to a system', and the name of God only 'a vague word that men have continually on their lips without being able to attach to it any ideas . . .'. Locke never dared, or was never disposed to draw such conclusions from his epistemology.

The Encyclopedists were also followers of Locke in their political philosophy, which resembled their epistemology in taking the individual subject as its central concept. Social and political institutions were to be judged by the liberty they allowed the individual to dispose himself and his property as he pleased, within the law. The authority of the state was conditional upon the consent of the subjects, sovereign and subjects alike being bound by a social contract whose existence was the sole source of political authority and of civil society itself. But this classical liberal-democratic political philosophy was by no means without its internal problems. A central source of intellectual difficulty and (later, when the philosophy became transformed into a programme for action) of political schism, was that the rights to liberty and property (these rights were hardly distinguished from one another) were seen to conflict with the ideals of democracy and equality once these ideals were conceived in anything more than purely formal or juridical terms. A constitutional monarchy, with a limited property-franchise, on the English pattern, was the political form which most nearly realised the aspirations of these liberal theorists. Others, most notably Rousseau, who came close to producing a critique of the Enlightenment in its own terms, insisted upon the need to restrict the liberty to accumulate wealth in the interests of equality. Though generally regarded as a radical Rousseau was quite ambiguous in his political thought. His conception of economic equality (inequalities should never be so great as to permit of the citizen's selling himself, or being bought by another) implied hostility to the capitalist development of industry, aided by scientific advance, upon which the Enlightenment, following both Locke and Bacon, had based its firm conviction of the inevitability of human progress. Further, in some places Rousseau makes it clear that he favours economic equality less as a desirable end in itself than as a condition whose absence is a threat to the more important end of social order. Rousseau also made a profound break with the individualism of the Enlightenment in his notion of the 'general will' which was to serve as an important source both of French conservative thought and of later socialist and communist political thought.

In England, a century before, the empiricist theory of knowledge, together with the science it defended, had played a part in preparing the intellectual conditions for the English revolution. In France, science and empiricism, together with the political philosophy of liberalism which had also been established by the British empiricists, played their part in preparing the way for the yet more profound revolution of 1789–94. In both revolutions empiricism, science and religious unorthodoxy were partisan forces. They favoured (and, in general, were favoured by) the newly forming bourgeoisie, the merchants, the manufacturers, the artisans and craftsmen, not to mention the professionals, the shopkeepers and the urban and rural labouring poor: in short, they favoured those classes whose political alliance broke the power of the old feudal order, and established the conditions for the development of the capitalist mode of production and distribution, and the social order based upon it.[10]

But in the English case the revolutionary cutting-edge of empiricism became blunted with the achievement of this task — even prior to it. The English compromise between aristocracy and bourgeoisie is mirrored in Locke's compromise in epistemology. In France, the initial phases of revolution seemed set to replace absolute monarchy with a compromise on the English model. But the contradictions in the French social structure, and the exigencies of its international situation, would not allow of this. In the defence of their newly won liberties against international counter-revolution the French bourgeoisie had to call upon and mobilise ever broader and deeper layers of the French masses. But the very extent of this mobilisation, and the far greater differentiation of the 'Third Estate' in France meant that the liberal bourgeois leadership of the French revolution met with a more rapid and far more powerful challenge from below than had been experienced by their counterparts in the English revolution. Those who risked their lives to defend the property-rights of the bourgeoisie felt entitled to their share. Never again, after the experience of the radical-petit bourgeois Jacobin dictatorship of 1793/4 did French bourgeois thought return to the confident liberal individualism of the Enlightenment. The ruling currents in French social thought during the nineteenth century, in contrast to both the Enlightenment and English social philosophy, were preoccupied with the problem of subordination of the individual to the social whole, with the problem of maintaining social order. Only the British ruling class retained the self-confidence to dispense — in theory, at least — with the aid of the state to defend it against the claims of the lower orders.

Notes

1. Descartes, *Discourse on Method*, trans. Wollaston (Harmondsworth, Penguin, 1964), p. 47.

2. Ibid., p.36.

3. Ibid., p. 47.

4. W. V. Quine, 'Two Dogmas of Empiricism' in *From A Logical Point of View* (New York, Harper & Row, 1961), pp. 20-46.

5. In the writing of this section I have depended very heavily on Christopher Hill's *Intellectual Origins of the English Revolution* (London, Panther, 1972). L. Kolakowski's *Positivist Philosophy* (Harmondsworth, Penguin, 1972), is also a useful introductory

work. George Novack's *Empiricism and its Evolution, a Marxist View* (New York, Pathfinder, 1971) is of some interest, but is far less reliable than the above works. The standard histories of philosophy by Russell and Copleston are also worth consulting, particularly the latter.

6. Hill, op. cit., p. 29.

7. A useful introduction to this debate can be gained from the earlier contributions in *Science and Religious Belief*, ed. C. A. Russell (Open University, 1973). See also Christopher Hill, *Puritanism and Revolution* (London, Panther, 1968).

8. See R. H. Popkin (ed.), *The Philosophy of the 16th and 17th Centuries* (London, Collier-Macmillan, 1968), p. 85.

9. The body of literature on the Enlightenment is enormous. Of the introductory material available, the collection *The Enlightenment*, edited by J. F. Lively (London, Longmans, 1966), provides a helpful diversity of brief extracts from primary sources, which can be followed up according to the student's interest. Ernst Cassirer's *The Philosophy of the Enlightenment* (Princeton University Press, 1951) is a classic secondary work, whilst Lucien Goldmann *The Philosophy of the Enlightenment* (London, Routledge & Kegan Paul, 1973) and Eric Hobsbawm *The Age of Revolution, 1798-1848* (London and New York, Mentor, 1962) provides useful analyses of Enlightenment and post-Enlightenment thought in its social and historical importance. E. Barker's *Social Contract* (London, Oxford University Press, 1971) brings together three important texts of Enlightenment political philosophy.

10. See Maurice Dobb, *Studies in the Development of Capitalism* (London, Routledge & Kegan Paul, 1963), especially chapter 4.

'Social Integration' and
the Rise of Industrial Society:
The Division of Labour,
Anomie and Suicide

19. Forms of Social Solidarity
and
The Division of Labour and Social Differentiation
Emile Durkheim

Restitutive sanctions and the relationship between mechanical and organic solidarity

What distinguishes [the restitutive] sanction is that it is not expiatory but consists of a simple return in state. The person who violates or disregards the law is not made to suffer in relation to his wrongdoing; he is simply sentenced to comply. If certain things have already been done, the judge reinstates them as they should have been. He speaks of law; he says nothing of punishment. Damage payments have no penal character; they are only a means of reviewing the past in order to reinstate it, as far as possible, in its normal form. . .

Neglect of these rules is not even punished diffusely. The defendant who has lost in litigation is not disgraced, his honour is not smirched. We can even imagine these rules differing from how they are now without any feeling of distaste. The idea of tolerating murder makes us indignant, but we quite easily accept modification of the law of inheritance, and can even conceive of its possible abolition. It is at least a question which we do not refuse to discuss. In the same way, we readily accept that the law of easements or that of usufructs may be organised differently, that the obligations of vendor and purchaser may be determined in another way, or that administrative functions may be distributed according to different principles. As these prescriptions do not correspond to any sentiment in us, and as we generally do not know scientifically the reasons for their existence, since this science does not exist, they have no roots in the majority of us. Of course, there are exceptions. We do not tolerate the idea that a contract, contrary to custom or obtained either through force or fraud, can bind the contracting parties. Thus, when public opinion finds itself in the presence of a case of this sort, it shows itself less indifferent than we have previously said, and it increases the legal sanction by its censure. The different domains of moral life are not radically separated one from another; on the contrary, they are continuous, and accordingly they contain marginal regions where these different characteristics are found at the same time. However, the preceding proposition remains true in the great majority of cases. It is proof that rules with a restitutive sanction either do not at all derive from the *conscience collective*, or are only feeble states of it. Repressive law corresponds to the heart, the centre of the common conscience; purely moral rules are already a less central part; finally, restitutive law originates in very marginal regions, spreading well beyond. The more it becomes truly itself, the more removed it becomes.

'Forms of Social Solidarity' and 'The Divison of Labour and Social Differentiation' from *EMILE DURKHEIM: SELECTED WRITINGS*, edited, translated, and with an introduction by Anthony Giddens (Cambridge University Press, 1972), pp. 135-154.

This characteristic is, moreover, manifest in the manner of its functioning. While repressive law tends to remain diffuse within society, restitutive law creates organs which are increasingly specialised: commercial courts, councils of arbitration, administrative courts of many kinds. Even in its most general part, that which pertains to civil law, it is exercised only through particular functionaries: magistrates, lawyers, etc., who are able to fill this role in virtue of very specialised training.

But, although these rules are to some degree outside the *conscience collective*, they do not refer only to individuals. If this were so, restitutive law would have nothing in common with social solidarity, for the relations that it regulates would bind individuals to one-another without binding them to society. These would simply be happenings in private life, as friendly relations are. But it is necessarily the case that society is far from being absent in this sphere of legal life. It is true that, generally, it does not intervene directly and actively; it must be solicited by the interested parties. But in being called forth, its intervention is nonetheless the essential cog in the machine, since it alone makes it function. It propounds the law through the organ of its representatives.

It has been contended, however, that this role has nothing properly social about it, but reduces itself to that of a conciliator of private interests; that, consequently, any individual can fill it, and that, if society is in charge of it, it is only for reasons of convenience. But nothing is more incorrect than to consider society as a sort of third-party arbitrator. When it is led to intervene, it is not to rectify individual interests. It does not seek to discover what may be the most advantageous solution for the adversaries and does not propose a compromise for them. Rather it applies to the particular case which is submitted to its general and traditional rules of law. Now law is, above all, a social thing, the objective of which is something other than the interest of the litigants. The judge who examines a request for divorce is not concerned with knowing whether this separation is truly desirable for the married parties, but rather whether the causes which are adduced come under one of the categories embodied in the law. . .

Since rules with restitutive sanctions are foreign to the *conscience collective*, the ties that they determine are not those which relate indiscriminately to everyone. That is to say, they are established, not between the individual and society, but between restricted, specific parts of society, whom they link to one-another. But, on the other hand, since society is not absent, it must be more or less directly interested, and it must feel the repercussions. Thus, according to the force with which society feels them, it intervenes more or less directly and actively, through the intermediary of special organs charged with representing it. These relations are, then, quite different from those which repressive law regulates, for the latter attach the particular individual to the *conscience collective* directly and without mediation: that is, the individual to society. . .

To sum up: the relations governed by co-operative law with restitutive sanctions, and the solidarity which they express, result from the division of social labour. We have explained, moreover, that, in general, co-operative relations do not convey other sanctions. In fact, it is in the nature of specialised tasks to escape the action of the *conscience collective*, for, in order for a thing to be the object of common sentiments, it must necessarily be shared: that is to say, it must be present in all minds such that everyone can represent it in one and the same manner. To be sure, in so far as functions have a certain generality, everybody can have some idea of them. But the more specialised they are, the more restricted the number of individuals who know each of them; consequently, the more marginal they are to the *conscience collective*. The rules which determine them cannot have that dominating force and transcendent authority which, when offended, demands expiation. It is also from public opinion that their authority derives, as with penal rules, but from such opinion localised in restricted regions of society.

Moreover, even in the special circles where they apply and where, consequently, they are represented in man's minds, they do not correspond to very active sentiments, nor even very often to any type of emotional state. For, as they fix the manner in which the different functions ought to concur in diverse combinations of circumstances which can arise, the objects to which they are connected are not always present in consciousness. We are not constantly called upon to administer guardianship, trusteeship, or exercise the rights of creditor or buyer, etc., or, more important, to exercise them in such and such a situation. Now, states of consciousness are strong only in so far as they are permanent. The violation of these rules reaches neither the common spirit of society, nor even, generally speaking, that of special groups, and consequently it can stimulate only a very moderate reaction. All that is necessary is that the functions concur in a regular manner. If this regularity is disrupted, it is sufficient for us to re-establish it. Assuredly, this is not to say that the development of the division of labour cannot influence penal law. There are, as we already know, administrative and governmental functions in which certain relations are regulated by repressive law, because of the particular character of this agency of the *conscience collective* and everything connected with it. In still other cases, the links of solidarity which unite certain social functions can be such that their breach stimulates repercussions which are sufficiently extensive to provoke a penal reaction. But, for the reason we have given, these reactions are exceptional. . .[thus] we recognise only two kinds of positive solidarity, which are distinguishable by the following qualities:

1. The first ties the individual directly to society without any intermediary. In the second, he depends upon society, because he depends upon the parts which compose it.

2. Society is not seen in the same aspect in the two cases. In the first, what we call 'society' is a more or less closely organised totality of beliefs and sentiments common to all the members of the group: it is the collective type. By contrast, the society to which we are bound in the second instance is a system of differentiated and specialised functions which are united in definite relationships. These two societies really make up only one. They are two aspects of one and the same reality, but nonetheless they must be distinguished.

3. From this second difference there arises another which helps us to characterise and name the two kinds of solidarity.

The first can be strong only to the degree that the ideas and tendencies common to all the members of the society are greater in number and intensity than those which pertain to each individual member. Its strength is determined by the degree to which this is the case. But what makes our personality is how many particular characteristics we possess which distinguish us from others. This solidarity thus can grow only in inverse ratio to personality. There are in each of us, as we have said, two forms of consciousness: one which is common to our group as a whole, which, consequently, is not ourself, but society living and acting within us; the other, on the other hand, represents that in us which is personal and distinct, that which makes us an individual. Solidarity which comes from resemblance is at its maximum when the *conscience collective* completely envelops our whole consciousness and coincides in all points with it. But, at that moment, our individuality is nil. It can develop only if the community takes a lesser part of us. There are, here, two contrary forces, one centripetal, the other centrifugal, which cannot flourish at the same time. We cannot, at one and the same time, develop ourselves in two opposite senses. If we have a strong inclination to think and act for ourselves, we cannot be as strongly inclined to think and act as others do. If our ideal is to present a unique and personal appearance, we cannot resemble everybody else. Moreover, at the moment when this latter solidarity exercises its force, our personality vanishes, by definition, one might say, for we are no longer ourselves, but the collective being.

The social molecules which cohere in this way can act together only in so far as they have no action of their own, as with the molecules of inorganic bodies. That is why we propose to call this form of solidarity 'mechanical'. The term does not signify that it is produced by mechanical and artificial means. We call it that only by analogy to the cohesion which unites the elements of an inorganic body, as contrasted to that which forms a unity out of the elements of a living body. What finally justifies this term is that the link which thus unites the individual to society is wholly comparable to that which attaches a thing to a person. The individual consciousness, considered in this light, is a simple appendage of the collective type and follows all of its actions, as the possessed object follows those of its owner. In societies where this type of solidarity is highly developed, the individual is not his own master, as we shall see later; solidarity is, literally something which the society possesses. Thus, in these types of society, personal rights are not yet distinguished from real rights.

It is quite different with the solidarity which the division of labour produces. Whereas the previous type implies that individuals resemble each other, this latter presumes that they differ. The former is possible only in so far as the individual personality is absorbed into the collective personality; the latter is possible only if each one has a sphere of action which is peculiar to him — that is, if he possesses a personality. It is necessary, then, that the *conscience collective* leave open a part of the individual consciousness in order that special functions may be established there, functions which it cannot regulate. The more this region is extended, the stronger is the cohesion which results from this solidarity. In fact, on the one hand, every individual depends more directly on society as labour becomes more divided; and, on the other, the activity of every individual becomes more personalised to the degree that it is more specialised. No doubt, as circumscribed as it is, it is never completely original; even in the exercise of our occupation, we conform to conventions and practices which are common to our whole occupational group. But, in this instance, the yoke that we submit to is much less heavy than when society completely controls us, and it leaves much more place open for the free play of our initiative. Here, then, the individuality of all grows at the same time as that of its parts. Society becomes more capable of collective action, at the same time that each of its elements has more freedom of action. This solidarity resembles that which we observe among the higher animals. Each organ, in effect, has its special character and autonomy; and yet the unity of the organism is as great as the individuation of the parts is more marked. Because of this analogy, we propose to call the solidarity which is due to the division of labour, 'organic'.

DTS, pp. 79, 80–2, 83, 96–101

THE DIVISION OF LABOUR AND SOCIAL DIFFERENTIATION

The growth of structural differentiation in social development

Thus, it is an historical law that mechanical solidarity, which first stands alone, or nearly so, progressively loses ground, and that organic solidarity gradually becomes preponderant. But when the mode of solidarity becomes changed, the structure of societies cannot but change. The form of a body is necessarily transformed when the molecular relationships are no longer the same. Consequently, if the preceding proposition is correct, there must be two social types which correspond to these two types of solidarity.

If we try to construct hypothetically the ideal type of a society whose cohesion were exclusively the result of resemblance, we should have to conceive it as an absolutely homogeneous mass whose parts were not distinguished from one another, and which consequently had no structure. In short, it would be devoid of all definite form and all organisation. It would be the actual social protoplasm, the germ out of which all social types would develop. We propose to call the aggregate thus characterised, a *horde*.

It is true that we have not yet, in any completely authenticated fashion, observed societies which complied in all respects with this definition. What gives us the right to postulate their existence, however, is that the lower societies, those which are closest to this primitive stage, are formed by a simple repetition of aggregates of this kind. We find an almost perfectly pure example of this social organisation among the Indians of North America. Each Iroquois tribe, for example, is composed of a certain number of partial societies (the largest ones comprise eight) which present all the characteristics we have just mentioned. The adults of both sexes are equal to each other. The *sachems* and chiefs, who are at the head of each of these groups and by whose council the common affairs of the tribe are administered, do not enjoy any superiority. Kinship itself is not organised, for we cannot give this name to the distribution of the population in layers of generations. In the late epoch in which these peoples have been studied, there were, indeed, some special obligations which bound the child to its maternal relatives, but these are of little consequence, and are not perceptibly distinct from those which link the child to other members of society. . .

We give the name *clan* to the horde which has ceased to be independent by becoming an element in a more extensive group, and that of *segmental societies with a clan-base* to societies which are formed by an association of clans. We call societies 'segmental' in order to indicate that they are characterised by the repetition of similar groupings, rather like the rings of an earthworm, and we call this fundamental element a 'clan', because this word well expresses its mixed nature, at once familial and political. It is a family in the sense that all the members who compose it consider themselves relatives, and they are, in fact, for the most part consanguineous. The affinities that are created by these blood-ties are those which principally keep them united. In addition, they sustain relationships which we can term domestic, since we also find them in societies whose familial character is indisputable: I am referring to collective punishment, collective responsibility, and, as soon as private property makes its appearance, common inheritance. But, on the other hand, it is not a family in the proper sense of the word, for in order to belong to it, it is not necessary to have any definite relations of consanguinity with other members of the clan. It is enough to possess an external quality, which generally consists in having the same name. Although this sign is thought to denote a common origin, such a civil status really constitutes very inconclusive proof, and is very easy to copy. Thus, the clan contains a great many strangers, and this permits it to attain dimensions such as a family, properly speaking, never has. It often comprises several thousand persons. Moreover, it is the fundamental political unit; the heads of clans are the only social authorities.

We can thus label this organisation 'politico-familial'. Not only has the clan consanguinity as its basis, but different clans within the same society are often considered as kin to one-another. . .

This organisation, just like the horde, of which it is only an extension, evidently carries with it no other solidarity than that derived from resemblance, since the society is formed of similar segments and these in their turn enclose only homogeneous elements. No doubt, each clan has its own character and is thereby distinguished from others; but the solidarity is proportionally weaker as they are more heterogeneous, and vice versa. For segmental organisation to be possible, the segments must resemble one another: without that, they would not be united. And they must differ; without this, they would lose themselves in each other and be effaced. These two contrasting prerequisites are found in varying ratio in different societies, but the type of society remains the same. . .

The structure of societies where organic solidarity is preponderant is quite different.

These are formed, not by the repetition of similar, homogeneous segments, but by a system of different organs each of which has a special role, and which are themselves formed of differentiated parts. Not only are social elements not of the same nature, but they are not distributed in the same way. They are not juxtaposed in a linear fashion as the rings of an earthworm, nor entwined one with another, but co-ordinated and subordinated one to another around the same central organ which exercises a moderating action over the rest of the organism. This organ itself no longer has the same character as in the preceding case, for, if the others depend upon it, it, in its turn, depends upon them. No doubt, it still enjoys a special situation, a privileged position, but that is due to the nature of the role that it fills and not to some cause foreign to its functions, to some force communicated to it externally. Thus, there is no longer anything about it that is not temporal and human; between it and other organs, there is no longer anything but differences in degree. This is comparable to the way in which, in the animal, the dominance of the nervous system over other systems is reduced to the right, if one may speak thus, of obtaining the best food and of having its fill before the others. But it needs them, just as they have need of it.

This social type rests on principles so different from the preceding that it can develop only in proportion to the effacement of that type. In this type, individuals are no longer grouped according to their relations of lineage, but according to the particular nature of the social activity to which they devote themselves. Their natural and necessary milieu is no longer that given by birth, but that given by occupation. It is no longer real or fictitious blood-ties which mark the place of each one, but the function which he fills. No doubt, when this new form of organisation begins to appear, it tries to utilise and to take over the existing one. The way in which functions are divided thus follows, as faithfully as possible, the way in which society is already divided. The segments, or at least the groups of segments united by special affinities, become organs. It is thus that the clans which together formed the tribe of the Levites appropriated priestly functions for themselves among the Hebrew people. In a general way, classes and castes probably derive their origin and their character in this way; they arise from the numerous occupational organisations which spring up within the pre-existing familial organisation. But this mixed arrangement cannot endure, for between the two conditions that it attempts to reconcile, there is an antagonism which necessarily ends in a break. It is only a very rudimentary division of labour which can adapt itself to those rigid, defined moulds which were not made for it. It can grow only by freeing itself from the framework which encloses it. As soon as it has passed a certain stage of development, there is no longer any connection either between the given number of segments and the steady growth of functions which are becoming specialised, or between the hereditarily fixed properties of the first and the new aptitudes that the second calls forth. The substance of social life must enter into entirely new combinations in order to organise itself upon completely different foundations. But the old structure, so far as it persists, is opposed to this. That is why it must disappear.

DTS, pp. 148–51, 152 and 157–9

The decline of mechanical solidarity and emergence of moral individualism

Not only, in a general way, does mechanical solidarity link men less strongly than organic solidarity, but also, as we advance in the scale of social evolution, it becomes increasingly weak.

The strength of the social ties which have this origin differ in relation to the three following conditions:

1. The relation between the volume of the *conscience collective* and that of the individual mind. The links are stronger the more the first completely envelops the second.

177

2. The average intensity of the states of the *conscience collective*. The relation between volumes being equal, it has as much power over the individual as it has vitality. If, on the other hand, it consists of only weak forces, it can move the individual only weakly in the collective direction. He will the more easily be able to pursue his own course, and solidarity will thus be less.

3. The greater or lesser the fixity of these same states the more defined are beliefs and practices which exist, and the less place they leave for individual differences. They are uniform moulds within which all our ideas and actions are formed. Consensus is then as perfect as possible; all minds move in unison. Conversely, the more abstract and indeterminate the rules of conduct and thought, the more conscious direction must intervene to apply them to particular cases. But the latter cannot awaken without dissensions occurring, for as it varies from one man to another in quality and quantity, it inevitably leads to this result. Centrifugal tendencies thus multiply at the expense of social cohesion and the harmony of actions.

On the other hand, strong and defined states of the *conscience collective* are the basis of penal law. But we shall see that the number of these is less today than previously, and that it diminishes progressively as societies approach our social type. Thus it is the case that the average intensity and degree of fixity of collective states have themselves diminished. From this fact, it is true, we cannot conclude that the total extent of the *conscience collective* has narrowed, for it may be that the region to which penal law corresponds has contracted, and that the remainder, by contrast, has expanded. It may manifest fewer strong and defined states, but compensate with a greater number of others. But this growth, if it is real, is at most equivalent to that which is produced in the individual mind, for the latter has, at least, grown in the same proportions. If there are more things common to all, there are far more that are personal to each. There is, indeed, every reason to believe that the latter have increased more than the former, for the differences between men become more pronounced in so far as they are more educated. We have just seen that specialised activities have developed more than the *conscience collective*. It is, therefore, at least probable that, in each individual mind, the personal sphere has grown more than the other. In any case, the relation between them has at most remained the same. Consequently, from this point of view, mechanical solidarity has gained nothing, even if it has not lost anything. If therefore, from another aspect, we discover that the *conscience collective* has become weaker and more ill-defined, we can rest assured that there has been a weakening of this solidarity, since, in respect of the three conditions upon which its power of action rests, two, at least, are losing their intensity, while the third remains unchanged. . .

This is not to say, however, that the *conscience collective* is likely to disappear completely. Rather it increasingly comes to consist of very general and indeterminate ways of thought and sentiment, which leaves room open for a growing variety of individual differences. There is even a place where it is strengthened and made precise: this is, in the way in which it regards the individual. As all the other beliefs and all the other practices take on a less and less religious character, the individual becomes the object of a sort of religion. We have a cult of personal dignity which, as with every strong cult, already has its superstitions. It is, thus, we may say, a common faith but it is possible only by the ruin of all others and, consequently, cannot produce the same effects as this mass of extinguished beliefs. There is no compensation for these. Moreover, if it is common in so far as it is shared by the community, it is individual in its object. If it turns all wills towards the same end, this end is not social. It thus occupies a completely exceptional place in the *conscience collective*. It is still from society that it takes all its force, but it is not to society that it attaches us; it is to ourselves. Hence, it does not constitute a true social bond. That is why we have been justly able to criticise the theorists who have made this sentiment the only fundamental element in their moral doctrine with the ensuing dissolution of society. We can then conclude by saying that all social links which result from likeness progressively slacken.

DTS, 124–6 and 146–7

[Written in review of Tönnies' *Gemeinschaft und Gesellschaft*.]

Like the author I believe that there are two major types of society, and the words which he uses to designate them indicate their nature fairly well; it is a pity that they are untranslatable. I accept, in common with him, that *Gemeinschaft* is the original phenomenon, and *Gesellschaft* the end result which derives from it. Lastly I agree with the general lines of analysis and the description of *Gemeinschaft* which he has given us.

The point over which I diverge from him, however, concerns the theory of *Gesellschaft*. If I have properly understood his thought, *Gesellschaft* is supposed to be characterised by a progressive development of individualism, the dispersive effects of which can only be prevented for a time, and by artificial means, by the action of the state. It is seen essentially as a mechanical aggregate; what there is that remains of truly collective life is presumed to result, not from an internal spontaneity, but from the wholly external stimulus of the state. In short. . .it is society such as Bentham conceived of it. Now I believe that the life of large social agglomerations is just as natural as that of small groupings. It is no less organic and no less internal. Outside of these purely individual actions there is a collective activity in our contemporary societies which is just as natural as that of the smaller societies of previous ages. It is certainly different; it constitutes a distinct type, but however different they may be, there is no difference in nature between these two varieties of the same genus. If in order to prove this, it would need a book; I can do no more than state the proposition. Is it likely, moreover, that the evolution of a single entity, society, begins by being organic only to subsequently become purely mechanical? There is such a chasm between these two modes of existence that it is impossible to see how they could form part of the same development. To reconcile the theory of Aristotle with that of Bentham in this way is simply to juxtapose opposites. We have to choose: if society is originally a natural phenomenon, it stays such until the end of its life.

But what does this collective life of *Gesellschaft* consist in? The procedure followed by the author does not allow an answer to this question, because it is completely ideological. In the second part of his work, Tönnies devotes more time to the systematic analysis of concepts than to the observation of facts. He proceeds by conceptual argument; we find in his writing the distinctions and symmetrical classifications which are so beloved of German logicians. The only way to avoid this would have been to proceed inductively, that is, to study *Gesellschaft* through the law and the mores which correspond to it, and which reveal its structure.

RP, 1889, pp. 421–2

The condemnation of individualism has been facilitated by its confusion with the narrow utilitarianism and utilitarian egoism of Spencer and the economists. But this is very facile. It is not hard, to be sure, to denounce as a shallow ideal that narrow commercialism which reduces society to nothing more than a vast apparatus of production and exchange; and it is perfectly clear that all social life would be impossible if there did not exist interests superior to the interests of individuals. It is wholly correct that such doctrines should be treated as anarchical, and we fully agree with this view. But what is unacceptable is that this individualism should be presented as the only one that there is, or even could be. Quite the contrary; it is becoming increasingly rare and exceptional. The practical philosophy of Spencer is of such moral poverty that it now has hardly any supporters. As for the economists, even if they once allowed themselves to be seduced by the simplicity of this theory, they have for a long time now felt the need to modify the severity of their primitive orthodoxy and to open their minds to more generous sentiments. M. de Molinari is almost alone, in France, in remaining intractable and I am not aware that he has exercised a significant influence on the ideas of our time. Indeed, if individualism had not other representatives, it would be quite pointless to move heaven and earth in this way to combat an enemy who is in the process of quietly dying a natural death.

However, there exists another individualism over which it is less easy to triumph. It has been upheld for a century by the great majority of thinkers: it is the individualism of Kant and Rousseau and the spiritualists, that which the Declaration of the Rights of Man sought, more or less successfully, to translate into formulae, which is now taught in our schools and which has become the basis of our moral catechism. It is true that it has been thought possible to attack this individualism by reference to the first type; but the two are fundamentally different, and the criticisms which apply to the one could not be appropriate to the other. It is so far from making personal interest the aim of human conduct that it sees personal motives as the very source of evil. According to Kant, I am only certain of acting properly if the motives that influence me relate, not to the particular circumstances in which I am placed, but to my equality as a man in *abstracto*. Conversely, my action is wrong when it cannot be justified logically except by reference to the situation I happen to be in and my social condition, class or caste interests, my emotions, etc. Hence immoral conduct is to be recognised by the sign that it is closely linked to the individuality of the agent and cannot be universalised without manifest absurdity. Similarly, if Rousseau sees the general will, which is the basis of the social contract, as infallible, as the authentic expression of perfect justice, this is because it is a resultant of the totality of particular wills; consequently it constitutes a kind of impersonal average from which all individual considerations have been eliminated, since, being distinct from and even antagonistic to one-another, they are neutralised and cancel each other out. Thus, for both these thinkers, the only modes of conduct that are moral are those which are applicable to all men equally: that is to say, which are implied in the notion of man in general.

This is indeed far removed from that apotheosis of pleasure and private interest, the egoistic cult of the self for which utilitarian individualism has validly been criticised. Quite the contrary: according to these moralists, duty consists in turning our attention from what concerns us personally, from all that relates to our empirical individuality, so as to pursue solely that which is demanded by our human condition, that which we hold in common with all our fellow men. This ideal goes so far beyond the limit of utilitarian ends that it appears to those who aspire to it as having a religious character. The human person, by reference to the definition of which good must be distinguished from evil, is considered as sacred, in what can be called the ritual sense of the word. It has something of that transcendental majesty which the churches of all times have accorded to their gods. It is conceived as being invested with that mysterious property which creates a vacuum about holy objects, which keeps them away from profane contacts and which separates them from ordinary life. And it is exactly this characteristic which confers the respect of which it is the object. Whoever makes an attempt on a man's life, on a man's liberty, on a man's honour, inspires us with a feeling of revulsion, in every way comparable to that which the believer experiences when he sees his idol profaned. Such a morality is therefore not simply a hygienic discipline or a wise principle of economy. It is a religion of which man is, at the same time, both believer and god.

But this religion is individualistic, since it has man as its object; man is, by definition, an individual. Indeed there is no system whose individualism is more uncompromising. Nowhere are the rights of man affirmed more energetically, since the individual is here placed on the level of sacrosanct objects; nowhere is he more jealously protected from external encroachments, whatever their source.

A verbal similarity has made possible the belief that *individualism* necessarily resulted from *individual*, and thus egoistic, sentiments. In reality, the religion of the individual is a social institution like all known religions. It is society which provides us with this ideal as the only common end which is today able to offer a focus for men's wills. To remove this ideal, without replacing it with any other, is therefore to plunge us into that very moral anarchy which it is sought to avoid.

Nonetheless we must not consider as perfect and definitive the formula with which the eighteenth century gave expression to individualism, a formula which we have made the mistake of maintaining in an almost unchanged form. Although it was adequate a century ago, it today needs to be enlarged and completed. It presented individualism only in its most negative aspect. Our forerunners were concerned solely with freeing the individual from the political shackles which hampered his development. Thus they regarded freedom of thought, freedom to write, and freedom to vote as the primary values that it was necessary to achieve — and this emancipation was indeed the precondition of all subsequent progress. However, carried away by the enthusiasm of the struggle, and concerned only with the objective they pursued, in the end they no longer saw beyond it, and made into something of an ultimate goal what was merely the next stage in their efforts. Now, political freedom is a means, not an end. It is worth no more than the manner in which it is put to use. If it does not serve something which exists beyond it, it is not merely fruitless, it becomes dangerous. If those who handle this weapon do not know how to use it in productive struggles, they will not be slow in turning it against themselves.

It is precisely for this reason that it has fallen today into a certain discredit. Men of my generation recall how great our enthusiasm was when, twenty years ago, we finally succeeded in toppling the last barriers which we impatiently confronted. But alas! disenchantment came quickly; for we soon had to admit that no one knew what use should be made of this freedom that had been so laboriously achieved. Those to whom we owed it only made use of it in internecine conflicts. And it was from that moment that one felt the growth in the country of this current of gloom and despondency, which became stronger with each day that passed, the ultimate result of which must inevitably be to break the spirit of those least able to resist.

Thus, we can no longer subscribe to this negative ideal. We must go beyond what has been achieved, if only to preserve it. Indeed, if we do not learn to put to use the means of action that we have in our hands, it is inevitable that they will become less effective. Let us therefore use our freedoms to discover what must be done and in order to do it. Let us use them in order to soften the functioning of the social machine, still so harsh to individuals, so as to put at their disposal all possible means for the free development of their faculties in order finally to progress towards making a reality of the famous precept: to each according to his works!

RB, 1898, pp. 7–8 and 12–13

The causes of the development of the division of labour

We have seen that the organised structure, and thus the division of labour, develop correspondingly as the segmental structure disappears. Thus either this disappearance is the cause of the development, or the development is the cause of the disappearance. The latter hypothesis is unacceptable, for we know that the segmental arrangement is an unsurmountable obstacle to the division of labour, and must at least partially have become dissolved for the division of labour to emerge. The latter can only develop in so far as the former ceases to exist. To be sure, once the division of labour appears, it can contribute towards the hastening of the other's regression, but it only comes into being once this regression has begun. The effect reacts upon the cause, but never loses its quality of effect; its action, consequently, is secondary. The growth of the division of labour is thus brought about by the social segments losing their individuality, as the boundaries between them become less marked. In short, a merging takes place which makes it possible for social life to enter into new combinations.

But the disappearance of this type can have this consequence for only one reason. That is because it produces a coming together between individuals who were separated — or, at least, a closer relationship than existed previously. Consequently, there is an interchange of action between parts of the social mass which, until then, had no effect upon one another. The more pronounced the segmental system, the more are our relations enclosed within the limits of the segment to which we belong. There are, as it were, moral gaps between the different segments. By contrast, these gaps are filled in as the system becomes levelled out. Social life, instead of being concentrated in a large number of separate, small centres, each of which resembles the other, is generalised. Social relations — or more correctly, intra-social relations — consequently become more numerous, since they extend, on all sides, beyond their original limits. The division of labour develops, therefore, as there are more individuals sufficiently in contact to be able to act and react upon one-another. If we agree to call this coming together, and the active commerce resulting from it, 'dynamic' or 'formal' density, we can say that the progress of the division of labour is in direct ratio to the moral or dynamic density of society.

But this moral relationship can only produce its effect if the real distance between individuals has itself diminished in some way. Moral density cannot grow unless material density grows at the same time, and the latter can be used to measure the former. It is useless, moreover, to try to find out which has determined the other; it is enough to state that they are inseparable.

The progressive condensation of societies in the course of historical development is produced in three principal ways:

1. Whereas lower societies are spread over immense areas relative to the size of their populations, among more advanced peoples population tends to become more and more concentrated. . . The changes brought about in the industrial life of nations prove the universality of this transformation. The productive activity of nomads, hunters, or shepherds implies the absence of all concentration, dispersion over the largest possible surface. Agriculture, since it necessitates a life in a fixed territory, presupposes a certain tightening of the social tissues, but is still incomplete, for there are stretches of land between each family. In the city, although the condensation was greater, the houses were not contiguous, for joint property was no part of the Roman law. It grew up on our soil, and demonstrates that the social web has become tighter. On the other hand, from their origins, the European societies have witnessed a continuous growth in their density, short-lived regressions notwithstanding.

2. The formation of towns and their development is an even more characteristic symptom of the same phenomenon. The increase in average density may be due to the material increase of the birth-rate, and, consequently, can be reconciled with a very weak concentration, whereby the segmental type remains prevalent. But towns always result from the need of individuals to put themselves constantly in the closest possible contact with each other. There are so many points where the social mass is contracted more strongly than elsewhere. Thus when they multiply and expand the moral density must become raised. We shall see, moreover, that they receive a source of recruitment from immigration, something which is only possible when the fusion of social segments is advanced.

As long as social organisation is essentially segmental, towns do not exist. There are none in lower societies. They did not exist among the Iroquois, nor among the ancient Germans. It was the same with the primitive populations of Italy. . .But towns did not take long to appear. Athens and Rome are or become towns, and the same transformation occurred throughout Italy. In our Christian societies, the town is in evidence from the beginning, for those left by the Roman empire did not disappear with it. Since then, they have increased and multiplied. The tendency of the country to stream into the town, so general in the civilised world, is only a consequence of this movement. It is not of recent origin; from the seventeenth century, statesmen have been preoccupied with it.

Because societies generally begin with an agricultural period, there has sometimes been the temptation to regard the development of urban centres as a sign of old age and decadence. But we must not lose sight of the fact that the length of this agricultural phase is shorter the more advanced the society. Whereas in Germany, among the Indians of America, and with all primitive peoples, it lasts for the duration of their existence, in Rome and Athens, it ends fairly quickly; and, with us, we can say that it never existed in pure form. On the other hand, urban life begins earlier and consequently expands further. The constantly increasing acceleration of this development proves that, far from constituting a sort of pathological phenomenon, it comes from the very nature of higher social types. The supposition that this movement has attained alarming proportions in our societies today, which perhaps are no longer flexible enough to adapt themselves to it, will not prevent this movement from continuing either within our societies, or after them; and the social types which will be formed after ours will probably be distinguished by a still more complete and rapid contraction of rural life.

3. Finally, there are the number and rapidity of the means of communication and transportation. By suppressing or diminishing the gaps which separate social segments, they increase the density of society. It is not necessary, however, to prove that they become more numerous and perfected in societies of a more developed type.

Since this visible and measurable symbol reflects the variations of what we have called 'moral density' we can substitute it for this latter in the formula we have proposed. Moreover, we must repeat here what we said before. If society, in concentrating, determines the development of the division of labour, the latter, in its turn, increases the concentration of society. But this is not important, for the division of labour remains the derived fact, and, consequently, the advances which it has made are due to parallel advances of social density, whatever may be the causes of the latter. That is all we wished to prove. . .

If work becomes progressively divided as societies become more voluminous and dense, it is not because external circumstances are more varied, but because struggle for existence is more acute.

Darwin quite correctly observed that the struggle between two organisms is as active as they are similar. Having the same needs and pursuing the same aims, they are in rivalry everywhere. So long as they have more resources than they need, they can still live side by side, but if their number increases to such proportions that their needs can no longer all be adequately satisfied, war breaks out, and it is the more violent the more marked this scarcity; that is to say, as the number of participants increase. It is quite otherwise if the co-existing individuals are of different species or varieties. As they do not feed in the same manner, and do not lead the same kind of life, they do not disturb each other. What is advantageous to one is without value to the others. The occasions for conflict thus diminish with occasions of confrontation, and this happens increasingly as the species or varieties become more distant from one-another. . .

Men obey the same law. In the same city, different occupations can co-exist without being obliged mutually to destroy one another, for they pursue different objectives. The soldier seeks military glory, the priest moral authority, the statesman power, the businessman riches, and the scholar scientific renown. Each of them can attain his end without preventing the others from attaining theirs. It is still the same even when the functions are less separated from one another. The occulist does not compete with the psychiatrist, the shoemaker with the hatter, the mason with the cabinet maker, the physicist with the chemist, etc. Since they perform different services, they can perform them together.

The closer functions approach one-another, however, the more points of contact they have; the more, consequently, they are exposed to conflict. As in this case they satisfy similar needs by different means, they inevitably seek to curtail the other's development. The judge never is in competition with the businessman, but the brewer and the wine-grower, the clothier and the manufacturer of silks, the poet and the musician, often try to supplant each other. As for those who have exactly the same function, each can prosper only to the detriment of the others. If, then, these different functions are pictured as a series of branches issuing from a common trunk, the struggle is at its minimum between the extreme points, whereas it increases steadily as we approach the centre. It is so, not only inside each city, but in all society. Similar occupations located at different points are as competitive as they are alike, provided the difficulty of communication and transport does not restrict the circle of their action.

This having been said, it is easy to understand that any condensation of the social mass, especially if it is accompanied by an increase in population, necessarily stimulates an advance in the division of labour.

DTS, pp. 273–8, 239–41 and 248–50

20. The Anomic Division of Labor
Emile Durkheim

Up to now, we have studied the division of labor only as a normal phenomenon, but, like all social facts, and, more generally, all biological facts, it presents pathological forms which must be analyzed. Though normally the division of labor produces social solidarity, it sometimes happens that it has different, and even contrary results. Now, it is important to find out what makes it deviate from its natural course, for if we do not prove that these cases are exceptional, the division of labor might be accused of logically implying them. Moreover, the study of these devious forms will permit us to determine the conditions of existence of the normal state better. When we know the circumstances in which the division of labor ceases to bring forth solidarity, we shall better understand what is necessary for it to have that effect. Pathology, here as elsewhere, is a valuable aid of physiology.

One might be tempted to reckon as irregular forms of the division of labor criminal occupations and other harmful activities. They are the very negation of solidarity, and yet they take the form of special activities. But to speak with exactitude, there is no division of labor here, but differentiation pure and simple. The two terms must not be confused. Thus, cancer and tuberculosis increase the diversity of organic tissues without bringing forth a new specialization of biologic functions.[1] In all these cases, there is no partition of a common function, but, in the midst of the organism, whether individual or social, another is formed which seeks to live at the expense of the first. In reality, there is not even a function, for a way of acting merits this name only if it joins with others in maintaining general life. This question, then, does not enter into the body of our investigation.

We shall reduce to three types the exceptional forms of the phenomenon that we are studying. This is not because there can be no others, but rather because those of which we are going to speak are the most general and the most serious.

I

The first case of this kind is furnished us by industrial or commercial crises, by failures, which are so many partial breaks in organic solidarity. They evince, in effect, that at certain points in the organism certain social functions are not adjusted to one another. But, in so far as labor is divided more, these phenomena seem to become more frequent, at least in certain cases. From 1845 to 1869, failures increased 70%.[2] We cannot, however, attribute this fact to the growth in economic life, since enterprises have become a great deal more concentrated than numerous.

The conflict between capital and labor is another example, more striking, of the same phenomenon. In so far as industrial functions become more specialized, the conflict becomes more lively, instead of solidarity increasing. In the middle ages, the worker

Reprinted with permission of The Free Press, an imprint of Simon & Schuster from *THE DIVISION OF LABOR IN SOCIETY* by Emile Durkheim, translated by George Simpson. Copyright © 1964 by The Free Press.

everywhere lived at the side of his master, pursuing his tasks "in the same shop, in the same establishment".[3] Both were part of the same corporation and led the same existence. "They were on an almost equal footing; whoever had served his apprenticeship could, at least in many of the occupations, set himself up independently if he had the means."[4] Hence, conflicts were wholly unusual. Beginning with the fifteenth century things began to change. "The occupational circle is no longer a common organization; it is an exclusive possession of the masters, who alone decided all matters. . . . From that time, a sharp line is drawn between masters and workers. The latter formed, so to speak, an order apart; they had their customs, their rules, their independent associations".[5] Once this separation was effected, quarrels became numerous. "When the workers thought they had a just complaint, they struck or boycotted a village, an employer, and all of them were compelled to obey the letter of the order. . . . The power of association gave the workers the means of combating their employers with equal force."[6] But things were then far from reaching "the point at which we now see them. Workers rebelled in order to secure higher wages or some other change in the condition of labor, but they did not consider the employer as a permanent enemy who one obeyed because of his force. They wished to make him concede a point, and they worked energetically towards that end, but the conflict was not everlasting. The workshops did not contain two opposing classes. Our socialist doctrines were unknown".[7] Finally, in the seventeenth century, the third phase of this history of the working classes begins: the birth of large-scale industry. The worker is more completely separated from the employer. "He becomes somewhat regimented. Each has his function, and the system of the division of labor makes some progress. In the factory of Van-Robais, which employed 1692 workers, there were particular shops for wheelwrighting, for cutlery, for washing, for dyeing, for warping, and the shops for weaving themselves contained several types of workers whose labor was entirely distinct."[8] At the same time that specialization becomes greater, revolts become more frequent. "The smallest cause for discontent was enough to upset an establishment, and cause a worker unhappiness who did not respect the decision of the community".[9] We well know that, since then, the warfare has become ever more violent.

To be sure, we shall see in the following chapter that this tension in social relations is due, in part, to the fact that the working classes are not really satisfied with the conditions under which they live, but very often accept them only as constrained and forced, since they have not the means to change them. This constraint alone, however, would not account for the phenomenon. In effect, it does not weigh less heavily upon all those generally bereft of fortune, and yet this state of permanent hostility is wholly special to the industrial world. Then, in the interior of this world, it is the same for all workers indiscriminately. But, small-scale industry, where work is less divided, displays a relative harmony between worker and employer.[10] It is only in large-scale industry that these relations are in a sickly state. That is because they depend in part upon a different cause.

Another illustration of the same phenomenon has often been observed in the history of sciences. Until very recent times, science, not being very divided, could be cultivated almost entirely by one and the same person. Thus was had a very lively sense of its unity. The particular truths which composed it were neither so numerous nor so heterogeneous that one could not easily see the tie which bound them in one and the same system. Methods, being themselves very general, were little different from one another, and one could perceive the common trunk from which they imperceptibly diverged. But, as specialization is introduced into scientific work, each scholar becomes more and more enclosed, not only in particular science, but in a special order of problems. Auguste Comte had already complained that, in his time, there were in the scientific world "very few minds embracing in the conception the total scope of even a single science, which is, however, in turn, only a part of a greater whole. The greater part were already occupied with some isolated consideration of a more or less extensive section of one certain science, without being very much concerned with the relation of the particular labors to the general system of positive knowledge."[11] But then, science, parcelled out into a multitude of detailed studies which are not joined together, no longer forms a solidary whole. What best manifests, perhaps, this absence of concert and unit is the theory, so prevalent, that each particular science has an absolute value, and that the scholar ought to devote himself to his special researches without bothering to inquire whether they serve some purpose and lead anywhere. "This division of intellectual labor," says Schaeffle, "offers good reason for fearing that this return to a new Alexandrianism will lead once again to the ruin of all science."[12]

II

What makes these facts serious is that they have sometimes been considered a necessary effect of the division of labor after it has passed beyond a certain stage of development. In this case, it is said, the individual, hemmed in by his task, becomes isolated in a special activity. He no longer feels the idea of common work being done by those who work side by side with him. Thus, the division of labor could not be pushed farther without becoming a source of disintegration. "Since all such decomposition,"says Auguste Comte, "necessarily has the tendency to determine a corresponding dispersion, the fundamental partition of human labors cannot avoid evoking, in a proportionate degree, individual divergences, both intellectual and moral, whose combined influence must, in the same measure, demand a permanent discipline able to prevent or unceasingly contain their discordant flight. If, on the one hand, indeed, the separation of social functions permits a felicitous development of the spirit of detail otherwise impossible, it spontaneously tends, on the other hand, to snuff out the spirit of togetherness or, at least, to undermine it profoundly. Likewise, from the moral point of view, at the same time that each is thus placed in strict dependence upon the mass, he is naturally deterred by the peculiar scope of his special activity which constantly links him to his own private interest whose true relation with the public interest he perceives but very vaguely. . . . Thus it is that the same principle which has alone permitted the development and the extension of general society threatens, in a different aspect, to decompose it into a multitude of incoherent corporations which almost seem not to be of the same species".[13] Expinas has expressed himself almost in the same terms: "Division," he says, "is dispersion."[14]

The division of labor would thus exercise, because of its very nature, a dissolving influence which would be particularly obvious where functions are very specialized. Comte, however, does not conclude from his principle that societies must be led to what he himself calls the age of generality, that is, to that state of indistinctness and homogeneity which was their point of departure. The diversity of functions is useful and necessary, but as unity, which is no less indispensable, does not spontaneously spring up, the care of realizing it and of maintaining it would constitute a special function in the social organism, represented by an independent organ. This organ is the State or government. "The social destiny of government," says Comte, "appears to me to consist particularly in sufficiently containing, and preventing, as far as possible, this fatal disposition towards a fundamental dispersion of ideas, sentiments, and interests, the inevitable result of the very principle of human development, and which, if it could follow its natural course without interruption, would inevitably end by arresting social progress in all important respects. This conception, in my eyes, constitutes the first positive and rational basis of an elementary and abstract theory of government properly so called, seen in its noblest and greatest scientific extension, as characterized in general by a universal and necessary reaction, at first spontaneous and then regulated, of the totality of the parts that go to make it up. It is clear, in effect, that the only real means of preventing such a dispersion consists in this indispensable reaction in a new and special function, susceptible of fittingly intervening in the habitual accomplishment of all the diverse functions of social economy, so as to recall to them unceasingly the feeling of unity and the sentiment of common solidarity."[15]

What government is to society in its totality philosophy ought to be to the sciences. Since the diversity of science tends to disrupt the unity of science, a new science must be set up to re-establish it. Since detailed studies make us lose sight of the whole vista of human knowledge, we must institute a particular system of researches to retrieve it and set it off. In other words, "we must make an even greater specialty of the study of scientific generalities. A new class of scholars, prepared by suitable education, without devoting themselves to a special culture of any particular branch of natural philosophy, will busy themselves with considering the various positive sciences in their present state, with exactly determining the spirit of each of them, with discovering their relations and their continuity, with summing up, if possible, all their principles in a very small number of principles common to all, and the division of labor in the sciences will be pushed, without any danger, as far as the development of the various orders of knowledge demand." [16]

Of course, we have ourselves shown[17] that the governmental organ develops with the division of labor, not as a repercussion of it, but because of mechanical necessity. As organs are rigorously solidary where functions are very divided, what affects one affects the others, and social events take on a more general interest. At the same time, with the effacement of the segmental type, they penetrate more easily throughout the extent of the same tissue or the same system. For these two reasons, there are more of them which are retained in the directive organ whose functional activity, more often exercised, grows with the volume. But its sphere of action does not extend further.

But beneath this general, superficial life there is an intestine, a world of organs which, without being completely independent of the first, nevertheless function without its intervention, without its even being conscious of them, at least normally. They are free from its action because it is too remote for them. The government cannot, at every instant, regulate the conditions of the different economic markets, fixing the prices of their commodities and services, or keeping production within the bounds of consumptionary needs, etc. All these practical problems arise from a multitude of detail, coming from thousands of particular circumstances which only those very close to the problems know about. Thus, we cannot adjust these functions to one another and make them concur harmoniously if they do not concur of themselves. If, then, the division of labor has the dispersive effects that are attributed to it, they ought to develop without resistance in this region of society, since there is nothing to hold them together. What gives unity to organized societies, however, as to all organisms, is the spontaneous consensus of parts. Such is the internal solidarity which not only is as indispensable as the regulative action of higher centres, but which also is their necessary condition, for they do no more than translate it into another language and, so to speak, consecrate it. Thus the brain does not make the unity of the organism, but expresses and completes it. Some speak of the necessity of a reaction of the totality of parts, but it still is necessary for this totality to exist; that is to say, the parts must be already solidary with one another for the whole to take conscience of itself and react in this way. Else, as work is divided, one would see a sort of progressive decomposition produced, not only at certain points, but throughout society, instead of the even stronger concentration that we really observe.

Notes

1. This is a distinction that Spencer does not make. It seems that, for him, the two terms are synonymous. The differentiation, however, which disintegrates (cancerous, microbic, criminal) is very different from that which brings vital forces together (division of labor).

2. Block, *Statistique de la France*.

3. Levasseur, *Less classes ouvrières en France jusqu' à la Révolution*, II, p. 315.

4. *Ibid.*, I, p. 496.

5. Levasseur, I, p. 496.

6. *Ibid.*, I, p. 504.

7. Hubert Vallerous, *Les Corporations d'arts et de métiers*, p. 49.

8. Levasseur, II, p. 315.

9. *Ibid.*, p. 319.

10. See Cauwes, *Précis d'économie politique*, II p. 39.

11. *Cours de philosophie*, I, p. 27.

12. *Bau und Leben des sozialen Körpers*, IV, p.113.

13. *Cours*, IV, p. 429.

14. *Sociétés animales*, conclusion, IV.

15. *Cours de Philosophie positive*, IV, pp. 430-431.

16. This bringing together of government and philosophy ought not to surprise us, for, in Comte's eyes, the two institutions are inseparable. Government, as he conceives it, is possible only upon the institution of the positive philosophy.

17. See above, Book I, ch. vii, § 3.

21. 'Introduction' to Suicide: A Study in Sociology

Emile Durkheim

I

Since the word "suicide" recurs constantly in the course of conversation, it might be thought that its sense is universally known and that definition is superfluous. Actually, the words of everyday language, like the concepts they express, are always susceptible of more than one meaning, and the scholar employing them in their accepted use without further definition would risk serious misunderstanding. Not only is their meaning so indefinite as to vary, from case to case, with the needs of argument, but, as the classification from which they derive is not analytic, but merely translates the confused impressions of the crowd, categories of very different sorts of fact are indistinctly combined under the same heading, or similar realities are differently named. So, if we follow common use, we risk distinguishing what should be combined, or combining what should be distinguished, thus mistaking the real affinities of things, and accordingly misapprehending their nature. Only comparison affords explanation. A scientific investigation can thus be achieved only if it deals with comparable facts, and it is the more likely to succeed the more certainly it has combined all those that can be usefully compared. But these natural affinities of entities cannot be made clear safely by such superficial examination as produces ordinary terminology; and so the scholar cannot take as the subject of his research roughly assembled groups of facts corresponding to words of common usage. He himself must establish the groups he wishes to study in order to give them the homogeneity and the specific meaning necessary for them to be susceptible of scientific treatment. Thus the botanist, speaking of flowers or fruits, the zoologist of fish or insects, employ these various terms in previously determined senses.

Our first task then must be to determine the order of facts to be studied under the name of suicides. Accordingly, we must inquire whether, among the different varieties of death, some have common qualities objective enough to be recognizable by all honest observers, specific enough not to be found elsewhere and also sufficiently kin to those commonly called suicides for us to retain the same term without breaking with common usage. If such are found, we shall combine under that name absolutely all the facts presenting these distinctive characteristics, regardless of whether the resulting class fails to include all cases ordinarily included under the name or includes others usually otherwise classified. The essential thing is not to express with some precision what the average intelligence terms suicide, but to establish a category of objects permitting this classification, which are objectively established, that is, correspond to a definite aspect of things.

Reprinted with the permission of The Free Press, an imprint of Simon & Schuster, and Routledge, from *SUICIDE: A STUDY IN SOCIOLOGY* by Emile Durkheim, translated by John A. Spaulding and George Simpson. Copyright © 1951, copyright renewed 1979 by The Free Press.

Among the different species of death, some have the special quality of being the deed of the victim himself, resulting from an act whose author is also the sufferer; and this same characteristic, on the other hand, is certainly fundamental to the usual idea of suicide. The intrinsic nature of the acts so resulting is unimportant. Though suicide is commonly conceived as a positive, violent action involving some muscular energy, it may happen that a purely negative attitude or mere abstention will have the same consequence. Refusal to take food is as suicidal as self-destruction by a dagger or fire-arm. The subject's act need not even have been directly antecedent to death for death to be regarded as its effect; the causal relation may be indirect without that changing the nature of the phenomenon. The iconoclast, committing with the hope of a martyr's palm the crime of high treason known to be capital and dying by the executioner's hand, achieves his own death as truly as though he had dealt his own death-blow; there is, at least, no reason to classify differently these two sorts of voluntary death, since only material details of their execution differ. We come then to our first formula: the term suicide is applied to any death which is the direct or indirect result of a positive or negative act accomplished by the victim himself.

But this definition is incomplete; it fails to distinguish between two very different sorts of death. The same classification and treatment cannot be given the death of a victim of hallucination, who throws himself from an upper window thinking it on a level with the ground, and that of the sane person who strikes while knowing what he is doing. In one sense, indeed, few cases of death exist which are not immediately or distantly due to some act of the subject. The causes of death are outside rather than within us, and are effective only if we venture into their sphere of activity.

Shall suicide be considered to exist only if the act resulting in death was performed by the victim to achieve this result? Shall only he be thought truly to slay himself who has wished to do so, and suicide be intentional self-homicide? In the first place, this would define suicide by a characteristic which, whatever its interest and significance, would at least suffer from not being easily recognizable, since it is not easily observed. How discover the agent's motive and whether he desired death itself when he formed his resolve, or had some other purpose? Intent is too intimate a thing to be more than approximately interpreted by another. It even escapes self-observation. How often we mistake the true reasons for our acts! We constantly explain acts due to petty feelings or blind routine by generous passions or lofty considerations.

Besides, in general, an act cannot be defined by the end sought by the actor, for an identical system of behavior may be adjustable to too many different ends without altering its nature. Indeed, if the intention of self-destruction alone constituted suicide, the name suicide could not be given to facts which, despite apparent differences, are fundamentally identical with those always called suicide and which could not be otherwise described without discarding the term. The soldier facing certain death to save his regiment does not wish to die, and yet is he not as much the author of his own death as the manufacturer or merchant who kills himself to avoid bankruptcy? This holds true for the martyr dying for his faith, the mother sacrificing herself for her child, etc. Whether death is accepted merely as an unfortunate consequence, but inevitable given the purpose, or is actually itself sought and desired, in either case the person renounces existence, and the various methods of doing so can be only varieties of a single class. They possess too many essential similarities not to be combined in one generic expression, subject to distinction as the species of the genus thus established. Of course, in common terms, suicide is pre-eminently the desperate act of one who does not care to live. But actually life is none the less abandoned because one desires it at the moment of renouncing it; and there are common traits clearly essential to all acts by which a living being thus renounces the possession presumably most precious of all. Rather, the diversity of motives capable of actuating these resolves can give rise only to secondary differences. Thus, when resolution entails certain sacrifice of life, scientifically this is suicide; of what sort shall be seen later.

The common quality of all these possible forms of supreme renunciation is that the determining act is performed advisedly; that at the moment of acting the victim knows the certain result of his conduct, no matter what reason may have led him to act thus. All mortal facts thus characterized are clearly distinct from all others in which the victim is either not the author of his own end or else only its unconscious author. They differ by an easily recognizable feature, for it is not impossible to discover whether the individual did or did not know in advance the natural results of his action. Thus, they form a definite, homogeneous group, distinguishable from any other and therefore to be designated by a special term. Suicide is the one appropriate; there is no need to create another, for the vast majority of occurrences customarily so-called belong to this group. We may then say conclusively: the term *suicide is applied to all cases of death resulting directly or indirectly from a positive or negative act of the victim himself, which he knows will produce this result.* An attempt is an act thus defined but falling short of actual death.

This definition excludes from our study everything related to the suicide of animals. Our knowledge of animal intelligence does not really allow us to attribute to them an understanding anticipatory of their death nor, especially, of the means to accomplish it. Some, to be sure, are known to refuse to enter a spot where others have been killed; they seem to have a presentiment of death. Actually, however, the smell of blood sufficiently explains this instinctive reaction. All cases cited at all authentically which might appear true suicides may be quite differently explained. If the irritated scorpion pierces itself with its sting (which is not at all certain), it is probably from an automatic, unreflecting reaction. The motive energy aroused by his irritation is discharged by chance and at random; the creature happens to become its victim, though it cannot be said to have had a preconception of the result of its action. On the other hand, if some dogs refuse to take food on losing their masters, it is because the sadness into which they are thrown has automatically caused lack of hunger; death has resulted, but without having been foreseen. Neither fasting in this case nor the wound in the other have been used as means to a known effect. So the special characteristics of suicide as defined by us are lacking. Hence in the following we shall treat human suicide only.[1]

But this definition not only forestalls erroneous combinations and arbitrary exclusions; it also gives us at once an idea of the place of suicide in moral life as a whole. It shows indeed that suicides do not form, as might be thought, a wholly distinct group, an isolated class of monstrous phenomena, unrelated to other forms of conduct, but rather are related to them by a continuous series of intermediate cases. They are merely the exaggerated form of common practices. Suicide, we say, exists indeed when the victim at the moment he commits the act destined to be fatal, knows the normal result of it with certainty. This certainty, however, may be greater or less. Introduce a few doubts, and you have a new fact, not suicide but closely akin to it, since only a difference of degree exists between them. Doubtless, a man exposing himself knowingly for another's sake but without the certainty of a fatal result is not a suicide, even if he should die, any more than the daredevil who intentionally toys with death while seeking to avoid it, or the man of apathetic temperament who, having no vital interest in anything, takes no care of health and so imperils it by neglect. Yet these different ways of acting are not radically distinct from true suicide. They result from similar states of mind, since they also entail mortal risks not unknown to the agent, and the prospect of these is no deterrent; the sole difference is a lesser chance of death. Thus the scholar who dies from excessive devotion to study is currently and not wholly unreasonably said to have killed himself by his labor. All such facts form a sort of embryonic suicide, and though it is not methodologically sound to confuse them with complete and full suicide, their close relation to it must not be neglected. For suicide appears quite another matter, once its unbroken connection is recognized with acts, on the one hand, of courage and devotion, on the other of imprudence and clear neglect. The lesson of these connections will be better understood in what follows.

II

But is the fact thus defined of interest to the sociologist? Since suicide is an individual action affecting the individual only, it must seemingly depend exclusively on individual factors, thus belonging to psychology alone. Is not the suicide's resolve usually explained by his temperament, character, antecedents and private history?

The degree and conditions under which suicides may be legitimately studied in this way need not now be considered, but that they may be viewed in an entirely different light is certain. If, instead of seeing in them only separate occurrences, unrelated and to be separately studied, the suicides committed in a given society during a given period of time are taken as a whole, it appears that this total is not simply a sum of independent units, a collective total, but is itself a new fact *sui generis*, with its own unity, individuality and consequently its own nature — a nature, furthermore, dominantly social. Indeed, provided too long a period is not considered, the statistics for one and the same society are almost invariable, as appears in Table 1. This is because the environmental circumstances attending the life of peoples remain relatively unchanged from year to year. To be sure, more considerable variations occasionally occur; but they are quite exceptional. They are also clearly always contemporaneous with some passing crisis affecting the social state.[2] Thus, in 1848 there occurred an abrupt decline in all European states.

If a longer period of time is considered, more serious changes are observed. Then, however, they become chronic; they only prove that the structural characteristics of society have simultaneously suffered profound changes. It is interesting to note that they do not take place with the extreme slowness that quite a large number of observers has attributed to them, but are both abrupt and progressive. After a series of years, during which these figures have varied within very narrow limits, a rise suddenly appears which, after repeated vacillation, is confirmed, grows and is at last fixed. This is because every breach of social equilibrium, though sudden in its appearance, takes time to produce all its consequences. Thus, the evolution of suicide is composed of undulating movements, distinct and successive, which occur spasmodically, develop for a time, and then stop only to begin again. On the [below] table one of these waves is seen to have occurred almost throughout Europe in the wake of the events of 1848, or about the years 1850–1853 depending on the country; another began in Germany after the war of 1866, in France somewhat earlier, about 1860 at the height of the imperial government, in England about 1868, or after the commercial revolution caused by contemporary commercial treaties. Perhaps the same cause occasioned the new recrudescence observable in France about 1865. Finally, a new forward movement began after the war of 1870 which is still evident and fairly general throughout Europe.[3]

Table I **Stability of suicide in the principal European countries (absolute figures)**

Years	France	Prussia	England	Saxony	Bavaria	Denmark
1841	2,814	1,630		290		377
1842	2,866	1,598		318		317
1843	3,020	1,720		420		301
1844	2,973	1,575		335	244	285
1845	3,082	1,700		338	250	290
1846	3,102	1,707		373	220	376
1847	(3,647)	(1,852)		377	217	345
1848	(3,301)	(1,649)		398	215	(305)
1849	3,583	(1,527)		(328)	(189)	337
1850	3,596	1,736		390	250	340
1851	3,598	1,809		402	260	401
1852	3,676	2,073		530	226	426
1853	3,415	1,942		431	263	419
1854	3,700	2,198		547	318	363
1855	3,810	2,351		568	307	399
1856	4,189	2,377		550	318	426
1857	3,967	2,038	1,349	485	286	427
1858	3,903	2,126	1,275	491	329	457
1859	3,899	2,146	1,248	507	387	451
1860	4,050	2,105	1,365	548	339	468
1861	4,454	2,185	1,347	(643)		
1862	4,770	2,112	1,317	557		
1863	4,613	2,374	1,315	643		
1864	4,521	2,203	1,240	(545)		411
1865	4,946	2,361	1,392	619		451
1866	5,119	2,485	1,329	704	410	443
1867	5,011	3,625	1,316	752	471	469
1868	(5,547)	3,658	1,508	800	453	498
1869	5,114	3,544	1,588	710	425	462
1870		3,270	1,554			486
1871		3,135	1,495			
1872		3,467	1,514			

At each moment of its history, therefore, each society has a definite aptitude for suicide. The relative intensity of this aptitude is measured by taking the proportion between the total number of voluntary deaths and the population of every age and sex. We will call this numerical datum *the rate of mortality through suicide, characteristic of the society under consideration*. It is generally calculated in proportion to a million or a hundred thousand inhabitants.

Not only is this rate constant for long periods, but its invariability is even greater than that of leading demographic data. General mortality, especially, varies much more often from year to year and the variations it undergoes are far greater. This is shown assuredly by comparing the way in which both phenomena vary in several periods. This we have done in Table II. To manifest the relationship, the rate for each year of both deaths and suicides, has been expressed as a proportion of the average rate of the period, in percentage form. Thus the differences of one year from another or with reference to the average rate are made comparable in the two columns. From this comparison it appears that at each period the degree of variation is much greater with respect to general mortality than to suicide; on the average, it is twice as great. Only the minimum difference between two successive years is perceptibly the same in each case during the last two periods. However, this minimum is exceptional in the column of mortality, whereas the annual variations of suicides differ from it rarely. This may be seen by a comparison of the average differences.[4]

Table II   Comparative variations of the rate of mortality by suicide and the rate of general mortality

A. ABSOLUTE FIGURES

Period 1841–46	Suicides per 100,000 inhabitants	Deaths per 1,000 inhabitants	Period 1849–55	Suicides per 100,000 inhabitants	Deaths per 1,000 inhabitants	Period 1856–60	Suicides per 100,000 inhabitants	Deaths per 1,000 inhabitants
1841	8.2	23.2	1849	10.0	27.3	1856	11.6	23.1
1842	8.3	24.0	1850	10.1	21.4	1857	10.9	23.7
1843	8.7	23.1	1851	10.0	22.3	1858	10.7	24.1
1844	8.5	22.1	1852	10.5	22.5	1859	11.1	26.8
1845	8.8	21.2	1853	9.4	22.0	1860	11.9	21.4
1846	8.7	23.2	1854	10.2	27.4			
			1855	10.5	25.9			
Averages	8.5	22.8	Averages	10.1	24.1	Averages	11.2	23.8

B. ANNUAL RATE RELATED TO THE AVERAGE IN PERCENTAGE FORM

1841	96	101.7	1849	98.9	113.2	1856	103.5	97
1842	97	105.2	1850	100	88.7	1857	97.3	99.3
1843	102	101.3	1851	98.9	92.5	1858	95.5	101.2
1844	100	96.9	1852	103.8	93.3	1859	99.1	112.6
1845	103.5	95.9	1853	93	91.2	1860	106.0	89.9
1846	102.3	101.7	1854	100.9	113.6			
			1855	103	107.4			
Averages	100	100	Averages	100	100	Averages	100	100

C. DEGREE OF DIFFERENCE

	Between two consecutive years			Above and below the average	
	Greatest difference	Least difference	Average difference	Greatest below	Greatest above
			Per. 1841–46		
General mortality	8.8	2.5	4.9	7.1	4.0
Suicide-rate	5.0	1	2.5	4	2.8
			Per. 1849–55		
General mortality	24.5	0.8	10.6	13.6	11.3
Suicide-rate	10.8	1.1	4.48	3.8	7.0
	Per. 1856–60				
General mortality	22.7	1.9	9.57	12.6	10.1
Suicide-rate	6.9	1.8	4.82	6.0	4.5

To be sure, if we compare not the successive years of a single period but the averages of different periods, the variations observed in the rate of mortality become almost negligible. The changes in one or the other direction occurring from year to year and due to temporary and accidental causes neutralize one another if a more extended unit of time is made the basis of calculation; and thus disappear from the average figures which, because of this elimination, show much more invariability. For example, in France from 1841 to 1870, it was in each successive ten-year period 23.18; 23.72; 22.87. But, first, it is already remarkable that from one year to its successor suicide is at least as stable, if not more so, than general mortality taken only from period to period. The average rate of mortality, furthermore, achieves this regularity only by being general and impersonal, and can afford only a very imperfect description of a given society. It is in fact substantially the same for all peoples of approximately the same degree of civilization; at least, the differences are very slight. In France, for example, as we have just seen, it oscillates, from 1841 to 1870, around 23 deaths per 1,000 inhabitants; during the same period in Belgium it was successively 23.93, 22.5, 24.04; in England, 22.32, 22.21, 22.68; in Denmark, 22.65 (1845–49), 20.44 (1855–59), 20.4 (1861–68). With the exception of Russia, which is still only geographically European, the only large European countries where the incidence of mortality differs somewhat more widely from the above figures are Italy, where even between 1861 and 1867 it rose to 30.6, and Austria, where it was yet greater (32.52).[5] On the contrary, the suicide-rate, while showing only slight annual changes, varies according to society by doubling, tripling, quadrupling, and even more (Table III below). Accordingly, to a much higher degree than the death-rate, it is peculiar to each social group where it can be considered as a characteristic index. It is even so closely related to what is most deeply constitutional in each national temperament that the order in which the different societies appear in this respect remains almost exactly the same at very different periods. This is proved by examining this same table. During the three periods there compared, suicide has everywhere increased, but in this advance the various peoples have retained their respective distances from one another. Each has its own peculiar coefficient of acceleration.

Table III Rate of suicides per million inhabitants in the different European countries

	Period			Numerical Position in the		
	1866–70	1871–75	1874–78	1 period	2 period	3 period
Italy	30	35	38	1	1	1
Belgium	66	69	78	2	3	4
England	67	66	69	3	2	2
Norway	76	73	71	4	4	3
Austria	78	94	130	5	7	7
Sweden	85	81	91	6	5	5
Bavaria	90	91	100	7	6	6
France	135	150	160	8	9	9
Prussia	142	134	152	9	8	8
Denmark	277	258	255	10	10	10
Saxony	293	267	334	11	11	11

The suicide-rate is therefore a factual order, unified and definite, as is shown by both its permanence and its variability. For this permanence would be inexplicable if it were not the result of a group of distinct characteristics, solidary one with another, and simultaneously effective in spite of different attendant circumstances; and this variability proves the concrete and individual quality of these same characteristics, since they vary with the individual character of society itself. In short, these statistical data express the suicidal tendency with which each society is collectively afflicted. We need not state the actual nature of this tendency, whether it is a state *sui generis* of the collective mind,[6] with its own reality, or represents merely a sum of individual states. Although the preceding considerations are hard to reconcile with the second hypothesis, we reserve this problem for treatment in the course of this work.[7] Whatever one's opinion on this subject, such a tendency certainly exists under one heading or another. Each society is predisposed to contribute a definite quota of voluntary deaths. This predisposition may therefore be the subject of a special study belonging to sociology. This is the study we are going to undertake.

We do not accordingly intend to make as nearly complete an inventory as possible of all the conditions affecting the origin of individual suicides, but merely to examine those on which the definite fact that we have called the social suicide-rate depends. The two questions are obviously quite distinct, whatever relation may nevertheless exist between them. Certainly many of the individual conditions are not general enough to affect the relation between the total number of voluntary deaths and the population. They may perhaps cause this or that separate individual to kill himself, but not give society as a whole a greater or lesser tendency to suicide. As they do not depend on a certain state of social organization, they have no social repercussions. Thus they concern the psychologist, not the sociologist. The latter studies the causes capable of affecting not separate individuals but the group. Therefore among the factors of suicide the only ones which concern him are those whose action is felt by society as a whole. The suicide-rate is the product of these factors. This is why we must limit our attention to them.

Such is the subject of the present work, to contain three parts.

The phenomenon to be explained can depend only on extra-social causes of broad generality or on causes expressly social. We shall search first for the influence of the former and shall find it non-existent or very inconsiderable.

Next we shall determine the nature of the social causes, how they produce their effects, and their relations to the individual states associated with the different sorts of suicide.

After that, we shall be better able to state precisely what the social element of suicide consists of; that is, the collective tendency just referred to, its relations to other social facts, and the means that can be used to counteract it.[8]

Notes

1. A very small but highly suspicious number of cases may not be explicable this way. For instance as reported by Aristotle, that of a horse, who, realizing that be had been made to cover his dam without knowing the fact and after repeated refusals, flung himself intentionally from a cliff (*History of Animals*, IX, 47). Horse-breeders state that horses are by no means averse to incest. On this whole question see Westcott, *Suicide*, p. 174–179.

2. The numbers applying to these exceptional years we have put in parentheses.

3. In the table, ordinary figures and heavy type figures represent respectively the series of numbers indicating these different waves of movement, to make each group stand out in its distinctiveness.

4. Wagner had already compared mortality and marriage in this way *(Die Gesetzmässigkeit, etc.*, p. 87.)

5. According to Bertillon, article *Mortalité* in the *Dictionnaire Encyclopedique des sciences medicals*, V. LXI, p. 738.

6. By the use of this expression we of course do not at all intend to hypostasize the collective conscience. We do not recognize any more substantial a soul in society than in the individual. But we shall revert to this point.

7. Bk. III, Chap. I.

8. Whenever necessary, the special bibliography of the particular questions treated will be found at the beginning of each chapter. Below are the references on the general bibliography of suicide:

I. Official statistical publications forming our principal sources: Oesterreichische Statistik (Statistik des Sanitätswesens).—Annuaire statistique de la Belgique.— Zeitschrift des Koeniglisch Bayerischen statistischen Bureau.—Preussische Statistik (Sterblichkeit nach Todesursachen und Altersklassen der Gestorbenen).—Würtembürgische Jahrbücher für Statistik und Landeskunde.—Badische Statistik.—Tenth Census of the United States. Report on the mortality and vital statistics of the United States, 1880, 11th part.—Annuario statistico Italiano.—Statistica delle cause delle Morti in tutti i communi del Regno.—Relazione medico-statistica sulle conditione sanitarie dell' Exercito Italiano.—Statistische Nachrichten des Grossherzogthums Oldenburg.—Compte-rendu general de l'administration de la justice criminelle en France.

Statistisches Jahrbuch der Stadt Berlin.—Statistik der Stadt Wien.—Statistisches Handbuch für den Hamburgischen Staat.—Jahrbuch für die amtliche Statistik der Bremischen Staaten.— Annuaire statistique de la ville de Paris.

Other useful information will be found in the following articles: Platter, *Ueber die Selbstmorde in Oesterreich in den Jahren 1819–1872*. In *Statist. Monatsh*, 1876.—Brattassevic, *Die Selbstmorde in Oesterreirch in den Jahren 1873–77*, in *Stat. Monatsh.*, 1878, p. 429.—Ogle, *Suicides in England and Wales in relation to Age, Sex, Season and Occupation*. In *Journal of the Statistical Society*, 1886.—Rossi, *Il Suicidio nella Spagna nel 1884. Arch di psychiatria*, Turin, 1886.

II. Studies on suicide in general: De Guerry, *Statistique morale de la France*, Paris, 1835, and *Statistique morale comparée de la France et de l'Angleterre*, Paris, 1864.— Tissot, *De la manie du suicide et de l'esprit de révolte, de leurs causes et de leurs remèdes*, Paris, 1841.— Etoc-Demazy, *Recherehes statistiques sur le suicide*, Paris 1844.—Lisle, *Du suicide*, Paris, 1856.—Wappäus, *Allgemeine Bevölkerungsstatistik*, Leipzig, 1861.—Wagner, *Die Gesetzmässigkeit in den scheinbar willkürlichen menschlichen Handlungen*, Hamburg, 1864, Part 2.—Brierre de Boismont, *Du suicide et de la folie-suicide*, Paris, Germer Bailliere, 1865.— Douay, *Le suicide ou la mort volontaire*, Paris, 1870.—Leroy, *Etude sur le suicide et les maladies mentales dans le department de Seine-et-Marne*, Paris, 1870.—Oettingen, *Die Moralstatistik*, 3rd Ed., Erlangen, 1882, p. 786–832 and accompanying tables 103–120.—By the same, *Ueber acuten und chronischen Selbstmord*, Dorpat, 1881.—Morselli, *Il suicidio*, Milan, 1879.—Legoyt, *Le suicide ancien et moderne*, Paris, 1881.—Masaryk, *Der Selbtsmord als sociale Massenerscheinung*, Vienna, 1881.—Westcott, *Suicide, its history, literature*, etc., London, 1885.—Motta, *Bibliografia del Suicidio*, Bellinzona, 1890.—Corre, *Crime et suicide*, Paris, 1891.—Bonomeli, *Il suicido*, Milan, 1892.—Mayr, *Selbstmordstatistik*, In *Handwörterbuch der Staatswissenschafen, berausgegeben von Conrad, Erster Supplementband*, Jena, 1895.— Hauviller, D., *Suicide*, thesis, 1898–99.

22. The Moral Meanings of Suicide
Jack D. Douglas

A man who kills himself is now increasingly seen as "victim" rather than "evil-doer."
Suicides themselves, in the notes they leave, tend to blame other people.

Suicide is no longer classed as a crime in Britain, though it still sometimes elicits moral judgments among, for example, coroners. It is one form of social action, and interpretations of it have varied with time. But anyone attempting to study it as a form of action must start with Emile Durkheim's great book, *Suicide*, published 60 years ago.

Durkheim's book attempted to reconcile French analyses of the official statistics on suicide with the prevailing "egoistic" explanation of suicide. The official suicide rates had been found to be stable: so writers like Guerry (*Statistique morale de la France*, 1833) and, more importantly, Quetelet *(Sur l'homme*, 1835) felt that something external to individuals must be causing them to commit suicide; no individual factors would account for such stability.

Members of this statistical school of thought concluded — at any rate by the time of Monselli's work on *Suicide* (1879) — that the egoism of modern man must be primarily responsible. They felt there had to be something "wrong" in the relations between an individual and society before he would commit suicide. The rather unclear argument was than an individual would kill himself only when in some way he was not paying sufficient heed to his social obligations, when he was being "immoral," or — more especially — "egoistic." Durkheim's great contribution was his attempt to demonstrate much more systemetically that suicide is primarily a social phenomenon. But there are two great weaknesses in his work.

Inaccurate statistics

First of all, Durkheim didn't give enough thought to how the official statistics on suicide are collected. Most previous students of suicide realised that the statistics had gross inaccuracies. (In *Suicide and Insanity*, Strahan had estimated that in England the real suicide rate was sometimes probably twice that shown by the official statistics. An error of this sort would make any statistics meaningless.)

Durkheim's second error also came from his statistical approach. Because he had no information, other than his own common sense, on the meanings given to suicide by the individuals who committed suicide or who observed suicide, he decided what the social meanings of the statistics were entirely by common sense or by preconceived theoretical explanations. This basic failure was especially clear in Durkheim's assumption that suicide was considered equally immoral in all the nations and groups of Europe.

Jack D. Douglas: 'The Moral Meanings of Suicide' in *NEW SOCIETY* (July 1967). Reproduced by permission of New Statesman and Society.

In one of the great works in the history of ideas and morality, *Le suicide et la morale* (1922), Albert Bayet criticised Durkheim's approach. Recognising the need for actual observation of what people said and did about suicide, he analysed a huge number of these observations taken from the history of France. He concluded that there was a fundamental division in the moral attitudes toward suicide. The lower class, rural, relatively uneducated groups seemed to have a rather "simple" moral abhorrence for suicide. On the other hand, the upper class, urban, educated groups had a far more complicated, "nuanced" moral attitude toward suicide. For them the moral meaning of a case of suicide depended on the *situation* in which it occurred. Some suicides were heroic, some cowardly; some were damnable, some laudable.

Bayet showed that, at least for the relatively small group of the educated upper class, there has been this same moral relativism for centuries. And though he did show that there was among some other groups a moral abhorrence for suicide, he did not consider how far the people involved could control what category the action fell in. For some European societies it has long been the practice to avoid legal, and possibly moral, consequences of suicide by avoiding this categorisation. In England, for well over 100 years juries refused to categorise the cause of death as "suicide" because they wanted to avoid the legal consequences for the family. And there are even more effective means of avoiding this categorisation of a death.

An "accident"

When we look at cases of suicide today, we find that the individuals committing the act as well as the other people involved, especially the family, almost always manage the action in such a way that the observers will give certain meanings to it. One kind of management that is still very common is the attempt to hide the suicidal cause of death — i.e., to make the cause of death seem due to something other than suicide, an "accident" perhaps. It is impossible to say how often this succeeds, but my impression from many individual cases is that it succeeds fairly often. In the 19th century and before (the source of Durkheim's statistics), it must have been still easier. There was almost no systematic medical examination of the dead until the latter part of the 19th century and even then, as Maurice Halbwachs showed for France, medical examination was much less frequent and less professional in the more rural areas. All of this, however, simply means that the negative moral judgments were rarely imposed because suicide was rarely discovered.

Today there is little evidence of any general negative moral attitude toward suicide when one observes actual cases of suicide. If we ask individuals what they think of suicide in the *abstract* — as, for instance, in a public opinion poll — we still find that a high percentage of people consider suicide to be wrong in some way, though no attempt has yet been made to determine specifically what people mean by this. But even here we find many people holding a highly libertarian view of suicide. When we look at what people say and do about an actual case of suicide in which they are involved we rarely see any moral judgments made. When there are reproaches, they are almost always because of the "foolishness" of it, the "senselessness" of it, and so on. Though there may be some tinge of moral feeling involved, it seems reasonably clear that these are primarily statements about the irrationality of suicide. This is a very different idea and one which is generally shared in western societies today.

Today, with probably only minor exceptions, people judge suicide in terms of the situation in which it is committed, and these situations rarely lead actual observers to condemn it morally. The difficult thing is to explain why this change in moral judgments has occurred since Durkheim's forerunners saw it as a wrongful action.

The most important reason seems to be a change in the commonsense ideas people have about the causes of individual actions. For centuries men in the western world explained human action primarily in terms of the inner forces of the will and the choices of the soul. Suicide was seen as a very wilful action, an "egoistic" action. It was believed that the individual committed suicide because of his own choice and in opposition to the interests of others. Over the last century this commonsense theory has been increasingly displaced by the externalistic theory of action (in which the 19th century interpreters, being in a bridging position, played an originating role). The actions of individuals have been increasingly explained in terms of what happens outside them. Economic determinism, psychiatric theories of mental illness and sociology itself have all been both the results and further causes of this. One of the most common themes now in the notes of suicides is the idea that "I couldn't stand it any more" or "I couldn't stop myself."

As people have come to see the causes of suicidal actions as external to the individual, they have seen the moral *responsibility* for them as also external. The idea of external causation and moral responsibility is now so strong that it is common to speak of the suicide as the "victim" rather than the "evil-doer" or some such thing.

This explanation of the decrease in the moral denunciation of suicide leads one next to expect that at the same time the moral denunciation of external forces would increase, because these external forces are the cause — hence morally responsible. And this seems to be what has happened. It has probably always been possible to some degree to manage one's suicide so that others, especially those closest to you, since they are believed to have the greatest causal effect on you, will be blamed for it (Phaedra did just this). But such revenge suicides seem far more common in the 20th century and certainly far more successful. Notes such as the following, by a young clerk, are common and very effective:

> "To whom it may interest: The cause of it all: I loved and trusted my wife and trusted my brother. Now I hate my wife, despise my brother and sentence myself to die for having been fool enough to have ever loved anyone as contemptible as my wife has proven to be. Both she and her lover (my brother) knew this afternoon that I intended to die tonight. They were quite pleased at the prospect and did not trouble to conceal their elation. They had good reason to know that I was not jesting"
> (quoted from Dublin and Bunzel, *To Be or Not To Be*).

Marilyn Monroe's suicide was used by writers and philosophers to blame many different aspects of her life — Hollywood, the supposed envy of Americans for anyone above the mediocrity, and so on. No one blamed her for it. The "victim" gets sympathy. Rather than blame, the observers now feel greater warmth — and love. Consequently, attempted suicide and its possible outcome, suicide, have become increasingly effective ways to "cry for help," as E. Shneidman and N. Farberow have called it (*The Cry for*

Help, McGraw-Hill), or to get others to change their way of acting towards the individual.

Perhaps the one significant bit of evidence that would seem to contradict this analysis is the derision which is frequently shouted at people who threaten to commit suicide in a dramatic, public way, usually by jumping from a high building. The officials who are trying to save the potential "victim" and newspaper accounts very often condemn these bystanders who seem to be blaming the suicide and telling him to go ahead and do it. The officials and newspapers are expressing sympathy for him and blaming the blamers, whom they see as potentially responsible in part for his suicide. They are clearly expressing the view we have been led by the above analysis to expect. The negative judgments of the bystanders, however, are probably not directed at the potential suicide. Since they are taunting him to leap, it seems apparent that they do not believe he will.

It is a strong belief in general that people who threaten suicide do not mean it — a belief which psychiatrists are now trying to change. The reason for the belief is almost obvious: all of us have known people who spoke of or threatened suicide, yet we also know that few, if any, of these people ever committed suicide. And, in fact, very few of the people who take part in the drama of the suicide rescue actually leap, even when people are taunting them to do so. Consequently, the bystanders are probably blaming the person for making a show of his threat without actually intending to do it. If the person actually jumps to his death, the above analysis would lead us to expect that they would feel great sympathy for him and blame or guilt for themselves.

Though it is difficult to predict changes in patterns of social meanings and actions, this revolution in the patterns of suicide is an excellent chance for testing some such predictions. The externalistic theories of man have been spreading. We can expect an ever greater spread of the commonsense theory of external causation of suicide, with a consequent further decrease in the blaming of the suicide and increase in the blaming of the people and situations with which the suicide "victim" is involved.

One of the things that we must also expect is an increasing formalisation of the methods of blaming others for one's death by the ways in which one kills himself. We can predict along these lines that distinct patterns of revenge suicide will develop throughout western societies, somewhat comparable in their purposes and effects to the ancient patterns of revenge suicide found throughout Asia. Such formalised patterns already seem to be developing in the public dramas of the suicide rescue and in the ever-present threat of suicide which patients hold over the heads of psychiatrists on whom they seem to be completely dependent. Moreover, the use of the suicide note as a means of *pointing out* who is to blame for one's suicide already is becoming quite formalised. Considering the fundamental importance of such states as "rejection," "desertion," "loneliness," "alienation" in our western societies, it would also seem likely that there will be an increasing use of such devices — by committing suicide just after a separation and so on — to point out who is to blame for one's suicide.

As always, there are contrary currents of thought in the western world. More especially, the rise of phenomenological and existential thought among intellectuals has led to a greater emphasis among these groups on the internal aspects of man and on the individual's responsibility for his own actions. If Camus's *Myth of Sisyphus* is any indication of their line of thought concerning suicide, and there is plenty of reason to think it is, then this will move in an opposite direction to the externalistic theories of man. In the 19th century the intellectuals concerned with society insisted on man's lack of freedom. Now the great mass of men have come around to this way of thinking and the intellectuals have returned, though only roughly, to where the mass of men were in the 19th century. It may be that, in the long run, the current of thought about suicide supported by these intellectuals will become stronger and greatly influence the everyday patterns of meanings and actions associated with suicide. But in the shorter run it seems very weak in comparison with the rising tide of the externalistic theories of man.

Weber and the Search for 'Interpretation' and 'Understanding'

23. Fundamental Concepts of Sociology and Types of Authority

Max Weber

The types of social action

Social action, like other forms of action, may be classified in the following four types according to its mode of orientation: (1) in terms of rational orientation to a system of discrete individual ends (*zweckrational*), that is, through expectations as to the behaviour of objects in the external situation and of other human individuals, making use of these expectations as 'conditions' or 'means' for the successful attainment of the actor's own rationally chosen ends; (2) in terms of rational orientation to an absolute value (*wertrational*); involving a conscious belief in the absolute value of some ethical, aesthetic, religious, or other form of behaviour, entirely for its own sake and independently of any prospects of external success; (3) in terms of affectual orientation, especially emotional, determined by the specific affects and states of feeling of the actor; (4) traditionally oriented, through the habituation of long practice.[38]

1. Strictly traditional behaviour, like the reactive type of imitation discussed above, lies very close to the borderline of what can justifiably be called meaningfully oriented action, and indeed often on the other side. For it is very often a matter of almost automatic reaction to habitual stimuli which guide behaviour in a course which has been repeatedly followed. The great bulk of all everyday action to which people have become habitually accustomed approaches this type. Hence, its place in a systematic classification is not merely that of a limiting case because, as will be shown later, attachment to habitual forms can be upheld with varying degrees of self-consciousness and in a variety of senses. In this case the type may shade over into number two (*Wertrationalität*).

2. Purely affectual behaviour also stands on the borderline of what can be considered 'meaningfully' oriented, and often it, too, goes over the line. It may, for instance, consist in an uncontrolled reaction to some exceptional stimulus. It is a case of sublimation when affectually determined action occurs in the form of conscious release of emotional tension. When this happens it is usually, though not always, well on the road to rationalization in one or the other or both of the above senses.

3. The orientation of action in terms of absolute value is distinguished from the affectual type by its clearly self-conscious formulation of the ultimate values governing the action and the consistently planned orientation of its detailed course to these values. At the same time the two types have a common element, namely that the meaning of the action does not lie in the achievement of a result ulterior to it, but in

Reprinted with the permission of The Free Press, an imprint of Simon and Schuster from *THE THEORY OF SOCIAL AND ECONOMIC ORGANIZATION* by Max Weber, translated by A.M. Henderson and Talcott Parsons. Edited by Talcott Parsons. Copyright © 1947, copyright renewed 1975 by Talcott Parsons.

carrying out the specific type of action for its own sake. Examples of affectual action are the satisfaction of a direct impulse to revenge, to sensual gratification, to devote oneself to a person or ideal, to contemplative bliss, or, finally, toward the working off of emotional tensions. Such impulses belong in this category regardless of how sordid or sublime they may be.

Examples of pure rational orientation to absolute values would be the action of persons who, regardless of possible cost to themselves, act to put into practice their convictions of what seems to them to be required by duty, honour, the pursuit of beauty, a religious call, personal loyalty, or the importance of some 'cause' no matter in what it consists. For the purposes of this discussion, when action is oriented to absolute values, it always involves 'commands' or 'demands' to the fulfilment of which the actor feels obligated. It is only in cases where human action is motivated by the fulfilment of such unconditional demands that it will be described as oriented to absolute values. This is empirically the case in widely varying degrees, but for the most part only to a relatively slight extent. Nevertheless, it will be shown that the occurrence of this mode of action is important enough to justify its formulation as a distinct type; though it may be remarked that there is no intention here of attempting to formulate in any sense an exhaustive classification of types of action.

4. Action is rationally oriented to a system of discrete individual ends (*zweckrational*) when the end, the means, and the secondary results are all rationally taken into account and weighed. This involves rational consideration of alternative means to the end, of the relations of the end to other prospective results of employment of any given means, and finally of the relative importance of different possible ends. Determination of action, either in affectual or in traditional terms, is thus incompatible with this type. Choice between alternative and conflicting ends and results may well be determined by considerations of absolute value. In that case, action is rationally oriented to a system of discrete individual ends only in respect to the choice of means. On the other hand, the actor may, instead of deciding between alternative and conflicting ends in terms of a rational orientation to a system of values, simply take them as given subjective wants and arrange them in a scale of consciously assessed relative urgency. He may then orient his action to this scale in such a way that they are satisfied as far as possible in order of urgency, as formulated in the principle of 'marginal utility.' The orientation of action to absolute values may thus have various different modes of relation to the other type of rational action, in terms of a system of discrete individual ends. From the latter point of view, however, absolute values are always irrational. Indeed, the more the value to which action is oriented is elevated to the status of an absolute value, the more 'irrational' in this sense the corresponding action is. For, the more unconditionally the actor devotes himself to this value for its own sake, to pure sentiment or beauty, to absolute goodness or devotion to duty, the less is he influenced by considerations of the consequences of his action. The orientation of action wholly to the rational achievement of ends without relation to fundamental values is, to be sure, essentially only a limiting case.

5. It would be very unusual to find concrete cases of action, especially of social action, which were oriented *only* in one or another of these ways. Furthermore, this classification of the modes of orientation of action is in no sense meant to exhaust the

possibilities of the field, but only to formulate in conceptually pure form certain sociologically important types, to which actual action is more or less closely approximated or, in much the more common case, which constitute the elements combining to make it up. The usefulness of the classification for the purposes of this investigation can only be judged in terms of its results.

*   *   *

Types of solidary social relationships

A social relationship will be called 'communal'[65] if and so far as the orientation of social action — whether in the individual case, on the average, or in the pure type — is based on a subjective feeling of the parties, whether affectual or traditional, that they belong together. A social relationship will, on the other hand, be called 'associative' if and in so far as the orientation of social action within it rests on a rationally motivated adjustment of interests or a similarly motivated agreement, whether the basis of rational judgment be absolute values or reasons of expediency. It is especially common, though by no means inevitable, for the associative type of relationship to rest on a rational agreement by mutual consent. In that case the corresponding action is, at the pole of rationality, oriented either to a rational belief in the binding validity of the obligation to adhere to it, or to a rational expectation that the other party will live up to it.[66]

1. The purest cases of associative relationships are: (a) rational free market exchange, which constitutes a compromise of opposed but complementary interests; (b) the pure voluntary association based on self-interest,[67] a case of agreement as to a long-run course of action oriented purely to the promotion of specific ulterior interests, economic or other, of its members; (c) the voluntary association of individuals motivated by an adherence to a set of common absolute values,[68] for example, the rational sect, in so far as it does not cultivate emotional and affective interests, but seeks only to serve a 'cause.' This last case, to be sure, seldom occurs in anything approaching the pure type.

2. Communal relationships may rest on various types of affectual, emotional, or traditional bases. Examples are a religious brotherhood, an erotic relationship, a relation of personal loyalty, a national community, the *esprit de corps* of a military unit. The type case is most conveniently illustrated by the family. But the great majority of social relationships has this characteristic to some degree, while it is at the same time to some degree determined by associative factors. No matter how calculating and hard-headed the ruling considerations in such a social relationship — as that of a merchant to his customers — may be, it is quite possible for it to involve emotional values which transcend its utilitarian significance. Every social relationship which goes beyond the pursuit of immediate common ends, which hence lasts for long periods, involves relatively permanent social relationships between the same persons, and these cannot be exclusively confined to the technically necessary activities. Hence in such cases as association in the same military unit, in the same school class, in the same workshop or office, there is always some tendency in this direction, although the degree, to be sure, varies enormously.[69] Conversely, a social relationship which is normally considered primarily communal may involve action on the part of some or

even all of the participants, which is to an important degree oriented to considerations of expediency. There is, for instance, a wide variation in the extent to which the members of a family group feel a genuine community of interests or, on the other hand, exploit the relationship for their own ends. The concept of communal relationship has been intentionally defined in very general terms and hence includes a very heterogeneous group of phenomena.

3. The communal type of relationship is, according to the usual interpretation of its subjective meaning, the most radical antithesis of conflict. This should not, however, be allowed to obscure the fact that coercion of all sorts is a very common thing in even the most intimate of such communal relationships if one party is weaker in character than the other. Furthermore, a process of the selection of types leading to differences in opportunity and survival, goes on within these relationships just the same as anywhere else. Associative relationships, on the other hand, very often consist only in compromises between rival interests, where only a part of the occasion or means of conflict has been eliminated, or even an attempt has been made to do so. Hence, outside the area of compromise, the conflict of interests, with its attendant competition for supremacy, remains unchanged. Conflict and communal relationships are relative concepts. Conflict varies enormously according to the means employed, especially whether they are violent or peaceful, and to the ruthlessness with which they are used. It has already been pointed out that any type of order governing social action in some way leaves room for a process of selection among various rival human types.

4. It is by no means true that the existence of common qualities, a common situation, or common modes of behaviour imply the existence of a communal social relationship. Thus, for instance, the possession of a common biological inheritance by virtue of which persons are classified as belonging to the same 'race,' naturally implies no sort of communal social relationship between them. By restrictions on social intercourse and on marriage persons may find themselves in a similar situation, a situation of isolation from the environment which imposes these distinctions. But even if they all react to this situation in the same way, this does not constitute a communal relationship. The latter does not even exist if they have a common 'feeling' about this situation and its consequences. It is only when this feeling leads to a mutual orientation of their behaviour to each other that a social relationship arises between them, a social relationship to each other and not only to persons in the environment. Furthermore, it is only so far as this relationship involves feelings of belonging together that it is a 'communal' relationship. In the case of the Jews, for instance, except for Zionist circles and the action of certain associations promoting specifically Jewish interests, there thus exist communal relationships only to a relatively small extent; indeed, Jews often repudiate the existence of a Jewish 'community.'

Community of language, which arises from a similarity of tradition through the family and the surrounding social environment, facilitates mutual understanding, and thus the formation of all types of social relationships, in the highest degree. But taken by itself it is not sufficient to constitute a communal relationship, but only for the facilitation of intercourse within the groups concerned, thus for the development of associative relationships. In the first place, this takes place between *individuals,* not because they speak the same language, but because they have other types of interests. Orientation to the rules of a common language is thus primarily important as a means of communication, not as the content of a social relationship. It is only with the emergence of a consciousness of difference from third persons who speak a different language that the fact that two persons speak the same language, and in that respect share a common situation, can lead them to a feeling of community and to modes of social organization consciously based on the sharing of the common language.

Participation in a 'market'[70] is of still another kind. It encourages association between the individual parties to specific acts of exchange and a social relationship, above all that of competition, between the individual participants who must mutually orient their action to each other. But no further modes of association develop except in cases where certain participants enter into agreements in order to better their competitive situations, or where they all agree on rules for the purpose of regulating transactions and of securing favourable general conditions for all. It may further be remarked that the market and the competitive economy resting on it form the most important type of the reciprocal determination of action in terms of pure self-interest, a type which is characteristic of modern economic life.

* * *

THE TYPES OF AUTHORITY AND IMPERATIVE CO-ORDINATION

I. The basis of legitimacy[1]

1. The definition, conditions, and types of imperative control

'Imperative co-ordination' was defined above[2] as the probability that certain specific commands (or all commands) from a given source will be obeyed by a given group of persons. It thus does not include every mode of exercising 'power' or 'influence' over other persons. The motives of obedience to commands in this sense can rest on considerations varying over a wide range from case to case; all the way from simple habituation to the most purely rational calculation of advantage. A criterion of every true relation of imperative control, however, is a certain minimum of voluntary submission; thus an interest (based on ulterior motives or genuine acceptance) in obedience.

Not every ease of imperative co-ordination makes use of economic means; *still less* does it always have economic objectives. But normally (not always) the imperative co-ordination of the action of a considerable number of men requires control of a staff of persons.[3] It is necessary, that is, that there should be a relatively high probability that the action of a definite, supposedly reliable group of persons will be primarily oriented to the execution of the supreme authority's general policy and specific commands.

The members of the administrative staff may be bound to obedience to their superior (or superiors) by custom, by affectual ties, by a purely material complex of interests, or by ideal *(wertrational)* motives. *Purely* material interests and calculations of advantage as the basis of solidarity between the chief and his administrative staff result, in this as in other connexions, in a relatively unstable situation. Normally other elements, affectual and ideal, supplement such interests. In certain exceptional, temporary cases the former may be alone decisive. In everyday routine life these relationships, like others, are governed by custom and in addition, material calculation of advantage. But these factors, custom and personal advantage, purely affectual or ideal motives of solidarity, do not, even taken together, form a sufficiently reliable basis for a system of imperative co-ordination. In addition there is normally a further element, the belief in legitimacy.

It is an induction from experience that no system of authority voluntarily limits itself to the appeal to material or affectual or ideal motives as a basis for guaranteeing its continuance. In addition every such system attempts to establish and to cultivate the belief in its 'legitimacy.' But according to the kind of legitimacy which is claimed, the type of obedience, the kind of administrative staff developed to guarantee it, and the mode of exercising authority, will all differ fundamentally. Equally fundamental is the variation in effect. Hence, it is useful to classify the types of authority according to the kind of claim to legitimacy typically made by each. In doing this it is best to start from modern and therefore more familiar examples.

1. The choice of this rather than some other basis of classification can only be justified by its results. The fact that certain other typical criteria of variation are thereby neglected for the time being and can only be introduced at a later stage is not a decisive difficulty. The 'legitimacy' of a system of authority has far more than a merely 'ideal' significance, if only because it has very definite relations to the legitimacy of property.

2. Not every 'claim' which is protected by custom or by law should be spoken of as involving a relation of authority. Otherwise the worker, in his claim for fulfilment of the wage contract, would be exercising 'authority' over his employer because his claim can, on occasion, be enforced by order of a court. Actually his formal status is that of party to a contractual relationship with his employer, in which he has certain 'rights' to receive payments. At the same time the concept of a relation of authority naturally does not exclude the possibility that it has originated in a formally free contract. This is true of the authority of the employer over the worker as manifested in the former's rules and instructions regarding the work process; and also of the authority of a feudal lord over a vassal who has freely entered into the relation of fealty. That subjection to military discipline is formally 'involuntary' while that to the discipline of the factory is voluntary does not alter the fact that the latter is also a case of subjection to authority. The position of a bureaucratic official is also entered into by contract and can be freely resigned, and even the status of 'subject' can often be freely entered into and (in certain circumstances) freely repudiated. Only in the limiting case of the slave is formal subjection to authority absolutely involuntary.

Another case, in some respects related, is that of economic 'power' based on monopolistic position; that is, in this case, the possibility of 'dictating' the terms of exchange to contractual partners. This will not, taken by itself, be considered to constitute 'authority' any more than any other kind of 'influence' which is derived from some kind of superiority, as by virtue of erotic attractiveness, skill in sport or in discussion. Even if a big bank is in a position to force other banks into a cartel arrangement, this will not alone be sufficient to justify calling it a relation of imperative co-ordination. But if there is an immediate relation of command and obedience such that the management of the first bank can give orders to the others with the claim that they shall, and the probability that they will, be obeyed purely as such regardless of particular content, and if their carrying out is supervised, it is another matter. Naturally, here as everywhere the transitions are gradual; there are all sorts of intermediate steps between mere indebtedness and debt slavery. Even the position of a 'salon' can come very close to the borderline of authoritarian domination and yet not necessarily constitute a system of authority. Sharp differentiation in concrete fact is often impossible, but this makes clarity in the analytical distinctions all the more important.

3. Naturally, the legitimacy of a system of authority may be treated sociologically only as the probability that to a relevant degree the appropriate attitudes will exist, and the corresponding practical conduct ensue. It is by no means true that every case of submissiveness to persons in positions of power is primarily (or even at all) oriented to this belief. Loyalty may be hypocritically simulated by individuals or by whole groups on purely opportunistic grounds, or carried out in practice for reasons of material self-interest. Or people may submit from individual weakness and helplessness because there is no acceptable alternative. But these considerations are not decisive for the classification of types of imperative co-ordination. What is important is the fact that in a given case the particular claim to legitimacy is to a significant degree and according to its type treated as 'valid'; that this fact confirms the position of the persons claiming authority and that it helps to determine the choice of means of its exercise.

Furthermore a system of imperative co-ordination may — as often occurs in practice — be so completely assured of dominance, on the one hand by the obvious community of interests between the chief and his administrative staff as opposed to the subjects (bodyguards, Pretorians, 'red' or 'white' guards), on the other hand by the helplessness of the latter, that it can afford to drop even the pretence of a claim to legitimacy. But even then the mode of legitimation of the relation between chief and his staff may vary widely according to the type of basis of the relation of authority between them, and, as will be shown, this variation is highly significant for the structure of imperative co-ordination.

4. 'Obedience' will be taken to mean that the action of the person obeying follows in essentials such a course that the content of the command may be taken to have become the basis of action for its own sake. Furthermore, the fact that it is so taken is referable only to the formal obligation, without regard to the actor's own attitude to the value or lack of value of the content of the command as such.

5. Subjectively, the causal sequence may vary, especially as between 'submission' and 'sympathetic agreement.' This distinction is not, however, significant for the present classification of types of authority.

6. The scope of determination of social relationships and cultural phenomena by authority and imperative co-ordination is considerably broader than appears at first sight. For instance, the authority exercised in the school has much to do with the determination of the forms of speech and of written language which are regarded as orthodox. The official languages of autonomous political units, hence of their ruling groups, have often become in this sense orthodox forms of speech and writing and have even led to the formation of separate 'nations' (for instance, the separation of Holland

from Germany). The authority of parents and of the school, however, extends far beyond the determination of such cultural patterns which are perhaps only apparently formal, to the formation of the character of the young, and hence of human beings generally.

7. The fact that the chief and his administrative staff often appear formally as servants or agents of those they rule, naturally does nothing whatever to disprove the authoritarian character of the relationship. There will be occasion later to speak of the substantive features of so-called 'democracy.' But a certain minimum of assured power to issue commands, thus of 'authority,' must be provided for in nearly every conceivable case.

2. The three pure types of legitimate authority

There are three pure types of legitimate authority. The validity of their claims to legitimacy may be based on:

1. Rational grounds — resting on a belief in the 'legality' of patterns of normative rules and the right of those elevated to authority under such rules to issue commands (legal authority).

2. Traditional grounds — resting on an established belief in the sanctity of immemorial traditions and the legitimacy of the status of those exercising authority under them (traditional authority); or finally,

3. Charismatic grounds — resting on devotion to the specific and exceptional sanctity, heroism or exemplary character of an individual person, and of the normative patterns or order revealed or ordained by him (charismatic authority).

In the case of legal authority, obedience is owed to the legally established impersonal order. It extends to the persons exercising the authority of office under it only by virtue of the formal legality of their commands and only within the scope of authority of the office. In the case of traditional authority, obedience is owed to the *person* of the chief who occupies the traditionally sanctioned position of authority and who is (within its sphere) bound by tradition. But here the obligation of obedience is not based on the impersonal order, but is a matter of personal loyalty within the area of accustomed obligations. In the case of charismatic authority, it is the charismatically qualified leader as such who is obeyed by virtue of personal trust in him and his revelation, his heroism or his exemplary qualities so far as they fall within the scope of the individual's belief in his charisma.

1. The usefulness of the above classification can only be judged by its results in promoting systematic analysis. The concept of 'charisma' ('the gift of grace') is taken from the vocabulary of early Christianity. For the Christian religious organization Rudolf Sohm, in his *Kirchenrecht,* was the first to clarify the substance of the concept, even though he did not use the same terminology. Others (for instance, Hollin, *Enthusiasmus und Bussgewalt*) have clarified certain important consequences of it. It is thus nothing new.

2. The fact that none of these three ideal types, the elucidation of which will occupy the following pages, is usually to be found in historical cases in 'pure' form, is naturally not

a valid objection to attempting their conceptual formulation in the sharpest possible form. In this respect the present case is no different from many others. Later on (§ 11 ff.) the transformation of pure charisma by the process of routinization will be discussed and thereby the relevance of the concept to the understanding of empirical systems of authority considerably increased. But even so it may be said of every empirically historical phenomenon of authority that it is not likely to be 'as an open book.' Analysis in terms of sociological types has, after all, as compared with purely empirical historical investigation, certain advantages which should not be minimized. That is, it can in the particular case of a concrete form of authority determine what conforms to or approximates such types as 'charisma,' 'hereditary charisma' (§ 10, 11), 'the charisma of office,' 'patriarchy' (§ 7), 'bureaucracy' (§ 4), the authority of status groups,[4] and in doing so it can work with relatively unambiguous concepts. But the idea that the whole of concrete historical reality can be exhausted in the conceptual scheme about to be developed is as far from the author's thoughts as anything could be.

LEGAL AUTHORITY WITH A BUREAUCRATIC ADMINISTRATIVE STAFF[5]

3. Legal authority: the pure type with employment of a bureaucratic administrative staff

The effectiveness of legal authority rests on the acceptance of the validity of the following mutually inter-dependent ideas.

1. That any given legal norm may be established by agreement or by imposition, on grounds of expediency or rational values or both, with a claim to obedience at least on the part of the members of the corporate group. This is, however, usually extended to include all persons within the sphere of authority or of power in question — which in the case of territorial bodies is the territorial area — who stand in certain social relationships or carry out forms of social action which in the order governing the corporate group have been declared to be relevant.

2. That every body of law consists essentially in a consistent system of abstract rules which have normally been intentionally established. Furthermore, administration of law is held to consist in the application of these rules to particular cases; the administrative process in the rational pursuit of the interests which are specified in the order governing the corporate group within the limits laid down by legal precepts and following principles which are capable of generalized formulation and are approved in the order governing the group, or at least not disapproved in it.

3. That thus the typical person in authority occupies an 'office.' In the action associated with his status, including the commands he issues to others, he is subject to an impersonal order to which his actions are oriented. This is true not only for persons exercising legal authority who are in the usual sense 'officials,' but, for instance, for the elected president of a state.

4. That the person who obeys authority does so, as it is usually stated, only in his capacity as a 'member' of the corporate group and what he obeys is only 'the law.' He may in this connexion be the member of an association, of a territorial commune, of a church, or a citizen of a state.

5. In conformity with point 3, it is held that the members of the corporate group, in so far as they obey a person in authority, do not owe this obedience to him as an individual, but to the impersonal order. Hence, it follows that there is an obligation to obedience only within the sphere of the rationally delimited authority which, in terms of the order, has been conferred upon him.

The following may thus be said to be the fundamental categories of rational legal authority:—

(1) A continuous organization of official functions bound by rules.

(2) A specified sphere of competence. This involves (a) a sphere of obligations to perform functions which has been marked off as part of a systematic division of labour. (b) The provision of the incumbent with the necessary authority to carry out these functions. (c) That the necessary means of compulsion are clearly defined and their use is subject to definite conditions. A unit exercising authority which is organized in this way will be called an 'administrative organ.'[6]

There are administrative organs in this sense in large-scale private organizations, in parties and armies, as well as in the state and the church. An elected president, a cabinet of ministers, or a body of elected representatives also in this sense constitute administrative organs. This is not, however, the place to discuss these concepts. Not every administrative organ is provided with compulsory powers. But this distinction is not important for present purposes.

(3) The organization of offices follows the principle of hierarchy; that is, each lower office is under the control and supervision of a higher one. There is a right of appeal and of statement of grievances from the lower to the higher. Hierarchies differ in respect to whether and in what cases complaints can lead to a ruling from an authority at various points higher in the scale, and as to whether changes are imposed from higher up or the responsibility for such changes is left to the lower office, the conduct of which was the subject of complaint.

(4) The rules which regulate the conduct of an office may be technical rules or norms.[7] In both cases, if their application is to be fully rational, specialized training is necessary. It is thus normally true that only a person who has demonstrated an adequate technical training is qualified to be a member of the administrative staff of such an organized group, and hence only such persons are eligible for appointment to official positions. The administrative staff of a rational corporate group thus typically consists of 'officials,' whether the organization be devoted to political, religious, economic — in particular, capitalistic — or other ends.

(5) In the rational type it is a matter of principle that the members of the administrative staff should be completely separated from ownership of the means of production or administration. Officials, employees, and workers attached to the administrative staff do not themselves own the non-human means of production and administration. These are rather provided for their use in kind or in money, and the official is obligated to render an accounting of their use. There exists, furthermore, in principle complete separation of the property belonging to the organization, which is controlled within the sphere of office, and the personal property of the official, which

is available for his own private uses. There is a corresponding separation of the place in which official functions are carried out, the 'office' in the sense of premises, from living quarters.

(6) In the rational type case, there is also a complete absence of appropriation of his official position by the incumbent. Where 'rights' to an office exist, as in the case of judges, and recently of an increasing proportion of officials and even of workers, they do not normally serve the purpose of appropriation by the official, but of securing the purely objective and independent character of the conduct of the office so that it is oriented only to the relevant norms.

(7) Administrative acts, decisions, and rules are formulated and recorded in writing, even in cases where oral discussion is the rule or is even mandatory. This applies at least to preliminary discussions and proposals, to final decisions, and to all sorts of orders and rules. The combination of written documents and a continuous organization of official functions constitutes the 'office'[8] which is the central focus of all types of modern corporate action.

(8) Legal authority can be exercised in a wide variety of different forms which will be distinguished and discussed later. The following analysis will be deliberately confined for the most part to the aspect of imperative co-ordination in the structure of the administrative staff. It will consist in an analysis in terms of ideal types of officialdom or 'bureaucracy.'

In the above outline no mention has been made of the kind of supreme head appropriate to a system of legal authority. This is a consequence of certain considerations which can only be made entirely understandable at a later stage in the analysis. There are very important types of rational imperative co-ordination which, with respect to the ultimate source of authority, belong to other categories. This is true of the hereditary charismatic type, as illustrated by hereditary monarchy and of the pure charismatic type of a president chosen by plebiscite. Other cases involve rational elements at important points, but are made up of a combination of bureaucratic and charismatic components, as is true of the cabinet form of government. Still others are subject to the authority of the chief of other corporate groups, whether their character be charismatic or bureaucratic; thus the formal head of a government department under a parliamentary regime may be a minister who occupies his position because of his authority in a party. The type of rational, legal administrative staff is capable of application in all kinds of situations and contexts. It is the most important mechanism for the administration of everyday profane affairs. For in that sphere, the exercise of authority and, more broadly, imperative co-ordination, consists precisely in administration.

4. Legal authority: the pure type with employment of a bureaucratic administrative staff — (Continued)

The purest type of exercise of legal authority is that which employs a bureaucratic administrative staff. Only the supreme chief of the organization occupies his position of authority by virtue of appropriation, of election, or of having been designated for the succession. But even *his* authority consists in a sphere of legal 'competence.' The whole administrative staff under the supreme authority then consists, in the purest type, of individual officials who are appointed and function according to the following criteria:[9]

(1) They are personally free and subject to authority only with respect to their impersonal official obligations.

(2) They are organized in a clearly defined hierarchy of offices.

(3) Each office has a clearly defined sphere of competence in the legal sense.

(4) The office is filled by a free contractual relationship. Thus, in principle, there is free selection.

(5) Candidates are selected on the basis of technical qualifications. In the most rational case, this is tested by examination or guaranteed by diplomas certifying technical training, or both. They are *appointed*, not elected.

(6) They are remunerated by fixed salaries in money, for the most part with a right to pensions. Only under certain circumstances does the employing authority, especially in private organizations, have a right to terminate the appointment, but the official is always free to resign. The salary scale is primarily graded according to rank in the hierarchy; but in addition to this criterion, the responsibility of the position and the requirements of the incumbent's social status may be taken into account.[10]

(7) The office is treated as the sole, or at least the primary, occupation of the incumbent.

(8) It constitutes a career. There is a system of 'promotion' according to seniority or to achievement, or both. Promotion is dependent on the judgment of superiors.

(9) The official works entirely separated from ownership of the means of administration and without appropriation of his position.

(10) He is subject to strict and systematic discipline and control in the conduct of the office.

This type of organization is in principle applicable with equal facility to a wide variety of different fields. It may be applied in profit-making business or in charitable organizations, or in any number of other types of private enterprises serving ideal or material ends. It is equally applicable to political and to religious organizations. With varying degrees of approximation to a pure type, its historical existence can be demonstrated in all these fields.

1. For example, this type of bureaucracy is found in private clinics, as well as in endowed hospitals or the hospitals maintained by religious orders. Bureaucratic organization has played a major role in the Catholic Church. It is well illustrated by the administrative role of the priesthood[11] in the modern church, which has expropriated almost all of the old church benefices, which were in former days to a large extent subject to private appropriation. It is also illustrated by the conception of the universal Episcopate, which is thought of as formally constituting a universal legal competence in religious matters. Similarly, the doctrine of Papal infallibility is thought of as in fact involving a universal competence, but only one which functions

'ex cathedra' in the sphere of the office, thus implying the typical distinction between the sphere of office and that of the private affairs of the incumbent. The same phenomena are found in the large-scale capitalistic enterprise; and the larger it is, the greater their role. And this is not less true of political parties, which will be discussed separately. Finally, the modern army is essentially a bureaucratic organization administered by that peculiar type of military functionary, the 'officer.'

2. Bureaucratic authority is carried out in its purest form where it is most clearly dominated by the principle of appointment. There is no such thing as a hierarchy of elected officials in the same sense as there is a hierarchical organization of appointed officials. In the first place, election makes it impossible to attain a stringency of discipline even approaching that in the appointed type. For it is open to a subordinate official to compete for elective honours on the same terms as his superiors, and his prospects are not dependent on the superior's judgment.[12]

3. Appointment by free contract, which makes free selection possible, is essential to modern bureaucracy. Where there is a hierarchical organization with impersonal spheres of competence, but occupied by unfree officials — like slaves or dependents, who, however, function in a formally bureaucratic manner — the term 'patrimonial bureaucracy' will be used.

4. The role of technical qualifications in bureaucratic organizations is continually increasing. Even an official in a party or a trade-union organization is in need of specialized knowledge, though it is usually of an empirical character, developed by experience, rather than by formal training. In the modern state, the only 'offices' for which no technical qualifications are required are those of ministers and presidents. This only goes to prove that they are 'officials' only in a formal sense, and not substantively, as is true of the managing director or president of a large business corporation. There is no question but that the 'position' of the capitalistic entrepreneur is as definitely appropriated as is that of a monarch. Thus at the top of a bureaucratic organization, there is necessarily an element which is at least not purely bureaucratic. The category of bureaucracy is one applying only to the exercise of control by means of a particular kind of administrative staff.

5. The bureaucratic official normally receives a fixed salary. By contrast, sources of income which are privately appropriated will be called 'benefices.'[13] Bureaucratic salaries are also normally paid in money. Though this is not essential to the concept of bureaucracy, it is the arrangement which best fits the pure type. Payments in kind are apt to have the character of benefices, and the receipt of a benefice normally implies the appropriation of opportunities for earnings and of positions. There are, however, gradual transitions in this field with many intermediate types. Appropriation by virtue of leasing or sale of offices or the pledge of income from office are phenomena foreign to the pure type of bureaucracy.

6. 'Offices' which do not constitute the incumbent's principal occupation, in particular 'honorary' offices, belong in other categories, which will be discussed later.[14] The typical 'bureaucratic' official occupies the office as his principal occupation.

7. With respect to the separation of the official from ownership of the means of administration, the situation is essentially the same in the field of public administration and in private bureaucratic organizations, such as the large-scale capitalistic enterprise.

8. Collegial bodies will be discussed separately below.[15] At the present time they are rapidly decreasing in importance in favour of types of organization which are in fact, and for the most part formally as well, subject to the authority of a single head. For instance, the collegial 'governments' in Prussia have long since given way to the monocratic 'district president.'[16] The decisive factor in this development has been the need for rapid, clear decisions, free of the necessity of compromise between different opinions and also free of shifting majorities.

9. The modern army officer is a type of appointed official who is clearly marked off by certain class distinctions. This will be discussed elsewhere.[17] In this respect such officers differ radically from elected military leaders, from charismatic condottieri,[18] from the type of officers who recruit and lead mercenary armies as a capitalistic enterprise, and, finally, from the incumbents of commissions which have been purchased.[19] There may be gradual transitions between these types. The patrimonial 'retainer,' who is separated from the means of carrying out his function, and the proprietor of a mercenary army for capitalistic purposes have, along with the private capitalistic entrepreneur, been pioneers in the organization of the modern type of bureaucracy. This will be discussed in detail below.[20]

Notes

38. The two terms *zweckrational* and *wertrational* are of central significance to Weber's theory, but at the same time present one of the most difficult problems to the translator. Perhaps the keynote of the distinction lies in the absoluteness with which the values involved in *Wertrationalität* are held. The sole important consideration to the actor becomes the realization of the value. In so far as it involves ends, rational considerations, such as those of efficiency, are involved in the choice of means. But there is no question either of rational weighing of this end against others, nor is there a question of 'counting the cost' in the sense of taking account of possible results other than the attainment of the absolute end. In the case of *Zweckrationalität,* on the other hand, Weber conceives action as motivated by a plurality of relatively independent ends, none of which is absolute. Hence, rationality involves on the one hand the weighing of the relative importance of their realization, on the other hand, consideration of whether undesirable consequences would outweigh the benefits to be derived from the projected course of action. It has not seemed possible to find English terms which would express this distinction succinctly. Hence the attempt has been made to express the ideas as clearly as possible without specific terms.

It should also be pointed out that as Weber's analysis proceeds, there is a tendency of the meaning of these terms to shift so that *Wertrationalität* comes to refer to a system of ultimate ends, regardless of the degree of their absoluteness, while *Zweckrationalität* refers primarily to considerations respecting the choice of means and ends which are in turn means to further ends, such as money. What seems to have happened is that Weber shifted from a classification of ideal types of action to one of elements in the structure of action. In the latter context 'expediency' is often an adequate rendering of *Zweckrationalität*. This process has been analysed in the editor's *Structure of Social Action,* chap. xvi.

The other two terms *affektuell* and *traditional* do not present any difficulty of translation. The term affectual has come into English psychological usage from the German largely through the influence of psychoanalysis.

* * *

65. The two types of relationship which Weber distinguishes in this section he himself calls *Vergemeinschaftung* and *Vergesellschaftung*. His own usage here is an adaptation of the well-known terms of Tönnies, *Gemeinschaft* and *Gesellschaft,* and has been directly influenced by Tönnies' work. Though there has been much discussion of them in English, it is safe to say that no satisfactory equivalent of Tönnies' terms have been found. In particular 'community' and either 'society' or 'association' are unsatisfactory since these terms have quite different connotations in English. In the context, however, in which Weber uses his slightly altered terms, that of action within a social relationship, the adjective forms 'communal' and 'associative' do not seem to be objectionable. Their exact meanings should become clear from Weber's definitions and comments (ed).

66. This terminology is similar to the distinction made by Ferdinand Tönnies in his pioneering work *Gemeinschaft und Gesellschaft;* but for his purposes, Tönnies has given this distinction a rather more specific meaning than would be convenient for purposes of the present discussion.

67. *Zweckverein.*

68. *Gesinnungsverein.*

69. Weber's emphasis on the importance of these communal elements even within functionally specific formal organizations like industrial plants has been strongly confirmed by the findings of research since this was written. One important study which shows the importance of informal social organization on this level among the workers of an industrial plant is reported in Roethlisberger and Dickson, *Management and the Worker* (ed).

70. For definition. See chap. ii, p. 181 ff.

* * *

1. In this chapter Weber departs from his previous practice and, in addition to the usual division into numbered sections, has a system of somewhat more comprehensive subdivisions. These will be designated by capital letters (ed).

2. Chap. i, p. 152. The translation problem raised by the term *Herrschaft* was commented on at that point (ed).

3. An 'administrative staff.' See chap i, 12.

4. *Ständische.* There is no really acceptable English rendering of this term (ed).

5. The specifically modern type of administration has intentionally been taken as a point of departure in order to make it possible later to contrast the others with it.

6. *Behörde.*

7. Weber does not explain this distinction. By a 'technical rule' he probably means a prescribed course of action which is dictated primarily on grounds touching efficiency of the performance of the immediate functions, while by 'norms' he probably means rulers which limit conduct on grounds other than those of efficiency. Of course, in one sense all rules are norms in that they are prescriptions for conduct, conformity with which is problematical (ed).

8. *Bureau*. It has seemed necessary to use the English word 'office' in three different meanings which are distinguished in Weber's discussion by at least two terms. The first is *Amt*, which means 'office' in the sense of the institutionally defined status of a person. The second is the 'work premises' as in the expression 'he spent the afternoon in his office.' For this Weber uses *Bureau* as also for the third meaning which he has just defined, the 'organized work process of a group.' In this last sense an office is a particular type of 'organization' or *Betrieb* in Weber's sense. This use is established in English in such expressions as 'the District Attorney's Office has such and such functions.' Which of the three meanings is involved in a given case will generally be clear from the context (ed).

9. This characterization applies to the 'monocratic' as opposed to the 'collegial' type, which will be discussed below.

10. See below, chap. iv.

11. *Kaplanokratie.*

12. On elective officials, see below, sec. 14.

13. *Pfründen.* On this concept, see below, sec. 7 (ed).

14. See below, sec. 14.

15. See sec. 15.

16. *Regierungs präsident.*

17. See chap. iv. As has already been remarked, chap. iv was left incomplete and the part which is available contains no discussion of this subject (ed).

18. See sec. 10.

19. See sec. 8.

20. The parts of Weber's work included in this translation contain only fragmentary discussions of military organization. It was a subject in which Weber was greatly interested and to which he attributed great importance for social phenomena generally. This factor is one in which, for the ancient world, he laid great stress in his important study, *Agrärverhältnisse im Altertum.* Though at various points in the rest of *Wirtschaft und Gesellschaft* the subject comes up, it is probable that he intended to treat it systematically but that this was never done (ed).

24. Fundamental Concepts of Sociology
Anthony Giddens

Interpretative sociology

Weber's methodological essays were mostly written within the context of the specific problems which occupied him in his early empirical works; they document a struggle to break out of the intellectual confines of the traditions of legal, economic and historical thought within which he was originally trained. In the methodological essays, sociology is treated as subordinate to history: the main problems of interest in the social sciences are deemed to be those concerned with questions possessing definite cultural significance. Weber rejects the view that generalisation is impossible in the social sciences, but treats the formulation of general principles mainly as a means to an end.

The very direction in which Weber's own empirical writings led, especially as manifest in the massive *Economy and Society*, caused a certain change in emphasis in this standpoint. Weber did not relinquish his fundamental stand upon the absolute logical disjunction between factual and value-judgements, nor the correlate thesis that the analysis of unique historical configurations cannot be carried through solely in terms of general principles, these latter being only of prefatory significance to such a task. In *Economy and Society*, however, the focus of Weber's interest moves more towards a direct concern with the establishment of uniformities of social and economic organisation: that is, towards sociology.

Sociology, Weber says, is concerned with the formulation of general principles and generic type concepts in relation to human social action; history, by contrast, 'is directed towards the causal analysis and explanation of particular, culturally significant, actions, structures, and personalities'.[1] This, of course, reiterates the basic position established in the methodological essays, and it may be said that in general the shift in Weber's concerns in the direction of sociology is a change of emphasis in his own personal interests rather than a modification of his basic methodological views. The degree to which *Economy and Society* represents a new departure in Weber's thinking has often been exaggerated in secondary accounts of Weber's thought. *Economy and Society* forms part of a large-scale collaborative work on different aspects of political economy: Weber intends his own contribution to provide a preface to the more specialised volumes written by his collaborating authors.[2] In describing his objectives in writing *Economy and Society* Weber indicates that the sociological analysis contained in it performs a task of 'very modest preparation' which is necessary to the study of specific historical phenomena. 'It is then the concern of history to give a causal explanation of these particular characteristics.' [3]

Anthony Giddens: 'Fundamental Concepts of Sociology' from *CAPITALISM AND MODERN SOCIAL THEORY: AN ANALYSIS OF THE WRITINGS OF MARX, DURKHEIM AND MAX WEBER* (Cambridge University Press, 1971), pp. 145-168.

In his essay on 'objectivity', Weber emphasises that 'in the social sciences we are concerned with mental phenomena the empathic "understanding" of which is naturally a task of a specifically different type from those which the schemes of the exact natural sciences in general can or seek to solve'.[4] One of the main steps to the analysis of social phenomena, therefore, is that of 'rendering intelligible' the subjective basis upon which it rests; a principal theme of the essay, of course, is that the possibility of the 'objective' analysis of social and historical phenomena is not precluded by the fact that human activity has a 'subjective' character. On the other hand, this subjectivity cannot simply be eschewed from consideration by conflating natural and social science. In outlining his conception of 'interpretative sociology' in *Economy and Society*, Weber preserves this stress upon the significance of the subjective for sociological analysis.[5]

'In the sense in which this highly ambiguous word is used here', Weber says, sociology 'shall be taken to refer to a science concerning itself with the interpretive understanding of social action and thereby with a causal explanation of its course and consequences'.[6] Social action or conduct (*soziales Handeln*) is that in which the subjective meaning involved relates to another individual or group. There are two senses in which the meaning of action may be analysed: either in reference to the concrete meaning which action has for a given individual actor, or in relation to an ideal type of subjective meaning on the part of a hypothetical actor.

There is no clear-cut separation in reality between action thus defined, and behaviour which is purely unthinking or automatic. Large sectors of human activity which are important for sociological purposes lie on the margins of meaningful action: this is especially true of behaviour of a traditional kind. Moreover, the same empirical activity may involve a fusion of understandable and non-understandable elements. This may be the case, for instance, in some forms of religious activity, which may involve mystical experiences which are only partially understandable to a social scientist who has not experienced them. The full recapitulation of an experience is, of course, not necessary to this task of rendering it analytically intelligible: ' "one need not have been Caesar in order to understand Caesar"'.[7]

It is important to capture the main drift of Weber's argument here. While he accepts that subjective meaning is a basic component of much human conduct, Weber's point is that intuitionism is not the only doctrine which can offer the possibility of studying this; on the contrary, interpretative sociology can and must be based upon techniques of the interpretation of meaning which are replicable, and thus are verifiable according to the conventional canons of scientific method. This can be accomplished, according to Weber, either by rational understanding of logical relationships which form part of the subjective framework of the actor, or by understanding of a more emotive-sympathetic kind. Rational understanding is most complete and precise in the instance of the use by the actor of mathematical reasoning or formal logic. 'We have a perfectly clear understanding of what it means when somebody employs the proposition $2 \times 2 = 4$ or the Pythagorean theorem in reasoning or argument, or when someone correctly carries out a logical train of reasoning according to our accepted modes of thinking.'[8] But there is no absolutely clear line between the comprehension of propositions of logic in this strict sense, and the manner in which we understand the actions of a man who rationally selects and employs a given means to reach a practical end. While empathy is an important means of obtaining understanding of action which takes place in an emotive context, it is mistaken to identify empathy, and understanding: the latter demands not merely a sentiment of emotional sympathy on the part of the sociologist, but the grasping of the subjective intelligibility of action. In general, however, it is true that the more the ideals towards which human activity is directed are foreign to those which govern our own conduct, the harder it is to understand the meaning they have for those who hold them. We must accept, in these circumstances, that only partial comprehension is possible, and when even this cannot be attained, we have to be content to treat them as 'given data'.

Sociology, must of course, take account of objects and events which influence human activity, but which are devoid of subjective meaning. These phenomena (which include, for example, climatic, geographical and biological factors) are 'conditions' of human behaviour, but do not necessarily have any relationship to any human purpose. But in so far as such phenomena do become involved with human subjective ends, they take on meaning, and become elements within social action. An artifact such as a machine 'can be understood only in terms of the meaning (*Sinn*) which its production and use have had or were intended to have. . .'.[9]

The scientific analysis of social action, in so far as it proceeds beyond mere description, proceeds through the construction of ideal types: and, given the difficulties involved in the understanding of many forms of value-directed or emotively influenced action, it is normally useful to construct rational types. Having specified in the ideal type what constitutes rational action, deviation from it can be examined in terms of the influence of irrational elements. The main advantage of rational ideal types has already been demonstrated, Weber considers, in economics: they are precise in formulation and unambiguous in application. Weber emphasises this as a procedural point; it is a methodological device the use of which does not in any sense imply the existence of a 'rationalist bias'.

Weber distinguishes two basic kinds of interpretative grasp of meaning, each of which may be subdivided according to whether it involves the understanding of rational or of emotive actions. The first kind is 'direct understanding'. In this case, we understand the meaning of an action through direct observation: the rational subdivision of direct understanding can be illustrated by the example quoted previously, of the comprehension of a mathematical proposition. We understand the meaning of the sum $2 \times 2 = 4$ at once if we hear it spoken, or see it written. Direct understanding of irrational conduct, on the other hand, is shown, for example, where we 'understand an outbreak of anger as manifested by facial expression, exclamations or irrational emotional reactions'. The second kind of understanding, 'explanatory understanding' (*erklärendes Verstehen*) differs from this in that it involves the elucidation of an intervening motivational link between the observed activity and its meaning to the actor. Here there are similarly two subsidiary forms. The rational form consists in the understanding of action where an individual is engaged in an activity which involves the use of a given means to realise a particular purpose. Thus, in the example which Weber adduces, if an observe sees a man chopping wood, and knows that he wishes to get some fuel in to light his fire, he is able without difficulty to grasp the rational content of the other's action. The same sort of indirect process of motivational inference can be made in relation to irrational conduct. So, for instance, we are able to understand, in this sense, the response of a person who bursts into tears if we know that he has just suffered a bitter disappointment.

In explanatory understanding, the particular action concerned is 'placed in an understandable sequence of motivation, the understanding of which can be treated as an explanation of the actual course of behaviour. Thus for a science which is concerned with the subjective meaning of action, explanation requires a grasp of the complex of meaning (*Sinnzusammenhang*) in which an actual course of understandable action thus interpreted belongs.' [10] This is extremely important in Weber's conception of the application of interpretative sociology to empirical analysis. The understanding of 'motivation' always involves relating the particular conduct concerned to a broader normative standard with reference to which the individual acts. In order to reach the level of causal explanation, a distinction has to be made between 'subjective' and 'causal' adequacy. The interpretation of a given course of action is subjectively adequate (adequate 'on the level of meaning') if the motivation which is attributed to it accords with recognised or habitual normative patterns. This entails showing, in other words, that the action concerned is meaningful in that it 'makes sense' in terms of accepted norms. But this is not enough, in itself, to provide a viable explanation of the particular action. Indeed, it is the basic fallacy of idealist philosophy to identify subjective adequacy with causal adequacy. The essential flaw in this view is that there is no direct and simple relationship between 'complexes of meaning', motives, and conduct. Similar actions on the part of several individuals may be the result of a diversity of motives and, conversely, similar motives can be linked to different concrete forms of behaviour. Weber does not attempt to deny the complex character of human motivation. Men often experience conflicts of motives; and those motives of which a man is consciously aware may be largely rationalisations of deeper motives of which he is unconscious. The sociologist must be cognisant of these possibilities, and ready to deal with them on an empirical level — although, of course, the more it is the case that an activity is the result of impulses that are not accessible to consciousness, the more this becomes a marginal phenomenon for the interpretation of meaning.

For these reasons, 'causal' adequacy demands that it should be possible 'to determine that there is a probability, which in the rare ideal case can be numerically stated, but is always in some sense calculable, that a given observable event (overt or subjective) will be followed or accompanied by another event'.[11] Thus, in order to demonstrate explanatory significance, there must be an established empirical generalisation which relates the subjective meaning of the act to a specified range of determinable consequences. It follows from the intrinsic suppositions of Weber's method, of course, that if any such generalisation, however precisely verified, lacks adequacy on the level of meaning, then it remains a statistical correlation outside the scope of interpretative sociology:

> Only those statistical regularities are thus sociological generalisations which correspond to an understandable common meaning of a course of social action, and constitute understandable types of action, in the sense of the term used here. Only those rational formulations of subjectively

understandable action which can at least with some degree of closeness be observed in reality, constitute sociological types relating to real events. It is by no means the case that the actual likelihood of the occurrence of a given course of overt action is always proportional to the clarity of subjective interpretation.[12]

There are many sorts of statistical data which, while they may relate to phenomena which conceivably influence human behaviour, are not meaningful in Weber's sense of that term. But meaningful action is not refractory to statistical treatment: sociological statistics in this sense include, for example, crime rates or statistics of the distribution of occupations.

Weber does not limit the range of information which is of value in the study of human social conduct to that which can be analysed according to the method of interpretative sociology. There are many sorts of processes and influences which have causal relevance for social life which are not ' understandable', but the importance of which Weber by no means discounts. It is essential to stress this, since it has become commonplace to suppose that, according to Weber, interpretative sociology is the sole basis of generalisation in relation to human social conduct. Weber is conscious that his own limitation of the term 'sociology' to the analysis of subjectively meaningful action cross-cuts other conceptions of the range of the field which are often applied: 'sociology in our sense . . . is restricted to "interpretative sociology" (*verstehende Soziologie*) — a usage which no-one else should or can be compelled to follow.'[13]

Weber's specific reference to organicist sociology, such as represented by Schäffle's *Bau und Leben des Socialen Körpers* — which Weber calls a 'brilliant work' — is of relevance here. Functionalism, Weber notes, has a definite utility in approaching the study of social life: as a means of 'practical illustration and for provisional orientation . . . it is not only useful but indispensable'.[14] Just as in the case of the study of organic systems, in the social sciences functional analysis allows us to identify which units within the 'whole' [society] it is important to study. But at a certain point the analogy between society and organism breaks down, in that in the analysis of the former it is possible, and also necessary, to go beyond the establishment of functional uniformities. Rather than being a barrier to scientific knowledge, however, the achievement of interpretative understanding should be regarded as offering explanatory possibilities which are unavailable in the natural sciences. This does not come wholly without cost though: it is paid for by the lower level of precision and certainty of findings characteristic of the social sciences.

Where Weber does differ sharply with Schäffle is on the issue of the logical status of holistic concepts. Those sociologists who take their point of departure from the 'whole' and from thence approach the analysis of individual behaviour are easily lured into the hypostatisation of concepts. Thus 'society', which is never more than the multitudinous interactions of individuals in particular milieux, takes on a reified identity of its own, as if it were an acting unit which has its own peculiar consciousness. Weber admits, of course, that it is necessary in the social sciences to use concepts which refer to collectivities, such as states, industrial firms, etc. But it must not be forgotten that these collectives are 'solely the resultants and modes of organisation of the specific acts of *individual* men, since these alone are for us the agents who carry out subjectively understandable action'.[15] There is another respect, however, in which such collective agencies are of vital importance in interpretative sociology: this is, that they form realities from the subjective standpoint of individual actors, and are frequently represented by them as autonomous unities. Such representations may play an important causal role in influencing social conduct.

Interpretative sociology, according to Weber, does not involve the connotation that social phenomena can be explained reductively in psychological terms.[16] The findings of psychology are certainly relevant to all the social sciences, but no more so than those of those of other borderline disciplines. The sociologist is not interested in the psychological make-up of the individual *per se*, but in the interpretative analysis of social action. Weber rejects unequivocally the notion that social institutions can be 'derived', in an explanatory sense, from psychological generalisations. Since human life is primarily shaped by socio-cultural influences, it is in fact more likely that sociology has more to contribute to psychology than *vice versa*:

> the procedure does not begin with the analysis of psychological qualities, moving then to the analysis of social institutions . . .on the contrary, insight into the psychological preconditions and consequences of institutions presupposes a precise knowledge of the latter and the scientific analysis of their structure. . . We will not however deduce the institutions from psychological laws or explain them by elementary psychological phenomena.[17]

Social relationships and the orientation of social conduct

Social action covers any sort of human conduct which is meaningfully 'oriented to the past, present, or expected future behaviour of others'.[18] A social 'relationship' exists whenever there is reciprocity on the part of two or more individuals, each of whom relates his action to acts (or anticipated acts) of the other. This does *not* necessarily imply, however, that the meanings involved in the relationship are shared: in many cases, such as in a 'love' relationship which conforms to the proverb *il y a un qui aime et un qui se laisse aimer*, the attitudes held by one party are not at all the same as those held by the other. Nevertheless in such relationships, if they are continued over time, there are mutually complementary meanings which define for each individual what is 'expected' of him. Following Simmel, Weber speaks of *Vergesellschaftung*, which carries the sense of the formation of relationships and means literally 'societalisation', rather than of *Gesellschaft* (society). Many of the relationships of which social life is compounded are of a transitory character, and are constantly in the process of formation and dissolution. Nor, of course, is it implied that the existence of a social relationship presupposes co-operation between those involved. As Weber is careful to point out, conflict is a characteristic of even the most permanent of relationships.

Not all types of contact between individuals constitute, in Weber's terms, a social relationship. If two men walking along the street collide with each other without having noticed the other prior to the collision, their interaction is not a case of social action: it would become so if they should subsequently argue over who was to blame for the mishap. Weber also mentions the case of interaction in crowds: if Le Bon is correct, membership of a crowd group can give rise to collective moods which are stimulated by subconscious influences over which the individual has little control. Here the behaviour of the individual is causally influenced by that of others, but this is not action which is oriented to others on the level of meaning, and hence is not 'social action' in Weber's terminology.

Weber distinguishes four types of orientation of social conduct. In 'purposively rational' conduct, the individual rationally assesses the probable results of a given act in terms of the calculation of means to an end. In securing a given objective, a number of alternative means of reaching that end usually exist. The individual faced with these alternatives weighs the relative effectiveness of each of the possible means of attaining the end, and the consequences of securing it for other goals which the individual holds. Here Weber applies the schema, already formulated with regard to the rational application of social scientific knowledge, to the paradigm of social action in general. 'Value rational' action, by contrast, is directed towards an overriding ideal, and takes no account of any other considerations as relevant. 'The Christian does rightly and leaves the results to the Lord.'[19] This is nonetheless rational action, because it involves the setting of coherent objectives to which the individual channels his activity. All actions which are solely directed to overriding ideals of duty, honour, or devotion to a 'cause', approximate to this type. A primary distinction between a value rational action and the third type, which is 'affective' action, is that, whereas the former presupposes that the individual holds a clearly defined ideal which dominates his activity, in the latter case this characteristic is absent. Affective action is that which is carried out under the sway of some sort of emotive state, and as such is on the borderline of meaningful and non-meaningful conduct. It shares with value rational action the characteristic that the meaning of the action is not located, as in purposively rational conduct, in the instrumentality of means to ends, but in carrying out the act for its own sake.

The fourth type of orientation of action, 'traditional' action, also overlaps the margins of meaningful and non-meaningful conduct. Traditional action is carried out under the influence of custom and habit. This applies to the 'great bulk of all everyday action to which people have become habitually accustomed. .'.[20] In this type, the meaning of action is derived from ideals or symbols which do not have the coherent, defined form of those which are pursued in value rationality. In so far as traditional values become rationalised, traditional action merges with value rational action.

This fourfold typology which Weber delineates underlies the empirical substance of *Economy and Society*, but it is not intended as an overall classification of social action; it is an ideal typical schema which provides a mode of applying Weber's stated dictum that the analysis of social action can best be pursued through the use of rational types against which irrational deviations can be measured. Thus a particular empirical instance of human conduct can be interpreted according to which of the four types of action it most closely approximates. But very few empirical cases will not in fact include, in varying combinations, a mixture of elements from more than one type.

In his discussion of the difficulties posed by the problem of verification in interpretative sociology, Weber stresses that causal adequacy always is a matter of degrees of probability. Those who have argued that human behaviour is 'unpredictable' are demonstrably mistaken: 'the characteristic of "incalculability" . . . is the privilege of — the insane'.[21] But the uniformities which are found in human conduct are expressible only in terms of the probability that a particular act or circumstance will produce a given response from an actor. Every social relationship thus may be said to rest upon the 'probability' (which must not be confused with 'chance' in the sense of 'accident') that an actor or plurality of actors will direct their action in a specified manner. To affirm the element of contingency in human conduct, in Weber's view, is not to deny its regularity and predictability; but it is to emphasise once again the contrast between meaningful conduct and the invariant response characteristic of, for example, a subconsciously mediated withdrawal reaction to a painful stimulus.

In setting out a conceptual taxonomy of the principal types of social relationship and more inclusive forms of social organisation, Weber thus couches his description in terms of probability. Every social relationship which is of a durable character presupposes uniformities of conduct which, at the most basic level, consist in what Weber calls 'usage' (Brauch) and 'custom' (Sitte). A uniformity in social action is a usage 'in so far as the probability of its existence within a group is based on nothing but actual practice'.[22] A custom is simply a usage which is long established. A usage or custom is any form of 'usual' conduct which, while it is neither expressly approved or disapproved of by others, is habitually followed by an individual or number of individuals. Conformity to it is not backed by any kind of sanctions, but is a matter of the voluntary accord of the actor. 'Today it is customary every morning to eat a breakfast which, within limits, conforms to a certain pattern. But there is no obligation to do so (except in the case of hotel guests); and it was not always a custom.' [23] The social importance of usage and custom must not be under-estimated. Consumption habits, for example, which are usually customary, have great economic significance. Uniformity of conduct founded upon usage or custom contrasts with that associated with the ideal type of rational action where individuals, subjectively pursue their own self-interest. The attitude of the capitalist entrepreneur in a free market is the prototypical case of this.[24] Where uniformity of conduct is adhered to from motives of self-interest — in other words, approximates to this type — a social relationship is usually much more unstable than one resting upon custom.

Legitimacy, domination, and authority

The most stable forms of social relationship are those in which the subjective attitudes of the participating individuals are directed towards the belief in a *legitimate order*. In order to illustrate the distinctions at issue here, Weber gives the following examples:

> If furniture movers regularly advertise at the time many leases expire, this uniformity is determined by self-interest. If a salesman visits certain customers on particular days of the month or the week, it is either a case of customary behaviour or a product of self-interested orientation. However, when a civil servant appears in his office daily at a fixed time, he does not act only on the basis of custom or self-interest which he could disregard if he wanted to; as a rule, his action is also determined by the validity of an order (viz., the civil service rules), which he fulfils partly

because disobedience would be disadvantageous to him but also because its violation would be abhorrent to his sense of duty (of course, in varying degrees).[25]

Action may be guided by the belief in a legitimate order in other ways than through adherence to the tenets of that order. Such is the case with a criminal, who, while violating laws, recognises and adapts his conduct to their existence by the very measures he takes to plan his criminal activity. In this instance, his actions are governed by the fact that violation of the legal order is punished, and he wishes to avoid the punishment. But his acceptance of the validity of the order purely as a 'fact' is only at one extreme of many sorts of violations in which individuals make some attempt to claim legitimate justification for their acts. Moreover, it is extremely important to note that the same legitimate order may be interpreted in differing ways. This is something which can be readily illustrated from Weber's empirical analyses of the sociology of religion: thus the Protestantism of the Reformation was a radicalisation of the very same Christian order as was claimed by the Catholic church as the basis of its legitimacy.

There is no clear empirical line between usage and custom, and what Weber calls 'convention'. Conformity is not, in this case, a matter of the voluntary disposition of the individual. If, for example, a member of a high-ranking status group departs from the conventions governing appropriate standards of politeness, the probability is that he will be ridiculed or ostracised by the rest of the group. The mobilisation of such sanctions is often an extremely powerful mode of securing compliance to an established order. 'Law' exists where a convention is backed, not simply by diffuse informal sanctions, but by an individual, or more usually a group, who has the legitimate capacity and duty to apply sanctions against transgressors.[26] The law-enforcement agency need not necessarily involve the sort of specialised professional body of judiciary and police found in modern societies; in the blood feud, for example, the clan group fulfils an equivalent task as a sanctioning agency. The empirical relationship between custom, convention and law is an intimate one. Even the hold of sheer usage may be very strong. Those who frame laws to cover conduct which was formerly merely 'usual' frequently discover that very little additional conformity to the prescription in question is attained. However, usage and custom do in most cases provide the origin of rules which become laws. The reverse also occurs, although less frequently: the introduction of a new law may eventuate in new modes of habitual conduct. Such a consequence may be direct or indirect. Thus one indirect consequence of the laws which allow the free formation of contracts, for example, is that salesmen spend much of their time travelling to solicit and maintain orders from buyers; this is not enforced by the laws of contract, but nevertheless is conditional upon their existence.

Weber does not hold that we can only speak of the existence of 'law' where the coercive apparatus involved is a political agency. A legal order exists in any circumstance in which a group — such as a kinship group or a religious body — assumes the task of applying sanctions to punish transgressions. In fact, the influence of religious groups upon the rationalisation of law is a main theme in Weber's empirical writings. In more general terms, the inter-relationships between the 'legal', 'religious' and 'political' are of decisive significance to economic structures and economic development. Weber defines a 'political' society as one whose 'existence and order is continuously safeguarded within a given territorial area by the threat and application of physical force on the part of the administrative staff'. This does not imply, of course, that political organisations exist only through the continual use of force, merely that the threat or actual employment of force is used as an ultimate sanction, which may be utilised when all else fails. A political organisation becomes a 'state' where it is able successfully to exercise a legitimate monopoly over the organised use of force within a given territory.[27]

Weber defines 'power' (*Macht*) as the probability that an actor will be able to realise his own objectives even against opposition from others with whom he is in a social relationship. This definition is very broad indeed: in this sense, every sort of social relationship is, to some degree and in certain circumstances, a power relationship. The concept of 'domination' (*Herrschaft*) is more specific: it refers only to those cases of the exercise of power where an actor obeys a specific command issued by another.[28] Acceptance of domination may rest upon quite different motives, ranging from sheer habit to the cynical promotion of self-advantage. The possibility of obtaining material rewards and of securing social esteem, however, are two of the most pervasive forms of tie binding leader and follower.[29] But no stable system of domination is based purely upon either automatic habituation or upon the appeal to self-interest: the main prop is belief by subordinates in the legitimacy of their subordination.

Weber distinguishes three ideal types of legitimacy upon which a relationship of domination may rest: traditional, charismatic, and legal. Traditional authority is based upon the belief in the 'sanctity of age-old rules and powers'.[30] In the most elementary kinds of traditional domination, those who rule have no specialised administrative staff through which they exercise their authority. In many small rural communities, authority is held by the village elders: those who are oldest are considered to be most steeped in traditional wisdom and thereby qualified to hold authority. A second form of traditional domination, which in fact often exists in combination with gerontocracy, is patriarchalism. In this form, which is normally based upon a household unit, the head of the family possesses authority which is transmitted from generation to generation by definite rules of inheritance. Where an administrative staff exists, subordinated by ties of personal allegiance to a master, patrimonialism develops.

Patrimonialism is the characteristic form of domination in the traditional despotic governments of the Orient, as well as in the Near East and in mediaeval Europe. In contrast to the less complex patriarchal form, patrimonialism is marked by a clear distinction between ruler and 'subjects': in simple patriarchalism 'domination, even though it is an inherent traditional right of the master, must definitely be exercised as a joint right in the interest of all members and is thus not freely appropriated by the incumbent'.[31] Patrimonial authority is rooted in the household administration of the ruler; the intermingling of courtly life and governmental functions is its distinctive feature, and officials are first recruited from the personal retainers or servants of the ruler. Where patrimonial domination is exerted over large territories, however, a broader basis of recruitment is necessary, and frequently a tendency towards decentralisation of administration develops, providing a basis for a variety of tensions and conflicts between ruler and local patrimonial officials or 'notables'.

While in historical reality numerous mixtures of types are possible and have existed, the pure type of traditional organisation offers a contrast with the ideal type of rational bureaucracy, which is founded upon legal domination. In traditional organisations, the tasks of members are ambiguously defined, and privileges and duties are subject to modification according to the inclination of the ruler; recruitment is made on the basis of personal affiliation; and there is no rational process of 'law-making': any innovations in administrative rules have to be made to appear to be rediscoveries of 'given' truths.

Weber sets out the pure type of legal authority as follows.[32] In this type, an individual who holds authority does so in virtue of impersonal norms which are not the residue of tradition, but which have been consciously established within a context of either purposive or value rationality. Those who are subject to authority obey their superordinate, not because of any personal dependence on him, but because of their acceptance of the impersonal norms which define that authority; 'thus the typical person holding legal authority, the "superior", is himself subject to an impersonal order, and orients his actions to it in his own dispositions and commands'.[33] Those subject to legal authority owe no personal allegiance to a superordinate, and follow his commands only within the restricted sphere in which his jurisdiction is clearly specified.

The pure type of bureaucratic organisation shows the following characteristics. The activities of the administrative staff are carried out on a regular basis, and thus constitute well-defined official 'duties'. The spheres of competence of the officials are clearly demarcated, and levels of authority are delimited in the form of a hierarchy of offices. The rules governing conduct of the staff, their authority and responsibilities, are recorded in written form. Recruitment is based upon demonstration of specialised competence via competitive examinations or the possession of diplomas or degrees giving evidence of appropriate qualifications. Office property is not owned by the official, and a separation is maintained between the official and the office, such that under no conditions is the office 'owned' by its incumbent. This type of organisation has distinct consequences for the position of the official: (1) The career of the official is governed by an abstract conception of duty; the performance of official tasks in a faithful manner is an end in itself rather than a means of obtaining personal material gain through rents, etc. (2) The official obtains his position through being appointed, on the basis of his technical qualifications, by a higher authority; he is not elected. (3) He normally holds a tenured position. (4) His remuneration takes the shape of a fixed and regular salary. (5) The occupational position of the official is such as to provide for 'career' involving movement up the hierarchy of authority; the degree of progression achieved is determined either by manifest ability or seniority, or by a combination of the two.

It is only within modern capitalism that organisations are found which approximate to this ideal typical form. The main examples of developed bureaucracies, prior to the emergence of modern capitalism, were those of ancient Egypt, China, the later Roman principate, and the mediaeval Catholic church. These bureaucracies, particularly the first three, were essentially patrimonial, and were based largely upon the payment of officials in kind. This shows that the prior formation of a money economy is not an essential prerequisite to the emergence of bureaucratic organisation, although it has been of great importance in facilitating the growth of modern rational bureaucracy. The advance of bureaucratisation in the modern world is directly associated with the expansion of the division of labour in various spheres of social life. It is basic to Weber's sociology of modern capitalism that the phenomenon of specialisation of occupational function is by no means limited to the economic sphere. The separation of the labourer from control of his means of production which Marx singled out as the most distinctive feature of modern capitalism is not confined to industry, but extends throughout the polity, army, and other sectors of society in which large-scale organisations become prominent.[34] In post-mediaeval western Europe, the bureaucratisation of the state has preceded that in the economic sphere. The modern capitalist state is completely dependent upon bureaucratic organisation for its continued existence. 'The larger the state, or the more it becomes a great power state, the more unconditionally is this the case...'[35] While sheer size of the administrative unit is a major factor determining the spread of rational bureaucratic organisation — as in the case of the modern mass political party — there is not a unilateral relationship between size and bureaucratisation.[36] The necessity of specialisation to fulfil specific administrative tasks is as important as size in promoting bureaucratic specialisation. Thus in Egypt, the oldest bureaucratic state, the development of bureaucracy was primarily determined by the need for the regulation of irrigation by a centralised administration. In the modern capitalist economy, the formation of a supra-local market is a major condition stimulating the development of bureaucracy, since it demands the regular and co-ordinated distribution of goods and services.[37]

The efficiency of bureaucratic organisation in the performance of such routinised tasks is the main reason for its spread.

> The fully developed bureaucratic apparatus compares with other organisations exactly as does the machine with the non-mechanical modes of production. Precision, speed, unambiguity, knowledge of the files, continuity, discretion, unity, strict subordination, reduction of friction and of material and personal costs — these are raised to the optimum point in the strictly bureaucratic organisation...[38]

These qualities are demanded above all by the capitalist economy, which requires that economic operations be discharged with speed and precision. Weber's position on this point has often been misunderstood. Weber was obviously aware of the view — common since the turn of the nineteenth century — that bureaucracy is associated with 'red tape', and 'inefficiency'.[39] Nor was Weber ignorant of the importance in the substantive operation of bureaucratic organisations of the existence of informal contacts and patterns of relationship which overlap with the formally designated distribution of authority and responsibilities.[40] Bureaucratic organisation may produce 'definite impediments for the discharge of business in a manner best adapted to the individuality of each case'.[41] It is from this latter fact that the concern with 'red tape' derives, and it is not wholly misplaced, because by its very nature as a rationalised structure, bureaucracy operates according to systematised rules of conduct. It is entirely conceivable, according to Weber, that prior forms of administrative organisation may be superior in terms of dealing with a given particular case. This can be illustrated by the instance of judicial decisions. In traditional legal practice, a patrimonial ruler intervenes at will in the dispensation of justice, and consequently may sometimes be able to render a verdict on the basis of his own personal knowledge of a defendant which is more 'just' than a judgement returned in a similar case in a modern law-court, because in the latter instance 'only unambiguous general characteristics of the facts of the case are taken into account'.[42]

But this would certainly not happen in the majority of cases, and it is precisely the element of 'calculability' involved in rational legal domination which makes bureaucratic administration quite distinct from prior types: indeed, it is the only form of organisation which is capable of coping with the immense tasks of co-ordination necessary to modern capitalism. Weber states the point as follows:

> however many people may complain about the 'bureaucracy', it would be an illusion to think for a moment that continuous administrative work can be carried out in any field except by means of officials working in offices. The whole pattern of everyday life is cut to fit this framework. If bureaucratic administration is, *ceteris paribus*, always the most rational type from a formal, technical point of view, the needs of mass administration (of people or of things) make it today completely indispensable.[43]

Charismatic domination, Weber's third type, is wholly distinct from the other two. Both traditional and legal domination are permanent systems of administration, concerned with the routine tasks of everyday life. The pure type of charismatic domination is, by definition, an extraordinary type. Charisma is defined by Weber as 'a certain quality of an individual personality by virtue of which he is considered extraordinary and treated as endowed with supernatural, superhuman, or at least specifically exceptional powers or qualities'.[44] A charismatic individual is, therefore, one whom others believe to possess strikingly unusual capacities, often thought to be of a supernatural kind, which set him apart from the ordinary. Whether a man "really" possesses any or all of the characteristics attributed to him by his followers is not at issue; what matters is that extraordinary qualities should be attributed to him by others. Charismatic domination can arise in the most varied social and historical contexts, and consequently charismatic figures range from political leaders and religious prophets whose actions have influenced the course of development of whole civilisations, through to many sorts of petty demagogue in all walks of life who have secured for themselves a temporary following. The claim to legitimacy in charismatic authority, in whatever context it is found, is thus always founded upon the belief of both leader and followers in the authenticity of the leader's mission. The charismatic figure normally supplies 'proof' of his genuineness through the performance of miracles or the issuing of divine revelations. While these are signs of the validity of his authority, however, they are not as such the basis upon which it rests, which 'lies rather in the conception that it is the duty of those subject to charismatic authority to recognise its genuineness and to act accordingly'.[45]

Membership of secondary authority positions in a charismatic movement is not based upon privileged selection through personal ties, nor upon the possession of technical qualifications. There is no fixed hierarchy of subordination, nor is there a 'career' such as exists in bureaucratic organisations. The charismatic leader simply has an indeterminate number of intimates who share in his charisma or who possess charisma of their own. Unlike the permanent forms of organisation, a charismatic movement has no systematically organised·means of economic support: its income is either received from donations of some kind or another, or is acquired by plunder. The charismatic movement is not organised around fixed juridical principles of a general kind, such as are found, with different content, in both traditional and legal domination; judgements are made in relation to each particular case, and are presented as divine revelations. 'The genuine prophet, like the genuine military leader and every true leader in this sense, preaches, creates, or demands *new* obligations. . .'[46]

This is symptomatic of the break with the accepted order which the emergence of charismatic domination represents. 'Within the sphere of its claims, charismatic authority rejects the past, and is in this sense specifically revolutionary.' [47] Charisma is a driving, creative force which surges through the established rules, whether traditional or legal, which govern an existing order. It is, according to Weber, a specifically irrational phenomenon. This is indeed essential to Weber's very definition of charisma, since the sole basis of charismatic authority is the recognition of the authenticity of the claims of the leader: the ideals of the charismatic movement are consequently in no way necessarily bound to those of the existing system of domination. Charisma is thus particularly important as a revolutionary force within traditional systems of domination, where authority is tied to precedents which have been handed down in a relatively unchanging form from the past. 'In prerationalistic periods, tradition and charisma between them have almost exhausted the whole of the orientation of action.' [48] With the advance of rationalisation, however, the rational implementation of social change (e.g., through the application of scientific knowledge to technological innovation) becomes increasingly significant.

Because of its antipathy to the routine and the everyday, charisma necessarily undergoes profound modification if it survives into anything like permanent existence. The 'routinisation' (*Veralltäglichung*) of charisma hence involves the devolution of charismatic authority in the direction of either traditional or legal organisation. Since charismatic authority is focused upon the extraordinary qualities of a particular individual, a difficult problem of succession is posed when that person dies or is in some other way removed from the scene. The type of authority relationship which emerges as a consequence of routinisation is determined in large degree by how the 'succession problem' is resolved. Weber distinguishes several possible avenues whereby this may take place.

One historically important solution to the succession problem is where the charismatic leader, or his disciples who share in his charisma, designates his successor. The successor is not elected; he is shown to possess the appropriate charismatic qualifications for authority. According to Weber, this was the original significance of the coronation of monarchs and bishops in western Europe.[49] Charisma may also be treated as a quality which is passed on through heredity, and is consequently possessed by the closest relatives of the original bearer. It is mainly in feudal Europe and Japan, however, that this has become linked with the principle of primogeniture. When charismatic domination is transmuted into a routine, traditional form, it becomes the sacred source of legitimation for the position of those holding power; in this way charisma forms a persisting element in social life. While this is 'alien to its essence', there is still justification, Weber says, for speaking of the persistence of 'charisma', since as a sacred force it maintains its extraordinary character. However, once charisma has in this way become an impersonal force, it no longer is necessarily regarded as a quality which cannot be taught, and the acquisition of charisma may come to depend partly upon a process of education.

The routinisation of charisma demands that the activities of the administrative staff be placed upon a regular basis, which may be achieved through either the formation of traditional norms or the establishment of legal rules. If charisma becomes transmitted through heredity, the officialdom is likely to become a traditional status group, with recruitment to positions itself being based primarily upon inheritance. In other cases, criteria for admission to office may become determined by tests of qualification, thus tending to the rational legal type. Regardless of which of these lines of development is followed, routinisation always requires the setting up of a regular series of economic arrangements which, if the trend is towards traditionalism, will be benefices or fiefs, and if it is towards the legal type, will take the shape of salaried positions.

The content of the ideals promoted by the emergence of a charismatic movement cannot be directly inferred from the pre-existing system of domination. This does not mean to say that the claims of the charismatic movement are not influenced by the symbols of the order in reaction to which it arises, nor that economic or 'material' interests are not important in affecting the growth of a charismatic movement. It does mean, however, that the content of the charismatic 'mission' is not to be explained away as an ideal 'reflection' of material processes which are effecting social changes. The revolutionary dynamic, for Weber, is not to be pinned to any rational sequence of overall historical development. This preserves on a more empirical level the dismissal of developmental theories which Weber reaches according to purely theoretical considerations.

The influence of market relationships: classes and status groups

Weber's rejection of overall theories of historical development applies equally to Hegelianism and Marxism. But a further basic conceptual and empirical line of thought in Weber's work is particularly relevant to the claims of Marxism. If 'theories of history' as a whole are impossible, it follows on the more specific level that any theory which attempts to tie historical development to the universal causal predominance of economic or class relationships is doomed to failure. Weber's discussion of 'class', 'status' and 'party' thus establishes these as three 'dimensions' of stratification, each of which is conceptually separate from the others, and specifies that, on an empirical level, each may causally influence each of the others.

Economy and Society contains two sections dealing with class and status groups.[50] Both sections, however, are short, and are incommensurate with the importance of the concepts in Weber's historical writings. Like Marx, Weber did not complete a detailed analytical account of the notion of class and its relationship to other bases of stratification in society. Weber's conception of class takes its point of departure from his more generalised analysis of economic action in a market. Economic action is defined by Weber as conduct which seeks, through peaceful means, to acquire control of desired utilities.[51] In Weber's usage, utilities include both goods and services. A market is distinguished from direct reciprocal exchange (barter) in so far as it involves speculative economic action oriented towards the securing of profit through competitive trading. 'Classes' can only exist when such a market — which may take numerous concrete forms — has come into existence, and this in turn presupposes the formation of a money economy.[52] Money plays an extremely important part in this because it makes possible the estimation of the values exchanged in quantitative and fixed, rather than in subjective, terms. Economic relationships thus free themselves from the particular ties and obligations of local community structure, and become fluidly determined by the material chances which individuals have of using property, goods or services which they possess for exchange on the competitive market. 'Therewith', Weber says, ' "class struggles" begin'. [53]

The 'market situation' of any object of exchange is defined as 'all the opportunities of exchanging it for money which are known to the participants in exchange relationships and aid their orientation in the competitive price struggle.' [54] Those who own comparable objects of exchange (both goods and services) share 'in common a specific causal component of their life chances'.[55] That is to say, those who share the same market or 'class situation' are all subject to similar economic exigencies, which causally influence both the material standards of their existence, and what sorts of personal life experiences they are able to enjoy. A 'class' denotes an aggregate of individuals who thus share the same class situation. In these terms, those who are propertyless, and who can only offer services on the market, are divided according to the kinds of services they can offer, just as those who own property can be differentiated according to what they own and how they use it for economic ends.

Weber admits, with Marx, that ownership versus non-ownership of property is the most important basis of class division in a competitive market. He also follows Marx in distinguishing, among those who possess property, rentier classes and entrepreneurial classes, which Weber calls respectively 'ownership classes' (*Besitzklassen*) and 'commercial classes' (*Erwerbsklassen*). Ownership classes are those in which owners of property receive rents through their possession of land, mines, etc. These rentiers are 'positively advantaged' ownership classes. 'Negatively advantaged' ownership classes include all those without either property or skills to offer (for example, the *déclassé* Roman proletarians). Between the positively and the negatively advantaged groups fall a range of middle classes who either own small properties or who possess skills which can be offered as marketable services. These include such categories of persons as officials, artisans and peasants. Commercial classes are those where the positively advantaged groups are either entrepreneurs offering goods for sale on the market, or those who participate in the financing of such operations, such as bankers.[56] Wage-labourers constitute the negatively advantaged commercial classes. The middle classes include the petty bourgeoisie and administrative officials in government or in industry.

Most secondary discussions of Weber's conception of class have concentrated upon his earlier discussion (see below, note 59), and have neglected this second formulation. This is unfortunate, since it gives the impression that Weber's conception is less unified than in fact is the case. While in principle, according to the identification of class situation with market situation, there could be as many class divisions as there are minute gradations of economic position, in fact Weber regards only certain definite combinations, organised around the ownership and non-ownership of property, as historically significant. In his later exposition, besides differentiating ownership classes and commercial classes, Weber also distinguishes what he calls simply 'social' classes. In so far as individuals may move freely within a common cluster of class situations (e.g., a man may move without difficulty from a clerical job in the civil service to one in a business firm), they form a definite social class. Compressing some of the divisions which compose the commercial classes, Weber describes the social class composition of capitalism as consisting of the following: (1) The manual working class. The existence of skill differentials — especially where they are controlled as monopolies — is a major factor threatening the unity of the working class. But the increasing mechanisation of industry is pushing a large proportion of workers into the semi-skilled category. (2) The petty bourgeoisie. (3) Propertyless white-collar workers, technicians and intelligentsia. (4) The dominant entrepreneurial and propertied groups, who also tend to share a privileged access to educational opportunities.[57]

The relationship between the existence of similar class interests, and the occurrence of manifest class conflict, is historically contingent. Groups of individuals may share a similar class situation without being aware of it, and without forming any organisation to further their common economic interests. It is not always the most marked inequalities in the distribution of property which lead to class struggles. Class conflict is likely to develop only where the unequal distribution of life-chances comes to be perceived as not an 'inevitable fact': in many periods of history, the negatively advantaged classes accept their position of inferiority as legitimate. Class consciousness most readily becomes developed in circumstances where: (1) The class enemy is a group in visible and direct economic competition: in modern capitalism, for example, the working class can more readily be organised to fight against the industrial entrepreneur or manager, rather than against the more remote financier or shareholder. 'It is not the rentier, the shareholder, and the banker who suffer the ill will of the worker, but almost exclusively the manufacturer and the business executives who are the direct opponents of workers in wage conflicts.'[58]. (2) There is a large number of people who share the same class situation. (3) Communication and assembly are simple to organise: as where, for instance, in modern factory production, the workers are concentrated together in large-scale productive units. (4) The class in question is provided with leadership — such as from the intelligentsia — which supplies clear and comprehensible goals for their activity.

'Class' refers to the objective attributes of the market situation of numbers of individuals, and as such the influence of class upon social action operates independently of any valuations these individuals might make of themselves or others. Since Weber rejects the notion that economic phenomena directly determine the nature of human ideals, it follows that such valuations have to be conceptualised independently of class interests. Weber therefore distinguishes class situation from 'status situation' (*ständische Lage*). The status situation of an individual refers to the evaluations which others make of him or his social position, thus attributing to him some form of (positive or negative) social prestige or esteem. A status group is a number of individuals who share the same status situation. Status groups, unlike classes, are almost always conscious of their common position. 'In relation to classes, the status group comes closest to the "social" class and is most unlike the "commercial" class.'[59] However, there is no necessary or universal connection between status situation and any of the three types of class which Weber distinguishes. Property classes often, but by no means always, constitute definite status groups; commercial classes rarely do so.

Status groups normally manifest their distinctiveness through following a particular life-style, and through placing restrictions upon the manner in which others may interact with them. The enforcement of restrictions upon marriage, sometimes involving strict endogamy, is a particularly frequent way in which this may be achieved. Caste represents the most clear-cut example of this; here the distinctive character of the status group is held to rest upon ethnic factors, and is enforced by religious prescriptions as well as by legal and conventional sanctions. While it is only in traditional India that a whole society is organised according to strict caste principles, caste-like properties are also characteristic of the position of 'pariah' peoples. These are ethnic minorities, the most notable historical example of which is that of the Jews, whose economic activities are limited to a particular occupation or range of occupations, and whose contacts with the 'host' population are limited.

Stratification by status is not, for Weber, simply a 'complication' of class hierarchies: on the contrary, status groups, as differentiated from classes, are of vital significance in numerous phases of historical development. Moreover, status groups may act to influence in a direct way the operation of the market, and so may causally affect class relationships. One historically important way in which this has occurred is through the restriction of the spheres of economic life which are permitted to become governed by the market:

> For example, in many Hellenic cities during the 'status era' and also originally in Rome, the inherited estate (as is shown by the old formula for placing spendthrifts under a guardian) was monopolised, as were the estates of knights, peasants, priests, and especially the clientele of the craft and merchant guilds. The market is restricted, and the power of naked property *per se*, which gives its stamp to class formation, is pushed into the background.[60]

Many instances can be adduced in which men draw clear distinctions between economic possession and status privilege. The possession of material property is not by any means always a sufficient basis for entry into a dominant status group. The claims of *nouveaux riches* for entry to an established status group are not likely to be accepted by those within it, although the individual can ordinarily use his wealth to ensure that his offspring can acquire the necessary criteria for membership. Nevertheless, Weber does stress that, while status group membership 'normally stands in sharp opposition to the pretensions of sheer property', it is still the case that property is 'in the long run' recognised 'with extraordinary regularity' as a status qualification.[61] The degree to which status stratification is prevalent in any given social order is influenced by how far the society in question is subject to rapid economic transformation. Where marked economic changes are occurring, class stratification is a more pervasive determinant of action than in a situation where there is little change. In the latter case, status differentials come increasingly to the fore.

Both class and status group membership may be a basis of social power; but the formation of political parties is a further, analytically independent, influence upon the distribution of power. A 'party' refers to any voluntary association which has the aim of securing directive control of an organisation in order to implement certain definite policies within that organisation. In this definition, parties can exist in any form of organisation in which the formation of freely recruited groupings is permitted: from a sports club up to the state.[62] The bases for the establishment of parties, even of modern political parties, are diverse. A common class or status situation may provide the sole source of recruitment to a political party but this is fairly rare. 'In any individual case, parties may represent interests determined through class situation or status situation. . . . But they need be neither purely class nor purely status parties; in fact, they are more likely to be mixed types, and sometimes they are neither.' [63]

The growth of the modern state has brought with it the development of mass political parties, and the emergence of professional politicians. A man whose occupation is concerned with the struggle for political power may either live 'for' politics or 'off' politics. An individual who relies upon his political activities to supply his main source of income lives 'off' politics; a man who engages in full-time political activities, but who does not receive his income from this source, lives 'for' politics. A political order in which recruitment to positions of power is filled by those who live 'for' politics is necessarily drawn from a propertied elite, who are usually rentiers rather than entrepreneurs. This does not imply that such politicians will pursue policies which are wholly directed towards favouring the interests of the class or status group from which they originate.[64]

Notes

1. *ES*, vol. 1, p. 19; *WuG*, vol. 1. p. 9.

2. The collection of volumes as a whole is entitled *Grundriss der Sozialökonomik*. Authors include Sombart, Michels, Alfred Weber, and Schumpeter. The first contributions were published in 1914, and others appeared up until 1930, when the collection was terminated. See Johannes Winckelmann: 'Max Weber's Opus Post humum', *Zeitschrift für die gesamten Staatswissenschaften*, vol. 105. 1949, pp. 368–87.

3. Letter to Georg von Below, June 1914, quoted in von Below: *Der deutsche Staat des Mittelalters* (Leipzig, 1925), p. xxiv.

4. *MSS*, p. 74; *GAW*, p. 173.

5. The account presented in the first volume of *ES* is a revised version of an earlier essay 'Über einige Kategorien der verstehenden Soziologie', *GAW*, pp. 427–74 (originally published in 1913).

6. *ES*, vol. 1, p. 4; *WuG*, vol. 1, p. 1. cf. Julien Freund: *The Sociology of Max Weber* (London, 1968), pp. 90–1.

7. *ES*, vol. 1, p. 5. Carlo Anloni: *From History to Sociology* (London, 1962), p. 170.

8. *ES*, vol. 1, p. 5.

9. *ES*, vol. 1. p. 7; *WuG*, vol. 1, p. 3.

10. *ES*, vol. 1, p. 9. For an analysis of the theoretical significance of this, see Parsons, pp. 635ff.

11. *ES*, vol. 1, pp. 11–12. Given this condition, as Weber makes clear in his critique of Roscher and Knies, 'The "interpretative" motive-research of the historian is causal attribution in exactly the same sense as the causal interpretation of any individual process in nature. . .'. *GAW*, p. 134.

12. *ES*, vol. 1, p. 12; *WuG*, vol. 1, p. 6.

13. *ES*, vol. 1, pp. 12–13; *WuG*, vol. 1, p. 6.

14. *ES*, vol. 1, p. 15.

15. *ES*, vol. 1, p. 13; *WuG*, vol. 1, p. 6. For an extensive critical consideration of this and other points in Weber's outline of interpretative sociology, see Alfred Schutz: *The Phenomenology of the Social World* (Evanston, 1967).

16. *ES*, vol. 1, p. 19.

17. *MSS*, pp. 88–9.

18. *ES*, vol. 1, p. 22.

19. *FMW*, p. 120.

20. *ES*, vol. 1, p. 25.

21. *MSS*, p. 124. See also *GAW*, pp. 65ff, where Weber discusses in detail the relationship between 'irrationality', 'unpredictability' and 'freedom of will'.

22. *ES*, vol. 1, p. 29.

23. *ES*, vol. 1, p. 29; *WuG*, vol. 1, p. 15.

24. It might be pointed out that Weber here is speaking of empirical cases which approximate to purposively rational action. This is not, therefore, the equivalent of Durkheim's 'egoism', since in Weber's instance the subjective pursuit of self-interest is 'oriented towards identical expectations' (*ES*, vol. 1, pp. 29–30).

25. *ES*, vol. 1, p. 31.

26. Weber distinguishes at one point between 'guaranteed' law and 'indirectly guaranteed' law. The first type is backed directly by a coercive apparatus. The second type refers to the case of a norm the transgression of which is not legally punished, but has the consequence of infringing other norms which are guaranteed laws. But Weber normally uses 'law' without qualification to denote guaranteed law.

27. Compare Durkheim's divergent conceptualisation, above, p. 100. Neither the possession of a fixed territory nor the capability of applying force appears in Durkheim's definition.

28. For a summary of issues relevant to the terminological debate over whether *Herrschaft* should be translated as 'domination' or 'authority', see Roth's annotation in *ES*, vol. 1, pp. 61–2 (note 31). I have used the term 'domination' as broader in denotation than 'authority' (*legitime Herrschaft*).

29. *FMW*, pp. 80–1.

30. *ES*, vol. 1, p. 226.

31. *ES*, vol. 1, p. 231. I have also used here Weber's earlier account of patrimonialism in *ES*, vol. 3, pp. 1006–10

32. Weber's alternative exposition is to be found in *ES*, vol. 3, pp. 956–1005; the later version is in vol. 1, pp. 217–26.

33. *ES*, vol. 1, p. 217; *WuG*, vol. 1, p. 125.

34. cf. *GASS*, pp. 498ff. The importance of this point is amplified, in relation to Marx's position, see below, pp. 234–8.

35. *ES*, vol. 3, p. 971; *WuG*, vol. 2, p. 568.

36. Weber thus criticises Michels for exaggerating the 'iron' character of the tendency towards the formation of oligarchy in bureaucracies. *ES*, vol. 3, pp. 1003–4.

37. It is important to emphasise that the modern state and economy do not become totally bureaucratised. For those at 'the top', specialised qualifications of a technical kind are not required. Ministerial and presidential positions are filled through some kind of electoral process, and the industrial entrepreneur is not appointed by the bureaucracy he heads. 'Thus at the top of a bureaucratic organisation, there is necessarily an element which is at least not purely bureaucratic.' *ES*, vol. 1, p. 222.

38. *ES*, vol. 3, p. 973.

39. cf. Martin Albrow: *Bureaucracy* (London, 1970), pp. 26–54.

40. cf. Weber's contributions to the discussions of the *Verein für Sozialpolitzk* in 1909, *GASS*, pp. 412–16.

41. *ES*, vol. 3, pp. 974–5.

42. *ES*, vol. 2, pp. 656–7.

43. *ES*, vol. 1, p. 223; *WuG*, vol. 1, p. 128.

44. *ES*, vol. 1, p. 241.

45. *ES*, vol. 1, p. 242.

46. *ES*, vol. 1, p. 243. 'Kadi-justice' is administered in this way, in principle; in practice, Weber says, it was actually closely bound to traditional precedent.

47. *ES*, vol. 1, p. 244; *WuG*, vol. 1, p. 141.

48. *ES*. vol. 1, p. 245

49. *ES*, vol. 1, pp. 247–8.

50. The earlier rendition is in *ES*, vol. 2, pp. 926–40; the later analysis is to be found in *ES*, vol. 1, pp. 302–7.

51. *ES*, vol. 1, p. 63. For an earlier formulation of the concept of the 'economic', see *MSS*, p. 65.

52. *ES*, vol. 1, pp. 80–2.

53. *ES*, vol. 2, p. 928.

54. *ES*, vol. 1, p. 82.

55. ES, vol. 2, p. 927.

56. Positively advantaged commercial classes also sometimes include those who are able to control a monopoly of particular skills, such as professionals and craft workers. *ES*, vol. 1, p. 304.

57. *ES*, vol. 1, p. 305. cf. Paul Mombert: 'Zum Wesen der sozialen Klasse', in Melchior Palyi: *Erinnerungsgabe für Max Weber* (Munich and Leipzig, 1923), pp. 239–75.

58. *ES*, vol. 2, p. 931. It is this fact, Weber points out, which has made possible the growth of patriarchal socialism. Similarly, in the army, the soldier resents the corporal rather than the higher echelons of command. *GASS*, p. 509.

59. *ES*, vol. 1, pp. 306–7; *WuG*, vol. 1, p. 180. For Marx's use of the term *Stand*, see above, p. 6, n. 22.

60. *ES*, vol. 2, p. 937.

61. *ES*, vol. 2, p. 932.

62. *ES*, vol. 1, pp. 284–6.

63. *ES*, vol. 2, p. 938

64. *FMW*, pp. 85–6.

25. The Weberian Project

Terry Johnson, Christopher Dandeker and Clive Ashworth

Elements of Husserlian phenomenology have come to influence sociology through a number of routes: directly, through the attempts of Schutz to apply phenomenology to the problems of the social sciences, and indirectly through the Husserlian influence on the Frankfurt School of critical theory and what have become known as the phenomenological marxists. Central to each of these projects has been the Husserlian contention that the sciences should be founded in the 'constitutive operations' of the subject, a strategy that would confront all forms of objectivism, reification and alienation in the social sciences.

Schutz embarked upon a phenomenological social science by way of a critique of what he regarded as the major attempt in classical theory to construct sociology from a subjectivist point of view: the methodological work of Max Weber. As in Schutz's own work (see Johnson, Dandeker, Ashworth, pp. 94–100), Weber's subjectivism is characterised by two distinct but related ways of viewing the emergent properties of social structure. Weber accepts the subjectivist proposition that the subject-matter of social science is not given to the observer in any direct fashion, but results from the scientist's *interpretative selection*: that is, his own 'constitutive operations'. In addition, social phenomena are not themselves 'finished productions', objectively existing, but are in a continual process of being produced and reproduced by the interpretative activities of social actors. For Weber, then, structure is an emergent property; it emerges out of the doings of human subjects and the conceptualisations of professional observers.

Two sets of methodological distinctions are utilised by Weber in order to distinguish the social sciences from the natural sciences. First of all, he distinguished between the two on the basis of the different properties of their subject-matter: inanimate nature on the one hand, and mental and spiritual life on the other. The natural sciences may, in attempting to explain the relations between 'things', use theory and observation to generate *causal laws*, so calculating the regular occurrence of physical events. While Weber considers that causal laws are not, in principle, impossible in the social sciences, these sciences have what he regards as an additional advantage — that is, of being able to penetrate historical events through an *understanding* of their meaning; by discovering the human intentions lying behind such events. Weber's point is that social and historical events have 'authors' — intentional participants, who, because they are similar to ourselves, allow for the possibility of *understanding*. This procedure, which Weber refers to as *Verstehen*, is denied to us in our attempts to gain knowledge of the natural world.

Copyright © 1984 Johnson, T., Dandeker, C. and Ashworth, C., from *THE STRUCTURE OF SOCIAL THEORY*. Reprinted with permission of Macmillan Press Limited and St Martin's Press, Incorporated.

The second distinction used by Weber, which does not entirely coincide with the natural/social distinction, is based, not on any inherent property of scientific objects, but on the type of abstraction or frame of reference that may be brought to bear on the phenomenal worlds of men and nature. In general, these frames of reference are of two kinds: the *individualising*, which involves a focus on the unique, concrete aspects of phenomena, or the *generalising*, which seeks to establish the regular law-like relationships between phenomena. That these two forms of abstraction are not meant by Weber to refer to the natural-science/social-science distinction is clear in so far as he considered psychology to be a generalising science. Nevertheless the cultural or social sciences are seen to be primarily the study of those unique processes through which social reality is constructed. There is no distinction in Weber, between individualising history and generalising sociology. They are part of the same intellectual project.

It is within these broad subjectivist parameters that Weber critically confronted a number of objectivist traditions in the German cultural sciences — particularly the substantialism of Marx and the rationalism of the Hegelian tradition. He constructed a project, however, poised precariously between subjectivism and empiricism, continually drifting in one or other of these directions.

The historical observer

For Weber all reality, including the social world, comprises an infinite flux of events over time and in space. It is a reality that defies any final, exhaustive description or summary, allowing only for incomplete and partial accounts which abstract from that reality in a number of different ways. All knowledge, he argues, involves both selection and abstraction even where the knowledge results from studies concerned with the details of concrete historical events. The form of abstraction that is used is not determined by the fact that the research is being carried out by a sociologist or historian or even physicist, but is determined by the nature of the research problem confronted. Thus, both 'generalising' and 'individualising' abstractions are used by all sciences. It is, then, the way in which these methods relate to one another rather than their distinctiveness that is important in understanding the scientific process. A significant aspect of this relationship as far as Weber's conception of sociology is concerned is the link between abstraction and values. For Weber rejects the empiricist assumption that generalisations about history refer to objective events that are reflected in the senses of detached observers. It is Weber's contention that the events about which we generalise are the product of value-selection by human beings. For example, the study of the history of a particular economic organisation or institution, such as production relations within the weaving industry, already presupposes such generalising concepts as *economic* and *industry* without which the study could not proceed. The possibility of abstracting such a particular process from the myriad events of history is a product of the selectivity of human beings who thereby endow their study with particular cultural significance. In short, it is a value-laden process. Social scientists, then, like all human subjects, endow events with meaning and it is only once they have generalised on such a basis that any causal analysis is possible. Causal statements in social science are, according to Weber, impossible without value orientations.

Weber does attempt, however, to maintain a distinction between value orientation, which involves determining the significance of historical events as worthy of study, and value judgements, which entail committing oneself to a positive or negative moral evaluation of the events themselves. Value orientation appears to operate at a number of levels, incorporating the values of a culture (what is deemed significant or otherwise), the values of a discipline such as sociology, and the values of the observer such as a sociologist.[4] The implications of this position include the view that what is conceived of as historical reality changes as a result of cultural change, and that the field of knowledge in social science changes with the historical process itself. Weber's position departs radically from the positivist view that social science is a linear, cumulative process. Far from value orientation creating a subjective barrier to the acquisition of valid historical knowledge, it is the indispensable means of acquiring any historical knowledge at all.

In committing himself to the view that our socio-historical knowledge is *created* by the social scientist in a cultural context of shifting values, Weber comes up against one of the major problems of the subjectivist strategy. What prevents the constitutive operations of subjectivity from merely inventing history? Surely, there is nothing to stop us making up nice *histories* which accord with our own values? It is at this point that the major tension in Weber's project arises. The constraints on story-telling are a set of procedures that Weber derives from a broadly empiricist strategy, and these lay the foundations of what emerges as an unstable synthesis of subjectivism and empiricism.

Let us briefly consider these procedures. It is through value orientation that the social scientist constitutes his object of study — he selectively detaches a set of events from the totality of history. In this process the scientist must further refine his concepts through abstraction; that is to say, certain distinguishing features of the phenomenon or set of events are selected as its most important characteristics from a particular point of view. It is this process of abstraction that involves the construction of an ideal type. The purpose of the ideal type is not to explain or even to describe social reality but to *prepare* abstracted historical individuals or configurations for causal explanation. They are 'conceptual utopias' through which we may analyse social reality by examining the precise extent to which reality approximates to or departs from their pure form. Thus, one can construct an ideal type of the protestant ethic by conceptually arranging certain traits actually found in an unclear, impure form in various protestant beliefs into a consistent ideal-construct which accentuates its essential tendencies. From that point on, historical research involves determining in each case the extent to which this ideal-construct approximates to or diverges from reality; to what extent are its features found in Calvinism, Methodism, etc.

However, while conceptual constructs in social science derive from subjective points of view,

> In the mode of their *use* . . . the investigator is obviously bound by the norms of our thought just as much here as elsewhere. For scientific truth is precisely what is *valid* for all who seek the truth.[5]

What Weber has in mind here are the canons of logical consistency, care in the use of evidence, and publication of sources, which are the institutionalised bases of all scientific knowledge. At the same time, however, he suggests that without a prior value commitment the validity of the social science project cannot be defended. Thus, while we cannot sustain the empiricist belief that reality is reflected in our concepts, nevertheless an ideal type that is merely the 'creation of fantasy', remote from objective possibility, will be of little use in empirical research.

The ideal type is central to Weber's attempt at causal analysis. He poses the question: what mental operations do we perform when we argue that one event is causally more important than another in determining a particular historical outcome. Weber draws on the example of the battle of Marathon between the Greeks and Persians, suggesting that the significance of the battle lies in the contention that it probably was significant in determining the subsequent course of Western history.[6] He is careful to point out that this does not mean that Western history would have been totally different had the battle not occurred, but that it would have been significantly different. Again, 'significant' in this context means in relation to certain selected aspects (via abstraction) of particular cultural events. Thus Marathon was significant in relation to the causal origins of aspects of Hellenistic culture which characterise the political and other institutions of modern Western Europe. How the battle is causally imputed as a 'significant event' involves the creation of ideal-type courses of events through what Weber terms 'thought experiments'. In the case of Marathon, its causal significance derives from the probability that if the outcome of the battle had been a Persian victory, then our knowledge of the ways in which Persians acted in relation to other subjugated peoples would suggest that certain aspects of Hellenistic culture would have been weakened in ways that might well have affected the course of Western history 'significantly'. The general implication of this argument is that the estimation of causal significance rests upon the construction of ideal types of alternative possibilities or counter factuals. This is the meaning of Weber's view that in respect of both the conceptualisation of events and their causal explanation we must create unreal events in order to study real ones.

An uneasy synthesis between subjectivism and empiricism emerges in Weber's work. This is the product of a form of analysis which although based on the constituting operations of subjectivity, achieves 'objectivity' as a result of the operation of the canons of scientific method rather than a direct confrontation with empirical reality. Weberian methodology never allows the observer to encounter the empirical world directly — the traditional hope of the empiricist. Rather it provides the observer with a means of estimating the extent to which his unreal idealisations have grasped aspects of events, through systematic historical research. The problem remains, however, that while Weber is aware that history is not comprised of pre-given data but is constituted by the historian, he sometimes does appear to countenance the possibility of directly confronting 'real events'.

Weber regards the relations between ideal types and concrete reality as including the possibility that items within an ideal type will reflect aspects of reality. For example, when studying belief systems such as Calvinism, in so far as various aspects of such beliefs are explicitly formulated by a religious thinker or organisation, they may be drawn on directly in forming ideal-typical constructs by the observer. Thus our *own* conceptual imaginations in forming ideal types are heightened to the extent to which the main principles of an ideology 'have either only very imperfectly or not at all been raised to the level of explicit consciousness, or at least not have taken the form of explicitly elaborated complexes of ideas'.[7]

The problems and strains that emerge in Weber's work as a result of this tension between the dual strategies of subjectivism and empiricism become the starting-point of the critique of Weber's project developed by the more thoroughgoing subjectivism of phenomenology. Weber's debts to empiricism are expressed in two aspects of his methodology. First, they are expressed in his argument that the procedures of scientific verification and the logic of historical explanation prevent a drift into subjectivist fantasy. Second, his nominalist position involves the claim that value-selection and abstraction create one-sided models of social events which can provide useful tools of analysis, but that these should not be mistaken for reality. This ideal-typical procedure can be applied to particular types of social relation, such as charismatic authority. It can be applied to holistic models of social structure, such as 'rational bourgeois capitalism', and it can even be applied to developmental schemes, such as the 'rationalisation of the West'. But in all cases he presents us with 'conceptual utopias' devised by the investigator for specific purposes. Such a procedure involves an absolute rejection of the view that these concepts refer to some underlying reality of history; thus it is a rejection of any Marxist developmentalism which conceives of real societies developing through feudalism, capitalism and socialism. There are no 'key factors' of history. In short, there is no way in which social reality could be deduced from the conceptual models we apply to it.

Subjectivity and social life

In Weber's methodology, then, social structure is always constituted through the ideal types of the historical observer. However, the raw materials of these types — historical events — are not equivalent to the events studied by the natural sciences; they are meaningful. They arise out of the courses of social action undertaken by individual human subjects. Weber's analysis of historical events as social actions, and of structures emerging from courses of action, provides a further context for his synthesis of the disparate sociological traditions of subjectivism and empiricism. Just as the historical observer engages in subjective selection from the events of history, so those events are made up of actors' interpretations and meanings. In the social sciences, therefore, the observer enters into a meaningful dialogue with the subject-matter itself. It is an interpretative process. However, Weber's debt to empiricism remains, in so far as his view of history as made up of meaningful acts is modified by the claim that such social acts take place under conditions of scarcity, and that interpretation of meaning cannot be dissociated from the empirical observation of human behaviour. Through such claims Weber distances himself from the pure subjectivism that was to be taken up by phenomenology.

Weberian interpretative sociology is, therefore, rooted not simply in the constitutive operations of the observer but in the relationship between these operations and the meaningful acts he is attempting to explain. The possibility of an 'objective' analysis of these subjective meanings lies in Weber's conception of the instrumental rationality of human action — its means end character — which is present, he argues, in a heightened form in modern capitalist societies, dominated as they are by technical reason.[8] For Weber, the act of understanding action presupposes the investigator's ability to place meanings in context: that is, contexts that are sufficiently close to the observer's own way of thinking to make sense. It is in modern 'rational' societies, where instrumental action is transparent to the observer's understanding, that Weber's ideal types are of especial explanatory significance.

Crucial to the process of understanding is the fact that human action is motivated. Such motivations are potentially objects of self-consciousness — we are able to reflect on why we and others act in particular ways — and this consciousness provides a basis for the systematic analysis of action in the form of chains or interconnected systems of practical reasoning. Implicit in this concept of action is the actor's capacity to choose between various means in order to achieve given ends. It is this possibility of human choice that, for Weber, explains the basis of human 'free will', and explains why human action is never fully determined, and why history is an open-ended sequence of events — human behaviour is not reducible to the material conditions of action. However, far from such freedom of action leading to the conclusion that human action is not amenable to the logic of scientific rationality or calculation, Weber claims the reverse is the case, for the motivated means–end character of action links it indissolubly with rationality and calculability. The very texture of our commonsense understanding of social relationships depends on the concept of rational action, which is, in turn, a condition of orderly social existence, including the planning of one's actions in relation to others.

The means–end character of action makes it susceptible to ideal-type analysis, argues Weber, and he distinguishes four basic types of action, although only two are clearly genuine examples of rationality as he understands the term.[9] First, *purposive rational action* involves the self-conscious assessment of the probable outcomes of a number of strategies available to the actor, in terms of some calculus of costs and benefits. Second, *value-rational action* involves the single-minded pursuit of a paramount goal no matter what the consequences for other goals, which are, therefore, marginal with respect to the organisation of an actor's resources. Both types are regarded as rational because they involve conscious planning of the use of resources in pursuit of ends. It must be remembered here that the availability of resources is important for Weber's analysis, for his interpretative sociology is firmly rooted in a context of the scarcity of material and cultural resources. Action is always conceived of, therefore, as occurring within variable resource contexts such as 'life-chances' in relation to a market, a context that informs his analysis of class action.

The other two types of action are marginal to the concept of rationality and are not, therefore, strictly speaking, types of action at all. Weber's type of *traditional action* refers to an unthinking obedience to the demands of custom or habit. It is marginal because its 'unthinkingness' renders it opaque to an observer who wishes to make it an object of his understanding. It is an orientation to social norms rather than a process of practical reasoning. Finally, *affectual action*, which is even more marginal to rationality, involves a behavioural response to emotive states. Such action can be simply illustrated by contrasting a 'blink' with a 'wink'. Depending on the social context, a wink may be part of a chain of purposive or value-rational actions; it may denote an informal understanding in the course of a business meeting or initiate a sexual encounter; whereas a blink does not involve such social significance, except where it is misinterpreted.

Concrete actions are constituted by complex combinations of these ideal types, and this confronts Weber with the problem of how we are to use the ideal type in the analysis of such reality. Part of this problem involves, for Weber, relating the 'direct' subjective meaning of action to a broader context of meaning. By 'direct understanding' Weber refers to the immediate comprehension of an action, such as understanding a grimace of pain, or understanding that the numerical calculation 2 x 2 = 4. Such meanings may be further understood by placing them in a broader context in which their performance makes sense. For example, the grimace of pain may be meaningful within the context of a legally regulated system of corporal punishment, while the numerical calculation may have significance within the context of capitalist accounting procedures such as double-entry book-keeping.

Weber's notion of direct understanding here, raises again the main tension in his work — the attempt to synthesise subjectivism and empiricism. Weber grapples with the difficult problem of how the meaning of an action can be grasped without at the same time understanding the context in which it *makes* sense. Weber's attempt to combine empiricist procedures with interpretative understanding in this case appears to lead to the empiricist conclusion that meaning can be *first* directly observed and then contextualised. As we shall see below, a fully subjectivist strategy would stand on the principle that all meaning is contextual and that any departure from such a principle involves a collapse into empiricist error.

A second problem relating to the use of the ideal types of action is how they can be used in the *explanation* of a course of action. In effect, how does Weber adjudicate between competing plausible accounts of the 'real' meaning of a course of action? While, for Weber, the reasons actors give for their actions are an important component of the causal analysis of such action, there is no principled reason why these actors' accounts should be preferred to those of the observer's interpretation. For just as Weber argues that inequalities in the distribution of means are a constraint upon the realisation of meaningful acts, so too does he emphasise that actors are often unaware of the 'real' reason for their actions. On the other hand, actions that appear to an observer to be identical may have quite different meanings from the point of view of the actors. Also, motives and meanings may be mixed complexly in respect of particular courses of action. How, then, can the observer be reasonably sure that his account is an adequate one?

Weber offers two related procedures: adequacy at the level of reasoning, and causal adequacy. [10] Given the constraints imposed by our own position in historical space and time, he suggests that we may grasp meaning adequately at the first level if we are able to reconstruct the *rules* of, or 'ways of going about', the activity that interests us. The construction of these rules will involve repeated recourse to examples in order to finally grasp a typical complex of meanings: i.e. we must repeatedly observe the rules in operation. The limitation on such a procedure is that certain 'rules' will escape us if they are beyond 'our habitual modes of thought and feeling'.

Causal adequacy refers to establishing the conditions under which a particular course of conduct or action will or will not actually take place. If we take the example of 'shooting in self-defence', using Weberian procedures, we would first develop a set of criteria or rules through a process of repeated observation, so generating a typical meaning complex of 'self defence'. The determination of causal adequacy would once again involve placing this ideal type within a broader context, say the political and military situation in Northern Ireland, and considering the conditions that led to the person with the gun using it under specified circumstances.

Of central interest here is that Weber comes to the conclusion that meaning and motive can only in the end be determined adequately by recourse to the empirical, 'objective' events which are its context; the meaning can be found in the field of response or behaviour. The whole interpretative superstructure is undercut by recourse to direct empirical observation of the facts, as the procedure that clinches the determination of adequacy. Indeed, some critics have suggested that Weber's methodological concern with meaning and motive is best thought of as rather an elaborate means of generating useful hypotheses from which the observer can derive probabilistic statements about behaviour which are then subject to empirical test.[11] Such interpretations of Weber have the paradoxical consequence of marginalising the whole concern with meaning; it is no longer a distinguishing feature of the subject-matter of social science. Weber invites such interpretation of his work by seeking to make the analysis of motive as 'objective' as possible. Nevertheless, as we have seen, his central concern with the subjective nature of the social world would lead him to reject such interpretations.

Weber's attempt to construct a theoretical project that integrates a subjectivist view of social reality with a methodology constituting that reality as the subject-matter of an 'objective' science, is in the end indecisive. His efforts to place meaningful action in a context that includes the material conditions of action, lead to a conception of causal adequacy that would be regarded as unexceptional as a statement of empiricist epistemology. The case for subjectivism is undermined by Weber himself.

This drift toward objectivism does not, however, lead Weber to subordinate the meaningful act to *material* conditions of life; a feature of Marxist analysis that he rejected. For Weber, meanings were never to be conceived of as disembodied 'cultural values' but were accounts embodied in practical material life. What Weber sought to eradicate was a materialism which reduced ideas and values to a reflection of the material conditions of social existence. In his sociology of religion, for example, he was at pains to stress the association between material conditions and religious attachment, while also stressing the contingent character of that relationship.[12] He posits a connection between 'this worldly' ascetic religious beliefs and the conditions of life of an emergent, urban bourgeoisie. Protestant beliefs, he argued, provided a meaningful framework which had an affinity with the material position of these protocapitalist businessmen and manufacturers. However, not all such groups turn to such a form of religious belief as the appropriate symbolic expression of their material position; nor is it possible to deduce the existence of such beliefs from a knowledge of their material conditions. The affinity between beliefs and their material conditions is, therefore, in part, a *creative* process in which specific groups seek out meaningful explanations for their lives. The beliefs themselves are not spontaneously generated by the situation but have their own history of determinations, often arising in quite other contexts.

Weber, then, focusses on the interplay of meaning and conditions of action, and the concrete, contingent nature of that relation. In stressing that the properties of social structure are emergent out of concrete and contingent historical situations, Weber wishes to emphasise the creative aspect of human action. In this, Weber rejects any rationalist view of meaning as residing in 'mind' or 'culture' and expressing itself as a universal structure of rules. He would, therefore, reject the very possibility of completely describing the semantic structure of a language according to some analytical schema. The meaning-relations between words are not fixed by objective rules in some final way, but are the outcome of the genuinely creative activities of individuals in changing historical circumstances. Weber does not deny the structural properties of meaning; rather he suggests that these are emergent from the relations between actors in an historical process, which itself offers genuine opportunities for creative action.

Weber's attachment to such a view arises substantively in his work in the concept of charisma.[13] He defines charisma in terms of the way in which the personal qualities of an individual may be seen by others as in some way exceptional or even supernatural. Such qualities exist so long as the person concerned can sustain a belief in them among his followers. Weber argues that charisma can operate as a revolutionary force in human affairs, in so far as the charismatic individual is able to inspire his followers to break with established routines and in so doing found novel normative orders not on the basis of instrumental calculation but of moral inspiration. While suggesting that there are general preconditions for such charismatic eruptions, it follows that the emergence of a new normative order from such a source cannot be deduced from any structural theory of history or developmental scheme, neither of which can recognise the specific significance of a charismatic break with the past. In consequence such developmental schemes may only have a heuristic value for Weber, for history has no determinate structure other than that imposed on it by such schemes for the purposes of analysis. The concept of charisma is, then, a reminder that history is the contingent outcome of actors' interpretations and is not susceptible to explanation in terms of 'laws of development'.

Weber's analysis presents itself as a continuous attempt to establish an empirically contingent relationship between types of action, specified through a process of abstraction and selection, and actual, concrete courses of action. This process is clearly illustrated by his account of the relationship between class position and action.[14] The starting-point for Weber's analysis of class is the distribution of life-chances in the market. He employs the term 'class situation' as applying to the probability that a given state of (a) provision with goods, (b) external conditions of life, and (c) subjective satisfactions or frustrations, will be possessed by an individual or group. A class is, then, a group of persons whose shared life-chances cluster in terms of the differential distribution of chances or exploitable market chances, and on the basis of personal and social ties, over the course of several generations. Certain typical social actions may flow from such structural locations but these are contingent and not necessary effects — the actions of actual class actors are not predictable. As Weber argues:

> . . . the concept of class interest is an ambiguous one as soon as one understands by it something other than the factual direction of interests following with a certain probability for a certain average of those people subjected to the class situation. The class situation and other circumstances remaining the same, the direction in which the individual worker, for instance, is likely to pursue his interests may vary widely . . . The emergence of an association or even of more social action from a common class situation is by no means a universal phenomenon.[15]

Class situations are, then, positions upon which coherent class actions may be based, but the specific forms of these actions can in no way be deduced from a concept of class and its 'real interests' as is the case in some of the Marxist formulations to which Weber objected. The indeterminacy of the view that there are as many class situations as there are clusters of life-chances is reinforced by Weber's commitment to historical research founded in value orientations. The analyst may choose to focus on certain class situations and actions rather than others, because of their significance for a particular historical problem. Also, in an examination of the concepts of group, class, and interests, Weber rejects the 'misuse' of all collective concepts whereby the capacity to act is attributed to a collectivity. The individual, he argues, is the 'sole bearer of meaningful conduct'. The observer may legitimately focus on class interests only in so far as they are closely specified by the analytical constraints of a particular research problem, and only then if we remain aware of the great whirlpool of antagonistic and contradictory value relations which actually characterise concrete situations.

For Weber, social reality is 'doubly created' by the constructions of the historical observer's shifting value orientations and the meaningful acts of historical actors under conditions of scarcity. The nature of, and constraints on, social action can only be known from one-sided points of view. Such constraints (for example, the 'iron cage' of bureaucratised systems of domination in modern capitalism with its associated ethos of 'disenchantment' and instrumental rationality) relate to Weber's particular interpretation of history from the standpoint of the values of Western individualism, to which he subscribed and which he also regarded as under threat in the modern world.[16] For all Weber's emphasis on, and analysis of, objective institutional structures in his work, this objectivism — the tendency toward substantialism and rationalism — is undercut by his subjectivist understanding of the basis of social structure (rooted in social action) and sociological knowledge (value orientation and ideal types).

Indeed, Weber's historical sociology only escapes from the charge that it is no more than story-telling by subscribing to empiricist canons of proof and demonstration; in particular by drawing on John Stuart Mill's conception of causal explanation in science (as in the example of the battle of Marathon). Yet these canons are not seen as reflections of reality, but as values; a belief in which is a precondition for scientific work. A subjective and evaluative rather than a rational basis is given as a *raison d'être* for science. In addition Weber is not content with the empiricist concept of historical 'facts' — 'interpretation-free' data — yet we have seen he countenances such an idea in discussing how ideal types connect with reality, and more generally in his idea of 'direct understanding' of, for example, a grimace of pain.

Weber's subjectivism, the belief that social reality is the double creation of historical observer and actor, can and has been criticised from the point of view of the very subjectivist strategy in which his analysis is rooted. When Weber establishes his rules for the observer, and an analysis of social action that supposes that actors attach meaning to what they do, he takes for granted that the social world is *there* for both the observer and actor. He says little about how actors actually sustain the sense of an objective world 'out there'; what procedures they use. In addition, Weber presumes that the observer is outside such procedures, and can therefore devote his energies to constructing historical methodologies without enquiring how he *too*, along with everyone else, sustains a sense of that objective social world. It is Weber's failure to recognise the significance of such procedures for the construction of a subjectivist project that led to Schutz's critique of Weber; a critique that drew upon the arguments that Husserl had marshalled in rejecting all forms of objectivist social science.

4. M. Weber, *Methodology of the Social Sciences* (Glencoe, Ill.: Free Press, 1949) pp. 72–112; M. Weber, 'Science as a Vocation', in H. Gerth and C. W. Mills, *From Max Weber: Essays in Sociology* (London: Routledge & Kegan Paul, 1970) pp. 142–56.

5. Weber, *Methodology of the Social Sciences*, p. 84.

6. Ibid, pp. 171–6.

7. Ibid, p. 97.

8. M. Weber, *Economy and Society* (Berkeley: University of California Press, 1978) pp. 22–31; A. Giddens, *Positivism and Sociology* (London: Heinemann, 1974) pp. 23–31.

9. Weber, *Economy and Society*, pp. 24–6.

10. Ibid, pp. 8–22.

11. For example, T. Abel, 'The Operation Called Verstehen', *American Journal of Sociology*, 59, pp. 211-18.

12. Weber, *Economy and Society*, pp. 468–500.

13. Ibid, pp. 241–54, 1111–56.

14. Ibid, pp. 302-7, 926–39.

15. Ibid, pp. 928–9.

16. Max Weber, *The Protestant Ethic and the Spirit of Capitalism* (London: Allen & Unwin, 1968) pp. 24–8.

Economy and Society:
Marx, Historical Materialism
and Class Analysis

26. Preface to *A Contribution to the Critique of Political Economy*

Karl Marx

I examine the system of bourgeois economics in the following order: *capital, landed property, wage labour; state, foreign trade, world market*. Under the first three headings, I investigate the economic conditions of life of the three great classes into which modern bourgeois society is divided; the interconnection of the three other headings is obvious at a glance. The first section of the first book, which deals with capital, consists of the following chapters: 1. Commodities; 2. Money, or simple circulation; 3. Capital in general. The first two chapters form the contents of the present part. The total material lies before me in the form of monographs, which were written at widely separated periods, for self-clarification, not for publication, and whose coherent elaboration according to the plan indicated will be dependent on external circumstances.

I am omitting a general introduction which I had jotted down because on closer reflection any anticipation of results still to be proved appears to me to be disturbing, and the reader who on the whole desires to follow me must be resolved to ascend from the particular to the general. A few indications concerning the course of my own politico-economic studies may, on the other hand, appear in place here.

I was taking up law, which discipline, however, I only pursued as a subordinate subject along with philosophy and history. In the years 1842–3, as editor of the *Rheinische Zeitung*, I experienced for the first time the embarrassment of having to take part in discussions on so-called material interests. The proceedings of the Rhenish Landtag on thefts of wood and parcelling of landed property, the official polemic which Herr von Schaper, then *Oberpräsident* of the Rhine Province, opened again the *Rheinische Zeitung* on the conditions of the Moselle peasantry, and finally debates on free trade and protective tariffs provided the first occasions for occupying myself with economic questions. On the other hand, at that time when the good will "to go further" greatly outweighed knowledge of the subject, a philosophically weakly tinged echo of French socialism and communism made itself audible in the *Rheinische Zeitung*. I declared myself against this amateurism, but frankly confessed at the same time in a controversy with the *Allgemeine Augsburger Zeitung* that my previous studies did not permit me even to venture any judgement on the content of the French tendencies. Instead, I eagerly seized on the illusion of the managers of the *Rheinische Zeitung*, who thought that by a weaker attitude on the part of the paper they could secure a remission of the death sentence passed upon it, to withdraw from the public stage into the study.

The first work which I undertook for a solution of the doubts which assailed me was a critical review of the Hegelian philosophy of right[1], a work the introduction[2] to which appeared in 1844 in the *Deutsch-Französiche Jahrbücher*, published in Paris. My

Karl Marx: 'Preface' to *A CRITIQUE OF POLITICAL ECONOMY (1859)*. (Lawrence and Wishart, 1970), pp. 502-506.

investigation led to the result that legal relations as well as forms of state are to be grasped neither from themselves nor from the so-called general development of the human mind, but rather have their roots in the material conditions of life, the sum total of which Hegel, following the example of the Englishmen and Frenchmen of the eighteenth century, combines under the name of "civil society," that, however, the anatomy of civil society is to be sought in political economy. The investigation of the latter, which I began in Paris, I continued in Brussels, whither I had emigrated in consequence of an expulsion order of M. Guizot. The general result at which I arrived and which, once won, served as a guiding thread for my studies, can be briefly formulated as follows: In the social production of their life, men enter into definite relations that are indispensable and independent of their will, relations of production which correspond to a definite stage of development of their material productive forces. The sum total of these relations of production constitutes the economic structure of society, the real foundation, on which rises a legal and political superstructure and to which correspond definite forms of social consciousness. The mode of production of material life conditions the social, political and intellectual life process in general. It is not the consciousness of men that determines their being, but, on the contrary, their social being that determines their consciousness. At a certain stage of their development, the material productive forces of society come in conflict with the existing relations of production, or — what is but a legal expression for the same thing — with the property relations within which they have been at work hitherto. From forms of development of the productive forces these relations turn into their fetters. Then begins an epoch of social revolution. With the change of the economic foundation the entire immense superstructure is more or less rapidly transformed. In considering such transformations a distinction should always be made between the material transformation of the economic conditions of production, which can be determined with the precision of natural science, and the legal, political, religious, aesthetic or philosophic — in short, ideological forms in which men become conscious of this conflict and fight it out. Just as our opinion of an individual is not based on what he thinks of himself, so can we not judge of such a period of transformation by its own consciousness; on the contrary, this consciousness must be explained rather from the contradictions of material life, from the existing conflict between the social productive forces and the relations of production. No social order ever perishes before all the productive forces for which there is room in it have developed; and new, higher relations of production never appear before the material conditions of their existence have matured in the womb of the old society itself. Therefore mankind always sets itself only such tasks as it can solve; since, looking at the matter more closely, it will always be found that the task itself arises only when the material conditions for its solution already exist or are at least in the process of formation. In broad outlines Asiatic, ancient, feudal, and modern bourgeois modes of production can be designated as progressive epochs in the economic formation of society. The bourgeois relations of production are the last antagonistic form of the social process of production — antagonistic not in the sense of individual antagonism, but of one arising from the social conditions of life of the individuals; at the same time the productive forces developing in the womb of bourgeois society create the material conditions for the solution of that antagonism. This social formation brings, therefore, the prehistory of human society to a close.

Frederick Engels, with whom, since the appearance of his brilliant sketch on the criticism of the economic categories[3] (in the *Deutsch-Französische Jahrbücher),* I maintained a constant exchange of ideas by correspondence, had by another road (compare his *The Condition of the Working Class in England in 1844*) arrived at the same result as I, and when in the spring of 1845 he also settled in Brussels, we resolved to work out in common the opposition of our view to the ideological view of German philosophy, in fact, to settle accounts with our erstwhile philosophical conscience. The resolve was carried out in the form of a criticism of post-Hegelian philosophy[4]. The manuscript, two large octavo volumes, had long reached its place of publication in Westphalia when we received the news that altered circumstances did not allow of its being printed. We abandoned the manuscript to the gnawing criticism of the mice all the more willingly as we had achieved our main purpose — self-clarification. Of the scattered works in which we put our views before the public at that time, now from one aspect, now from another, I will mention only the *Manifesto of the Communist Party,* jointly written by Engels and myself, and *Discours sur le libre échange* published by me. The decisive points of our view were first scientifically, although only polemically, indicated in my work published in 1847 and directed against Proudhon: *Misère de la Philosophie,* etc. A dissertation written in German on *Wage Labour*[5], in which I put together my lectures on this subject delivered in the Brussels German Workers' Society, was interrupted, while being printed, by the February Revolution and my consequent forcible removal from Belgium.

The editing of the *Neue Rheinische Zeitung* in 1848 and 1849, and the subsequent events, interrupted my economic studies which could only be resumed in the year 1850 in London. The enormous material for the history of political economy which is accumulated in the British Museum, the favourable vantage point afforded by London for the observation of bourgeois society, and finally the new stage of development upon which the latter appeared to have entered with the discovery of gold in California and Australia, determined me to begin afresh from the very beginning and to work through the new material critically. These studies led partly of themselves into apparently quite remote subjects on which I had to dwell for a shorter or longer period. Especially, however, was the time at my disposal curtailed by the imperative necessity of earning my living. My contributions, during eight years now, to the first English-American newspaper, the *New York Tribune,* compelled an extraordinary scattering of my studies, since I occupy myself with newspaper correspondence proper only in exceptional cases. However, articles on striking economic events in England and on the Continent constituted so considerable a part of my contributions that I was compelled to make myself familiar with practical details which lie outside the sphere of the actual science of political economy.

This sketch of the course of my studies in the sphere of political economy is intended only to show that my views, however they may be judged and however little they coincide with the interested prejudices of the ruling classes, are the result of conscientious investigation lasting many years. But at the entrance to science, as at the entrance to hell, the demand must be posted:

Qui si convien lasciare ogni sospetto;
Ogni viltà convien che qui sia morta.[6]

Notes

1. K. Marx, *Contribution to the Critique of Hegel's Philosophy of Right.*

2. K. Marx, *Contribution to the Critique of Hegel's Philosophy of Right. Introduction* (see Marx and Engels, *On Religion*, Moscow, 1962, pp. 41–58).

3. F. Engels, *Outlines of a Critique of Political Economy* (see K. Marx, *Economic and Philosophic Manuscripts of 1844*, Moscow, 1959, pp. 175–209).

4. Marx and Engels, *The German Ideology.*

5. K. Marx, *Labour and Capital.*

6. Here all mistrust must be abandoned and here must perish every craven thought. [Danke, *The Divine Comedy*].

27. Marx and the Critique of Political Economy

David Lee and Howard Newby

Among all the major founding fathers of modern sociology there are, by general agreement, three who stand out — Marx, Weber and Durkheim. The following three parts will deal with each of these in turn. We will describe the main ideas of each author and at the same time give some indication of their continuing relevance to the analysis of contemporary social problems.

In this chapter we will introduce the first of the three: Karl Marx. Because of the voluminous nature of Marx's writings, and also because of the intrinsic importance of his work, we shall take two chapters to give even a modest outline of his theories. In a third we shall attempt to apply some of his insights to the analysis of inequality in modern Britain.

We hope we need hardly stress the importance of Marxist thought in the modern world. Karl Marx is probably the single most influential figure in the history of ideas since Jesus Christ. Today hundreds of millions of people live in societies which bear an allegiance, however nominal this may be, to the system of political ideas which bears his name. This indicates that Marx was, of course, much more than a sociologist. Indeed to call him a sociologist would be in many ways to trivialize his thought. Marx developed a body of ideas and theory which encompass the whole of the social sciences and the humanities. Marx's thought is therefore an 'ism' — a systematic doctrine of ideas and, not least, a moral guide to *action*. Marx paid no heed to the irrelevant artificialities of disciplinary boundaries. His work encompasses philosophy, economics, politics, sociology and history. Its intellectual power and its intuitive appeal lie partly in the fact that it offers such a *total* world-view. Its scope is therefore enormous and its complexity is immense. It was developed over four decades in response to changing social and political conditions in Europe and it is not, therefore, an easy or glib philosophy which can be reduced to a few easily grasped nostrums. Moreover, Marxism has developed a language which has to be understood before the full significance of Marx's ideas can be assimilated.

In this part, therefore, we can only introduce Marx's writings in a very sketchy way. We shall be offering not only an introduction to, but also a commentary on, Marx — a few edited highlights and after-the-event summaries, and no more. Those readers who are already politically committed Marxists will have to excuse the superficiality of this. And those who, by contrast, are totally unfamiliar with Marx must *not* take our interpretation — any more than anyone else's — as gospel. The interpretations of Marx's thought are legion and some of them are mischievously misleading. It is *always* better, wherever possible, to read Marx in the original and make one's own judgement,

David Lee and Howard Newby: 'Marx and the Critique of Political Economy' in *THE PROBLEM OF SOCIOLOGY: AN INTRODUCTION TO THE DISCIPLINE* (Hutchinson, 1983), pp. 113-123. Reproduced by permission of Routledge.

rather than rely on someone else's (including ours). This is important not only in a purely academic sense, but because different interpretations of Marx have very different political implications — as any superficial perusal of those societies which are organized politically according to the application of Marxist principles will make clear.

Historical materialism

We shall begin our discussion of Marx by outlining the methodological basis of Marxist theory — historical materialism.

Marx refused to recognize the distinction between what we now label as 'philosophy' and 'sociology'. He believed, like most other nineteenth-century social thinkers, that philosophy and sociology constituted a single field of enquiry. On the one hand philosophy provided a conceptual framework for the investigation of society, while on the other sociological enquiry helped to resolve some philosophical problems which would otherwise be intractable for as long as we relied upon what Marx calls 'speculative reason'. For Marx, the two are inseparable. The investigation of society could never be a uniquely empirical matter of gathering 'facts', for 'facts' only make sense in relation to the presuppositions made within a body of *theory*. In other words, as in any science, the 'science of society' rests upon the sort of concepts that are used, what they mean and how they stand in relation to one another *as much as* the evidence which we collect. Conversely, Marx believed that as long as questions like, 'What is human motive?', and, 'What is society?', were dealt with purely speculatively (that is, without *any* empirical substantiation whatsoever) then there would be no solution to them. Marx is insistent (along with other classical sociologists) that a true 'science of society' cannot be allowed to descend into mere metaphysics. Marx, of all the nineteenth-century sociological theorists, was not going to surrender sociology to mere armchair theorizing.

For this reason, among others, Marx refuted the philosophical tradition of *idealism*, which had been most influentially expounded by the German philosopher, Hegel, in the eighteenth century. Idealism was an attempt to explain the nature of society in terms of the development of human consciousness, of 'ideas'. For Hegel society was guided by, and had limits placed on its development by, the human 'spirit' (or *Geist*), a kind of quintessence of, and abstraction from, human culture. This 'spirit' was — literally — meta-physical. But where, Marx asked, does this 'spirit' come from? And how could Hegel's claims be substantiated? Neither Hegel nor any other idealist philosopher could, Marx believed, satisfactorily answer these kinds of questions. Their statements were matters of pure metaphysical speculation which could not be investigated scientifically. So Marx, in his early work, in a famous phrase 'turned Hegel on his head'. Ideas, Marx argued, were a *product* of society rather than the other way round. And this simple inversion of Hegel is the starting-point for Marx's historical materialism. For Marx, the doctrine of historical materialism enabled society to be studied empirically and scientifically, rather than speculatively and by purely metaphysical deduction.

This 'Hegelian inversion' was not a new 'discovery' of Marx. The German philosopher, Feuerbach, had already made this criticism of Hegel. It was Marx's brilliant contribution to develop the implications of Feuerbach's critique in his work, *The*

268

German Ideology, which Marx wrote between 1845 and 1847. As in so many other of his theoretical writings, however, Marx took the ideas of a very heterodox group of writers — Scottish political economists, English political philosophers, French 'physiocrats', German philosophers — reworked and developed them with wonderful facility and produced something that was entirely and uniquely Marxist. In *The German Ideology* Marx combined Feuerbach's critique of Hegel with the work of the French utopian socialist, Claude de Saint-Simon, whom we have already encountered in [Chapter 2]. Marx shared Saint-Simon's basic assumption that *the* most fundamental aspect of human existence is the absolute necessity to *produce* the means of subsistence (initially food and shelter). It is the most fundamental aspect of human existence because the production of the means of subsistence is prior to *all* other human activities. Unless a society is able to organize the production of its subsistence needs there would be no society at all. Hence, according to Marx, the way production is organized determines human existence *in the last analysis*. (The latter qualification is, as we shall see, very important.) Ideas, consciousness, culture, the 'spirit: all are in the last analysis dependent upon the prior capacity of societies to organize the production of the means of their subsistence. Hegel's idealism as a philosophy of human history is therefore inverted by Marx to become his *historical materialism*.

There is a further aspect of historical materialism which needs to be emphasized at this point. Marx not only believed that the way in which production is organized accounts for all the other facets of society. He also argued strongly that this productive activity is impossible without human beings entering into relationships with other human beings. The isolated individual producer, who, as we have seen, was much admired by the utilitarians like Adam Smith, was, Marx believed, a figment of their imagination. Humans were never anything other than *social* beings and in order to overcome the forces of nature they entered into relationships with one another. Work — that is, production — is therefore always a collective social activity. Individuals produce only by cooperating and mutually exchanging their products. Thus the social world is created by interacting productive individuals and the science of society is the study of this process. Therefore an analysis of what Marx calls the 'mode of production' is where an analysis of society must begin. Hence, Marx's philosophy of history is called materialism.

The base/superstructure distinction

The considerations which inform Marx's historical materialism lead him to enunciate his famous distinction between the 'base' and the 'superstructure' of society. The base is the sum total of what we might loosely call the productive activities of society or the 'mode of production.' It is, in the broadest possible sense, the sphere of economic relationships. The superstructure consists of the cultural ideas, or 'ideological' aspects, of society (including politics and the law), The superstructure is, *in the last analysis*, determined by the base.

This base/superstructure distinction lies at the heart of Marx's sociology. It is something which is entirely distinctive about Marx's contribution to sociological theory and is therefore an approach which is uniquely Marxist. Marx himself refers to the base/superstructure distinction as the 'guiding thread for my studies'. Partly as a consequence it is a distinction which is surrounded by intense controversy, as much within Marxism as outside. This is what Marx himself had to say about it in two frequently cited passages:

> In the social production of their life, men enter into definite relations that are indispensable and independent of their will, relations of production which correspond to a definite stage of development of their material productive forces. The sum total of these relations of production constitutes the economic structure of society, the real foundation on which rises a legal and political superstructure and to which correspond definite forms of social consciousness. The mode of production of material life conditions the social, political and intellectual life process in general. It is not the consciousness of men that determines their being, but, on the contrary, their social being that determines their consciousness. (Marx 1975, p. 452)

> The specific economic form, in which unpaid surplus is pumped out of direct producers, determines the relationship of rulers and ruled, as it grows directly out of production itself and, in turn, reacts upon it as a determining element. Upon this, however, is founded the entire formation of the economic community which grows out of the productive relations themselves, thereby simultaneously its specific political form. It is always the direct relationship of the owners of the conditions of production to the direct producers — a relation always naturally corresponding to a definite stage in the development in the methods of labour and thereby its social productivity — which reveals the innermost secret, the hidden basis of the entire social structure, and with it the political form of the relation of sovereignty and dependence, in short, the corresponding specific form of the state. (Marx 1972, p. 791)

For such an important element in Marx's theory, it is a pity that his own writings on the base/superstructure distinction are so tantalizingly obscure — although, it should be added, he himself attached no particular significance to these passages; this has been confirmed by subsequent scholars. In the first passage, for example, *precisely* what does Marx mean by his statement that the mode of production 'conditions' social, political and intellectual life? Does he mean 'causes', 'determines', 'reflects', 'places limits on', 'specifies', or what? What, for that matter, does the phrase, guiding thread for my studies' signify? Does it mean that Marx regards the base/superstructure distinction as absolutely crucial or merely a handy metaphor?

Questions like these have been a source of lively (to put it mildly) debate within Marxism since Marx's death. If Marx meant that the base *determines* or *causes* the superstructure this would amount to a theory of *economic determinism* — that all social, political and intellectual development is caused by economic changes and even that all human action is economically motivated. Since this is patently not true the charge of economic determinism has long been something of an embarrassment to Marxism. But note that Marx also states that forms of 'social consciousness' merely 'correspond' to the economic structure — that is, there is an affinity but not necessarily a direct relationship of cause and effect. As these ambiguities began to be debated after Marx's death, his collaborator, Friedrich Engels, attempted to clarify matters in a letter written in 1894:

> Political, juridical, philosophical, religious, literary, artistic, etc, development is based on economic development. But all these react upon one another and also upon the economic basis. It is not that the economic situation is *cause, solely active*, while everything else is only passive effect. There is, rather, interaction on the basis of economic necessity, which *ultimately* always asserts itself. . . . So it is not as people try here and there conveniently to imagine that the economic situation produces an automatic effect. No. Men make their history themselves, only they do so in a given environment, which conditions them, and so on the basis of actual relations already existing, among which economic relations, however much they may be influenced by the other — the political and ideological relations — are still ultimately the decisive ones, forming the keynote which runs through everything and alone leads to understanding

Engels's interpretation is one which has subsequently received widespread acceptance. Engels is trying to draw a careful distinction between historical materialism and economic determinism. He is arguing that the base is only *ultimately* determinant — or, as we emphasized above, determinant *in the last analysis*. This does *not* mean that *at any particular point in time* the whole of social life is economically determined or that everyone is guided by economic motives in their actions. Indeed Marx himself regarded the latter as a trivialization of his views, scolding his 'Marxist' followers who had adopted this interpretation by telling them, 'Je ne suis pas un Marxiste' ('I am not a Marxist'). For Marx such 'economic reductionism' was *not* historical materialism and neither was Marxism a dehumanizing theory which reduced all individuals to economic automata and denied them any free will.

What Marx did mean, then, was that, viewed historically, the laws which governed the development of society were *ultimately* determined by material productive forces. Human beings did *not* have complete freedom of action to create a society based solely on their own ideas. This freedom of action was always constrained within certain limits by the level of development of the mode of production. It was this to which Marx was referring in his famous statement that:

> Men make their own history, but not under circumstances of their own choosing.

There are certain ascertainable laws — material laws — of social development that provide limits upon what individuals can achieve on the basis of ideas. *The base is restrictive, not prescriptive.*

It should already be apparent that historical materialism rides roughshod over some of the most cherished assumptions of liberal individualism. According to Marx individuals do not possess complete freedom of action — indeed, taking the long-term historical view this is quite severely circumscribed by forces beyond their individual control. Even Engels's attempt at a helpful clarification does not entirely remove the

271

taint of economic reductionism, for at times it looks merely like a 'sooner-or-later' kind of argument: superstructural factors may have a transient importance, but sooner or later the base will determine the nature of social development. Numerous critics of Marx have found this a depressing and dehumanizing philosophy of history, and by no means all of them have been unsympathetic to the political ideals of Marxism. The problem is that to call into question the base/superstructure distinction and the determinacy of the base in the last analysis tends to result in a sanitized version of Marxism which is less distinctively Marxist. On the other hand, attempts to assert the centrality of the base/superstructure distinction, while preserving the distinctive contribution of a Marxist sociology, lay the theory open to the charge of economic determinism.

This argument can be illustrated by referring, very schematically and somewhat over-simplistically, to two 'schools' of Marxist thought which have received considerable attention in the twentieth century.

Humanist Marxism

The so-called 'humanist' Marxists tend to deny the importance of the base/superstructure distinction. They believe that Marx used it as a metaphor and little more. Humanist Marxists tend to emphasize the libertarian aspects of Marx's writings — specifically Marx's analysis of the dehumanizing consequences of the rise of a capitalist society. They are concerned with Marxism as a *method* of analysing and transcending this dehumanization, thereby opening up the possibility of liberating the true productive potential of humanity through political 'praxis' (the unity of theory and action). In particular humanist Marxists pay attention to Marx's writings on *alienation*.

Alienation refers to the process, endemic to capitalism, whereby the products of human labour become expropriated from and appear as opposed — 'alien' — to those who produce them. Workers, indeed, not only become alienated from the products of their labour, but from the labour process itself, from each other and ultimately from themselves. The emphasis placed upon Marxist analysis as a means of enabling workers to overcome their alienation is what designates those who subscribe to this interpretation of Marx as 'humanist' Marxists. Their adoption of Marx's analysis is in order to develop further his critique of the dehumanizing aspects of capitalism. They regard too great an emphasis on the base/superstructure distinction as leading to an equally dehumanizing form of Marxism.

The most polemical of the humanist Marxists was the Hungarian philosopher and critic George Lukacs, especially in his 1934 work *History and Class Consciousness* (1971). Others have included Antonio Gramsci, the founder of the Italian Communist Party, and more recently the historian E. P. Thompson, whose essay *The Poverty of Theory* (1978) is a polemic against recent anti-humanist interpretations of Marx (see below).

Scientific Marxism

This is associated with the French philosopher Louis Althusser and has been extremely influential in the decade after 1968. Scientific Marxists emphasize the capacity of

Marx's theory to be truly scientific. They regard humanism as an ideology and therefore 'unscientific'. They acknowledge the existence of Marx's early writings on alienation but attribute this to an immature flirtation with humanistic ideology. They argue that an important 'break' occurred in Marx's work around 1844: thereafter Marx became less concerned with alienation and more concerned with *exploitation* (see Althusser 1969). The exploitation of workers can be measured objectively and, moreover, is not based upon speculative notions concerning the essence of humanity. It consists of the value of the productive activity of workers — or their 'labour power' — which is not retained by them but is taken away and retained by another individual or group. Scientific Marxists argue that as Marx moved away from a concern with alienation to this new 'problematic' of how a proportion of the value of labour power ('surplus value') is removed and retained by non-labourers, so he developed a truly scientific form of historical materialism.

It follows from this that scientific Marxists pay particular attention to the economic 'base' where these exploitative mechanisms are located. It is the 'mode of production' which is given primacy over all elements of the superstructure. While superstructural elements like politics or ideology are granted a degree of 'relative autonomy', it is the 'mode of production' which determines the level of social development. It therefore becomes crucial to define the 'mode of production' in a manner which leaves it untainted by superstructural elements and, *ipso facto*, to draw a clear line between 'base' and 'superstructure'. Thus, for scientific Marxists the base/superstructure distinction is of paramount importance — it renders Marxism a scientifically valid method of analysis.

Scientific Marxists thus shift the emphasis in Marx's work 'from alienation to surplus value'. In doing so they leave themselves open to the charge of economic determinism and although they would hotly deny this, much recent Marxist debate has involved attempts by scientific Marxists to extricate themselves from this accusation. Simultaneously, in placing so much emphasis on the 'mode of production' or 'base' they have been forced to seek a definition which does not risk superstructural contamination. As we shall now see, this has not been easy.

The mode of production

What actually constitutes the 'mode of production' which forms the base? As the preceding section has already indicated this also tends to be a vexed issue among Marxist scholars, partly because Marx himself was never entirely clear or consistent in what he meant by it. The term itself comes from Adam Smith and, like him, Marx occasionally uses the term very loosely to describe 'how people make things'. This loose meaning can, however, cause confusion. For example, people make things by using tools or machinery — 'the instruments of labour' — which may or may not be defined as their 'property'. Property relationships are clearly part of the mode of production, therefore, for they literally help to define 'how people make things'. Yet 'property' is also a legal matter — and therefore part of the ideological superstructure of society. Can a rigid division between base and superstructure therefore be maintained and with it a clear definition of the mode of production? As we have seen this is clearly important if one takes a view of Marx's work which states that what is uniquely scientific about it is the base/superstructure distinction.

Consequently recent Marxist scholars, especially Althusser, have attempted to offer a much more specific definition of the mode of production. For them the mode of production consists of the following:

1. The *forces* of production — this refers to broader historical factors in the development of human knowledge which can be applied to productive activity. For example, the growth of science and technology would constitute forces of production which have in turn determined the development of new means of production.

2. The forces of production also include the *means* of production — broadly speaking the tools and machines which people use in order to produce, or the 'instruments of labour'.

3. Social *relations* of production — the way in which the labour process is socially organized.

Scattered through Marx's later work, and especially in *Capital*, there are passages where this schema can be clearly discerned. The general argument is that as the forces of production constantly develop, so the means of production are improved and the social relations of production are constantly changed. Human inventiveness grows and expands as people rise to the challenges inherent in the conquest of nature and the pressure of circumstances which have been handed down through history. New means of production, such as the change in the late eighteenth century from water power to steam power, promote new relations of production, such as the change from handicraft to the factory system, and it is the contradiction between the means of production and the social relations of production which eventually brings about the transformation of the entire *mode* of production.

Marx's theory is therefore a *dynamic* one. He is less concerned to offer a static description of any particular mode of production than to offer a theory of how it changes and is eventually superseded. Marx offers a theory of social development and change rather than a theory of what society is. This, as we have seen in previous chapters, was a common nineteenth-century concern. And in common with many of his contemporaries, Marx accepted the idea that societies develop through an evolutionary process — evolution in Marx's case meaning the progressive human domination over the forces of nature.

But the *logic* of evolutionary development was quite different to the theories we discussed in [Chapter 5]. The logic of evolution was of a kind which Marx took from Hegel — the *dialectic*. Marx may have 'turned Hegel on his head' by rejecting Hegelian idealism, but he retained Hegel's analytical method. The dialectic is therefore Marx's *method* of analysis. The Hegelian notion of the dialectic holds that all matter (or the *thesis*) always and inevitably creates its own opposite (or *antithesis*). From the contradiction between thesis and antithesis there emerges a transformation which becomes the new thesis, which creates its own antithesis, and so on. *Change therefore results from contradiction* — and, in the case of human social development, human attempts to overcome contradiction.

This dialectical scheme is applied by Marx to his analysis of the mode of production. The mode of production contains inherent contradictions which produce its transformation and ensure the continuity of social evolution. Here is Marx using this dialectical method in another famous passage from his *Preface to the Critique of Political Economy*:

> At a certain stage of their development the material productive forces of society come in conflict with the existing relations of production. . . . From forms of development of the productive forces these relations turn into their fetters. Then begins an epoch of social revolution. With the change of the economic foundation the entire immense superstructure is more or less rapidly transformed. (Marx 1975, pp. 425-6)

So the focal point of Marx's thought is the dialectic between the material world and people in society. People progressively subordinate the material world to their purposes but in so doing transform those purposes and generate new needs which require a transformation of their relationships to the material world — and so on. Thus a level of material development which began as liberatory turns into a constraint — 'a fetter' — which must be overcome. In other words, one mode of production which, in the historical evolution of mankind, was once emancipatory must be itself transformed in order to ensure the continuation of the evolutionary process.

Thus, history is divided by Marx into separate epochs (albeit with periods of transition in between), according to the dominant mode of production in each. These are in chronological order:

(a) primitive communism (or tribal society);
(b) ancient society (based upon slavery);
(c) feudalism;
(d) capitalism; and eventually
(e) socialism.

(Later Marx also added an 'Asiatic mode of production' which emerged out of tribal societies in the Orient.)

Each epoch is marked by a distinctive mode of production and the transition from one to the next is marked by a social revolution and the transformation of productive relationships. Marx, however, devoted most of his attention to capitalism. His interest in pre-capitalist modes of production was somewhat perfunctory and even his writings on socialism were sketchy and somewhat utopian. Nevertheless Marx regarded capitalism as merely one stage in the evolutionary development of mankind. Just as it had emerged out of the contradictions inherent in feudalism, so capitalism was doomed by its own eventual contradictions. Such teleology is now rather frowned upon among Marxist scholars, for, as we shall see in the [Chapter 16, (pp. 276ff.)], the philosophical foundations of teleological explanations are, to say the least, shaky. Nevertheless, the view that capitalism contained 'the seeds of its own destruction' was quite central to Marx's analysis. The development of capitalism, like all hitherto existing modes of production, would lead eventually to the revolutionary transformation of the entire society and its material base. How was this to occur? Through the social activity which is absolutely central to Marx's analysis of society: the class struggle.

Marxism and class analysis

It has become commonplace to remark that while Marx never developed a systematic analysis of class, it is nevertheless central to Marx and to Marxism. As Tom Bottomore has pointed out, all of Marx's writings were concerned with class, either implicitly or explicitly (Bottomore 1965. p. 17). Frustratingly, however, the manuscript of *Capital* breaks off at precisely the point at which Marx was beginning to set out in detail his theory of social class. So we are left to infer such a theory from the remainder of Marx's writings. Thus although the concept of class has become an indispensable component of sociological analysis, the precise meaning which Marx gives to it is by no means unambiguous. What is clear is the place of class, and the struggle between classes, in Marx's overall theoretical scheme. For classes perform a decisive function in the evolution of human history: it is through the class struggle that society transforms itself. Every significant social change is therefore related in one way or another to the class struggle. It is in this sense that Marx and Engels assert, in the opening sentence of *The Manifesto of the Communist Party*, that:

> The history of all hitherto existing society is the history of class struggles.
>
> (Marx and Engels 1969)

What, then, does Marx mean by the term 'class'? In order fully to appreciate his use of the concept, it is necessary first to understand that Marx employed it in two different ways — in a *theoretical*, *sociological* sense; and in a *descriptive*, *historical* sense.

Sociologically, class is defined as 'relation to the means of production' — although Marx himself never used these words (they are Lenin's). Classes, that is, are defined according to the positions which they occupy in the process of production. Under capitalism, for example, one class, the owners of the means of production, is the bourgeoisie: the other, which does *not* own the means of production, is the proletariat. These classes are fundamentally opposed to one another *because* of their different position within the mode of production. The bourgeoisie, as we have seen, *exploits* the proletariat by retaining part of the 'surplus value' of the production which the proletariat creates. Thus their different relationship to the means of production creates inherently antagonistic class interests. Moreover, class conflict occurs not only over the division between wages and profits, but over the labour process itself and the authority relations associated with it. It is this class struggle, then, which provides the driving force of social and economic development. Hence a sociological analysis of (capitalist) society is *reducible to* a class analysis: society can be explained by the variety of ways in which the class struggle manifests itself.

A number of important points follow from this schema which need to be considered in more detail:

1. First, it is important to note that this is a genuinely *sociological* usage of the concept of class by Marx. 'Class', in this context, refers to a *relationship* based upon the position occupied in the productive process. It is, by definition, an exploitative and an antagonistic relationship. Indeed what makes the relationship a *class* relationship is that it is based upon contradictory interests which stem from differing relations to the means of production.

2. It follows from this that no single 'class' can stand on its own. A class is forged out of its relationship (exploitative, antagonistic) with *another* class, to whose interests it is opposed. There can be no bourgeoisie without a proletariat and vice versa. A society in which there is only one 'class' is a society in which the concept of class is meaningless.

3. The implications of this line of reasoning go even further, however. Class, in this sociological sense, is used as an explanatory concept. Class *explains* the relationship between bourgeoisie and proletariat — and with it the nature of capitalist society. *Thus 'class' is not a group of people*. We could not possibly round up 'the proletarian class' or 'the working class' in some gigantic sports stadium and believe that we had observed 'class'. Class, in this sociological sense, is used as a theoretical *concept* in order to *explain* a certain kind of relationship regarded as central to the historical evolution of society.

4. Because class is here used in this conceptual sense, statements like 'the proletariat is a revolutionary class' are *theoretical*, and not empirical, statements. This does *not* mean that each and every proletarian is a revolutionary. Rather it means that it is the destiny of the proletariat to become the revolutionary class in the overthrow of capitalism, a role which it will assume when the contradictions in the capitalist mode of production cannot be resolved without their fundamental transformation.

It should now be possible to see how Marx is able to reduce a sociological analysis of society to a class analysis. Somewhat over-schematically, Marx's reasoning runs as follows. Class is an antagonistic relationship defined by the relation to the means of production. The ability of one class to exploit the other is to a large degree defined by the capacity of the exploited class to prevent it: hence the class struggle determines the development of the mode of production. Yet the mode of production, as the economic 'base' of society, is what in turn determines (in the last analysis) the superstructure. Thus the totality of society, and the pattern of its historical development, can be understood through an analysis of the class struggle.

We can now turn to the second meaning of 'class' which Marx employed — the purely *descriptive* sense. Here he used the term 'class' simply as a classificatory device — that is, he classified people like so many butterflies according to some relevant criterion, usually an economic characteristic such as income or wealth. Thus in *Revolution and Counter-Revolution in Germany*, Marx distinguishes seven classes — feudal landlords, the bourgeoisie, petty bourgeoisie, rich and middle peasants, poor peasants, the proletariat and the lumpenproletariat — and in *The Class Struggles in France* he refers to six. Here we *are* dealing with actual groups of people. These are simply listed as major social groups, the chief actors on the historical stage. Classes in this sense are bound to be numerous and their number will vary according to the historical situation which is being described. As the above list indicates these classes are to some extent merely subgroupings, or *fractions*, of the sociological classes referred to earlier in this section (bourgeoisie and proletariat): others may be transitional classes destined to become absorbed into one or other of the sociological classes; still others, such as the peasantry, seem to stand outside the major division between bourgeoisie and proletariat. One problem with Marx's writing on class — and one reason why the fact that *Capital* breaks off at this point is so tantalizing — is that it is not clear how class in this descriptive sense is reconcilable with class in the theoretical sense and we do not know how Marx would have tried to square the circle. It was fundamental to Marx's analysis of capitalism that in the final stages only two classes would remain — the bourgeoisie and the proletariat. Marx believed that all intermediate and transitional classes would disappear and that the class struggle would take this form.

Thus only in the period immediately prior to the revolutionary transformation of society would the two meanings of 'class' elide. Then the two contending classes would become polarized and the class struggle would become a naked conflict between two groups of people defined by their relation to the mode of production. Indeed the observation of a society in this polarized condition would lead one to conclude that a revolution was imminent. It goes without saying that most societies most of the time do not correspond to this form. The class struggle is not, therefore, always directly observable in this sense. For the most part, Marx invites us to look behind the multitude of social groupings and the confusing complexity of the social world in order to comprehend the underlying contradictions which will *eventually* produce a revolutionary transformation. Such a class analysis is therefore a gigantic gamble on the outcome of history. Marx's theory is vindicated not by a description of what society *is*, but by what society *will become*.

It is therefore in no way a test of Marx's theory to discover how many non-owners of the mean of production, *here and now*, recognize that they have interests opposed to the bourgeoisie, are exploited by them and are locked into a class struggle which will result in the overthrow of capitalism. It is fair to say, however, that Marx would regard such data as interesting indicators of how the class struggle was proceeding. In fact at one stage Marx even devised his own (unintentionally hilarious) questionnaire as the basis of an enquiry into the state of proletarian politics — or *enquête ouvrière* (see Bottomore and Rubel 1962). This is not to say then, that contemporary evidence is irrelevant to Marxism — for this would be tantamount to stating that Marxism is irrelevant to an understanding of contemporary society — but that its relevance is somewhat limited. Marxist theory legitimately abjures the narrowly immediate in favour of the broad historical sweep. The ambiguities in the concept of class derive in part from Marx's own attempts to describe existing social reality *and* explain the past and future course of social evolution.

Marx himself was not entirely unaware of this ambiguity. He proposed a twofold distinction:

1. A class-in-itself (*Klasse an sich*) — a class consisting of those people occupying the same relation to the means of production, irrespective of their acknowledgement or awareness of this. They are lacking in any common class identity, political mobilization or other ideological bonds.

2. A class-for-itself (*Klasse für sich*) — a fully fledged conscious class pursuing its own interests against those of the opposing class, aware of their common identity and organized politically.

The observable proliferation of classes, in the descriptive sense, was evidence of a low level of *class consciousness* and an indication of a class (in the sociological sense) existing merely 'in itself'. The key question, of course, was how a class in itself could be transformed into a class 'for itself' and thereby engender the evolutionary transformation from one mode of production to another. Marx never satisfactorily answered this question. In part the contradictions inherent in the mode of production would ensure these changes. Yet Marx was not prepared to regard them as inevitable. They had to be gained through conscious organization and struggle. Marxism has never been merely a desiccated alternative to classical economics — it has also been a rallying cry for political *action*. Capitalism, however, has endured. Does this mean that Marx's gamble on the outcome of history has failed? We can evaluate this question more thoroughly on the basis of Marx's own theory of capitalist development.

28. Historical Materialism
Anthony Giddens

The first fruit of Marx's association with Engels was the heavily polemical *The Holy Family*, which was begun in the latter part of 1844, and was published towards the end of 1845. The bulk of the book is the work of Marx, and it documents Marx's final break with the rest of the Young Hegelians. It was followed shortly afterwards by *The German Ideology*, written in 1845–6, also primarily a critical work, but one in which Marx for the first time outlines a general statement of the tenets of historical materialism. From this time onwards, Marx's general outlook changed little, and the rest of his life was devoted to the theoretical exploration and the practical application of the views set out in this latter work.

The full text of *The German Ideology* was not published in the lifetime of Marx or Engels. In 1859, looking back to the period at which *The German Ideology* was written, Marx wrote that he and Engels were not disappointed that they could not get the work published: they 'abandoned the work to the gnawing criticism of the mice all the more willingly', since the main purpose — 'self-clarification' — had been achieved.[1] Nonetheless, Marx explicitly refers to his 'Critique' of Hegel, and to the year 1844, as marking the most significant line of demarcation in his intellectual career. It was the analysis of Hegel's philosophy of the state, Marx wrote in his preface to *A Contribution to the Critique of Political Economy*, which led him to the conclusion 'that legal relations as well as forms of State are to be grasped neither from themselves nor from the so-called general development of the human mind (*Geist*), but rather are rooted in the material conditions of life'.[2]

Engels later remarked of *The German Ideology* that the exposition of the materialistic conception of history presented therein 'proves only how incomplete our knowledge of economic history still was at that time'.[3] But, although Marx's knowledge of economic history was indeed thin at this period — the scheme of 'stages' of the development of productive systems set out there was subsequently considerably overhauled — the account of historical materialism which is given in the work accords closely with that later portrayed by Marx on other occasions. All precise dividing lines are arbitrary; but while *The German Ideology* is sometimes regarded as part of Marx's 'early' period, it is more appropriate to regard it as the first important work representing Marx's mature position.

Debate over the relevance of Marx's writings of 1843 and 1844 to his mature conception of historical materialism has simmered continuously since their publication in 1929–32. The controversy has obvious ramifications of a directly political nature, and it is difficult to suppose that the points at issue are likely to be resolved to the satisfaction of all parties involved. But in fact the main lines of continuity between the

Anthony Giddens: 'Historical Materialism' from *CAPITALISM AND MODERN SOCIAL THEORY: AN ANALYSIS OF THE WRITINGS OF MARX, DURKHEIM AND MAX WEBER* (Cambridge University Press, 1971), pp. 18-34.

'Critique' of Hegel, the 1844 *Manuscripts*, and Marx's mature thought, are evident enough. The most important themes which Marx developed in the early writings and embodied within his later works, are the following:

1. The conception, for which Marx was heavily indebted to Hegel, of the progressive 'self-creation' of man. As Marx expresses it in the 1844 *Manuscripts*, 'the *whole of what is called world history* is nothing but the creation of man by human labour. . .'.[4]

2. The notion of alienation. One reason why Marx largely dropped the term 'alienation' from his writings after 1844 was certainly his desire to separate his own position decisively from abstract philosophy. Thus in *The Communist Manifesto* (1848), Marx writes derisively of the 'philosophical nonsense' of the German philosophers who write of the 'alienation of the human essence'.[5] The main implication of the views which, although they were substantially present in the *Manuscripts*, were not fully worked out until the writing of *The German Ideology*, is that alienation must be studied as an historical phenomenon, which can only be understood in terms of the development of specific social formations. Marx's studies of the stages of historical development trace the growth of the division of labour and the emergence of private property, culminating in the process of the alienation of the peasantry from control of their means of production with the disintegration of European feudalism. This latter process, the creation of a large mass of propertyless wage-labourers, is portrayed in *Capital* as a necessary precondition for the rise of capitalism.[6]

3. The kernel of the theory of the state, and its supersession in the future form of society, as set out in Marx's 'Critique' of Hegel's philosophy of the state. While Marx had, at the time of the writing of the 'Critique', only a rudimentary conception of the sort of social order which he hoped and expected would replace capitalism, the thesis that the abolition of the state can be achieved through the elimination of the separate sphere of the 'political' remains intrinsic to his later views upon this issue.

4. The main rudiments of historical materialism as a perspective for the analysis of social development. In spite of the fact that Marx frequently writes in the language of Hegel and Feuerbach in his early works, it is very clear that Marx's emergent standpoint constitutes a decisive epistemological break with these writers, and especially with Hegel. It is not a new philosophy which Marx seeks to substitute for the older views; Marx repudiates philosophy in favour of an approach which is social and historical. Thus Marx already stresses in the 1844 *Manuscripts* that capitalism is rooted in a definite form of society, the main structural characteristic of which is a dichotomous class relation between capital and wage-labour.

5. A summary conception of the theory of revolutionary *Praxis*. Marx's comments on Strauss and Bauer (that they substitute 'the "self-consciousness" of abstract man for the substance of "abstract nature" ')[7] anticipate the views stated at length in *The Holy Family* and *The German Ideology*, that critical philosophy is irrelevant to anything but the very early stages of a revolutionary movement.

Only by the union of theory and practice, by the conjunction of theoretical understanding and practical political activity, can social change be effected. This means integrating the study of the emergent transformations potential in history with a programme of practical action which can actualise these changes.

The crux of the transition between the 1844 *Manuscripts* and *The German Ideology* is to be found in the short set of critical propositions on Feuerbach which Marx wrote in March 1845, and which have since become famous as the *Theses on Feuerbach*.[8] Marx makes several criticisms of Feuerbach. In the first place, Feuerbach's approach is unhistorical. Feuerbach conceives of an abstract 'man' prior to society: he not only reduces man to religious man, but fails to see 'that "religious feeling" is itself a social product and that the abstract individual he analyses belongs to a particular form of society'.[9] Secondly, Feuerbach's materialism remains at the level of a philosophical doctrine, which simply regards ideas as 'reflections' of material reality. There is, in fact, a constant reciprocity between the consciousness and human *Praxis*. Feuerbach, in common with all previous materialist philosophers, treats 'material reality' as the determinant of human activity, and does not analyse the modification of the 'objective' world by the 'subject', i.e., by the activity of men. Marx also makes this extremely important point in another way. Feuerbach's materialistic doctrine, he states, is unable to deal with the fact that revolutionary activity is the outcome of the conscious, willed acts of men, but instead portrays the world in terms of the 'one-way' influence of material reality over ideas. However, Marx points out, 'circumstances are changed by men and. . . the educator must himself be educated . . .'.[10]

In Marx's eyes, Feuerbach has made a contribution of decisive importance in showing that 'philosophy [i.e., Hegel's philosophy] is nothing more than religion brought into thought and developed by thought, and that it is equally to be condemned as another form and mode of existence of human alienation'.[11] But, in so doing, Feuerbach sets out a 'contemplative' or passive materialism, neglecting Hegel's emphasis upon 'the dialectic of negativity as the moving and creating principle. . .'.[12] It is this dialectic between the subject (man in society) and object (the material world), in which men progressively subordinate the material world to their purposes, and thereby transform those purposes and generate new needs, which becomes focal to Marx's thought.

The materialist thesis

The general conception of historical materialism which is established in *The German Ideology* and subsequent writings is hence very different from that of Feuerbach, and from earlier traditions of philosophical materialism. As Marx employs it, 'materialism' does not refer to the assumption of any logically argued ontological position.[13] Marx undoubtedly accepts a 'realist' standpoint, according to which ideas are the product of the human brain in sensory transaction with a knowable material world; ideas are not founded in immanent categories given in the human mind independently of experience. But this definitely does not involve the application of a deterministic philosophical materialism to the interpretation of the development of society. Human consciousness is conditioned in dialectical interplay between subject and object, in which man actively shapes the world he lives in at the same time as it shapes him. This can be illustrated by Marx's observation, developing a point made in the *Theses on*

Feuerbach, that even our perception of the material world is conditioned by society. Feuerbach does not see that sensory perception is not fixed and immutable for all time, but is integrated within a phenomenal world which is:

> an historical product, the result of the activity of a whole succession of generations, each standing on the shoulders of the preceding one, developing further its industry and its intercourse, modifying its social order according to the changed needs. Even the objects of the simplest 'sensuous certainty' are only given him through social development, industry and commercial intercourse.[14]

For Marx, history is a process of the continuous creation, satisfaction and re-creation of human needs. This is what distinguishes men from the animals, whose needs are fixed and unchanging. This is why labour, the creative interchange between men and their natural environment, is the foundation of human society. The relation of the individual to his material environment is mediated by the particular characteristics of the society of which he is a member. In studying the development of human society, we must start from an empirical examination of the concrete processes of social life which are the *sine qua non* of human existence. As Marx expresses it in a passage worth quoting at length:

> This method of approach is not devoid of premises. It starts out from the real premises and does not abandon them for a moment. Its premises are men, not in any fantastic isolation and rigidity, but in their actual, empirically perceptible process of development under definite conditions. As soon as this active life-process is described, history ceases to be a collection of dead facts as it is with the materialists (themselves still abstract), or an imagined activity of imagined subjects, as with the idealists.
>
> Where speculation ends — in real life — there real, positive science begins: the representation of the practical activity, of the practical process of development of men. Talk about consciousness ceases, and real knowledge has to take its place. When reality is depicted, philosophy as an independent branch of knowledge loses its medium of existence. At most its place can be taken by a synthesis of the most general results, that may be abstracted from observation of the historical development of men. Separated from actual history, these abstractions have in themselves no value whatsoever. They can only serve to facilitate the ordering of historical materials, to indicate the sequence of its separate layers. But they by no means provide a recipe or scheme, as does philosophy, for neatly trimming the epochs of history. On the contrary, the difficulties only first begin when we set about the observation and the arrangement — the real depiction — of the materials, whether it be of a past epoch or of the present.[15]

In this resonant phraseology, Marx proclaims the need for an empirical science of society which will be founded upon the study of the creative and dynamic interaction between man and nature, the generative process whereby man makes himself.

Marx's conception of the main 'stages' in the development of society, in common with several other basic areas within his works, has to be reconstructed from fragmentary materials. Apart from the scheme given in *The German Ideology*, Marx nowhere makes an integrated exposition of the main types of society which he distinguished. Nevertheless the general principles which inform Marx's interpretation of social development are clear. Each of the various types of society which Marx identifies has its own characteristic internal dynamics or 'logic' of development. But these can only be discovered and analysed by *ex post facto* empirical analysis. This is emphasised both as a broad theoretical principle and more specifically in tracing the process of development from one type of society to another. 'History is nothing', Marx affirms, 'but the succession of the separate generations, each of which exploits the materials, the capital funds, the productive forces handed down to it by all preceding generations, and thus, on the one hand, continues the traditional activity in completely changed circumstances and, on the other, modifies the old circumstances with a completely changed activity.' [16] It is simply a teleological distortion to attribute 'goals' to history, such that 'later history is made the goal of earlier history'.[17]

Marx expresses the same views when, commenting upon the assertion that a capitalist stage is a necessary prerequisite to the establishment of communism in every modern society, he rejects a unilinear standpoint. Taking an earlier period of history as illustrative, he cites the case of Rome. Certain of the conditions which were to play an essential role in the formation of capitalism in western Europe at a later period already existed in Rome, but instead of giving rise to capitalist production, the Roman economy disintegrated internally. This shows 'that events of a striking similarity, but occurring in different historical contexts, produced quite different results'. This can be understood, Marx continues, if one studies these situations separately, 'but we shall never succeed in understanding them if we rely upon the *passe par-tout* of a historical-philosophical theory whose chief quality is that of being supra-historical'.[18]

Marx's typology of society is based upon tracing the progressive differentiation of the division of labour. As he states in the 1844 *Manuscripts*, the expansion of the division of labour is synonymous with the growth of alienation and private property. The formation of class society out of the original undifferentiated system of communal property is, of course, contingent upon specialisation in the division of labour; and it is the division of labour which by identifying men with their particular occupational specialisation (e.g., 'wage-labourer') negates their range of capacities as 'universal' producers. Thus: 'The various stages of development in the division of labour are just so many different forms of ownership; i.e., the existing stage in the division of labour determines also the relations of individuals to one another with reference to the material, instrument, and product of labour.' [19]

Pre-class systems

Every form of human society presupposes some rudimentary division of labour. But in the simplest type of society, tribal society, this is minimal, involving a broad division between the sexes: women, being largely occupied with the rearing of children, play a lesser productive role than men. Man is at first a wholly communal being; individualisation is a historical product, associated with an increasingly complex and specialised division of labour. A progressively more complicated division of labour goes hand in hand with the capacity to produce a surplus over and above what is necessary to satisfy basic wants. This in turn entails the exchange of goods; exchange in its turn produces the progressive individualisation of men — a process which reaches its apex under capitalism, with the development of a highly specialised division of labour, a money economy, and commodity production. Men thus only become individualised through the process of history: '[Man] originally appears as a *species-being*, a *tribal being*, a *herd animal*. . . Exchange itself is a major agent of this individualisation.' [20] Property is also at first communal; private property does not derive from a state of nature, but is the outcome of later social development. It is nonsense, Marx asserts, to conceive of human society as originally existing in conditions where separate individuals, each owning his little piece of private property, at some date came together to form a community through some kind of contractual agreement. 'An isolated individual could no more possess property in land than he could speak. At most he could live off it as a source of supply, like the animals.' [21] An individual's relation to the land he works, Marx emphasises, is mediated *through* the community. 'The producer exists as part of a family, a tribe, a grouping of his people, etc. — which assumes historically differing forms as the result of mixture with, and opposition to, others.' [22]

The simplest form of tribal society is that which follows a migratory existence, involving either hunting and gathering, or pastoralism. The tribe is not settled in any one fixed area, and exhausts the resources in one place before moving on to another. Men are not settled as part of their nature; they only become so when at a certain stage the nomadic group becomes a stable agricultural community. Once this transition has occurred, there are many factors which influence how the community henceforth develops, including both the physical conditions of the environment, and the internal structure of the tribe, the 'tribal character'. Further differentiation in the division of labour develops through the related processes of population increase, conflicts between tribes thus forced into contact, and the subjugation of one tribe by another.[23] This tends to produce an ethnically-based slavery system, part of a differentiated stratification system involving 'patriarchal family chieftains; below them the members of the tribe; finally slaves'.[24] Contact between societies stimulates trade as well as war. Since 'different communities find different means of production, and different means of subsistence in their natural environment',[25] exchange of products develops, stimulating further specialisation in the occupational sphere, and providing the first origin of the production of commodities: that is, products intended for sale on an exchange market. The first commodities include such things as slaves, cattle, metals, which are originally exchanged in direct barter. As such exchanges proliferate, and as they encompass a wider variety of commodities, the use of some form of money begins to occur. Exchange relations thus set up promote the interdependence of larger units, and thus make for societies of an expanded size.

While in Marx's earlier works a single line of development is portrayed, simply using historical materials from Europe, from tribal society to ancient society (Greece and Rome), Marx later distinguishes more than one line of development out of tribalism. This includes particularly oriental society (India and China), but Marx also distinguishes a specific type of tribal society, the Germanic, which in conjunction with the disintegrating Roman Empire formed the nexus out of which feudalism developed in western Europe.

Marx's views on the nature of the 'Asiatic mode of production' (oriental society) underwent some change. In his articles in the *New York Daily Tribune*, beginning in 1853, Marx places considerable stress upon factors of climate and geography which made centralised irrigation important in agriculture, and thus led to strong central government, or 'oriental despotism'.[26] However, Marx's later view is that this is rooted in more integral characteristics of this type of society, generic to the local community itself. Oriental society is highly resistant to change; this tendency to stagnation does not derive solely from the rigid despotic control of the centralised agency of government, but also (and primarily) from the internally self-sufficient character of the village commune. The small village community is 'entirely self-sustaining and contains within itself all conditions of production and surplus production'.[27] The historical origins of this phenomenon are not at all clear, but however this came about originally, the result is a 'self-sustaining unity of manufactures and agriculture', which leads to no impetus to further differentiation.

Population increase in oriental society tends only to produce 'a new community ... on the pattern of the old one, on unoccupied land'.[28] An essential factor in this is the lack of private property in land. Where private ownership of landed property does develop, as in parts of Europe and particularly in Rome, population growth leads to increasing pressure for proprietorship and consequently a constant tendency to expansion. However, in oriental society the individual 'never becomes an owner but only a possessor'. This type of society is not necessarily despotic; small village communes may exist as a segmentalised loosely associated grouping. However, the communities may devote part of their surplus product, often under the inspiration of religion, the 'imagined tribal entity of the god', as tribute to a despot. But the unity of the ruler with his subjects is not based upon an integrated society bound together by extensive economic interdependence; it remains a society composed basically of segmental units connected by a religious affiliation to the person of the despot.

The self-sufficient character of the local village communities definitely limits the growth of cities, and the latter never came to play a dominant role in either India or China.[29] In the type of society represented by Greece and Rome, on the other hand, the city becomes of central importance. Marx lays considerable stress upon the growth of urbanisation generally as marking the clearest index of differentiation within the division of labour. 'The opposition between town and country begins with the transition from barbarism to civilisation, from tribe to state, from locality to nation, and runs through the whole history of civilisation up to the present day. . .'.[30] The division of city and country provides the historical conditions for the growth of capital, which first begins in the city, and its separation from landed property. In the cities we find the 'beginning of property having its basis only in labour and exchange'.[31]

Ancient society, a city-based civilisation, is the first definite form of class society. Although the Asiatic societies show a certain development of state organisation, they are not regarded by Marx as involving a developed class system, since property remains wholly communal at the local level.[32] Classes only come into existence when the surplus of privately appropriated wealth becomes sufficient for an internally self-recruiting grouping to be clearly set off from the mass of the producers. Even in ancient society — and particularly in Greece — private property is still overshadowed by 'communal and public property'.

The ancient world

Ancient society results 'from the union of several tribes into a city, either by agreement or conquest'.[33] Unlike in the East, the city is an economic whole. The original tribes composing the city-states were aggressive and warlike. The cities were first organised around the military, and throughout their history both Greece and Rome preserved an expansionist character. Marx's analysis of ancient society concentrates upon the case of Rome. While Rome is an urban society, it is by no means completely separated from the influence of landed property. The private landed proprietor is at the same time an urban citizen. Marx describes this as 'a form in which the agriculturalist lives in a city'.[34] The ruling class is founded, during all periods of Roman history, upon ownership of landed property. Precisely because of this, population growth produces pressure for territorial expansion; and this is the main source of change in Roman society, the main 'contradiction' built into its structure: 'While . . . this is an essential part of the economic conditions of the community itself, it breaks the real bond on which the community rests.' [35] Population expansion, and the militaristic adventures which this promotes, serve to produce an extension of slavery and an increasing concentration of landed property. The wars of conquest and colonisation lead to the emergence of more sharply drawn lines of social differentiation, causing a swelling of the ranks of the slaves.[36] The slaves come to bear the full brunt of the productive labour, while the patrician landlords emerge as an increasingly separate ruling class monopolising public funds and the organisation of warfare. 'The whole system . . . was founded on certain limits of the numbers in the population, which could not be surpassed without endangering the conditions of antique civilisation itself.' This caused the pressure to what Marx calls 'compulsory emigration', in the shape of the periodical setting-up of colonies, which ' formed a regular link in the structure of society'.[37]

The pressure deriving from shortage of land is so strong because there is no motivation to increase productivity from existing resources. There exists no ideology which would 'push' toward an interest in maximising profits:

> Wealth does not appear as the aim of production, although Cato may well investigate the most profitable cultivation of fields, or Brutus may even lend money at the most favourable rate of interest. The enquiry is always about what kind of property creates the best citizens. Wealth as an end in itself appears only among a few trading peoples. . .[38]

Wealth is not valued for its own sake, but the 'private enjoyment' it brings; commerce and manufacture are thus looked upon by the ruling class with suspicion and even scorn. Moreover, labour in general is regarded with contempt, and as not worthy of free men.

By the end of the Republic, the Roman state is already founded on 'the ruthless exploitation of the conquered provinces',[39] a process which is regularised openly under the emperors. Class conflict inside Roman society centres around a struggle between patricians and plebeians. The former exploit the plebeians shamelessly, primarily through usury, which reaches a high development in Rome although never forming part of a general process of capital accumulation. In discussing the role of usury, in the third volume of *Capital*, Marx indicates that while usurers' capital plays an important part in the development of capitalism in combination with other conditions, without these conditions it serves only as a debilitating influence in the economy. This is what happens in Rome; usury exerts an undermining influence upon the small peasantry, since, instead of replenishing the real needs of the plebeians who are continually facing ruin through being forced to serve in wars, the patricians lend money at exorbitant rates of interest. 'As soon as the usury of the Roman patricians had completely ruined the Roman plebeians, the small peasants, this form of exploitation came to an end and a pure slave economy replaced the small peasant economy.' [40]

Slavery as an institution passes through various stages in Roman history. Beginning as a patriarchal system where slaves assist the small producers, the increasing depression of the plebeians themselves into slavery leads to the growth of large estates, the *latifundiae*, where agricultural production for a market is practised on a large scale. But the failure of commerce and industry to develop beyond a certain point, combined with the exploitative depression of the majority of the population into poverty, means that the *latifundiae* eventually themselves become uneconomical. A further decline in trade sets in, together with the decay of the towns. What commerce survives is reduced to ruin by the taxation imposed by state officials seeking to prop up a disintegrating state. Slavery itself begins to be abolished, and the large plantations are broken up and leased to hereditary tenants in small farms. Small-scale farming again becomes predominant.

Thus Rome, at its height a great empire producing a concentration of enormous wealth, eventually decays; while a considerable development of productive forces is attained, the internal composition of the society prevents growth beyond a certain point. The expropriation of large numbers of peasants from their means of production — a process upon which Marx lays great stress in discussing the origins of capitalism — does not lead to the development of capitalist production, but instead to a system based on slavery, which eventually disintegrates from within.

Feudalism and the origins of capitalist development

The barbarian onslaught upon Rome, therefore, was only the precipitating condition of the fall of the ancient world: the real causes derive from the internal development of Rome itself. Marx apparently does not regard ancient society as a *necessary* stage in the development of feudalism;[41] but in western Europe at any rate the disintegration of the Roman Empire forms the basis for the emergence of feudal society. Marx nowhere discusses the early phases of feudalism in any detail. But it is probable that he would accept the substance of the views set out by Engels in his *Origin of the Family, Private Property and the State*, according to which the barbarians, faced with the task of administering the territories they have acquired, are forced to modify their own system of government and adopt elements of the Roman legacy. This new social order centres upon the dominant position of the military commander, and eventuates in the transformation of military leadership into monarchy.[42] A new nobility thus forms itself around a personal retinue of military retainers, and supplemented by an educated elite drawn from Romanised officials and scholars. Several centuries of continual warfare and civil disorder in western Europe lead to the permanent impoverishment of the free peasant farmers, who make up the core of the barbarian armies, and to their consequent enserfment to local noble landlords. By the ninth century selfdom becomes predominant. Marx does say in one place, however, that throughout the feudal period a substructure of the old barbarian (Germanic) form of social organisation remains, evinced concretely in the survival of communal property on the local level. This substructure 'remained throughout the Middle Ages the unique stronghold of popular liberty and popular life'.[43]

Marx has no great interest in delineating the characteristics of feudal society, concentrating more of his attention upon the process of transition from feudalism to capitalism — although even here there are large gaps and obscurities in his treatment. What can be gleaned of Marx's view of the mature period of feudal society in Europe follows the standard conceptions in the economic history of his day. The basis of feudal economy consists in small-scale peasant agriculture involving the bonded serf; this is supplemented by domestic industry and by handicraft production in the towns. But the feudal system is basically a rural one: 'If Antiquity started out from the *town* and its little territory, the Middle Ages started out from the *country*.'[44] In serfdom, although the worker must surrender a certain amount of his produce to the lord, there is only a low degree of alienation between the producer and his product. The serf is his own proprietor, by and large producing for the needs of himself and his family. 'The lord does not try to extract the maximum profit from his estate. He rather consumes what is there, and tranquilly leaves the care of producing it to the serfs and tenant farmers.'[45] The history of the early stages of capitalism is, for Marx, very largely a history of the progressively increasing alienation of the small producer from control of his product: in other words, of his expropriation from his means of production, and his consequent dependence upon the sale of his labour on the market.

The disintegration of feudalism, and the early development of capitalism, is bound up with the growth of towns. Marx emphasises the importance of the emergence of the municipal movements in the twelfth century, which had a 'revolutionary character', and as a result of which the urban communities eventually secure a high degree of administrative autonomy.[46] As in Antiquity, the development of urban centres goes hand in hand with the formation of mercantile and usurers' capital, and a monetary system in terms of which they operate, which act as a force undermining the system based upon agricultural production.[47] While a few towns probably did persist from the period of the Roman Empire, the development of urban centres into wealthy commercial and manufacturing centres only really begins in the twelfth century; these are populated mainly by freed serfs. The growth of commerce stimulates an ever-widening extension of the use of money, and consequently of commodity exchange, into the formerly self-sufficient rural feudal economy. This facilitates the growth of usury in the towns, stimulates a decline in the fortunes of the land-owning aristocracy and allows the more prosperous peasant to discharge his obligations to the lord in monetary form, or to free himself from the latter's control altogether. In England, by the conclusion of the fourteenth century, serfdom has virtually disappeared. Whatever their feudal title, the vast mass of the labouring population in that country are by that date free peasant proprietors. The fate of serfdom, of course, varies greatly in different parts of Europe, and in some areas serfdom undergoes periods of 'revival'.[48]

Although as early as the fourteenth century we find 'the beginnings of capitalist production' in Italy,[49] and in the fifteenth century in England, these are very restricted in scope. The towns are dominated by strong guild organisations which strictly limit the number of journeymen and apprentices whom a master may employ, and the guilds keep themselves separate from mercantile capital, 'the only form of free capital with which they came into contact'.[50] Moreover, there is no possibility of capitalism developing while the majority of the labouring population consists of independent peasantry. The process of 'primary accumulation' [51] — that is, the initial formation of the capitalist mode of production — involves, as Marx stresses many times, the expropriation of the peasant from his means of production, a set of events which 'is written in the annals of mankind in letters of blood and fire'.

This process occurs at divergent periods, and in various ways, in different countries, and Marx concentrates upon the example of England, where it appears in 'classic form'. In England, the transformation of independent peasant into wage-labourer begins in earnest in the late fifteenth century.[52] By this time, the great feudal wars have sapped the resources of the nobility. The first 'mass of free proletarians' is thrown onto the market through the disbanding of retainers by the impoverished aristocracy, and the declining position of the feudal aristocracy is hastened by the growing power of the monarchy. The land-owning aristocracy is increasingly drawn into an exchange economy. The result is the enclosure movement, to which the rise of Flemish wool manufacture, leading to a sharp rise in the price of wool in England, gives a further impetus. In 'defiant opposition to King and Parliament' the feudal lords uproot large numbers of the peasantry, forcibly driving them from their land. Arable land is turned into pasture, which only requires a few herdsmen. This whole process of expropriation receives in the sixteenth century 'a new and frightening impulse' from the Reformation; the extensive church lands are handed out to royal favourites or sold cheaply to speculators who drive out the hereditary tenants and consolidate their holdings into large units. The expropriated peasantry are 'turned *en masse* into beggars, vagabonds, partly from inclination, in most cases from stress of circumstances'.[53] This is met with fierce legislation against vagrancy, by which means the vagabond population is subjected to 'the discipline necessary for the wage system'.[54]

By the early period of the sixteenth century then, there exists in England the beginnings of a proletariat — a stratum of dispossessed peasants who are a 'floating', mobile group, separated from their means of production, and thrown onto the market as 'free' wage-labourers. Marx notes scornfully that political economists interpret this in a purely positive light, speaking of the liberation of men from feudal ties and restrictions, neglecting altogether the fact that this freedom entails 'the most shameless violation of the "sacred rights of property" and the grossest acts of violence to persons'.[55]

In themselves, however, these events cannot, Marx indicates, be regarded as sufficient conditions for the rise of capitalism. At the turn of the sixteenth century, the decaying remnants of feudalism are poised between further disintegration and a movement into a more advanced productive form: capitalism. A factor of some importance in stimulating the latter development is the rapid and vast expansion of overseas commerce which develops as a result of the startling geographical discoveries made in the last part of the fifteenth century. These include principally the discovery of America and the rounding of the Cape, which 'gave to commerce, to navigation, to industry, an impulse never before known, and thereby, to the revolutionary element in the tottering feudal society, a rapid development'.[56] The rapid influx of capital deriving from this mushrooming trade, plus the flood of precious metals coming into the country following the discovery of gold and silver in America, cuts through the existing social and economic arrangements in England. New manufacturers become established at the sea-ports, and at inland centres outside the control of the older corporate towns and their guild organisations. The former undergo rapid growth, in spite of 'an embittered struggle of the corporate towns against these new industrial nurseries'.[57] Modern capitalism thus begins away from the older centres of manufacture, 'on the basis of large-scale maritime and overland trade',[58] Organised manufacture does not originate in the craft industries controlled by the guilds, but in what Marx calls the 'rural subsidiary operations' of spinning and weaving, which need little technical training. While rural society is the last place where capitalism develops in its 'purest and most logical form', the initial impetus is located there.[59] Not before this stage is reached is capital a revolutionary force. While the previous development of mercantilism beginning in the eleventh century acts as a major factor in dissolving feudal structures, the towns which develop are essentially dependent upon the old system, and play an essentially conservative role once they attain a certain level of power.

The ascendency of those who control capital, the emergent bourgeoisie, develops progressively from the opening of the sixteenth century onwards. The influx of gold and silver produces a sharp increase in prices. This acts to offer large profits in trade and manufacturing, but is a source of ruination to the great landlords, and swells the number of wage-labourers. The fruit of all this in the political sphere is the first English revolution, which is one moment in a rapid extension of state power. The developing mechanisms of centralised administration and consolidated political power are used 'to hasten, hothouse fashion, the process of transformation of the feudal mode of production into the capitalist mode, and to shorten the transition'.[60]

Not a great deal is known, even today, of the specific origins of the first capitalists, and Marx has little in the way of concrete historical material to offer on this matter. He does indicate, however, that there are two contrasting historical modes of progression into capitalist production. The first is where a segment of the merchant class moves over from purely trading operations to take a direct hand in production. This occurred in the early development of capitalism in Italy, and is the main source of recruitment of capitalists in England in the late fifteenth and early sixteenth centuries. However, this form of capitalist formation soon becomes 'an obstacle to a real capitalist mode of production and declines with the development of the latter'.[61] The second avenue of capitalist development is, according to Marx, 'the really revolutionary way'. Here individual producers themselves accumulate capital, and move from production to expand the sphere of their activities to include trade. They therefore from the very beginning operate outside the guilds and in conflict with them. While Marx gives only a few hints of how this second mode of development occurs in manufacture, he does specify some aspects of the process as it occurs in farming in England. By the middle of the seventeenth century much of the land is owned by capitalist farmers employing wage-labour and producing for a commodity market. Their property is considerably augmented by their forcible usurpation of those common lands which still survive from the feudal period. But this latter process is an extended one, not completed until the second half of the eighteenth century. Its completion is contemporaneous with the final disappearance of the independent peasantry, 'incorporating land as capital' and creating for the industries of the town 'the necessary supply of an outlawed proletariat'.[62]

Marx distinguishes two broad stages of productive organisation in the capitalist period. The first stage is dominated by manufacture. The distinctive characteristic of this form is that it involves the breaking-down of craft skills into various specialised tasks carried out by a number of workers, who accomplish collectively what one skilled man would do under the guild system. Manufacture is more efficient than handicraft production, not because of any technical advances, but because the division of labour it involves makes it possible to produce more units per man-hour. This form of production, which is predominant from the sixteenth century until the concluding part of the eighteenth in England, has definite limitations. The expansion of markets by the end of the eighteenth century is so great that manufacture is insufficiently productive to meet the demands placed upon it. As a consequence, a strong pressure builds up to create technically more efficient means of production; 'the development of machinery was a necessary consequence of the needs of the market'.[63] The result is the 'industrial revolution'.[64] Mechanisation henceforth dominates the capitalist mode of production. There is set in motion the constant impetus towards technological modification which becomes a hallmark of capitalism. The development of increasingly more complicated and expensive machinery is a primary factor in the centralisation of the capitalist economy upon which Marx lays so much stress in *Capital* in discussing the predicted dissolution of capitalism.

Notes

Marx and Engels: *Werke*. Vols. 1–41, plus supplementary volumes. Berlin, 1956–67.

T.B. Bottomore: *Karl Marx, Early Writings*, New York, 1964.

Loyd D. Easton and Kurt H. Guddat: *Writings of the Young Marx on Philosophy and Society*, New York, 1967.

Marx and Engels: *Selected Works*. Vols. 1–2. Moscow, 1958.

Capital. Vols. 1–3. Vol. 1, London, 1970; Vol. 2, Moscow, 1957; Vol. 3, Moscow, 1962.

The German Ideology. London, 1965.

The Communist Manifesto. New York, 1967 (Laski's edition).

1. *SW*, vol. 1, p. 364. For Engels' subsequent appraisal of the significance of the early writings, up to and including *The German Ideology*, see A. Voden: 'Talks with Engels', in *Reminiscences of Marx and Engels* (Moscow, n.d.), pp. 330ff.

2. *SW*, vol 1, p. 362, *We*, vol. 13, p. 8.

3. *SW*, vol. 2, p. 359.

4. *EW*, p. 166. On Marx's concept of 'labour', see Helmut Klages: *Technischer Humanismus* (Stuttgart, 1964), pp. 11-128.

5. *CM*, p. 168; *We*, vol. 4, p. 486.

6. The view that Marx eliminated the concept of 'alienation' from his later writings, and therefore that there is a major break in continuity between Marx's early and later works, is expressed by Louis Feuer: 'What is alienation? The career of a concept', *New Politics*, 1962, pp. 116–34; and by Daniel Bell: 'The debate on alienation', in Leopold Labedz: *Revisionism* (London, 1963), pp. 195–211. For a comparable statement, but from an opposed political perspective, cf. Louis Althusser: *For Marx* (London, 1969), pp. 51–86 and passim.

7. *EW*, p. 195.

8. The *Theses on Feuerbach* were first published in 1888 by Engels, who remarks that they contain 'the brilliant germ of a new world outlook' (*SW*, vol. 2, p. 359). Here I quote from the translation in *WYM*, pp. 400–2.

9. *WYM*, p. 402.

10. *WYM*, p. 401.

11. *EW*, p. 197, my parenthesis.

12. *EW*, p. 202. For an expanded treatment of the significance of this point, see below, pp. 403–6.

13. Which is not to say, of course, that Marx's position does not imply definite ontological assumptions. cf. H. B. Acton: *The Illusion of the Epoch* (London, 1955). For a convincing refutation of the view that Marx is a 'materialist' in the traditional sense, see Alfred Schmidt: *Der Begriff der Natur in der Lehre von Marx* (Frankfurt, 1962); also Z. A. Jordan: *The Evolution of Dialectical Materialism* (London, 1967).

14. *GI*, p. 57; *We*, vol. 3, p. 43.

15. *GI*, pp. 38–9; *We*, vol. 3, p. 27.

16. *GI*, p. 60. cf. also *The Holy Family, or Critique of Critical Critique* (Moscow, 1956), p. 125.

17. *GI*, p. 60. Marx makes the same criticism in reference to Proudhon's use of Hegel's dialectic. Proudhon simply substitutes economic categories for the Hegelian succession of ideas, and thus is absolved from studying historical development in detail. 'M. Proudhon considers economic relations as so many social phases engendering one another resulting from one another like antithesis from thesis, and realising in their logical sequence the impersonal reason of humanity.' *The Poverty of Philosophy* (London, n.d.), p. 93.

18. Letter to the editor of *Otyecestvenniye Zapisky*, translation after T. B. Bottomore and Maximilien Rubel: Karl Marx: *Selected Writings in Sociology and Social Philosophy* (London, 1963), p. 38.

19. *GI*, p. 33.

20. *Pre-Capitalist Economic Formations* (London, 1964), p. 96; *Gru*, pp. 395–6.

21. *Economic Formations*, p. 81.

22. *Ibid.* p. 87; *Gru*, p. 389

23. cf. *Cap*, vol. 1, pp. 87–9. The similarity to Durkheim may be noted.

24. *Pre-Capitalist Economic Formations*, pp. 122–3.

25. *Cap* vol. 1, p. 351.

26. *The American Journalism of Marx and Engels* (New York, 1966); *Articles on India* (Bombay, 1951); *Marx on China* 1853–60 (London, 1968).

27. *Pre-Capitalist Economic Formations*, p. 70.

28. *Cap*, vol. 1, p. 358. The structure of the Asian mode of production is eventually undermined by the impact of western colonialism.

29. This is a point later made by Weber, with reference to both India and China.

30. *GI*, p. 65; *We*, vol. 3, p. 50.

31. *GI*, p. 66.

32. Wittfogel has argued that Marx 'failed to draw a conclusion, which from the standpoint of his own theory seemed inescapable — namely, that under conditions of the Asiatic mode of production the agro-managerial bureaucracy constituted the ruling class'. Karl A. Wittfogel: *Oriental Despotism* (New Haven, 1957), p. 6. Since Marx refers to Russia as a 'semi-Asiatic' society, the class character of the 'Asian mode of production' has considerable political ramifications. Wittfogel gives an (unsympathetic) account of the debate on Asian society among Russian scholars (*ibid.* chapter 9). cf. George Lichtheim: 'Marx and the "Asiatic mode of production" ', *St Anthony's Papers*, No. 14, 1963, pp. 86–112.

33. *GI*, p. 33.

34. *Pre-Capitalist Economic Formations*, pp. 79–80.

35. *Ibid.* p. 83.

36. *Ibid.* pp 92–3.

37. *American Journalism of Marx and Engels*, p. 77.

38. *Pre-Capitalist Economic Formations*, p. 84. Marx notes that the outlook prevailing in the ancient world, although existing in alienated form — in terms of a 'narrowly national, religious, or political' world-view — still places man very much at the centre of things as compared to *bourgeois* society, where human ends become subordinated to production and the accumulation of wealth. But Marx continues: 'In fact, however, when the narrow *bourgeois* form has been peeled away, what is wealth, if not the universality of needs, capacities, enjoyments, productive powers, etc., of individuals, produced in universal exchange?' Thus while the 'childish world of the Ancients' is in one aspect superior to the modern world, it is so only in terms of a relatively narrow range of human potentialities. *Ibid.* pp. 84–5.

39. The phrase is Engels', *SW*, vol. 2, p. 299.

40. *Cap.* vol. 3, p. 582.

41. *Pre-Capitalist Economic Formations*, p. 70.

42. Marx does in one place refer briefly to the system following Rome in Europe as a 'synthesis' in which 'two systems mutually modified each other'. *A Contribution to the Critique of Political Economy* (Chicago, 1904), p. 288.

43. *Pre-Capitalist Economic Formations*, pp. 144–5. (From the third draft of Marx's letter to Zasulich.)

44. *GI*, p. 35.

45. *EW*, p 115.

46. Marx quotes Thierry to the effect that the word *capitalia* first appears with the rise of the autonomous urban communes. Letter from Marx to Engels, July 1854, *Selected Correspondence* (London, 1934), p. 72.

47. Dobb has argued that the primary factor producing the decay of feudalism 'was the inefficiency of feudalism as a system of production, coupled with the growing needs of the ruling class for revenue. . .'. Maurice Dobb: *Studies in the Development of Capitalism* (London, 1963), p. 42. For a discussion of Dobb's book see Paul M. Sweezy: *The Transition from Feudalism to Capitalism* (London, 1954).

48. A phenomenon to which Engels gives some attention, speaking of the rise of a 'second serfdom' in eastern parts of Europe in the fifteenth century. Letter to Marx, December 1882, *Selected Correspondence*, pp. 407–8.

49. Marx mentions that, in Italy, where the earliest development of capitalist production occurs, 'the dissolution of serfdom also took place earlier than elsewhere'. *Cap*, vol. 1, p. 716.

50. *Cap*, vol. 1, p. 358.

51. The phrase is usually rendered 'primitive accumulation'. Here I follow Sweezy (p. 17) and others in translating *ursprünglich* as 'primary', which avoids the potentially misleading implications of the usual rendering.

52. *Cap*, vol. 1, pp. 718ff.

53. *Cap*, vol. 1, pp. 718, 721 & 734; *We*, vol. 23, pp. 746, 748 & 762.

54. *Cap* vol. 1, p. 737.

55. *Cap* vol. 1, p. 727.

56. *CM*, p. 133: *GI*, p. 73.

57. *Cap*, vol. 1, p. 751.

58. *Pre-Capitalist Economic Formations*, p. 116.

59. *Ibid*. p. 116. Marx adds: 'Hence the ancients, who never advanced beyond specifically urban craft skill and application, were never able to achieve large-scale industry' (p. 117).

60. *Cap*, vol. 1, p. 751.

61. *Cap*, vol. 3, p. 329.

62. *Cap*, vol. 1, p. 733; *We*, vol. 23, p. 761.

63. Letter to Annenkov, quoted in *Poverty of Philosophy*, p. 156.

64. Engels used this term before Marx. See the former's *Condition of the Working Class in England in 1844* (Oxford, 1968), pp. 9–26. There is some dispute over the origin of the term 'industrial revolution'. cf. Dobb, p. 258.

29. Manifesto of the Communist Party

Karl Marx and Frederick Engels

Preface to the German edition of 1872

The Communist League, an international association of workers, which could of course be only a secret one under the conditions obtaining at the time, commissioned the undersigned, at the Congress held in London in November 1847, to draw up for publication a detailed theoretical and practical programme of the Party. Such was the origin of the following Manifesto, the manuscript of which travelled to London, to be printed, a few weeks before the February Revolution. First published in German, it has been republished in that language in at least twelve different editions in Germany, England and America. It was published in English for the first time in 1850 in the *Red Republican*, London, translated by Miss Helen Macfarlane, and in 1871 in at least three different translations in America. A French version first appeared in Paris shortly before the June insurrection of 1848 and recently in *Le Socialiste* of New York. A new translation is in the course of preparation. A Polish version appeared in London shortly after it was first published in German. A Russian translation was published in Geneva in the sixties. Into Danish, too, it was translated shortly after its first appearance.

However much the state of things may have altered during the last twenty-five years, the general principles laid down in this Manifesto are, on the whole, as correct today as ever. Here and there some detail might be improved. The practical application of the principles will depend, as the Manifesto itself states, everywhere and at all times, on the historical conditions for the time being existing, and, for that reason, no special stress is laid on the revolutionary measures proposed at the end of Section II. That passage would, in many respects, be very differently worded today. In view of the gigantic strides of Modern Industry in the last twenty-five years, and of the accompanying improved and extended party organisation of the working class, in view of the practical experience gained, first in the February Revolution, and then, still more, in the Paris Commune, where the proletariat for the first time held political power for two whole months, this programme has in some details become antiquated. One thing especially was proved by the Commune, *viz.*, that "the working class cannot simply lay hold of the ready-made State machinery, and wield it for its own purposes." (See *The Civil War in France; Address of the General Council of the International Working Men's Association*, London, Truelove, 1871, p. 15, where this point is further developed.) Further, it is self-evident that the criticism of socialist literature is deficient in relation to the present time, because it comes down only to 1847; also, that the remarks on the relation of the Communists to the various opposition parties (Section IV), although in principle still correct, yet in practice are antiquated, because the political situation has been entirely changed, and the progress of history has swept from off the earth the greater portion of the political parties there enumerated.

Karl Marx and Frederick Engels: Extract from *MANIFESTO OF THE COMMUNIST PARTY (1888)* (Lawrence & Wishart, 1983), pp. 31-46.

But, then, the Manifesto has become a historical document which we have no longer any right to alter. A subsequent edition may perhaps appear with an introduction bridging the gap from 1847 to the present day; this reprint was too unexpected to leave us time for that.

Karl Marx   *Frederick Engels*

London, June 24,1872

Written by Marx and Engels
for the German edition which
appeared in Leipzig in 1872

Printed according to
the 1872 edition
Translated from the German

From the Preface to the German edition of 1890

The Manifesto has had a history of its own. Greeted with enthusiasm, at the time of its appearance, by the then still not at all numerous vanguard of scientific socialism (as is proved by the translations mentioned in the first preface), it was soon forced into the background by the reaction that began with the defeat of the Paris workers in June 1848, and was finally excommunicated "according to law" by the conviction of the Cologne Communists in November 1852. With the disappearance from the public scene of the workers' movement that had begun with the February Revolution, the Manifesto too passed into the background.

When the working class of Europe had again gathered sufficient strength for a new onslaught upon the power of the ruling classes, the International Working Men's Association came into being. Its aim was to weld together into *one* huge army the whole militant working class of Europe and America. Therefore it could not *set out* from the principles laid down in the Manifesto. It was bound to have a programme which would not shut the door on the English trade unions, the French, Belgian, Italian and Spanish Proudhonists and the German Lassalleans[1]. This programme — the preamble to the Rules of the International[2] — was drawn up by Marx with a master hand acknowledged even by Bakunin and the Anarchists. For the ultimate triumph of the ideas set forth in the Manifesto Marx relied solely and exclusively upon the intellectual development of the working class, as it necessarily had to ensue from united action and discussion. The events and vicissitudes in the struggle against capital, the defeats even more than the successes, could not but demonstrate to the fighters the inadequacy hitherto of their universal panaceas and make their minds more receptive to a thorough understanding of the true conditions for the emancipation of the workers. And Marx was right. The working class of 1874, at the dissolution of the International, was altogether different from that of 1864, at its foundation. Proudhonism in the Latin countries and the specific Lassalleanism in Germany were dying out, and even the then arch-conservative English trade unions were gradually approaching the point where in 1887 the chairman of their Swansea Congress[3] could say in their name: "Continental Socialism has lost its terrors for us." Yet by 1887 Continental Socialism was almost exclusively the theory heralded in the Manifesto. Thus, to a certain extent, the history of the Manifesto reflects the history of the modern working-class movement since 1848. At present it is doubtless the most widely circulated, the most international product of all socialist literature, the common programme of many millions of workers of all countries, from Siberia to California.

Nevertheless, when it appeared we could not have called it a *Socialist* Manifesto. In 1847 two kinds of people were considered Socialists. On the one hand were the adherents of the various Utopian systems, notably the Owenites in England and the Fourierists in France, both of whom at that date had already dwindled to mere sects gradually dying out. On the other, the manifold types of social quacks who wanted to eliminate social abuses through their various universal panaceas and all kinds of patchwork, without hurting capital and profit in the least. In both cases, people who stood outside the labour movement and who looked for support rather to the "educated" classes. The section of the working class, however, which demanded a radical reconstruction of society, convinced that mere political revolutions were not enough, then called itself *Communist*. It was still a rough-hewn, only instinctive, and frequently somewhat crude communism. Yet it was powerful enough to bring into being two systems of Utopian Communism — in France the "Icarian" communism of Cabet, and in Germany that of Weitling. Socialism in 1847 signified a bourgeois movement, communism a working-class movement. Socialism was, on the Continent at least, quite respectable, whereas communism was the very opposite. And since we were very decidedly of the opinion as early as then that "the emancipation of the workers must be the act of the working class itself," we could have no hesitations as to which of the two names we should choose. Nor has it ever occurred to us since to repudiate it.

"Working men of all countries, unite!" But few voices responded when we proclaimed these words to the world forty-two years ago, on the eve of the first Paris Revolution in which the proletariat came out with demands of its own. On September 28, 1864, however, the proletarians of most of the Western European countries united to form the International Working Men's Association of glorious memory. True, the International itself lived only nine years. But that the eternal union of the proletarians of all countries created by it is still alive and lives stronger than ever, there is no better witness than this day. Because today, as I write these lines, the European and American proletariat is reviewing its fighting forces, mobilised for the first time, mobilised as one army, under one flag, for one immediate aim: the standard eight-hour working day, to be established by legal enactment, as proclaimed by the Geneva Congress of the International in 1866, and again by the Paris Workers' Congress in 1889. And today's spectacle will open the eyes of the capitalists and landlords of all countries to the fact that today the working men of all countries are united indeed.

If only Marx were still by my side to see this with his own eyes!

F. Engels

London, May 1,1890

Written by Engels for the German
edition which appeared in London
in 1890

Printed according to the
1890 edition
Translated from the German

MANIFESTO OF THE COMMUNIST PARTY

A spectre is haunting Europe — the spectre of Communism. All the Powers of old Europe have entered into a holy alliance to exorcise this spectre: Pope and Czar, Metternich and Guizot, French Radicals and German police-spies.

Where is the party in opposition that has not been decried as Communistic by its opponents in power? Where the Opposition that has not hurled back the branding reproach of Communism, against the more advanced opposition parties, as well as against its reactionary adversaries?

Two things result from this fact.

I. Communism is already acknowledged by all European Powers to be itself a Power.

II. It is high time that Communists should openly, in the face of the whole world, publish their views, their aims, their tendencies, and meet this nursery tale of the Spectre of Communism with a Manifesto of the party itself.

To this end, Communists of various nationalities have assembled in London, and sketched the following Manifesto, to be published in the English, French, German, Italian, Flemish and Danish languages.

I

Bourgeois and Proletarians[4]

The history of all hitherto existing society[5] is the history of class struggles.

Freeman and slave, patrician and plebeian, lord and serf, guildmaster[6] and journeyman, in a word, oppressor and oppressed, stood in constant opposition to one another, carried on an uninterrupted, now hidden, now open fight, a fight that each time ended, either in a revolutionary re-constitution of society at large, or in the common ruin of the contending classes.

In the earlier epochs of history, we find almost everywhere a complicated arrangement of society into various orders, a manifold gradation of social rank. In ancient Rome we have patricians, knights, plebeians, slaves; in the Middle Ages, feudal lords, vassals, guild-masters, journeymen, apprentices, serfs; in almost all of these classes, again, subordinate gradations.

The modern bourgeois society that has sprouted from the ruins of feudal society has not done away with class antagonisms. It has but established new classes, new conditions of oppression, new forms of struggle in place of the old ones.

Our epoch, the epoch of the bourgeoisie, possesses, however, this distinctive feature: it has simplified the class antagonisms. Society as a whole is more and more splitting up into two great hostile camps, into two great classes directly facing each other: Bourgeoisie and Proletariat.

From the serfs of the Middle Ages sprang the chartered burghers of the earliest towns. From these burgesses the first elements of the bourgeoisie were developed.

The discovery of America, the rounding of the Cape, opened up fresh ground for the rising bourgeoisie. The East-Indian and Chinese markets, the colonisation of America, trade with the colonies, the increase in the means of exchange and in commodities generally, gave to commerce, to navigation, to industry, an impulse never before known, and thereby, to the revolutionary element in the tottering feudal society, a rapid development.

The feudal system of industry, under which industrial production was monopolised by closed guilds, now no longer sufficed for the growing wants of the new markets. The manufacturing system took its place. The guild-masters were pushed on one side by the manufacturing middle class; division of labour between the different corporate guilds vanished in the face of division of labour in each single workshop.

Meantime the markets kept ever growing, the demand ever rising. Even manufacture no longer sufficed. Thereupon, steam and machinery revolutionised industrial production. The place of manufacture was taken by the giant, Modern Industry, the place of the industrial middle class, by industrial millionaires, the leaders of whole industrial armies, the modern bourgeois.

Modern industry has established the world-market, for which the discovery of America paved the way. This market has given an immense development to commerce, to navigation, to communication by land. This development has, in its turn, reacted on the extension of industry; and in proportion as industry, commerce, navigation, railways extended, in the same proportion the bourgeoisie developed, increased its capital, and pushed into the background every class handed down from the Middle Ages.

We see, therefore, how the modern bourgeoisie is itself the product of a long course of development, of a series of revolutions in the modes of production and of exchange.

Each step in the development of the bourgeoisie was accompanied by a corresponding political advance of that class. An oppressed class under the sway of the feudal nobility, an armed and self-governing association in the mediaeval commune[7]; here independent urban republic (as in Italy and Germany), there taxable "third estate" of the monarchy (as in France), afterwards, in the period of manufacture proper, serving either the semi-feudal or the absolute monarchy as a counterpoise against the nobility, and, in fact, corner-stone of the great monarchies in general, the bourgeoisie has at last, since the establishment of Modern Industry and of the world-market, conquered for itself, in the modern representative State, exclusive political sway. The executive of the modern State is but a committee for managing the common affairs of the whole bourgeoisie.

The bourgeoisie, historically, has played a most revolutionary part.

The bourgeoisie, wherever it has got the upper hand, has put an end to all feudal, patriarchal, idyllic relations. It has pitilessly torn asunder the motley feudal ties that bound man to his "natural superiors," and has left remaining no other nexus between man and man than naked self-interest, than callous "cash payment." It has drowned the most heavenly ecstasies of religious fervour, of chivalrous enthusiasm, of philistine sentimentalism, in the icy water of egotistical calculation. It has resolved personal worth into exchanges value, and in place of the numberless indefeasible chartered freedoms, has set up that single, unconscionable freedom — Free Trade. In one word, for exploitation, veiled by religious and political illusions, it has substituted naked, shameless, direct, brutal exploitation.

The bourgeoisie has stripped of its halo every occupation hitherto honoured and looked up to with reverent awe. It has converted the physician, the lawyer, the priest, the poet, the man of science, into its paid wage-labourers.

The bourgeoisie has torn away from the family its sentimental veil, and has reduced the family relation to a mere money relation.

The bourgeoisie has disclosed how it came to pass that the brutal display of vigour in the Middle Ages, which Reactionists so much admire, found its fitting complement in the most slothful indolence. It has been the first to show what man's activity can bring about. It has accomplished wonders far surpassing Egyptian pyramids, Roman aqueducts, and Gothic cathedrals; it has conducted expeditions that put in the shade all former Exoduses of nations and crusades.

The bourgeoisie cannot exist without constantly revolutionising the instruments of production, and thereby the relations of production, and with them the whole relations of society. Conservation of the old modes of production in unaltered form, was, on the contrary, the first condition of existence for all earlier industrial classes. Constant revolutionising of production, uninterrupted disturbance of all social conditions, everlasting uncertainty and agitation distinguish the bourgeois epoch from all earlier ones. All fixed, fast-frozen relations, with their train of ancient and venerable prejudices and opinions, are swept away, all newformed ones become antiquated before they can ossify. All that is solid melts into air, all that is holy is profaned, and man is at last compelled to face with sober senses, his real conditions of life, and his relations with his kind.

The need of a constantly expanding market for its products chases the bourgeoisie over the whole surface of the globe. It must nestle everywhere, settle everywhere, establish connexions everywhere.

The bourgeoisie has through its exploitation of the world-market given a cosmopolitan character to production and consumption in every country. To the great chagrin of Reactionists, it has drawn from under the feet of industry the national ground on which it stood. All old-established national industries have been destroyed or are daily being destroyed. They are dislodged by new industries, whose introduction becomes a life and death question for all civilised nations, by industries that no longer work up indigenous raw material, but raw material drawn from the remotest zones; industries whose products are consumed, not only at home, but in every quarter of the globe. In place of the old wants, satisfied by the productions of the country, we find new wants, requiring for their satisfaction the products of distant lands and climes. In place of the old local and national seclusion and self-sufficiency, we have intercourse in every direction, universal inter-dependence of nations. And as in material, so also in intellectual production. The intellectual creations of individual nations become common property. National one-sidedness and narrow-mindedness become more and more impossible, and from the numerous national and local literatures, there arises a world literature.

The bourgeoisie, by the rapid improvement of all instruments of production, by the immensely facilitated means of communication, draws all, even the most barbarian, nations into civilisation. The cheap prices of its commodities are the heavy artillery with which it batters down all Chinese walls, with which it forces the barbarians' intensely obstinate hatred of foreigners to capitulate. It compels all nations, on pain of extinction, to adopt the bourgeois mode of production; it compels them to introduce what it calls civilisation into their midst, i.e., to become bourgeois themselves. In one word, it creates a world after its own image.

The bourgeoisie has subjected the country to the rule of the towns. It has created enormous cities, has greatly increased the urban population as compared with the rural, and has thus rescued a considerable part of the population from the idiocy of rural life. Just as it has made the country dependent on the towns; so it has made barbarian and semi-barbarian countries dependent on the civilised ones, nations of peasants on nations of bourgeois, the East on the West.

The bourgeoisie keeps more and more doing away with the scattered state of the population, of the means of production, and of property. It has agglomerated population, centralised means of production, and has concentrated property in a few hands. The necessary consequence of this was political centralisation. Independent, or but loosely connected provinces, with separate interests, laws, governments and systems of taxation, became lumped together into one nation, with one government, one code of laws, one national class-interest, one frontier and one customs-tariff.

The bourgeoisie, during its rule of scarce one hundred years, has created more massive and more colossal productive forces than have all preceding generations together. Subjection of Nature's forces to man, machinery, application of chemistry to industry and agriculture, steam-navigation, railways, electric telegraphs, clearing of whole continents for cultivation, canalisation of rivers, whole populations conjured out of the ground — what earlier century had even a presentiment that such productive forces slumbered in the lap of social labour?

We see then: the means of production and of exchange, on whose foundation the bourgeoisie built itself up, were generated in feudal society. At a certain stage in the development of these means of production and of exchange, the conditions under which feudal society produced and exchanged, the feudal organisation of agriculture and manufacturing industry, in one word, the feudal relations of property became no longer compatible with the already developed productive forces; they became so many fetters. They had to be burst asunder; they were burst asunder.

Into their place stepped free competition, accompanied by a social and political constitution adapted to it, and by the economical and political sway of the bourgeois class.

A similar movement is going on before our own eyes. Modern bourgeois society with its relations of production, of exchange and of property, a society that has conjured up such gigantic means of production and of exchange, is like the sorcerer, who is no longer able to control the powers of the nether world whom he has called up by his spells. For many a decade past the history of industry and commerce is but the history of the revolt of modern productive forces against modern conditions of production, against the property relations that are the conditions for the existence of the bourgeoisie and of its rule. It is enough to mention the commercial crises that by their periodical return put on its trial, each time more threateningly, the existence of the entire bourgeois society. In these crises a great part not only of the existing products, but also of the previously created productive forces, are periodically destroyed. In these crises there breaks out an epidemic that, in all earlier epochs, would have seemed an absurdity — the epidemic of over-production. Society suddenly finds itself put back into a state of momentary barbarism; it appears as if a famine, a universal war of devastation had cut off the supply of every means of subsistence; industry and commerce seem to be destroyed; and why? Because there is too much civilisation, too much means of subsistence, too much industry, too much commerce. The productive forces at the disposal of society no longer tend to further the development of the conditions of bourgeois property; on the contrary, they have become too powerful for these conditions, by which they are fettered, and so soon as they overcome these fetters, they bring disorder into the whole of bourgeois society, endanger the existence of bourgeois property. The conditions of bourgeois society are too narrow to comprise the wealth created by them. And how does the bourgeoisie get over these crises? On the one hand by enforced destruction of a mass of productive forces; on the other, by the conquest of new markets, and by the more thorough exploitation of the old ones. That is to say, by paving the way for more extensive and more destructive crises, and by diminishing the means whereby crises are prevented.

The weapons with which the bourgeoisie felled feudalism to the ground are now turned against the bourgeoisie itself.

But not only has the bourgeoisie forged the weapons that bring death to itself; it has also called into existence the men who are to wield those weapons — the modern working class — the proletarians.

In proportion as the bourgeoisie, *i.e.,* capital, is developed, in the same proportion is the proletariat, the modern working class, developed — a class of labourers, who live only so long as they find work, and who find work only so long as their labour increases capital. These labourers, who must sell themselves piecemeal, are a commodity, like every other article of commerce, and are consequently exposed to all the vicissitudes of competition, to all the fluctuations of the market.

Owing to the extensive use of machinery and to division of labour, the work of the proletarians has lost all individual character, and, consequently, all charm for the workman. He becomes an appendage of the machine, and it is only the most simple, most monotonous, and most easily acquired knack, that is required of him. Hence, the cost of production of a workman is restricted, almost entirely, to the means of subsistence that he requires for his maintenance, and for the propagation of his race. But the price of a commodity, and therefore also of labour, is equal to its cost of production. In proportion, therefore, as the repulsiveness of the work increases, the wage decreases. Nay more, in proportion as the use of machinery and division of labour increases, in the same proportion the burden of toil also increases, whether by prolongation of the working hours, by increase of the work exacted in a given time or by increased speed of the machinery, etc.

Modern industry has converted the little workshop of the patriarchal master into the great factory of the industrial capitalist. Masses of labourers, crowded into the factory, are organised like soldiers. As privates of the industrial army they are placed under the command of a perfect hierarchy of officers and sergeants. Not only are they slaves of the bourgeois class, and of the bourgeois State; they are daily and hourly enslaved by the machine, by the overlooker, and, above all, by the individual bourgeois manufacturer himself. The more 'openly this despotism proclaims gain to be its end and aim, the more petty, the more hateful and the more embittering it is.

The less the skill and exertion of strength implied in manual labour, in other words, the more modern industry becomes developed, the more is the labour of men superseded by that of women. Differences of age and sex have no longer any distinctive social validity for the working class. All are instruments of labour, more or less expensive to use, according to their age and sex.

No sooner is the exploitation of the labourer by the manufacturer so far, at an end, and he receives his wages in cash, than he is set upon by the other portions of the bourgeoisie, the landlord, the shopkeeper, the pawnbroker, etc.

The lower strata of the middle class — the small tradespeople, shopkeepers, and retired tradesmen generally, the handicraftsmen and peasants — all these sink gradually into the proletariat, partly because their diminutive capital does not suffice for the scale on which Modern Industry is carried on, and is swamped in the competition with the large capitalists, partly because their specialised skill is rendered worthless by new methods of production. Thus the proletariat is recruited from all classes of the population.

The proletariat goes through various stages of development. With its birth begins its struggle with the bourgeoisie. At first the contest is carried on by individual labourers, then by the workpeople of a factory, then by the operatives of one trade, in one locality, against the individual bourgeois who directly exploits them. They direct their attacks not against the bourgeois conditions of production, but against the instruments of production themselves; they destroy imported wares that compete with their labour, they smash to pieces machinery, they set factories ablaze, they seek to restore by force the vanished status of the workman of the Middle Ages.

At this stage the labourers still form an incoherent mass scattered over the whole country, and broken up by their mutual competition. If anywhere they unite to form more compact bodies, this is not yet the consequence of their own active union, but of the union of the bourgeoisie, which class, in order to attain its own political ends, is compelled to set the whole proletariat in motion, and is moreover yet, for a time, able to do so. At this stage, therefore, the proletarians do not fight their enemies, but the enemies of their enemies, the remnants of absolute monarchy, the landowners, the non-industrial bourgeois, the petty bourgeoisie. Thus the whole historical movement is concentrated in the hands of the bourgeoisie; every victory so obtained is a victory for the bourgeoisie.

But with the development of industry the proletariat not only increases in number; it becomes concentrated in greater masses; its strength grows, and it feels that strength more. The various interests and conditions of life within the ranks of the proletariat are more and more equalised, in proportion as machinery obliterates all distinctions of labour, and nearly everywhere reduces wages to the same low level. The growing competition among the bourgeois, and the resulting commercial crises, make the wages of the workers ever more fluctuating. The unceasing improvement of machinery, ever more rapidly developing, makes their livelihood more and more precarious; the collisions between individual workmen and individual bourgeois take more and more the character of collisions between two classes. Thereupon the workers begin to form combinations (Trades' Unions) against the bourgeois; they club together in order to keep up the rate of wages; they found permanent associations in order to make provision beforehand for these occasional revolts. Here and there the contest breaks out into riots.

Now and then the workers are victorious, but only for a time. The real fruit of their battles lies, not in the immediate result, but in the ever-expanding union of the workers. This union is helped on by the improved means of communication that are created by modern industry and that place the workers of different localities in contact with one another. It was just this contact that was needed to centralise the numerous local struggles, all of the same character, into one national struggle between classes. But every class struggle is a political struggle. And that union, to attain which the burghers of the Middle Ages, with their miserable highways, required centuries, the modern proletarians, thanks to railways, achieve in a few years.

This organisation of the proletarians into a class, and consequently into a political party, is continually being upset again by the competition between the workers themselves. But it ever rises up again, stronger, firmer, mightier. It compels legislative recognition of particular interests of the workers, by taking advantage of the divisions among the bourgeoisie itself. Thus the ten-hours' bill in England was carried.

Altogether collisions between the classes of the old society further, in many ways, the course of development of the proletariat. The bourgeoisie finds itself involved in a constant battle. At first with the aristocracy; later on, with those portions of the bourgeoisie itself, whose interests have become antagonistic to the progress of industry; at all times, with the bourgeoisie of foreign countries. In all these battles it sees itself compelled to appeal to the proletariat, to ask for its help, and thus, to drag it into the political arena. The bourgeoisie itself, therefore, supplies the proletariat with its own elements of political and general education, in other words, it furnishes the proletariat with weapons for fighting the bourgeoisie.

Further, as we have already seen, entire sections of the ruling classes are, by the advance of industry, precipitated into the proletariat, or are at least threatened in their conditions of existence. These also supply the proletariat with fresh elements of enlightenment and progress.

Finally, in times when the class struggle nears the decisive hour, the process of dissolution going on within the ruling class, in fact within the whole range of old society, assumes such a violent, glaring character, that a small section of the ruling class cuts itself adrift, and joins the revolutionary class, the class that holds the future in its hands. Just as, therefore, at an earlier period, a section of the nobility went over to the bourgeoisie, so now a portion of the bourgeoisie goes over to the proletariat, and in particular, a portion of the bourgeois ideologists, who have raised themselves to the level of comprehending theoretically the historical movement as a whole.

Of all the classes that stand face to face with the bourgeoisie today, the proletariat alone is a really revolutionary class. The other classes decay and finally disappear in the face of Modern Industry; the proletariat is its special and essential product.

The lower middle class, the small manufacturer, the shopkeeper the artisan, the peasant, all these fight against the bourgeoisie, to save from extinction their existence as fractions of the middle class. They are therefore not revolutionary, but conservative. Nay more, they are reactionary, for they try to roll back the wheel of history. If by chance they are revolutionary, they are so only in view of their impending transfer into the proletariat, they thus defend not their present, but their future interests, they desert their own standpoint to place themselves at that of the proletariat.

The "dangerous class," the social scum, that passively rotting mass thrown off by the lowest layers of old society, may, here and there, be swept into the movement by a proletarian revolution, its conditions of life, however, prepare it far more for the part of a bribed tool of reactionary intrigue.

In the conditions of the proletariat, those of old society at large are already virtually swamped. The proletarian is without property; his relation to his wife and children has no longer anything in common with the bourgeois family-relations; modern industrial labour, modern subjection to capital, the same in England as in France, in America as in Germany, has stripped him of every trace of national character. Law, morality, religion, are to him so many bourgeois prejudices, behind which lurk in ambush just as many bourgeois interests.

All the preceding classes that got the upper hand, sought to fortify their already acquired status by subjecting society at large to their conditions of appropriation. The proletarians cannot become masters of the productive forces of society, except by abolishing their own previous mode of appropriation, and thereby also every other previous mode of appropriation. They have nothing of their own to secure and to fortify; their mission is to destroy all previous securities for, and insurances of, individual property.

All previous historical movements were movements of minorities, or in the interests of minorities. The proletarian movement is the self-conscious, independent movement of the immense majority, in the interests of the immense majority. The proletariat, the lowest stratum of our present society, cannot stir, cannot raise itself up, without the whole superincumbent strata of official society being sprung into the air.

Though not in substance, yet in form, the struggle of the proletariat with the bourgeoisie is at first a national struggle. The proletariat of each country must, of course, first of all settle matters with its own bourgeoisie.

In depicting the most general phases of the development of the proletariat, we traced the more or less veiled civil war, raging within existing society, up to the point where that war breaks out into open revolution, and where the violent overthrow of the bourgeoisie lays the foundation for the sway of the proletariat.

Hitherto, every form of society has been based, as we have already seen, on the antagonism of oppressing and oppressed classes. But in order to oppress a class, certain conditions must be assured to it under which it can, at least, continue its slavish existence. The serf, in the period of serfdom, raised himself to membership in the commune, just as the petty bourgeois, under the yoke of feudal absolutism, managed to develop into a bourgeois. The modern labourer, on the contrary, instead of rising with the progress of industry, sinks deeper and deeper below the conditions of existence of his own class. He becomes a pauper, and pauperism develops more rapidly than population and wealth. And here it becomes evident, that the bourgeoisie is unfit any longer to be the ruling class in society, and to impose its conditions of existence upon society as an over-riding law. It is unfit to rule because it is incompetent to assure an existence to its slave within his slavery, because it cannot help letting him sink into such a state, that it has to feed him, instead of being fed by him. Society can no longer live under this bourgeoisie, in other words, its existence is no longer compatible with society.

The essential condition for the existence, and for the sway of the bourgeois class, is the formation and augmentation of capital; the condition for capital is wage-labour. Wage-labour rests exclusively on competition between the labourers. The advance of industry, whose involuntary promoter is the bourgeoisie, replaces the isolation of the labourers, due to competition, by their revolutionary combination, due to association. The development of Modern Industry, therefore, cuts from under its feet the very foundation on which the bourgeoisie produces and appropriates products. What the bourgeoisie, therefore, produces, above all, is its own grave-diggers. Its fall and the victory of the proletariat are equally inevitable.

Notes

1. Lassalle personally, to us, always acknowledged himself to be a "disciple" of Marx, and, as such, stood, of course, on the ground of the Manifesto. Matters were quite different with regard to those of his followers who did not go beyond his demand for producers' co-operatives supported by state credits and who divided the whole working class into supporters by state credits and who divided the whole working class into supporters of state assistance and supporters of self-assistance. [*Note by Engels.*]

2. K. Marx, *General Rules of the International Working Men's Association* (see Marx and Engels, *Selected Works*, Moscow, 1962, Vol. I, pp. 386-89).—*Ed.*

3. W. Bevan.—*Ed.*

4. By bourgeoisie is meant the class of modern Capitalists, owners of the means of social production and employers of wage-labour. By proletariat, the class of modern wage-labourers who, having no means of production of their own, are reduced to selling their labour-power in order to live. [*Note by Engels to the English edition of 1988*].

5. That is, all *written* history. In 1847, the pre-history of society, the social organisation existing previous to recorded history, was all but unknown. Since then, Haxthausen discovered common ownership of land in Russia, Maurer proved it to be the social foundation from which all Teutonic races started in history, and by and by village

communities were found to be, or to have been the primitive form of society everywhere from India to Ireland. The inner organisation of this primitive Communistic society was laid bare, in its typical form, by Morgan's crowning discovery of the true nature of the *gens* and its relation to the *tribe*. With the dissolution of these primaeval communities society begins to be differentiated into separate and finally antagonistic classes. I have attempted to retrace this process of dissolution in: "Der Ursprung der Familie, des Privateigenthums und des Staats" [*The Origin of the Family, Private Property and the State*. See pp. 455-593 of this volume.—*Ed.*], 2nd edition, Stuttgart 1886. [*Note by Engels to the English edition of 1888*].

6. Guild-master, that is, a full member of the a guild, a master within, not a head of a guild. [*Note by Engels to the English edition of 1888.*]

7. "Commune" was the name taken, in France, by the nascent towns even before they had conquered from their feudal lords and masters local self-government and political rights as the "Third Estate". Generally speaking, for the economical development of the bourgeoisie, England is here taken as the typical country; for its political development, France. [*Note by Engels to the English edition of 1888.*]

This was the name given their urban communities by the townsmen of Italy and France, after they had purchased or wrested their initial rights of self-government from their feudal lords. [*Note by Engels to the German edition of 1890.*]

30. Marxist Class Analysis

Barry Hindess

This chapter presents an outline of the basic features of marxist class analysis and an indication of the range of theoretical and political differences that can occur within it. It is organized in three sections. The first introduces some of Marx's programmatic statements of his general approach and, by way of illustration, looks briefly at an example of his class analysis of French politics. The other two take up some influential debates within marxism to show that marxism is very far from being a monolithic theoretical position. One looks at the debates between Lenin and Kautsky, around the time of the Russian revolution, concerning the class character of parliamentary democracy; the other considers differences between 'structuralist' and 'sociological' styles of marxist class analysis, taking as an illustration the debate between Poulantzas and Miliband.

Marx's theory of history and class struggle

> In the social production of their existence, men inevitably enter into definite relations, which are independent of their will, namely relations of production appropriate to a given stage in the development of their material forces of production. The totality of these relations of production constitutes the economic structure of society, the real foundation, on which arises a legal and political superstructure and to which correspond definite forms of social consciousness. The mode of production of material life conditions the general process of social, political and intellectual life. It is not the consciousness of men that determines their existence, but their social existence that determines their consciousness. At a certain stage of development, the material productive forces of society come into conflict with the existing relations of production or — this merely expresses the same thing in legal terms — with the property relations within the framework of which they have operated hitherto. From forms of development of the productive forces these relations turn into their fetters. Then begins an era of social revolution. The changes in the economic foundation lead sooner or later to the transformation of the whole immense superstructure . . . (Marx, 1971, p. 21)

Two of the best known shorter excerpts from Marx's work are the passage just quoted from the Preface to *A Contribution to the Critique of Political Economy* and the following two sentences from the first section of *The Communist Manifesto:*

> The history of all hitherto existing society is the history of class struggles. Freeman and slave, patrician and plebeian, lord and serf, guild-master and journeyman, in a word, oppressor and oppressed, stood in constant opposition to one another, carried on an uninterrupted, now hidden, now

Barry Hindess: 'Marxist Class Analysis' from *POLITICS AND CLASS ANALYSIS* (Basil Blackwell Limited, 1987), pp. 11-33.

> open fight, a fight that each time ended, either in a revolutionary
> re-constitution of society at large, or in the common ruin of the contending
> classes. (Marx and Engels, 1968, pp. 35–6)

In other writings Marx and subsequent marxists have provided more sophisticated accounts of various aspects of their approach, but these passages nevertheless give a good concise statement of the most basic features of Marx's theory of history. The Preface gives a schematic outline of the structure of society and the mechanisms of social change, and the passage from *The Communist Manifesto* is a polemical assertion of the role of class struggle in history. I will consider these issues in turn.

In the Preface, Marx presents a model of society as structured by three loosely defined parts or levels, namely, 'the economic foundation', 'a legal and political superstructure' and 'definite forms of social consciousness'. Together these define a mode of production, and its parts are said to be related in such a way that the first plays a primary role, in the sense that changes in the economic foundation of society lead to corresponding changes elsewhere. The economic foundation itself is further divided into 'relations of production' and 'material forces of production'. 'Relations of production' involve definite forms of possession of, or separation from, the means of production. Some examples of different relations of production will be considered in a moment. 'Forces of production' is a loose term referring to forms of organization and integration of distinct labour processes and to various other features that affect the level of productivity of a society. The forces of production of capitalist society would include the complex division of labour, the use of machinery and mechanized transmission within the workplace (as distinct from the limited division of labour characteristic of handicraft production), and the integration of workplaces through market exchanges (as distinct from state planning and other forms of non-market distribution).

The Preface indicates that the relationship between the relations and forces of production provides the general mechanism of social change. Marx suggests that the forces of production have an immanent tendency to develop which inevitably brings them into conflict with existing relations of production (or property relations). This contradiction generates a period of acute social conflict, culminating in the overthrow of the existing relations of production and the formation of a new mode of production. History therefore moves from one mode of production to another, with capitalism representing, in Marx's time, the highest stage of development of the productive forces. Later in the Preface Marx refers to capitalist relations of production as 'the last antagonistic form'. This means that after a period of transition the overthrow of capitalism will lead to a classless society in which productive property is held in common and there are no further contradictions between relations and forces of production.

This model of the structure of society and of historical change may seem straightforward enough at first sight, but it is important to recognize that there are several respects in which it remains obscure. Marx does not clearly define the connections between the three parts of society which he refers to with the words 'on which arises' and 'to which corresponds'. Or again, the assertion that changes in the economic foundation 'lead sooner or later' to transformations elsewhere in society suggests that there may well be periods in which politics, law and 'forms of social thought' do not correspond to the foundation on which they are supposed to arise.

More seriously, perhaps, this general model (of the structure of society and the mechanisms of historical development) is not the product of any systematic demonstration in Marx's work. The Preface states a position, but does not argue for it. In *The German Ideology* (Marx and Engels, 1976) and other works Marx argues strongly for a materialist approach to history, in which material conditions rather than ideas are the starting point of social explanation. There is more than an echo of that position in the Preface. Unfortunately, materialism in that general sense does not explain why the economy rather than, say, politics or kinship and gender relations should be regarded as the 'real foundation on which arises' the rest of society. It is of course trivially true that social life depends on production: those who do not eat do not live to engage in politics. But that truism does not tell us how the economic structure of society is supposed to determine the character of the rest.

In Marx's basic model of society and of societal change the major structural components of society and the relations between them are not rigorously defined, and they are obviously open to a variety of interpretations. This lack of precision in what Marx describes as 'the guiding principle of my studies' is a problem in Marx's theory of history, but it is not a good reason for rejecting it. Theoretical work has to start somewhere, and positions that prove to be inadequate at one stage can always be refined or discarded in later investigations. Marx himself regarded his work as being open to correction. His theories have been the subject of vigorous criticism and equally vigorous defence (for examples, see Cutler *et al.*, 1977, 1978 and Cohen, 1978), and we will consider some of the criticisms below. But few of Marx's most severe critics would deny that his approach has been extraordinarily productive. What should be noted here, however, is an important consequence of Marx's lack of precision. Marxists can agree about the basic model of society and societal change while disagreeing about how exactly it is to be understood, about how precisely law and politics are related to the economic foundation, and how these are related to 'definite forms of social consciousness'. Examples of such disagreements will be considered in later sections of this chapter.

Now, although Marx talks of social revolution in the Preface, he does not refer directly to classes as such or to class struggle. Nevertheless, it is clear from *The Communist Manifesto* and Marx's other writings that class struggle plays a major part in his account of historical change. How do classes fit in to the model of the structure of society sketched in the Preface? That question can be approached from two directions, which indicates a considerable ambiguity in Marx's conceptualization of classes. First, class struggle is the agency of social change: classes are conceived as social forces, as participants in a struggle that takes political and ideological forms. In this sense classes are, or are represented by, political organizations and institutions (political parties, trade unions, state apparatuses) and cultural and ideological forms (for example, by socialist or conservative political doctrines).

Secondly, classes are defined by reference to relations of production. Relations of production involve positions of possession or non-possession of the means of production. Classes consist of those who occupy these positions. In this book we are

313

concerned with classes in capitalist societies, and therefore with capitalist relations of production, but it will be helpful to contrast these with two other kinds of relations of production. Capitalist relations of production define two basic classes: capitalists and workers. Members of the capitalist class possess the means of production in the form of commodities — that is, the land, buildings, machinery and raw materials involved in production are actual or potential objects of commercial transactions. Non-possessors have access to production by means of wage-labour contracts, that is, they sell their labour-power as a commodity. This means that control over production is in the hands of capitalists, since all elements of the production process, including labour-power, are their property. Distribution of the product takes place by means of commodity exchanges between capitalist and capitalist, capitalists and workers (in the exchange of labour-power) and workers and capitalists (in the exchange of consumption goods). Workers are seen as subject to *control* by capitalists and as engaged in *production*. We shall see that this approach leaves considerable room for dispute concerning the class position of employees (i.e. non-possessors) whose job is to control the labour of others and of workers engaged in distribution and financial transactions.

Now consider two other sorts of relations of production. First, in feudal relations of production there are again two basic classes, landowners and serfs. Possession involves the monopoly control of land, and non-possessors have access to land in return for rent (in the form of labour, produce or money). The landowner is therefore in the position of the manager of an estate, controlling both the provision of mills, drainage and other facilities and the use of portions of the land by allocating them to serfs in return for various kinds and levels of rent or by farming them directly with the use of serf labour. Secondly, in petty-commodity production the labourers are also possessors of the means of production, so in this case the relations of production define only one class position. Independent artisans, self-employed professionals and peasants in some societies are engaged in such relations of production.

In Marx's approach to class analysis the forms of possession and non-possession of the means of production have a central place in the identification of classes. Market relations do play an important part in class relations in capitalist societies, but they do so as a consequence of the form in which the means of production are possessed as commodities in capitalist relations of production. Market relations may or may not be present in feudal societies but, on Marx's account, they are not an integral feature of feudal relations of production. We shall see that the market has a very different place in weberian approaches to the identification of classes.

Antagonistic relations of production involve two basic classes, whose different relations to the means of production inevitably create conflicting interests. When Marx refers to bourgeois relations as 'the last antagonistic form', he has in mind the antagonism between the two great classes defined by those relations: the bourgeoisie, who possess the means of production; and the proletariat, who do not. It is the *last* antagonistic form because, in Marx's view, capitalist relations of production will be superseded by possession of the means of production in common. Once that is achieved there is no possibility of antagonism between a class that possesses the means of production and another class that does not.

I will return to some of the problems with this way of identifying classes with particular reference to modern capitalism. For the moment, notice the ambiguity of Marx's discussion of classes. On the one hand, they are defined in terms of opposing positions specified in particular relations of production: bourgeoisie and proletariat, lord and serf, slave-owner and slave, etc. On the other, classes are social forces — in fact the major social forces in history. Why should we identify social forces with the occupants of certain positions in the relations of production? Why should things that are clearly not classes in the latter sense, like political parties, trade unions or newspapers, be treated as if they ultimately represented particular classes and their interests?

These queries reproduce in relation to class the issues raised above in relation to Marx's basic model of society and historical change. In both cases Marx and marxism assume a fundamental relationship between the economy and other features of society — between the 'economic foundation' and other parts of society, and between class in the sense of the occupants of a certain position and class in the sense of a major social force. Just as marxists disagree over the precise interpretation of Marx's model of the structure of society, so they disagree over the precise definition of classes and the connections that are supposed to hold between classes, as defined by relations of production, and the forces engaged in politics and culture. Indeed, different positions on this last issue can be found throughout Marx's own work.

An example of Marx's class analysis: 'The Eighteenth Brumaire'

'The Eighteenth Brumaire of Louis Bonaparte' (Marx, 1968) is an outstanding example of Marx's political analysis. It surveys French political history from the overthrow of Louis-Philippe in 1848 to Louis Bonaparte's *coup d'état* in December 1851. Throughout Europe, 1848 was a year of revolutionary insurrection in the name of constitutional democracy, national self-determination, the abolition of serfdom, and the conversion of all men from subjects of the sovereign into free citizens. With the exception of the emancipation of the serfs in parts of the Austrian empire, the revolution was an almost universal failure. In France, the overthrow of the monarchy in February was followed by crushing defeats for both democratic and revolutionary socialism and then for republicanism. The working class revolt was suppressed, and the victory of the 'party of order' ended in the elevation of Bonaparte to Emperor of France. Marx's discussion of the course of the revolution in France was intended to show that momentous political events could be understood only in terms of their underlying material conditions.

This is not the place for an extended discussion of Marx's classic text, and I use it here simply to introduce two problem areas within marxist class analysis. The first concerns the relations between the economy and the forces engaged in political struggle.

Consider first Marx's comments on what he calls 'the republican faction of the bourgeoisie':

> It was not a faction of the bourgeoisie held together by great common interests and marked off by specific conditions of production. It was a clique of republican-minded bourgeois, writers, lawyers, officers and

315

officials that owed its influence to the personal antipathies of the country against Louis Phillipe, to memories of the old republic, to the republican faith of a number of enthusiasts, above all, however, to French nationalism . . . (Marx, 1968, p. 105)

The two points to notice here are Marx's explicit recognition that this faction is not to be identified by reference to economic conditions, and that the conditions introduced to account for its strength are manifestly non-economic in character. In effect, Marx recognizes the existence of political forces and a field of political conflict that is not immediately explicable in terms of the effects of economic relations.

So far, so good. Unfortunately his treatment of the two Royalist factions is utterly different, openly disparaging any explanation of their differences in terms of principles and the like:

> what kept the two factions apart was not any so-called principles, it was their material conditions of existence, two different kinds of property . . . That at the same time old memories . . . convictions, articles of faith, and principles bound them to one or the other royal house, who is there to deny this? Upon the different forms of property, upon the social conditions of existence, arises an entire superstructure of distinct and peculiarly formed sentiments, illusions, modes of thought and views of life. (pp. 118–19)

Of course, principles are involved, but only because they are themselves the effects of material conditions, of different forms of property. The difficulty raised by the contrast between these passages is clear. If political conditions are not explicable in terms of material conditions (as the treatment of the republican faction suggests) then 'two different kinds of property' cannot account for what kept the Royalist factions apart. If, on the other hand, political forces are reducible to the effects of material conditions, then Marx has no business treating the republican faction as a real and distinct political force.

What is at issue here is the question of reductionism. It is not a serious problem for the overall argument of 'The Eighteenth Brumaire', but it has been a perpetual source of dispute within marxism. I return to the issue of reductionism in [chapter 6], but briefly what is at stake is the question of how far politics, law and culture are explicable in terms of an economic foundation — in terms of classes and the conflicts between them. How far, in other words, does class analysis take us in the understanding of political institutions, ideologies and conflicts? We shall see that the problem of reductionist political analysis is by no means restricted to marxism.

The second problem area to be considered here concerns the tension in the marxist tradition between what might be called 'sociological' and 'structuralist' approaches to class analysis. The first approach operates in terms of a distinction between an objective determination of class position (by reference to relations of production), on the one hand, and a subjective unity of class consciousness, on the other. The point of the distinction can be seen by comparing Marx and Engels's discussion of the proletariat in *The Communist Manifesto* with Marx's comments on the French peasantry in 'The Eighteenth Brumaire'. *The Communist Manifesto* describes the proletariat as developing through various stages, starting with the struggle of individual labourers or of workers in a single factory against their employers, and gradually building up to the class-conscious organization of struggle at a national or even international level by the working class as a whole against the bourgeoisie. At one extreme, the class exists merely as a category of individuals organized, if they are organized at all, into a multitude of local groups. But the growth of capitalist industry leads to a growth in the size of the proletariat, to its concentration in large workplaces and communities and to improved means of communication, which allow for the growth of contacts between different communities of workers. These factors, together with their own experience of struggle against employers and the capitalist state, eventually lead to the integration of the workers into a class-conscious and politically organized collectivity. The proletariat is not a static entity: it is transformed by the dynamics of the capitalist economy, and it transforms itself through the experience of struggle.

Compare that account of the proletariat with the description of the French peasantry in 'The Eighteenth Brumaire':

> The small-holding peasants form a vast mass, the members of which live in similar conditions but without entering into manifold relations with one another. Their mode of production isolates them from one another instead of bringing them into mutual intercourse . . . In so far as there is merely local interconnection among these small-holding peasants, and the identity of their interests begets no community, no national bond and no political organization among them, they do not form a class. They are consequently incapable of enforcing their class interests in their own name, whether through parliament or through a convention. They cannot represent themselves, they must be represented. (1968, p. 171)

The place of the proletariat in the capitalist organization of production, and the development of capitalism itself, leads in the long run to the class-conscious political organization of the working class as a whole. The character of small-holding peasant production and poor communication between peasant communities effectively rule out the possibility of political organization and collective action by the class as a whole.

What these and other passages suggest is a conceptualization of classes as, first, a category of similarly situated individuals, and secondly, under suitable conditions, as a collective social actor — a cultural and political agency. A class *in itself* is defined by the fact that its members occupy a common position in the organization of production. It becomes a class *for itself* only as a consequence of the members' growing awareness of a community of interests. This awareness would be facilitated by some social conditions and by the experience of collective action, and it would be inhibited by other social conditions. The connection between class as defined by relations of production and class as a social force is made in terms of social conditions leading to collective awareness and the formation of ties of solidarity as the basis of communal action.

Such an account of classes has a clear affinity with the weberian approach considered in the [next chapter]. Although they define class situation rather difirerently, both accounts treat it as providing a possible basis for collective action. It is not surprising that many sociologists have been attracted to this version of marxist class analysis, looking for explanations of collective action in terms of awareness of common interests and ties of solidarity.

In sharp contrast to this 'sociological' approach is what might be called the 'structuralist' style of marxist analysis. The term 'structuralism' is used in a variety of different ways in the social sciences. Probably the most common usage refers to a general methodological approach based on features of modern linguistics and widely employed in literary criticism, aesthetic theory and anthropology, especially in France and the USA. In linguistics, 'structuralism' refers to the description and analysis of linguistic features in terms of structures and systems. In its more general usage, 'structuralism' is characterized not simply by a preoccupation with structure, but also with the identification of structures that are supposed to underlie and generate the phenomena under investigation. The best known 'structuralist' in the social sciences is probably the anthropologist Claude Lévi-Strauss. In his analyses of kinship systems and mythology (eg. 1966, 1969), 'structure' refers not to a web of directly observable social relationships, but rather to an underlying reality which constitutes the hidden logic of a social system. 'Structuralism' then is a methodological approach to the analysis of phenomena which refers us to the actions of structures rather than the intentional actions of individuals. Where Lévi-Strauss ultimately refers us to the structures of the human mind, marxist 'structuralism' refers us to the underlying structure of the social formation. Thus the 'structuralist' approach to class analysis subordinates the conceptualization of classes to thc basic model of society as a unity of three levels organized around the primacy of the economy. Classes are defined primarily by reference to the economy, but they are represented in other levels, in politics, law and culture, as a consequence of the relations of determination between the superstructures and the economic foundation on which they are supposed to be based.

I will return to the tension between 'sociological' and 'structuralist' class analysis later in this chapter in connection with the debate between Miliband and Poulantzas. What should be noted for the moment is that 'structuralist' positions suggest ways of treating political organizations, ideologies and cultural forms as *representing* classes and their interests, even in the absence of class consciousness and ties of solidarity. The closing sentences of the passage on the French peasantry quoted above suggest that Marx regards the peasantry as having a decisive political impact, in spite of the fact that they are not in a position to form a collectivity or an organized political force.

The discussion so far has briefly considered Marx's theory of class and history. It involves a model of society and societal change and an insistence on the importance of class struggle in history. That model and that insistence are the common currency of marxism; it is the acceptance of that currency that identifies a distinctively marxist approach to class analysis. But I have also indicated that there are significant ambiguities which allow for different interpretations of the precise definition of classes and the relations that are supposed to hold between classes on the one hand and politics and culture on the other. The common currency of marxism can be put to radically different theoretical and political uses. The remaining sections of this chapter take up two examples of these differences: one a debate over the class character of parliamentary democracy and the other a dispute between 'sociological' and 'structuralist' approaches to the analysis of the capitalist state. The aim is not to take sides in these debates, but rather to clarify what the differences are between the opposed positions and to establish that marxism is far from being a monolithic theoretical or political approach.

The class character of the democratic state

Since their development around the end of the nineteenth century, the representative institutions of mass electoral democracy have posed a problem for marxist class analysis. On the one hand, the democratic state is seen as a capitalist state, that is, as a state serving to reproduce capitalist relations of production and furthering the interests of the capitalist ruling class. On the other hand, the growth of a large and organized working class (the largest section of the population in the more advanced capitalist economies) suggests the possibility of the working class voting its own representatives into power. In effect, class analysis can lead to radically different assessments of the nature of parliamentary regimes. On one side, the democratic state is essentially *capitalist,* indeed in Lenin's view it is 'the best possible shell' for capitalism. On the other side, and precisely because it is democratic, it contains the possibility of a peaceful transfer of state power from the capitalists to the working class.

These opposing interpretations of parliamentary democracy are well represented in a long-running dispute between Kautsky and Lenin in the years before and after the Russian revolutions of 1917. Lenin was a powerful advocate of the 'revolutionary' position, arguing that the capitalist state (democratic or not) must be smashed if the working class is to seize power. This view was opposed by Kautsky well before the Russian revolution, and one of Lenin's best-known books, *The State and Revolution* (1964), written in 1917, has substantial sections devoted to polemics against Kautsky's brand of socialist politics.

Kautsky was an important figure in the German Social Democratic Party, the largest and best-organized socialist party in the late nineteenth and early twentieth centuries. He worked with Marx and Engels and was widely regarded as the third leading figure in marxist theory. He was an early advocate of what later became known as the strategy of the 'parliamentary road to socialism', a strategy that has been taken up by most of the western communist parties in the post-war period. Kautsky wrote *The Dictatorship of the Proletariat* (1964) shortly after the Russian revolution. He regarded the Bolshevik seizure of power in 1917 as a betrayal of democracy and therefore of socialism and, since it associated socialism with dictatorship, as a major obstacle to democratic socialist politics in the rest of Europe. Lenin responded with another polemical book, *The Proletarian Revolution and the Renegade Kautsky* (1964). Although the prestige of Kautsky and the German Social Democratic Party had been damaged by splits over participation in the First World War, Lenin still had good reason to fear the effects of criticism from someone of Kautsky's stature.

The dispute is significant for the present discussion because both Lenin and Kautsky write as convinced marxists, and they make considerable use of the writings of Marx and Engels in support of their arguments. In particular, they both refer to Marx and Engels's comment on the lessons of the Paris Commune in their Preface to the 1872 edition of *The Communist Manifesto*. This suggests that the experience of the Commune, 'where the proletariat for the first time held power for two whole months' makes some details of the *Manifesto* appear dated: 'One thing especially was proved by the Commune, viz., that the working class cannot simply lay hold of the ready made state machinery, and wield it for its own purposes' (Marx and Engels, 1968, p. 99). In Kautsky's view the principal lesson of the Commune is that democracy is an indispensable prerequisite for socialism. The Parisian working class could not simply lay hold of the existing state machine because it was not democratic. They therefore set out to construct a democratic state machine of their own. Lenin counters with the argument that there is democracy and democracy: there is parliamentary democracy, which is an instrument of bourgeois rule, and there is proletarian democracy, democracy for the working class. This dispute raises important issues of democratic theory, some of which I have discussed elsewhere (Hindess, 1983). What matters for present purposes is to see how marxist class analysis can give rise to such radically opposed interpretations of parliamentary democracy.

The validity of a class analysis of politics or of Marx's general model of society is not at issue between Kautsky and Lenin. Rather, it is the question of how precisely politics and the state are to be analysed in class terms. For Kautsky, politics is class struggle: the working class struggles first to obtain democracy, and then uses it to effect the transfer of state power and the socialist transformation of society. Democracy for Kautsky is not just a matter of universal suffrage; it also requires the state machine (the police, the military and the civil bureaucracy) to be subject to parliamentary control, competition between parties for popular support, and freedom of speech and organization. An elected assembly is necessary to secure popular control over central government, and party competition and basic political liberties allow political differences and alliances to be worked out in a relatively open way — they also allow for changes in the party of government. Kautsky therefore insists on the difference between parties and classes: working class power is not to be identified with the rule of a single party claiming to represent the working class.

Kautsky goes on to argue that the capacity of parliament to dominate the state machine varies according to the balance of political forces outside parliament, and especially according to the strength of the organized working class. Where the working class is weak the capacity of parliament to control the activities of the state will be very limited. But, in Kautsky's view, the effects of capitalist economic development will ensure that there is a substantial working class majority in the population. Given universal suffrage, the experience of working class struggle will eventually ensure a parliamentary majority for socialism backed by a powerful and well-organized working class. On this account of the development of politics under capitalism, democracy is the product of popular struggle and once achieved, it provides the institutional conditions in which state power may be held by the bourgeoisie or by the proletariat. Kautsky does not, of course, deny that politics in capitalist democracies is loaded against the left, or that elected parliaments are limited in their capacity to control the state. His argument is that these problems can be overcome by a numerically strong and well-organized working class.

Lenin disputes this possibility. He too sees politics as class struggle, but he also maintains that the institutional conditions of parliamentary democracy provide an arena of political struggle that only appears to be free and open. In fact it is heavily weighted against the interests of the working class. Important sections of the state machine are not within the effective control of parliament; the political freedoms and competition that Kautsky makes such a fuss over in fact work to the benefit of the bourgeoisie through their ownership of the media, control over meeting places, etc. As for the protection of the rights of individuals and political minorities, this is always partial and selective: in practice, in Lenin's view, it favours the parties of the bourgeoisie and the 'democratic' state rarely hesitates to suppress militant organizations of the left. For Lenin democracy is a form of dictatorship by a class: it is always democracy for one class and against another. Parliamentary democracy is democracy for the capitalists and must be overthrown and replaced by popular democracy, the institutional reflection of the interests of the working class and working people generally. On this view, to argue (as Kautsky does) that state power in a democracy may be held by the bourgeoisie or by the proletariat is to ignore the fundamental class determinants of the institutional forms of political life.

A final thing to notice about this dispute is that it is very different in tone from normal academic argument. *The Dictatorship of the Proletariat* is a sustained attack on the Bolsheviks' seizure of state power in 1917 and on their subsequent use of that power. For that reason alone the bitterness of Lenin's response is not surprising. However, there is a more general point to be made here. Lenin and Kautsky were political leaders, not academic social scientists. Indeed, the most influential marxists thinkers – Kautsky, Lenin, Gramsci, Mao — have all been important political figures, and their major political analyses have been developed in the context of strategic political argument. In that sense marxism has never been just another tradition of academic work — throughout most of its history, theoretical work and social analysis within the marxist tradition have been closely tied to problems of political practice. This link has shown significant signs of weakening over the last 30 years or so as a growing proportion of influential marxists have been in academic positions. Nevertheless disagreements within marxism still frequently carry political overtones that are generally absent from debates within other intellectual traditions in the humanities and social sciences.

'Structuralism' and the human subject

Our second debate concerning the class analysis of the state has a very different character from that between Kautsky and Lenin. It consists of Poulantzas's review of Miliband's book, *The State in Capitalist Society* and a reply by Miliband (both reprinted in Blackburn, 1972). The central issue between them is not so much the class character of the state but rather the methodological question of how it should be analysed. In terms of our earlier discussion of different approaches to marxist class analysis, Poulantzas's argument here is militantly 'structuralist', while Miliband's approach is more nearly sociological in character. Consideration of their arguments will reveal some striking differences regarding the place of the human subject in social analysis.

Poulantzas's argument is organized around two central themes. The first of these is epistemological: it concerns the difference between science and ideology. Briefly, Poulantzas's position is that marxism is a science and that the non-marxist social sciences — economics, sociology, political science — are ideologies. They may be more or less rigorous in their arguments and demonstrations, but they are fundamentally and systematically misleading in their accounts of capitalist society. I have argued elsewhere that such distinctions between marxist 'science' and bourgeois 'ideologies' cannot be sustained (Hindess, 1977), but that argument need not concern us here. It is sufficient to note Poulantzas's view on this point in order to understand his insistence that marxism should have no truck with the 'ideological' concepts of bourgeois social science — for example in his comments on 'elites'. A secondary theme here concerns the alleged effects of theoretical contamination in marxist thought. It leads to theoretical deviations and therefore to political errors, for example, to reformism or a confusion between socialism and trade-unionism.

But it is the second central theme that is important for present purposes. Poulantzas advocates a particularly clear and systematic version of what might be called the 'structuralist' approach to marxist class analysis. I suggested that 'structuralism' provides a way of analysing politics, law or culture in terms of classes and their interests, without assuming class consciousness on the part of the individuals involved. In this loose sense, 'structuralism' is an element in most marxist work: marxist analyses and explanations generally go beyond the consciousnesses of individuals in their discussions of how organizations and ideologies 'represent' the interests of particular classes or fractions of classes.

Marxist 'structuralism' is based on a particular interpretation of the model of society sketched by Marx in the 1859 Preface. It is his elaboration of that model that allows Poulantzas to discuss the position of managers or the role of the state in terms of objective functions rather than in terms of intersubjective relations. Marx refers to the economy as the foundation of the whole superstructure of society. This is what Poulantzas refers to as 'the role of determinant in the last instance': the economic base determines (but only 'in the last instance') the general character of the different parts of society and the relations between them. What these relations are will still vary from one mode of production to another, so that in some cases politics or ideology may play a more important role than the economy in the day-to-day life of the society. That is what Poulantzas calls the dominant role.

On this account, then, we have a complex structure of three levels: an economic base, a political and legal superstructure, and 'forms of social consciousness' (or ideology), interacting with each other in ways that vary from one mode of production to another. Although the economy plays the ultimately determining role, the other levels are nevertheless supposed to have some real effectiveness of their own. That is the point of the qualification, determinant *in the last instance*. What Poulantzas in the first part of his review refers to as 'economism' is the mistake of treating the rest of society as simply reflecting the economic base, forgetting that the other levels are 'relatively autonomous', that is, that they have real effects of their own. Some critics have argued that these notions of 'determination in the last instance' and 'relative autonomy' cannot be coherently sustained. We leave that issue for discussion in [chapter 6].

Poulantzas's fundamental argument against Miliband is that a marxist analysis should begin by locating its object within the marxist model of society as a complex structured whole. To neglect that starting point is to allow the ideological concerns of marxism's intellectual opponents to dominate the analysis, and thereby to expose marxism to contamination by bourgeois ideology. For example, in his discussion of Miliband's account of the state bureaucracy, Poulantzas argues that he concedes too much to the opponents of marxism. By concentrating on providing a direct rebuttal of their arguments, Miliband concedes the terms in which they approach the analysis of the state. In effect, he investigates the origins of the leading members of the state machine and tries to demonstrate their social and cultural links with the ruling class.

It is all very well, in Poulantzas's view to collect such information, but it doesn't address the most important question. The relation between the state and the ruling class is an objective relation that arises as a consequence of the structure of capitalist society, not as an effect of the social composition and conduct of the members of the state machine. The latter is really an effect of the structure, not an explanation of it. Poulantzas argues that Miliband should have established the function of the state within capitalist societies before he investigated the members of the state bureaucracy. Starting from a clear recognition of the function of the state it would then be possible to determine the significance of the social background and other characteristics of the state bureaucracy for the performance of that function. Poulantzas suggests, for example, that it is precisely the fact that the state bureaucracy is not operated directly by capitalists themselves that allows the state to serve the interests of the capitalist class as a whole.

Poulantzas's objection to analysis of the state in terms of the background, values and interpersonal relations of individuals is that it concedes too much to the 'problematic of the subject'. In other words it proceeds as if the human individual were the origin of action, so that explanation has to be grounded in the motivations of individuals. Poulantzas objects that that approach contradicts a principle which he regards as fundamental to marxism, namely, that classes and the state are bearers of objective functions determined by their location in the structure of society. To characterize the class position of managers, for example: 'one need not refer to the motivations of their conduct, but only to their place in production and their relationship to the ownership of the means of production' (Poulantzas, 1972, p. 244). On that view, the action of the structure is the ultimate source of explanation; human individuals are merely its 'bearers'.

I have suggested that marxist analysis always goes beyond the consciousnesses of individuals to locate its analyses and explanations in some discussion of material conditions. Poulantzas' comments on the place of the human subject in marxist theory takes this 'structuralist' tendency to a particularly clear extreme. He dismisses the 'problematic of the subject', in which the individual's will and consciousness appear as the origin of social action, as belonging to the ideological theories of the bourgeois social sciences. He insists that, on the contrary, people are to be treated as bearers of the objective structures and systems of relations in which they are located. The consciousness of individuals cannot explain their actions. They are merely the products of their objective locations and of the part they play in the reproduction of capitalist social relations.

Miliband has little time for such a complete relegation of the individual to an effect of its place in the structure, and he responds by accusing his critic of 'superstructuralism'. Miliband argues that because Poulantzas appears to reduce everything to a matter of objective structures, he ends up with little more than a complicated version of the 'economism' that he condemns in his opening paragraphs. In Miliband's view, the relationship between the state and the various classes is more complex than Poulantzas's 'structural determinism' allows. The values and concerns of managers or of the state elites play an important part in Miliband's account of their behaviour, and he is concerned to investigate the features of their social backgrounds and patterns of social life that sustain those values.

But the supposed effects of the structure nevertheless continue to play an essential part in Miliband's argument. To take just one example, consider what *The State in Capitalist Society* refers to as 'the process of legitimation'. Miliband follows Gramsci in maintaining that the survival of modern capitalist societies depends to a considerable extent on the 'consent' of an overwhelming majority whose real interests lie in the overthrow of capitalism. The real interests of the working class and other oppressed groups are given by their position in the structure of capitalist social relations. In other words, their interests are determined by their position in the structure, and what has to be explained is their failure to recognise those interests and act on them.

The role of consent in this argument follows from the observation that the repressive apparatuses of the state, that is, the police and the military, are not enough to account for the relative political stability of the advanced capitalist societies. The vast majority of the population are very far from a socialist politics committed to the overthrow of capitalism. Yet marxist class analysis tells us that the working class, who form a majority in the advanced capitalist economies, have an objective interest in the overthrow of capitalism, and that they share that interest with other oppressed groups who may not themselves be directly exploited by capitalists. The continued survival of capitalism must therefore be explained by a combination of repression and 'consent'. It is in order to explain that consent that *The State in Capitalist Society* devotes so much attention to what Miliband calls 'the process of legitimation'.

The important points to notice here are first that the problem of consent arises in this form only because Miliband's marxist analysis of capitalism identifies the real interests of the working class and other groups quite independently of any recognition of those interests on the part of the individuals concerned. Miliband disputes Poulantzas's 'superstructuralism' but his own argument is crucially dependent on another structural account of classes and their real interests. Given that account 'the process of legitimation' is brought in to explain why workers (and others) fail to pursue their real interests. It works by inculcating the bulk of the population with ideologies representing the interests of the capitalist ruling class through the actions of a variety of organizations and institutions — churches, political parties, schools, etc. Poulantzas and Miliband disagree over whether these should all be included within the concept of the state, but they agree on their basic function in the maintenance of capitalism.

Secondly, for all the striking differences between them, these arguments of Poulantzas and Miliband clearly exhibit the characteristic promise of class analysis. Different versions of class analysis present their premise in rather different terms, but in all cases it involves the claim that crucial features of the parties, movements, ideologies and other elements of political life can be understood by reference to something more fundamental. My [closing chapters] argue that this claim is nothing more than a gesture, and that it cannot be substantiated.

Developments in
Interpretative Sociology

31. Society as a Conspiracy: Phenomenological Sociology and Ethnomethodology

Ian Craib

Symbolic interactionism is the longest-standing sociological tradition concerned with looking at day-to-day social interactions. I have suggested that it can fairly easily be built into a macro-sociology that makes social action its starting point. An alternative — and in many ways very different — concern with interaction emerged during the late 1960s. This chapter will be primarily concerned with ethnomethodology, just one of a number of approaches that emerged during that period and later — phenomenological sociology, existential sociology, the sociology of everyday life — none of which really consolidated itself as a major school, although many of their insights have become common currency. I think this flourish can be seen as part of the general trend that I have already mentioned: away from any attempt to conceive of society as an 'entity' over and above individuals and towards an emphasis — what I regard as a gross overemphasis — on the ways in which human beings create their social worlds: a response to modern conditions that ignores what it is unpleasant to see. Ethnomethodology and the others are part of a swing to 'social constructionism' over the past quarter-century. Many of these approaches were motivated by a general and rather vague humanist and liberationist spirit, and it is interesting that — at the moment, at any rate — the most rigorous and least political one has proved most hardy. I will approach ethnomethodology initially through its philosophical background — European phenomenology and linguistic philosophy.

The philosophical background

Phenomenology

The founding father of phenomenological philosophy was Edmund Husserl, whose most important work was published in the last decade of the nineteenth century and the first decades of this century. Husserl was concerned to develop a radical philosophy in a literal sense of the word: a philosophy that goes to the roots of our knowledge and experience. In particular, he argued that scientific knowledge had become divorced from the everyday experience and activities in which it is rooted, and he saw the task of phenomenology as restoring that connection. Half a century later, sociologists were to use the same argument against established social theory, in particular structural-functionalism: it had become divorced from everyday social experience.

Phenomenology is concerned solely with the structures and workings of human consciousness, and its basic — though often implicit — presupposition is that the world we live in is created in consciousness, in our heads. Of course, it would be absurd to deny that there is any external world, but the argument is that the outside world has

Copyright © 1992 Craib, Ian. Reproduced from *MODERN SOCIAL THEORY: FROM PARSONS TO HABERMAS*. Reprinted with permission of Harvester Wheatsheaf and St Martin's Press, Incorporated.

meaning only through our consciousness of it. The sociologist — or any scientist, for that matter — is interested only in the world in so far as it is meaningful, and she must therefore understand how we make it meaningful. This is achieved through setting aside what we normally assume we know and tracing the process of coming to know it. This setting aside of our knowledge is referred to sometimes as the 'phenomenological reduction', sometimes as 'bracketing', and in the more technical literature as the *époché*.

Phenomenological sociology

To begin with, I want to make two points. First, I must emphasise the similarity between the approaches I have discussed so far and the concerns of phenomenology. They all see meanings — norms, values beliefs, etc. — as the central focus of the sociological enterprise. They are all theories of persons and of action. Secondly, I think that phenomenology, in its sociological form, loses some of its most interesting aspects. I have discussed it so far purely as a theory of cognition, of knowing: many phenomenological philosophers, including Husserl, have concerned themselves with a much wider range of experience — with emotions, the imagination, hallucination and so on. This side has been lost in phenomenological sociology.

The most prominent phenomenological sociologist was Alfred Schutz, a pupil of Husserl who emigrated to the USA after the rise of fascism in Europe and made a career as a banker and part-time teacher. He came under the influence of pragmatist philosophy and symbolic interactionism, and his classic work, *The Phenomenology of the Social World* (1972), was concerned with combining the insights of phenomenology with sociology through a philosophical critique of the work of Max Weber. He attempted to show how we build our knowledge of the social world from a basic stream of incoherent and meaningless experience. We do this through a process of 'typification', which involves building up classes of experience through similarity. Thus, in my stream of experience, I notice that certain objects have particular features in common — that they move from place to place, perhaps, whilst their surroundings remain constant. This gives me the most abstract category of 'living beings'; then I notice that amongst these there are some who emit consistent noises of a type of which I am capable; thus, from 'living beings' I sort out 'other people'. I then distinguish different classes of other people: blacks and whites, men and women. Finally, I identify those characteristics which distinguish specific others: my mother, my friend. Thus we build up what Schutz calls 'meaning contexts', sets of criteria by means of which we organise out sense experience into a meaningful world and stocks of knowledge, which are not stocks of knowledge *about* the world but, for all practical purposes, the world itself. Action and social action thus become things that happen in consciousness: we are concerned with acts of consciousness rather than action in the world, and the social world is something which we create together.

This is the basis of our social world: taken-for-granted, common-sense knowledge. We each organise the world of common-sense knowledge on the basis of the 'here and now', of what we are doing in a particular time and place, or — to use another of Schutz's terms — on the basis of our 'project'. The sociologist is distinguished from other people by her own project and consequent organisation of the shared stocks of knowledge. Her project is to construct a rational, and therefore objective, account of the social world. To do this, she must construct 'second-order typifications': typifications of out common-sense typifications which order the social world in a rational way; we can then use this rational model to predict how people behave if they behave rationally, and to indicate the irrationality of their action if it does not fit the model. Schutz talks about social theory as creating a world of rational puppets who can be manipulated by the theorist to provide knowledge about the real world: we can say that if people have certain goals and behave rationally, then they will act in such a way; if the situation changes, then their action will change in this or that way. Again the cognitive emphasis of Schutz's work is clear, and, paradoxically, we arrive at a version of rational choice theory. It is, however, a more complete version, showing how the situation of choice is constructed and giving a more elaborate analysis of motivation: Schutz, for example, distinguishes between 'because motives', what we know might happen on the basis of experience, and 'in order to' motives, the state of affairs we want to achieve.

Generally Schutz's work has been used to provide further sensitising concepts, often implicitly. I am not aware of any one empirical study that uses it systematically except through the development of ethnomethodology, which I will be discussing shortly. There is, however, one writer, Peter Berger, who has made systematic attempts to extend phenomenology to a theory of society. The central work, which he wrote with Thomas Luckman, is *The Social Construction of Reality* (1967), which explicitly sets out to combine a holistic and individualistic analysis. Berger and Luckman still see shared, taken-for-granted, common-sense meanings as the basis of social organisation, but they are more concerned with shared and explicit overarching meanings that develop out of common-sense meanings. They argue that human beings have very few stable and specific instincts; the stability of social life must therefore come from the social environment which they themselves create, and in this environment it is the overarching values and meanings, initially religious, which provide the real focus of social organisation and are shared by everybody. Berger and Luckman are concerned with the way in which these meanings develop and are 'objectivated' in social institutions, and thus socialise new members of a society. Overall, this leaves us with an approach similar to structural-functionalism. Ideas, cultural values and norms are seen as the centre of social organisation, into which new members are socialised. Berger and Luckman spend rather more time talking about the development of these values out of the social interaction of individuals, but the end-picture of social organisation is the same. The crucial difference is that structural-functionalism has a great deal to say about institutional organisations and the systematic relationships between institutions, whereas for Berger and Luckman these tend to be secondary. It is fairly simple to place this approach in a structural-functionalist context as yet another fragment, concerned with the cultural system, which for Parsons is one of four systems, even if it is the most important. I said above that once phenomenology has placed action 'inside the head', it finds it difficult to break out again; and indeed, in the sociological literature Berger is regarded primarily as a sociologist of knowledge, rather than a theorist of society.

Linguistic philosophy

Ethnomethodology provides our first encounter with what has become known as the 'linguistic turn' in modern philosophy: an increasing concern with the nature of language as somehow providing the key to the world; in different ways, British analytical philosophy and European philosophy have focused on language, and this concern has fed through to sociology — primarily through ethnomethodology and Giddens's structuration theory, but also in the form of post-structuralism.

Here I am concerned with the former, and I will approach it through the work of Peter Winch, whose *The Idea of a Social Science* (1958) has had a sort of underground influence in sociology, rarely acknowledged by sociologists. For Winch, society — or social relations — and the way we conceive of social relations are the same thing; the task of philosophy and of social science is the same: to elaborate the 'form of life' of a particular society, the way in which that society conceives of its social relations. He employs a now popular analogy with language, taken here from Wittgenstein. What is interesting about language is that there is no substantive definition of a word which covers all its uses. Wittgenstein talked about 'language games', and the word 'game' is a good example. Netball is a game, so is chess and so is Snakes and Ladders; but I can also talk about the 'sociology game'; people can 'play games' with me, or vice versa, and — at least during the 1960s — a 'game bird' could mean, in different contexts, a pheasant, a partridge, a grouse, or a woman who was willing to engage in sexual intercourse. There is no definition of the word that could link all these usages. Rather, there are rules which govern the use of the word, implicit rules which we none the less all share — rules which, for example, would leave people looking puzzled if I talked about having had a 'game shave' this morning.

We can look at social action in the same way: it is rule-following, and the elaboration of a 'form of life' is the elaboration of the rules governing a culture or subculture, the rules governing the way we conceive of — effectively, the way we create — our world. This leads to a fairly thoroughgoing relativism. No one form of life takes priority over another, none is more 'true' — in the classic argument, science and witchcraft are alternative forms of life, there are no external standards by which we can judge one to be better than another. However, the fact that we are all human, that all cultures have to deal with the fact that we are born, we die, and we have to organise our sexual relations, means that there is a basis for mutual understanding.

Ethnomethodology: doing

For some time, ethnomethodology was a thorn in the side of the sociological establishment; it appeared to undermine all existing forms of sociological work and indirectly challenge the integrity of established sociologists. There was a period at the beginning of the 1970s when a number of sociology departments in universities in the USA and Britain were split by arguments, and there are stories of ethnomethodologists being fired from their jobs simply because they were ethnomethodologists. After an initial cult popularity the movement subsided somewhat, and although a number of sociologists still identify themselves with the approach, it has settled into being another of the discipline's many aspects. The analogy I drew with viewing society as a conspiracy is even more apt in the case of ethnomethodology. Like phenomenology, ethnomethodology sees social organisation as something which has to be established out of different individuals' different experiences. However, whereas Schutz would argue that order is the result of shared common-sense knowledge, ethnomethodology argues that such knowledge is itself inherently unstable, something which is created anew in each new encounter. We conspire together to create the impression of shared common-sense knowledge. In a classroom we all assume that we are reasonably intelligent people engaged in a process of learning and teaching and rarely, if at all, do we need to articulate those assumptions. For Schutz the existence of such assumptions explains the orderly proceeding of the class. For an ethnomethodologist, such assumptions do not exist in any substantial way, and in each and every class we are conspiring together — of necessity in a taken-for-granted way — to give each other the impression that they do exist. We are 'doing' a class — my students are 'doing' being students and I am 'doing' being a teacher. Every stable social interaction is an *achievement*, something done, and ethnomethodology seeks to discover how it is done. Hence the name: *ology*, the study of, *ethno*, peoples, *method*, methods — for creating social order.

It used to be common to distinguish between 'situational' and 'linguistic' ethnomethodology, but I think such a distinction is misleading, since the central insights of the approach have to do with our use of language to make situations stable, although certainly linguistic concerns have tended to be more narrow and have less connection with sociology in a wider sense. Paradoxically, the clarity of expression associated with linguistic philosophy is transformed by ethnomethodology into the most convoluted jargon to have appeared in an area where jargon is the norm. As time has passed, it has become clear that all this verbiage hides two important ideas which have led to some interesting work and a lot of nonsense — or, more charitably, a lost of routine work dressed up in a jargon that makes it seem nonsense. These ideas are built into a criticism of established sociology, and this provides a good entry to the substantive contribution of ethnomethodology.

The usual way of putting this criticism is that conventional sociology takes as a resource what should be taken as a topic. At some level, different in each case, the meanings employed by those we study — their norms, values, attitudes and beliefs; the rules which govern their conduct — are treated as if their meaning were unproblematic. The work of explanation then employs those very same meanings as its basis — the sociologist conspires with the people she studies to produce yet another impression of social order. This is where the important insights of ethnomethodology come into play. The first is the inherent *indexicality* of meaning. Language works rather like an indexing system in a library, constantly referring us to other works on the same topic, works by the same author, and so on; the meaning of each term in a language refers us to its context, the situation in which it is used and the words around it. This is most obvious with pronouns such as 'you' — which 'you' I am talking about is clear only in the situation in which I use it. However, the same is true of any word or statement; when we listen to somebody talk, we are always having to wait to understand what they are saying: if you go back and read the first sentence of this paragraph, it is by no means clear what I am talking about; in the process of reading you suspend judgement until I explain what I mean. However, the same is true of any sentence or phrase taken in isolation, and the process of explanation has no end. It is always possible to ask, 'What do you mean?' to any reply you get. We cannot, therefore, take any meaning for granted, yet we all behave as though we can. This is essentially the same insight into the nature of language as that provided by Peter Winch.

The second significant idea approaches the question of how we can behave as though meaning were clear: it points to the *reflexivity* of our talk about our actions and situations. When we describe a situation, we are simultaneously creating it, making it appear solid, meaningful and rational. When I write: 'I am writing a book on sociological theory', I am not just describing what I am doing, I am simultaneously justifying what I am doing, telling myself and others how to approach what I am doing, removing areas of doubt and uncertainty. The term 'reflexivity' sums up the activities that we employ in everyday interaction, to correct 'indexicality' and establish a sense of social stability. Harold Garfinkel, the generally recognised founder of ethnomethodology, first followed Schutz in referring to them as 'background expectancies', taken-for-granted forms of common-sense knowledge. His earlier work took the form of experiments to establish the existence of such expectations, and of indexicality. He would send his students out to do things that would challenge background expectations — for example, to go into a department store and try to bargain for goods, or to go back to their family home and behave as if they were lodgers. He regarded the resulting social disorder as proving his claim. To demonstrate indexicality he asked them to clarify the meaning of a transcribed conversation between a husband and wife, and of course no complete clarification was possible. He could always ask, 'What do you mean by this?'

Later he came to talk less about background expectations and more about 'practices' and rules, emphasising the point that maintaining an impression of social order is a never-ceasing activity. Such activities are difficult to grasp at first, simply because they are, in Garfinkel's view, a taken-for-granted basis to all our actions; it is rather like paying constant attention to the process of breathing or the way in which we put one foot in front of another. A couple of examples should suffice. The first is 'glossing'. If we use the word at all in our everyday speech, glossing usually refers to something like 'avoiding the issue', trying to talk our way around the issue. The first part of this paragraph is glossing — I could not give a literal definition of these practices, so I talked about how hard it is to understand them. If the argument about indexicality is correct, then all talking is glossing. One of the most interesting ethnomethodologists, Aaron Cicourel, sums it up thus:

> We can perhaps achieve glimpses of our glossing activity by making it clear that every attempt to stimulate or avoid the glossing activity is itself a glossing operation. This means showing the absurdity of efforts to be uncompromisingly literal in our description of observed events or activities in which we participate. (Cicourel, 1973: 109)

In the process of glossing, it seems we have recourse to certain implicit and taken-for-granted rules (as opposed to taken-for-granted substantive knowledge). An example of such a rule is the *et cetera* clause, an addendum to all rules of social behaviour which says something like 'except in reasonable circumstances'. For example, when I give a lecture, there is an informal (and sometimes formal) rule that I am the one who does the talking and everybody else keeps quiet. The *et cetera* rule allows people to break the first rule 'in reasonable circumstances': by asking a question, perhaps, or carrying on a short whispered conversation with a neighbour, or pointing out that the room is on fire. The next step would be to look at ways in which the *et cetera* rule is invoked.

Again we are left with a low-level theory — a few theoretical insights which point towards empirical investigation. Although there have been attempts to develop the theory further — I shall look at these shortly — the emphasis of ethnomethodology has been on empirical work. It involves a sort of empirical application of the phenomenological reduction: the researcher pays no attention to the substance of what people say (that would be to engage in the conspiracy of giving an impression of social order) but looks at the way they say it, trying to identify the rule and practices by means of which the impression of order is given. The result is a startling departure from what we would normally expect. Another early ethnomethodologist, Harvey Sacks, employed his research time in a Suicide Prevention Centre studying the way in which people opened telephone conversations. Much ethnomethodological research seems to spend a great deal of time and energy to come up with taken-for-granted rules that are, in fact, no surprise to anyone: amongst Sacks's conclusions, for example, were the propositions that in conversations, generally only one person speaks at a time and when more than one person speaks at a time, it will be only briefly. There are, I think, good reasons for this comparative poverty of research findings: reflexivity refers to a process in which the product is a sense of order, of apparently substantive meanings, and the starting point is the absence of that sense. We can find out very little about the process itself without already knowing about the starting point and the end-point. To try would be like trying to understand the production process in a factory without bothering to find out what raw materials are used and ignoring the finished product; and in this case there would appear to be no raw material. This is precisely what a lot of empirical ethnomethodology manages to do, and for this reason a lot of sociologists dismiss it. I think this is a mistake: like any other theory, ethnomethodology opens some doors and closes others. I want now to examine its theoretical status rather more closely.

The way out of cognition

I think the best way to approach ethnomethodology is as a theory of 'social cognition', which in turn must have its place in a general theory of persons or actions. It is a theory of the way in which we come to agree on what makes up the social world. Aaron Cicourel seems to me to have made the most theoretical progress in this direction, and his work points to more interesting possibilities. He argues that the sense of social structure we seek to establish in our interaction is the product of what he calls 'surface' and 'interpretive' or 'deep' rules (drawing here on the work of the linguist, Noam Chomsky). Surface rules are the norms of social life that the other theoretical approaches have taken for granted. Ethnomethodology has, I think, established conclusively that such rules cannot be taken for granted but are at least interpreted and reconstructed in different ways in different situations. This reconstruction is carried out by an underlying structure of interpretative rules which, Cicourel seems to think, are innate properties of human beings. We do not learn them; instead, they are the basis for learning. This in itself is sufficiently interesting, but Cicourel goes further in indicating why such an underlying structure of interpretative rules should be necessary. Our perception of the world works through all our five senses: we can see the world, hear, feel, taste and smell all at the same time, and the things and events of the world are perceived simultaneously. Language, however, enables us only to talk about one thing at a time, and there is a process of translation from our other non-linguistic experiences of the world into our descriptions. This is why describing an event is always creating that event, never simply a matter of recording it. Here, at last, there is a pointer out of cognition, since not just our minds but our emotions are involved in our experience of the world. The connections between the word and the perception, and the world and the feeling, have been barely touched on by social theory; yet all empirical investigations concerned with what people say assume that these relations present no problems.

Conclusion

One of the points to emerge from phenomenological sociology in general, and from Cicourel's work in particular, refers to another part of the social world which seems to comprise a separate area of study: the realm of general meanings. The existence of such a realm is disputed by ethnomethodology in some of its forms; to accept a realm of general meanings is seen as entering into the conspiracy to give an impression of social order. However, whilst it might be true to say that an impression of social order is constructed afresh in each social interaction, we do not invent meaning each time; what we do is give a specific situation-related version of a general meaning. General meanings are tools we employ in different ways in different circumstances, rather as we might use a hammer for knocking in a nail, pulling out a nail, or smashing a window to escape from a fire. These general meanings are Cicourel's surface rules of Berger and Luckman's overarching symbols, socially shared and established, similar to language itself. Thus ethnomethodology, if it does not exactly point beyond cognition in this respect, again indicates an area of investigation and a problem for action theory: what is involved in employing a general meaning in a particular way. Again we find that a theory of action, without a theory of society or culture, nevertheless assumes a theory of culture.

Having said all this, it is still true that ethnomethodology closes some extremely important doors. In the case of symbolic interactionism, I argued that to assume that there may be no such thing as a society when the experience of those we study suggests that there is such a thing is to do violence to the experience of those we study. Ethnomethodology deliberately sets out to do such violence: the perception of 'society' as a social structure over and above social interactions is a result of conspiracy. To investigate society in such a sense is simply to take part in the conspiracy. For reasons I have already suggested, it seems to me that we can accept that social interaction involves creating an impression of social order, but this in no way invalidates the arguments I used in the [Introduction to Part II] about the existence of societies as separate and different objects of study. If we accept the ethnomethodological argument on this point, then we cannot approach any of the major social problems, such as unemployment, crime or war, that are crucial features of our lives. It is not helpful if opening the door to the indexical and reflexive features of interaction closes the door to more conventional forms of sociological study; rather, it should add a new dimension to them.

In redefining social action as *activity*, as what people actually do and how they organise what they do, ethnomethodology does focus attention on areas often ignored by sociologists. As Sharrock and Anderson (1986) point out, most sociology of medicine says very little about what doctors actually do — in Goffman's essay on surgeons, for example, we learn nothing about surgery. Ethnomethodology focuses precisely on the activity of surgery and its organisation. Empirical work on ethnomethodology over the past decade has focused on, for example, what scientists, including mathematicians, *do* in the day-to-day organisation of their activities. It is in the making of these activities rationally accountable that we find the answer to Parsons's problem of order; indeed, Sharrock and Anderson present Garfinkel as radicalising Parsons, looking at day-to-day interaction and not finding the common values that Parsons suggests should be there: finding, instead, that the social is a constant creation; this is, indeed a new dimension to sociology, but in its implicit presupposition of a culture and a shared language and meanings, it still presupposes Parsons.

Further reading

On phenomenological sociology

The two books co-authored by Peter Berger are very readable starting points, but Schutz provides the real flavour of the approach. The other works listed are mainly introductory articles or readers (Psathas is more advanced) and there is little to choose between them.

Berger, P. and Kellner, H. (1974) *The Homeless Mind*, Penguin, Harmondsworth.

Berger, P. and Luckman, T. (1967) *The Social Construction of Reality*, Allen Lane, London.

Filmer, P. *et al* (1972) *New Directions in Sociological Theory*, Collier Macmillan, London.

Lassman, P. (1974) 'Phenomenological perspectives in sociology', in Rex, J. (ed.), *Approaches in Sociology*, Routledge & Kegan Paul, London, pp. 125–44.

Psathas, G. (1973) *Phenomenological Sociology: Issues and Applications*, John Wiley, New York.

Schutz, A. (1962–6) *Collected Papers* (2 vols), Martinus Nijhoff, The Hague.

Schutz, A. (1972) *The Phenomenology of the Social World*, Heinemann, London.

Winch, P. (1958) *The Idea of a Social Science*, Routledge & Kegan Paul, London.

Wolff, K. H. (1978) 'Phenomenology and sociology', in Bottomore, T. B. and Nisbet, R. (eds), *A History of Sociology Analysis*, Heinemann, London, pp. 499–556.

Ethnomethodology

Of the following introductions, Sharrock and Anderson and Livingston stand out, but all are adequate:

Attewell, P. (1974) 'Ethnomethodology since Garfinkel', *Theory and Society*, vol. 1, pp. 179–210.

Benson, D. and Hughes, J. H. (1983) *The Perspective of Ethnomethodology*, Longman, London.

Heritage, J. (1984) *Garfinkel and Ethnomethodology*, Cambridge University Press, Cambridge.

Leiter, K. (1980) *A Primer on Ethnomethodology*, Oxford University Press, Oxford.

Livingston, E. (1987) *Making Sense of Ethnomethodology*, Routledge & Kegan Paul, London.

Sharrock, W. and Anderson, B. (1986) *The Ethnomethodologists*, Ellis Horwood, Chichester/Tavistock, London.

Useful classical texts:

Atkinson, M. and Heritage, J. (1984) *Structures of Social Action*, Cambridge University Press, Cambridge.

Cicourel, A. V. (1964) *Method and Measurement in Sociology*, The Free Press, New York.

Cicourel, A. V. (1973) *Cognitive Sociology*, Penguin, Harmondsworth.

Douglas, J. D. (1971) *Understanding Everyday Life*, Routledge & Kegan Paul, London.

Garfinkel, H. (1967) *Studies in Ethnomethodology*, Prentice Hall, Englewood Cliffs, NJ.

Psathas, G. (ed.) (1979) *Everyday Language*, Irvington Press, New York.

Schenkein, J. (ed.) (1978) *Studies in the Organization of Conversational Interaction*, Academic Press, New York.

Sudnow, D. (ed.) (1972) *Studies in Social Interaction*, The Free Press, Glencoe, NJ.

Turner, R. (1974) *Ethnomethodology*, Penguin, Harmondsworth.

Recent empirical work:

Garfinkel, H. (1986) *Ethnomethodological Studies of Work*, Routledge & Kegan Paul, London.

Lieberman, K. (1985) *Understanding Interaction in Central Australia*, Routledge & Kegan Paul, London.

Livingston, E. (1986) *The Ethnomethodological Foundations of Mathematics*, Routledge & Kegan Paul, London.

Lynch, M. (1985) *Art and Artefact in Laboratory Science*, Routledge & Kegan Paul, London.

A useful summary:

Atkinson, P. (1988) 'Ethnomethodology: A critical review', *Annual Review of Sociology*, Annual Reviews Inc., Palo Alto, CA, pp. 441–65.

Useful critical studies:

Giddens, A. (1976) *New Rules of Sociological Method*, Hutchinson, London (Chapter 1).

Goldthorpe, J. H. (1973) 'A revolution in sociology', *Sociology*, vol. 7, pp. 449–62.

32.

The Stranger:
An Essay in Social Psychology
Alfred Schutz

The present paper intends to study in terms of a general theory of interpretation the typical situation in which a stranger finds himself in his attempt to interpret the cultural pattern of a social group which he approaches and to orient himself within it. For our present purposes the term "stranger" shall mean an adult individual of our times and civilization who tries to be permanently accepted or at least tolerated by the group which he approaches. The outstanding example for the social situation under scrutiny is that of the immigrant, and the following analyses are, as a matter of convenience, worked out with this instance in view. But by no means is their validity restricted to this special case. The applicant for membership in a closed club, the prospective bridegroom who wants to be admitted to the girl's family, the farmer's son who enters college, the city-dweller who settles in a rural environment, the "selectee" who joins the Army, the family of the war worker who moves into a boom town — all are strangers according to the definition just given, although in these cases the typical "crisis" that the immigrant undergoes may assume milder forms or even be entirely absent. Intentionally excluded, however, from the present investigation are certain cases the inclusion of which would require some qualifications in our statements: (a) the visitor or guest who intends to establish a merely transitory contact with the group; (b) children or primitives; and (c) relationships between individuals and groups of different levels of civilization, as in the case of the Huron brought to Europe — a pattern dear to some moralists of the eighteenth century. Furthermore, it is not the purpose of this paper to deal with the processes of social assimilation and social adjustment which are treated in an abundant and, for the most part, excellent literature [1] but rather with the situation of approaching which precedes every possible social adjustment and which includes its prerequisites.

As a convenient starting-point we shall investigate how the cultural pattern of group life presents itself to the common sense of a man who lives his everyday life within the group among his fellow-men. Following the customary terminology, we use the term "cultural pattern of group life" for designating all the peculiar valuations, institutions, and systems of orientation and guidance (such as the folkways, mores, laws, habits, customs, etiquette, fashions) which, in the common opinion of sociologists of our time, characterize — if not constitute — any social group at a given moment in its history. This cultural pattern, like any phenomenon of the social world, has a different aspect for the sociologist and for the man who acts and thinks within it.[2] The sociologist (as sociologist, not as a man among fellow-men which he remains in his private life) is the disinterested scientific onlooker of the social world. He is disinterested in that he

Alfred Schutz: 'The Stranger: An Essay in Social Psychology' from COLLECTED PAPERS II: STUDIES IN SOCIAL THEORY, edited and introduced by Arvid Brodersen (Martinus Nijhoff, 1971), pp. 91–105. Copyright © 1971 Martinus Nijhoff Publishers, The Hague. Reprinted by permission of Kluwer Academic Publishers.

intentionally refrains from participating in the network of plans, means-and-ends relations, motives and chances, hopes and fears, which the actor within the social world uses for interpreting his experiences of it; as a scientist he tries to observe, describe, and classify the social world as clearly as possible in well-ordered terms in accordance with the scientific ideals of coherence, consistency, and analytical consequence. The actor within the social world, however, experiences it primarily as a field of his actual and possible acts and only secondarily as an object of his thinking. In so far as he is interested in knowledge of his social world, he organizes this knowledge not in terms of a scientific system but in terms of relevance to his actions. He groups the world around himself (as the center) as a field of domination and is therefore especially interested in that segment which is within his actual or potential reach. He singles out those of its elements which may serve as means or ends for his "use and enjoyment," [3] for furthering his purposes, and for overcoming obstacles. His interest in these elements is of different degrees, and for this reason he does not aspire to become acquainted with all of them with equal thoroughness. What he wants is *graduated knowledge* of relevant elements, the degree of desired knowledge being correlated with their relevance. Otherwise stated, the world seems to him at any given moment as stratified in different layers of relevance, each of them requiring a different degree of knowledge. To illustrate these strata of relevance we may — borrowing the term from cartography — speak of "isohypses" or "hypsographical contour lines of relevance," trying to suggest by this metaphor that we could show the distribution of the interests of an individual at a given moment with respect both to their intensity and to their scope by connecting elements of equal relevance to his acts, just as the cartographer connects points of equal height by contour lines in order to reproduce adequately the shape of a mountain. The graphical representation of these "contour lines of relevance" would not show them as a single closed field but rather as numerous areas scattered over the map, each of different size and shape. Distinguishing with William James [4] two kinds of knowledge, namely, "*knowledge of acquaintance*" and "*knowledge about*," we may say that, within the field covered by the contour lines of relevance, there are centers of explicit knowledge *of* what is aimed at; they are surrounded by a halo knowledge *about* what seems to be sufficient; next comes a region in which it will do merely "to put one's trust"; the adjoining foothills are the home of unwarranted hopes and assumptions; between these areas, however, lie zones of complete ignorance.

We do not want to overcharge this image. Its chief purpose has been to illustrate that the knowledge of the man who acts and thinks within the world of his daily life is not homogeneous; it is (1) incoherent, (2) only partially clear, and (3) not at all free from contradictions.

1. It is incoherent because the individual's interests which determine the relevance of the objects selected for further inquiry are themselves not integrated into a coherent system. They are only partially organized under plans of any kind, such as plans of life, plans of work and leisure, plans for every social role assumed. But the hierarchy of these plans changes with the situation and with the growth of the personality; interests are shifted continually and entail an uninterrupted transformation of the shape and density of the relevance lines. Not only the selection of the objects of curiosity but also the degree of knowledge aimed at changes.

2. Man in his daily life is only partially — and we dare say exceptionally — interested in the clarity of his knowledge, i.e., in full insight into the relations between the elements of his world and the general principles ruling those relations. He is satisfied that a well-functioning telephone service is available to him and, normally, does not ask how the apparatus functions in detail and what laws of physics make this functioning possible. He buys merchandise in the store, not knowing how it is produced, and pays with money, although he has only a vague idea of what money really is. He takes it for granted that his fellow-man will understand his thought if expressed in plain language and will answer accordingly, without wondering how this miraculous performance may be explained. Furthermore, he does not search for the truth and does not quest for certainty. All he wants is information on likelihood and insight into the chances or risks which the situation at hand entails for the outcome of his actions. That the subway will run tomorrow as usual is for him almost of the same order of likelihood as that the sun will rise. If by reason of a special interest he needs more explicit knowledge on a topic, a benign modern civilization holds ready for him a chain of information desks and reference libraries.

3. His knowledge, finally, is not consistent. At the same time he may consider statements as equally valid which in fact are incompatible with one another. As a father, a citizen, an employee, and a member of his church he may have the most different and the least congruent opinions on moral, political, or economic matters. This inconsistency does not necessarily originate in a logical fallacy. Men's thinking is distributed over subject matters located within different and differently relevant levels, and they are not aware of the modifications they would have to make in passing from one level to another. This and similar problems would have to be explored by a logic of everyday thinking, postulated but not attained by all the great logicians from Leibniz to Husserl and Dewey. Up to now the science of logic has primarily dealt with the logic of science.

The system of knowledge thus acquired — incoherent, inconsistent, and only partially clear, as it is — takes on for the members of the in-group the appearance of a *sufficient* coherence, clarity, and consistency to give anybody a reasonable chance of understanding and of being understood. Any member born or reared within the group accepts the ready-made standardized scheme of the cultural pattern handed down to him by ancestors, teachers, and authorities as an unquestioned and unquestionable guide in all the situations which normally occur within the social world. The knowledge correlated to the cultural pattern carries its evidence in itself — or, rather, it is taken for granted in the absence of evidence to the contrary. It is a knowledge of trustworthy *recipes* for interpreting the social world and for handling things and men in order to obtain the best results in every situation with a minimum of effort by avoiding undesirable consequences. The recipe works, on the one hand, as a precept for actions and thus serves as a scheme of expression: whoever wants to obtain a certain result has to proceed as indicated by the recipe provided for this purpose. On the other hand, the recipe serves as a scheme of interpretation: whoever proceeds as indicated by a specific recipe is supposed to intend the correlated result. Thus it is the function of the cultural pattern to eliminate troublesome inquiries by offering ready-made directions for use, to replace truth hard to attain by comfortable truisms, and to substitute the self-explanatory for the questionable.

This "thinking as usual," as we may call it, corresponds to Max Scheler's idea of the "relatively natural conception of the world" (*relativ naturliche Weltanschauung*); [5] it includes the "of-course" assumptions relevant to a particular social group which Robert S. Lynd describes in such a masterly way — together with their inherent contradictions and ambivalence — as the "Middletown-spirit." [6] Thinking-as-usual may be maintained as long as some basic assumptions hold true, namely: (1) that life and especially social life will continue to be the same as it has been so far; that is to say, that the same problems requiring the same solutions will recur and that, therefore, our former experiences will suffice for mastering future situations; (2) that we may rely on the knowledge handed down to us by parents, teachers, governments, traditions, habits, etc., even if we do not understand its origin and its real meaning; (3) that in the ordinary course of affairs it is sufficient to know something *about* the general type or style of events we may encounter in our life-world in order to manage or control them; and (4) that neither the systems of recipes as schemes of interpretation and expression nor the underlying basic assumptions just mentioned are our private affair, but that they are likewise accepted and applied by our fellow-men.

If only one of these assumptions ceases to stand the test, thinking-as-usual becomes unworkable. Then a "crisis" arises which, according to W. I. Thomas' famous definition, "interrupts the flow of habit and gives rise to changed conditions of consciousness and practice"; or, as we may say, it overthrows precipitously the actual system of relevances. The cultural pattern no longer functions as a system of tested recipes at hand; it reveals that its applicability is restricted to a specific historical situation.

Yet the stranger, by reason of his personal crisis, does not share the above-mentioned basic assumptions. He becomes essentially the man who has to place in question nearly everything that seems to be unquestionable to the members of the approached group.

To him the cultural pattern of the approached group does not have the authority of a tested system of recipes, and this, if for no other reason, because he does not partake in the vivid historical tradition by which it has been formed. To be sure, from the stranger's point of view, too, the culture of the approached group has its peculiar history, and this history is even accessible to him. But it has never become an integral part of his biography, as did the history of his home group. Only the ways in which his fathers and grandfathers lived become for everyone elements of his own way of life. Graves and reminiscences can neither be transferred nor conquered. The stranger, therefore, approaches the other group as a newcomer in the true meaning of the term. At best he may be willing and able to share the present and the future with the approached group in vivid and immediate experience; under all circumstances, however, he remains excluded from such experiences of its past. Seen from the point of view of the approached group, he is a man without a history.

To the stranger the cultural pattern of his home group continues to be the outcome of an unbroken historical development and an element of his personal biography, which for this very reason has been and still is the unquestioned scheme of reference for his "relatively natural conception of the world." As a matter of course, therefore, the stranger starts to interpret his new social environment in terms of his thinking as usual. Within the scheme of reference brought from his home group, however, he finds a ready-made idea of the pattern supposedly valid within the approached group — an idea which necessarily will soon prove inadequate. [7]

First, the idea of the cultural pattern of the approached group which the stranger finds within the interpretive scheme of his home group has originated in the attitude of a disinterested observer. The approaching stranger, however, is about to transform himself from an unconcerned onlooker into a would-be member of the approached group. The cultural pattern of the approached group, then, is no longer a subject matter of his thought but a segment of the world which has to be dominated by actions. Consequently, its position within the stranger's system of relevance changes decisively, and this means, as we have seen, that another type of knowledge is required for its interpretation. Jumping from the stalls to the stage, so to speak, the former onlooker becomes a member of the cast, enters as a partner into social relations with his co-actors and participates henceforth in the action in progress.

Second, the new cultural pattern acquires an environmental character. Its remoteness changes into proximity; its vacant frames become occupied by vivid experiences; its anonymous contents turn into definite social situations; its ready-made typologies disintegrate. In other words, the level of environmental experience of social objects is incongruous with the level of mere beliefs about unapproached objects; by passing from the latter to the former, any concept originating in the level of departure becomes necessarily inadequate if applied to the new level without having been restated in its terms.

Third, the ready-made picture of the foreign group subsisting within the stranger's home-group proves its inadequacy for the approaching stranger for the mere reason that it has not been formed with the aim of provoking a response or a reaction from the members of the foreign group. The knowledge which it offers serves merely as a handy scheme for interpreting the foreign group and not as a guide for interaction between the two groups. Its validity is primarily based on the consensus of those members of the home group who do not intend to establish a direct social relationship with members of the foreign group. (Those who intend to do so are in a situation analogous to that of the approaching stranger). Consequently, the scheme of interpretation refers to the members of the foreign group merely as objects of this interpretation, but not beyond it, as addressees of possible acts emanating from the outcome of the interpretive procedure and not as subjects of anticipated reactions toward those acts. Hence, this kind of knowledge is, so to speak, insulated; it can be neither verified nor falsified by responses of the members of the foreign group. The latter, therefore, consider this knowledge — by a kind of "looking-glass" effect [8] — as both irresponsive and irresponsible and complain of its prejudices, bias, and misunderstandings. The approaching stranger, however, becomes aware of the fact that an important element of his "thinking as usual," namely, his ideas of the foreign group, its cultural pattern, and its way of life, do not stand the test of vivid experience and social interaction.

The discovery that things in his new surroundings look quite different from what he expected them to be at home is frequently the first shock to the stranger's confidence in the validity of his habitual "thinking as usual." Not only the picture which the stranger has brought along of the cultural pattern of the approached group but the whole hitherto unquestioned scheme of interpretation current within the home group becomes invalidated. It cannot be used as a scheme of orientation within the new social surroundings. For the members of the approached group *their* cultural pattern fulfills the functions of such a scheme. But the approaching stranger can neither use it simply as it is nor establish a general formula of transformation between both cultural patterns permitting him, so to speak, to convert all the co-ordinates within one scheme of orientation into those valid within the other — and this for the following reasons.

First, any scheme of orientation presupposes that everyone who uses it looks at the surrounding world as grouped around himself who stands at its center. He who wants to use a map successfully has first of all to know his standpoint in two respects: its location on the ground and its representation on the map. Applied to the social world this means that only members of the in-group, having a definite status in its hierarchy and also being aware of it, can use its cultural pattern as a natural and trustworthy scheme of orientation. The stranger, however, has to face the fact that he lacks any status as a member of the social group he is about to join and is therefore unable to get a starting-point to take his bearings. He finds himself a border case outside the territory covered by the scheme of orientation current within the group. He is, therefore, no longer permitted to consider himself as the center of his social environment, and this fact causes again a dislocation of his contour lines of relevance.

Second, the cultural pattern and its recipes represent only for the members of the in-group a unit of coinciding schemes of interpretation as well as of expression. For the outsider, however, this seeming unity falls to pieces. The approaching stranger has to "translate" its terms into terms of the cultural pattern of his home group, provided that, within the latter, interpretive equivalents exist at all. If they exist, the translated terms may be understood and remembered; they can be recognized by recurrence; they are at hand but not in hand. Yet, even then, it is obvious that the stranger cannot assume that his interpretation of the new cultural pattern coincides with that current with the members of the in-group. On the contrary, he has to reckon with fundamental discrepancies in seeing things and handling situations.

Only after having thus collected a certain knowledge of the interpretive function of the new cultural pattern may the stranger start to adopt it as the scheme of his own expression. The difference between the two stages of knowledge is familiar to any student of a foreign language and has received the full attention of psychologists dealing with the theory of learning. It is the difference between the passive understanding of a language and its active mastering as a means for realizing one's own acts and thoughts. As a matter of convenience we want to keep to this example in order to make clear some of the limits set to the stranger's attempt at conquering the foreign pattern as a scheme of expression, bearing in mind, however, that the following remarks could easily be adapted with appropriate modifications to other categories of the cultural pattern such as mores, laws, folkways, fashions, etc.

Language as a scheme of interpretation and expression does not merely consist of the linguistic symbols catalogued in the dictionary and of the syntactical rules enumerated in an ideal grammar. The former are translatable into other languages; the latter are understandable by referring them to corresponding or deviating rules of the unquestioned mother-tongue.[9] However, several other factors supervene.

1. Every word and every sentence is, to borrow again a term of William James, surrounded by "fringes" connecting them, on the one hand, with past and future elements of the universe of discourse to which they pertain and surrounding them, on the other hand, with a halo of emotional values and irrational implications which themselves remain ineffable. The fringes are the stuff poetry is made of; they are capable of being set to music but they are not translatable.

2. There are in any language terms with several connotations. They, too, are noted in the dictionary. But, besides these standardized connotations, every element of speech acquires its special secondary meaning derived from the context or the social environment within which it is used and, in addition, gets a special tinge from the actual occasion in which it is employed.

3. Idioms, technical terms, jargons, and dialects, whose use remains restricted to specific social groups, exist in every language, and their significance can be learned by an outsider too. But, in addition, every social group, be it ever so small (if not every individual), has its own private code, understandable only by those who have participated in the common past experiences in which it took rise or in the tradition connected with them.

4. As Vossler has shown, the whole history of the linguistic group is mirrored in its way of saying things.[10] All the other elements of group life enter into it — above all, its literature. The erudite stranger, for example, approaching an English-speaking country is heavily handicapped if he has not read the Bible and Shakespeare in the English language, even if he grew up with translations of those books in his mother-tongue.

All the above-mentioned features are accessible only to the members of the in-group. They all pertain to the scheme of expression. They are not teachable and cannot be learned in the same way as, for example, the vocabulary. In order to command a language freely as a scheme of expression, one must have written love letters in it; one has to know how to pray and curse in it and how to say things with every shade appropriate to the addressee and to the situation. Only members of the in-group have the scheme of expression as a genuine one in hand and command it freely within their thinking as usual.

Applying the result to the total of the cultural pattern of group life, we may say that the member of the in-group looks in a single glance through the normal social situations occurring to him and that he catches immediately the ready-made recipe appropriate to its solution. In those situations his acting shows all the marks of habituality, automatism, and half-consciousness. This is possible because the cultural pattern provides by its recipes typical solutions for typical problems available for typical actors. In other words, the chance of obtaining the desired standardized result by applying a standardized recipe is an objective one; that is open to everyone who conducts himself like the anonymous type required by the recipe. Therefore, the actor who follows a recipe does not have to check whether this objective chance coincides with a subjective chance, that is, a chance open to him, the individual, by reason of his personal circumstances and faculties which subsists independently of the question whether other people in similar situations could or could not act in the same way with the same likelihood. Even more, it can be stated that the objective chances for the efficiency of a recipe are the greater, the fewer deviations from the anonymous typified behavior occur, and this holds especially for recipes designed for social interaction. This kind of recipe, if it is to work, presupposes that any partner expects the other to act or to react typically, provided that the actor himself acts typically. He who wants to travel by railroad has to behave in that typical way which the type "railroad agent" may reasonably expect as the typical conduct of the type "passenger," and vice versa. Neither party examines the subjective chances involved. The scheme, being designed for everyone's use, need not be tested for its fitness for the peculiar individual who employs it.

For those who have grown up within the cultural pattern, not only the recipes and their possible efficiency but also the typical and anonymous attitudes required by them are an unquestioned "matter of course" which gives them both security and assurance. In other words, these attitudes by their very anonymity and typicality are placed not within the actor's stratum of relevance which requires explicit knowledge *of* but in the region of mere acquaintance in which it will do to put one's trust. This interrelation between objective chance, typicality, anonymity, and relevance seems to be rather important.[11]

For the approaching stranger, however, the pattern of the approached group does not guarantee an objective chance for success but rather a pure subjective likelihood which has to be checked step by step, that is, he has to make sure that the solutions suggested by the new scheme will also produce the desired effect for him in his special position as outsider and newcomer who has not brought within his grasp the whole system of the cultural pattern but who is rather puzzled by its inconsistency, incoherence, and lack of clarity. He has, first of all, to use the term of W. I. Thomas, to *define* the situation. Therefore, he cannot stop at an approximate acquaintance with the new pattern, trusting in his vague knowledge *about* its general style and structure but needs an explicit knowledge of its elements, inquiring not only into their *that* but into their *why*. Consequently, the shape of his contour lines of relevance by necessity differs radically from those of a member of the in-group as to situations, recipes, means, ends, social partners, etc. Keeping in mind the above-mentioned interrelationship between relevance, on the one hand, and typicality and anonymity, on the other, it follows that he uses another yardstick for anonymity and typicality of social acts than the members of the in-group. For to the stranger the observed actors within the approached group are not — as for their co-actors — of a certain presupposed anonymity, namely, mere performers of typical functions, but individuals. On the other hand, he is inclined to take mere individual traits as typical ones. Thus he constructs a social world of pseudo-anonymity, pseudo-intimacy, and pseudo-typicality. Therefore, he cannot integrate the personal types constructed by him into a coherent picture of the approached group and cannot rely on his expectation of their response. And even less can the stranger himself adopt those typical and anonymous attitudes which a member of the in-group is entitled to expect from a partner in a typical situation. Hence the stranger's lack of feeling for distance, his oscillating between remoteness and intimacy, his hesitation and uncertainty, and his distrust in every matter which seems to be so simple and uncomplicated to those who rely on the efficiency of unquestioned recipes which have just to be followed but not understood.

In other words, the cultural pattern of the approached group is to the stranger not a shelter but a field of adventure, not a matter of course but a questionable topic of investigation, not an instrument for disentangling problematic situations but a problematic situation itself and one hard to master.

These facts explain two basic traits of the stranger's attitude toward the group to which nearly all sociological writers dealing with this topic have rendered special attention, namely, (1) the stranger's objectivity and (2) his doubtful loyalty.

1. The stranger's objectivity cannot be sufficiently explained by his critical attitude. To be sure, he is not bound to worship the "idols of the tribe" and has a vivid feeling for the incoherence and inconsistency of the approached cultural pattern. But this attitude originates far less in his propensity to judge the newly approached group by the standards brought from home than in his need to acquire full knowledge *of* the elements of the approached cultural pattern and to examine for this purpose with care and precision what seems self-explanatory to the in-group. The deeper reason for his objectivity, however, lies in his own bitter experience of the limits of the "thinking as usual," which has taught him that a man may loose his status, his rules of guidance, and even his history and that the normal way of life is always far less guaranteed than it seems. Therefore, the stranger discerns, frequently with a grievous clear-sightedness, the rising of a crisis which may menace the whole foundation of the "relatively natural conception of the world," while all those symptoms pass unnoticed by the members of the in-group, who rely on the continuance of their customary way of life.

2. The doubtful loyalty of the stranger is unfortunately very frequently more than a prejudice on the part of the approached group. This is especially true in cases in which the stranger proves unwilling or unable to substitute the new cultural pattern entirely for that of the home group. Then the stranger remains what Park and Stonequist have aptly called a "marginal man," a cultural hybrid on the verge of two different patterns of group life, not knowing to which of them he belongs. But very frequently the reproach of doubtful loyalty originates in the astonishment of the members of the in-group that the stranger does not accept the total of its cultural pattern as the natural and appropriate way of life and as the best of all possible solutions of any problem. The stranger is called ungrateful, since he refuses to acknowledge that the cultural pattern offered to him grants him shelter and protection. But these people do not understand that the stranger in the state of transition does not consider this pattern as a protecting shelter at all but as a labyrinth in which he has lost all sense of his bearings.

As stated before, we have intentionally restricted our topic to the specific attitude of the approaching stranger which precedes any social adjustment and refrained from investigating the process of social assimilation itself. A single remark concerning the latter may be permitted. Strangeness and familiarity are not limited to the social field but are general categories of our interpretation of the world. If we encounter in our experience something previously unknown and which therefore stands out of the ordinary order of our knowledge, we begin a process of inquiry. We first define the new fact; we try to catch its meaning; we then transform step by step our general scheme of interpretation of the world in such a way that the strange fact and its meaning become compatible and consistent with all the other facts of our experience and their meanings. If we succeed in this endeavor, then that which formerly was a strange fact and a puzzling problem to our mind is transformed into an additional element of our warranted knowledge. We have enlarged and adjusted our stock of experiences.

What is commonly called the process of social adjustment which the newcomer has to undergo is but a special case of this general principle. The adaptation of the newcomer to the in-group which at first seemed to be strange and unfamiliar to him is a continuous process of inquiry into the cultural pattern of the approached group. If this process of inquiry succeeds, then this pattern and its elements will become to the newcomer a matter of course, an unquestionable way of life, a shelter, and a protection. But then the stranger is no stranger any more, and his specific problems have been solved.

Notes

1. Instead of mentioning individual outstanding contributions by American writers, such as W. G. Sumner, W. I. Thomas, Florian Znaniecki, R. E. Park, H. A. Miller, E. V. Stonequist, E. S. Bogardus, and Kimball Young, and by German authors, especially Georg Simmel and Robert Michels, we refer to the valuable monograph by Margaret Mary Wood, *The Stranger: A Study in Social Relationship*, New York, 1934, and the bibliography quoted therein.

2. This insight seems to be the most important contribution of Max Weber's methodological writings to the problems of social science. Cf. the present writer's *Der sinnhafte Aufbau der sozialen Welt*, Vienna, 1932, 2nd ed. 1960.

3. John Dewey, *Logic, the Theory of Inquiry*, New York, 1938, Chap. iv.

4. For the distinction of these two kinds of knowledge cf. William James, *Principles of Psychology*, New York, 1890, Vol. I, pp. 221–22.

5. Max Scheler, "Probleme einer Soziologie des Wissens," *Die Wissensformen und die Gesellschaft*, Leipzig, 1926, pp. 58ff.; cf. Howard Becker and Hellmuth Otto Dahlke, "Max Scheler's Sociology of Knowledge," *Philosophy and Phenomenological Research*, Vol. II, 1942, pp. 310–22, esp. p. 315.

6. Robert S. Lynd, *Middletown in Transition*, New York, 1937, Chap. xii, and *Knowledge for What?*, Princeton, 1939, pp. 58–63.

7. As one account showing how the American cultural pattern depicts itself as an "unquestionable" element within the scheme of interpretation of European intellectuals we refer to Martin Gumpert's humorous description in his book, *First Papers*, New York, 1941, pp. 8–9. Cf. also books like Jules Romains, *Visite chez les Americains*, Paris, 1930, and Jean Prevost Usonie, *Esquisse de la civilisation americaine*, Paris, 1939, pp. 245–66.

8. In using this term, we allude to Cooley's well-known theory of the reflected or looking-glass self (Charles H. Cooley, *Human Nature and the Social Order* [rev. ed.; New York, 1922], p. 184).

9. Therefore, the learning of a foreign language reveals to the student frequently for the first time the grammar rules of his mother-tongue which he has followed so far as "the most natural thing in the world," namely, as recipes.

10. Karl Vossler, *Geist und Kultur in der Sprache*, Heidelberg, 1925, pp. 117ff.

11. It could be referred to a general principle of the theory of relevance, but this would surpass the frame of the present paper. The only point for which there is space to contend is that all the obstacles which the stranger meets in his attempt at interpreting the approached group arise from the incongruence of the contour lines of the mutual relevance systems and, consequently, from the distortion the stranger's system undergoes within the new surrounding. But any social relationship, and especially any establishment of new social contacts, even between individuals, involves analogous phenomena, although they do not necessarily lead to a crisis.

33. Performance

Erving Goffman

Belief in the part one is playing

When an individual plays a part he implicitly requests his observers to take seriously the impression that is fostered before them. They are asked to believe that the character they see actually possesses the attributes he appears to possess, that the task he performs will have the consequences that are implicitly claimed for it, and that, in general, matters are what they appear to be. In line with this, there is the popular view that the individual offers his performance and puts on his show 'for the benefit of other people'. It will be convenient to begin a consideration of performances by turning the question around and looking at the individual's own belief in the impression of reality that he attempts to engender in those among whom he finds himself.

At one extreme, one finds that the performer can be fully taken in by his own act; he can be sincerely convinced that the impression of reality which he stages is the real reality. When his audience is also convinced in this way about the show he puts on — and this seems to be the typical case — then for the moment at least, only the sociologist or the socially disgruntled will have any doubts about the 'realness' of what is presented.

At the other extreme, we find that the performer may not be taken in at all by his own routine. This possibility is understandable, since no one is in quite as good an observational position to see through the act as the person who puts it on. Coupled with this, the performer may be moved to guide the conviction of his audience only as a means to other ends, having no ultimate concern in the conception that they have of him or of the situation. When the individual has no belief in his own act and no ultimate concern with the beliefs of his audience, we may call him cynical, reserving the term 'sincere' for individuals who believe in the impression fostered by their own performance. It should be understood that the cynic, with all his professional disinvolvement, may obtain unprofessional pleasures from his masquerade, experiencing a kind of gleeful spiritual aggression from the fact that he can toy at will with something his audience must take seriously.[1]

It is not assumed, of course, that all cynical performers are interested in deluding their audiences for purposes of what is called 'self-interest' or private gain. A cynical individual may delude his audience for what he considers to be their own good, or for the good of the community, etc. For illustrations of this we need not appeal to sadly enlightened showmen such as Marcus Aurelius or Hsun Tzû. We know that in service occupations practitioners who may otherwise be sincere are sometimes forced to delude their customers because their customers show such a heartfelt demand for it. Doctors who are led into giving placebos, filling station attendants who resignedly

From *THE PRESENTATION OF SELF IN EVERYDAY LIFE* by Erving Goffman. Copyright © 1959 by Erving Goffman. Used by permission of Doubleday, a division of Bantam Doubleday Dell Publishing Group, Inc.

check and recheck tyre pressures for anxious women motorists, shoe clerks who sell a shoe that fits but tell the customer it is the size she wants to hear — these are cynical performers whose audiences will not allow them to be sincere. Similarly, it seems that sympathetic patients in mental wards will sometimes feign bizarre symptoms so that student nurses will not be subjected to a disappointingly sane performance.[2] So also, when inferiors extend their most lavish reception for visiting superiors, the selfish desire to win favour may not be the chief motive; the inferior may be tactfully attempting to put the superior at ease by simulating the kind of world the superior is thought to take for granted.

I have suggested two extremes: an individual may be taken in by his own act or be cynical about it. These extremes are something a little more than just the ends of a continuum. Each provides the individual with a position which has its own particular securities and defences, so there will be a tendency for those who have travelled close to one of these poles to complete the voyage. Starting with lack of inward belief in one's role, the individual may follow the natural movement described by Park:

> It is probably no mere historical accident that the word person, in its first meaning, is a mask. It is rather a recognition of the fact that everyone is always and everywhere, more or less consciously, playing a role. . . . It is in these roles that we know each other; it is in these roles that we know ourselves.[3]

> In a sense, and in so far as this mask represents the conception we have formed of ourselves — the role we are striving to live up to — this mask is our truer self, the self we would like to be. In the end, our conception of our role becomes second nature and an integral part of our personality. We come into the world as individuals, achieve character, and become persons.[4]

This may be illustrated from the community life of Shetland.[5] For the last four or five years the island's tourist hotel has been owned and operated by a married couple of crofter origins. From the beginning, the owners were forced to set aside their own conceptions as to how life ought to be led, displaying in the hotel a full round of middle-class services and amenities. Lately, however, it appears that the managers have become less cynical about the performance that they stage; they themselves are becoming middle class and more and more enamoured of the selves their clients impute to them.

Another illustration may be found in the raw recruit who initially follows army etiquette in order to avoid physical punishment and eventually comes to follow the rules so that his organization will not be shamed and his officers and fellow soldiers will respect him.

As suggested, the cycle of disbelief-to-belief can be followed in the other direction, starting with conviction or insecure aspiration and ending in cynicism. Professions which the public holds in religious awe often allow their recruits to follow it in this direction not because of a slow realization that they are deluding their audience — for by ordinary social standards the claims they make may be quite valid — but because they can use this cynicism as a means of insulating their inner selves from contact with the audience. And we may even expect to find typical careers of faith, with the individual starting out with one kind of involvement in the performance he is required to give, then moving back and forth several times between sincerity and cynicism before completing all the phases and turning-points of self-belief for a person of his station. Thus, students of medical schools suggest that idealistically oriented beginners in medical school typically lay aside their holy aspirations for a period of time. During the first two years the students find that their interest in medicine must be dropped that they may give all their time to the task of learning how to get through examinations. During the next two years they are too busy learning about diseases to show much concern for the persons who are diseased. It is only after their medical schooling has ended that their original ideals about medical service may be reasserted.[6]

While we can expect to find natural movement back and forth between cynicism and sincerity, still we must not rule out the kind of transitional point that can be sustained on the strength of a little self-illusion. We find that the individual may attempt to induce the audience to judge him and the situation in a particular way, and he may seek this judgement as an ultimate end in itself, and yet he may not completely believe that he deserves the valuation of self which he asks for or that the impression of reality which he fosters is valid. Another mixture of cynicism and belief is suggested in Kroeber's discussion of shamanism:

> Next, there is the old question of deception. Probably most shamans or medicine men, the world over, help along with sleight-of-hand in curing and especially in exhibitions of power. This sleight-of-hand is sometimes deliberate; in many cases awareness is perhaps not deeper than the foreconscious. The attitude, whether there has been repression or not, seems to be as towards a pious fraud. Field ethnographers seem quite generally convinced that even shamans who know that they are frauds nevertheless also believe in their powers, and especially in those of other shamans: they consult them when they themselves or their children are ill.[7]

Front

I have been using the term 'performance' to refer to all the activity of an individual which occurs during a period marked by his continuous presence before a particular set of observers and which has some influence on the observers. It will be convenient to label as 'front' that part of the individual's performance which regularly functions in a general and fixed fashion to define the situation for those who observe the performance. Front, then, is the expressive equipment of a standard kind intentionally or unwittingly employed by the individual during his performance. For preliminary purposes, it will be convenient to distinguish and label what seem to be the standard parts of front.

First, there is the 'setting', involving furniture, décor, physical layout, and other background items which supply the scenery and stage props for the spate of human action played out before, within, or upon it. A setting tends to stay put, geographically speaking, so that those who would use a particular setting as part of their performance cannot begin their act until they have brought themselves to the appropriate place and must terminate their performance when they leave it. It is only in exceptional circumstances that the setting follows along with the performers; we see this in the funeral cortège, the civic parade, and the dream-like processions that kings and queens are made of. In the main, these exceptions seem to offer some kind of extra protection for performers who are, or who have momentarily become, highly sacred. These worthies are to be distinguished, of course, from quite profane performers of the pedlar class who move their place of work between performances, often being forced to do so. In the matter of having one fixed place for one's setting, a ruler may be too sacred, a pedlar too profane.

In thinking about the scenic aspects of front, we tend to think of the living-room in a particular house and the small number of performers who can thoroughly identify themselves with it. We have given insufficient attention to assemblages of sign-equipment which large numbers of performers can call their own for short periods of time. It is characteristic of Western European countries, and no doubt a source of stability for them, that a large number of luxurious settings are available for hire to anyone of the right kind who can afford them. One illustration of this may be cited from a study of the higher civil servant in Britain:

> The question how far the men who rise to the top in the Civil Service take on the 'tone' or 'colour' of a class other than that to which they belong by birth is delicate and difficult. The only definite information bearing on the question is the figures relating to the membership of the great London clubs. More than three-quarters of our high administrative officials belong to one or more clubs of high status and considerable luxury, where the entrance fee might be twenty guineas or more, and the annual subscription from twelve to twenty guineas. These institutions are of the upper class (not even of the upper-middle) in their premises, their equipment, the style of living practised there, their whole atmosphere. Though many of the members would not be described as wealthy, only a wealthy man would unaided provide for himself and his family space, food and drink, service, and other amenities of life to the same standard as he will find at the Union, the Travellers', or the Reform.[8]

Another example can be found in the recent development of the medical profession where we find that it is increasingly important for a doctor to have access to the elaborate scientific stage provided by large hospitals, so that fewer and fewer doctors are able to feel that their setting is a place that they can lock up at night.[9]

If we take the term 'setting' to refer to the scenic parts of expressive equipment, one may take the term 'personal front' to refer to the other items of expressive equipment, the items that we most intimately identify with the performer himself and that we naturally expect will follow the performer wherever he goes. As part of personal front we may include: insignia of office or rank; clothing; sex, age, and racial characteristics; size and looks; posture; speech patterns; facial expressions; bodily gestures; and the like. Some of these vehicles for conveying signs such as racial characteristics, are relatively fixed and over a span of time do not vary for the individual from one situation to another. On the other hand, some of these sign vehicles are relatively mobile or transitory, such as facial expression, and can vary during a performance from one moment to the next.

It is sometimes convenient to divide the stimuli which make up personal front into 'appearance' and 'manner', according to the function performed by the information that these stimuli convey. 'Appearance' may be taken to refer to those stimuli which function at the time to tell us of the performer's social statuses. These stimuli also tell us of the individual's temporary ritual state: that is, whether he is engaging in formal social activity, work, or informal recreation; whether or not he is celebrating a new phase in the season cycle or in his life-cycle. 'Manner' may be taken to refer to those stimuli which function at the time to warn us of the interaction role the performer will expect to play in the oncoming situation. Thus a haughty, aggressive manner may give the impression that the performer expects to be the one who will initiate the verbal interaction and direct its course. A meek, apologetic manner may give the impression that the performer expects to follow the lead of others, or at least that he can be led to do so.

We often expect, of course, a confirming consistency between appearance and manner; we expect that the differences in social statuses among the interactants will be expressed in some way by congruent differences in the indications that are made of an expected interaction role. This type of coherence of front may be illustrated by the following description of the procession of a mandarin through a Chinese city:

> Coming closely behind . . . the luxurious chair of the mandarin, carried by eight bearers, fills the vacant space in the street. He is mayor of the town, and for all practical purposes the supreme power in it. He is an ideal-looking official, for he is large and massive in appearance, whilst he has that stern and forbidding aspect, as though he were on his way to the execution ground to have some criminal decapitated. This is the kind of air that the mandarins put on when they appear in public. In the course of many years' experience, I have never once seen any of them, from the highest to the lowest, with a smile on his face or a look of sympathy for the people whilst he was being carried officially through the streets.[10]

But, of course, appearance and manner may tend to contradict each other, as when a performer who appears to be of higher estate than his audience acts in a manner that is unexpectedly equalitarian, or intimate, or apologetic, or when a performer dressed in the garments of a high position presents himself to an individual of even higher status.

In addition to the expected consistency between appearance and manner, we expect, of course, some coherence among setting, appearance, and manner.[11] Such coherence represents an ideal type that provides us with a means of stimulating our attention to and interest in exceptions. In this the student is assisted by the journalist, for exceptions to expected consistency among setting, appearance and manner provide the piquancy and glamour of many careers and the saleable appeal of many magazine articles. For example, a *New Yorker* profile on Roger Stevens (the real-estate agent who engineered the sale of the Empire State Building) comments on the startling fact that Stevens has a small house, a meagre office, and no letterhead stationery.[12]

355

In order to explore more fully the relations among the several parts of social front, it will be convenient to consider here a significant characteristic of the information conveyed by front, namely, its abstractness and generality.

However specialized and unique a routine is, its social front, with certain exceptions, will tend to claim facts that can be equally claimed and asserted of other, somewhat different, routines. For example, many service occupations offer their clients a performance that is illuminated with dramatic expressions of cleanliness, modernity, competence, and integrity. While in fact these abstract standards have a different significance in different occupational performances, the observer is encouraged to stress the abstract similarities. For the observer this is a wonderful, though sometimes disastrous, convenience. Instead of having to maintain a different pattern of expectation and responsive treatment for each slightly different performer and performance, he can place the situation in a broad category around which it is easy for him to mobilize his past experience and stereotypical thinking. Observers then need only be familiar with a small and hence manageable vocabulary of fronts, and know how to respond to them, in order to orient themselves in a wide variety of situations. Thus in London the current tendency for chimney sweeps[13] and perfume clerks to wear white lab coats tends to provide the client with an understanding that the delicate tasks performed by these persons will be performed in what has become a standardized, clinical, confidential manner.

There are grounds for believing that the tendency for a large number of different acts to be presented from behind a small number of fronts is a natural development in social organization. Radcliffe-Brown has suggested this in his claim that a 'descriptive' kinship system which gives each person a unique place may work for very small communities, but, as the number of persons becomes large, clan segmentation becomes necessary as a means of providing a less complicated system of identifications and treatments.[14] We see this tendency illustrated in factories, barracks, and other large social establishments. Those who organize these establishments find it impossible to provide a special cafeteria, special modes of payment, special vacation rights, and special sanitary facilities for every line and staff status category in the organization, and at the same time they feel that persons of dissimilar status ought not to be indiscriminately thrown together or classified together. As a compromise, the full range of diversity is cut at a few crucial points, and all those within a given bracket are allowed or obliged to maintain the same social front in certain situations.

In addition to the fact that different routines may employ the same front, it is to be noted that a given social front tends to become institutionalized in terms of the abstract stereotyped expectations to which it gives rise, and tends to take on a meaning and stability apart from the specific tasks which happen at the time to be performed in its name. The front becomes a 'collective representation' and a fact in its own right.

When an actor takes on an established social role, usually he finds that a particular front has already been established for it. Whether his acquisition of the role was primarily motivated by a desire to perform the given task or by a desire to maintain the corresponding front, the actor will find that he must do both.

Further, if the individual takes on a task that is not only new to him but also unestablished in the society, or if he attempts to change the light in which his task is viewed, he is likely to find that there are already several well-established fronts among which he must choose. Thus, when a task is given a new front we seldom find that the front it is given is itself new.

Since fronts tend to be selected, not created, we may expect trouble to arise when those who perform a given task are forced to select a suitable front for themselves from among several quite dissimilar ones. Thus, in military organizations, tasks are always developing which (it is felt) require too much authority and skill to be carried out behind the front maintained by one grade of personnel and too little authority and skill to be carried out behind the front maintained by the next grade in the hierarchy. Since there are relatively large jumps between grades, the task will come to 'carry too much rank' or to carry too little.

An interesting illustration of the dilemma of selecting an appropriate front from several not quite fitting ones may be found today in American medical organizations with respect to the task of administering anaesthesia.[15] In some hospitals anaesthesia is still administered by nurses behind the front that nurses are allowed to have in hospitals regardless of the tasks they perform — a front involving ceremonial subordination to doctors and a relatively low rate of pay. In order to establish anaesthesiology as a speciality for graduate medical doctors, interested practitioners have had to advocate strongly the idea that administering anaesthesia is a sufficiently complex and vital task to justify giving to those who perform it the ceremonial and financial reward given to doctors. The difference between the front maintained by a nurse and the front maintained by a doctor is great; many things that are acceptable for nurses are *infra dignitatem* for doctors. Some medical people have felt that a nurse 'under-ranked' for the task of administering anaesthesia and that doctors 'over-ranked'; were there an established status midway between nurse and doctor, an easier solution to the problem could perhaps be found.[16] Similarly, had the Canadian Army had a rank half-way between lieutenant and captain, two and a half pips instead of two or three, then Dental Corps captains, many of them of a low ethnic origin, could have been given a rank that would perhaps have been more suitable in the eyes of the Army than the captaincies they were actually given.

I do not mean here to stress the point of view of a formal organization or a society; the individual, as someone who possesses a limited range of sign-equipment, must also make unhappy choices. Thus, in the crofting community studied by the writer, hosts often marked the visit of a friend by offering him a shot of hard liquor, a glass of wine, some home-made brew, or a cup of tea. The higher the rank or temporary ceremonial status of the visitor, the more likely he was to receive an offering near the liquor end of the continuum. Now one problem associated with this range of sign-equipment was that some crofters could not afford to keep a bottle of hard liquor, so that wine tended to be the most indulgent gesture they could employ. But perhaps a more common difficulty was the fact that certain visitors, given their permanent and temporary status at the time, outranked one potable and under-ranked the next one in line. There was often a danger that the visitor would feel just a little affronted or, on the other hand, that the host's costly and limited sign-equipment would be misused. In our middle classes a similar situation arises when a hostess has to decide whether or not to use the good silver, or which would be the more appropriate to wear, her best afternoon-dress or her plainest evening-gown.

I have suggested that social front can be divided into traditional parts, such as setting, appearance, and manner, and that (since different routines may be presented from behind the same front) we may not find a perfect fit between the specific character of a performance and the general socialized guise in which it appears to us. These two facts, taken together, lead one to appreciate that items in the social front of a particular routine are not only found in the social fronts of a whole range of routines but also that the whole range of routines in which one item of sign-equipment is found will differ from the range of routines in which another item in the same social front will be found. Thus a lawyer may talk to a client in a social setting that he employs only for this purpose (or for a study), but the suitable clothes he wears on such occasions he will also employ, with equal suitability, at dinner with colleagues and at the theatre with his wife. Similarly, the prints that hang on his wall and the carpet on his floor may be found in domestic social establishments. Of course, in highly ceremonial occasions, setting, manner, and appearance may all be unique and specific, used only for performances of a single type of routine, but such exclusive use of sign-equipment is the exception rather than the rule.

Notes

1. Perhaps the real crime of the confidence man is not that he takes money from his victims but that he robs all of us of the belief that middle-class manners and appearance can be sustained only by middle-class people. A disabused professional can be cynically hostile to the service relation his clients expect him to extend to them; the confidence man is in a position to hold the whole 'legit' world in this contempt.

2. See Taxel, 'Authority Structure in a Mental Hospital Ward', page 4. Harry Stack Sullivan has suggested that the tact of institutionalized performers can operate in the other direction, resulting in a kind of *noblesse-oblige* sanity. See his 'Socio-Psychiatric Research', *American Journal of Psychiatry*, x, pages 987–8:

   'A study of "social recoveries" in one of our large mental hospitals some years ago taught me that patients were often released from care because they had learned not to manifest symptoms to the environing persons; in other words, had integrated enough of the personal environment to realize the prejudice opposed to their delusions. It seemed almost as if they grew wise enough to be tolerant of the imbecility surrounding them, having finally discovered that it was stupidity and not malice. They could then secure satisfaction from contact with others, while discharging a part of their cravings by psychotic means.'

3. Robert Ezra Park, *Race and Culture* (Glencoe, Illinois: The Free Press 1950), page 249.

4. ibid., page 250.

5. Shetland Isle study.

6. H. S. Becker and Blanche Greer, 'The Fate of Idealism in Medical School', *American Sociological Review, 23,* pages 50–56.

7. A. L. Kroeber, *The Nature of Culture* (Chicago: University of Chicago Press, 1952), page 311.

8. H. B. Dale, *The Higher Civil Service of Great Britain* (Oxford: Oxford University Press, 1941) page 50.

9. David Solomon, 'Career Contingencies of Chicago Physicians' (unpublished Ph.D. dissertation, Department of Sociology, University of Chicago, 1952), page 74.

10. J. Macgowan, *Sidelights on Chinese Life* (Philadelphia: Lippincott, 1908), page 187.

11. cf. Kenneth Burke's comments on the 'scene-act-agent ratio', *A Grammar of Motives* (New York: Prentice-Hall, 1945), pages 6–9.

12. E. J. Kahn, Jr, 'Closings and Openings', *New Yorker,* 13 and 20 February 1954.

13. See Mervyn Jones, 'White as a Sweep', *New Statesman and Nation,* 6 December 1952.

14. A. R. Radcliffe-Brown, 'The Social Organization of Australian Tribes', *Oceania,* 1, page 440.

15. See the thorough treatment of this problem in Dan C. Lortie, 'Doctors without Patients: The Anesthesiologist, a New Medical Speciality' (unpublished Master's thesis, Department of Sociology, University of Chicago 1950). See also Mark Murphy's three-part Profile of Dr Rovenstine, 'Anesthesiologist', *New Yorker,* 25 October and 1 and 8 November 1947.

16. In some hospitals the intern and the medical student perform tasks that are beneath a doctor and above a nurse. Presumably such tasks do not require a large amount of experience and practical training, for while this intermediate status of doctor-in-training is a permanent part of hospitals, all those who hold it do so temporarily.

34.   The Life-World
Alfred Schutz

The world of the natural attitude

We begin with an analysis of the world of daily life which the wide-awake, grown-up man who acts in it and upon it amidst his fellow-men experiences with the natural attitude as a reality.

"World of daily life" shall mean the intersubjective world which existed long before our birth, experienced and interpreted by others, our predecessors, as an organized world. Now it is given to our experience and interpretation. All interpretation of this world is based upon a stock of previous experiences of it, our own experiences and those handed down to us by our parents and teachers, which in the form of "knowledge at hand" function as a scheme of reference.

To this stock of experiences at hand belongs our knowledge that the world we live in is a world of well circumscribed objects with definite qualities, objects among which we move, which resist us and upon which we may act. To the natural attitude the world is not and never has been a mere aggregate of colored spots, incoherent noises, centers of warmth and cold. Philosophical or psychological analysis of the constitution of our experiences may afterwards, retrospectively, describe how elements of this world affect our senses, how we passively perceive them in an indistinct and confused way, how by active apperception our mind singles out certain features from the perceptional field, conceiving them as well delineated things which stand out over against a more or less inarticulated background or horizon. The natural attitude does not know these problems. To it the world is from the outset not the private world of the single individual, but an intersubjective world, common to all of us, in which we have not a theoretical but an eminently practical interest. The world of everyday life is the scene and also the object of our actions and interactions. We have to dominate it and we have to change it in order to realize the purposes which we pursue within it among our fellow-men. Thus, we work and operate not only within but upon the world. Our bodily movements — kinaesthetic, locomotive, operative — gear, so to speak, into the world, modifying or changing its objects and their mutual relationships. On the other hand, these objects offer resistance to our acts which we have either to overcome or to which we have to yield. In this sense it may be correctly said that a pragmatic motive governs our natural attitude toward the world of daily life. World, in this sense, is something that we have to modify by our actions or that modifies our actions.

Biographically determined situation

Man finds himself at any moment of his daily life in a biographically determined situation, that is, in a physical and sociological environment as defined by him, within which he has his position, not merely his position in terms of physical space and outer

Alfred Schutz: 'The Life-World' from ON PHENOMENOLOGY AND SOCIAL RELATIONS (University of Chicago Press, 1970), pp. 72-76.

time or of his status and role within the social system but also his moral and ideological position. To say that this definition of the situation is biographically determined means to say that it has its history; it is the sedimentation of all of man's previous experiences, organized in the habitual possessions of his stock of knowledge, at hand, and as such his unique possession, given to him and to him alone. This biographically determined situation includes certain possibilities of future practical or theoretical activities which shall be briefly called the "purpose at hand." It is this purpose at hand which defines those elements among all the others contained in such a situation which are relevant for this purpose. This system of relevances in turn determines what elements have to be made a substratum of generalizing typification, what traits of these have to be selected as characteristically typical and what others as unique and individual. . . .

Stock of knowledge

Man in daily life . . . finds at any given moment a stock of knowledge at hand that serves him as a scheme of interpretation of his past and present experiences, and also determines his anticipations of things to come. This stock of knowledge has its particular history. It has been constituted in and by previous experiencing activities of our consciousness, the outcome of which has now become our habitual possession. Husserl, in describing the constituting process that is here involved, speaks graphically of the "sedimentation" of meaning.

On the other hand, this stock of knowledge at hand is by no means homogenous, but shows a particular structure. I have already alluded to William James' distinction between "knowledge about" and "knowledge of acquaintance." There is a relatively small kernel of knowledge that is clear, distinct, and consistent in itself. This kernel is surrounded by zones of various gradations of vagueness, obscurity, and ambiguity. These follow zones of things just taken for granted, blind beliefs, bare suppositions, mere guesswork, zones in which it will do merely to "put one's trust." And finally, there are regions of our complete ignorance . . .

First, let us consider what determines the structurization of the stock of knowledge at a particular Now. A preliminary answer is that it is the system of our practical or theoretical interest at this specific moment which determines not only what is problematic and what can remain unquestioned but also what has to be known and with what degree of clarity and precision it has to be known in order to solve the emergent problem. In other words, it is the particular problem we are concerned with that subdivides our stock of knowledge at hand into layers of different relevance for its solution, and thus establishes the borderlines of the various zones of our knowledge just mentioned, zones of distinctness and vagueness, of clarity and obscurity, of precision and ambiguity. Here is the root of the pragmatistic interpretation of the nature of our knowledge, the relative validity of which has to be recognized even by those who reject the other tenets of pragmatism, especially its theory of truth. To be sure, even within the restricted limits of commonsense knowledge of everyday life, the reference to "interests," "problems," "relevances" is not a sufficient explanation. All these terms are merely headings of highly complicated subject matters for further research.

Secondly, it must be emphasized that the stock of knowledge is in a continual flux, and changes from any Now to the next one not only in its range but also in its structure. It is clear that any supervening experience enlarges and enriches it. By reference to the stock of knowledge at hand at that particular Now, the actually emerging experience is found to be a "familiar" one if it is related by a "synthesis of recognition" to a previous experience in the modes of "sameness," "likeness," "similarity," "analogy," and the like. The emerging experience may, for example, be conceived as a pre-experienced "same which recurs" or as a pre-experienced "same but modified" or as of a type similar to a pre-experienced one, and so on. Or the emergent experience is found to be "strange" if it cannot be referred, at least as to its type, to pre-experiences at hand. In both cases it is the stock of knowledge at hand that serves as the scheme of interpretation for the actually emergent experience. This reference to already experienced acts presupposes memory and all of its functions, such as retention, recollection, recognition.

The character of practical knowledge

. . . the knowledge of the man who acts and thinks within the world of his daily life is not homogeneous: it is (1) incoherent, (2) only partially clear, and (3) not at all free from contradictions.

1. It is incoherent because the individual's interests which determine the relevance of the objects selected for further inquiry are themselves not integrated into a coherent system. They are only partially organized under plans of any kind, such as plans of life, plans of work and leisure, plans for every social role assumed. But the hierarchy of these plans changes with the situation and with the growth of the personality; interests are shifted continually and entail an uninterrupted transformation of the shape and density of the relevance lines. Not only the selection of the objects of curiosity but also the degree of knowledge aimed at changes.

2. Man in his daily life is only partially — and we dare say exceptionally — interested in the clarity of his knowledge, i.e., in full insight into the relations between the elements of his world and the general principles ruling those relations. He is satisfied that a well-functioning telephone service is available to him and, normally, does not ask how the apparatus functions in detail and what laws of physics make this functioning possible. He buys merchandise in the store, not knowing how it is produced, and pays with money, although he has only a vague idea what money really is. He takes it for granted that his fellow-man will understand his thought if expressed in plain language and will answer accordingly, without wondering how this miraculous performance may be explained. Furthermore, he does not search for the truth and does not quest for certainty. All he wants is information on likelihood and insight into the chances or risks which the situation at hand entails for the outcome of his actions. That the subway will run tomorrow as usual is for him almost of the same order of likelihood as that the sun will rise. If by reason of special interest he needs more explicit knowledge on a topic, a benign modern civilization holds ready for him a chain of information desks and reference libraries.

3. His knowledge, finally, is not a consistent one. At the same time he may consider statements as equally valid which in fact are incompatible with one another. As a

father, citizen, an employee, and a member of his church he may have the most different and the least congruent opinions on moral, political, or economic matters. This inconsistency does not necessarily originate in a logical fallacy. Men's thought is just spread over subject matters located within different and differently relevant levels, and they are not aware of the modifications they would have to make in passing from one level to another.

35.   Self

George Herbert Mead

The self is something which has a development; it is not initially there at birth but arises in the process of social experience and activity, that is, develops in the given individual as a result of his relations to that process as a whole and to other individuals within that process. The intelligence of the lower forms of animal life, like a great deal of human intelligence, does not involve a self. In our habitual actions, for example, in our moving about in a world that is simply there and to which we are so adjusted that no thinking is involved, there is a certain amount of sensuous experience such as persons have when they are just waking up, a bare 'thereness' of the world. Such characters about us may exist in experience without taking their place in relationship to the self. One must, of course, under those conditions, distinguish between the experience that immediately takes place and our own organization of it into the experience of the self. One says upon analysis that a certain item had its place in his experience, in the experience of his self. We inevitably do tend at a certain level of sophistication to organize all experience into that of a self. We do so intimately identify our experiences, especially our affective experiences, with the self that it takes a moment's abstraction to realize that pain and pleasure can be there without being the experience of the self. Similarly, we normally organize our memories upon the string of our self. When we date things we always date them from the point of view of our past experiences. We frequently have memories that we cannot date, that we cannot place. A picture comes before us suddenly, and we are at a loss to explain when that experience originally took place. We remember perfectly distinctly the picture, but we do not have it definitely placed, and until we can place, it in terms of our past experience we are not satisfied. Nevertheless, I think it is obvious, when one comes to consider it, that the self is not necessarily involved in the life of the organism, nor involved in what we term our sensuous experience, that is, experience in a world about us for which we have habitual reactions.

We can distinguish very definitely between the self and the body. The body can be there and can operate in a very intelligent fashion without there being a self involved in the experience. The self has the characteristic that it is an object to itself, and that characteristic distinguishes it from other objects and from the body. It is perfectly true that the eye can see the foot, but it does not see the body as a whole. We cannot see our backs; we can feel certain portions of them, if we are agile, but we cannot get an experience of our whole body. There are, of course, experiences which are somewhat vague and difficult of location, but the bodily experiences are for us organized about a self. The foot and hand belong to the self. We can see our feet, especially when we look at them from the wrong end of an opera glass, as strange things which we have

Excerpts from George Herbert Mead, *MIND, SELF AND SOCIETY FROM THE STANDPOINT OF A SOCIAL BEHAVIORIST*, with an introduction by Charles W. Morris (University of Chicago Press, 1934; 1962). Copyright © University of Chicago Press 1934, 1962. Reprinted in Anselm L. Strauss (ed), *THE SOCIAL PSYCHOLOGY OF GEORGE HERBERT MEAD* (University of Chicago Press, 1956), pp. 199-246.

difficulty in recognizing as our own. The parts of the body are quite distinguishable from the self. We can lose parts of the body without any serious invasion of the self. The mere ability to experience different parts of the body is not different from the experience of a table. The table presents a different feel from what the hand does when one hand feels another, but it is an experience of something with which we come definitely into contact. The body does not experience itself as a whole, in the sense in which the self in some way enters into the experience of the self.

It is the characteristic of the self as an object to itself that I want to bring out. This characteristic is represented in the word 'self', which is a reflexive, and indicates that which can be both subject and object. This type of object is essentially different from other objects, and in the past it has been distinguished as conscious, a term which indicates an experience with, an experience of, one's self. It was assumed that consciousness in some way carried this capacity of being an object to itself. In giving a behavioristic statement of consciousness we have to look for some sort of experience in which the physical organism can become an object to itself.

When one is running away from someone who is chasing him, he is entirely occupied in this action, and his experience may be swallowed up in the objects about him, so that he has, at the time being, no consciousness of self at all. We must be, of course, very completely occupied to have that take place, but we can, I think, recognize that sort of a possible experience in which the self does not enter. We can, perhaps, get some light on that situation through those experiences in which during very intense action there appear in the experience of the individual, back of this intense action, memories and anticipations. Tolstoy as an officer in the war gives an account of having pictures of his past experience in the midst of his most intense action. There are also the pictures that flash into a person's mind when he is drowning. In such instances there is a contrast between an experience that is absolutely wound up in outside activity in which the self as an object does not enter, and an activity of memory and imagination in which the self is the principal object. The self is then entirely distinguishable from an organism that is surrounded by things and acts with reference to things, including parts of its own body. These latter may be objects like other objects, but they are just objects out there in the field, and they do not involve a self that is an object to the organism. This is, I think, frequently overlooked. It is that fact which makes our anthropomorphic reconstructions of animal life so fallacious. How can an individual get outside himself (experientially) in such a way as to become an object to himself? This is the essential psychological problem of selfhood or of self-consciousness; and its solution is to be found by referring to the process of social conduct or activity in which the given person or individual is implicated. The apparatus of reason would not be complete unless it swept itself into its own analysis of the field of experience or unless the individual brought himself into the same experiential field as that of the other individual selves in relation to whom he acts in any given social situation. Reason cannot become impersonal unless it takes an objective, non-affective attitude toward itself; otherwise we have just consciousness, not *self*-consciousness. And it is necessary to rational conduct that the individual should thus take an objective, impersonal attitude toward himself, that he should become an object to himself. For the individual organism is obviously an essential and important fact or constituent element of the empirical situation in which it acts; and without taking objective account of itself as such, it cannot act intelligently or rationally.

The individual experiences himself as such, not directly, but only indirectly, from the particular standpoints of other individual members of the same social group or from the generalized standpoint of the social group as a whole to which he belongs. For he enters his own experience as a self or individual, not directly or immediately, not by becoming a subject to himself, but only in so far as he first becomes an object to himself just as other individuals are objects to him or are in his experience; and he becomes an object to himself only by taking the attitudes of other individuals toward himself within a social environment or context of experience and behavior in which both he and they are involved.

The importance of what we term 'communication' lies in the fact that it provides a form of behavior in which the organism or the individual may become an object to himself. It is that sort of communication which we have been discussing — not communication in the sense of the cluck of the hen to the chickens, or the bark of a wolf to the pack, or ' the lowing of a cow, but communication in the sense of significant symbols, communication which is directed not only to others but also to the individual himself. So far as that type of communication is a part of behavior, it at least introduces a self. Of course, one may hear without listening; one may see things that he does not realize; do things that he is not really aware of. But it is when one does respond to that which he addresses to another and when that response of his own becomes a part of his conduct, when he not only hears himself but responds to himself, talks and replies to himself as truly as the other person replies to him, that we have behavior in which the individuals become objects to themselves.

Such a self is not, I would say, primarily the physiological organism. The physiological organism is essential to it, but we are at least able to think of a self without it. Persons who believe in immortality, or believe in ghosts, or in the possibility of the self leaving the body, assume a self which is quite distinguishable from the body. How successfully they can hold these conceptions is an open question, but we do, as a fact, separate the self and the organism. It is fair to say that the beginning of the self as an object, so far as we can see, is to be found in the experiences of people that lead to the conception of a 'double'. Primitive people assume that there is a double, located presumably in the diaphragm, that leaves the body temporarily in sleep and completely in death. It can be enticed out of the body of one's enemy and perhaps killed. It is represented in infancy by the imaginary playmates which children create and through which they come to control their experiences in their play.

The self, as that which can be an object to itself, is essentially a social structure, and it arises in social experience. After a self has arisen, it in a certain sense provides for itself its social experiences, and so we can conceive of an absolutely solitary self. But it is impossible to conceive of a self arising outside of social experience. When it has arisen, we can think of a person in solitary confinement for the rest of his life, but who still has himself as a companion and is able to think and to converse with himself as he had communicated with others. That process to which I have just referred, of responding to one's self as another responds to it, taking part in one's own conversation with others, being aware of what one is saying and using that awareness of what one is saying to determine what one is going to say thereafter — that is a process with which we are all familiar. We are continually following up our own address to other persons by an understanding of what we are saying and using that understanding in the direction of our continued speech. We are finding out what we are going to say, what we are going to do, by saying and doing, and in the process we are continually controlling the process itself. In the conversation of gestures what we say calls out a certain response in another and that in turn changes our own action, so that we shift from what we started to do because of the reply the other makes. The conversation of gestures is the beginning of communication. The individual comes to carry on a conversation of gestures with himself. He says something and that calls out a certain reply in himself which makes him change what he was going to say. One starts to say something, we will presume an unpleasant something, but when he starts to say it he realizes it is cruel. The effect on himself of what he is saying checks him; there is here a conversation of gestures between the individual and himself. By significant speech we mean that the action is one that affects the individual himself and that the effect upon the individual himself is part of the intelligent carrying-out of the conversation with others. Now we, so to speak, amputate that social phase and dispense with it for the time being, so that one is talking to one's self as one would talk to another person.

This process of abstraction cannot be carried on indefinitely. One inevitably seeks an audience, has to pour himself out to somebody. In reflective intelligence one thinks to act and to act solely so that this action remains a part of a social process. Thinking becomes preparatory to social action. The very process of thinking is, of course, simply an inner conversation that goes on, but it is a conversation of gestures which in its completion implies the expression of that which one thinks to an audience. One separates the significance of what he is saying to others from the actual speech and gets it ready before saying it. He thinks it out and perhaps writes it in the form of a book; but it is still a part of social intercourse in which one is addressing other persons and at the same time addressing one's self, and in which one controls the address to other persons by the response made to one's own gesture. That the person should be responding to himself is necessary to the self, and it is this sort of social conduct which provides behavior within which that self appears. I know of no other form of behavior than the linguistic in which the individual is an object to himself, and, so far as I can see, the individual is not a self in the reflective sense unless he is an object to himself. It is this fact that gives a critical importance to communication, since this is a type of behavior in which the individual does so respond to himself.

We realize in everyday conduct and experience that an individual does not mean a great deal of what he is doing and saying. We frequently say that such an individual is not himself. We come away from an interview with a realization that we have left out important things, that there are parts of the self that did not get into what was said. What determines the amount of the self that gets into communication is the social experience itself. Of course, a good deal of the self does not need to get expression. We carry on a whole series of different relationships to different people. We are one thing to one man and another thing to another. There are parts of the self which exist only for the self in relationship to itself. We divide ourselves up in all sorts of different selves with reference to our acquaintances. We discuss politics with one and religion with another. There are all sorts of different selves answering to all sorts of different social reactions. It is the social process itself that is responsible for the appearance of the self; it is not there as a self apart from this type of experience. [. . .]

Play, the game and the generalized other

[. . .] The organized community or social group which gives to the individual his unity of self can be called 'the generalized other'. The attitude of the generalized other is the attitude of the whole community. Thus, for example, in the case of such a social group as a ball team, the team is the generalized other in so far as it enters — as an organized process on social activity — into the experience of any one of the individual members. [. . .]

If the given human individual is to develop a self in the fullest sense, it is not sufficient for him merely to take the attitudes of other human individuals toward himself and toward one another within the human social process and to bring that social process as a whole into his individual experience merely in these terms. He must also, in the same way that he takes the attitudes of other individuals toward himself and toward one another, take their attitudes toward the various phases or aspects of the common social activity or set of social undertakings in which, as members of an organized society or social group, they are all engaged. He must then, by generalizing these individual attitudes of that organized society or social group itself as a whole, act toward different social projects which at any given time it is carrying out, or toward the various larger phases of the general social process which constitutes the group's life and of which these projects are specific manifestations. Getting these broad activities of any given social whole or organized society within the experiential field of any one of the individuals involved or included in that whole is, in other words, the essential basis and prerequisite of the fullest development of that individual's self — only in so far as he takes the attitudes of the organized social group to which he belongs toward the organized, cooperative social activity or set of such activities in which that group as such is engaged, does he develop a complete self or possess the sort of complete self he has developed. And on the other hand, the complex cooperative processes and activities and institutional functionings of organized human society are also possible only in so far as every individual involved in them or belonging to that society can take the general attitudes of all other such individuals with reference to these processes and activities and institutional functionings and to the organized social whole of experiential relations and interactions thereby constituted — and can direct his own behavior accordingly.

It is in the form of the generalized other that the social process influences the behavior of the individuals involved in it and carrying it on, that is, that the community exercises control over the conduct of its individual members; for it is in this form that the social process or community enters as a determining factor into the individual's thinking. In abstract thought the individual takes the attitude of the generalized other toward himself, without reference to its expression in any particular other individuals; and in concrete thought, he takes that attitude in so far as it is expressed in the attitudes toward his behavior of those other individuals with whom he is involved in the given social situation or act. But only by taking the attitude of the generalized other toward himself, in one or another of these ways, can he think at all; for only thus can thinking — or the internalized conversation of gestures which constitutes thinking — occur. And only through the taking by individuals of the attitude or attitudes of the generalized other toward themselves is the existence of a universe of discourse, as that system of common or social meanings which thinking presupposes as its context, rendered possible.

The self-conscious human individual, then, takes or assumes the organized social attitudes of the given social group or community (or of some one section thereof) to which he belongs, toward the social problems of various kinds which confront that group or community at any given time and which arise in connection with the correspondingly different social projects or organized cooperative enterprises in which that group of community as such is engaged; and as an individual participant in these social projects or cooperative enterprises, he governs his own conduct accordingly. In politics, for example, the individual identifies himself with an entire political party and takes the organized attitudes of that entire party toward the rest of the given social community and toward the problems which confront the party within the given social situation; and he consequently reacts or responds in terms of the organized attitudes of the party as a whole. He thus enters into a special set of social relations with all the other individuals who belong to that political party; and in the same way he enters into various other special sets of social relations, with various other classes of individuals respectively, the individuals of each of these classes being the other members of some one of the particular organized subgroups (determined in socially functional terms) of which he himself is a member within the entire given society, or social community. In the most highly developed, organized and complicated human social communities — those evolved by civilized man — these various socially functional classes or subgroups of individuals to which any given individual belongs (and with the other individual members of which he thus enters into a special set of social relations) are of two kinds. Some of them are concrete social classes or subgroups, such as political parties, clubs, corporations, which are all actually functional social units, in terms of which their individual members are directly related to one another. The others are abstract social classes or subgroups, such as the class of debtors and the class of creditors, in terms of which their individual members are related to one another only more or less indirectly and which only more or less indirectly function as social units, but which afford or represent unlimited possibilities for the widening and ramifying and enriching of the social relations among all the individual members of the given society as an organized and unified whole. The given individual's membership in several of these abstract social classes or subgroups makes possible his entrance into definite social relations (however indirect) with an almost infinite number of other individuals who also belong to or are included within one or another of these abstract social classes or subgroups cutting across functional lines of demarcation which divide different human social communities from one another, and including individual members from several (in some cases from all) such communities. Of these abstract social classes or subgroups of human individuals the one which is most inclusive and extensive is, of course, the one defined by the logical universe of discourse (or system of universally significant symbols) determined by the participation and communicative interaction of individuals; for all such classes or subgroups, it is the one which claims the largest number of individual members and which enables the largest conceivable number of human individuals to enter into some sort of social relation, however indirect or abstract it may be, with one another — a relation arising from the universal functioning of gestures as significant symbols in the general human social process of communication.

I have pointed out, then, that there are two general stages in the full development of the self. At the first of these stages, the individual's self is constituted simply by an organization of the particular attitudes of other individuals toward himself and toward one another in the specific social acts in which he participates with them. But at the second stage in the full development of the individual's self, that self is constituted not only by an organization of these particular individual attitudes, but also by an organization of the social attitudes of the generalized other or the social group as a whole to which he belongs. These social or group attitudes are brought within the individual's field of direct experience and are included as elements in the structure or constitution of his self, in the same way that the attitudes of particular other individuals are; and the individual arrives at them, or succeeds in taking them, by means of further organizing, and then generalizing, the attitudes of particular other individuals in terms of their organized social bearings and implications. So the self reaches its full development by organizing these individual attitudes of others into the organized social or group attitudes, and by thus becoming an individual reflection of the general systematic pattern of social or group behavior in which it and the others are all involved — a pattern which enters as a whole into the individual's experience in terms of these organized group attitudes which, through the mechanism of his central nervous system, he takes toward himself, just as he takes the individual attitudes of others.

The game has a logic, so that such an organization of the self is rendered possible. There is a definite end to be obtained; the actions of the different individuals are all related to each other with reference to that end so that they do not conflict; one is not in conflict with himself in the attitude of another man on the team. If one has the attitude of the person throwing the ball, he can also have the response of catching the ball. The two are related so that they further the purpose of the game itself. They are interrelated in a unitary, organic fashion. There is a definite unity, then, which is introduced into the organization of other selves when we reach such a stage as that of the game, as against the situation of play where there is a simple succession of one role after another, a situation which is, of course, characteristic of the child's own personality. The child is one thing at one time and another at another, and what he is at one moment does not determine what he is at another. That is both the charm of childhood as well as its inadequacy. You cannot count on the child; you cannot assume that all the things he does are going to determine what he will do at any moment. He is not organized into a whole. The child has no definite character, no definite personality.

The game is then an illustration of the situation out of which an organized personality arises. In so far as the child does take the attitude of the other and allows that attitude of the other to determine the thing he is going to do with reference to a common end,

371

he is becoming an organic member of society. He is taking over the morale of that society and is becoming an essential member of it. He belongs to it in so far as he does allow the attitude of the other that he takes to control his own immediate expression. What is involved here is some sort of an organized process. That which is expressed in terms of the game is, of course, being continually expressed in the social life of the child, but this wider process goes beyond the immediate experience of the child himself. The importance of the game is that it lies entirely inside the child's own experience, and the importance of our modern type of education is that it is brought as far as possible within this realm. The different attitudes that a child assumes are so organized that they exercise a definite control over his response, as the attitudes in a game control his own immediate response. In the game we get an organized other, a generalized other, which is found in the nature of the child itself, and finds its expression in the immediate experience of the child. And it is that organized activity in the child's own nature controlling the particular response which gives unity, and which builds up his own self.

What goes on in the game goes on in the life of the child all the time. He is continually taking the attitudes of those about him, especially the roles of those who in some sense control him and on whom he depends. He gets the function of the process in an abstract sort of way at first. It goes over from the play into the game in a real sense. He has to play the game. The morale of the game takes hold of the child more than the larger morale of the whole community. The child passes into the game, and the game expresses a social situation in which he can completely enter; its morale may have a greater hold on him than that of the family to which he belongs or the community in which he lives. There are all sorts of social organizations, some of which are fairly lasting, some temporary, into which the child is entering, and he is playing a sort of social game in them. It is a period in which he likes 'to belong', and he gets into organizations which come into existence and pass out of existence. He becomes a something which can function in the organized whole, and thus tends to determine himself in his relationship with the group to which he belongs. That process is one which is a striking stage in the development of the child's morale. It constitutes him a self-conscious member of the community to which he belongs.

Such is the process by which a personality arises. I have spoken of this as a process in which a child takes the role of the other and said that it takes place essentially through the use of language. Language is predominantly based on the vocal gesture by means of which cooperative activities in a community are carried out. Language in its significant sense is that vocal gesture which tends to arouse in the individual the attitude which it arouses in others, and it is this perfecting of the self by the gesture which mediates the social activities that gives rise to the process of taking the role of the other. The latter phrase is a little unfortunate because it suggests an actor's attitude which is actually more sophisticated than that which is involved in our own experience. To this degree it does not correctly describe that which I have in mind. We see the process most definitely in a primitive form in those situations where the child's play takes different roles. Here the very fact that he is ready to pay money, for instance, arouses the attitude of the person who receives money, the very process is calling out in him the corresponding activities of the other person involved. The individual stimulates himself to the response which he is calling out in the other person, and then acts in some degree in response to that situation. In play the child does definitely act the role which he himself has aroused in himself. It is that which gives, as I have said, a definite content in the individual which answers to the stimulus that affects him as it affects somebody else. The content of the other that enters into one personality is the response in the individual which his gesture calls out in the other. [. . .]

I have so far emphasized what I have called the structures upon which the self is constructed, the framework of the self, as it were. Of course we are not only what is common to all: each one of the selves is different from everyone else; but there has to be such a common structure as I have sketched in order that we may be members of a community at all. We cannot be ourselves unless we are also members in whom there is a community of attitudes which control the attitudes of all. We cannot have rights unless we have common attitudes. That which we have acquired as self-conscious persons makes us members of society and gives us selves. Selves can only exist in definite relationships to other selves. No hard-and-fast line can be drawn between our own selves and the selves of others, since our own selves exist and enter as such into our experience only in so far as the selves of others exist and enter as such into our experience also. The individual possesses a self only in relation to the selves of the other members of his social group; and the structure of his self expresses or reflects the general behavior pattern of this social group to which he belongs, just as does the structure of the self of every other individual belonging to this social group.

The self and the subjective

Emphasis should be laid on the central position of thinking when considering the nature of the self. Self-consciousness, rather than affective experience with its motor accompaniments, provides the core and primary structure of the self, which is thus essentially a cognitive rather than an emotional phenomenon. The thinking or intellectual process — internalization and inner dramatization, by the individual, of the external conversation of significant gestures which constitutes his chief mode of interaction with other individuals belonging to the same society — is the earliest experiential phase in the genesis and development of the self. Cooley and James, it is true, endeavor to find the basis of the self in reflexive affective experiences, that is, experiences involving 'self-feeling'; but the theory that the nature of 'the self is to be found in such experiences does not account for the origin of the self or of the self-feeling which is supposed to characterize such experiences. The individual need not take the attitudes of others toward himself in these experiences, since these experiences merely in themselves do not necessitate his doing so, and unless he does so, he cannot develop a self; and he will not do so in these experiences unless his self has already originated otherwise, namely, in the way we have been describing. The essence of the self, as we have said, is cognitive. It lies in the internalized conversation of gestures which constitutes thinking or in terms of which thought or reflection proceeds. And hence the origin and foundations of the self, like those of thinking, are social.

The 'I' and the 'me'

We have discussed at length the social foundations of the self and hinted that the self does not consist simply in the bare organization of social attitudes. We may now explicitly raise the question as to the nature of the 'I' which is aware of the social 'me'. [. . .]

The simplest way of handling the problem would be in terms of memory. I talk to myself, and I remember what I said and perhaps the emotional content that went with it. The 'I' of this moment is present in the 'me' of the next moment. There again I cannot turn around quick enough to catch myself. I become a 'me' in so far as I remember what I said. [. . .]

The 'I' is the response of the organism to the attitudes of the others; the 'me' is the organized set of attitudes of others which one himself assumes. The attitudes of the others constitute the organized 'me', and then one reacts toward that as an 'I'. [. . .]

A contrast of individualistic and social theories of the self

The differences between the type of social psychology which derives the selves of individuals from the social process in which they are implicated and in which they empirically interact with one another and the type of social psychology which instead derives that process from the selves of the individuals involved in it are clear. The first type assumes a social process or social order as the logical and biological precondition of the appearance of the selves of the individual organisms involved in that process or belonging to that order. The other type, on the contrary, assumes individual selves as the presuppositions, logically and biologically, of the social process or order within which they interact.

The difference between the social and the individual theories of the development of mind, self and the social process of experience or behavior is analogous to the difference between the evolutionary and the contract theories of the state as held in the past by both rationalists and empiricists. The latter theory takes individuals and their individual experiencing — individual minds and selves — as logically prior to the social process in which they are involved, and explains the existence of that social process in terms of them; whereas the former takes the social process of experience or behavior as logically prior to the individuals and their individual experiencing which are involved in it, and explains their existence in terms of that social process. But the latter type of theory cannot explain that which is taken as logically prior at all, cannot explain the existence of minds and selves; whereas the former type of theory can explain that which it takes as logically prior, namely, the existence of the social process of behavior, in terms of such fundamental biological or physiological relations and interactions as reproduction, or the cooperation of individuals for mutual protection or for the securing of food.

Our contention is that mind can never find expression, and could never have come into existence at all, except in terms of a social environment; that an organized set or pattern of social relations and interactions (especially those of communication by means of gestures functioning as significant symbols and thus creating a universe of discourse) is necessarily presupposed by it and involved in its nature. And this entirely social theory or interpretation of mind — this contention that mind develops and has its being only in and by virtue of the social process of experience and activity, which it hence presupposes, and that in no other way can it develop and have its being — must be clearly distinguished from the partially (but only partially) social view of mind. On this view, though mind can get expression only within or in terms of the environment of an organized social group, yet it is nevertheless in some sense a native endowment — a congenital or hereditary biological attribute — of the individual organism and could not otherwise exist or manifest itself in the social process at all; so that it is not itself essentially a social phenomenon, but rather is biological both in its nature and in its origin and is social only in its characteristic manifestations or expressions. According to this latter view, moreover, the social process presupposes, and in a sense is a product of, mind; in direct contrast is our opposite view that mind presupposes, and is a product of, the social process. The advantage of our view is that it enables us to give a detailed account and actually to explain the genesis and development of mind; whereas the view that mind is a congenital biological endowment of the individual organism does not really enable us to explain its nature and origin at all — neither what sort of biological endowment it is, nor how organisms at a certain level of evolutionary progress come to possess it. Furthermore, the supposition that the social process presupposes, and is in some sense a product of, mind seems to be contradicted by the existence of the social communities of certain of the lower animals, especially the highly complex social organizations of bees and ants, which apparently operate on a purely instinctive or reflex basis, and do not in the least involve the existence of mind or consciousness in the individual organisms which form or constitute them. And even if this contradiction is avoided by the admission that only at its higher levels — only at the levels represented by the social relations and interactions of human beings — does the social process of experience and behavior presuppose the existence of mind or become necessarily a product of mind, still it is hardly plausible to suppose that this already ongoing and developing process should suddenly, at a particular stage in its evolution, become dependent for its further continuance upon an entirely extraneous factor, introduced into it, so to speak, from without.

The individual enters as such into his own experience only as an object, not as a subject; and he can enter as an object only on the basis of social relations and interactions, only by means of his experiential transactions with other individuals in an organized social environment. It is true that certain contents of experience (particularly kinaesthetic) are accessible only to the given individual organism and not to any others; and that these private or 'subjective', as opposed to public or 'objective', contents of experience are usually regarded as being peculiarly and intimately connected with the individual's self or as being in a special sense self-experiences. But this accessibility solely to the given individual organism of certain contents of its experience does not affect, nor in any way conflict with, the theory as to the social nature and origin of the self that we are presenting. Existence of private or 'subjective' contents of experience does not alter the fact that self-consciousness involves the individual's becoming an object to himself by taking the attitudes of other individuals toward himself within an organized setting of social relationships, and that unless the individual had thus become an object to himself he would not be self-conscious or have a self at all. Apart from his social interactions with other individuals, he would not relate the private or 'subjective' contents of his experience to himself and he could not become aware of himself as such, that is, as an individual, a person, merely by means or in terms of these contents of his experience; for in order to become aware of himself as such he must, to repeat, become an object to himself, or enter his own experience as an object, and only by social means — only by taking the attitudes of others toward himself — is he able to become an object to himself.

It is true, of course, that once mind has arisen in the social process it makes possible the development of that process into much more complex forms of social interaction among the component individuals than was possible before it had arisen. But there is nothing odd about a product of a given process contributing to, or becoming an essential factor in, the further development of that process. The social process, then, does not depend for its origin or initial existence upon the existence and interactions of selves, though it does depend upon the latter for the higher stages of complexity and organization which it reaches after selves have arisen within it.

Developments in the Concern with Structure

36. Parsons: Theory as a Filing System
Ian Craib

STRUCTURAL-FUNCTIONALISM

Introduction

Talcott Parsons dominated English-language social theory from the end of World
War II until the mid 1960s. He produced an immense theoretical framework that
claimed, in principle, to be capable of embracing everything in the social world. The
basis of the system was laid during the economic crises of the 1930s. Alvin Gouldner,
in *The Coming Crisis of Western Sociology* (1970), argues that in fact it was developed
as a response to the challenge of Marxism: whereas Marxism was a general theory of
society which condemned capitalism, structural-functionalism was to become a general
theory of society which did not so much justify capitalism (although it often did) as
offer an explanation and understanding of its difficulties without condemning it. As we
shall see, this is achieved by seeing difficulties as part of an evolutionary process
leading to greater stability and integration. Perhaps luckily for Parsons, capitalism
responded in an appropriate way after World War II, and the period during which he
dominated sociology corresponded with a period of comparative stability and economic
expansion. Both the theory and capitalism began to run into difficulties again in the
late 1960s, and within ten years it seemed that Parsons's theory was of purely
historical interest. Since Parsons's death in 1979, however, there has been a major
revival of interest amongst younger American sociologists in the United States, and
there is now a flourishing 'neo-functionalist' school in existence.

Parson's work is notoriously difficult to understand — because of its complication
rather than its profundity, I would suggest. Reading him, I am sometimes made to
think of a filing clerk who is too intelligent for his work. To exercise his intelligence
and overcome his frustration, he develops a new and complicated system which has a
place for every document ever used by his firm. The problem is that he is the only
person who can work it, and without him nothing can be found.

In his early work Parsons set out to bring together the different streams of nineteenth-
and early-twentieth-century social thought into one comprehensive synthesis. There
are still debates about the accuracy of his interpretations, and critics frequently point
out that he barely mentioned Marx. For our present purposes the most important
feature of this synthesis is that it brings together the 'holistic' and 'individualistic'
theories of social action associated with the names of Durkheim and Weber,
respectively, amongst the founding fathers of sociology. For Weber, sociology should be
concerned with the actions of individuals directed towards each other (i.e. social
action). Such action can be seen as sets of means employed to achieve particular goals
— practical purposes or the realisation of some ultimate value, or a combination of
both. It must be understood in terms of the meanings which individuals give to it.

Copyright © 1992 Craib, Ian. Reproduced from *MODERN SOCIAL THEORY: FROM PARSONS TO
HABERMAS*. Reprinted with permission of Harvester Wheatsheaf and St Martin's Press, Incorporated.

Durkheim was also concerned with meanings, but he saw the most important meanings as having an existence over and above individuals. They comprised a 'collective conscience' into which individuals had to be socialised. Thus both are concerned with meanings — with people's ideas — but one starts with the individual, one with the social whole. Both are theories of ideas and actions — of persons.

Here we can find Parsons's main themes. First, he sees the social world in terms of people's ideas, particularly their norms and values. Norms are the socially accepted rules which people employ in deciding on their actions; values can best be described as their beliefs about what the world should be like, and they too have a determining effect on people's actions. The most important social processes are seen as the communication of meaning, of symbols and information. Secondly, he is concerned with the organisation of individual actions into systems of action, with employing the holistic and individualistic approaches at the same time.

The idea of a system gives us the crucial analogy or metaphor in Parsons's theory: that of the biological organism or living system. He pushes this further than a simple analogy: he does not stop at saying that social life is *like* a living system, he says that it *is* a living system of a particular type. The problem with this will emerge later, but it is fair to say that it is always dangerous to push an analogy too far: there is a world of difference between saying 'My love is *like* a red, red rose' and saying 'My love *is* a red, red rose.' The idea of social life as a system — a network of different parts — explains the 'structural' part of the structural-functionalist label that is usually attached to Parsons's work. The analogy with a biological system explains the 'functionalist' part. If we take the human body as a system, it can be seen as having certain needs — for example, food — and a number of interrelated parts (the digestive system, the stomach, the intestines, etc) which function to meet those needs. Parsons sees a social system of action as having needs which must be met if it is to survive, and a number of parts which function to meet those needs. All living systems are seen as tending towards equilibrium, a stable and balanced relationship between the different parts, and maintaining themselves separately from other systems (a tendency to 'boundary maintenance').

Parsons's emphasis is always on stability and order, and indeed, he sees social theory as attempting to answer the question 'How is social order possible?' — a problem often associated with the philosopher Thomas Hobbes, who formulated it in its clearest form. It presupposes that in the 'natural state' human beings are entirely self-seeking, that there is a war of all against all, and this natural tendency has to be moulded and limited by social organisation.

The Grand Theory

Parsons's idea of theory

Parsons describes himself as an 'incurable theorist'; certainly his style conveys the sense of a terminal case. He has a particular idea of what a theory is, and this explains some of the difficulty. The world we can see is confused and confusing, and to make sense of it we must use our general ideas to organise it. Assuming that the real world is a system, the first step is to organise our general ideas into a systematic and ordered body of abstract concepts. Only after we have done this will we be able to make propositions about the world. An abstract concept is a generalisation which emphasises something important about the world. Such concepts abound in everyday life. The concept of 'red', for example, can be seen as an abstraction from all the red things we see around us. Now the logical ordering of abstract concepts is not the same thing as talking about the world we can see around us, and if this is kept in mind, then Parsons becomes marginally easier to read. From Parsons's point of view, the first test for such a theory is its logical coherence. If it is, as he intends it to be, a logically coherent theory of social science, then it should bring together all that we already know about the social world, and much of his work is concerned with translating other theories and research results into his own terms, to show that they fit. The assumption is one we will meet again: that despite appearances the social world is organised in a logical, rational way, and a logical, rational theory is therefore most likely to be right. Eventually, this can be confirmed by developing testable propositions from the theory, but that stage is some way off.

The unit act and the system of action: institutionalisation

In *The Structure of Social Action*, originally published in 1937, Parsons argued that all the major theorists he examined could be seen as moving towards what he called a 'voluntaristic theory of action', in which human beings were conceived of as making choices about — deciding between — different goals and means to achieve them. Such a conception could be the foundation of all the human sciences, and he suggested that it was possible to distil from their work a basic model of human action, defining all its components in abstract terms. This model comprises, first, the human actor and, second, a range of goals or ends between which the actor must choose, and different means by which these ends may be reached — again, the actor has to choose between them. However, the choices are not made in a vacuum. The environment is made up of a number of physical and social factors which limit the range of choices: for example, my eyesight is not good enough to enable me to become an airline pilot, and in the current economic situation I cannot choose to be an engineer because no engineering jobs are available. Most important of all, the environment includes generally accepted norms and values and other ideas which influence our choice of goals and means. If I am a Roman Catholic and a gynaecologist I will not specialise in abortion, even if the option is open to me; similarly, I am not able to break the informal rules that govern relationships with my colleagues (e.g. about attendance at the university) without suffering punitive criticism. The most formal and universal norms are set out in a society's legal system — I always have the option of murdering my students when they hand in late work, but I am unlikely to take it, not only because I think it is morally wrong, but because there is a likelihood of severe punishment.

The 'unit act', then, is made up of an actor, means, goals, and an environment which comprises physical and social objects and norms and values. This is an abstract description of all action and the starting point of Parsons's immense scheme, most of which can be unravelled from here. The task of the social scientist is to make sense of the ways choices are made within the contraints I have just discussed. Now Parsons is not concerned just with individual action but also with systems of action, and as his theory developed, so did his idea of a system. Amongst the social objects in the actors' environment are other actors, and for Parsons a system of action is made up of relationships between actors. The emphasis of Parsons's work here changes from voluntarism, from looking at the individual actors' choices, to looking at the way systems of action limit and even determine individual choices. This has been the focus for a number of criticisms, to which I will return later. For the moment, I want to look at the way in which Parsons develops the idea of the unit act to a conception of the *social system*. This is built up around the norms and values that together with other actors, make up part of the actors' environment. He assumes that each actor aims for maximum gratification, and if she engages in interaction with another and receives gratification, the interaction will be repeated. Each actor will come to expect certain responses from the other, and so social rules or norms will develop, together with generally accepted values, which help to guarantee those responses. A simple example would be a love affair which develops into a marriage. As the partners gain gratification from each other, so they come to expect each other to continue to act in the way which supplies gratification. The marriage will develop its own informal, and perhaps even formal, rules of behaviour. Each may come to expect the other to tolerate minor adulteries, or to share equally in the household chores, and each will come to regard this as an obligation. Both may come to believe in the 'sanctity of marriage', although before the wedding, both may have laughed at the idea.

Reverting to Parsons's terminology, a system of 'status roles' develops — a network of positions to which expectations of behaviour (and rewards and sanctions for fulfilling or not fulfilling those expectations) are attached. This process is called *institutionalisation* — a solidifying of relationships over time in such a way that the behaviour attached to each status role remains constant whoever is occupying it. Society as a whole, and different institutions in society, may be considered as a network of status roles, each governed by established norms and values.

The social system is not the only system contained in embryonic form in the unit act. The description of the process of institutionalisation and the development of the social system which I have just described presupposes three other systems. It presupposes an actor who aims for maximum gratification (i.e. a personality system); it presupposes, as far as society as a whole is concerned, a system of wider values which give coherence to the different norms attached to different status roles (i.e. a cultural system); and it presupposes a physical environment to which society must adapt (i.e. a biological organism). This is where the filing system requires at least sixty-four new filing cabinets. I will not bother with all of them.

Systems and subsystems: functional prerequisites

For Guy Rocher (1974) Parsons's theory is like 'a set of Chinese boxes — when one is opened, it contains a smaller one, which contains a smaller one still, and so on'. This is an apt description. I said above that Parsons's concepts — unit, act, status roles, social system, etc — were abstractions, and there are different levels of abstraction. Going back to the example of red: there is a higher-level abstraction ('colour') of which red is one type, lower-level abstractions (dark red, light red, pink, etc), and lower-lower-level abstractions, which involve adding other qualities (dark red and round). The process can be continued until we are describing a unique object (the dark red round rubber object of six inches in diameter on the floor in front of me — in other words, 'this ball'). Here there is an insight into the difficulty of Parsons's theory — much of it is equivalent to describing this ball as 'the dark red . . . etc.' .

By talking about the development of status role and the social system, we have arrived somewhere above the middle level of abstraction. It is possible to distinguish at least the following levels:

1. The highest level: all living systems. Sometimes Parsons writes as if living systems are a subsystem of *all* systems (i.e. everything), but that is not important for our present purposes.

2. Second-highest level: systems of action, including everything in the unit act.

3. Third-highest level: the subsystems of action; the personality, cultural, biological and social systems.

4. Fourth-highest level: subsystem of subsystems. The subsystems of the social system are the political system, the socialisation system, the economy and the 'societal community' (I will explain this shortly).

5. Fifth-highest level: subsystems of subsystems of subsystems. The most clearly worked out at this level belong to the economy: the economic commitments subsystem, the capitalisation subsystem, the production subsystem, the organisational subsystem.

Presumably the process could go on *ad infinitum*, but I will concern myself only with levels 3 and 4. The first question to ask is why at each stage we find four new subsystems, and the answer brings Parsons's functionalism into play. He argues that any system, at whatever level, must satisfy four needs or requirements if it is to survive, and in each case a specialist subsystem is developed to meet each requirement. These four requirements, or *functional prerequisities*, are as follows:

1. Each system must adapt to its environment (*adaptation*).

2. Each system must have a means of mobilising its resources in order to achieve its goals and thus obtain gratification (*goal attainment*).

3. Each system must maintain the internal co-ordination of its parts and develop ways of dealing with deviance — in other words, it must keep itself together (*integration*).

4. Each system must maintain itself as nearly as possible in a state of equilibrium — the examples below and later should distinguish this from 3 above (*pattern maintenance*).

Table 1 shows which subsystem fulfils which functional prerequisite for the general system of action and the social system.

To sum up: the unit act contains, in embryonic form, four subsystems which can be seen as developing through a process of institutionalisation; each subsystem has further subsystems of its own. At each level, the subsystems develop to meet four needs or functional prerequisites which must be met if the system is to survive. It is more important to get the general idea of all this rather than the detail.

Table 1   Subsystems fulfilling functional prerequisites

Major system	Adaptation	Goal attainment	Integration	Pattern maintenance
The general system of action (described in the 'unit act')	The *biological organism*, which provides the link between the physical world and the meanings (norms, values, etc.) that make up the world of action	The *personality* system which is formed by socialisation in such a way that it internalises general cultural values and societal norms. It thus becomes the instrument through which the major system achieves its goals	The *social system* of status roles governed by norms which define which actions are or are not allowable	The *cultural system* — the most general ideas, ideals and values of the major system, made more concrete in the norms of the social system and internalised in the personality system
The social system	The *economy*, the link between social organisation and the physical world or nature	The *political system* — including *all* forms of decision-making and resource mobilisation	The *'societal community'* — the institutions of social control - ranging from the legal system to informal rule of conduct	The *socialisation processes*, by means of which individuals are educated into the cultural values and societal norms of the system

Ways of analysing action: the pattern variables

Before moving on to look at how all this works, I want to deal briefly with one other set of variables — what Parsons calls the *pattern variables*. These illustrate even more emphatically the classifying power of his thought — on my tentative calculation, we now need 512 filing cabinets and we have not yet reached the lowest level of abstraction, and no information about the real world has yet been collected. More importantly, they bring together two different concerns in his work: the voluntaristic theory of action, concerned with individual choices, and systems theory. Both individual actions and system organisation can be seen as choosing between alternatives; remember from the original discussion of the unit act that all action involves choice. There are four major pairs of alternatives:

1.   Particularism-universalism: I may treat an object as a specific, unique object, or as one of a general class — the difference between the way I treat my children and my students.

2. Affective-affectively neutral: I may allow the full range of my feelings to come into play in a relationship (my children) or I might maintain neutral feelings (my students).

3. Quality-performance: I might value an object for its own sake (my children) or what can be done with it, its instrumental potentiality (my students).

4. Diffuseness-specificity: I might be involved in a total relationship to all aspects of an object (my children) or I might be concerned with only one activity in the relationship (my students).

This is as far as I want to go in elaborating the filing system as such; the pattern variables will not reappear until I discuss the criticisms that can be made of structural-functionalism. I have included them because they illustrate certain important features of Parsons's theory. For the time being, I want to return to systems and the relationships between them.

The cybernetic hierarchy

I said in the [Introduction to Part II] that Parsons's theory of social action is also a theory of meanings — of norms, values, symbols and communication. For Parsons the various systems are related through the exchange of symbolic information. A symbol is seen as something valuable not in itself but because of what can be done with it. Money is the clearest example: a coin is near to worthless as a metal object; it is valuable only because we can use it to buy things. Each subsystem of the social system has its equivalent symbol: the economy itself deals in money, the political system in power, in the societal community it is influence, and in the socialisation system, commitment. Through exchanging symbolic resources, each system remains in equilibrium with the others, whilst maintaining its own identity — maintaining its boundaries.

There is more than this to the exchanges between systems, however. Here we go back to the analogy between systems of action and all living systems — in fact *all* systems, because Parsons draws on cybernetics, the science of systems. This suggests that any system is controlled by that subsystem which is the highest on information and lowest on energy, and we can thus construct a hierarchy of subsystems, the lowest being that which has most energy but least information. Parsons himself provides the useful example of a washing machine in which the controlling timing mechanism, which has a great deal of programmed information, uses very little energy (electricity) compared with the working parts it controls. Thus the lower subsystems push energy up through the system, the higher controlling subsystems pass information back down. We can thus order the different subsystems described in Table 1 in the manner shown in Table 2.

Table 2   The cybernetic hierarchy

The general system of action		The social system
The cultural system	High on information	The socialisation system
The social system	High on information	The societal community
The personality system	High on energy	The political system
The biological organism	High on energy	The economic system

This ordering of systems, together with the postulate that all systems tend towards equilibrium, does — finally — enable us to approach the real world and organise it to some effect. We can put the filing system to work. We can also talk about causal mechanisms: first, the idea of a 'homeostatic loop', where change in one subsystem affects the others, which in turn react back on the first and restore the original situation. And, secondly, a 'feedback' mechanism, whereby those subsystems 'high' on information use that information selectively to control subordinate subsystems.

I have not described Parsons's system in anything like its full complexity — a number of the subsystems that I have only mentioned are analysed in much greater detail, and there are other aspects to the theory. However, I hope I have dealt with enough aspects to convey a general idea of the enterprise without causing too many nervous breakdowns.

Structural-functionalist explanations: change and modernity

In the following examples, I will be using the term 'explain' loosely; it will emerge later that the ability of Parsons's system to explain rather than describe is a major issue for critics. Parsons presents an evolutionary theory of change, drawing again on the analogy with biological organisms, this time on the way a cell divides and multiplies. Most people will have seen, at some time, a film taken through a microscope of a cell dividing into two and then four, and so on. For Parsons, the development of human society can be seen in the same way. Simple societies can be regarded as the single cell, which divides first into the four subsystems of the general system of action and then, in turn, each of these divides. This process involves three stages: the new subsystem differentiates itself, the new arrangement goes through a process of adaptation and reintegration, and finally there is the establishment of a more general system of values at the highest cybernetic level — a system of values which embraces the new subsystem.

A more specific example can be taken from Parsons himself: the transition from agriculture-based peasant societies to industrial societies. This involves the separation of the economic from the socialisation system. Whereas in pre-industrial societies the family unit was also the main unit of production, the family holding and working the land together — albeit with some division of labour — industrialisation separated work in factories and offices whilst family life became confined to the home. For this separation to be successful, Parsons argues that it must have greater adaptive capacity; work is carried out more efficiently and rationally in the new industrial units and productivity increases, whilst the family fulfils its socialisation functions more efficiently when it is stripped of its economic functions. The process of integration involves the co-ordination of the two subsystems (presumably such developments as the laws prohibiting women and children from certain occupations) and the development of a new economic hierarchy of control, since the father of the family no longer fulfils that role.[1] Both subsystems must be integrated into the wider societal and political communities, and finally the value system must develop to include the new status roles: the father stripped of some previous power, the new industrial managers, and so on.

A more recent example comes from an article Parsons wrote on American youth and youth and youth subcultures (1964). In general terms he argues that the twentieth century is a period of remarkable historical change, and there are reasons why youth in particular should experience the strains of such change. The strains are seen in terms of *anomie* — a state in which values and norms are no longer clear, or have lost their relevance. The explanation begins with the cultural: a paradoxical feature of the American value system is that at its centre is the value of individual success and achievement. The paradox is that in the pursuit of this value, structural differentiation is hastened, society becomes more complex more quickly, and lower-level value patterns become outdated. At the same time, increased complexity means that individual achievement has to be limited by specialisation and co-operation.

There are various ways in which youth is made problematic by this process. Training and education take much longer, so during the period when they might once have moved into adulthood, young people are kept dependent on the family, despite the fact that at the centre of their lives are people of the same age outside the family, the 'peer group'. The increased specialisation has isolated the nuclear family and young children are thus made more dependent on it, and this can create problems later when it is time to begin leaving the family. Traditional ties are weakened by the increased complexity of social relations, and this is reflected in changes in sexual behaviour, where the contrast with traditional values is most marked.

In this context, youth subcultures have destructive and progressive functions. On the one hand they can be simply rebellious, rejecting traditional values and the central value system and offering nothing in their place. They can also be means by which the traditional value systems are transformed and brought up to date and new values established, and they provide social support for the individual in the long period when she has outgrown her own family but is not in a position to form a family of her own. Most youth subcultures in fact display both aspects, and both are likely to entail conflict.

Thus change and conflict are explained in terms of continuing evolutionary adjustment of different subsystems to each other. This analysis encapsulates the tensions of the modern world: it involves living in larger and larger communities, undergoing constant differentiation and acting rationally, orientated only be the most universal norms and values; the attempt to find a specific individual and communal identity in this context is not only a explanation of youth culture.

Cracks in the Grand Theory

I said above that Parsons developed the most comprehensive and worked-out form of action theory, and there is a sense in which the other variants may be seen as fragments of his system. Now I want to look at the main fault lines along which this fragmentation occurs. In the period up to his death, there were three main lines of criticism. Many critics distinguish between the logical and substantive problems with the theory, but I do not think this is very helpful: a logical problem in a theory's explanation is also a sign that it misconceives what it is trying to explain. There are also a number of common criticisms that boil down to saying that the theory does not generate testable propositions about the world; this might be true, but as I have pointed out before, this is not the only criterion by which theories can be judged, and in the case of the social world, complexity and the inability to experiment make the formation of testable hypotheses very difficult.

Here, I will concentrate on the imaginative or creative aspect of the theory, the employment of the biological systems analogy, on the generalisation from action (persons) to system (societies) and the explanatory power of the theory.

Structural-functionalism as Utopia: the problems of conflict and change

It was often argued that Parsons's model of social life, with its emphasis on equilibrium, balanced exchange and functional relationships, cannot make sense of social change and conflict. Dahrendorf likened it to a literary Utopia, a vision of a perfectly good or perfectly bad society, a world of balance, with no sense of history and without any source of change inside the society. Such criticism is frequently extended to argue that the theory has an in-built conservative bias: inequalities of wealth (social stratification) are seen as functional, an efficient way of keeping the system going, as are differences in status; power is distributed in the way that is most functional for achieving the system's goals; everything is perfect.

I deliberately employed the example of historical change and youth subcultures to illustrate that this sort of criticism is misguided. In fact, throughout the time when Parsons was writing, others were using the same framework to understand change. Robert Merton, for example, argued that the emphasis on functional unity and equilibrium tends to direct attention away from questions about the *degree* of unity and equilibrium and the processes by which they come about. He also made important distinctions between manifest and latent functions (similar to that between intended and unintended consequences) and function and dysfunction (the opposite of function), both of which can be deployed to make sense of change and conflict. Alvin Gouldner (1970) pointed out that system integration may involve anything from complete dependence of the parts on each other to comparative independence. Both writers tended towards a less general level of theorising than Parsons. Merton called it middle-range theory, dealing with different parts of the system rather than the system as a whole. Finally, Lewis Coser, in *The Functions of Social Conflict* (1956), argues that the occurrence of social conflict can be seen as having a vital integrating effect through releasing tension and setting in motion a chain of adjustments; this is along the same lines as the youth-culture example.

If Parsons takes the analogy between a social system and a biological system to its extreme, these criticisms — particularly those of Merton and Gouldner — can be seen as drawing back from identifying the two and exploring the differences.

Teleological and functional explanations

The important criticisms seem to me to have to do with structural-functionalism's failure, at least in Parsons's theory, to explore the differences between biological, living systems and social systems: it results precisely in a generalisation of a theory of persons to a theory of societies. Persons are, amongst other things, biological organisms; it does not automatically follow that the same is true of societies.

One line of argument is that we cannot claim that social systems have needs which must be met in order to survive. Parsons's critics argue that in practice this is meaningless. To establish that it is true, we would need examples of societies which did not survive and we would have to show that they did not meet all the functional requisites. Now excluding very simple societies, it is difficult to find an example. It seems that what usually happens is that a society less well adapted to its environment is absorbed through military or economic conquest by a better-adapted society. It does not disappear but remains, perhaps in a modified form, as part of the better-adapted society. Thus some native American tribes were wiped out by military conquest, but others remain today as a clearly identifiable part of American society. The difference between those that were wiped out and those that survived seems to depend as much on the political processes of the conquering whites as on anything else; and the sense in which those that remain have 'survived' is itself debatable. An even clearer example is the way in which peasant agriculture in South and Latin America has been integrated into the industrial system of North America and Europe. In fact the Parsonian position would be tenable only if different societies were like different animal species battling for survival: only the fittest would survive.

Second, the critics argue that to say that a social system has needs does not explain how those needs are met. It might be true, for example, that modern industrial societies need complicated education systems. Yet Britain, France and America, all societies at approximately the same evolutionary stage, have different education systems. A need can be met in any number of ways, and simply starting its existence does not explain anything about how it is met. Third, Anthony Giddens argues, against functionalism, that proper explanations involve reference to actors and actions, and the functionalist explanations can be rewritten in such terms. Thus, to explain the existence of something by the function it fulfils is to make a nonsense of the idea of cause. A function is not fulfilled until something exists. If the function is the cause of its existence, then the effect — existence — must come before the cause — the function. In other words, time seems to be reversed.

I said that the first criticism would not apply if social systems were like animal species. The second and third would not apply if social systems really were like individual actors. If a social system had sense organs that could experience the need for, say, an education system as the body can experience hunger; if the experience could be communicated to a system brain, translated into symbolic thought, pondered and analysed; if the social brain could decide what sort of education system it wants and then transmit the appropriate messages along its nervous system so that an education system were constructed, then — and only then — would these criticisms not apply. But social systems do not have needs and goals like individuals.

The difference is that the human organism is made up of parts which are not capable of independent reflective thought and are controlled by a part that is. It is only in *Peanuts* cartoons that the stomach argues with the feet and the tail demands higher status. Social systems are — according to Parsons himself — made up of parts which are capable of reflective thought as they occupy their status roles; the organic link is very different to that between parts of the body. Yet the implication that a social system is consequently different from other living systems is not taken up.

Material and normative interests

Here I want to draw on two papers by David Lockwood, written during the period when Parsons was the dominant figure in sociology. In the present context, they emphasise the difference between persons and societies by pointing to features of the social world which exist but cannot be understood by structural–functionalism.

I have emphasised throughout that at the centre of Parsons's theory are meanings: norms and values, around which the action system and the social system are organised. Lockwood suggests that there is another factor at work in social life, what he calls the 'material substratum':

> the factual disposition of means in the situation of action which structures differential (life-chances) and produces interests of a non-normative kind — that is interests other than those which actors have in conforming with the normative definition of the situation. (Lockwood, 1964: 284)

Thus social life is structured by people's access to goods and property and the life which goes with the possession of goods and property. For example, it is possible to argue that the distribution of property (including skills) is such in both Britain and the USA that blacks have different material interests to whites. The white material interest might be in maintaining a system of racial discrimination which keeps blacks out of certain types of jobs, and this might outweigh adherence to a core system of social values which includes racial equality. Similarly it might be suggested, with some evidence in support, that people go to work not because they adhere to a system of norms and values that says work is a good thing, but because they have a material interest — at the lowest level, that of not starving. Think about it: why do *you* work?

In a second article, Lockwood (1964) distinguishes between what he calls *social* integration, which is a matter of relationships between actors, and *system* integration, relationships between different parts of the system. We can talk about societies manifesting social or normative integration, but not manifesting system integration. An economic crisis, for example, may certainly be taken as an indication of a system imbalance, a lack of integration; however, people may still adhere to the values and norms of the society, despite the economic hardship they suffer. We can add to this the idea of material interests, and it becomes apparent that the normative system may be used to achieve certain material interests. It may be in the material interests of large business corporations to reduce the taxes they pay, necessitating cuts in government expenditure on social services. The central normative and value system — which, for example, may involve a strong belief in private enterprise and the absence of state interference — may persuade those who suffer from the cuts that those cuts are justified.

Parsons's theory, and structural-functionalism in general, seems to me to be incapable of grasping such eventualities, despite the fact that they are immediately plausible. It can see social life only as a normative and value-controlled system, not as also a 'material' system. To do that, to make a distinction between social and system integration, it is necessary to make a distinction between persons and societies.

Can structural-functionalism explain?

When I gave some examples of structural-functionalist explanation, I said that I was using the term 'explain' loosely. I have indicated some problems with functional explanation, and now I want to suggest that by its very nature the theory is descriptive rather than explanatory. This is indicated by the possibility of writing out vast complicated passages of Parsons's work and then rewriting them in common-sense language, adding to the clarity, not losing any ideas, and taking up only a few lines. C. Wright Mills does this brilliantly in *The Sociological Imagination*. It seems to me that this is possible because of the very meaning Parsons gives to theory — we break everything down into its component parts and then add them together: 'this ball' becomes the dark red round rubber object on the floor. My relationship with employer is particularistic, affectively negative, performance-orientated and specific: I don't like her, but I'm having an affair with her in the hope of promotion.

If an explanation involves identifying causal processes and causal mechanisms, then the theory cannot explain. Its concepts — systems, subsystems, and so on — are abstractions; causal processes and mechanisms are real. If you go back to my earlier 'explanations', I think it should be clear that they are really elaborate descriptions with an element of explanation provided by the idea of a cybernetic hierarchy and a process of evolution attached to it. It might be said that Parsons is a 'cultural determinist' as opposed to Marx's economic determinism. On closer examination, however, even this is ambiguous. Wolf Heydebrand points out (1972) that the flow is two-way: energy from below, information from above; and both could be regarded as determining or causing. Taking Heydebrand's example of the police force: this must be geared to enforcing the cultural values and social norms of a society (i.e. controlled from above). At the same time its very existence depends upon an economic system which produces enough to keep a police force in existence. We cannot assign any causal priority.

I think this throws light on another criticism of Parsons already touched on several times: that as his theory develops, it changes from an individualist theory talking about actors' choices, as in the model of the unit act, to a holistic one dealing with the way systems determine actors' choices. The vast majority of his ideas, and most of his work, have been concerned with systems rather than individuals, and the criticism is usually made from the point of view of an action theory which concentrates on individual action and interaction. However, I do not think this criticism is justified. Parsons deals with both, and the importance of the pattern variables — the reason why

391

I listed them earlier — is that they enable him to deal with both. However, he cannot do so at the same time — he must switch from one point of view to the other — and this is precisely what the different variants of action theory do: structural-functionalism and conflict theory are concerned in different ways with systems of action; symbolic interactionism and more recent variants with individual interactions. Parsons cannot give priority to one or the other; in one sense, the system is the individual writ large; in another, the individual is the system writ small. No causal priority is, or can be, assigned. Consequently, it is possible for variants of action theory to emphasise either side over the other and, indeed, for Parsons to do the same at different stages in his career.

Notes

1. As far as I know, Parsons mentions only the second of these.

Further reading

Very little of Parson's own mammoth output makes easy reading; I have found the following comparatively accessible and, at least, comparatively short:

Parsons, T. (1961) 'An outline of the social system', in Parsons, T., Shils, E., Naegele, A. and Pitts, J. (eds), *Theories of Society: Foundations of modern sociological theory*, The Free Press, New York, pp. 30–79.

Parsons, T. (1964) *Social Structure and Personality*, The Free Press, Glencoe, NJ.

Parsons, T. (1966) *Societies: Evolutionary and comparative perspectives*, Prentice Hall, Englewood Cliffs, NJ.

Parsons, T. (1970) 'Some problems of General Theory in sociology', in McKinney, J. C. and Tyriakian, E. A. (eds), *Theoretical Sociology: Perspectives and developments*, Appleton-Century-Crofts, New York, pp. 27-68.

Parsons, T. (1971) *The System of Modern Societies*, Prentice Hall, Englewood Cliffs, NJ.

His most important books are:

Parsons, T. (1949) *The Structure of Social Action*, The Free Press, New York.

Parsons, T. (1951) *The Social System*, The Free Press, New York.

Parsons, T. and Shils, E. (1951) *Toward a General Theory of Action*, Harvard University Press, Cambridge, MA.

The following are secondary; Rocher is the clearest:

Adriaansens, H. P. M. (1980) *Talcott Parsons and the Conceptual Dilemma*, Routledge & Kegan Paul, London.

Bourricaud, F. (1981) *The Sociology of Talcott Parsons*, University of Chicago Press, Chicago.

Colomy, P. (ed) (1990) *Functionalist Sociology*, Edward Elgar, Aldershot, Hants.

Devereux, E. C. (1961) 'Parsons' sociological theory', in Black, M. (ed), *The Social Theories of Talcott Parsons*, Prentice Hall, Englewood Cliffs, NJ, pp. 1-63.

Hamilton, P. (1983) *Talcott Parsons*, Ellis Horwood, Chichester/Tavistock, London.

Holton, R. J. and Turner, B. S. (1986) *Talcott Parsons on Economy and Society*, Routledge & Kegan Paul, London.

Merton, R. K. (1968) *Social Theory and Social Structure*, The Free Press,Glencoe, NJ.

Mills, C. Wright (1980) *The Sociological Imagination*, Penguin, Harmondsworth.

Moore, W. E. (1978) 'Functionalism', in Bottomore, T. and Nisbet, R. (eds), *History of Sociological Analysis*, Heinemann, London, pp. 321-61.

Robertson, R. and Turner, B. S. (1991) *Talcott Parsons, Theorist of Modernity*, Sage, London.

Rocher, G. (1974) *Talcott Parsons and American Sociology*, Nelson, London.

The most useful critical essays are:

Burger, T. (1977) 'Talcott Parsons, the problem of order in society, and the program of analytic sociology', *American Journal of Sociology*, vol. 81, pp. 320-34, plus the following debate: Parsons's 'Comment', ibid., pp. 335-9; Burger's reply in vol. 83, no. 2, (1978), pp. 983-6.

Coser, I. (1956) *The Functions of Social Conflict*, The Free Press, Glencoe, NJ.

Dahrendorf, R. (1964) 'Out of Utopia: Toward a reconstruction of sociological analysis', in Coser, I. and Rosenburg, B. (eds), *Sociological Theory*, Macmillan, New York, pp. 209-27.

Demereth, N. J. and Peterson, R. A. (eds), (1967) *System, Change and Conflict: A reader on contemporary sociological theory and the debate over functionalism*, The Free Press, New York.

Giddens, A. (1977) 'Functionalism: Après la lutte', in *Studies on Social and Political Theory*, Heinemann, London, pp. 96-134.

Gouldner, A. W. (1970) *The Coming Crisis of Western Sociology*, Heinemann, London.

Heydebrand, W. and Toby, J. (1972) 'Review symposium on Parsons' *The System of Modern Societies*', *Contemporary Sociology*, vol. 1, pp. 387-401.

Homans, G. C. (1964) 'Bringing men back in', *American Sociological Review*, vol. 29, pp. 809-18.

Lockwood, D. (1964) 'Social integration and system integration', in Zollschan, G. K. and Hirsch, W. (eds), *Explanations in Social Change*, Routledge & Kegan Paul, London, pp. 244-57.

Lockwood, D. (1964) 'Some remarks on *The Social System*', in Demereth, N. J. and Peterson, R. A. (eds), pp. 281-57.

Schwanenberg, E. (1970/71) 'The two problems of order in Parsons' theory: An analysis from within', *Social Forces*, vol. 49, pp. 569-81.

Turner, J. H. (1978) *The Structure of Sociological Theory*, Dorsey Press, Homewood, H.

37. Meaning and Communicative Intent
Anthony Giddens

So far, I have been concerned only with problems of the 'meaning' of doings. When, in ordinary English usage, we refer to purposiveness we often talk about what a person 'means to do'; just as, in reference to utterances, we talk about what he or she 'means to say'. From this it would seem to be but a short step to the proposition, or the assumption, that to 'mean something' in doing is the same as to 'mean something' in saying. Here Austin's notions of illocutionary acts and illocutionary forces have done perhaps as much harm as good. Austin was struck by the fact that to say something is not always simply to state something. The utterance, 'With this ring I thee wed', is not a description of an action, but the very action (of marrying) itself. If, in such instances, to mean something in saying is *ipso facto* to mean something in doing, it would seem as though there is a single and sovereign form of meaning which does not necessitate making any differentiation between doing something and saying something. But this is not so. For virtually all utterances, with the exception of involuntary exclamations, cries of pain or ecstasy, have a communicative character. Some sorts of verbal communication, including ritual utterances such as 'With this ring I thee wed', are proclamatory in form, but this does not affect the point. In such cases the utterance is both a 'meaningful act' in itself, and is at the same time a mode of communicating a message or a meaning to others: the meaning in this case being perhaps something of the order 'the union of marriage is hereby sealed and made binding', as understood by the marital pair and others present on the scene.

The meaning of utterances as 'communicative acts' (if they have one) can thus always in principle be distinguished from the meaning of action, or the identification of action as particular acts. A communicative act is one in which an actor's purpose, or one of an actor's purposes, is linked to the achievement of passing on information to others. Such 'information', of course, does not have to be solely of a propositional sort, but can be comprised within an attempt to persuade or influence others to respond in a particular way. Now just as utterance may be both an act — something which is 'done' — and a 'communicative act', so something which is 'done' may also have communicative intent. The efforts that actors make to create specific sorts of impressions on others from the cues which they engineer their actions to 'give off' are well analysed in the writings of Erving Goffman, who is interested in comparing and contrasting such forms of communication with those conveyed in utterances. But again this does not detract from the point: chopping wood, and many other forms of action, are not communicative acts in this sense. There is, in sum, a difference between making sense of what someone is doing when she or he is doing something (including making ritual utterances in marriage ceremonies), and making sense of how others make sense of what she or he says or does in efforts at communication. I have noted

Anthony Giddens: 'Meaning and Communicative Intent' from *NEW RULES OF SOCIOLOGICAL METHOD: A POSITIVE CRITIQUE OF INTERPRETATIVE SOCIOLOGIES* (2nd revised edition, Polity Press, 1993), pp. 93-98. Reproduced by permission of Basil Blackwell Limited.

that when actors or social scientists ask why-questions about actions, they may be asking either 'what' the action is, or for an explanation of why the actor should be inclined to conduct herself or himself in a particular way. We may ask such why-questions about utterances but when we want to know why a man said something in particular, rather than why he did something in particular, we are asking about his *communicative intent*. We may be asking what he meant, the first type of why-question; or we may be asking something such as 'What impelled him to say that to me in a situation when he knew it would embarrass me?'

Some, although only some, aspects of communicative intent in utterances have been explored by Strawson, Grice, Searle and others. The attempt to break away from older theories of meaning, represented by Wittgenstein's later studies, and by Austin's concentration on the instrumental uses of words, has undoubtedly had some welcome consequences. There is an obvious convergence between recent work in the philosophy of language and the ideas developed by Chomsky and his followers on transformational grammars. Both see language-use as a skilled and creative performance. But in some philosophical writings the reaction against the assumption that all utterances have some form of propositional content has led to an equally exaggerated emphasis in which 'meaning' comes to be regarded as exhausted by communicative intent.

In concluding this section, I want now to show that the work of the authors mentioned at the beginning of the previous paragraph leads us back to considerations given great prominence by Schutz and Garfinkel: the role of 'common-sense understandings', or what I shall later refer to as taken-for-granted *mutual knowledge*, in human social interaction. The most influential analysis of meaning as communicative intent ('non-natural meaning') is that given by Grice. In his original formulation, Grice put forward the view that the statement that an actor S 'meant so-and-so by X' is usually expressible as 'S intended the utterance X to produce an effect upon another or others by means of their recognizing this to be his intention'. But this will not do as it stands, he later pointed out, because it may include cases which would not be examples of (non-natural) meaning. A person may discover that whenever he or she makes a certain sort of exclamation another collapses in agony, and once having made the discovery, intentionally repeats the effect; if, however, when the first person makes the exclamation, the other collapses, having recognized the exclamation, and with it the intention, we should not want to say that the exclamation 'meant' something. Thus Grice reaches the conclusion that the effect which S intends to produce 'must be something which in some sense is within the control of the audience, or that in some sense of "reason" the recognition of the intention behind X is for the audience a reason and not merely a cause'.[11]

Various ambiguities and difficulties have been exposed in this account by critics. One of these is that it seems to lead to an infinite regress, in which what S_1 intends to produce as an effect upon S_2 depends upon S_1 intending S_2 to recognize his or her intention to get S_1 to recognize his or her intention to get S_2 to recognize his or her intention. . . In his later discussion, Grice claims that the possibility of such a regress creates no particular problems, since in any actual situation the refusal, or incapacity, of an actor to proceed very far along the line of regressive knowledge of intentions will impose practical limits.[12] But this is not very satisfactory, since the problem of regress is a logical one; the regress can only be escaped, I think, by introducing an element that does not directly figure in Grice's own discussions. This element is precisely that of the 'common-sense understandings' possessed by actors within shared cultural milieux — or, to adopt a different terminology, what one philosopher has called 'mutual knowledge'. (He says in fact that the phenomenon has no accepted name, and that hence he has to coin one.)[13] There are many things that an actor will assume or take for granted that any other competent agent will know when he addresses an utterance to her, and he will also take for granted that the other knows that he assumes this. This does not, I believe, introduce another infinite regress of 'knowing that the other knows that one knows that the other knows. . .'. The infinite regress of 'knowing that the other knows one knows. . .' threatens only in strategic circumstances, such as a poker game, in which the people involved are trying to out-manoeuvre or out-guess one another: and here it is a practical problem for the actors, rather than a logical one to puzzle the philosopher or social scientist. The 'common-sense understanding' or mutual knowledge relevant to the theory of communicative intent involves, first, 'what any competent actor can be expected to know (believe)' about the properties of competent actors, including both herself or himself and others, and second, that the particular situation in which the actor is at a given time, and the other or others to whom an utterance is addressed, together comprise examples of a specific type of circumstance to which the attribution of definite forms of competence is therefore appropriate.

The view has been strongly urged, by Grice and others, that communicative intent is the fundamental form of 'meaning', in the sense that giving a satisfactory account of it will allow us to understand the (conventional) meanings of utterance types. In other words, 'S-meaning' (what an actor means in making an utterance) is the key to explicating 'X-meaning' (what a specific mark or symbol means).[14] I want to deny that this is so. 'X-meaning' is both sociologically and logically prior to 'S-meaning'. Sociologically prior, because the framework of symbolic capacities necessary to the very existence of most human purposes, as these are acted upon by any individual person, presupposes the existence of a linguistic structure which mediates cultural forms. Logically prior, because any account which begins from 'S-meaning' cannot explain the origin of 'common-sense understandings' or mutual knowledge, but must assume them as givens. This can be made clear by looking at certain philosophical writings that mesh fairly closely with and have similar shortcomings to, Grice's theory of meaning.[15]

One such account, trimmed to its essentials, runs as follows. The meaning of a word in a linguistic community depends upon the norms or conventions which prevail in that community, to the effect that 'the word is conventionally accepted to mean p'. A convention can be understood as a resolution of a co-ordination problem, as the latter is defined in game-theory. In a co-ordination problem, two or more people have a shared end that they wish to bring about, to do which each has to select from a series of alternative, mutually exclusive means. The means selected have no significance in themselves, save that, combined with those chosen by the other or others, they serve to bring about what is mutually desired; the mutual responses of the actors are in equilibrium when there is an equivalence of outcomes, regardless of *what* means are used. Thus suppose two groups of individuals, one of whom is used to driving on the left, the other of whom is accustomed to driving on the right, come together to form a community in a new territory. The co-ordination problem is that of achieving the outcome that everyone drives on the same side of the road. There are two sets of equilibria that represent successful outcomes: where everyone drives on the right-hand side of the road, and where everyone drives on the left, and in terms of the initial problem as a problem of the co-ordination of actions, each is equally 'successful'. The significance of this is that it seems to indicate how communicative intent might be tied in with convention. For the actors involved in a co-ordination problem — at least, in so far as they conduct themselves 'rationally' — will all act in a way that they expect the others will expect that they will act.

But this view, while having a certain formal symmetry that is not unattractive, is misleading as an account of convention in general and as a theory of conventional aspects of meaning in particular. It is sociologically lacking, and I think logically untenable — in the latter respect in so far, at least, as it is focused on meaning conventions. In the first place, it seems evident that some sorts of norm or convention do not involve co-ordination problems at all. It is conventional in our culture, for example, for women to wear skirts and for men not to do so; but co-ordination problems are only associated with conventional styles of dress with regard to such matters in so far as, say, the fact that women now increasingly wear trousers rather than skirts creates a difficulty in telling the sexes apart, so that the achievement of mutually desired outcomes in sexual relationships may be compromised! More important, even in those conventions which might be said to involve co-ordination problems, the aims and expectations of those who are party to the conventions are characteristically defined *by* acceptance of the convention, rather than the convention being reached as an outcome of them. Co-ordination problems, as problems for *actors* (rather than for the social-scientific observer attempting to understand how the co-ordination of the actions of members is concretely realized), arise only in the circumstances I have already noted: when people are trying either to guess or to out-guess what others are going to do, having at their disposal the information that others are also trying to do the same with regard to their own likely actions. But in most circumstances in social life, actors do not (consciously) have to do this, in large part precisely *because* of the existence of conventions in terms of which 'appropriate' modes of response are taken for granted; this applies to norms as a whole, but with particular force to meaning conventions. When a person says something to another person, her or his aim is not that of co-ordinating her or his action to those of others, but of communicating with the other in some way, by the use *of* conventional symbols.

Notes

11. Grice, H. P., 'Meaning', *Philosophical Review*, Vol. 66, 1957, p. 385.

12. Grice, 'Utterer's meaning and intentions', *Philosophical Review*, Vol. 78, 1969.

13. Schiffer, Stephen R., *Meaning*, Oxford, 1972, pp. 30–42.

14. Ibid., pp. 1–5 and *passim*.

15. Lewis, David K., *Convention*, Cambridge (Mass.), 1969.

38.   Grand Theory

C. Wright Mills

Let us begin with a sample of grand theory, taken from Talcott Parsons' *The Social System* — widely regarded as a most important book by a most eminent representative of the style.

> An element of a shared symbolic system which serves as a criterion or standard for selection among the alternatives of orientation which are intrinsically open in a situation may be called a value. . . But from this motivational orientation aspect of the totality of action it is, in view of the role of symbolic systems, necessary to distinguish a 'value-orientation' aspect. This aspect concerns, not the meaning of the expected state of affairs to the actor in terms of his gratification-deprivation balance but the content of the selective standards themselves. The concept of value-orientations in this sense is thus the logical device for formulating one central aspect of the articulation of cultural traditions into the action system.
>
> It follows from the derivation of normative orientation and the role of values in action as stated above, that all values involve what may be called a social reference. . . It is inherent in an action system that action is, to use one phrase, 'normatively oriented.' This follows, as was shown, from the concept of expectations and its place in action theory, especially in the 'active' phase in which the actor pursues goals. Expectations then, in combination with the 'double contingency' of the process of interaction as it has been called, create a crucially imperative problem of order. Two aspects of this problem of order may in turn be distinguished, order in the symbolic systems which make communication possible, and order in the mutuality of motivational orientation to the normative aspect of expectations, the 'Hobbesian' problem of order.
>
> The problem of order, and thus of the nature of the integration of stable systems of social interaction, that is, of social structure, thus focuses on the integration of the motivation of actors with the normative cultural standards which integrate the action system, in our context interpersonally. These standards are, in the terms used in the preceding chapter, patterns of value-orientation, and as such are a particularly crucial part of the cultural tradition of the social system.[1]

Perhaps some readers will now feel a desire to turn to the next chapter; I hope they will not indulge the impulse. Grand Theory — the associating and dissociating of concepts — is well worth considering. True, it has not had so important an effect as the methodological inhibition that is to be examined in the [next chapter], for as a style of work its spread has been limited. The fact is that it is not readily understandable;

From *THE SOCIOLOGICAL IMAGINATION* by C. Wright Mills. Copyright © 1959 by Oxford University Press, Inc.; renewed 1987 by Yaraslava Mills. Reprinted by permission of the publisher.

the suspicion is that it may not be altogether intelligible. This is, to be sure, a protective advantage, but it is a disadvantage in so far as its *pronunciamentos* are intended to influence the working habits of social scientists. Not to make fun but to report factually, we have to admit that its productions have been received by social scientists in one or more of the following ways:

To at least some of those who claim to understand it, and who like it, it is one of the greatest advances in the entire history of social science.

To many of those who claim to understand it, but who do not like it, it is a clumsy piece of irrelevant ponderosity. (These are rare, if only because dislike and impatience prevent many from trying to puzzle it out.)

To those who do not claim to understand it, but who like it very much — and there are many of these — it is a wondrous maze, fascinating precisely because of its often splendid lack of intelligibility.

Those who do not claim to understand it and who do not like it — if they retain the courage of their convictions — will feel that indeed the emperor has no clothes.

Of course there are also many who qualify their views, and many more who remain patiently neutral, waiting to see the professional outcome, if any. And although it is, perhaps, a dreadful thought, many social scientists do not even know about it, except as notorious hearsay.

Now all this raises a sore point — intelligibility. That point, of course, goes beyond grand theory,[2] but grand theorists are so deeply involved in it that I fear we really must ask: Is grand theory merely a confused verbiage or is there, after all, also something there? The answer, I think, is: Something is there, buried deep to be sure, but still something is being said. So the question becomes: After all the impediments to meaning are removed from grand theory and what is intelligible becomes available, what, then, is being said?

1

There is only one way to answer such a question: we must translate a leading example of this style of thought and then consider the translation. I have already indicated my choice of example. I want now to make clear that I am not here trying to judge the value of Parsons' work as a whole. If I refer to other writings of his, it is only in order to clarify, in an economical way, some point contained in this one volume. In translating the contents of *The Social System* into English, I do not pretend that my translation is excellent, but only that in the translation no explicit meaning is lost. This — I am asserting — contains all that is intelligible in it. In particular, I shall attempt to sort out statements about something from definitions of words and of their wordy relations. Both are important; to confuse them is fatal to clarity. To make evident the sort of thing that is needed, I shall first translate several passages; then I shall offer two abbreviated translations of the book as a whole.

To translate the example quoted at the opening of this chapter: People often share standards and expect one another to stick to them. In so far as they do, their society may be orderly. (end of translation)

Parsons has written:

> There is in turn a two-fold structure of this 'binding in.' In the first place, by virtue of internalization of the standard, conformity with it tends to be of personal, expressive and/or instrumental significance to ego. In the second place, the structuring of the reactions of alter to ego's action as sanctions is a function of his conformity with the standard. Therefore conformity as a direct mode of the fulfilment of his own need-dispositions tends to coincide with conformity as a condition of eliciting the favorable and avoiding the unfavorable reactions of others. In so far as, relative to the actions of a plurality of actors, conformity with a value-orientation standard meets *both* these criteria, that is from the point of view of any given actor in the system, it is both a mode of the fulfilment of his own need-dispositions and a condition of 'optimizing' the reactions of other significant actors, that standard will be said to be 'institutionalized.'

> A value pattern in this sense is always institutionalized in an *interaction* context. Therefore there is always a double aspect of the expectation system which is integrated in relation to it. On the one hand there are the expectations which concern and in part set standards for the behavior of the actor, ego, who is taken as the point of reference; these are his 'role-expectations.' On the other hand, from his point of view there is a set of expectations relative to the contingently probable *reactions* of others (alters) — these will be called 'sanctions,' which in turn may be subdivided into positive and negative according to whether they are felt by ego to be gratification-promoting or depriving. The relation between role-expectations and sanctions then is clearly reciprocal. What are sanctions to ego are role-expectations to alter and vice versa.

> A role then is a sector of the total orientation system of an individual actor which is organized about expectations in relation to a particular interaction context, that is integrated with a particular set of value-standards which govern interaction with one or more alters in the appropriate complementary roles. These alters need not be a defined group of individuals, but can involve any alter if and when he comes into a particular complementary interaction relationship with ego which involves a reciprocity of expectations with reference to common standards of value-orientation.

> The institutionalization of a set of role-expectations and of the corresponding sanctions is clearly a matter of degree. This degree is a function of two sets of variables; on the one hand those affecting the actual sharedness of the value-orientation patterns, on the other those determining the motivational orientation or commitment to the fulfilment of the relevant expectations. As we shall see a variety of factors can influence this degree of institutionalization through each of these channels. The polar antithesis of full institutionalization is, however, *anomie*, the absence of structured complementarity of the interaction

process or, what is the same thing, the complete breakdown of normative order in both senses. This is, however, a limiting concept which is never descriptive of a concrete social system. Just as there are degrees of institutionalization so are there also degrees of *anomie*. The one is the obverse of the other.

An *institution* will be said to be a complex of institutionalized role integrates which is of strategic structural significance in the social system in question. The institution should be considered to be a higher order unit of social structure than the role, and indeed it is made up of a plurality of interdependent role-patterns or components of them.[3]

Or in other words: Men act with and against one another. Each takes into account what others expect. When such mutual expectations are sufficiently definite and durable, we call them standards. Each man also expects that others are going to react to what he does. We call these expected reactions sanctions. Some of them seem very gratifying, some do not. When men are guided by standards and sanctions, we may say that they are playing roles together. It is a convenient metaphor. And as a matter of fact, what we call an institution is probably best defined as a more or less stable set of roles. When within some institution — or an entire society composed of such institutions — the standards and sanctions no longer grip men, we may speak, with Durkheim, of *anomie*. At one extreme, then, are institutions, with standards and sanctions all neat and orderly. At the other extreme, there is *anomie*: as Yeats says, the center does not hold; or, as I say, the normative order has broken down. (end of translation)

In this translation, I must admit, I have not been altogether faithful; I have helped out a little because these are very good ideas. In fact, many of the ideas of grand theorists, when translated, are more or less standard ones available in many textbooks of sociology. But in connection with 'institutions' the definition given above is not quite complete. To what is translated, we must add that the roles making up an institution are not usually just one big 'complementarity' of 'shared expectations.' Have you ever been in an army, a factory — or for that matter a family? Well, those are institutions. Within them, the expectations of some men seem just a little more urgent than those of anyone else. That is because, as we say, they have more power. Or to put it more sociologically, although not yet altogether so: an institution is a set of roles graded in authority.

Parsons writes:

Attachment to common values means, motivationally considered, that the actors have common 'sentiments' in support of the value patterns, which may be defined as meaning that conformity with the relevant expectations is treated as a 'good thing' relatively independently of any specific instrumental 'advantage' to be gained from such conformity, e.g., in the avoidance of negative sanctions. Furthermore, this attachment to common values, while it may fit the immediate gratificational needs of the actor, always has also a 'moral' aspect in that to some degree this conformity defines the 'responsibilities' of the actor in the wider, that is, social action systems in which he participates. Obviously the specific focus of responsibility is the collectivity which is constituted by a particular common value-orientation.

Finally, it is quite clear that the 'sentiments' which support such common values are not ordinarily in their specific structure the manifestation of constitutionally given propensities of the organism. They are in general learned or acquired. Furthermore, the part they play in the orientation of action is not predominantly that of cultural objects which are cognized and 'adapted to' but the culture patterns have come to be internalized; they constitute part of the structure of the personality system of the actor itself. Such sentiments or 'value-attitudes' as they may be called are therefore genuine need-dispositions of the personality. It is only by virtue of internalization of institutionalized values that a genuine motivational integration of behavior in the social structure takes place, that the 'deeper' layers of motivation become harnessed to the fulfilment of role-expectations. It is only when this has taken place to a high degree that it is possible to say that a social system is highly integrated, and that the interests of the collectivity and the private interests of its constituent members can be said to approach* coincidence.

This integration of a set of common value patterns with the internalized need-disposition structure of the constituent personalities is the core phenomenon of the dynamics of social systems. That the stability of any social system except the most evanescent interaction process is dependent on a degree of such integration may be said to be the fundamental dynamic theorem of sociology. It is the major point of reference for all analysis which may claim to be a dynamic analysis of social process.[4]

Or in other words: When people share the same values, they tend to behave in accordance with the way they expect one another to behave. Moreover, they often treat such conformity as a very good thing — even when it seems to go against their immediate interests. That these shared values are learned rather than inherited does not make them any the less important in human motivation. On the contrary, they become part of the personality itself. As such, they bind a society together, for what is socially expected becomes individually needed. This is so important to the stability of any social system that I am going to use it as my chief point of departure if I ever analyze some society as a going concern. (end of translation)

In a similar fashion, I suppose, one could translate the 555 pages of *The Social System* into about 150 pages of straightforward English. The result would not be very impressive. It would, however, contain the terms in which the key problem of the book, and the solution it offers to this problem, are most clearly statable. Any idea, any book can of course be suggested in a sentence or expounded in twenty volumes. It is a

* Exact coincidence should be regarded as a limiting case like the famous frictionless machine. Though complete integration of a social system of motivation with a fully consistent set of cultural patterns is empirically unknown, the conception of such an integrated social system is of high theoretical significance. (Parsons' footnote: CWM).

question of how full a statement is needed to make something clear and of how important that something seems to be: how many experiences it makes intelligible, how great a range of problems it enables us to solve or at least to state.

To suggest Parsons' book, for example, in two or three phrases: 'We are asked: How is social order possible? The answer we are given seems to be: Commonly accepted values.' Is that all there is to it? Of course not, but it is the main point. But isn't this unfair? Can't any book be treated this way? Of course. Here is a book of my own treated in this way: 'Who, after all, runs America? No one runs it altogether, but in so far as any group does, the power elite.' And here is the book in your hand: 'What are the social sciences all about? They ought to be about man and society and sometimes they are. They are attempts to help us understand biography and history, and the connections of the two in a variety of social structures.'

Here is a translation of Parsons' book in four paragraphs:

Let us imagine something we may call 'the social system,' in which individuals act with reference to one another. These actions are often rather orderly, for the individuals in the system share standards of value and of appropriate and practical ways to behave. Some of these standards we may call norms; those who act in accordance with them tend to act similarly on similar occasions. In so far as this is so, there are 'social regularities,' which we may observe and which are often quite durable. Such enduring and stable regularities I shall call 'structural.' It is possible to think of all these regularities within the social system as a great and intricate balance. That this is a metaphor I am now going to forget, because I want you to take as very real my Concept: The social equilibrium.

There are two major ways by which the social equilibrium is maintained, and by which — should either or both fail — disequilibrium results. The first is 'socialization,' all the ways by which the newborn individual is made into a social person. Part of this social making of persons consists in their acquiring motives for taking the social actions required or expected by others. The second is 'social control,' by which I mean all the ways of keeping people in line and by which they keep themselves in line. By 'line' of course, I refer to whatever action is typically expected and approved in the social system.

The first problem of maintaining social equilibrium is to make people want to do what is required and expected of them. That failing, the second problem is to adopt other means to keep them in line. The best classifications and definitions of these social controls have been given by Max Weber, and I have little to add to what he, and a few other writers since then, have said so well.

One point does puzzle me a little: given this social equilibrium, and all the socialization and control that man it, how is it possible that anyone should ever get out of line? This I cannot explain very well, that is, in the terms of my Systematic and General Theory of the social system. And there is another point that is not as clear as I should like it to be: how should I account for social change — that is, for history? About these two problems, I recommend that whenever you come upon them, you undertake empirical investigations. (end of translation)

Perhaps that is enough. Of course we could translate more fully, but 'more fully' does not necessarily mean 'more adequately,' and I invite the reader to inspect *The Social System* and find more. In the meantime, we have three tasks: first, to characterize the logical style of thinking represented by grand theory; second, to make clear a certain generic confusion in this particular example; third, to indicate how most social scientists now set up and solve Parsons' problem of order. My purpose in all this is to help grand theorists get down from their useless heights.

2

Serious differences among social scientists occur not between those who would observe without thinking and those who would think without observing; the differences have rather to do with what kinds of thinking, what kinds of observing, and what kinds of links, if any, there are between the two.

The basic cause of grand theory is the initial choice of a level of thinking so general that its practitioners cannot logically get down to observation. They never, as grand theorists, get down from the higher generalities to problems in their historical and structural contexts. This absence of a firm sense of genuine problems, in turn, makes for the unreality so noticeable in their pages. One resulting characteristic is a seemingly arbitrary and certainly endless elaboration of distinctions, which neither enlarge our understanding nor make our experience more sensible. This in turn is revealed as a partially organized abdication of the effort to describe and explain human conduct and society plainly.

When we consider what a word stands for, we are dealing with its *semantic* aspects; when we consider it in relation to other words, we are dealing with its *syntactic* features.[5] I introduce these shorthand terms because they provide an economical and precise way to make this point: Grand theory is drunk on syntax, blind to semantics. Its practitioners do not truly understand that when we define a word we are merely inviting others to use it as we would like it to be used; that the purpose of definition is to focus argument upon fact, and that the proper result of good definition is to transform argument over terms into disagreements about fact, and thus open arguments to further inquiry.

The grand theorists are so preoccupied by syntactic meanings and so unimaginative about semantic references, they are so rigidly confined to such high levels of abstraction that the 'typologies' they make up — and the work they do to make them up — seem more often an arid game of Concepts than an effort to define systematically — which is to say, in a clear and orderly way — the problems at hand, and to guide our efforts to solve them.

One great lesson that we can learn from its systematic absence in the work of the grand theorists is that every self-conscious thinker must at all times be aware of — and hence be able to control — the levels of abstraction on which he is working. The capacity to shuttle between levels of abstraction, with ease and with clarity, is a signal mark of the imaginative and systematic thinker.

Around such terms as 'capitalism' or 'middle class' or 'bureaucracy' or 'power elite' or 'totalitarian democracy,' there are often somewhat tangled and obscured connotations, and in using these terms, such connotations must be carefully watched and controlled. Around such terms, there are often 'compounded' sets of facts and relations as well as merely guessed-at factors and observations. These too must be carefully sorted out and made clear in our definition and in our use.

To clarify the syntactic and the semantic dimensions of such conceptions, we must be aware of the hierarchy of specificity under each of them, and we must be able to consider all levels of this hierarchy. We must ask: Do we mean by 'capitalism,' as we are going to use it, merely the fact that all means of production are privately owned? Or do we also want to include under the term the further idea of a free market as the determining mechanism of price, wages, profit? And to what extent are we entitled to assume that, by definition, the term implies assertions about the political order as well as economic institutions?

Such habits of mind I suppose to be the keys to systematic thinking and their absence the keys to the fetishism of the Concept. Perhaps one result of such an absence will become clearer as we consider, more specifically now, a major confusion of Parsons' book.

3

Claiming to set forth 'a general sociological theory,' the grand theorist in fact sets forth a realm of concepts from which are excluded many structural features of human society, features long and accurately recognized as fundamental to its understanding. Seemingly, this is deliberate in the interest of making the concern of sociologists a specialized endeavor distinct from that of economists and political scientists. Sociology, according to Parsons, has to do with 'that aspect of the theory of social systems which is concerned with the phenomena of the institutionalization of patterns of value-orientation in the social system, with the conditions of that institutionalization; and of changes in the patterns, with conditions of conformity with and deviance from a set of such patterns, and with motivational processes in so far as they are involved in all of these.'[6] Translated and unloaded of assumption, as any definition should be, this reads: Sociologists of my sort would like to study what people want and cherish. We would also like to find out why there is a variety of such values and why they change. When we do find a more or less unitary set of values, we would like to find out why some people do and others do not conform to them. (end of translation)

As David Lockwood has noted,[7] such a statement delivers the sociologist from any concern with 'power,' with economic and political institutions. I would go further than that. This statement, and, in fact, the whole of Parsons' book, deals much more with what have been traditionally called 'legitimations' than with institutions of any sort. The result, I think, is to transform, by definition, all institutional structures into a sort of moral sphere — or more accurately, into what has been called 'the symbol sphere.'[8] In order to make the point clear, I should like first to explain something about this sphere; second to discuss its alleged autonomy; and third, to indicate how Parsons' conceptions make it quite difficult even to raise several of the most important problems of any analysis of social structure.

406

Those in authority attempt to justify their rule over institutions by linking it, as if it were a necessary consequence, with widely believed-in moral symbols, sacred emblems, legal formulae. These central conceptions may refer to a god or gods, the 'vote of the majority,' 'the will of the people,' 'the aristocracy of talent or wealth,' to the 'divine right of kings,' or to the allegedly extraordinary endowment of the ruler himself. Social scientists, following Weber, call such conceptions 'legitimations,' or sometimes 'symbols of justification.'

Various thinkers have used different terms to refer to them: Mosca's 'political formula' or 'great superstitions,' Locke's 'principle of sovereignty,' Sorel's 'ruling myth,' Thurman Arnold's 'folklore,' Weber's 'legitimations,' Durkheim's 'collective representations,' Marx's 'dominant ideas,' Rousseau's 'general will,' Lasswell's 'symbols of authority,' Mannheim's 'ideology,' Herbert Spencer's 'public sentiments' — all these and others like them testify to the central place of master symbols in social analysis.

Similarly in psychological analysis, such master symbols, relevant when they are taken over privately, become the reasons and often the motives that lead persons into roles and sanction their enactment of them. If, for example, economic institutions are publicly justified in terms of them, then references to self-interest may be acceptable justification for individual conduct. But, if it is felt publicly necessary to justify such institutions in terms of 'public service and trust,' the old self-interest motives and reasons may lead to guilt or at least to uneasiness among capitalists. Legitimations that are publicly effective often become, in due course, effective as personal motives.

Now, what Parsons and other grand theorists call 'value-orientations' and 'normative structure' has mainly to do with master symbols of legitimation. This is, indeed, a useful and important subject. The relations of such symbols to the structure of institutions are among the most important problems of social science. Such symbols, however, do not form some autonomous realm within a society; their social relevance lies in their use to justify or to oppose the arrangement of power and the positions within this arrangement of the powerful. Their psychological relevance lies in the fact that they become the basis for adherence to the structure of power or for opposing it.

We may not merely assume that some such set of values, or legitimations, *must* prevail lest a social structure come apart, nor may we assume that a social structure must be made coherent or unified by any such 'normative structure.' Certainly we may not merely assume that any such 'normative structure' as may prevail is, in any meaning of the word, autonomous. In fact, for modern Western societies — and in particular the United States — there is much evidence that the opposite of each of these assumptions is the more accurate. Often — although not in the United States since World War II — there are quite well organized symbols of opposition which are used to justify insurgent movements and to debunk ruling authorities. The continuity of the American political system is quite unique, having been threatened by internal violence only once in its history; this fact may be among those that have misled Parsons in his image of The Normative Structure of Value-Orientation.

'Governments' do not necessarily, as Emerson would have it, 'have their origin in the moral identity of men.' To believe that government does is to confuse its legitimations with its causes. Just as often, or even more often, such moral identities as men of some society may have rest on the fact that institutional rulers successfully monopolize, and even impose, their master symbols.

Some hundred years ago, this matter was fruitfully discussed in terms of the assumptions of those who believe that symbol spheres are self-determining, and that such 'values' may indeed dominate history: The symbols that justify some authority are separated from the actual persons or strata that exercise the authority. The 'ideas,' not the strata or the persons using the ideas, are then thought to rule. In order to lend continuity to the sequence of these symbols, they are presented as in some way connected with one another. The symbols are thus seen as 'self-determining.' To make more plausible this curious notion, the symbols are often 'personalized' or given 'self-consciousness.' They may then be conceived of as The Concepts of History or as a sequence of 'philosophers' whose thinking determines institutional dynamics. Or, we may add, the Concept of 'normative order' may be fetishized. I have, of course, just paraphrased Marx and Engels speaking of Hegel.[9]

Unless they justify institutions and motivate persons to enact institutional roles, 'the values' of a society, however important in various private milieux, are historically and sociologically irrelevant. There is of course an interplay between justifying symbols, institutional authorities, and obedient persons. At times we should not hesitate to assign causal weight to master symbols — but we may not misuse the idea as *the* theory of social order or of the unity of society. There are better ways to construct a 'unity,' as we shall presently see, ways that are more useful in the formulation of significant problems of social structure and closer to observable materials.

So far as 'common values' interest us, it is best to build up our conception of them by examining the legitimations of each institutional order in any given social structure, rather than to *begin* by attempting first to grasp them, and in their light 'explain' the society's composition and unity.[10] We may, I suppose, speak of 'common values' when a great proportion of the members of an institutional order have taken over that order's legitimations, when such legitimations are the terms in which obedience is successfully claimed, or at least complacency secured. Such symbols are then used to 'define the situations' encountered in various roles and as yardsticks for the evaluations of leaders and followers. Social structures that display such universal and central symbols are naturally extreme and 'pure' types.

At the other end of the scale, there are societies in which a dominant set of institutions controls the total society and superimposes its values by violence and the threat of violence. This need not involve any breakdown of the social structure, for men may be effectively conditioned by formal discipline; and at times, unless they accept institutional demands for discipline, they may have no chance to earn a living.

> A skilled compositor employed by a reactionary newspaper, for example, may for the sake of making a living and holding his job conform to the demands of employer discipline. In his heart, and outside the shop, he may be a radical agitator. Many German socialists allowed themselves to become perfectly disciplined soldiers under the Kaiser's flag — despite the fact that their subjective values were those of revolutionary Marxism. It is a long way from symbols to conduct and back again, and not all integration is based on symbols.[11]

To emphasize such conflict of value is not to deny 'the force of rational consistencies.' The discrepancy between word and deed is often characteristic, but so is the striving for consistency. Which is predominant in any given society cannot be decided *a priori* on the basis of 'human nature' or on the 'principles of sociology' or by the fiat of grand theory. We might well imagine a 'pure type' of society, a perfectly disciplined social structure, in which the dominated men, for a variety of reasons, cannot quit their prescribed roles, but nevertheless share none of the dominator's values, and thus in no way believe in the legitimacy of the order. It would be like a ship manned by galley slaves, in which the disciplined movement of the oars reduces the rowers to cogs an a machine, and the violence of the whipmaster is only rarely needed. The galley slaves need not even be aware of the ship's direction, although any turn of the bow evokes the wrath of the master, the only man aboard who is able to see ahead. But perhaps I begin to describe rather than to imagine.

Between these two types — a 'common value system' and a superimposed discipline — there are numerous forms of 'social integration.' Most occidental societies have incorporated many divergent 'value-orientations'; their unities involve various mixtures of legitimation and coercion. And that, of course, may be true of any institutional order, not only of the political and economic. A father may impose demands upon his family by threatening to withhold inheritance, or by the use of such violence as the political order may allow him. Even in such sacred little groups as families, the unity of 'common values' is by no means necessary: distrust and hatred may be the very stuff needed to hold a loving family together. A society as well may of course flourish quite adequately without such a 'normative structure' as grand theorists believe to be universal.

I do not here wish to expound any solution to the problem of order, but merely to raise questions. For if we cannot do that, we must, as demanded by the fiat of quite arbitary definition, assume the 'normative structure' which Parsons imagines to be the heart of 'the social system.'

4

'Power,' as the term is now generally used in social science, has to do with whatever decisions men make about the arrangements under which they live, and about the events which make up the history of their period. Events that are beyond human decision do happen; social arrangements do change without benefit of explicit decision. But in so far as such decisions are made (and in so far as they could be but are not) the problem of who is involved in making them (or not making them) is the basic problem of power.

We cannot assume today that men must in the last resort be governed by their own consent. Among the means of power that now prevail is the power to manage and to manipulate the consent of men. That we do not know the limits of such power — and that we hope it does have limits — does not remove the fact that much power today is successfully employed without the sanction of the reason or the conscience of the obedient.

Surely in our time we need not argue that, in the last resort, coercion is the 'final' form of power. But then we are by no means constantly at the last resort. Authority (power justified by the beliefs of the voluntarily obedient) and manipulation (power wielded unbeknown to the powerless) must also be considered, along with coercion. In fact, the three types must constantly be sorted out when we think about the nature of power.

In the modern world, I think we must bear in mind, power is often not so authoritative as it appeared to be in the medieval period; justifications of rulers no longer seem so necessary to their exercise of power. At least for many of the great decisions of our time — especially those of an international sort — mass 'persuasion' has not been 'necessary'; the fact is simply accomplished. Furthermore, such ideologies as are available to the powerful are often neither taken up nor used by them. Ideologies usually arise as a response to an effective debunking of power; in the United States such opposition has not been recently effective enough to create a felt need for new ideologies of rule.

Today, of course, many people who are disengaged from prevailing allegiances have not acquired new ones, and so are inattentive to political concerns of any kind. They are neither radical nor reactionary. They are inactionary. If we accept the Greek's definition of the idiot as an altogether private man, then we must conclude that many citizens of many societies are indeed idiots. This — and I use the word with care — this spiritual condition seems to me the key to much modern malaise among political intellectuals, as well as the key to much political bewilderment in modern society. Intellectual 'conviction' and moral 'belief' are not necessary, in either the rulers or the ruled, for a structure of power to persist and even to flourish. So far as the role of ideologies is concerned, the frequent absence of engaging legitimation and the prevalence of mass apathy are surely two of the central political facts about the Western societies today.

In the course of any substantive research, many problems do confront those who hold the view of power that I have been suggesting. But we are not at all helped by the deviant assumptions of Parsons, who merely assumes that there is, presumably in every society, such a 'value hierarchy' as he imagines. Moreover, its implications systematically impede the clear formulation of significant problems.

To accept his scheme we are required to read out of the picture the facts of power and indeed of all institutional structures, in particular the economic, the political, the military. In this curious 'general theory,' such structures of domination have no place.

In the terms provided, we cannot properly pose the empirical question of the extent to which, and in what manner, institutions are, in any given case, legitimated. The idea of the normative order that is set forth, and the way it is handled by grand theorists, leads us to assume that virtually all power is legitimated. In fact: that in the social system, 'the maintenance of the complementarity of role-expectations, once established, is not problematical. . . . No special mechanisms are required for the explanation of the maintenance of complementary interaction-orientation.' [12]

In these terms, the idea of conflict cannot effectively be formulated. Structural antagonisms, large-scale revolts, revolutions — they cannot be imagined. In fact, it is assumed that 'the system,' once established, is not only stable but intrinsically harmonious; disturbances must, in his language, be 'introduced into the system.' [13] The idea of the normative order set forth leads us to assume a sort of harmony of interests as the natural feature of any society; as it appears here, this idea is as much a metaphysical anchor point as was the quite similar idea among the eighteenth century philosophers of natural order.[14]

The magical elimination of conflict, and the wondrous achievement of harmony, remove from this 'systematic' and 'general' theory the possibilities of dealing with social change, with history. Not only does the 'collective behavior' of terrorized masses and excited mobs, crowds and movements — with which our era is so filled — find no place in the normatively created social structures of grand theorists. But any systematic ideas of how history itself occurs, of its mechanics and processes, are unavailable to grand theory, and accordingly, Parsons believes, unavailable to social science: 'When such a theory is available the millennium for social science will have arrived. This will not come in our time and most probably never.'[15] Surely this is an extraordinarily vague assertion.

Virtually any problem of substance that is taken up in the terms of grand theory is incapable of being clearly stated. Worse: its statement is often loaded with evaluations as well as obscured by sponge-words. It is, for example, difficult to imagine a more futile endeavor than analyzing American society in terms of 'the value pattern' of 'universalistic-achievement' with no mention of the changing nature, meaning and forms of success characteristic of modern capitalism, or of the changing structure of capitalism itself; or, analyzing United States stratification in terms of 'the dominant value system' without taking into account the known statistics of life-chances based on levels of property and income.[16]

I do not think it too much to say that in so far as problems are dealt with realistically by grand theorists, they are dealt with in terms that find no place in grand theory, and are often contradictory to it. 'Indeed,' Alvin Gouldner has remarked, 'the extent to which Parsons' efforts at theoretical and empirical analysis of change suddenly lead him to enlist a body of Marxist concepts and assumptions is nothing less than bewildering. . . . It almost seems as if two sets of books were being kept, one for the analysis of equilibrium and another for the investigation of change.'[17] Gouldner goes on to remark how in the case of defeated Germany, Parsons recommends attacking the Junkers at their base, as 'a case of exclusive class privilege' and analyzes the civil service in terms of 'the class basis of recruitment.' In short, the whole economic and occupational structure — conceived in quite Marxian terms, not in terms of the normative structure projected by grand theory — suddenly rises into view. It makes one entertain the hope that grand theorists have not lost all touch with historical reality.

5

I now return to the problem of order, which in a rather Hobbesian version, seems to be the major problem in Parsons' book. It is possible to be brief about it because in the development of social science it has been re-defined, and in its most useful statement might now be called the problem of social integration; it does of course require a working conception of social structure and of historical change. Unlike grand theorists, most social scientists, I think, would give answers running something like this:

First of all, there is no *one* answer to the question, What holds a social structure together? There is no one answer because social structures differ profoundly in their degrees and kinds of unity. In fact, types of social structure are usefully conceived in terms of different modes of integration. When we descend from the level of grand theory to historical realities, we immediately realize the irrelevance of its monolithic Concepts. With these we cannot think about the human variety, about Nazi Germany in 1936, Sparta in seventh century B.C., the United States in 1836, Japan in 1866, Great Britain in 1950, Rome at the time of Diocletian. Merely to name this variety is surely to suggest that whatever these societies may have in common must be discovered by empirical examination. To predicate anything beyond the most empty formalities about the historical range of social structure is to mistake one's own capacity to talk for all that is meant by the work of social investigation.

One may usefully conceive types of social structure in terms of such institutional orders as the political and kinship, the military and economic, and the religious. Having defined each of these in such a way as to be able to discern their outlines in a given historical society, one asks how each is related to the others, how, in short, they are composed into a social structure. The answers are conveniently put as a set of 'working models' which are used to make us more aware, as we examine specific societies at specific times, of the links by which they are 'tied together.'

One such 'model' may be imagined in terms of the working out in each institutional order of a similar structural principle; think for example of Tocqueville's America. In that classical liberal society each order of institutions is conceived as autonomous, and its freedom demanded from any co-ordination by other orders. In the economy, there is *laissez faire*; in the religious sphere, a variety of sects and churches openly compete on the market for salvation; kinship institutions are set up on a marriage market in which individuals choose one another. Not a family-made man, but a self-made man, comes to ascendancy in the sphere of status. In the political order, there is party competition for the votes of the individual; even in the military zone there is much freedom in the recruitment of state militia, and in a wide sense — a very important sense — one man means one rifle. The principle of integration — which is also the basic legitimation of this society — is the ascendancy within each order of institutions of the free initiative of independent men in competition with one another. It is in this fact of correspondence that we may understand the way in which a classic liberal society is unified.

But such 'correspondence' is only one type, only one answer to the 'problem of order.' There are other types of unity. Nazi Germany, for example, was integrated by 'co-ordination.' The general model can be stated as follows: Within the economic order, institutions are highly centralized; a few big units more or less control all operations. Within the political order there is more fragmentation: Many parties compete to influence the state, but no one of them is powerful enough to control the results of economic concentration, one of these results — along with other factors — being the slump. The Nazi movement successfully exploits the mass despair, especially that of its lower middle classes, in the economic slump and brings into close correspondence the political, military, and economic orders. One party monopolizes and re-makes the political order, abolishing or amalgamating all other parties that might compete for power. To do this requires that the Nazi party find points of coinciding interest with monopolies in the economic order and also with certain elites of the military order. In these main orders there is, first, a corresponding concentration of power; then each of them coincides and co-operates in the taking of power. President Hindenburg's army is not interested in defending the Weimar Republic, or in crushing the marching columns of a popular war party. Big business circles are willing to help finance the Nazi party, which, among other things, promises to smash the labor movement. And the three types of elite join in an often uneasy coalition to maintain power in their respective orders and to co-ordinate the rest of society. Rival political parties are either suppressed and outlawed, or they disband voluntarily. Kinship and religious institutions, as well as all organizations within and between all orders, are infiltrated and co-ordinated, or at least neutralized.

The totalitarian party-state is the means by which high agents of each of the three dominant orders co-ordinate their own and other institutional orders. It becomes the over-all 'frame organization' which imposes goals upon all institutional orders instead of merely guaranteeing 'government by law.' The party extends itself, prowling everywhere in 'auxiliaries' and 'affiliations.' It either breaks up or it infiltrates, and in either case it comes to control all types of organizations, including the family.

The symbol spheres of all institutions are controlled by the party. With the partial exception of the religious order, no rival claims to legitimate autonomy are permitted. There is a party monopoly of formal communications, including educational institutions. All symbols are recast to form the basic legitimation of the co-ordinated society. The principle of absolute and magical leadership (charismatic rule) in a strict hierarchy is widely promulgated, in a social structure that is to a considerable extent held together by a network of rackets.[18]

But surely that is enough to make evident what I should think an obvious point: that there is no 'grand theory,' no one universal scheme in terms of which we can understand the unity of social structure, no one answer to the tired old problem of social order, taken *überhaupt*. Useful work on such problems will proceed in terms of a variety of such working models as I have outlined here, and these models will be used in close and empirical connection with a range of historical as well as contemporary social structures.

It is important to understand that such 'modes of integration' may also be conceived as working models of historical change. If, for example, we observe American society at the time of Tocqueville and again in the middle of the twentieth century, we see at once that the way the nineteenth century structure 'hangs together' is quite different from its current modes of integration. We ask: How have each of its institutional orders changed? How have its relations with each of the others changed? What have been the tempos, the varying rates at which these structural changes have occurred? And, in each case, what have been the necessary and sufficient causes of these changes? Usually, of course, the search for adequate cause requires at least some work in a comparative as well as an historical manner. In an over all way, we can summarize such an analysis of social change, and thus formulate more economically a range of larger problems, by indicating that the changes have resulted in a shift from one 'mode of integration' to another. For example, the last century of American history shows a transition from a social structure largely integrated by correspondence to one much more subject to co-ordination.

The general problem of a theory of history can not be separated from the general problem of a theory of social structure. I think it is obvious that in their actual studies, working social scientists do not experience any great theoretical difficulties in understanding the two in a unified way. Perhaps that is why one *Behemoth* is worth, to social science, twenty *Social Systems*.

I do not, of course, present these points in any effort to make a definitive statement of the problems of order and change — that is, of social structure and history. I do so merely to suggest the outlines of such problems and to indicate something of the kind of work that has been done on them. Perhaps these remarks are also useful to make more specific one aspect of the promise of social science. And, of course, I have set them forth here in order to indicate how inadequately grand theorists have handled one major problem of social science. In *The Social System* Parsons has not been able to get down to the work of social science because he is possessed by the idea that the one model of social order he has constructed is some kind of universal model; because, in fact, he has fetishized his Concepts. What is 'systematic' about this particular grand theory is the way it outruns any specific and empirical problem. It is not used to state more precisely or more adequately any new problem of recognizable significance. It has not been developed out of any need to fly high for a little while in order to see something in the social world more clearly, to solve some problem that can be stated in terms of the historical reality in which men and institutions have their concrete being. Its problem, its course, and its solutions are grandly theoretical.

The withdrawal into systematic work on conceptions should be only a formal moment within the work of social science. It is useful to recall that in Germany the yield of such formal work was soon turned to encyclopedic and historical use. That use, presided over by the ethos of Max Weber, was the climax of the classic German tradition. In considerable part, it was made possible by a body of sociological work in which general conceptions about society were closely joined with historical exposition. Classical Marxism has been central to the development of modern sociology; Max Weber, like so many other sociologists, developed much of his work in a dialogue with Karl Marx. But the amnesia of the American scholar has always to be recognized. In grand theory we now confront another formalist withdrawal, and again, what is properly only a pause seems to have become permanent. As they say in Spain, 'many can shuffle cards who can't play.'[19]

Notes

1. Talcott Parsons, *The Social System*, Glencoe, Illinois, The Free Press, 1951, pp. 12, 36–7.

2. See Appendix, section 5.

3. Parsons, op. cit. pp. 38–9

4. Ibid. pp. 41–2.

5. We can also consider it in relation to its users — the pragmatic aspect, about which we have no need to worry here. These are three 'dimensions of meaning' which Charles M. Morris has so neatly systematized in his useful 'Foundations of the Theory of Signs,' *International Encyclopedia of United Science*, Vol. I, No. 2. University of Chicago Press, 1938.

6. Parsons, op. cit. p. 552.

7. Cf. his excellent 'Some Remarks on "The Social System," ' *The British Journal of Sociology*, Vol. VII, 2 June 1956.

8. H. H. Gerth and C. Wright Mills, *Character and Social Structure*, New York, Harcourt, Brace, 1953, pp. 274–7, upon which I am drawing freely in this section and in section 5, below.

9. Cf. Karl Marx and Frederick Engels, *The German Ideology*, New York, International Publishers, 1939, pp. 42 ff.

10. For a detailed and empirical account of the 'values' which American businessmen, for example, seek to promulgate, see Sutton, Harris, Kaysen and Tobin, *The American Business Creed*, Cambridge, Mass., Harvard University Press, 1956.

11. Gerth and Mills, op. cit. p. 300.

12. Parsons, op. cit. p. 205.

13. Ibid. p. 262.

14. Cf. Carl Becker, *The Heavenly City*; and Lewis A. Coser, *Conflict*, Glencoe, Illinois, The Free Press, 1956.

15. Parsons, taken from Alvin W. Gouldner, 'Some observations on Systematic Theory, 1945–55,' *Sociology in the United States of America*, Paris, UNESCO, 1956, p. 40.

16. Cf. Lockwood, op. cit. p. 138.

17. Gouldner, op. cit. p. 41.

18. Franz Neumann, *Behemoth*, New York, Oxford, 1942, which is a truly splendid model of what a structural analysis of an historical society ought to be. For the above account, see Garth and Mills, op. cit. pp. 363 ff.

19. It must be evident that the particular view of society which it is possible to dig out of Parsons' texts is of rather direct ideological use; traditionally, such views have of course been associated with conservative styles of thinking. Grand theorists have not often descended into the political arena; certainly they have not often taken their problems to lie within the political contexts of modern society. But that of course does not exempt their work from ideological meaning. I shall not analyze Parsons in this connection, for the political meaning of *The Social System* lies so close to its surface, when it is adequately translated, that I feel no need to make it any plainer. Grand theory does not now play any direct bureaucratic role, and as I have noted, its lack of intelligibility limits any public favor it might come to have. This might of course become an asset: its obscurity does give it a great ideological potential.

The ideological meaning of grand theory tends strongly to legitimate stable forms of domination. Yet only if there should arise a much greater need for elaborate legitimations among conservative groups would grand theory have a chance to become politically relevant. I began this chapter with a question: Is grand theory, as represented in *The Social*

System, merely verbiage or is it also profound? My answer to this question is: It is only about 50 per cent verbiage; 40 per cent is well-known textbook sociology. The other 10 per cent, as Parsons might say, I am willing to leave open for your own empirical investigations. My own investigations suggest that the remaining 10 per cent is of possible — although rather vague — ideological use.

39. Social Structure and Dynamic Process: The Case of Modern Medical Practice
Talcott Parsons

In the most general terms medical practice may be said to be oriented to coping with disturbances to the "health" of the individual, with "illness" or "sickness." Traditionally the principal emphasis has been on "treatment" or "therapy," that is, on dealing with cases which have already developed a pathological state, and attempting to restore them to health or normality. Recently there has been increasing emphasis on "preventive medicine," that is, controlling the conditions which produce illness. For our purposes, however, the therapeutic functional context will present sufficient problems.

A little reflection will show immediately that the problem of health is intimately involved in the functional prerequisites of the social system as defined above. Certainly by almost any definition health is included in the functional needs of the individual member of the society so that from the point of view of functioning of the social system, too low a general level of health, too high an incidence of illness, is dysfunctional. This is in the first instance because illness incapacitates for the effective performance of social roles. It could of course be that this incidence was completely uncontrollable by social action, an independently given condition of social life. But in so far as it is controllable, through rational action or otherwise, it is clear that there is a functional interest of the society in its control, broadly in the minimization of illness. As one special aspect of this, attention may be called to premature death. From a variety of points of view, the birth and rearing of a child constitute a "cost" to the society, through pregnancy, child care, socialization, formal training and many other channels. Premature death, before the individual has had the opportunity to play out his full quota of social roles, means that only a partial "return" for this cost has been received.

All this would be true were illness purely a "natural phenomenon" in the sense that, like the vagaries of the weather, it was not, to our knowledge, reciprocally involved in the motivated interactions of human beings. In this case illness would be something which merely "happened to" people, which involved consequences which had to be dealt with and conditions which might or might not be controllable but was in no way an expression of motivated behavior.

This is in fact the case for a very important part of illness, but it has become increasingly clear, by no means for all. In a variety of ways motivational factors accessible to analysis in action terms are involved in the etiology of many illnesses, and conversely, though without exact correspondence, many conditions are open to therapeutic influence through motivational channels. To take the simplest kind of case, differential exposure, to injuries or to infection, is certainly motivated, and the role of unconscious wishes to be injured or to fall ill in such cases has been clearly

Reprinted with the permission of The Free Press, an imprint of Simon & Schuster, and Routledge, from *THE SOCIAL SYSTEM* by Talcott Parsons. Copyright © 1951, copyright renewed 1979 by Talcott Parsons.

demonstrated. Then there is the whole range of "psycho-somatic" illness about which knowledge has been rapidly accumulating in recent years. Finally, there is the field of "mental disease," the symptoms of which occur mainly on the behavioral level. Of course somatic states which are not motivationally determined may play a larger or smaller part in any or all of them, in some like syphilitic paresis they may be overwhelmingly predominant, but over the field as a whole there can be no doubt of the relevance of illness to the functional needs of the social system, in the further sense of its involvement in the motivated processes of interaction. At one time most medical opinion inclined to the "reduction" of *all* illness to a physiological and biological level in both the sense that etiology was always to be found on that level, and that only through such channels was effective therapy possible. This is certainly not the predominant medical view today. If it ever becomes possible to remove the hyphen from the term "psycho-somatic" and subsume all of "medical science" under a single conceptual scheme, it can be regarded as certain that it will not be the conceptual scheme of the biological science of the late nineteenth and early twentieth centuries. It is also certain that this conceptual scheme will prove applicable to a great deal of the range of social action in areas which extend well beyond what has conventionally been defined as the sphere of medical interests.

The fact that the relevance of illness is not confined to the non-motivated purely situational aspect of social action greatly increases its significance for the social system. It becomes not merely an "external" danger to be "warded off" but an integral part of the social equilibrium itself. Illness may be treated as one mode of response to social pressures, among other things, as one way of evading social responsibilities. But it may also, as will appear, have some possible positive functional significance.

Summing up, we may say that illness is a state of disturbance in the "normal" functioning of the total human individual, including both the state of the organism as a biological system and of his personal and social adjustments. It is thus partly biologically and partly socially defined. Participation in the social system is always potentially relevant to the state of illness, to its etiology and to the conditions of successful therapy, as well as to other things.

Medical practice as above defined is a "mechanism" in the social system for coping with the illnesses of its members. It involves a set of institutionalized roles which will be analyzed later. But this also involves a specialized relation to certain aspects of the general cultural tradition of a modern society. Modern medical practice is organized about the application of scientific knowledge to the problems of illness and health, to the control of "disease." Science is of course a very special type of cultural phenomenon and a really highly developed scientific level in any field is rare among known cultures, with the modern West in a completely unique position. It may also be noted that scientific advance beyond the level to which the Greeks brought it is, in the medical field, a recent phenomenon, as a broad cultural stream not much more than a century old.

We have dealt at some length in [Chapter VIII] with science as a general feature of the cultural tradition, and with some of the conditions of its application to practical affairs. This need not be repeated here. We need only note a few points particularly relevant to the medical field. First, it should be quite clear that the treatment of illness as a problem for applied science must be considered problematical and not taken for granted as "common sense." The comparative evidence is overwhelming that illness, even a very large part of what to us is obviously somatic illness, has been interpreted in supernatural terms, and magical treatment has been considered to be the appropriate method of coping with it. In non-literate societies there is an element of empirical lore which may be regarded as proto-scientific, with respect to the treatment of fractures for instance. But the prominence of magic in this field is overwhelmingly great.

This, however, is by no means confined to non-literate cultures. The examples of traditional China and our own Middle Ages will suffice. Where other features of the cultural tradition are not favorable to the traditionalized stereotyping which we think of as characteristic of magic in the full sense, we find a great deal, and sometimes predominance, of health "superstition" in the sense of pseudo rational or pseudo scientific beliefs and practices.

In the light of these considerations it is not surprising that in a society in which scientific medicine has come to be highly institutionalized, popular orientations toward the health problem are by no means confined to the scientific level. There is much popular health superstition, as evidenced by such things as the "patent medicines," for example the widely advertised "Dr. Pierce's Golden Medical Discovery," and many traditional "home remedies." Furthermore in the health field there is a considerable fringe of what are sometimes called "cults." Some religious denominations, of which Christian Science is perhaps the most conspicuous example, include a religious approach to health as an integral part of their general doctrine. Then there is a variety of groups which offer health treatments outside the medical profession and the professions auxiliary to it like dentistry and nursing. These are apt to include complex and bewildering mixtures of scientifically verifiable elements and various grades and varieties of pseudo-science.[3]

Finally the institutionalization of science is, as the analysis of [Chapter VIII] would lead us to expect, far from complete within the profession itself. There are many kinds of evidence of this, but for present purposes it is sufficient to cite the strong, often bitter resistance from within the profession itself to the acceptance of what have turned out to be critically important scientific advances in their own field. One of the classic cases is the opposition of the French Academy of Medicine to Pasteur, and for some time the complete failure to appreciate the importance of his discoveries. A closely related one is the opposition of the majority of the surgeons of the day to Lister's introduction of surgical asepsis. The conception of "laudable pus" is an excellent example of a medical "superstition."

It goes without saying that there is also an important involvement of expressive symbolism in medical practice. Rather, however, than attempting to review it at this point it will be better to call attention to certain aspects of it as we go along.

The social structure

The immediately relevant social structures consist in the patterning of the role of the medical practitioner himself and, though to common sense it may seem superfluous to analyze it, that of the "sick person" himself. There is also a range of important impingements of both roles on other aspects of the total structure of the social system which will have to be mentioned at the appropriate points.

The role of the medical practitioner belongs to the general class of "professional" roles, a sub-class of the larger group of occupational roles. Caring for the sick is thus not an incidental activity of other roles — though for example mothers do a good deal of it — but has become functionally specialized as a full-time "job." This, of course, is by no means true of all societies. As an occupational role it is institutionalized about the technical content of the function which is given a high degree of primacy relative to other status-determinants. It is thus inevitable both that incumbency of the role should be achieved and that performance criteria by standards of technical competence should be prominent. Selection for it and the context of its performance are to a high degree segregated from other bases of social status and solidarities. In common with the predominant patterns of occupational roles generally in our society it is therefore in addition to its incorporation of achievement values, universalistic, functionally specific, and affectively neutral. Unlike the role of the businessman, however, it is collectivity-oriented not self-oriented.

The importance of this patterning is, in one context, strongly emphasized by its relation to the cultural tradition. One basis for the division of labor is the specialization of technical competence. The role of physician is far along the continuum of increasingly high levels of technical competence required for performance. Because of the complexity and subtlety of the knowledge and skill required and the consequent length and intensity of training, it is difficult to see how the functions could, under modern conditions, be ascribed to people occupying a prior status as one of their activities in that status, following the pattern by which, to a degree, responsibility for the health of her children is ascribed to the mother-status. There is an intrinsic connection between achieved statuses and the requirements of high technical competence, as well as universalism and competence. In addition, of course, there is pressure in the society to assimilate the medical role to others of similar character in the total occupational system.

High technical competence also implies specificity of function. Such intensive devotion to expertness in matters of health and disease precludes comparable expertness in other fields. The physician is not, by virtue of his modern role, a generalized "wise man" or sage — though there is considerable folklore to that effect — but a specialist whose superiority to his fellows is confined to the specific sphere of his technical training and experience. For example one does not expect the physician as such to have better judgment about foreign policy or tax legislation than any other comparably intelligent and well-educated citizen. There are of course elaborate sub-divisions of specialization within the profession.

Affective neutrality is also involved in the physician's role as an applied scientist. The physician is expected to treat an objective problem in objective, scientifically justifiable terms. For example whether he likes or dislikes the particular patient as a person is supposed to be irrelevant, as indeed it is to most purely objective problems of how to handle a particular disease.

With regard to the pattern variable, self vs. collectivity-orientation, the physician's role clearly belongs to what, in our occupational system, is the "minority" group, strongly insisting on collectivity-orientation. The "ideology" of the profession lays great emphasis on the obligation of the physician to put the "welfare of the patient" above his personal interests, and regards "commercialism" as the most serious and insidious evil with which it has to contend. The line, therefore, is drawn primarily vis-à-vis "business." The "profit motive" is supposed to be drastically excluded from the medical world. This attitude is, of course, shared with the other professions, but it is perhaps more pronounced in the medical case than in any single one except perhaps the clergy.

In terms of the relation of the physician's occupational role to the total instrumental complex there is an important distinction between two types of physicians. One of the "private practitioner," the other the one who works within the context of organization. Be important thing about the former is that he must not only care for sick people in a technical sense, but must take responsibility for settlement of the terms of exchange with them because of his direct dependence on them for payment for his services, and must to a high degree also provide his own facilities for carrying on his function. It is a crucially important fact that expertness in caring for the sick does not imply any special competence one way or another in the settlement of terms of exchange. It may or may not be a good social policy to have the costs of medical care, the means of payment for it and so on settled by the members of the medical profession, as individuals or through organizations, but such a policy cannot be justified on the ground that their special training gives them as physicians a technical competence in these matters which others do not have.

An increasing proportion of medical practice is now taking place in the context of organization. To a large extent this is necessitated by the technological development of medicine itself, above all the need for technical facilities beyond the reach of the individual practitioner, and the fact that treating the same case often involves the complex cooperation of several different kinds of physicians as well as of auxiliary personnel. This greatly alters the relation of the physician to the rest of the instrumental complex. He tends to be relieved of much responsibility and hence necessarily of freedom, in relation to his patients other than in his technical role. Even if a hospital executive is a physician himself he is not in the usual sense engaged in the "practice of medicine" in performing his functions any more than the president of the Miners' Union is engaged in mining coal.

As was noted, for common sense there may be some question of whether "being sick" constitutes a social role at all — isn't it simply a state of fact, a "condition"? Things are not quite so simple as this. The test is the existence of a set of institutionalized expectations and the corresponding sentiments and sanctions.

There seem to be four aspects of the institutionalized expectation system relative to the sick role. First, is the exemption from normal social role responsibilities, which of course is relative to the nature and severity of the illness. This exemption requires legitimation by and to the various alters involved and the physician often serves as a court of appeal as well as a direct legitimatizing agent. It is noteworthy that like all institutionalized patterns the legitimation of being sick enough to avoid obligations can not only be a right of the sick person but an obligation upon him. People are often resistant to admitting they are sick and it is not uncommon for others to tell them that they *ought* to stay in bed. The word generally has a moral connotation. It goes almost without saying that this legitimation has the social function of protection against "malingering."

The second closely related aspect is the institutionalized definition that the sick person cannot be expected by "pulling himself together" to get well by an act of decision or will. In this sense also he is exempted from responsibility — he is in a condition that must "be taken care of." His "condition" must be changed, not merely his "attitude." Of course the process of recovery may be spontaneous but while the illness lasts he can't "help it." This element in the definition of the state of illness is obviously crucial as a bridge to the acceptance of "help."

The third element is the definition of the state of being ill as itself is undesirable with its obligation to want to "get well." The first two elements of legitimation of the sick role thus are conditional in a highly important sense. It is a relative legitimation so long as he is in this unfortunate state which both he and alter hope he can get out of as expeditiously as possible.

Finally, the fourth closely related element is the obligation — in proportion to the severity of the condition, of course — to seek *technically competent* help, namely, in the most usual case, that of a physician and to *cooperate* with him in the process of trying to get well. It is here, of course, that the role of the sick person as patient becomes articulated with that of the physician in a complementary role structure.

It is evident from the above that the role of motivational factors in illness immensely broadens the scope and increases the importance of the institutionalized role aspect of being sick. For then the problem of social control becomes much more than one of ascertaining facts and drawing lines. The privileges and exemptions of the sick role may become objects of a "secondary gain" which the patient is positively motivated, usually unconsciously, to secure or to retain. The problem, therefore, of the balance of motivations to recover, becomes of first importance. In general motivational balances of great functional significance to the social system are institutionally controlled, and it should, therefore, not be surprising that this is no exception.

A few further points may be made about the specific patterning of the sick role and its relation to social structure. It is, in the first place, a "contingent" role into which anyone, regardless of his status in other respects, may come. It is, furthermore, in the type case temporary. One may say that it is in a certain sense a "negatively achieved" role, through failure to "keep well," though, of course, positive motivations also operate, which by that very token must be motivations to deviance.

It is inherently universalistic, in that generalized objective criteria determine whether one is or is not sick, how sick, and with what kind of sickness; its focus is thus classificatory not relational. It is also functionally specific, confined to the sphere of health, and particular "complaints" and disabilities within that sphere. It is furthermore affectively neutral in orientation in that the expected behavior, "trying to get well," is focused on an objective problem not on the cathectic significance of persons,[4] or orientations to an emotionally disturbing problem, though this may be instrumentally and otherwise involved.

The orientation of the sick role vis-à-vis the physician is also defined as collectively-oriented. It is true that the patient has a very obvious self-interest in getting well in most cases, though this point may not always be so simple. But once he has called in a physician the attitude is clearly marked, that he has assumed the obligation to cooperate with that physician in what is regarded as a common task. The obverse of the physician's obligation to be guided by the welfare of the patient is the latter's obligation to "do his part" to the best of his ability. This point is clearly brought out, for example, in the attitudes of the profession toward what is called "shopping around." By that is meant the practice of a patient "checking" the advice of one physician against that of another without telling physician A that he intends to consult physician B, or if he comes back to A that he has done so or who B is. The medical view is that if the patient is not satisfied with the advice his physician gives him he may properly do one of two things, first he may request a consultation, even naming the physician he wishes called in, but in that case it is physician A not the patient who must call B in, the patient may not see B independently, and above all not without A's knowledge. The other proper recourse is to terminate the relation with A and become "B's patient." The notable fact here is that a pattern of behavior on the part not only of the physician, but also of the patient, is expected which is in sharp contrast to perfectly legitimate behavior in a commercial relationship. If he is buying a car there is no objection to the customer going to a number of dealers before making up his mind, and there is no obligation for him to inform any one dealer what others he is consulting, to say nothing of approaching the Chevrolet dealer only through the Ford dealer.

The doctor-patient relationship is thus focused on these pattern elements. The patient has a need for technical services because he doesn't — nor do his lay associates, family members, etc. — "know" what is the matter or what to do about it, nor does he control the necessary facilities. The physician is a technical expert who by special training and experience, and by an institutionally validated status, is qualified to "help" the patient in a situation institutionally defined as legitimate in a relative sense but as needing help. The intricacy of the social forces operating on this superficially simple sub-system of social relations will be brought out in the following analysis.

The situation of medical practice

A. The situation of the patient

The first step is to go more in detail into the analysis of relevant aspects of the situation in which the doctor and the patient find themselves. This will provide the setting in which the importance of the broad patterning of both physician's and patient's role can be interpreted, and will enable us to identify a series of mechanisms which, in addition to the physician's deliberate application of his technical knowledge, operate to facilitate his manifest functions in the control of disease, and to promote other, latent functions which are important to the social system.

First, it must be remembered that there is an enormous range of different types of illness, and of degrees of severity. Hence a certain abstraction is inevitable in any such general account as the present one. There is also a range of different types of physician. It will, therefore, be necessary to concentrate on what can be considered certain strategic and typical features of the situation of both.

It will be convenient first to take up the salient features of the situation of the patient and his "lay" associates, particularly members of his family. These may be classified under the three headings of helplessness and need of help, technical incompetence, and emotional involvement.

By institutional definition of the sick role the sick person is helpless and therefore in need of help. If being sick is to be regarded as "deviant" as certainly in important respects it must, it is as we have noted distinguished from other deviant roles precisely by the fact that the sick person is not regarded as "responsible" for his condition, "he can't help it." He may, of course, have carelessly exposed himself to danger of accident, but then once injured he cannot, for instance, mend a fractured leg by "will power." The exhortation to "try" has importance at many peripheral points in the handling of illness, but the core definition is that of a "condition" that either has to "right itself" or to be "acted upon," and usually the patient got into that condition through processes which are socially defined as "not his fault."

The urgency of the need of help will vary with the severity of the disability, suffering, and risk of death or serious, lengthy or permanent disablement. It will also vary inversely with the prospect, as defined in the culture, of spontaneous recovery in terms of certainty and duration. But a sufficient proportion of cases is severe in one or more of these senses, and unlikely to recover spontaneously, at least soon enough, so that the feeling of helplessness and the need of help are very real.

The sick person is, therefore, in a state where he is suffering or disabled or both, and possibly facing risks of worsening, which is socially defined as either "not his fault" or something from which he cannot be expected to extricate himself by his own effort, or generally both. He is also likely to be anxious about his state and the future. This is a very different kind of "need" from that of a person who merely "wants" something that he can be permitted to have if he can "swing" it independently, such as a new car, or even if he "needs something," such as adequate food, if he can reasonably be expected to procure it by his own efforts, as by working for it, and not being lazy or shiftless. In a special sense, the sick person is "entitled" to help.

By the same institutional definition the sick person is not, of course competent to help himself, or what he can do is, except for trivial illness, not adequate. But in our culture there is a special definition of the kind of help he needs, namely, professional, technically competent help. The nature of this help imposes a further disability or handicap upon him. He is not only generally not in a position to do what needs to be done, but he does not "know" what needs to be done or how to do it. It is not merely that he, being bedridden, cannot go down to the drug store to vet what is needed, but that he would, even if well, not be qualified to do what is needed, and to judge what needs to be done. There is, that is to say, a "communication gap."

Only a technically trained person has that qualification. And one of the most serious disabilities of the layman is that he is not qualified to judge technical qualifications, in general or in detail. Two physicians may very well give conflicting diagnoses of the same case, indeed often do. In general the layman is not qualified to choose between them. Nor is he qualified to choose the "best" physician among a panel. If he were fully rational he would have to rely on professional authority, on the advice of the professionally qualified or on institutional validation.

This disqualification is, of course, not absolute. Laymen do know something in the field, and have some objective bases of judgment. But the evidence is overwhelming that this knowledge is highly limited and that most laymen *think* they know more, and have better bases of judgment than is actually the case. For example the great majority of laymen think that *their* physician is either the best or one of the few best in his field in the community. It is manifestly impossible for the majority of such judgments to be objectively correct. Another type of evidence is the patterning of choice of physician. A very large proportion of people choose their physicians on the basis of the recommendations of friends or neighbors who "like Dr. X so much," without any sort of inquiry beyond that as to technical qualifications, even as to the medical school from which he holds a degree or the hospital at which he interned.[5] There must be some mechanisms to bridge this "gap." There must be some way of defining the situation to the patient and his family, as to what is "the matter with him" and why, what his prognosis is, what burdens will have to be assumed in recovery. There must be some mechanism for validating the "authority" of the physician, who only in special cases like the military services has any coercive sanctions at his command.

In this connection it should be noted that the burdens the physician asks his patients and their families to assume on his advice are often very severe. They include suffering — you "have to get worse before you can get better" as for instance in the case of a major surgical operation. They include risk of death, permanent or lengthy disablement, severe financial costs and various others. In terms of common sense it can always be said that the patient has the obvious interest in getting well and hence should be ready to accept any measures which may prove necessary. But there is always the question, implicit or explicit, "How do I know this will do any good?" The one thing certain seems to be that the layman's answer to this cannot, in the majority of severe and complex cases, i.e., the "strategic" ones, be based primarily on his own rational understanding of the factors involved and a fully rational weighing of them. The difference from the physician in this respect is often a matter of degree, but it is a crucially important difference of degree.

Finally, third, the situation of illness very generally presents the patient and those close to him with complex problems of emotional adjustment. It is, that is to say, a situation of strain. Even if there is no question of a "physic" factor in his condition, suffering, helplessness, disablement and the risk of death, or sometimes its certainty, constitute fundamental disturbances of the expectations by which men live. They cannot in general be emotionally "accepted" without the accompaniments of strain with which we are familiar and hence without difficult adjustments unless the patient happens to find positive satisfactions in them, in which case there is also a social problem. The significance of this emotional factor is magnified and complicated in so far as defensive and adjustive mechanisms are deeply involved in the pathological condition itself.

The range of possible complexities in this sphere is very great. The problems are, however, structured by the nature of the situation in certain relatively definite ways. Perhaps the most definite point is that for the "normal" person illness, the more so the greater its severity, constitutes a frustration of expectancies of his normal life pattern. He is cut off from his normal spheres of activity, and many of his normal enjoyments.

He is often humiliated by his incapacity to function normally. His social relationships are disrupted to a greater or a less degree. He may have to bear discomfort or pain which is hard to bear, and he may have to face serious alterations of his prospects for the future, in the extreme but by no means uncommon case the termination of his life.

For the normal person the direction of these alterations is undesirable, they are frustrations. Therefore it is to be expected that two types of reaction should be prominent, a kind of emotional "shock" at the beginning of illness, and anxiety about the future. In both cases there is reason to believe that most normal persons have an unrealistic bias in the direction of confidence that "everything will be all right," that is they are motivated to underestimate the chances of *their* falling ill, especially seriously ill (the minority of hypochondriacs is the obverse), and if they do they tend to overestimate the chances of a quick and complete recovery. Therefore even the necessary degree of emotional acceptance of the reality is difficult. One very possible reaction is to attempt to deny illness or various aspects of it, to refuse to "give in" to it. Another may be exaggerted self-pity and whining, a complaining demand for more help than is necessary or feasible, especially for incessant personal attention. In any case this factor reinforces the others. It makes it doubly difficult for the patient to have an objective judgment about his situation and what is needed. Whether they pay explicit attention to it in any technical sense or not, what physicians do inevitably influences the emotional states of their patients, and often this may have a most important influence on the state of their cases.

In this connection perhaps a few words may be said about the relation of the medical situation to death. As was noted in [Chapter VIII] death, and particularly premature death, is one of the most important situations in all societies, demanding complex emotional adjustments on the part of the dying person, if the probability is known to him in advance, and on the part of the survivors. This is so important that in no society is there an absence of both cultural and social structuring of ideas about death, attitudes toward it, or behavior in the presence of imminent death or its recent occurrences. Moreover the "death complex" is never purely instrumental in its patterning. It is a central focusing point for expressive symbolism.

American culture in general seems to have a strong "optimistic bias," one aspect of which is the "playing down" of death, the avoidance of too much concern with its prospect or its implications, and, when it must be faced, "getting it over with" as rapidly as possible. For example, we have relatively slight and probably decreasing emphasis on mourning. Our tendency is to "get on with living" as nearly in the usual pattern as possible. In the light of psychological knowledge and the evidence from comparative cultures it seems highly likely that this attitude is maintained only by virtue of strong disciplines which repress preoccupation with and anxiety about death. It may also mean that "grief reactions" are more frequently repressed than in other societies.

In a society normally at peace, death in most cases is preceded by illness, which links it very closely with the sick role. This is hence a point at which more or less free-floating anxieties about death have an opportunity to focus. Moreover, the physician is brought very closely into contact with death. He is often present at a death bed, and he is the first one to whom people look for structuring the situation in relation to their anxieties about the possibility of death; if the clergyman comes in it is usually later than the physician. It is striking that the medical is one of the few occupational groups which in our society have regular, expected contact with death in the course of their occupational roles, the clergyman, the undertaker, and in certain ways the police, being the other principal ones. The military in our society are a special, though sociologically extremely interesting case, because for us war is an exceptional "crisis" situation, not part of the normal life of the society.

It is to be presumed that this association with death is a very important factor in the emotional toning of the role of the physician. If he is not in general tending in our society to take the place formerly occupied by the clergy, an assertion often made, but subject to considerable qualifications, he at least has very important associations with the realm of the sacred. In this connection it is interesting to note that the dissection of a cadaver is included in the very first stage of formal medical training, and that it tends to be made both something of a solemn ritual, especially the first day, on the part of the medical school authorities, and medical students often have quite violent emotional reactions to the experience. It may hence be concluded that dissection is not only an instrumental means to the learning of anatomy, but is a symbolic act, highly charged with affective significance. It is in a sense the initiatory rite of the physician-to-be into his intimate association with death and the dead.

Indeed, this is confirmed by the fact that historically the medical profession had to wage a long and sometimes bitter struggle to secure the right to dissect cadavers as a regular part of medical training — at one time they secretly raided cemeteries for the purpose.[6] Even today some religious bodies strongly oppose autopsies except when they are required by the law of the state where there is suspicion of foul play.

To come back to the main theme. There are two particularly important broad consequences of the features of the situation of the sick person for the problem of the institutional structuring of medical practice. One is that the combination of helplessness, lack of technical competence, and emotional disturbance make him a peculiarly vulnerable object for exploitation. It may be said that the exploitation of the helpless sick is "unthinkable." That happens to be a very strong sentiment in our society, but for the sociologist the existence of this sentiment or that of other mechanisms for the prevention of exploitation must not be taken for granted. There is in fact a very real problem of how, in such a situation, the very possible exploitation is at least minimized.[7]

The other general point is the related one that the situation of the patient is such as to make a high level of rationality of judgment peculiarly difficult. He is therefore open to, and peculiarly liable to, a whole series of irr- and non-rational beliefs and practices. The world over the rational approach to health through applied science is, as we have noted, the exception rather than the rule, and in our society there is, even today, a very large volume of "superstition" and other non- or irrational beliefs and practices in the health field. This is not to say that the medical profession either has a monopoly of rational knowledge and techniques, or is free of the other type of elements, but the volume of such phenomena outside the framework of regular medical practice is a rough measure of this factor. This set of facts then makes problematical the degree to which the treatment of health problems by applied science has in fact come to be possible. It can by no means be taken for granted as the course which "reasonable men," i.e., the normal citizen of our society will "naturally" adopt.

The above discussion has been concerned primarily with the sick person himself. But in some cases, e.g., when he is an infant or is in a coma, the patient himself has nothing whatever to say about what is done to him. But short of this, the patient tends to be buttressed by family members and sometimes friends who are not sick. Does this not vitiate the whole argument of the above discussion? Definitely not. It may mitigate the severity of the impact of some of the features of the patient's situation, in fact, it often does. But in the first place laymen, sick or well, are no more technically competent in medical matters in one case than the other. The need of help is also just as strong because the solidarity of the family imposes a very strong pressure on the healthy members to see that the sick one gets the best possible care. It is, indeed, very common if not usual for the pressure of family members to tip the balance in the admission of being sick enough to go to bed or call a doctor, when the patient himself would tend to stand out longer. Furthermore the emotional relationships within the family are of such a character that the illness of one of its members creates somewhat different emotional problems from the patient's own to be sure, but nevertheless often very severe ones, and sometimes more severe, or more difficult for the physician to cope with. It is not, for instance, for nothing that pediatricians habitually mean the mother, not the sick child, when they say "my patient." To anyone schooled in modern psychology the emotional significance of a child's illness for the mother in our society scarcely needs further comment. Hence we may conclude that the basic problems of the role of the patient himself are shared by the others in his personal circle with whom the physician comes into contact in his practice. Sometimes the role of these others is to facilitate the work of the physician very significantly. But it would be rash to assert that this was true very much more often than the reverse. In any case it is quite clear that the role of family members does not invalidate the significance of the situation of the patient for the character of medical practice, as outlined above.

Notes

3. An excellent and very detailed analysis of one of these border-line groups is given in the study by Walter I. Wardwell, *Social Strain and Social Adjustment in the Marginal Role of the Chiropractor*, unpublished Ph.D. dissertation, Harvard University, 1951.

4. That it will appear later is particularly important to the therapeutic process. It is not to be interpreted either that the cathectic significance of persons has no part in the etiology of illness or that cathexis of the physician as an object does not occur — but it is controlled.

5. One physician, a suburban general practitioner, told that in several years of practice only one patient had asked him from what medical school he had graduated.

6. Cf. Shryock, Richard Harrison, *The Development of Modern Medicine*.

7. It is interesting to note that even leftist propaganda against the evils of our capitalistic society, in which exploitation is a major keynote, tends to spare the physician. The American Medical Association tends to be attacked, but in general not the ideal-typical physician. This is significant of the general public reputation for collectivity-orientation of the medical profession.

40. Saussure and the Origins of Structuralism

John Sturrock

We can say . . . that any word in a language is a sign, and that language functions as a system of signs.

Saussure analysed the sign into its two components: a sound or acoustic component which he called the *signifier* (*significant* in French), and a mental or conceptual component which he called the *signified* (*signifié*). In this analysis, be it noted, things themselves, for which linguistic signs can be asked to stand when we want to refer to the world around us, are ignored. The signified is not a thing but the notion of a thing, what comes into the mind of the speaker or hearer when the appropriate signifier is uttered. The signifier thus constitutes the material aspect of language: in the case of the spoken language a signifier is any meaningful sound which is uttered or heard, in the case of the written language it is a meaningful mark inscribed on the page. The signified is the mental aspect of language which we often deem to be immaterial, even though it is certain that within the brain a signified is also a neural event. Signifiers and signifieds can be separated in this way only by the theorist of language; in practice they are inseparable. A truly meaningless sound is not a signifier because it does not signify — there can be no signifier without a signified; correspondingly, no concept can be said to exist unless it has found expression, that is to say been materialized, either inwardly as a thought or outwardly in speech — there can be no signified without a signifier. . . .

The distinction between signifier and signified . . . can also be applied in situations other than the analysis of the constituent signs of natural language. We have experience in our daily lives of a great many signs that are not verbal ones: of pictures and diagrams, for instance. And it is a fact that any object whatsoever, be it natural or artificial, can become a sign provided that it is employed to communicate a message, i.e. to *signify*. The flower that grows only to blush unseen can never be a sign since there is no one present to turn it into one. But within a culture flowers can be and are used as signs: when they are made into a wreath and sent to a funeral, for example. In this instance, the wreath is the signifier whose signified is, let us say, 'condolence'. (There can be no precise signified for a wreath because the language of flowers is too loose, at any rate in our culture; but equally there can be no wreath without a significance of some kind.)

The nature of the message conveyed by signs such as wreaths of flowers is one determined by the culture in which the sender and recipient live. Flowers have no *natural* significance, only a cultural or conventional one. . . . When they are employed as signs they enter into what is often referred to as a *code*, a channel of communication linking the two parties to any such cultural transaction. . . . The study of signs in

© Oxford University Press 1979. Reprinted from *STRUCTURALISM AND SINCE: FROM LEVI-STRAUSS TO DERRIDA* by John Sturrock (1979) by permission of Oxford University Press.

general, and of the operation of the vast number of codes in any culture which enable us to interpret these signs satisfactorily, is now practised under the name of semiology in France and other European countries, and of semiotics in the United States. It was Saussure, again, who first called for the institution of such a general science of signs.

He also introduced two other pairs of contrasted terms which are important to any understanding of the style of thought we are faced with. In the study of language he distinguished first of all between what he called *langue* and *parole*, or 'language' and 'speech'. *Language* is the theoretical system or structure of a language, the corpus of linguistic rules which speakers of that language must obey if they are to communicate; *speech* is the actual day-to-day use made of that system by individual speakers. This distinction can usefully be compared to the rather better-known one popularized more recently by the American grammarian Noam Chomsky, who distinguishes between our linguistic *competence* and our linguistic *performance*, meaning respectively the theory of language we appear to be able to carry constantly in our heads and the practical applications we make of it. For Saussure the linguist's proper job was to study not speech but language, because it was only by doing so that he could grasp the principles on which language functions in practice. This same important distinction emerges, in the work examined in this book, as one between *structure* and *event*, that is to say between abstract systems of rules and the concrete, individual happenings produced within that system. The relation between one and the other, and the question of which should take precedence — do structures precede events? or events structures? — has been much debated.

A second and, for my purposes here, final Saussurian distinction is that between the *synchronic* and the *diachronic* axes of investigation. It is permissible to study language — to take Saussure's own subject — along two radically different axes: as a system functioning at a given moment in time, or as an institution which has evolved through time. Saussure himself advocated the synchronic study of language, by contrast with the diachronic studies of the linguists who were his predecessors in the nineteenth century. They had been preoccupied by the history of particular languages, by etymologies, phonetic change and the like, and had never stopped to try and work out the total structure of a language, freezing it at a set moment of its evolution the easier to comprehend the principles on which it functioned.

Synchronic, or structural, linguistics thus introduced a revolutionary shift in perspective. It would have recognized that a total study of language must combine both perspectives, but it was prepared to ignore the diachronic perspective in order to set linguistics on a sounder, more productive footing. Structuralism as a whole is necessarily synchronic; it is concerned to study particular systems or structures under artificial and ahistorical conditions, neglecting the systems or structures out of which they have emerged in the hope of explaining their present functioning. . . .

Another influence on structuralism to be traced to Saussure's linguistics is not a matter of vocabulary, but is the most profound — and also the most elusive — of all. A crucial premise of Saussure's theory of language is that the linguistic sign is 'arbitrary'. It is so in two ways: the signifier is arbitrary inasmuch as there is no natural, only a conventional, link between it and the thing it signifies (not the signified in this case). There is no property common to all trees, for instance, which makes it logical or necessary that we should refer to them as 'trees'. That is what we, as anglophone persons, call them by agreement among ourselves; the French choose differently, they refer to them as *'arbres'*. But language is arbitrary at the level of the signified also, for each native language divides up in different ways the total field of what may be expressed in words, as one soon finds out in the act of translating from one language to another. One language has concepts that are absent from another. The example which linguists like to give of such arbitrariness is that of colour terms, which vary greatly from one language to another, even though the colours themselves form a continuum and, being determined naturally by their wave frequency, are universal.

The extremely important consequence which Saussure draws from this twofold arbitrariness is that language is a system not of fixed, unalterable essences but of labile forms. It is a system of relations between its constituent units, and those units are themselves constituted by the differences that mark them off from other, related units. They cannot be said to have any existence within themselves, they are dependent for their identity on their fellows. It is the place which a particular unit, be it phonetic or semantic, occupies in the linguistic system which alone determines its value. Those values shift because there is nothing to hold them steady; the system is fundamentally arbitrary in respect of nature and what is arbitrary may be changed.

'Language is a form and not a substance' was Saussure's famous summation of this quite fundamental insight, an insight without which none of the work done by Lévi-Strauss, Barthes, and the others would have been feasible. Structuralism holds to this vital assumption that it studies relations between mutually conditioned elements of a system and not between self-contained essences. It is easiest once more to instantiate this from linguistics. There is nothing essential or self-contained about a given word; the word 'rock', let us take. That occupies a certain space, both phonetically and semantically. Phonetically it can only be defined by establishing what the limits of that space are: where the boundaries lie if it crosses which it changes from being the word 'rock' to being a different sign of the language — 'ruck', for instance, or 'wreck', which abut on it acoustically. Semantically, we can only delimit the meaning of the signifier 'rock' by differentiating it from other signs which abut on it semantically, such as 'stone', 'boulder', 'cliff'.

In short, without difference there can be no meaning. A one-term language is an impossibility because its single term could be applied to everything and differentiate nothing; it requires at least one other term to give it definition. It would be possible, if rudimentary, to differentiate the entire contents of the universe by means of a two-term code or language as being either *bing* or *bong* perhaps. But without the introduction of that small phonetic difference, between the two vowel sounds, we can have no viable language at all.

41. The World as a Logical Pattern: An Introduction to Structuralism

Ian Craib

The background

'Structuralism' is a form of theory which, during the 1960s and 1970s, became influential in a number of disciplines: philosophy, social theory, linguistics, literary criticism, cultural analysis, psychoanalysis, the history of ideas, the philosophy of science, anthropology, and others. It is difficult to provide an absolute definition, not least because for a while it achieved cult status. Originating in France, where intellectuals have generally played a greater part in public life than in Britain and America, and their work sometimes attracts a following amounting to a subculture, the movement also gained a following amongst young academics in Britain and America. Thus it took root in an intellectual climate very different to that of France. Traditionally, British (especially) and American universities have been suspicious of ideas originating from France and Germany; they are seen as vague and jargon-ridden speculations, and structuralism came under attack for precisely these reasons. The response of the disciples in these countries has been similar to the reactions I talked about in the [Introduction]: they retreated into their own world, made a virtue of jargon and complication, and tended towards dogmatism. As in the struggles over ethnomethodology, people lost their jobs.

As a school of thought, structuralism can trace several lines of descent. One line runs through British and French anthropology, and will be of comparatively little import for what I have to say here. Another runs through the central tradition of French sociology: Comte in the early nineteenth century, Durkheim around the beginning of this century, taking in particular the idea of society existing over and above the individual and 'social facts' as consisting of 'collective representations'. A third line is the philosophical tradition originating with Kant, whose crucial idea is that human beings possess rational faculties with which they impose order on the world. Yet another, and substantively the most important, is through the school of structural linguistics and the work of Ferdinand de Saussure and the Russian Formalist School of literary criticism. If there are many roots, I have already indicated that there are many branches, and the leading figures are still French: Claude Lévi-Strauss (anthropology), Louis Althusser (social theory and philosophy), Roland Barthes (literary criticism and cultural studies), Christian Metz (film criticism), Jacques Lacan (psychoanalysis), Michel Foucault (the history of ideas) and Jacques Derrida (philosophy).

Intellectual cults, like other modern cults, tend to pass quickly, and perhaps it was because of the intensity of the debate that the proponents of structuralism were the first to develop it in such a way as to undermine its own foundations. The names

Copyright © 1992 Craib, Ian. Reproduced from *MODERN SOCIAL THEORY: FROM PARSONS TO HABERMAS*. Reprinted with permission of Harvester Wheatsheaf and St Martin's Press Incorporated.

associated with what is now known as 'post-structuralism' are also associated with the original movement — Foucault and Derrida in particular. I will be following through one branch of this development in [Chapter 10] — in relation to the structuralist Marxism of Althusser. For the moment, however, I want to focus on structuralism as a theory of general meanings rather than of societies.

A first approximation

The model I will take throughout this chapter is language. Structuralism regards all human products as forms as language, and this includes what I called 'general ideas'. My argument in relation to ethnomethodology was that when we talk to other people we use terms which already have a general meaning, and give them a specific, context-bound meaning. I suggested that these general meanings might be considered another realm of social reality, and I want now to suggest that structuralism contributes to our understanding of this area. We can take a set of general ideas, a particular theory, or perhaps what we call 'common sense', and look for an underlying structure, a rationale or a logic to them. Hence the title of this chapter — the world as a logical pattern. Just as we might look at all the different actions and choices of a friend and seek an underlying logic in order to understand her, so we might do the same for all the different statements that, say, a Christian makes.

This is not to say that I think structuralism is unreservedly a good thing. I would like to make a distinction between structuralism as a method and as a set of metaphysical assumptions. By method I mean a procedure, a way of looking at or thinking about the world which enables us to discover things that we did not initially know were there. This sometimes involves making certain assumptions about the world. For example, if I am making a journey by train or plane and I want to discover how long the journey will take, I assume that the transport will run on time, that I won't be struck down by lightning when I leave, and so on. The assumptions become metaphysical if I assume that they *really* are the case, that all trains *do* leave on time, that I shall *never* be struck by lightning, and so on. As a method, I think structuralism is useful; it can tell us things about the world that we could not find without it. As a set of metaphysical assumptions, I think it is a disaster and an absurdity. Paradoxically, the metaphysical assumptions have become most closely identified with and most clearly distinguish the school as a whole, and I want to begin by looking at them — this will give us a view of the carcase of the animal; then I will look at the method, trying to distinguish the edible parts and the points at which they are connected to the carcase. From the point of view of many structuralists I *will* be doing a butchering job, since the metaphysical assumptions are the most vital part of the approach.

The metaphysical assumptions

By 'metaphysical assumptions', then, I mean statements about the nature of the world that cannot be proved and eventually have to be taken on faith, when in fact there are decisive arguments against taking them on faith.

The world as a product of ideas

I have mentioned several times the view that the world we see around us is a product of our ideas — this in turn has its roots in Kant's philosophy, or a distorted form of it.

This is very much an assumption of structuralism, and in claiming to show the underlying structure or logic of general ideas, it is also claiming to show how we — or rather, our ideas — produce the world we see. Thus when Lévi-Strauss, for example, claims to have discovered the underlying structure of kinship in tribal society, he is claiming to have discovered the underlying structure of kinship terminology, the ideas with which these societies talk about kinship. Again I must repeat the same argument: there is a degree of truth in this view — people with different ideas do, to some extent, live in different worlds. But the world always offers resistance to these ideas, and then it becomes a matter of approximating one to the other. Structuralism in its extreme form does not consider this resistance: it does not matter to Lévi-Strauss that kinship behaviour is different from what the terminology would lead us to expect.

This assumption often takes the form of an attack on any attempt to prove theories by testing them; after all, if our theories produce the world, there is no point in testing them against the world. We will find only what we have put there in the first place. Any approach which sees some form of empirical testing as playing a role (such as the view I am arguing for) is dismissed as 'empiricist', one of the dirtiest words in the structuralist vocabulary.

The world as a logical pattern

The structuralist emphasis is always on the logical order or structure underlying general meanings. It is sometimes assumed that this 'structure' — which I will discuss in more detail shortly — matches the 'structures' of the world, sometimes on the grounds that since the mind is part of the world, the ideas it produces will have the same structure as the world. This is a sort of wager which we must make against our intuition — since the real world gives evidence of being illogical — and it leaves structuralism open to what, in the [Introduction], I called the 'logical trap'. Any theory which is not entirely logical must be wrong, and since no theory is entirely logical, we fall into a bottomless pit.

'The death of the subject'

'The death of the subject' is the slogan most closely associated with structuralism. 'Subject' means what I have referred to as agency, actions and persons. The idea being attacked is that people are the authors of their thoughts and actions. It is assumed instead that people are the puppets of their ideas, and their actions are not determined by choice and decision but are the outcome of the underlying structure of ideas, the logic of these ideas. If, for example, I am a Christian, I do not speak about Christianity; rather, Christianity speaks through me; some structuralists reach the extreme of saying that people do not speak; rather, they are spoken (by the underlying structure of the language); that they do not read books, but are 'read' by books. They do not create societies, but are created by societies.

Again I can offer a 'moderate' argument: it is true that we are always limited by our ideas, that they stop us saying certain things and perhaps force us to say things that we do not exactly mean. We are all engaged in a constant struggle with our ideas. But it does not follow that our ideas — or rather, their underlying structure — turn us into puppets. Choice, intention, goals and values still have a role to play and need to be understood; they are not entirely predetermined.

I will now turn to structuralism as a method, showing the origins of each of these metaphysical assumptions but also distinguish the usefulness of the method. When we come to look at structuralist social theory in general, these assumptions will appear again frequently, as they generate the tensions and difficulties that lead to the fragmentation of the approach.

Structuralism as a method

By 'method' here I mean that structuralism can act as a guide to the analysis of general meanings: it gives us some idea of what to look for and how to find it. I will begin with linguistics as a basic model and go on to look at how the model has been extended.

The linguistic model

Ferdinand de Saussure is often regarded as the founding father of modern linguistics. Putting it oversimply, before Saussure, linguistics had been concerned with how a language develops over time; Saussure argued, like Durkheim in sociology, that we do not know how something works by tracing its history. Just as we can understand a society only by looking at the relationships between the different parts, so we need to look at the relationships between the different parts of language. The attempt to understand something by looking at its history has been labelled 'historicist' — after 'empiricist' the second -dirtiest word in the structuralist vocabulary.

Speech and language

The function of language is to enable people to communicate, and we need to look at the way in which the different elements of a language contribute to communication through their relationships to each other. We cannot do that by looking at individual acts of speech; we need to look at the language as a whole, hence the distinction between speech and language. The individual speech act, what I say when I open my mouth, is always to some extant unique, and it cannot, therefore, be the object of a science. Language, on the other hand, is constant and possessed by everybody who speaks it; it is the raw material out of which we form our sentences. Each language is made up of a finite number of sounds and rules about combining sounds, rather like the rules of grammar we learn at school. Speech refers to the apparently infinite numbers of sentences we may produce using these sounds and rules. Games provide helpful examples: the language of chess, for instance, consists of the board and the pieces and the rules of the game, and these are the same for every game; the speech act is the individual game, which is different from the other individual games.

The language, then, is the underlying structure or logic behind speech.

The sign

The elements of this structure or logic are 'signs'. In everyday life, we tend to use the word in different ways: a cross on a chain around my neck is a sign that I am a Christian; dark clouds are a sign of rain; a red light by the side of the road is a sign that traffic must stop. The American philosopher C. S. Peirce, one of the few non-

European ancestors of structuralism, distinguished three types of sign: the *icon*, where the relationship is based on similarity — the cross around my neck is similar to the cross on which Christ was crucified; the *index*, where the relationship is causal, such as that between clouds and rain; and the *symbol*, where the relationship is a matter of social convention or agreement. This is often called an *arbitrary* relationship, meaning that there is no necessary connection between, for example, the colour red and the instruction to traffic to stop. The colour could be blue, orange or purple; it just so happens that everyone agrees that red means stop or danger, and this is an external reality imposed on individual members of society. If I were to decide that, for me, red means go and green means stop, I would not remain a member of society for very long.

Signs, the basic units of language, are arbitrary. There is nothing intrinsic in the word 'dog' that means that it has to refer to some hairy four-legged creature; we might as well call such animals 'professors', be we don't. The sign has two aspects, a *signifier* and a *signified*; the relation between them is often likened to the one between two sides of a sheet of paper. The signifier is the 'material' element, the physical sound of 'dog', or the marks on a sheet of paper. This element is meaningless without the signified, which is the concept the sounds refer to. Both are necessary to each other: the concept cannot be articulated without the sound.

It is important to remember that the signified is the concept, not the object. We tend to assume that words are attached to objects like labels, but structural linguistics breaks this connection, insisting on the difference between the concept and the object. There are various pithy ways of pointing this out: the concept of a circle is not round; the concept of a dog does not bark. This is the first step along the road to the metaphysical assumption that the objects we see in the world are created by our language or ideas. It is, I think, a justified step, in that it is simply true that words do not 'grow out' of things naturally and are different from the things they denote.

Syntagm and paradigm

To say that the relationship between the sign and what it points to is arbitrary is only half the story. It is not a matter of agreeing the meaning of each sign in a language separately; rather, they are all agreed as a structure of a whole — the red of the traffic light is part of a structure that includes green; red means stop because green means go, and vice versa. *The meaning of a linguistic sign depends upon its relationship to other signs.* We know what 'three' means only because of its relationship to 'one', 'two', 'four', etc. If we regard a simple sound as a sign, in English the words 'dog' and 'god' are made up of the same signs, but they have different meanings because the sounds have different relationships to each other. Similarly, Althusser argues that the meaning of the word 'alienation' in Marx's later work is different from its meaning in his earlier work, because it is related to different concepts.

We find the significant elements of a language by a method of 'concomitant variation'. We take a sentence or a word, and in a sort of thought-experiment we vary each element, replacing one by another, and if there is a significant change in meaning, we have found a significant unit. If, taking the word dog, I substitute 'h' for 'd' and get hog, I have found a significant element. Structuralists often organise those elements as opposing pairs (binary oppositions) — d/h, for example. Lévi-Strauss would claim that the human mind is so constituted that it orders the whole world into such opposites. Whether this is true or not is less important than the fact that here already we are beginning to get to the rules which govern relationships between signs, and thus what meanings can be produced. They can be analysed on two levels, the *syntagm* and the *paradigm*, and the first is more clearly a matter of rules than the second.

The syntagmatic level refers to which sounds or signs can or cannot follow each other in the 'syntagmatic chain'. Thus in English we do not usually find the combination 'hd', though we might find 'dh'. Odd little rules at this level are sometimes taught at school as an aid to spelling: 'i before e except after c'. The rules of grammar are again the appropriate model. The syntagmatic level can be seen as a horizontal axis of language, the paradigmatic level is the vertical axis. The paradigm consists of the set of words connected with the word in question by rules of similarity of sound or meaning. In the same system as 'dog' we can find 'hog', 'bog', 'cur', 'bitch', 'golden retriever', and so on. Every time we use a word, we select from such a paradigm (see Figure 1).

This is as far as it is necessary to go with the linguistic model. We can see how the metaphysical assumptions are rooted in the method without following logically and necessarily from it. It seems to me justified to look at the language rather than speech, but it does not follow that speech is determined by language and that we must disregard the speaking subject. Similarly, it is reasonable to suggest that the meaning of a word or sign depends on its relationship to others, and that it stands for a concept rather than an object, but it does not follow that it has no relation to an external object or that it creates that object. So far, I hope, I have demonstrated that structuralism seeks the underlying structure of a language — the basic elements and the rules which govern their relationships: the logic underlying a language.

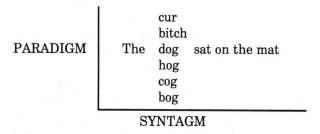

Figure 1. Sometimes the paradigm too may be described in terms of opposites (e.g. dog/cat, dog/bitch, etc.).